A History of England
in Eight Volumes
Founder Editor: SIR CHARLES OMAN

ENGLAND
UNDER THE TUDORS

A History of England
in Eight Volumes
Founder Editor: SIR CHARLES OMAN

* Replacing the original volume of the same title by A. D. Innes.
† Out of print.

England under the Tudors

by

G. R. ELTON

Fellow of Clare College, Cambridge

METHUEN & CO LTD
11 NEW FETTER LANE LONDON E.C.4.

First published September 8th 1955
Reprinted with minor corrections 1956, 1957 and 1958
Reprinted 1959 and 1960
Reprinted with a new bibliography 1962
Reprinted 1963, 1965 and 1967
Printed in Great Britain by
Cox & Wyman Ltd., London, Reading and Fakenham
and bound by James Burn and Co. Ltd., Esher

942.05

E 51e

CATALOGUE NO: 02/5780/33 [METHUEN]

I-II

PREFACE

THE writing of yet another history of the sixteenth century may seem to require justification; I can only say that I should not have written this book if I had thought so. There is much yet to discover about that well-worked period, and —more important—much of what has been discovered in the last thirty years has not yet reached the more general accounts. Only Professor Bindoff's brilliant short study of *Tudor England* provides an introduction to modern views; and he has left room for a book on a somewhat larger scale, with rather more detail in. Inevitably the different aspects of that crowded century could not all be given equal treatment: I can only hope that there is enough of them all to avoid at least the charge of deliberate obtuseness. To me it seems that what matters most in the story is the condition, reconstruction, and gradual moulding of a state—the history of a nation and its leaders in political action and therefore the history of government in the widest sense Other matters—economic, social, literary, military—are dealt with but more succinctly; this could not be helped. The needs of a book of this sort demanded a framework of fairly detailed narrative, and the analysis has had to concentrae on what seemed most important to the author. Tudor history can be written round such topics as religion, the maritime expansion, or Shakespeare, but I have chosen the constitutional problems of politics and government, in part because they attract me most and in part because I think that they involve less omission or falsification by emphasis than any other central theme.

More serious is the fact that in some parts of the story I have gone rather farther in being up-to-date than may be generally liked. I have come to some conclusions, especially about the place of Thomas Cromwell, the importance of the 1530s, and the nature of the Tudor polity, which—though by no means necessarily original—go counter to some accepted notions. I have elaborated some of these points elsewhere and hope to do so for others, but so far this has not been possible. I would therefore ask pardon for this preview, saying only that, confronted with a choice between writing what I think to be true and repeating what I believe to be doubtful, I could not but choose the former. The evidence exists, but much of it is not the kind that can be recited here.

Anyone who writes about the Tudor century puts his head into a number of untamed lions' mouths. Some of the issues—especially in religion—are still alive. Here dissension does not matter because agreement is impossible while people continue to be personally engaged. More troublesome are the difficulties which historians have created for themselves. Conflicts over the use of terms like modern and medieval, Renaissance and new learning, reflect a very real doubt as to the meaning of the century as a whole. I have tried to avoid the pitfalls, very probably without success: one may agree (as I am inclined to do) that modern and medieval are meaningless terms, but one cannot do without them. Where I have used them I have tried to make them say, respectively, 'more like what came after' and 'more like what came before', without prejudice as to what it was that came before and after. I happen to think that in my main theme—the nature of the English polity—changes took place in this period which cannot be described without the use of these terms, but I do not for one moment suppose that the differences between them are those between antitheses. If I speak of a 'Tudor revolution', I also know that the 'after' came out of the 'before'; but there was so much deliberate change crowded into the 1530s that a genuinely new state emerged, however closely it was linked to the old.

The fundamental difficulty arises from the attempt to treat the century as a unit, which it was not. In many ways the date 1485 matters less than almost any of the dates picked by historians as landmarks for guidance through the jungle and desert of events. It had only one real significance and that dynastic: it so happens that the family of Henry Tudor, unlike that of York which he overthrew or that of Lancaster which he claimed to represent, maintained itself on the throne for long enough to set its mark indelibly on the country over which it ruled. 1485 is the beginning of Tudor rule, and 1603 the end of it, and since the dates so conveniently circumscribe the life of one dynasty they have proved long-lived illusions. In the history of England nothing decisive happened in either 1485 or 1603. It may be natural to contrast 'the Tudors' with 'the Yorkists' who came before them and 'the Stuarts' who followed them, but once one can free oneself of these schematic dynastic preoccupations and look at events and people individually, one soon discovers that there are points of more profound significance in the sixteenth century than the accession of Henry VII or the death of Elizabeth. But it is better to accept these old categories and make them do new work than attempt to set up new categories which will only

create new confusions and quarrels. In 1485 Henry VII and no
one else ascended the throne, and in 1603 a foreign king full of a
kind of shrewd stupidity succeeded a wise and native queen: for
such not very deep reasons these two dates continue to have some
point as the limits of the tale. But let us remember that the
potentialities for change contained in so long a period as a hundred
and twenty years are not lessened by the simple device of giving
those years a family name.

I should like to record my very real gratitude to all those who
have helped in the writing of this book. In particular Dr P. J. Jones
is responsible for some of the above reflections, though he must not
be thought to agree with a word of them; Mr John Saltmarsh gave
me most generously of his precious time and great knowledge to
save Chapter IX from serious error, though, once again, he is not
in any way answerable for what I have there written; and I have
profited greatly from Mr J. J. Scarisbrick's unpublished researches
concerning the bishops of Henry VIII and from Dr W. Ullmann's
conversation on the subject of papal powers. Most of my many
debts to others are implicitly acknowledged in the Bibliography.

Cambridge, July 1954   G. R. E.

Though the occasion of an early reprint seemed hardly to call
for major alterations or revisions, it has given me the opportunity
of correcting some misprints and one or two errors of fact to
which reviewers have kindly drawn my attention. I have also
added a few items at the end of the Bibliography: in particular,
I am glad to be able to supply now two articles in which I have
given grounds for my interpretation of the career of Thomas
Cromwell, grounds whose absence I had to regret in my original
preface.

Cambridge, December 1955

This reprint includes an entirely revised bibliography, a step
made necessary by the recent flood of Tudor studies. I hope it
will not be regarded as arrogance or delusion if I say that nevertheless I cannot yet see any need to revise the book itself. Though
occasionally a minor point has been rendered doubtful by research,
and though I have changed my own mind on occasion, a real
reconsideration of the account and interpretation here put forward
does not, I think, seem so far to be called for.

Cambridge, October 1961

CONTENTS

MAPS AND DIAGRAMS

Chapter I

THE TUDOR PROBLEM

ON 22 August 1485 Henry, earl of Richmond, won one of the successive battles of the wars of the Roses near the Leicestershire township of Market Bosworth. His opponent, who commanded a stronger army halved by treason, was killed, and the throne thus left vacant by Richard III fell to the earl who became Henry VII. With this event, somewhat fortuitous in itself, there began the years of Tudor rule which were in the end to produce an England changed in many essentials—wealthier, more firmly unified, more fully national, more modern in her outlook, and properly equipped to play her part in the wider world which had also emerged in the course of the sixteenth century.

The England which Henry VII came to rule was the product of war and plague. Ever since Edward III set forth, in 1338, to claim the crown of France, Englishmen had been fighting—first the enemy on the continent and then, after a hundred years, each other in the squabbles for the English throne which really began with Richard II's deposition in 1399, burst into open war in 1450, and ended only when another Richard was killed on Bosworth Field. A period of war extending over nearly a century and a half was bound to leave a profound mark, though even by contemporary standards England suffered little in the fighting. The wars were far from continuous; even the thirty years' internecine struggle which we call the wars of the Roses was interrupted by long stretches of official peace. The war with France left that country exhausted and in misery, anxious for 'the naked, poor, and mangled Peace' for which Shakespeare's duke of Burgundy pleads so eloquently; the English, on the other hand, though they knew and disliked the noisy brawling soldier, back from France and eager to spend his loot on drink and women, were unacquainted with the real horrors of war—the ravaged countryside, the burning farm and town, the murder, rape, and brutalisation of the populace. They had, in fact, made considerable profit out of loot and ransoms, though more legitimate trading suffered. One might suppose that the civil wars had taught the country more of the realities, and indeed the wars of the Roses did cause distress here and there where marching columns passed or met for action; on the whole, however, events followed the pattern of English civil disturbances which tend to be transacted in a gentler fashion than those of other countries. The peasant and yeoman tilled the soil, the merchant—recovering from the trading depression of the mid-century—went about his business; life carried on in many parts of the country as though the kings and claimants, the great nobles and their riotous retainers, the politicians and soldiers, had not been busy cutting each other's throats on the public stage on which history must concentrate her attention.

The evil effects of the wars did not lie in material destruction or any stagnation of life. More subtle, less easily seen, and for that reason much more dangerous, they consisted in the growth of an unstable social structure thriving on disorder and lawlessness, and in the rapidly increasing weakness of the crown. The reign of Edward I (1272-1307) marked the transition from a society which was properly feudal to one which is now commonly described as bastard feudalism, a name which signifies not simply a corrupted or decaying form of feudalism but a social structure different and new in essentials. Feudalism embodied the link between lord and vassal in a system of land tenure; services were rendered in return for land held, and the tie was one carefully established in the law. The tenant had rights as well as duties, the lord duties as well as rights. Land is a real thing and does not move; a system taking it for its criterion is bound to have great fixity and stability. The feudal principle, evaded though it was, that land cannot be sold, though it can be granted away in return for services to be per-formed, added to this permanency. The origins of the system lay in the needs of military defence, but the military basis which had given it reality and strength vanished within a hundred years of the Norman Conquest. Men who owed services for the land they held were bound to be farmers or landlords before they were any-thing else; however loyal they might be to their lord, they had to see to the management of their estates. They might, reluctant and grumbling, come and do some military service if called upon to do so, but they could never become the nucleus of a private army.

In fact, they could not become the nucleus of any army, and as soon as the kings realised this fact they began to undermine the reality of feudalism by hiring their soldiers. This had happened as early as the middle of the twelfth century. A hundred years later Edward I unwittingly accelerated the break-up when he tried to safeguard the feudal rights of the crown by prohibiting

subinfeudation—the creation of new rungs in the feudal ladder—
which made it impossible for any man but the king to reward
services done, or ensure future services to be done, by the grant of
lands. The fourteenth century, from the Scottish wars of Edward I
through the civil wars of Edward II to the French wars of
Edward III, added the urgent problem of finding a military force
which could be relied upon against professional opponents, which
could be kept in the field, and which could be paid in some
fashion other than in land. Services were paid for as rendered—as
a rule in cash—instead of being incumbent upon certain units of
land whose tenant had to perform them. There grew up a system
by which men took service with someone—the king or a great
nobleman or, for that matter, any little knight. The nexus of lord
and vassal, whose means of exchange was land and whose essence
was direct and individual relationship between two men, was
replaced by that of master and man, whose means of exchange was
money and whose essence was patronage and affinity, that is
membership of a group gathered round one man. Feudalism,
stable on its basis of the land and firm in its scheme of known
rights and duties, gave way to the patronage system of bastard
feudalism where men's ambitions and needs were satisfied by him
who could pay for services and at whose order and discretion they
were done. It was essentially a less stable system, and at times it
grew frighteningly fluid.

Bastard feudalism began in military organisation, with the
indentures for service through which fourteenth-century armies
were recruited. The captains of the wars gathered round them
men eager to fight and make a profit, and they retained them by
indentures which specified the services to be done and rewards
to be given. In the course of time the system invaded other spheres,
and great nobles, from the king downwards, acquired ever growing
households of servants and retainers who held either indentures
or letters patent of grants outlining their rights and duties.
Superficially the relationship continued to be feudal, relying on
personal loyalties. In fact it was based on payment, though the
unstable tendencies inherent in it were balanced by the persistence
of personal and family ties; successive generations of one
family, or men of the same locality, would often adhere with
remarkable fidelity to the fortunes of one great house such as
Lancaster or York or Warwick. It was the military side of it which
made the arrangement really dangerous, for there it amounted to
the creation of private magnate armies within the kingdom. The
companies formed to fight in France were bound together by

service to the captain or patron whose retinue they composed;
when the wars in France were over, and chances of war offered in
England herself, it was fatally easy for these magnate employers of
armed bands to engage each other, in despite of the crown. But that
this chance offered was less the fault of bastard feudalism than of
that other consequence of the wars, the declining power and
authority of the crown.

The strength of her kings was once the special glory and distinction of England. No other country in the West achieved so early
the unification, the relative national consciousness, the common
law and common administration, the efficient and fatherly care,
which William I, Henry I, Henry II, and Edward I imposed on
their dominions. In the high middle ages England was almost the
model of a monarchy, resting indeed on a feudal social order and
animated by feudal concepts, but remarkably free from the
destructive centrifugal forces which feudalism released in France
and Germany. She owed this happy dispensation to the accident
of the Norman Conquest which made possible a virtually fresh
start; but even more she owed it to the kings who, intent on their
own interests, profited the country by the creation of a strong
central authority. From the land policy of the Conqueror to the
legislation of Edward I, English kings worked hard at preserving
the interests of the crown, and with it of the nation at large,
against the encroachments of individuals or classes whose potential
strength was kept in check only by the exercise of the royal prerogative in the hands of determined rulers. The death of Edward I
marked an epoch. His son was the worst king since the Conquest.
Richard I had been an absentee, John a man who made enemies
with undue ease, Henry III a near-mediocrity who never caught
up with the losses incurred in his minority. But Edward II was
vicious, unstable, and fatally given to favourites; also, he lacked
the warlike prowess which alone could control the incipient
phenomenon of bastard feudalism. In his reign, the killing of
Gaveston began the long series of political murders, the ambitions
of Thomas of Lancaster foreshadowed the future 'overmighty
subject', the Ordainers displayed the effective class opposition of
the baronage to the crown which was to end in the destruction of
Edward I's monarchy, the Dispensers and Mortimer introduced
the untamed passions and disorganised liberties of the Welsh
Marches into English politics which they were to dominate until
the accession of the Tudors, and Edward II's own deposition and
shameful death administered a profound shock to the concept of
kingship which his ancestors had represented.

In the rest of the fourteenth century things went from bad to worse. Edward III could maintain a pretence of strong kingship only by means of the wars which sidetracked turbulence but themselves gave the danger teeth when armed retainers were formed into small armies; moreover, his policy of lavish grants and generous patronage, while it saved the peace for a time, made sure that when trouble came the strength would not be on the king's side. It was unfortunate that Edward III lived too long and had too many children, that the Black Prince died before his father, that Richard II was a spoiled young man with high notions of his prerogative and little ability to support them. Such accidents shape history as much as the more majestic currents of economic forces or social changes. By endowing his family with the inheritance of the declining Norman nobility, by creating for them dukedoms and powers, Edward III called into being magnates related by blood to the king and ultimately intent on making their claim to the throne effective. The blood of Edward III ramified through too many veins; at the distance of two centuries it was still to prove fatal to the Pole family and the Courtenays in the reign of Henry VIII.

The weakness and arrogance of Richard II precipitated these latent troubles. The revolution of 1399 put on the throne a dynasty with a doubtful title and dependent on a party in the kingdom. In the reign of Henry IV the real power of the nobility came out in the influence of the great council of magnates whose virtual clients and spokesmen sat in the house of commons and gave to opposition that falsely modern air which led nineteenth-century historians to speak of the Lancastrian constitutional experiment. Henry V tried the old expedient of a French war; being himself an able soldier, and a strong man who could command violent men's loyalties, he had a measure of success, but he did nothing to solve the growing problems of the crown. His early death and Henry VI's long minority opened the flood gates. The magnates captured the king's permanent council, the very centre of the royal government; the wars went wrong, the house of Lancaster took the blame, and the house of York came forward to assert a claim which—according to the strict principles of inheritance—was slightly the better. And so the wars of the Roses followed upon the minority of Henry VI, to set the seal on the decay of royal power. The crown was a plaything of forces it did not control: when a great nobleman (of recent vintage) like the earl of Warwick disposed of the throne at his pleasure, English kingship had reached its nadir. For a time the house of York looked capable of restoring the position; that it failed was again due to a variety of largely personal reasons. Edward IV's character was one: his marriage to Elizabeth Woodville created the fatal divisions within his own party which led directly to the usurpation of Richard III and so to Henry Tudor's chance. More important, perhaps, was the accident of Edward's death before his heir was old enough to take over. The minority of Henry VI ruined Lancaster; that of Edward V ruined York. Finally, the Yorkist link with Burgundy and failure in European diplomacy preserved the life of the earl of Richmond, protected as he was by Brittany and France, and made possible the invasion of 1485.

Until then, the accession of Henry VII, the crown continued weak and uncertain, though both Yorkist kings had made quite a creditable start on restoring it to strength. The decline of English kingship in the fourteenth century ended in the wild murders and civil wars of the fifteenth, and no dynasty tied up with these excesses, and dependent for victory on its armed and rebellious followers, could hope to arrest the fatal movement. At the very time when the disruptive and anti-social forces inherent in the master-man relationship of bastard feudalism and nourished by war to extraordinary proportions were at their most dangerous, that part of the body politic which had both the interest and the potential power to control them was in decay. Government at the centre relinquished the reins, and the institutions of law and order fell under the sway of over-powerful individuals with armed men at their backs. The famous evils of the time were all the result of this. Livery (the equipping of armed retainers with their lord's uniform and badge to signify their sole allegiance), maintenance (the lord's support of his followers in courts of law; by force if necessary and irrespective of the merits of the case), embracery (the corruption or intimidation of juries)—these abuses undermined the whole system of law-enforcement and compelled men to resort to violence in order to fight violence. Not all retainers wielded the sword and buckler; others did as acceptable service by sitting on juries, acting as justices of the peace, or even as sheriffs, controlling commissions of enquiry and the like—all in the interest of the magnate to whose 'affinity' or following they belonged. The magnates did not destroy the system of law but perverted it to the service of injustice. Intimidation and chicanery supplanted impartiality and the king's peace.

These were the effects—in the last resort—of 150 years of war, and while they were very serious they were still restricted to those who had law suits to fight or happened to be involved in the faction struggles which spread from the centre outwards and alternatively from the shires inwards to the throne. A man might live a lifetime without coming in touch with these troubles, though he was very lucky if he did; nothing, however, could save him from the mysterious workings of the plague. The Black Death of 1349 was only the first, though also by far the most violent, of a recurring series of outbreaks; from the middle of the fourteenth century to about the middle of the seventeenth, bubonic plague was epidemic in England. As is the manner with the disease, its first onslaught proved the most killing; thereafter it occurred at gradually increasing intervals, withdrew from the countryside into the towns, and declined as a killer. But throughout the fourteenth and fifteenth centuries, men were dying from plague, and the mortality was sufficiently high to cause a permanent decline in population. This naturally had far-reaching economic effects. The increasing population of the thirteenth century had pressed hard on the available land, so that labour was cheap, lords found it easy to enforce the burdens of villeinage, and marginal land and waste were being broken up by the plough. In the fifteenth century the process was reversed. Much of the newly cultivated land was again given back to the wilderness; a land glut succeeded to the land hunger. Farming, with the market for produce declining, lost its attraction; lords preferred to let out their demesne lands rather than work them, but it was increasingly difficult to find tenants ready to enter upon the vacant holdings. Labour grew precious, and serfdom collapsed as lords found it impossible to enforce duties on men who could always escape elsewhere, for workmen were welcome and no one enquired too closely into antecedents. The payment of money wages—practised off and on for a long time—now became the rule, and the whole structure of rural society cracked. Lords who lived on rents from their lands lost contact both with the land and with the people; the old ties disappeared, and with them the basis of true feudalism—service in return for land, land granted in return for services.

Thus among the people who lived on and by the land—nine-tenths of the population—the long-term effects of the plague and the agricultural depression were to assist that change from feudalism to bastard feudalism which other factors in social and political life were producing. On the whole the upper classes suffered most; peasants and yeomen, exploiting their rarity value, could get land on very advantageous terms—easy rents, reduced fines on entry—and were emancipating themselves from legal bondage. During this period the foundations were being laid for many of the new fortunes of the next century; the great house of Russell rose from such humble villein origins. The lords, on the other hand, found their incomes decaying and their assets in land deteriorating, a fact which helps to explain their violent unrest, cut-throat competition, and lawless and ruthless fight for advantages. Long before the wars of the Roses reduced the numbers of the English aristocracy, the agricultural depression was at work sapping their strength and preparing their downfall. A new nobility grew up in the sixteenth century out of the gentry and merchants—or lesser men still—of the fifteenth: they had neither the same commitments nor the same expenses as their betters, and being better able to adjust themselves to the depression they survived more easily.

Trade, too, languished throughout most of the fifteenth century. It was a time when English merchants found their range contracting as the wars destroyed much of the important trade with France, and as the North German Hanse drove them from the Baltic and Iceland. The civil war completed the disaster both because trade always suffers worst from internecine disturbances, and because Edward IV only obtained the throne with the financial assistance of the Hanse who exacted valuable privileges in return. For a time, English merchants were at a disadvantage in their own country compared with the foreigner. The safe old stand-by, the export of wool, was stagnating in the hands of the Staplers of Calais who held a near-monopoly, while the trade in English cloth—mainly in the hands of the rising Merchant Adventurers of London—was still comparatively young and also more open to hazards. Wool was sold at Calais, that is in territory under English control; English cloth, on the other hand, had to fight competition in the markets of Flanders and Central Europe where English merchants were themselves foreigners and therefore at a disadvantage. England was in the awkward position of having relied on one main produce for her export trade; though she also sold tin, leather, hides, and some other goods, and though she imported wine and manufactures, it was on the sheep's backs that her prosperity grew. For that reason it was the more easily upset, and there is no need to look further than the war and the competition of foreign merchants for the cause of the slump which lasted till about 1475. It must be pointed out that the recovery began under Edward IV and was probably due to his restoration of peace; a country which produced the greater part of Europe's wool and exported it either raw or made up could not remain poor for long. But life was difficult at the best of times for the merchant with his overseas enterprises, and war made the risks of commerce impossibly great.

Henry VII thus succeeded to a much depleted inheritance. Just how depleted it was must now be discussed, if his achievement is to be seen in its true light. The country had been suffering from a gradually decreasing population for over a century, with all the depressing effects which such a development has on the spirit of a nation as well as, more obviously, on economic life. The despondent—one is tempted to say decadent—preoccupation with death indulged in by the fifteenth century, with the line 'Timor mortis conturbat me' running through many poems, is very different from the grim and often cynical interest in death displayed by the Elizabethans and Jacobeans. It mirrored a people who had found the medieval commonplace 'In media vita in morte sumus' only too true; they saw in recurrent plague the natural and inescapable punishment for sin, with the result that their spiritual needs found refuge in a rather spineless mysticism and resignation. One must be careful of generalising about the minds and morals of a whole people (even if there were barely three millions of them) and a whole century; there were many vigorous and crude characters about who paid no more regard to morbid fancies than their like in any generation. But it is hard to escape the conclusion that in the fifteenth century England displayed the characteristics of a stagnant and declining civilisation. The fundamental trouble was a spiritual malaise induced by plague and general uncertainty; among the more important symptoms were the disintegration of society, the violence of public life, the decay of law and order, and the weakness of the crown. But no one could cure the malaise—time and changing circumstances were miraculously to do that; it was to the symptoms that a ruler had to turn his attention.

There was, of course, nothing that anyone could then do about the epidemic disease which was undermining mental and physical resistance, but as it happened Henry VII came to the throne after the worst of it was over. Sporadic outbreaks were to recur until 1665: the Great Plague of London is so well remembered because it was the last fling of that particular plague cycle. But nothing like the disaster of the fourteenth-century Black Death, or the heavy mortality of the mid-fifteenth-century outbreak in London and other towns was to happen again. The decline in numbers was arrested and the nation recovering before the first Tudor won the crown. That it not to say that the problem was solved, but that the

Tudors found it at a stage when man-made solutions had a hope of succeeding.

However, it was on the effects of the wars that a strong king would have to start, and once peace was restored natural resilience could be trusted to look to the other matters. A poor and weak crown was confronted by wealthy and arrogant magnates: there lay the crux of the problem, as Edward IV, Richard III, and Henry VII after them, saw clearly enough.[1] The first cause of weakness at the top was the uncertainty of the succession; there was no hope of restoring an effective monarchy until the monarchs could feel reasonably safe on the throne. There had to be an end to dynastic war before any dynasty could set about rebuilding the kingdom. So much is obvious, and we shall see how Henry VII, and Henry VIII as well, were to deal with this question. Once firmly on the throne, what was to be the next step? Was it necessary to create a 'new monarchy', a name once fashionably bestowed on the Tudors, in order to produce an effective sort of kingship? That used to be the common view, and on the whole, with few exceptions, most books seem still to subscribe to it, only differing about the date of its inception and the name of its founder. Henry VII is to be displaced by Edward IV, incidentally a much more romantic figure; that one of them started something fresh—strong, energetic kingship with despotic leanings and practices (often deplorably enough graced with the quite meaningless title of a Renaissance kingship)—that is not doubted. This attitude is a relic of the view which saw in the fourteenth and fifteenth centuries a brave rehearsal of modern constitutionalism; if one believes that Edward III and Henry IV confronted parliaments like those faced by Charles I and James II, one must indeed speak of an incongruous period of despotism and the decline of parliament in the sixteenth century. But no one today seriously holds views on the 'Lancastrian Constitution' which make it necessary to speak of Yorkist or Tudor 'despotism'; those who have abandoned the first term should realise that the second has thereby become meaningless.

It is, thus, futile to argue whether Edward IV or Henry VII founded a monarchy new in that it displayed altogether new

[1] They did not need the teaching of the egregious Sir John Fortescue whose writings (recently at last described as 'overrated and misleading' by Mr K. B. Macfarlane) have for too long been allowed to usurp the credit for an analysis which statesmen could make for themselves. Historians, being literary craftsmen themselves, have a natural disposition to see undue importance in writers and writings. Few men of action ever learned their jobs or ideas from books.

tendencies of centralised control and royal power; there was nothing new in such attributes of kingship. We shall better understand what happened if we remember that the strong English monarchy had suffered first a decline and then a catastrophe in the waning middle ages, and that the task of the new dynasty essentially consisted in getting back to heights already reached 200 years earlier. Of course, the intervening centuries could not be wiped off the slate; in many ways Henry VII's monarchy differed from that of Edward I. But it was not essentially different: it fulfilled much the same ambitions and purpose with much the same instruments. The troubles of the fifteenth century had not destroyed the government of the country; they had merely overlaid it with an alluvial slime of individual lawlessness and general corruption. The weapons of the crown—the institutions through which the kings of England governed—had to be restored to their earlier effectiveness. The key to the problem was the personal action of the king and the ministers and agents who, surrounding him, formed the royal household. But if this is to be clear it will be necessary to give a very brief outline of English medieval government.

English government in the middle ages was truly the king's government. All action centred upon his person, and all action started from his court. The *curia regis* (king's court) of the Anglo-Norman kings contained the ministers, advisers, and servants on whom the king relied for the administration of revenue, the writing of letters and grants, the speaking of justice. But the king and his retinue were always moving about from place to place, while an ever more complicated machinery of government with its growing collections of archives and its need to be readily accessible to the king's subjects had to find some permanent residence. Thus departments began to specialise out of the *curia regis* and to acquire independent status: as the phrase goes, they 'went out of court'. The exchequer or financial department led the way in the middle of the twelfth century, to be followed by the courts of the common law (common pleas and king's bench) and the chancery in the course of the thirteenth. But this raised a new problem. A king who was very much the active ruler and administrator of his dominions now found himself often far from the instruments of his will. No document, for instance, was authentic unless issued under the great seal which was kept by the chancellor, but how was the king, writing perhaps from Chester or Carlisle, to convince a chancellor at Westminster of the genuineness of his instructions, especially since he himself could not write? The obvious answer was to evolve another seal—soon called the privy seal—with which all authorisations (warrants) sent to the chancery had to be sealed.

This process of duplication by which the royal household (as we call the king's retinue after the twelfth century) put out further institutions to supplement those which, having originally grown up in the same way, had already gone out of court and become departments of state, is the characteristic administrative development of the middle ages. The reason already mentioned— convenience and the king's uncertain movements—was reinforced from the thirteenth century onwards by the ambitions of the baronage to control the kingdom through control of the offices of state. When they succeeded in securing the appointment of chancellors, treasurers, and even keepers of the privy seal under their influence, the king could and did counter by developing such parts of his household as the wardrobe and chamber to do the work of departments of state. Henry III, for instance, employed his wardrobe in finance because the exchequer was in baronial hands, while Edward I greatly augmented its use because he found he could govern better through officials directly under his eye and entirely dependent upon him. The king remained the real ruler, in fact if he was capable, and in theory if he was not. Whatever departments might go out of court, there remained full power in the crown to create new instruments of government, and this power was naturally exercised through the king's immediate entourage, his household. Thus, the privy seal and later the signet came to take their place by the side of the great seal; the finances of the kingdom were often administered in wardrobe or chamber even when the official accounts were kept at the exchequer; the courts of common law were supplemented by the more elastic and adaptable jurisdiction of the king in his council, exercised either in ordinary council meetings, or (in the fourteenth century) when parliament met, or (in the fifteenth) by the chancellor who came to take over most of the council's judicial business.

Throughout the later middle ages, then, there were really two systems of administration, or—better—two layers to the royal administration, for both parts were very much the king's. Behind the obvious and manifest set of institutions which had left the retinue and become true departments of state there stood the royal household which not only did much independent work but actively inspired the official part of the administration. It was on these hidden springs that government really depended. The records of the offices of state show no decay or decline in the fifteenth century when the country was notoriously ill-governed or even ungoverned, but because the household did nothing government was in eclipse. As one would expect, the decline of the household went hand in hand with the decline of the crown; the king's increasing dependence on the power of his great nobles was displayed administratively in the gradual disappearance of that second layer of government from the reign of Henry IV onwards. Richard II had tried to set up a despotism through his signet and his chamber; naturally, the reaction against him stressed the need for the crown to work through those public seals and departments over which the magnates could exercise a measure of control. They came near to perfecting that control when during Henry VI's minority they captured the king's perpetual council, ordinarily a body of advisers chosen by the king and entirely his servants. But the household potential in government was not destroyed; it was only left to rust. The official parts of the machinery were in perfect working order even when they either did no effective work, or (like the exchequer) badly needed reconstructing to cope with new conditions, or (like the courts of law) needed supplementing with something less rigid if justice was to be done. Yet the motive power contained in the king's household—dormant not dead—only needed reviving. A new vigour of spirit was urgently necessary, but there was no call for a new kind of king or a new machinery of government.

This outline sketch has omitted two points—parliament, and the so-called franchises. We shall have more to say about parliament in the course of this book; here it will be enough to note that until the Tudor period parliament did not form a regular part of the government of the country. It met at the king's discretion and for his purposes. Its very composition was still in doubt. The clear distinction which the books make between great councils (of nobles, with no representatives from shires and boroughs) and parliaments proper does not appear to have been fully grasped even as late as the reign of Henry VII. The essence of parliament was the king and his council—his professional council, reinforced by such hereditary councillors (barons) as he chose to call, and if he liked by the commons. In practice, the commons were ordinarily necessary to make a parliament, and by the fifteenth century they had acquired sufficient corporateness to form a 'house'; the lords, on the other hand, were still simply a great council and not a 'house' of parliament. Edward III's wars and consequent need for money had promoted parliament to precocious importance; the weakness of the Lancastrian title and the magnates' influence in the great council and, through their clients, in the commons had continued its spuriously 'modern' activity. The need for taxation by parliamentary consent, in any case demanded by the practical problem of collection, was coming to be recognised, and by the late fifteenth century it was generally accepted that statutes enacted in parliament were laws of special authority. But these were vague gropings still. The old view which saw in the Tudor period an interruption to the natural growth of representative institutions in England is simply untenable, and most scholars now agree that parliament entered upon its proper career in the sixteenth century. Building upon medieval foundations but erecting something quite new on them, the Tudors and their ministers produced the composite sovereign body of the king in parliament which has ever since been the supreme authority in England.

Henry VII did not, then, take over a country without administrative institutions or the means of government; nor did he perhaps succeed to a parliamentary state which had broken down and needed rebuilding by despotism. He was faced with a machine which had been allowed to stop, though its components were sound, and these components consisted of departments of state in working order and departments of the royal household (including the council) which it needed only a strong king to revive. Only one problem could not be solved by mere restoration or revival, and that was the problem of franchises and feudal courts. All that has been said so far applies to the king's government only, but it was one of the leading medieval characteristics that the king's government did not cover everything. The state—for the king is only the embodiment of the state—had not yet entered upon its career of exclusive and all-embracing power; there were bodies and areas within the kingdom over which the king's control was limited or even nil. Some of these bodies with special rights were vexatious without being really objectionable, such as the municipal gilds whose regulations represented an obstacle to trade and industry, but an obstacle which the flood was certainly getting over and around. There was, however, nothing but trouble in the noble franchises—the special rights and immunities enjoyed by certain of the crown's subjects. There were palatinates like Durham and Lancaster, liberties like Ripon and Richmond, and plenty of smaller individual privileges and exemptions claimed by noblemen and knights, all of which limited the power of the crown. They involved rights to hold courts and rights to escape from the royal jurisdiction which made it very difficult to discipline the turbulent element. The biggest franchise of all was that of the Church, with its own system of courts, its rights of benefit of clergy which meant in effect that anyone in orders had his first crime free, its powers of granting sanctuary and staying the king's writ. The Church, subject to the international monarchy of the pope at Rome, formed a state within the state; how that problem came to a head in the reign of Henry VIII shall be shown later. In the reign of Henry VII the Church was loyal to the crown, the king a good son of the Church, and no problem arose.

The real trouble, then, were the franchises of the nobility. The early palatinates, Durham and Chester, had not mattered because Durham was episcopal (and bishops were chosen with the king's approval) and Chester soon fell to the crown. The same applied to the large franchise of Lancaster, united with the crown from 1399 when Henry of Lancaster became king. But there were many small franchises, and there were in particular the rights, privileges, and claims of the marcher lords. The powers of frontier nobles are always rather special; in this case, many of them also held lands and rights in Wales which had its own customs and was barely amenable to royal control at any time in the middle ages. The problem was complicated by the typical respect for property, or even mere possession, which the common law of the middle ages imposed upon the English mind until the early twentieth century. It was a principle of the law that no franchise was valid except by grant of the crown, but the reverse of this was that a franchise proven to be by grant of the crown was virtually indefeasible. In practice, it was very difficult to deal with a recalcitrant franchise holder who could prove crown grant. Edward I instituted proceedings known as *quo warranto*—by what warrant do you claim?—to enquire into the origins of rights asserted by his subjects; but the weaker kings who succeeded him could not hope to exercise such a measure of supervision. In the fifteenth century the decay of the crown and the disturbed state of the country produced, in practice, a vast increase in the independence and obstinacy of those claiming to hold franchises. The whole question of the medieval franchise was blown wide open by the abuses of the fifteenth century; ultimately there could be no solution except for the crown to assert the exclusive and general competence of the state. Though something may have been lost in variety and local independence, the gain in law-abiding orderliness and national unity produced by the centralising policy was enormous. It is easy to be romantic at this distance; the men of the sixteenth century who remembered the disturbed time, or remembered their fathers telling them about it, knew well enough why they allowed the Tudor kings to ride fairly roughshod over the petty kingdoms in the marches in the north and west, in Wales and Ireland.

These were the problems; what of the man who in 1485 took over the task of solving them? In many ways, Henry VII was eminently fitted for the job. Born in 1457, he was only twenty-eight when he came to the throne, and only fifty-two when he died in 1509; yet one never thinks of him as a young man. The common picture of him was painted by Francis Bacon in one of the great biographies in the language, and though Bacon wrote the book in a few weeks and without access to any material not now available his book has survived—perhaps too easily. Henry was undoubtedly shrewd, calculating, and long-headed; he seems never to have been overcome by passion. Yet if he had even a touch of the temper so noticeable in his descendants, this exercise of self-restraint must have cost him a great deal. Probably the hard training of a youth spent in wars, danger of execution, and long exile tamed the Tudor propensity to violence and taught the young earl of Richmond to hide his feelings and veil his purposes. That he was eager for money is certain; so, for that matter, were all the Tudors. He was not, however, a miser; where it served his purpose money was spent freely, and he saved and extorted only in the interests of a crown whose solvency was the basis of sound government and peace in the country. Some of the austerity which hangs about him may have been due to the school of exile; more, one suspects, came from the influence of that formidable old lady, his mother Margaret Beaufort, who ruled his court with a rod of iron.

Exile and his own patient nature seem to have taught Henry VII the most important lesson of all. If England was to recover order and the throne stability, the civil wars would have to be ended once and for all. That meant not only the cessation of hostilities, but the healing of wounds left by them, the assuaging of tempers heated by the long controversy. Perhaps the most important quality now required in a king, next to inflexible resolution, was judicious mercy, the mercy of head not heart. Henry VII was to display both resolution and clemency. It was remarked how hard the king was to persuade of conspiracies against him; no doubt the graduate of exile and conspiracies knew just how futile most of such enterprises were. But his reluctance to proceed to extremes and his readiness to accept old enemies into the fold display his determination to show that the wars were over. It is difficult to think that there was anything fundamentally kind-hearted about Henry VII, though he had a sly sardonic humour which both contemporaries and later historians have sometimes mistaken for spite. Perhaps we do him an injustice. If, as his honest partisans grumbled, he refused to listen to information and charged accusers with ill will and malice, it was not that he would not see the obvious but rather that he rated the danger at its true value and preferred to overlook any doings, however hostile, that did not constitute a present danger. Henry VII's famous mercy was the calculated product of statesmanlike common sense, and none the less creditable for that.

But—merciful, slow to wrath, hard-headed, and unemotional though he was—there was nothing at all of the procrastinator about this king. He proved himself a man of action and a soldier before he was twenty-eight, a fact which is commonly forgotten; if he refused to fight thereafter it was because he knew better than most that the need for peace overrode all other considerations. To the establishment of this peace, the preservation of law and order, the security of the realm, the creation of conditions in which men could follow their avocations in safety and with thought for the future, he applied all his high intelligence and tenacity of will, his shrewdness and his steady and daily interest in affairs. Like all his family he had an uncanny gift for picking men to serve him, and not even the great Elizabeth surrounded herself with a brighter galaxy of first-rate ministers than did her grandfather. Cardinal Morton, Bishop Fox, William Warham, Sir Reginald Bray, Sir Thomas Lovell, Sir John Heron, Sir Edward Belknap, Richard Empson, and Edmund Dudley—and others, many of whom are only now being painfully resuscitated by a process of historical exhumation—all these men were loyal and ardent servants of an exacting but worthy master. Much of what we have been accustomed to call the work of Henry VII probably sprang from the brains of these men, but the king himself was the active head of government, and in the last resort the recovery made must stand to his credit. The task was indeed formidable, but the intelligence, stubbornness, and sound sense assembled to deal with it were more formidable still.

Chapter II

HENRY VII: SECURING THE DYNASTY

1. HENRY'S CLAIM TO THE CROWN

WHEN victory was won at Bosworth, Lord Stanley, whose timely desertion of Richard III had made Henry's triumph possible, picked up the crown and put it on the victor's head; according to the chronicler, people rejoiced and clapped their hands and cried, 'King Henry, King Henry'. But while this acclamation must have been pleasant to his ears, it did not make the gold circlet sit any more securely on his head. Henry VII's first task was to convince the country and the world that he really was king. Though he could feel the task somewhat eased as his journey to London assumed the proportions of a triumph, there was probably no need to remind him of men's fickleness. The city of London, in particular, had distinguished itself by the readiness with which it had hailed each successive conqueror of the crown.

Henry's own claim to the crown was far from straightforward. Fifteenth-century England knew no proper law of succession. The judges had repeatedly declared that the common law did not extend to such exalted matters; they had, in fact, been too scared of the consequences to attempt a definition in the middle of the dynastic struggles. Henry IV, in 1399, had put forward a claim compounded of the (false) assertion that he represented the true line of succession, the proof of divine favour contained in his actual victory, and the duty of removing a lawless monarch like Richard II. There were points here which Henry VII might profitably remember. Richard, duke of York, in 1450, and his son Edward IV after him, opposed an out-and-out theory of legitimacy to the claims which the oath of allegiance gave to Henry VI, the king in possession. Legitimacy—the doctrine that the crown can descend only to one man at any given time and that this succession is determined by primogeniture—was the centre of the Yorkist position; being descended from John of Gaunt's elder brother, they found in it a useful weapon against Gaunt's issue. Richard III exploited it further when he took the crown by the simple step of declaring his nephews bastardised; this left him as the only legitimate heir of the only legitimate line. There was then in existence a general idea that the succession should pass to the eldest son, but the strict theory of legitimacy was still the property of a party, and the Lancastrians had never subscribed to it.

The theory was of no use at all to Henry VII. He claimed to represent the line of Lancaster; his mother Margaret was the last of the Beauforts, John of Gaunt's illegitimate descendants who had been legitimised by the pope and by Richard II. However, an insertion, itself of doubtful validity, in Henry IV's confirmation of his predecessor's grant had denied them the right to succeed to the crown. On the male side, Henry had no royal ancestry; if direct descent from Edward III was to be decisive, the young earl of Warwick, son of the late duke of Clarence, had undoubtedly the best claim. Legitimacy was thus valueless to the Tudor king. Nor did he intend to base his right on the much-mooted marriage to Elizabeth, daughter of Edward IV: it might be useful in appeasing the Yorkist faction, but Henry meant to be king in his own right. He therefore deliberately postponed the marriage until he had established himself on the throne. In actual fact, he adopted the simplest solution of all: he said that he was king. In November 1485 he told his first parliament that he had come to the crown by inheritance (leaving the details studiously vague) and by the proof of God's will expressed in his victory: his right was, in his own view, divine to this extent that divine approval had clearly been given on the field of battle. This Tudor kind of divine right is the exact opposite to the Stuart brand. The Tudors appealed to fact—God spoke through the arbitrament of war. The Stuarts believed in an indefeasible right which no amount of adverse circumstances could lessen or destroy.

Thus Henry certainly thought and acted as king of England as soon as Richard III was dead. Indeed, he arbitrarily fixed the beginning of his reign as the day before Bosworth, but this was only a typical piece of sharp practice designed to enable him to deal with Richard's supporters on that day as traitors to himself. There was no question of parliament conferring or even confirming his title. The very fact that the body which met in November 1485 counts as a real parliament is proof enough; only a true king can summon a true parliament, and the writs of summons went out early in September. Henry VII merely followed a precedent set in 1406 by Henry IV who had the succession after him registered in parliament, and he did it for the same reason—to avoid all ambiguity and pave the way for a stable continuance of his dynasty. It was 'ordained, established, and enacted' by the parliament, not that Henry was king, but that the inheritance of the crown of England, with every right and possession belonging to it, should remain and abide with 'our now sovereign lord king Henry' and his heirs. The act thus recognised that Henry was king, and that therefore rightly the succession must pass to his line; its purpose, like that of many Tudor acts, was to put a matter beyond doubt by putting it on record. It served the ends of propaganda the importance of which all the Tudors understood very well.

These were matters of theory, but of legal theory and therefore important. The care with which Henry made sure that his title should not rest on parliament, nor, on the other hand, be too thoroughly investigated, shows that he knew the value of theory. But practical considerations mattered even more. Henry might allege his claim to be beyond cavil, but there were others who would dispute this hotly. It was therefore only sound policy to make sure of all who could possibly raise a rival claim. Richard III had happily died without direct heirs and had—despite doubts, the point remains probable—eased Henry's way further by putting Edward IV's sons out of the way. There remained the daughters of Edward IV and the son of Clarence, the ten-year-old earl of Warwick. Henry dealt with the former by marrying Elizabeth, the eldest of them, in January 1486, and with the latter by securing his body in the Tower. The unfortunate boy was to live out his life there till the conspiracies of others of which he had neither knowledge nor part brought him to the block. There remained the claim of John de la Pole, earl of Lincoln, nephew of Edward IV and nominated as his successor by Richard III, but for the present he submitted to Henry. The marriage with Elizabeth of York also helped to keep quiet that section of Yorkists that had joined Henry against Richard III's usurpation and had made his victory possible; ultimately, in producing heirs to the claims of both Lancaster and York, it brought about that 'Union of the Two Noble and Illustrious Families' which the Tudor historian Edward Hall took for the subject of his discourse. For the moment, however, there remained many dissatisfied with the new king and many more to whom violent ups and downs in public life, with the chances they offered to the enterprising and unscrupulous, had become the normal state of things. Not until 1500 could the Spanish ambassador de Puebla report that no doubtful royal blood remained to unsettle the Tudor claim, and even a year or two later some royal officials at Calais, discussing politics and the king's illness, foresaw further dynastic difficulties. The reign was never quite free from the fact or threat of conspiracy, and for several years Henry VII had to defend his throne against the kind of enterprise which had secured it to him in the first place.

2. CONSPIRACIES

One of the purposes for which the parliament of November 1485 assembled was to dispose of the king's late adversaries. The usual crop of attainders[1] ruined a number of leading Yorkist supporters; so far, Henry VII showed no special mercy or any intention to end the wars by composing the feuds. There was, in any case, another good reason behind these acts which deprived some of the richest men in the kingdom of their property. The great act of resumption of the same year declared void all crown grants made since the death of Henry VI and recovered for Henry VII a vast deal of land; clearly, the king was from the first determined to improve his finances. In the true spirit of the civil wars, each stage of which had been signalled by the attainder of the defeated and the reversal of attainders previously inflicted on the victors, the parliament marked a Tudor, or even a Lancastrian, triumph. For the time being the Yorkists—even those who, hating Richard as a usurper, had supported Henry's bid for the crown—were left rather in the cold; the long overdue marriage to Elizabeth of York, so often promised, came none too soon to prevent the complete alienation of moderate Yorkist sentiment.

Moreover, there were still the extremists. In March 1486, having married his queen and seeing the south at peace, Henry travelled north into the Yorkist stronghold of Yorkshire, to show his face and overcome opposition. At Lincoln he heard that Francis, Lord Lovell, Richard III's friend and chamberlain, had broken sanctuary at Colchester, together with Humphrey and Thomas Stafford, and had fled to unknown parts. As the king continued into Yorkshire, news came in of armed bands raised by the fugitives and of threatened risings in Henry's path. But nothing happened. York, which recently had recorded an official lament at Richard III's overthrow, received his conqueror with pageantry and pomp; a local conspiracy was promptly scotched, and Lovell's forces melted away before the promise of a pardon. Lovell fled abroad; the Staffords, who had failed to raise the west country against the king, were dragged from sanctuary and taken to the Tower. The question arose whether they ought to escape justice because the Church's right of sanctuary had been violated. In his natural desire to prevent an acquittal, Henry tried to get the judges' opinion before the case came to trial, but since they were

---

[1] Attainders were acts of parliament registering somebody's conviction for treason and declaring all his property forfeit to the king and his blood 'corrupted'; only in 1539 did they come to be used in lieu of trials.

reluctant to commit themselves in advance he had to be content
with requesting a rapid decision. In the end the court of king's
bench decided that sanctuary was a common-law matter in which
the pope could not interfere—certainly a striking instance of the
growing spirit of resistance to ecclesiastical pretensions—and that
the privilege did not cover treasonable offences. Humphrey
Stafford was executed, though Thomas benefited from Henry
VII's awakening mercifulness. The rising itself was utterly insignificant, but the case deserves attention because it illustrates the
Tudor principle of relying on the decisions of common-law judges,
the Tudor readiness to respect the judges' independence, and the
Tudor disregard for ancient franchises and immunities.

In September 1486, Henry's heart was gladdened by the birth
of a son—Arthur (the revival of the ancient British name was
meant to be significant)—who seemed to make the dynasty secure.
The king himself was not yet thirty; there seemed no question that
he would live long enough to see his heir of age. However, just at
this juncture the first of the serious conspiracies of the reign came
into the open. The country was much unsettled by rumours: many
believed that the princes in the Tower were still alive and had
perhaps managed to escape, or that the earl of Warwick, the true
Yorkist claimant if Richard III had really disposed of Edward IV's
sons, was again at large. There was plenty of credulity, plenty of
Yorkist sentiment, and plenty of plain superstition for a skilful
man to exploit. An Oxford priest of no birth but some brains,
Richard Symonds, was the first to realise this. He planned to pass
off a pupil of his, a harmless gentle boy called Lambert Simnel, as
Richard of York, the younger of Edward's sons; soon after, when
it was rumoured that Warwick had died in the Tower, Simnel's
impersonation was changed to Warwick on the grounds that the
government would not be able to disprove the fraud by exhibiting
the real earl. The very fact that such a wildcat scheme could spring
from an obscure priest's brain—and that it came within measur-
able distance of success—indicates the state of the country and the
size of Henry's problem. Symonds found favour with the leaders
of the Yorkist party—Margaret, the dowager duchess of Burgundy,
sister of Edward IV and the centre of all the plots against
the Tudors, and the exiled Lord Lovell who had taken refuge
with her. John de la Pole, earl of Lincoln, Richard III's
successor-designate whom Henry VII had treated with kindness,
repaid the king by fleeing to join the rebels who had raised the
White Rose in Ireland. That country had always nursed Yorkist
sympathies, and its most powerful noble, the earl of Kildare,

welcomed any opportunity to throw off English control.
Thus Henry was suddenly faced with a major threat, all the
more dangerous in that it centred upon Ireland where he could
not touch it. Subsidiary moves in Lancashire and Cornwall could
be disregarded, but the menace from across the Irish channel
demanded immediate action. In vain the real Warwick was paraded
through London; in May 1487, the false Warwick was proclaimed
Edward VI in Dublin, and all Ireland except the city of Waterford
went over to him. His power rested on Kildare, the Yorkist
leaders Lincoln and Lovell, and 2,000 German mercenaries contributed by Margaret of Burgundy. In June they landed in
Lancashire and began their march on London. The familiar story
of the Wars of the Roses seemed about to re-open. However, the
country showed how tired it was of it all: even Yorkshire gave
little support to the White Rose, and the rest of the country
remained loyal to Henry. It is probable, also, that the inclusion in
Lincoln's army of many wild Irishmen served to lose him much
support. The decision came at Stoke, on 16 June 1487, where all
the Yorkist leaders were killed, or disappeared never to be heard
of again; Symonds and Simnel fell into the king's hands. Henry
proved merciful in a politic manner; his treatment of Simnel,
taken into the royal household where he made a career from scullion
to falconer, bore an air of sardonic but not unkindly humour.
Symonds was confined for life; there was no general proscription
or holocaust of executions such as was to disgrace later Tudor
victories, though a number of Simnel's followers paid for their
treason in sizeable fines. One of the victims of the affair, for
reasons which have remained obscure, was Henry's mother-in-
law, the foolish and meddling Elizabeth Woodville; she ended her
days in a convent. Throughout it is clear that Henry tried to play
down the whole business, an endeavour in which he succeeded.

Before the next serious threat to Henry's throne arose, England
became involved in a war with France. The full story is extremely
complicated, and almost equally immaterial. But its main lines are
important, for they indicate both Henry's VII's aims in foreign
affairs and the European diplomatic situation which was to
determine England's attitude to the continent until the fall of
Wolsey in 1529. In the last twenty years of the fifteenth century
Western Europe assumed a new aspect. France, consolidated by
Louis XI (who died in 1483), and Spain, created by the personal
union of Ferdinand of Aragon and Isabella of Castile (1469), took
over the leadership of affairs, and their quarrels form the story of
European diplomacy to which the machinations of Maximilian.

king of the Romans, of Italian princes including the pope, and of
the kings of England are quite subsidiary. Henry VII's immediate
attitude in 1487 was decided by several factors. The traditional
hostility to France was far from dead; indeed, it was kept alive
by the king's retention of a claim to the French throne which
feeling in the country would not have allowed him to surrender
even if he had felt so inclined. More materially, England's continued possession of Calais provided both a gateway into France
and a permanent irritant to relations between the two countries.
Furthermore, Henry earnestly wished to secure visible recognition
for his dynasty from some European power, and common interests,
mostly commercial, suggested the rising power of Spain. In 1488-9
he negotiated a treaty of marriage between his son Arthur and
Catherine, the younger daughter of Ferdinand and Isabella. In
return, Spain—who had ambitions for two French provinces in
the Pyrenees—secured a promise of English help against France.
The occasion of the quarrel was provided by the affairs of Brittany.
That duchy alone had escaped the centralising activities of Louis
XI, but his daughter (Anne of Beaujeu) and later his son (Charles
VIII) were determined to remedy the omission. Though the
French won a great victory in 1488 they lost its gains when the
duke of Brittany died soon after, to be succeeded by his daughter
Anne, aged twelve. Anne of Brittany was an important heiress
whose hand was worth fighting for; Spain saw a chance of embarrassing France, and Anne of Beaujeu a chance of asserting French
control of the duchy by claiming the wardship of the young
duchess; the war revived.

England's part was decided for her by the danger of letting the
Breton ports fall into French hands, by the fact that English
volunteers had been killed in hundreds in the previous Breton
defeat, and by Spanish pressure. In 1489 Henry prepared for war.
With some difficulty he obtained a parliamentary grant of £100,000,
only part of which was ever paid; its collection led to a major riot
in the north in which the king's lieutenant, the earl of Northumberland, was killed. The garrison at Calais was reinforced. The
treaty of Medina del Campo with Spain, in March 1489, bound
England to the war. Henry gained big trading concessions, but
Spain had much the best of the political bargain: either side could
withdraw when it had achieved its ends, but since Spain wanted
only the Pyrenean provinces while England spoke of recovering
Henry V's conquests, it is plain where the advantage lay. However,
Henry got what he wanted—trade on favoured terms and the
betrothal of Arthur and Catherine; as events were to show, he had

no intention of wasting blood or treasure over the affairs of Brittany or Spain. He fulfilled the terms of the treaty and assisted his other ally, Maximilian, in his struggle with Flemish rebels. Otherwise neither he nor anyone else made any move until in 1490 Maximilian suddenly married Anne of Brittany. Henry occupied 1491 in extracting money from his country by benevolences, that is, by forced gifts described as voluntary, a method declared illegal in 1484; but no one resisted Charles VIII when, stung to action by Anne's marriage, he proceeded gradually to conquer Brittany and in the end himself married Anne after she had secured the necessary dispensation from her non-consummated previous marriage.

The situation was now handsomely confused. Spain showed no intention of supporting her ally; not for the last time did kings of England regret an alliance with Ferdinand of Aragon. Brittany was irrevocably French, and the vast English ambitions for the recovery of Henry V's conquests were merely ridiculous. It need not be thought that the king shared them. But he could not afford to associate the Tudors with the surrender of claims so tenaciously held by Lancaster and York, nor did he wish to write off the considerable loans he had made to Brittany earlier in the war. He therefore spent 1492 in making demonstrations designed to impress France with the gravity of the English threat. He even crossed the channel in person and took an army to besiege Boulogne, an action which came to be considered the *sine qua non* of Tudor generalship in Northern France. Charles VIII had no reason for continuing the war, the more so as his restless ambition was turning to thoughts of Italy. Thus in December 1492 the two powers signed the treaty of Etaples by which Henry agreed to hold his claim to France in abeyance and received in return a sum which he could and did call a tribute, as well as repayment of the Breton debts. At relatively small expense he had obtained an honourable peace and a sizeable pension to compensate him for his outlay. He had thrown over Spain—but Ferdinand and Isabella had themselves been contemplating a separate peace, so that Henry had merely beaten them at their own game. His other ally, Maximilian, also felt himself deserted, but his own conduct had been extremely shifty, and no one ever at any time had any scruples in neglecting Maximilian. The war had demonstrated that England was once again a power to be reckoned with and entitled to play a part in European diplomacy. It had led to the official recognition of the Tudor dynasty by France and Spain, with both of whom Henry had concluded treaties. The king could feel that he had manoeuvred well in his first essay in this tricky game.

The treaty of Etaples came not a minute too soon, for Henry had to turn his attention to the most serious threat he was to face in his whole reign. In the year 1491, a young man of seventeen, servant to a Breton merchant, was walking up and down the streets of Cork, displaying on his person the silk clothes in which his master traded. His bearing and splendour made a great impression on the rather backward townsfolk, unsettled as they already were by tales of Plantagenet princes escaping hither and thither. They told the young man that he was the earl of Warwick, and when he denied this they obligingly changed him into a bastard of Richard III. He continued his denials, but they only turned him into Richard, duke of York, the younger son of Edward IV. Worn out by their importunity he agreed. This at least was the tale which the pretender later told in his confession which is now accepted as largely true, though it may still appear doubtful whether a man who for eight years pertinaciously maintained his identity as Richard of York really came by the imposture in so casual a manner. His real name was Perkin Warbeck—his parents were still alive in Tournai in 1497—and he had been travelling in the service of various merchants since he was eleven. The supposed miracle of his knowing the details which convinced others of his Plantagenet descent has been made too much of: it does not appear that he ever convinced anyone except people eager to use him against Henry VII. This also goes for his supposed aunt, Margaret of Burgundy, who was perfectly capable of taking up a pretender and swearing to his identity once she felt sure that no genuine Yorkist claimants survived at liberty. That she later coached him in his part is likely.

Warbeck's career as Richard of York was crowded and various; the story has been told often and at sufficient length, and only its salient points need concern us here. His appearance which had so impressed the Irish at Cork is known from a good drawing: his charm and intelligence cannot disguise a blatant weakness. Everything he undertook by himself ended in dismal failure; anyone less like the brutal and efficient Yorkist strain it is hard to imagine. It seems that of all the men who had to do with him only Henry VII, who treated him with weary contempt and almost offensive leniency, judged him fairly; others were too blinded by his usefulness to take his just measure. In consequence he served as the peg on which hung the events of eight disturbed years.

After the Irish lords had approved of him in their rough Irish fashion which counted not the truth when trouble could be stirred up against England, Warbeck's first protector was Charles

VIII of France, then at war with Henry VII. The treaty of
Etaples put a stop to this, and in 1493 Warbeck passed into
Burgundy, there to find favour with the dowager duchess Margaret and gather round him the Yorkist exiles and their hopes.
The support he received annoyed Henry VII to the point of
breaking off all trade with the Low Countries, a boycott which hit
the Flemish cloth industry very hard, dependent as it was on
English wool and unfinished cloth. However, the embargo was
naturally also unpopular with English merchants and could not
be prolonged unduly; it was lifted after two years though it had not
achieved the end for which it was imposed. Warbeck had sought
and found a better protector than Margaret; late in 1493 he was
at Vienna, winning over the unstable and foolish Maximilian who
saw a chance of paying Henry VII out for his alleged treachery in
the treaty of Etaples. Maximilian went so far as to recognise
Warbeck as Richard IV, the rightful king of England, and to
promise him full support in the recovery of the crown. In return,
Warbeck signed a document in January 1495 which made Maximilian his heir, so that—should Warbeck die in the attempt to win
the throne of England—the king of the Romans would succeed
to the full Yorkist claim. Maximilian was himself good at making
worthless promises, but one feels that on this occasion he had met
his match. However, the mere fact that the pretender found all
this support was significant. Maximilian and his son, the Archduke
Philip, ruler of the Netherlands, made the Low Countries the
centre of Warbeck's conspiracy to which many flocked even from
England in hopes of a Yorkist revival. By this time Warbeck knew
his part to perfection, and it is not surprising that he imposed on
those eager partisans of the White Rose.

More dangerous still was the fact that the conspiracy had developed a branch in England—indeed, in the very court itself. One
of those who had gone to Flanders to join Richard IV was Sir
Robert Clifford who, however, had second thoughts on arrival—
unless, as is possible, he was secretly in the service of Henry VII.
At any rate, in December 1494 he officially made his peace with
the king, received a pardon and reward, and returned to lay
detailed information against the heads of disaffection in England.
Probably Henry had had his eye on the men involved for some
time, and Clifford's testimony only served to clinch matters. A
number of lesser men, led by Lord Fitzwalter, died on block and
gallows, their property being subsequently confiscated and their
blood attainted in the parliament of 1495. One man fell with a
crash: Clifford accused Sir William Stanley, lord chamberlain of

the household and the man who had made the victory at Bosworth possible, of complicity in the plot. Nothing is known about the whole affair, but from the testimony of contemporaries we know that Henry VII was not easily persuaded of anyone's treasonable activity. It therefore seems likely that Stanley had aroused suspicion long before Clifford denounced him. After all, the Stanleys had changed sides in 1485 only after much hesitation; it is possible that Sir William did not think even a chamberlain's staff sufficient reward for his services.

The arrests and executions broke the conspiracy in England and made Warbeck's projected invasion hopeless. Nevertheless, it was attempted. In July 1495 he appeared off Deal and landed gradually the better part of his forces; he himself remained prudently on board ship. The royal officers were ready: the men who had landed were killed or taken, and the affair collapsed in ridicule as Warbeck sailed rapidly off to Ireland. Here he failed to take the loyal town of Waterford in an eleven days' siege and decided to try Scotland. King James IV had come to the throne as the head of the party bitterly hostile to England, after his mildly Anglophil father had been murdered. He was therefore more than ready to receive the pretender and offer him assistance. But this business too came to nothing. In January 1496 a Scottish force crossed the border and burnt and looted savagely—distressing Warbeck not a little, it must be added, much to the amazement of both Scots and English. They then withdrew again. Border raids were one thing; an expedition to put Richard IV on the throne of England was quite another. Henry VII was the less inclined to take serious countermeasures because his natural dislike of war was being encouraged by Spain who wanted his alliance against France (then too successful in Italy) and therefore tried to arrange peace between England and Scotland. Moreover, the heavy war taxation led to a really serious rising in Cornwall. The Cornishmen had no interest in Warbeck; what they wanted was relief from exactions demanded by affairs on the far northern border which they did not consider concerned them. They therefore rose in 1497, under the leadership of the blacksmith Joseph and the lawyer Flamank, to march to London and state their case. They were peaceable enough at first but killed a tax-collector at Taunton, probably thinking little of so obvious a deed. Then, led by Lord Audley, an impoverished peer, they marched right across England, for with the king's forces tied up on the border there was no one to oppose them. In June 1497 they sat down at Blackheath, but instead of being overawed—Henry never parleyed with rebels under arms—

the king proceeded to surround and attack them. Two thousand died on the day; of the survivors only the leaders were hanged. All this, however, did not make the problem of Perkin Warbeck easier for Henry.

In actual fact Perkin left Scotland, where he was kept as a potential but unused asset, in July 1497, hoping to try his luck once more in Ireland. But things had changed there; Kildare was, for the moment, loyal; and Warbeck thought it better to follow an invitation from Cornwall where the king's clemency had by some been misinterpreted as weakness. Opposed by the new lord chamberlain, Giles Lord Daubeney, Perkin once again lost heart; at Taunton he stole away at midnight with some sixty leading followers, leaving his forces unofficered. Though he reached sanctuary at Beaulieu monastery, he was persuaded to throw himself on Henry's mercy, and so in August 1497 the king at last had the troublesome adventurer in his hands. It was now that the famous confession appeared, telling of Warbeck's true identity and early life; but there is sound proof that Henry knew all these details as early as 1493, and corroborative evidence exists to establish the truth of the confession. Warbeck was kept at court in honourable custody; once again Henry VII refused to make martyrs. In 1498, however, he tried to escape and on his recapture suffered a harsher confinement. Finally, he made another attempt in November 1499, as is supposed with the king's connivance, for now the government hoped to get at the real Yorkist, the earl of Warwick, through the pretended one. Warwick seems to have been quite innocent of any attempt against Henry VII, but for some reason of which we are ignorant the government had decided that his very existence constituted a danger. Indeed, the career of Perkin Warbeck, and that of Lambert Simnel before him, gave grounds for such a belief, and it may be that diplomatic difficulties —the insistence of Spain on a safe Tudor title before they would let Catherine of Aragon go to England—forced Henry's hand. At any rate, the government produced some sort of evidence of a conspiracy; Warbeck was hanged and Warwick beheaded; and the Tudor could sleep more easily. There is nothing to be said in extenuation of such judicial murders of which the reign of Henry VIII was to produce many more, except that those who saw a danger in so perfectly innocent a man as Edward of Warwick were far from wrong. It was not what he did or thought but what he stood for in other men's minds that brought him to his death. For Warbeck one may feel sorry, but he had certainly earned his fate several times over.

3. IRELAND AND SCOTLAND

The stories of Lambert Simnel and Perkin Warbeck have served to underline an important truth: there was danger for the English crown within the British isles themselves. Ireland and Scotland were both trouble spots. The Norman conquest of Ireland in the twelfth century had imposed upon the native Celtic population a feudal ruling class, but though the kings of England might claim to be lords of Ireland they never, in fact, effectively ruled much of it. The so-called English Pale—a strip of coast stretching some 50 miles northwards from Dublin—was the real limit of English influence, though the few towns in the south, especially Waterford and Cork, also provided precarious centres of civilisation in a country not far removed from tribal barbarism. The Irish nobility, Anglo-Norman in origin, had long since suffered the common fate of English settlers in Ireland and become as Irish as the Irish, so that there was little to choose, from the king's point of view, between Anglo-Irish families like the Geraldines or Butlers and the purely Irish chieftains. Even within the Pale, Englishry was losing ground to Irish speech, dress, and habits. The wars of the Roses had further weakened the hold of the crown. The local feuds adopted the terminology of the English dynastic struggles: thus the Geraldines, led by the earls of Kildare and Desmond, championed the Yorkist cause, while their enemies, the Butlers under the earl of Ormond, espoused the side of Lancaster. The Geraldines won, with the result that Ireland became something of a Yorkist stronghold. But on the whole these were phrases rather than realities; what mattered to the Irish lords was independence from royal control and the fighting of their own internecine quarrels. The better part of the wild, wooded, boggy, and hilly country of the north and west had never so much as seen an English soldier or administrator.

The recovery and reduction of Ireland proved to be a general Tudor problem; to Henry VII its urgency was brought home by the fact that the country offered a safe and friendly springboard to any claimant, however absurd. In 1485 the power of Fitzgerald was paramount. The elder branch of the Butlers had moved to England, and though Henry VII restored them to their forfeited lands in Ireland, this did not affect the position of the great earl of Kildare whose many links with native families and wide personal possessions made him the virtual ruler of the country. He held the title of lord deputy and his brother was chancellor of Ireland; for the moment, Henry VII could not attempt to attack these strongholds of Geraldine power. Kildare was a curious character: arrogant and restless, he was yet gifted with some political skill, little rancour, and a roughish humour which, as it happened, appealed to the king. The support which the earl gave to Lambert Simnel was blatant and avowed, but Henry deliberately ignored it and permitted the two Fitzgeralds to continue in office when they admitted that they had been mistaken about the pretender. But forbearance was not the right treatment for a man who had earned the title of 'the great earl' by invariably getting his own way. In 1491, when Perkin Warbeck was acclaimed at Cork, Kildare showed himself cautiously ready to side with him, and in June 1492 Henry at last deprived him of the deputyship. Thomas Fitzgerald lost the great seal of Ireland, and the offices went instead to the archbishop of Dublin and Alexander Plunket, ancestor of a noble Irish line.

Kildare was sufficiently taken aback to seek the king's pardon, even asking his old enemy Ormond for help, but it was a full year before Henry would grant it (1493), and then only after the earl had come in person to seek it. The display of energy had at least produced signs of humility. Nothing, however, had been done to settle or even improve the state of Ireland. Government there was at the time managed at two removes: the king, as lord of Ireland, appointed a lord lieutenant (his uncle, the duke of Bedford) whose office was exercised for him by a lord deputy. More was required than the replacement of Kildare by a sequence of mediocrities, and in September 1494 Henry made his most determined attempt to solve the problem. He transferred the title of lord lieutenant to the infant prince Henry, his second son, so as to match in Ireland the nominal headship exercised by his elder son in Wales, and appointed as deputy Sir Edward Poynings, one of his most trusted and able ministers. The offices of chancellor and treasurer, too, were filled by Englishmen; the new policy announced itself from the first as hostile to all things Irish and determined to reduce the country to obedience to England.

Poynings was an experienced soldier and statesman, and the plan he had been sent to execute required the qualities of both. He was to conquer Ulster, the wildest part of the country where rebellion had always found safe refuge, and he was to impose on Ireland a constitution which would secure the full control of the English government. In the first he failed outright; in the second he succeeded after a fashion. His expedition against the tribesmen of the north got literally bogged down, and he had in the end to content himself with buying the clans off. The only positive result was the fall of Kildare, who had accompanied Poynings' forces, on a suspicion of treason to which his family's actions (Desmond assisted Warbeck in the siege of Waterford) and Ormond's whispers gave colour. The parliament of Drogheda, summoned by Poynings in December 1494, attainted him, thus mightily impressing the Irish to whom the earl had seemed an almost more than human figure. The deputy promptly arrested him and shipped him to the Tower. Some other acts of this parliament, commonly known as Poynings' laws, were designed to achieve the second of Henry's aims. Their total effect was to decree that an Irish parliament could only be summoned, and could only legislate, with the king's previous approval; no future laws were to be discussed unless first agreed to by the king in council. Furthermore, all laws made in England were automatically to apply to Ireland. Poynings' laws thus destroyed the legislative independence of the Irish parliament and, in law at least, gave the king vastly greater powers in Ireland than he had in England. It may be noticed that when these and other acts against the lawlessness and wild violence of Irish conditions were passed, they had the approval of the English colonist element which in later years was to be foremost in the attack on Poynings' laws.

However, Henry VII's success proved illusory. The failure to subdue the wild Irish increased the Irish budget enormously by forcing Poynings to pay blackmail for peace, and though he had been so far successful as to deal easily with Warbeck's attack on Waterford, the king was not satisfied. Henry VII now showed one side of the Tudor character not often in evidence in his reign. When new difficulties rendered a pre-arranged policy doubtful or expensive, these inspired opportunists were always ready to give up, even though in consequence the work already done might be put in jeopardy. In effect Henry despaired of the success of the measures initiated in 1494 when in 1496 he recalled Poynings and restored Kildare to favour and the office of deputy. If—as is reported—he answered the bishop of Meath's complaint that all Ireland could not rule Kildare by saying that in that case Kildare had better rule all Ireland, he may have proved his wit but hardly his sagacity. The problem of Ireland had turned out to be too big for solution; the return of Kildare meant the end of effective English control, despite the operation of Poynings' laws; and Henry VIII, Elizabeth, and Oliver Cromwell had to face a problem grown ever bigger in the interval. Henry VII had the best chance of all to win success, before the Reformation came to complicate matters; but parsimony (however necessary) and

opportunism triumphed. There were no claimants about to disturb
the peace from Ireland; why, then, waste good money on a probably
futile policy of direct rule? Henry VII was lucky to die before the
Irish problem revived, but revive it did—and largely because he
gave up the fight.

Scotland constituted a very different problem—more serious
and threatening on the face of it, though ultimately to prove much
less insidious. The presence on one small island of two hostile
powers had the most disastrous effects on both, but particularly on
the politically more advanced kingdom of England. Since Edward I's
ill-judged attempts to subdue Scotland, the northern kingdom
had been persistently opposed to its larger neighbour, and by dint
of its ancient alliance with France had managed to remain a very
painful thorn in England's side. The border from Berwick to
Carlisle was practically never at peace as raiding parties crossed
from either side, to kill, rob, and burn on the other. Far too often
these 'rodes' provided the ready pretext for more formal war.
Truce followed truce with monotonous and pointless regularity.
Compared with Scotland, harassed by perpetual feuds, gang
warfare, murders, and dynastic upsets, even the England of the
wars of the Roses was almost a law-abiding and peaceful state,
and in Scotland such troubles were considered by the nobility as
not only pleasurable but a necessity of life. One such conflagration
resulted, in 1488, in the overthrow and murder of king James III,
elevating to the throne a young king of romantically warlike
ambitions, James IV. Little purpose would be served by reciting
in detail his various attempts to instigate action on the border and
the repeated treaties for a cessation of the trouble, now for three
years and now for nine, none of which ever endured their appointed
length. The revolution which had put James IV on the throne left,
as was usual in Scotland, a powerful and dissatisfied opposition of
nobles who intrigued with England and afforded Henry VII an
opportunity to keep Scotland from getting dangerous. The French
war of 1489-92 passed off without active interference from the
north, but when Perkin Warbeck's wanderings took him to
Scotland James IV seized upon this providential opportunity of
embarrassing the enemy. The story of Scotland's share in Warbeck's Odyssey has already been told. At one time, in 1497, it
looked as though Henry VII would accept the challenge and
attempt serious war in the north, but the Cornish rebellion came
just in time to save James IV from his ill-regulated combativeness.
If one may judge from later events in Henry VIII's reign, the

Scottish army would have stood but a poor chance against the forces which the earl of Surrey was marshalling on the border.

As it was, Henry VII preserved his peaceful reputation unsullied, to prove once more how well he could exploit difficult situations without precipitating war. Surrey did cross the border once to teach James a sharp lesson, incidentally refusing a typically chivalrous but unrealistic offer of single combat. The end of Warbeck left James rather at a loss, and his own position in a country some of whose chief lords were ready to throw in their lot with the enemy was none too comfortable. Henry even hinted that two could play at the game of supporting pretenders and showed signs of adopting the cause of a Stuart claimant, the duke of Albany, then living in France. All these things working together, and Henry still continuing to offer real peace, an agreement was finally arrived at in December 1497. It was to endure as long as both sovereigns lived. But this truce suffered the common fate of these border treaties; it was broken in the following year by a Scottish raid and English counter-raid. Something more permanent was required, and Henry VII, seriously intent on settling these tiresome difficulties, therefore proposed to marry his daughter Margaret to the king of Scots. Margaret, born in 1490, was of course too young for a real marriage, and the negotiations were dragged out not only by James's reluctance to make peace but also by a chance he thought he had of marrying a Spanish princess of rather riper years. However, in the end things fell out as Henry had designed. In July 1499, a treaty of peace and alliance was concluded between England and Scotland, and in September serious negotiations began for the marriage. After further delays James IV finally agreed to it in January 1502. The dynastic marriages of the time were commonly concluded when one party or both were yet children; one result of this was the frequent annulment of such unions and remarriage of these diplomatic pawns. However, the union of James of Scotland and Margaret Tudor was destined to be successful. It turned into a proper marriage agreeable to both parties before James crowned a warlike life by getting killed at Flodden, in 1513, fighting his wife's brother as he had once fought his wife's father. The real significance of the marriage lay in the distant future. If Henry VII had hoped to settle Anglo-Scottish difficulties at once he was disappointed; Scotland continued persistently hostile, and Henry VIII was twice at war with her. In the end, however, the marriage provided England with her Stuart kings; though this was to prove anything but a blessing to her constitutional development, it did

end the ancient feud on the border and opened the way to a union
which was to be fruitful to both countries. Henry VII's Irish
policy was right but not pursued long enough; his policy towards
Scotland was wise and farseeing, and in the end completely
successful.

4. THE DYNASTY SECURED

As has been seen, the first year of the reign showed no indication
that Henry VII understood the necessity of ending the wars by
overlooking past differences, and of healing the breach by generous
and long-suffering mercy. But then the first few months after
victory in a ferocious enough struggle were hardly the time for
such statesmanlike forbearance; his own followers would not have
understood it, and Henry—even if he already desired it—could
not have afforded it. After the first proscriptions and attainders
his policy changed. For the rest of the reign he did his best to
make men forget the past and join as one nation under the Tudor
ægis; so far from suspiciously seeking out imaginary conspiracies
(as one might have expected), he proved uncommonly hard to
convince of real ones, and the statute book began to record the
reversal of past attainders rather than the further pursuit of vengeance. It was after the suppression of Simnel's revolt and
Warbeck's failure to land in Kent that Henry felt safe enough to
put the new policy into practice. The parliament of 1491 reversed
the attainder passed on the earl of Surrey, originally a Yorkist
supporter but now a loyal follower of Henry's whose best general
he proved to be; in 1495, the same was done for a number of
Yorkists or their heirs. Those who had shown themselves trust-
worthy were to be reprieved.

The parliament of 1495 went further: it passed an act designed
to draw a line under the past. This was the so-called *de facto* act
(11 Henry VII, c.1) which declared that no subject attending
upon a king of England 'for the time being' in a war and doing
him faithful service should suffer for it in his person or possessions,
any future act of parliament to the contrary notwithstanding. This
act was exaggerated by Bacon into a far-seeing major piece of
statesmanship, outlining a theory of kingship in that it made a
king *de facto* equivalent to one *de jure*. But the words *de facto* and
de jure do not occur in the document, in strong contrast to many
acts of the wars which were careful to refer to any defeated predecessor asking in deed though not of right. The distinction was
devised as a part of the struggle, and its omission in this act is

significant because it marks Henry's intention to let it be forgotten. The act's main purpose was to assure the yet unpunished members of the Yorkist faction that the past was dead; it was, in A. F. Pollard's words, a 'measure of temporary expediency very limited in scope'. It also served to reassure Henry's own followers about a possible reversal of fortune. No one ever invoked it on occasions when, on the common interpretation, it could have been useful. Nor did it make opposition to Henry VII himself venial in any circumstances, for a short but important proviso at the end excepted all men who would 'hereafter decline from his or their said allegiance'. The act was a notable step in closing the chapter of the wars, but no more. The attempt to bind future parliaments serves as a useful reminder that in 1495 the doctrine of parliament's omnicompetence was yet far from fully realised. In the cause of right reason one parliament could commit all its successors.

The policy of pacification continued through the rest of the reign, though interrupted at times by the activities of the irreconcilables. The last parliament of the reign (1504) empowered the king to reverse attainders made in his own reign and that of Richard III, on the grounds that parliamentary action was too dilatory; but this pointer towards Henry's real intentions was accompanied by an act attainting those who had been executed for their part in the Cornish rebellion and the treasons of Warbeck and Suffolk. Edmund de la Pole, earl of Suffolk, was the brother of that earl of Lincoln who had died in the battle of Stoke. A romantic but unimpressive figure, popular but without either sense or purpose, he was allowed to live at Henry's court—in comfort, but under the king's eye. After Warbeck's and Warwick's deaths he seems to have decided that the time had come for him to assert his own claims. In 1499 he fled abroad, without licence and therefore criminally. Though he returned when the king's messengers caught up with him and once more appeared at court, he finally broke with Henry when he absconded a second time, in the autumn of 1501, while assisting in the journey of Catherine of Aragon to England. He took refuge with Maximilian, now Holy Roman Emperor. But Maximilian was busy against the Turks and in Italy, and Henry experienced little difficulty in dealing with this last claimant of the reign. Indeed, one feels that he went through a familiar routine almost with an air of weariness. The normal by-plot in England was easily discovered and suppressed, with only a very few executions; among those to die was Sir James Tyrrell, the murderer of the princes in the Tower, who had since made a career as captain of Guisnes near Calais. Suffolk in exile

was soon surrounded by a band of genuine supporters among
whom there were also Henry's spies: the king knew all that went
on. In June 1502 Maximilian signed a treaty in which he agreed to
expel the earl from his dominions in return for £10,000. Suffolk
went to Aix-la-Chapelle, technically outside Maximilian's jurisdiction, where he lived miserably on borrowed money. But though
all Europe refused him countenance, Prince Arthur's death (1502)
and Prince Henry's youth were far from reassuring to the Tudor
dynasty, and the king could not feel safe until Suffolk was in his
hands. At last, by an agreement of 1506, the Archduke Philip of
Burgundy agreed to surrender the earl whose life Henry had
promised to spare. Suffolk continued in the Tower until, in 1513,
when Henry VIII undertook the first of his several clearances of
that depository of awkward personalities, another member of
the White Rose paid with his blood for his blood and the mistaken
ambitions it encouraged. His brother, Richard de la Pole, left
behind in Aix, managed with difficulty to get away from Suffolk's
creditors, travelled and fought all over Europe, persuaded France
to recognise him as king of England when war broke out again in
1512, and died at the battle of Pavia in 1525, fighting by the side
of Francis I of France. A strange and wonderful career ended in
an even stranger relief to the Tudor king who had no part in the
battle.

The ease with which Henry VII disposed of the earl of Suffolk
sufficiently illustrates the fact that the days of an uneasy crown
were over. Warbeck had been discredited and removed from the
neighbourhood of foreign kings who might use him as a pawn in
diplomacy; Warwick's death had ended the chances of further
impersonations; and now the last serious rival was lodged in the
Tower. The Tudor throne was pretty safe after some seventeen
years of Henry's rule. But there was every sign that its safety
depended too exclusively on Henry's own life. Prince Arthur died
suddenly in 1502, and—as if to underline the persistent and fatal
sickliness of the Tudor stock—the king himself fell ill soon after.
The continuance of the dynasty was suddenly in doubt; discussions
between great men centred on the subject of the succession and
the possibility of a dispute; and it is on record that on one occasion, when the problem was argued, people put forward the claims
of Buckingham and Suffolk, but ignored those of Prince Henry.
This sole male heir to an ailing king was born in 1491; no doubt
few wished to see the throne in the hands of a child of twelve or
thirteen. For Henry VII himself, assuring the succession after his
death had superseded the maintenance of his own rule as the

premier problem of his policy, and the diplomacy of his last ten years was dominated by matrimonial projects designed both to perpetuate the dynasty and to make capital out of the bridegrooms he had to offer. After the queen's death in 1503, these included even himself, an extravagance which has produced much moral censure and speculation as to his deteriorating character; yet he was only forty-six, and he may well have thought that with but one male heir he could not afford the luxury of widowerhood.

The triumph of Henry VII's earlier diplomacy was the marriage of Arthur to Catherine of Aragon. The project, first made part of the treaty which involved England in the French war of 1489-92, dragged on interminably. Both Henry and Ferdinand of Aragon were expert bargainers and chafferers; the negotiations over the bride's marriage portion and dower, and the commercial concessions to be made by England, were both lengthy and repellent. Agreement was also prevented by the Spanish ambition to turn Henry into an active ally against France, and by Spanish reluctance to commit the princess to a dynasty as yet threatened by pretenders. However, the two parties finally came to terms in October 1496; it was agreed that Catherine was to come to England in 1500, when Arthur would be fourteen, and that she would not lose her proper (though remote) claim to the throne of Castile if she were the only survivor of her family. The financial side of the transaction was complicated by Ferdinand's promise to pay Catherine's marriage portion in instalments; eighteen years later Henry VIII was still to try to secure payments due to England upon his wife's first marriage. Despite slight delays, the princess arrived in England in October 1501, and the marriage a month later was one of the occasions when Henry VII did not count the cost. For ten days the capital was the scene of festivities for all and sundry, with jousting and dancing, archery and fancy mermaids, singing and play-acting, and many other amusements provided to encourage proper rejoicing at so auspicious an event. Not only was there a prospect of the dynasty being propagated, thus ensuring a continuance of the peace and prosperity which Henry's reign had brought, but the king's son had been married to the daughter of one of the oldest houses in Europe and a princess from what was already obviously one of the great powers. No one could now call the Tudors upstart—or, if upstarts, they had arrived in society.

Five months after the marriage the young bridegroom died, and Catherine was left a widow in a foreign land, nothing now but a diplomatic counter to her unsympathetic father-in-law. Henry, who disliked waste, almost immediately proposed her remarriage to his other son Henry, and though Ferdinand haggled for some time the English king won his way. Since Henry VII would neither repay that part of the marriage portion which he had already received nor permit Catherine to leave the country, and since moreover Spain's affairs were going far from well in 1503, Ferdinand preferred to cut his losses. In June 1503 the younger Henry, now prince of Wales, was betrothed to his brother's widow; in December, the dispensation which their affinity by the bride's previous marriage necessitated was received from Pope Julius II; and though the wedding itself was to be postponed for another six years, with many tribulations to the unfortunate princess in the interval, the fateful union was in the end celebrated. It was delayed by a shift in the European system of alliances which ensued upon the death of Queen Isabella in 1504. The realm of Spain existed so far only through the personal union of the sovereigns of Castile and Aragon, and Isabella's demise threatened to dissolve it. The throne of Castile should have passed to her daughter Joanna, who was insane; Ferdinand, determined to preserve the achievements of a lifetime, made himself master of his late wife's kingdom, but found himself opposed by Joanna's husband, Archduke Philip of Burgundy, son of the Emperor Maximilian. In consequence the natural alliance between the Habsburgs and the house of Aragon, cemented by common hostility to France, collapsed, and in 1505 Ferdinand veered to the side of his old enemy, the king of France. This was to have far-reaching consequences in Italy where the Republic of Venice discovered, in 1508, that she could not withstand the joint forces of France and Spain, assisted by the papacy; in England, it led to some very peculiar twists and turns of matrimonial policy, much at variance with Henry VII's usual prudent treatment of such matters.

Henry intended to re-marry, or at least he said he did in order to attract allies. For it seems clear that after 1506, with Suffolk put away and the dynasty assured, the king desired to discard the self-restraint of earlier years and to play the game of diplomacy for its own sake. Now that he no longer needed to get his throne recognised by the powers, he wished to make the influence of England felt. It seems likely that the ambitious diplomacy later pursued by Wolsey and the young Henry VIII can be traced back to the last years of Henry VII. The habits of a lifetime and a proper regard for the value of money kept the older king from involving himself in wars, but at heart his policy was no less mistaken than Wolsey's because it overrated the weight he could put in the balance. Circumstances assisted him: like Wolsey, he found that the

idiotically complicated diplomacy of the powers made possible the
spinning of unsubstantial but strong-seeming webs, and like
Wolsey he was to discover their real weakness before he died. In
the process, however, he almost acquired a reputation either for
goatishness or for senility, for his projected marriages included,
at one time and another, his own daughter-in-law Catherine, the
young queen of Naples whose physical description he told his
ambassadors to list in great detail, the Habsburg princess Margaret
of Savoy, and her sister-in-law, the mad Joanna of Castile.
Whether he was serious in any of these approaches we cannot tell;
perhaps he still feared for his house, perhaps he was merely over-
stressing the common matrimonial aspect of contemporary diplomacy. At any rate, all his foreign policy from 1503 to 1509 was
marked by such futility that a very brief summary will be quite
sufficient.

The death of Isabella, and the rivalry of Ferdinand and Philip
for her inheritance, forced Henry to choose between his two allies.
Ordinarily, the king of Aragon—more reliable and powerful as
well as the father of Henry's prospective daughter-in-law—would
have had the higher claim, but in 1505, as things were going wrong
for him, his value as an ally grew doubtful. The marriage of Prince
Henry and Catherine was delayed, the prince even making a secret
certificate to the effect that he would disavow a contract made
during his minority. The presence of Suffolk in Burgundian lands
suggested the wisdom of keeping in with Philip, and the Franco-
Spanish alliance of October 1505 decided Henry's mind. An
accident enabled him to make the most of his new line of action.
In January 1506, Philip, on his way to Castile, was driven ashore on
the Dorset coast, and Henry at once enveloped his involuntary
guest in a mixture of lavish entertainment and diplomatic pressure.
In February, the king and archduke signed the treaty of Windsor
which renewed their alliance, gave Henry the body of Suffolk,
and guaranteed Philip English support against Ferdinand. But
when Philip died soon after arriving in Spain, Henry decided to
invade the field of Castilian castles himself. He ignored his Habsburg ties and resumed negotiations with Ferdinand, proposing
that he himself should marry Joanna; even Catherine was ordered
to recommend this fantastic match to her father, and—being little
better than a prisoner—she complied. It has been thought that
Henry toyed with a plan of ultimately pressing a claim to the
kingdom of Castile, a worse madness than any of his predecessors'
enterprises in France. To hurry up the hesitating Aragonese,
Henry succeeded in 1507 in concluding another alliance with

Maximilian by which the emperor's grandson Charles, heir to all Spanish and Habsburg dominions, was betrothed to Henry VII's daughter Mary. The Tudors were certainly aiming high. It looked as if Ferdinand, confronted by a general European coalition and the threat that Henry might seek another match for his son, would have to give way, agree to everything, pay what he owed of the old marriage portion, and even permit Henry VII's marriage with Joanna. But the whole wonderful structure collapsed at a touch when Pope Julius II, who cared only for Italian affairs, managed to combine France, the Empire, and Spain in the league of Cambrai against Venice (December 1508). So far from isolating Spain, Henry had only succeeded in demonstrating the essential isolation of England at a time when interests centred upon the Mediterranean. For the last half year of his life he played no part in European affairs, though the betrothal of Charles to Mary was celebrated—but only because Maximilian needed the 50,000 crowns which Henry was prepared to lend him in return.

The degree to which Henry's caution, parsimony, and sound sense had been affected by surprising dreams of European influence and ambitions is perhaps best indicated by this loan to a notoriously bad debtor. But Henry VII did not long survive the League of Cambrai and the collapse of his less reasonable hopes. He died on 21 April 1509, only fifty-two years old, and after twenty-four years of ruling as king of England. In those twenty-four years he had fought off all rivals, secured the recognition of his dynasty in Europe, and made its fortunes safe. This was achievement, but he deserves to be judged by his much more important work in restoring the king's government and the country's prosperity which went on behind these details of rebellions, diplomacy, and marriages.

Chapter III

HENRY VII: RESTORATION OF GOVERNMENT

1. HENRY VII'S KINGSHIP

AS has been seen, the decay of good government was not due to any fundamental troubles in the body politic: it sprang from no deep-seated social disruption, but only from the weakness of the crown. A king strong and independent enough to re-assert the inherent powers of the English crown would find the means all ready to hand, only waiting to be used. Henry VII was such a king, but it is not easy to say in what his strength lay. Certainly he did not, like the king of France and the sovereigns of Spain, dispose of an armed force on which to raise his pre-eminence; but then, unlike them, he did not have to create a united state out of militarily powerful particles, so that his need of an army was the less marked. Henry VII possessed the only siege-train of artillery in England, and though these guns were never used at home they had some value as a deterrent. But when rebellion had to be suppressed, Henry VII, with the military conservatism which characterised his house, preferred to rely on the bowmen of the shire levies and the forces raised by his supporters; that he could do so is in itself a sufficient commentary on the kind of opposition he had to overcome. The guard of 200 yeomen which he instituted on his accession (supposedly after the example of France) was never more than a ceremonial body useful in adding dignity to the royal person and in policing the court. Henry promoted the interests of his nascent navy, himself building six king's ships and encouraging the development of the merchant marine on which he depended in time of war, but the fleet was of little importance in the suppression of internal troubles. If Henry VII had depended for his success on physical force he would not have lasted many years.

Fundamental to his dynasty was, as is commonly recognised, the support of his people, a support which the Tudors rarely endangered and never lost. Most Englishmen had little interest in noble faction and were ready to welcome any king as long as he was king; those who suffered from the disturbed times only wanted a king who would restore order, no matter if his rose were white or red. The lesser gentry on their estates, the merchants and craftsmen in the towns, needed peace for their developing activities; what one can only call the middle sort of people—neither great landed magnates with their virtually dynastic politics, nor peasantry who played no part in affairs—were always to be the most reliable of Tudor subjects. To call them a middle class is to define them much more precisely than is proper for the fifteenth and sixteenth centuries; to lay the stress too heavily on the merchants is to forget that at least nine-tenths of England's population lived on and by the land. It was the landed gentry—a vague but unexceptionable term—who formed the bulk of the politically conscious and active population, and whose support had to be kept secure.

It would, however, be quite wrong to suppose, on the one hand, that Henry VII made himself a deliberately 'middle-class' king (though the books too readily suggest this), or—on the other—that he invariably deferred to the interests of gentry and merchants. The most obvious way in which Henry's kingship differed from that of his predecessors was in the greater stress he laid upon it. Even this far from impressive-looking man fostered the visible dignity of the office and took good care that the greatest of his subjects should appear small by his side. The Tudor court, with its red-coated guard and its vast expenditure on silks, satins, and velvets was always a gorgeous affair, and ceremonial was one thing on which Henry invariably spent in a prodigal manner. The feasts and joustings and displays which attended the visits of foreign potentates, the coronations and weddings of the reign, were things to marvel at, impressive even to the cynical eyes of Venetian and Milanese ambassadors. Henry also insisted on that special deference to the royal name which later deteriorated into the king-worship of Henry VIII's court and the Gloriana cult of Elizabeth's. He was still commonly 'his grace' and not yet 'his majesty', but his acts of parliament included references to 'his most gracious disposition', his 'most noble grace', and his 'great wisdom'. These touches were not altogether new—Richard II especially had anticipated the Tudor elevation of the estate of king—but Henry VII built up the formal and ceremonial element in medieval kingship to new heights, even as in other ways he greatly developed its practical attributes. The cheapening of the crown in the wars rendered such insistence on its dignity especially necessary and impressive.

The task was made easier by the relative decline of the nearest rivals, the great men of the kingdom. The nobility suffered a blood-letting in the wars of the Roses, though they were not (as is often assumed) virtually destroyed. Most significant was the disappearance of magnates closely related by blood to the ruling house, a disappearance which automatically increased the distance between the king and the highest rank of his subjects. Edward IV, with his marriage to Elizabeth Woodville, had protracted the entanglement of the royal family with the leading magnates; Henry VII made it quite plain that however magnificent a nobleman might be he could not compare with the blood royal. The Tudors might be upstart and *parvenu*, as indeed many of their deeds and attitudes proclaimed them to be, but by the simple fact of kingship they assumed an eminence which the oldest noble house in England must not rival. The economic decline of the baronage—more marked than the actual failure of lines—assisted further. Tudor society was not egalitarian, though it offered its chance to talent, of however humble an origin. Men who made a career aspired to the dignity and profits of nobility, and the Tudors were soon to surround themselves with many men of title. But the title was recent and conferred by the pre-eminent king, and men promoted at the king's pleasure knew where their loyalties must lie. The elevation of kingship made possible a greater fluidity in the ranks below: he whom the king delighted to honour could hold his own with the descendants of generations of nobility, whether they liked it or not. (They generally disliked it greatly.) What held society together, at the top as well as throughout all the layers of local and family loyalties, was the outstanding position of the king who personified the state. But it was still medieval kingship, no different in essence from that of Edward I and Richard II.

It is also commonly asserted that Henry VII innovated when he surrounded himself with a council of men from the 'middle class'. As a matter of fact, Henry's council included noblemen—Lancastrians like the earls of Oxford and Ormond, and reprieved Yorkists like the earl of Surrey. It included new creations like Giles Lord Daubeney who came from the upper ranks of the gentry. It included ecclesiastics like Cardinal Morton and Bishop Fox. The bulk of it was composed of new men, that is men whose families had not so far made an official career—gentlemen like Bray, Lovell, Poynings, and Belknap, though there were also men of humbler descent. Such a council was typical of nothing new, but of the older, pre-Lancastrian councils. While kings could pick their advisers—before, that is, the magnates conquered the king's council—they naturally picked men loyal to themselves who were useful for their practical qualities, and they had always had councils in which some nobles mixed with the churchmen and knights who supplied the administrative and professional elements of the middle ages. When Henry VII chose advisers from non-magnate ranks, he was following not only Yorkist example but the general practice which was only abandoned when the crown lost control of the government. There was no new kind of advisers—though new men there were inasmuch as they still had to make a name for themselves and their families—to serve a monarchy which it would be utterly misleading to describe as 'new'.

In any case, the prevalent impression that Henry VII, and the other Tudors after him, had only to suppress the nobility and elevate lesser men whose interests they protected, dangerously oversimplifies a pretty complex situation. The Tudors were not against aristocracy as such; they were against obstreperous men, whether noble or gentle or common. Henry VII's military commanders were mostly noblemen of pre-Tudor vintage—men like Oxford and Surrey—a detail which forcibly indicates how little the traditional view will explain. Nor could he rely on his so-called middle-class supporters with the certainty which that view supposes. Even among his immediate servants—that is, among those representatives of the lesser men who had the best reason to remain faithful—loyalty was inevitably tempered by self-interest. As late as 1503, the officers of Calais debated among themselves the best way of re-insuring against the king's death and the collapse of the Tudor dynasty. Sir James Tyrell, a typical 'new man' and as captain of Guisnes clearly a man trusted with a responsible task, deserted to the harebrained Suffolk at the first provocation, when none of the supposedly depressed nobility thought of raising a finger to assist their own return to power. Tudor legislation depended for its effectiveness on unpaid local gentlemen enforcing the law: this fact is taken to support the view that the kings depended on the wishes of that class. But (as we shall see) this dependence was much less than is supposed: in general even unpopular statutes were put into practice, though there were limits to what the crown could do.[1] Henry VII's policy of encouraging trade may have been intended to conciliate special interests, but it was also designed to advance national prosperity. In any case, the king was perfectly capable of using the diplomatic weapon of trade embargos, thus cutting off his merchants' noses to spite a foreign face. All told, the story of Henry VII's reign, like that of his successors', will not support the assumption that the Tudors had to defer to a class of their subjects on which they depended for power. Though they exercised great political skill in knowing the limits of their strength, they exercised as much in

[1] There always are.

going to those limits even against opposition from the very people
who ordinarily formed the safest support of the monarchy.

The truth is that Tudor kingship was strong in itself. To listen
to some historians, one might think that large-scale rebellion is
the kind of thing men devise over breakfast and carry out between
lunch and dinner. By being king, and by exploiting the great
inherent strength of that office, Henry VII put himself into a
position of such power that disagreement had to reach a very
considerable pitch before it would translate itself into resistance.
The name of king was great, and men obeyed whatever king there
was, unless they saw the chance of a better candidate or were
driven too far. Henry VII removed all other candidates, walked
with some delicacy to avoid driving anyone to extremes, and augmented his strength. He sought national support: he did not wish
to be ruler by the grace of any one class or section: and if the policy
he pursued suited and benefited especially the middle sort of
people, that was because it was a rational and national policy
bound to profit those who eschewed factious ambitions. The king
expected support from all layers of society, and he got it, though
some individuals in all layers he had to overcome. The power of
the king rested upon his rights and prerogatives. Not for nothing
did Henry VII elevate the word prerogative to the first place in his
political vocabulary, a habit which endured until the end of the
dynasty. No one could say exactly what the king's prerogative
amounted to, but all agreed that it included fixed rights and an
indefinite reserve of power vested in the crown. No Tudor wished
to define it: its vagueness was its worth. It was the essence of
regality, capable of acting in the interests of the state and equipped
with rights and privileges which none gainsaid because all understood their necessity and most approved their use. By making
himself king Henry VII had taken the longest step towards the
restoration of royal power; by putting himself upon his just
prerogative he made that power effective. It remains to see how he
used his prerogative to create strength out of wealth and to enforce
the law upon a violent and turbulent people.

2. REVENUE

The Lancastrians were weak, in great part at least, because they
were poor. Edward IV succeeded in returning to solvency, but no
more. The crown could not be strong while it had to seek financial
support from others, and while the resources of great nobles overshadowed its own. Henry VII realised from the start that in order

to be strong he had to be rich. The king came to the throne a poor man and heavily in debt to his French and Breton backers; he found it necessary at first to live on short-term loans contracted as best he might; yet within a few years he could lend sufficient money to Anne of Brittany to make the Breton debts a factor in the French war and the peace of Etaples. Henry understood the value of a good name and sound credit, and he scrupulously repaid the early loans taken up before he could tap the resources of the crown; he was able to do so because these resources were really very large. Once he had ascended the throne, a vast potential treasure-house opened to his touch; it only remained to secure all that was due to him, and to husband his resources in a sensible manner by careful management and controlled spending.

The kings of England disposed of an income derived from two basic sources. There was the ordinary revenue of the crown which came in year by year, and the extraordinary revenue from grants and loans made both in and out of parliament. The latter, however, was meant to assist only in emergencies. The famous theory that the king 'should live of his own'—that is, on his regular revenue and without recourse to special grants—found favour both with a people reluctant to part with its substance and with a king desirous of making himself independent. The politic Tudor reluctance to tax frequently helped to disguise what had already become fact. Most of the expenditure of the crown was no longer in any sense personal to the king; it was for purposes of state, and the nation in whose interests the money was spent ought to have contributed more formally to its supply. But since the Tudors did not wish to follow the Lancastrian precedent of surrendering freedom of action in exchange for votes of money, nor the Yorkist precedent of getting contributions without consent, the English people could continue to indulge their natural dislike of paying taxes and their predilection for starving government of the means to govern. The theory that the king was entitled to ask for money on special occasions was faithfully followed in the reign of Henry VII. Henry received votes after the battle of Stoke (1487) to cover that operation, in 1489 to assist in the French war, and in 1496 when he was preparing for action against Scotland; in 1491 he succeeded in having an illegal benevolence endorsed by parliament. The votes were as a rule for one or more 'tenths and fifteenths'; this, originally an assessment on moveables, had become a fixed sum of about £30,000 unconnected with the true distribution of property. It is difficult to say how much Henry received from parliamentary taxation since the money actually collected often bore little relation to that voted. For the French war, for instance, parliament voted about £100,000, but only something less than £60,000 ever came in, about enough to pay for the cost of the few weeks' invasion of France. This factor has to be taken into account when Henry is accused of cheating his subjects by demanding money for wars which he had no intention of undertaking. War was a terribly expensive business which no responsible king could face without the necessary ready cash in hand—and this he could never have saved from his ordinary revenue. Nevertheless, it is perfectly true that Henry turned the difficulty into an advantage when, for instance, he saved the whole grant for the Scottish war except the not inconsiderable sum spent in suppressing the Cornish rising, or when he allowed himself to be bought off at Etaples for an annual pension of £5,000.

These grants and pensions were only the decorative frills on Henry VII's revenue system: he naturally took what he could get, but as his finances grew sound, and as the danger of war or rebellion receded, he dispensed with parliamentary grants and relied exclusively on his proper revenue. Leaving aside some small and incidental items, the sources of this were four: the crown lands, the customs, profits of justice, and the profits of the feudal prerogative. Between them they yielded a large income capable of remarkable expansion, as Henry VII was to prove. Land he made the basis of his wealth; like any landowner of the age, he found it to be a safe and reliable source of income since it could be let at adequate rents which only needed collecting. Coming after the disturbances of the wars, Henry VII was in the happy position of inheriting from all sides. Repeated attainders and forfeitures had greatly increased even the Yorkist crown lands; these—with the earldoms of March and Warwick—now fell to the king by Richard III's overthrow, to be added to the inheritance of Lancaster (the great duchy) and of Tudor (the earldom of Richmond). As king, Henry VII automatically enjoyed the revenues of the duchy of Cornwall and the earldom of Chester. There were many other parcels of lands acquired through escheats—where men had died without heirs— and through the successive attainders of the reign. The fall of Sir William Stanley alone is supposed to have increased the royal revenues by £1,000 a year. Henry, being solvent, could reverse the earlier policy of alienation: where his predecessors had sold crown lands for ready cash, or granted them away as rewardsfor favours and services either received or solicited, he spent a profitable twenty-three years collecting land. In 1495 an act of parliament confirmed to him all the lands of Richard III, even where no special inquest had found that the lands claimed had ever in fact been Richard's, and various acts of resumption declared void grants of crown lands made as far back as the reign of Edward III. Though Henry's policy of mercy returned to private hands some lands which had been forfeited by attainder, this was a small matter compared with the acquisitions made. Thus the crown lands, once a meagre though sound source of revenue, soon took first place in the list. From a clear annual income[1] of about £10,000 in the early part of the reign, their yield rose to about £35,000. The duchy of Lancaster accounted separately; is, revenues went in the first place to pay for its own administratiount but the surplus available for general purposes grew from £650 to £6,500. This land revenue formed a solid and calculable foundation for the royal finances.

The customs, at first a larger part of the king's income, were in this reign just overtaken by the crown lands. The king enjoyed the export duties (*magna* and *parva custuma*) on wool, woolfells, and leather by virtue of his prerogative, while the import and export duties of tunnage (on wine) and poundage (on certain merchandise) were granted to him for life in the first parliament of the reign. The customs revenue was, however, never as great as it ought to have been. Collection in the various ports was difficult and smuggling flourished; especially in the more distant ports, the underpaid customs-service habitually joined in the illegal traffic. Henry tried several methods of increasing the yield: he vainly attempted by legislation to stop evasions, as by the act prohibiting coastal trading without customers' certificates (1487); he attempted to reduce some of the advantages which foreign merchants enjoyed by earlier treaties (1496); twice he revised the book of rates (1503 and 1507) to bring the assessment more into accord with contemporary conditions; and he encouraged trade for fiscal reasons. Medina del Campo (1491) remained the basis of Anglo-Spanish trade for forty years. The treaty known as the *Magnus Intercursus* of 1496 ended the embargo on trade with the Netherlands and put that vital commerce on a safe and permanent footing which profited both the countries concerned. An attempt of 1506 to take advantage of the Archduke Philip's predicament to extort concessions for the English cloth exporters (the *Malus Intercursus*) failed, but it showed whose interests Henry had at heart. The king assisted the merchants' struggles to break into the territories monopolised by

[1] Clear revenue means the sum left after payments charged on individual groups of lands in fees, wages, annuities, pensions, and expenses had been paid by the individual receivers.

the Hanse (the Baltic and north-eastern Europe) and Venice (Italy and the Mediterranean); commercial treaties concluded in 1490 with Denmark and Florence did something to open up those regions. As Henry's chief activity in foreign trade was to encourage the export of cloth, so he attempted to promote and protect the industry at home. Acts were passed to forbid the export of unfinished cloth by foreigners (1487), to encourage the weaving and finishing of cloth (1489), to prevent bad practices in the manufacture of fustian (1495), and to prohibit the import of silken goods (1504). Together with the navigation act of 1490, which in the interests of English shipping and the navy forbade the import of certain goods in foreign vessels, these statutes certainly amounted to a policy of protection. However, it must remain doubtful whether they were really the expression of a consistent policy of economic nationalism. The king did not interfere with the privileges of the Hanse in England and paid little attention to English interests when he used the cloth trade to put pressure on the Netherlands. His own chief interest lay in increasing the customs revenue: the more English trade flourished, the greater would be the cut enjoyed by the crown. The only thing he did not like about foreign merchants were the exemptions from customs payments they had extorted, and these he revoked; it did not concern him that they might perhaps deprive English merchants of some trade. Yet it is true that the measures of the reign greatly assisted commercial revival while their effect on the customs revenue was small. That revenue expanded immediately after Henry's accession, as one would expect at the conclusion of a civil war, and the average of just over £33,000 a year then attained was increased to no more than about £38,000 twenty years later. Smuggling, the difficulties of administration, and the occasional trade wars prevented the full exploitation of this source of money.

The revenue derived from the profits of justice and the feudal incidents is naturally less easily defined in accurate figures. It varied too much year by year, in accordance with events. However, it was here that an energetic king and council could apply the greatest pressure with the best hope of success, and it was here also that re-assertion of the king's rights was most necessary after the wars had lost the crown so much. The king's courts contributed in two ways to the king's finances. There were the fees paid for the writs without which no action could start or carry on; these, together with the fees payable on letters patent of grants and the like, were accounted for by the hanaper, the financial department of chancery, and formed a safe, continuous, and not inconsiderable income which an official of Henry VIII's time once described as a sheet-anchor. Secondly, there were the fines and amercements levied in the courts by way of punishment. Henry made it a general policy to punish by fine even those whose treasonable activities had earned them the death penalty, and each rising or disturbance in the reign was followed not by a forest of gallows but by an invasion of commissioners assessing and collecting fines. Great men paid heavily for contravening the laws against retainers, even though the story of £10,000 exacted from the earl of Oxford is probably apocryphal; merchants paid for attempts to smuggle goods; landed men were fined for breaches of the forest laws, and crown and borough officials for not doing their duty. New penal legislation punished offences by stated fines. In all this Henry VII did not revive obsolete legislation and rules, as Charles I was to do in a similar attempt to make lawlessness pay; in the later fifteenth century many laws had been disobeyed, but they had not become out of date. It is also certain that the policy of imposing heavy fines was, in part at least, political in intent and designed to weaken potential opponents: it was part of Henry VII's attack on overmighty subjects. Not uncommonly fines were remitted, wholly or in part, which shows that they were often intended to be deterrent rather than punitive. This fact makes it difficult to know what profit the king derived from them. They were not usually collected in cash: the victim gave a bond for his debt which he might take years to pay off. The policy was much resented, but it is by no means clear that it was unjust or even unduly harsh.

With it went the exploitation of the king's feudal rights. In the parliament of 1504 Henry managed to collect a feudal aid for the knighting of Prince Arthur (knighted long before and since dead) and for the marriage of his eldest daughter Margaret (married two years earlier). But this spectacular if belated revival of a legitimate claim was much less important than the searching out and enforcing of the rights which the king enjoyed over his tenants-in-chief. The feudal tenure by knight's service involved a number of financial commitments which lay heavily on the tenant and greatly profited the lord, and since the king was far and away the greatest lord his potential revenue from these rights was large. An heir, on taking over his lands, paid a fine known as relief. If he was under age, he and his lands were subject to wardship (that is, they were in the king's hands until he came of age) and livery (the fine paid to recover the lands out of wardship). An heiress's marriage, a marketable asset, was at the lord's disposal. Wardships could be sold for cash, often to the ward's family who wished to save them from the depredations which a temporary administrator would commonly inflict. Lands in the hands of widows and idiots, incapable of doing military service, also reverted to the lord for administration. No heir at all meant escheat—the complete return of the lands to the lord. Lands could not be alienated (sold) or granted in mortmain (to the Church) without royal licence, which had to be paid for. All these rights had one thing in common: it was in the tenant's interest to conceal their occurrence if he could. The disturbed times had given him his chance, and when Henry VII came to the throne the king's rights were generally speaking in a bad way. His first task was to establish what he could claim, and he therefore set up commissions which in the years 1486-92, and again later after the main attainders of the reign (1497-1500), investigated the king's rights by inquests on lands. Henry's careful attention to inquisitions *post mortem*, which established the possessions of a deceased tenant, was part of the same policy; as has been seen, the feudal incidents fell due when one tenant died and another took over. The work of these commissions was naturally much resented by those who had managed to break the law with impunity and were now forced to pay up. Together with the imposition of fines for breaches of statutes, these exactions created Henry VII's reputation for extortion and rapacity. Solidly entrenched though this reputation is, one may doubt whether it is borne out by the facts. He was getting his due at a time when that was difficult. It is argued that he acquired a liking for money for its own sake, but he never acted like a miser; his bad name grew out of the grouses of discovered offenders whose view prevailed with the chroniclers and was accepted by Bacon.[1] The simple truth is that Henry, faced with the task of replenishing an empty treasury and restoring the strength of royal government, from the beginning to the end of his reign enforced his feudal rights and punished offenders where they felt it most—in their pockets. It was the more necessary that he should do so because another period of evasions and concealments would have resulted in the obsolescence of just claims, the collapse of the royal finances, and consequently anarchy.

Among the lesser sources of revenue a few may be mentioned. The revenues of vacant episcopal sees came to the crown, and Henry only perfected an old policy when he habitually permitted such sees to remain vacant for one year. There are signs that

[1] We read such incredible sentimentalities as the view which ascribes an imaginary deterioration of the king to the death of his queen who played very little part in his life. The idea that Henry's policy turned from just to unjust exactions was based only on insufficient knowledge of the facts.

offices were sometimes sold, and that suitors offered money to buy the king's favour in law-suits; these methods would deserve all the execration heaped upon them if one could be sure of what was involved.[1] Henry sold pardons for offences, especially for murder, which, on the face of it, looks like a very bad practice indeed. But it probably meant only that he collected the fees due upon such pardons (as upon any document under the great seal), a practice common throughout the century and earlier; it need not mean that genuine criminals got off. In those violent times—and life was to remain violent well into the eighteenth century—many affrays ended in killings which resulted in accusations of murder when manslaughter or even self-defence would have been a more appropriate description. A pardon was thus commonly obtained before matters came to trial, not after conviction. One need only recall the affair in which Christopher Marlowe found his death; his killers were accused of murder but pardoned upon investigation by the council. Here, too, Henry's reputation has probably suffered through failure to grasp the meaning behind the phrases in the account books.

All this is not to deny that Henry VII eagerly augmented the royal revenues, as indeed he had to if he was to make his government effective, and that he husbanded his resources with the greatest care. Having started in debt, he balanced his accounts by about 1492 and began to show a sizeable surplus from about 1497 onwards. In the end the erstwhile debtor was making large loans to other European potentates and smaller ones to merchants and entrepreneurs. The total result may be summed up by quoting some more figures. Income rose in the reign from about £52,000 to about £142,000 a year; expenditure, which at first had greatly exceeded the regular revenue, was about £138,000 at the end. Much of this was in the nature of investment: money was freely spent on the jewels and plate in which the age generally laid up its treasure, and on loans and trading enterprises which would show a return in the future. Henry died possessed of a treasure worth between one and two millions; the evidence does not permit a more precise statement. Most of this was not in cash or bullion but in jewelry and plate. Such a reserve was essential in a period when

---

[1] Offices can only have been sold in the sense that people offered money for the appointment; one wants to know if they got it. And did the king favour those who offered him money? The taking of such sums was certainly undignified; whether it was corrupt is quite another question. One must also remember the circumstances of a time which habitually dealt in favours and rewards.

CET

the government's biggest problem was not how to increase its potential revenue but how to have cash in hand when it was needed. Difficulties arose when payments fell due and the money to pay them was not yet in, as happened constantly. The reserve itself was of course gratifying, but it may be doubted whether it really merits all the admiration which it has excited. After all, it took only two years of by no means extravagant war in the next reign to wipe it out. As always, war was far and away the most expensive of government activities, and Henry's pacifism is easily explained by his financial circumstances. The truth is that no government dependent on 'the king's own' and on ready cash could hope to be solvent for any length of time in the new conditions of European diplomacy and internal centralisation, but that problem—staved off with difficulty by the Tudors—was not solved until modern national methods of finance were developed after the Restoration.

3. FINANCIAL ADMINISTRATION

Henry VII's real difficulty was not to find new sources of revenue but to make sure that he got his due. He had to see that the revenues of his lands did not stick to the fingers of the various receivers, that customs were paid and handed over, that the law with its profitable by-products was enforced, and that the feudal rights of the crown were discovered and exacted. This problem of administration forms one of the most complicated and recondite, but also one of the fundamental, aspects of Tudor government; here it will not be possible to give more than a bare outline.

The financial department of state was the exchequer, developed as a separate institution in the later twelfth century and therefore already 300 years old when Henry VII came to the throne. Its two parts—the exchequer of receipt where the money was received, stored, and disbursed, and the exchequer of audit where accounts were audited and unpaid sums driven in—reflected a thorough desire for safety in bureaucracy. A multiplicity of officials and records, designed to prevent fraud and collusion, dealt with the finances. But while the king could be sure that the work of the exchequer was honest, he often had to wait a long time for the creaking machinery to do its work; accounts were audited years after they were due, and it took even longer to collect outstanding items. The records were so designed as to make knowledge of what was coming in, going out, or still in hand very hard to come by. These shortcomings had caused earlier kings to rival the exchequer machinery by financial departments developed in the royal

household where the king could exercise personal and direct supervision, keep clear of baronial interference which at times affected
offices of state, and handle the cash needed in daily administration
without recourse to the cumbersome machinery of the exchequer.
Henry III and Edward I had built up an office of finance out of the
wardrobe, the accounting department of the household, while
Edward II and Edward III had used the king's chamber, the
innermost part of the household out of which the exchequer had
originally grown. The decline of royal power in the fifteenth century was reflected in the decline of the dynamic household activity
in national government which characterised the middle ages;
wardrobe and chamber were reduced to purely household departments. Thus when Henry VII attacked the problem of a shrunken
revenue, he was confronted with an administration which could
be of little use in the expansion and exploitation of his resources.

Like the 'medieval' king that he was, Henry VII found the
answer to his problem in the household. Richard III, building up
on the rudimentary practice of his brother, had already outlined a
plan by which the king's chamber might become the centre of the
royal finances, and Henry VII adopted and developed the idea.
The details are unimportant: the result was to make the treasurer
of the chamber the chief financial officer of the crown from about
1487 onwards. The office was in the hands of such trained, loyal,
and efficient men as Sir Thomas Lovell (1485-92) and Sir John
Heron (1492-1524), and they were responsible solely to the king.
The basis of this 'chamber-system' was the transferring of the
crown-lands revenue from exchequer to chamber, local receivers
paying directly to its treasurer. In the course of time other items
were added, until the exchequer retained only the 'ancient
revenue' (the farms of the counties and towns collected by the
sheriffs) and the customs. The latter were left with the inefficient
old administration because their collection involved a detailed
knowledge and complicated array of officers and records not
available to the treasurer of the chamber. But everything else—
except the revenues of the self-administered duchy of Lancaster—
went to the chamber: land revenue, the profits of wardship and
other feudal dues, the profits of the hanaper, the fines and other
income from courts of law, the French pension—even parliamentary taxes, though their collection continued to be supervised by
the exchequer.

Before the end of the reign the treasurer of the chamber thus
handled an annual turnover of well over £100,000. He had taken
the place of the exchequer of receipt as the chief treasury of the

realm, but since he was not to be responsible to the exchequer of audit some other agency had to be created to supervise his affairs and scrutinise his accounts. In the reign of Henry VII, little progress was made in systematising this side of the new machinery, for the king took the responsibility largely upon himself. He personally checked the treasurer's account books, signing each page with his monogram, while for the periodic audit he appointed some of his councillors who were also to audit the accounts of other receivers of revenue removed from the survey of the exchequer. In course of time, the task came to be a specialised one, but there is no sign that anything like an organisation was set up; everything was still much too fluid and personal, in the true spirit of 'household' administration. The accession of Henry VIII, however, produced some changes which crystallised his father's system and allow one to see it more clearly. Unlike the old king, his successor did not wish to be bothered with the detailed work of government. Moreover, the change of ruler encouraged the exchequer to protest against the use of the chamber; attempts were made to distrain on revenue officials for sums they had long since paid to the chamber, but which in the view of the exchequer had never been officially received. A number of acts of parliament therefore appointed two general surveyors of crown lands to act as a department of audit. Therewith the so-called chamber-system was complete: a household treasurer as chief collector and paymaster of revenue, with a semi-household department of audit to supervise him and help in securing his revenues. The general surveyors were not as yet free of the household or given sufficient organisation to make them independent; the exchequer, a true department of state, kept their records and supplied means for legal process against defaulters.

Especially in the reign of Henry VII it was not enough to have a treasury and an audit office; equally necessary was an agency for the ascertaining of outstanding, and the discovery of concealed, sources of revenue. The commissions, already mentioned, which did this work early in the reign under the general supervision of Sir Reginald Bray were later superseded by more permanent officials. A master of the wards (Sir John Hussey) was appointed in 1503, to secure the revenue from wardships which he paid to the chamber. In 1508, in an attempt to exploit to the full the fiscal rights of the crown, the shortlived office of the surveyor of the king's prerogative was created and given to Sir Edward Belknap; again, the money was to go to the chamber. It is in connection with these agencies that one must explain the work of the notorious Richard Empson and Edmund Dudley. These men, crown officials who were trained lawyers rather than pure administrators like Bray or Lovell, formed the mainstay of the rather obscure 'king's legal counsel', organised under the chairmanship of the chancellor of the duchy of Lancaster, an office Empson held from 1504. Their task was in particular the taking of bonds (recognisances and obligations) in which men promised to pay fines imposed for breaches of the law, or debts contracted, or sums in case of non-performance of certain duties. It was a development of the earlier methods of Bray and Lovell, though the energy with which Empson and Dudley pursued their unpopular tasks gave them a worse reputation. It did not help matters that both men—unlike Bray—rapaciously lined their own pockets. Their activities do not deserve the name of extortion: this has already been explained. However, the fact that they acted as the agents of an energetic and pitiless financial policy left them wide open to attack when their royal protector died. Henry VIII found it an easy way to quick popularity to throw over his father's ministers, and it seems that people, happy to see Empson and Dudley die, overlooked the fact that Empson's and Dudley's policy was soon revived, though on the whole less stringently.

Apart from some small but useful changes in the exchequer of receipt, these were Henry VII's reforms in the financial machinery. He made no innovations in the means and principles employed, for chamber finance and the use of household officers had a long and respectable history. The degree to which he developed the system, however, was something new. No king before him had disposed of so efficient an agency so firmly under his personal control, for the collection of so large a revenue. But the system depended very much on his personal action; Henry VIII's lack of interest doomed it, though Wolsey continued to work a more bureaucratic form of it. In the last analysis, Henry VII, because he used the old household methods, failed to lay the foundations of a really reformed administration.

4. LAW AND ORDER

The financial measures of Henry VII restored strength to the crown, but what would ultimately matter was, of course, the use to which that strength was put. From the first the king took up the tasks of enforcing the law and suppressing those whose improper power had threatened the peace of the country. Some of the financial measures were themselves a means towards that end. The recovery of the king's feudal rights remedied one large-scale breach of the law, while the weapon of heavy fines proved most useful in breaking the power and spirit of 'overmighty subjects'. The turbulent noble and knight who had to redeem evasions of wardships and the like, and to pay for violent dispossessions or excessive retaining, were both taught the strength of the king's arm and rendered too weak to make their resentment felt. On the whole, the existing laws against violence sufficed: the courts needed only to be enabled to apply them sternly and impartially. Though Henry found it desirable to legislate against some symptoms of trouble, remarkably few statutes were passed providing against the kind of offences which had been common, in itself an indication that the disturbances grew out of weakness at the top, and arrogance and corruption lower down, and not out of any fundamental evils in the body politic. In 1485 hunting in disguise was prohibited, since it allegedly offered occasion for riots and murders. In 1487, several acts tightened up the procedure employed in catching and punishing murderers, stopped a gap by forbidding the taking away of women (heiresses) without their consent, and hoped to end the undermining of the king's own tenants' loyalty by forbidding other men to retain them for any service. Four separate acts of 1495 attempted to solve one of the greatest problems of all, the failure of a legal system which depended, both for evidence in property cases and for verdicts on crimes, on juries that had grown intimidated or—more commonly— corrupt. The returning of blatantly false verdicts by local juries, from which there was no appeal, continued to be the principal bane of Tudor law-enforcement, and the acts of 1495—though they spoke bravely against perjury, maintenance, and the empanelling of insufficient and thus easily corrupted jurors—achieved very little. One aspect of the problem lay in the powers of the sheriff whose connections with the local magnates tended to make him useless to the government. Sheriffs empanelled juries and kept prisoners in custody; in both they had often failed, and laws recalling them to their duty had to be passed in 1495 and 1504. In the end, the misdeeds of fifteenth-century sheriffs resulted in the fall from grace and power of their sixteenth-century successors.

In 1504 there was also passed Henry VII's great statute against retaining, not of course the first act against this fundamental evil, but rather a general codified statement on the subject. It ordered the enforcement of existing acts, appointed penalties both for those who retained men except as household servants and for those who allowed themselves to be so retained, placed the burden of searching out offenders on the justices of the peace, clarified the position

of the king's council in the enforcement of the law, and provided
a procedure which secured convictions even when juries refused to
indict patent transgressors.[1] The act remained the decisive pro-
nouncement on the subject; if enforced, it was bound to end the
existence of the armed bands on which the great supplanters of
royal authority had relied. But laws against retaining had been
passed before; what was needed was energetic enforcement. The
restoration of order depended not only on the suppression of the
overmighty subject; there had never been many of those, the wars
had thinned their ranks further, and the task was relatively
straightforward. It also required that the lesser men be taught to
take their quarrels to the law and not settle them by force. Until
the creation of a regular police force in the nineteenth century,
England remained a country of ready violence. Every dispute
turned too easily to bloodshed; in the Tudor age, men were far too
quick to draw daggers, wield clubs, break heads, and raise riots.
The sum of hundreds of such small affrays and quarrels year by
year was a far more pressing problem to the government than the
very occasional major risings or the remoter dangers of private
warfare, even though these latter could prove fatal. In the absence
of a police force there could be no hope of preventing trouble; one
could only make the consequences so unpleasant that people
would learn to curb their tempers and to seek satisfaction for their
claims and grievances in the long-drawn agony of the law courts
instead of the sharp exhilaration of the riot.

Henry VII found in existence a system of local government
which needed only fresh vigour and development. The justices of
the peace, local and (virtually) unpaid gentlemen appointed and
supervised by the crown, were the mainstay of the Tudor system of
law-enforcement. With the decline of the sheriff, the decay of the
old popular courts of hundred and shire, and the deliberate attack
made on the feudal and franchisal courts, they were rapidly
promoted to exclusive control of the countryside. Henry VII
legislated both to enlarge their duties and to keep them up to the
mark. They were empowered to take bail (1487) and to punish
on information without indictment (1495); disguised hunters,

---

[1] Strictly speaking, before the statute no man could be proceeded
against for illegal retaining unless he was indicted by a jury of present-
ment. These juries having failed in their duty, the council were to act on
information received (from J.Ps., as a rule), summoning offenders by
writs of *subpoena*; the chancellor could also order such *subpoenas* on his own
initiative, without formal information being laid. The procedure here
outlined was practised by the council before 1504; the act merely
legalised it.

vagabonds, thieves of swans' eggs, and many others were put under their jurisdiction; they were given special powers to investigate and punish the transgressions of sheriffs (1495). This was only the beginning of those 'stacks of statutes' whose execution, as the Elizabethan antiquary William Lambarde said, was laid upon their shoulders. Henry VII seems to have begun the practice of invariably including leading councillors in the commissions for the individual shires: this both raised the standing of the office and ensured that some of the justices at least would always be loyal servants of the royal will.

No system of local government is worth having unless it obeys the orders of the central government. The Tudor system suffered in any case from reliance on unpaid and therefore relatively independent agents; there was no choice in the matter. However, the independence of these J.Ps. has been greatly exaggerated. Legislation which went clean contrary to their sectional interests—the interests of the rural gentry—might, indeed, be difficult to enforce: enclosures of common land proceeded in the early Tudor period despite laws forbidding it, and in catholic Lancashire the recusancy laws of Elizabeth were readily flouted. On the other hand, the office of J.P. was not hereditary or held for life; the annual re-issue of the commission gave the government quite sufficient control, for no gentleman could afford being put out of it. With the commission he would lose his standing in his own county society; the consequences would be almost as bad for him as dismissal would be for a salaried official. If proof of their essential dependence and obedience to orders be sought, it will easily be found in the overbearing and peremptory manner in which the council addressed any justice who was thought to have failed in his duty. There was neither thought nor need of tact in these dealings. Henry VII could safely take up the office of justice of the peace, adapt it to his needs, and develop it into the mainstay of local government. But he could do so only because government at the centre fully recovered its vitality.

The centre of Henry VII's government, as of all medieval government, was the king himself, assisted by those with whom he chose to surround himself—that is, his council. The rather fluid permanent council of the fourteenth century consolidated in the reign of Richard II into an organised body. This council, with its small membership, its rules of procedure, and its regular term-time meetings, fell before the magnate onslaught under the Lancastrians; it ceased to be an instrument at the king's disposal. Following Yorkist practice, Henry VII, who chose a number of his own followers to be his councillors, reverted to a more primitive and less organised council. The number of the men described as councillors in his reign is large—over 150—and individual meetings could be attended, on occasion, by forty or more of them. They included great nobles like Oxford and Dorset, and later Surrey; great prelates like Morton and Fox and Warham; great administrators of the stamp of Bray and Lovell; but also the judges and legal advisers, and many lesser men whom one can at best describe as leading civil servants. Generally speaking, Henry's councillors were office-holders, but many of the offices held were minor, and Sir Reginald Bray's importance is not to be measured by the comparatively insignificant post of the chancellor of the duchy of Lancaster which he held.[1] The one qualification which embraces them all was that the king had chosen them; they were his men and did his will.

Naturally, however, there were grades and distinctions among them—even up to a point signs of differentiation in function. The legal council, who in Henry's last years employed themselves in collection of fines and bonds, are a case in point; the court of requests is another. Nevertheless it should be made plain once and for all that never in Tudor times was there more than one council in existence at the centre: there was always only one body to which men called councillors could belong. The separation of star chamber and privy council is hard to trace because in personnel no such separation ever took place. It is wrong to see in the council groupings of Henry VII's reign the origin of any subdivision of the council. In a body as large as this council there were, of course, some men of greater influence; some may be called ministers where others were only leading administrators. Naturally also, since the centre of government was with the king at court, the king tended to take his more important councillors with him on his travels; of all the peripatetic Tudor sovereigns, Henry VII was the most active. Thus there existed an 'inner ring' of more important, more influential, more powerful councillors, commonly in attendance on the king and forming the active ministry (as it were) within the larger body. The king's absence from the seat of the permanent departments of state at Westminister naturally suggested the advisability of leaving some councillors on call in the council room of that palace, the famous star chamber. It was desirable that his subjects or foreign visitors should at all times be able to find part of the government at Westminster. But the 'council attendant'

[1] This office enjoyed a temporary importance between 1485 and 1529 for which neither its earlier nor its later history seem to cast it.

and 'council at Westminster' of the books never existed, though councillors attendant or at Westminster there were. These terms describe the location of individuals, not the differentiation of institutions: a man would change his description as he travelled with the king or stayed behind, and there was no fixity about selection. If the king returned to Westminster all the councillors were there, except those detached on individual business and those away looking after their own affairs. Some men were apparently delegated during term to hear the petitions of poor persons and of the king's servants in the court specially developed for them by the reign of Richard III and known as that of requests; but even this differentiation was far from complete, and men technically allocated to the 'court' of requests are found at work in the 'court' of star chamber. Requests itself underwent frequent re-establishment until it emerged settled late in Henry VIII's reign.[1] Everything was very indeterminate: fluidity and lack of specialisation characterised Henry VII's council.

The council's function was threefold. It existed to advise the king in matters of policy, to administer the realm, and to adjudicate upon cases brought before it by petition. Of the first duty no evidence has survived, for advice was given by word of mouth after debate; the second has left a few traces here and there in writs and orders emanating from king and council; the third, however, is well-documented because it was essentially a task which called for record-keeping. In consequence, the importance of the council's functions has commonly been seen in inverse order to that which really applied, and its most formal business—judicial matters—has been allowed to obscure activities which have to be largely guessed at. In the reign of Henry VII this false stress is less injurious than later. The judicial work of the council was the centre and mainspring of that activity in restoring obedience to the law which gives the reign its chief claim to fame. However, if we are to understand the part the council played it will be necessary to outline briefly the regular courts of the realm—the courts of the common law.

Out of the undifferentiated *curia regis* of the twelfth century there grew, among other institutions, two courts of law which became established in Westminster Hall and separated from the king's entourage: the court of common pleas late in the twelfth century, and the court of king's bench early in the fourteenth. The first dealt with civil cases between party and party; the second with criminal matters and all cases affecting the king's interests.

[1] For the court of requests cf. also below, p. 83.

To them must be added the exchequer sitting as a court and handling revenue cases. These central courts made their influence felt by delegation. Civil cases were heard by justices doing circuits at regular intervals out of the legal terms; criminal jurisdiction was carried out locally by judges or justices of the peace armed with commissions of oyer and terminer and gaol delivery which were made out as need arose.[1] This system administered the common law of England, grown out of custom, judges' decisions (case law), and occasional acts of legislation like Henry II's 'assizes' or, later, parliamentary statutes. They were staffed by men trained at the inns of court who had made a career as counsel at the bar before promotion to the bench.

The common law is certainly one of the glories of England, and it was perhaps the chief legacy of the middle ages. But by the late fifteenth century the courts were in a bad way. The law had grown rigid while circumstances changed, and there were common and necessary practices in affairs of property which the courts did not recognise and therefore failed to protect. Their procedure was slow, highly technical, and very expensive: a trivial mistake in pleading could lose a good case, and a clever lawyer could drive a coach and four through the law by exploiting technicalities. Worst of all, in the wars the system failed because what is commonly regarded as its most praiseworthy component collapsed. The common law relied on the jury. In cases concerning property, for instance, there was no examination of witnesses; instead, a local jury would be empanelled to render a verdict on questions of just possession or rights of property from their own local knowledge. And juries could be intimidated or bribed or packed. In criminal matters, too, a defendant who 'put himself upon the country' (asked to be tried by a jury) could generally be sure of an acquittal if he knew the right people. With the jury proving an obstacle to justice, the whole common-law system, in any case careful rather to save the innocent than convict the guilty, was helpless in the face of the increasing violence.

But the growth of the common-law courts had not exhausted the reservoir of speaking justice which was the king's. The principle had always been that those who failed to get justice at law, or could not afford to seek it there, were entitled to appeal to the

---

[1] Oyer and terminer (to hear and determine) was originally issued for some specific case reported to the king's bench; gaol delivery was designed to deal with a number of men held in custody in a local gaol till one of the king's judges should arrive to dispose of them. By the sixteenth century the commissions were generally combined and tended to include one central judge together with several local J.Ps.

king for special intervention. In the reign of Edward I the practice grew up of collecting such petitions when the council met local representatives, that is in parliament. Parliaments soon became rather too busy with matters of general interest to attend to individual petitions; the council found their daily work hampered by this flood of requests for redress; and in the fifteenth century one of their number, the chancellor, began to specialise in dealing with petitions. Out of this activity, enormously increased when the chancellor let it be seen that he would enforce the contract known as 'feoffment to uses' or 'the use',[1] there grew the court of chancery, administering a system of law known as equity which was meant to supplement the common law. Thus, by the accession of Henry VII, the sphere of the chancellor in his nascent court of chancery was defined within wide limits: chancery as a court dealt only with civil cases. The judicial powers of the king's council remained untouched by its growth, and it was to them that Henry turned when he wished to enforce the law. People were encouraged to send their bills of complaint to the lords of the council—a technical term meaning councillors and nothing to do with peerage —though not much encouragement was in fact needed. Furthermore, the council began to act on its own initiative, either upon information being laid (usually by the king's attorney-general) or even without this. It enjoyed a number of advantages over the courts of the common law. It did not have to rely on juries but could summon witnesses to establish the truth, or have enquiries made by local magistrates. Plaintiff and defendant were upon oath, and there was no nonsense about allowing them to remain silent rather than incriminate themselves. The council represented the king; it naturally embodied the majesty of the law to a higher degree than the discredited common-law courts. Councillors were king's servants and amenable only to influence from the crown: towards all subjects, regardless of rank, they could be—and generally were—fearlessly impartial. The council could inflict penalties such as imprisonment and confiscation of property which were not open to the common law with its reliance on fines. On the other hand, felony and treason were beyond its competence

---

[1] Feoffment to uses was a device to transfer the legal property in land to a trustee, so as to avoid the feudal incidents which arose upon inheritance. If A wished his son B to succeed without payment of fines, etc., he would enfeoff C (the trustee) with his lands, to the use of B; the legal seisin (possession) would be in C when A died, though A and B enjoyed the profits from the land. There were more complicated forms of the use. Until the chancellor proved ready to protect such agreements, there was no remedy against defaulting trustees.

because it could not touch life or member—it could not order execution or mutilation.

In this judicial activity of the council lay the origin of the later court of star chamber. It was desirable that men should have some fixed place to resort to if the council was to act as a court, and in turn, once the council began to sit in one place at stated times and deal with judicial business in a regular manner, it developed all the characteristics of a court. It was the councillors at Westminster, meeting in the star chamber which had been the council room since Edward III's time, that dealt with the judicial work. But there was so far no division into court and council; there was only the council which—as it had done for at least a century—would meet in open session to adjudicate upon petitions. Henry VII only added pressure of work; the development into a court came later. The crown recovered strength; therefore the council, the crown's agent, also recovered strength; and thus it was able to deal with the pressing problem of disorder. But let it be noted that the councillors in the star chamber never administered a law of their own, as did chancery. They saw to it that the existing law was observed, a task they could discharge the more easily because their standing and procedure gave them marked advantages both over the ordinary courts and over the criminal. In consequence, the council in the star chamber—strong, impartial, energetic, and incorruptible—soon grew popular with suitors, and business increased steadily. In this reign it was largely concerned with matters of riot—any forcible breach of the peace, for whatever cause—and retained a touch of the tribunal of state, protecting the interests of the king and realm against law-breakers.

The conciliar principle which led to the growth of the court of requests and the development of the council in star chamber produced two more institutions which must be briefly mentioned. The country as a whole was lawless and disturbed enough, but this was as nothing compared with the state of the northern and Welsh borders. Scottish raids in the north, the franchises and violent practices of the marcher lords in the west, kept those parts in a turmoil of primitive lawlessness which the rest of the country had long outgrown. The ordinary institutions of local government exercised little influence in an area where violence was the order of the day and relations between men depended on personal allegiance to some great nobleman. The expansion of these conditions from the marches of Wales across the whole of England had put the country back into an anarchy unknown for centuries; now conditions returned to normal in the settled parts, but the borders remained anarchic. Henry VII produced no far-reaching solution. In the north, Richard III, as duke of Gloucester, had governed during his brother's reign, and like any great nobleman he had been surrounded by a council. After his death, and after the death of the earl of Northumberland (1487) on whom Henry had at first relied to keep the border country quiet, the king made the child Arthur warden of the Scottish marches with the earl of Surrey as his lieutenant. Surrey, too, had a council which, in the Tudor manner, was filled with officials rather than feudal retainers, and out of this the council of the north was ultimately to grow. In Wales and the Welsh marches, the Tudors were well placed by their descent; Henry found it unnecessary to do more than appoint a council technically in attendance on the prince of Wales who himself, of course, was a child and absent. This council administered the principality but played no part in the affairs of the marches where the organisation of the earldom of March (inherited from the Yorkists) was continued. Altogether, these gropings after administrative arrangements on the borders illustrate the conservatism of Henry VII's policy. Every baron had his council, and therefore the barons (or princes) appointed to local control had theirs; one might make sure that these councils were staffed by loyal and skilled administrators—as one made sure of the king's own council—but that was all. So far there was no sign of those later institutions, the council of the north and the council in the marches of Wales; old and tried expedients, personal and temporary in character, were the limits of Henry VII's inventiveness. He restored but did not innovate.

5. PARLIAMENT AND THE CHURCH

We have traced the government of the country from a crown rendered strong by financial independence, through the central council and courts, and through the local institution of justices of the peace; we have shown how Henry VII restored sound government by infusing new life into institutions which he found ready to hand, and in particular by restoring its earlier vigour to the royal household as an agency of national administration. In all this, we have had no occasion to say a word about parliament. The reason is simple: parliament, though by this time recognised as a specific institution, was not part of the ordinary government of the realm. It met when the king called it, and no king called it unless he had a special reason to do so, either to obtain supplies or to pass those formulations of existing or new law that are known as statutes.

Two things were already accepted about parliament: taxes could only be imposed with its consent, and the laws declared there were superior to all other laws. The first point arose originally from the convenience of getting the consent of the realm in one place and at one time; it was the more easily adhered to because a strong king like Henry VII preferred to 'live of his own' and not to trouble his parliaments. The second point arose out of parliament's character as a high court—the highest in the realm—whose decisions were binding on inferior courts; several times in the fifteenth century, the judges declared that certain matters were outside their competence, having been made the subject of parliamentary statute. The roots of parliament's two modern pillars—control of taxation and the supremacy of parliamentary legislation—had taken hold, though the institution was still very 'medieval'. The core of parliament was a meeting of the king with his council in the widest sense, a council consisting both of his barons and of his professional or permanent council. The parliament chamber, with its throne on the cloth of state, its benches for lords spiritual and temporal, and its woolsacks for councillors and judges, signified the true essence of parliament. In addition, there were the representatives of the communities—the knights of the shires and the burgesses of the boroughs. These had no right of access to the parliament chamber; they were outside the high court of parliament and for that very reason had organised themselves into a house of commons under the guidance of the Speaker who alone could address the king in his parliament. In the sixteenth century the meetings of the great council in the parliament were to develop into the house of lords, even as the meetings of the ordinary council in the star chamber developed into the court of star chamber. But this was yet in the future when Henry VII sat on the throne.

Henry VII's parliaments conformed generally to the medieval pattern. The Lancastrians in their weakness had had to rely on parliamentary support and taxes; the frequent meetings then held had certainly established the commons as an essential part of a proper parliament. But even the Lancastrian commons had appeared stronger than they were because the magnate opposition in the great council had employed them as mouthpieces. Henry VII had to fear no opposition from his lords of whom a majority (about forty) were bishops and abbots whose appointments he virtually controlled, while the lay peers were in part at least those he had promoted. Among the commons, too, there were never any signs of opposition. It was not fear, then, which caused Henry

VII to call but six parliaments in twenty-three years,[1] five of them
in the first ten years of his reign—a fact for which he claimed
credit, since he had thus saved his subjects' pockets. He looked on
parliament as a medieval king: it was a weapon he could employ
when he felt it to be useful, but with which he could dispense at
his pleasure. He would have to call it only if he needed taxes; but
he made his ordinary revenue suffice. It was a high court where the
grievances of the subject could find redress at the hands of king
and council; but the council sessions in the star chamber were
doing this more efficiently. It could declare what the law was (as
Henry's age still saw it) or, to our way of thinking, make laws by
its decisions; but he had little fresh law to make. Thus he called
only one parliament between 1497 and his death, and no one
thought anything of it. It is not true that this long break, after the
frequency of meetings early in the reign, in any way signified a
danger to the very existence of parliament: it was not wanted for
the present, but it would be called again if and when the king
should need it. In the meantime, there was reason to be pleased at
a policy which saved many men much bother and expense.

However, while Henry's attitude to parliament was essentially
medieval and shared by his subjects, there were signs that the
fifteenth-century development had not gone unnoticed and that
things might be different in the future. When the king tried to get
a money grant out of an irregular assembly called in 1496, he met
strenuous opposition on the grounds that only a proper parliament
could vote taxes; he called a parliament next year and got his supplies without difficulty. More important still, Henry exploited the
dominating position of the high court of parliament to attack the
lesser privileges and franchises which were so troublesome to the
Tudors. Some parts, such as Tynedale, had their rights taken
away by statute. An act of 1504 attacked the immunities of cor-
porations and gilds. Several acts defined the limits of 'benefit of
clergy'—the privilege enjoyed by those claiming to be members of
the Church to escape the consequences of wrongdoing. Parliament
interfered with an ordinance made by the city of London and
authorised (in the statute of retainers) the persecution of offenders
by methods unknown to the common law. All this legislation
purported to state what the true law ought to be and only to
clarify a position and elaborate details of procedure. As the phrase
goes, it was declaratory rather than legislative. The form was not
a disguise for deeper things; this was really the way in which both
king and nation looked upon the matter. Nevertheless, when such

[1] 1485, 1487, 1489, 1491, 1495, 1497, 1504.

plain law as accusation by indictment was set aside, when privileges grounded in good prescription were destroyed in a few words
without even the pretence that they had never existed, it is clear
that the modern doctrine of legislation by parliamentary statute
was on the way. These were the foundations, half-realised as yet,
on which the full Tudor doctrine of the sovereignty of the king in
parliament was to be built. But in the reign of the first Tudor,
parliament was still an occasional rather than a permanent part of
a government which was in the hands of the king and his courts—
institutions of which parliament, though the most solemn, was the
least frequent and in practice therefore the least important.

There remains one institution, the church. However, a full
discussion of this large subject had best be left till a later chapter.
In the reign of Henry VII the church enjoyed a kind of medieval
Indian summer. Relations with the lay power—the king—were
excellent; Henry was a pious son of the church, and the clergy
supplied many of his leading ministers and servants. The troubles
of the fourteenth century, to be discussed hereafter, were as if
forgotten by common consent. Henry's work in restoring order
necessitated a pruning of the privileges of benefit of clergy and
sanctuary of which unscrupulous men had taken undue advantage;
but the Church did not feel inclined to resent an invasion of its
rights which only promoted peace and good order. From these it
itself profited greatly. And so, while Henry stopped the violence
of greater and lesser troublemakers and asserted the supreme
authority of the crown over the laity, the problem of the relations
of Church and state never came up and remained unsolved. The
king was content to deal with the difficulties that existed, and in
this he was of course completely right. It was enough that he
should restore good and permanent government, an end he
achieved by putting new life into old institutions and, in particular,
by himself working night and day at the task of king. His reward
came when he could hand to his son a safe throne, a full treasury,
a functioning machine of government, and a reasonably ordered
and prosperous country.

Chapter IV

THE GREAT CARDINAL

THE reign of Henry VIII opened in a blaze of glory. Contemporaries were ready to be impressed; Henry VII had never been an inspiring figure, and in his later years—order having been restored—a cold, calculating, and cautious government held little to attract the livelier members of a nation which remembered an heroic past. Legitimate demands were termed exaction, and a foreign policy based on matrimony rather than war roused no enthusiasm. By contrast the new king, not quite eighteen when he ascended the throne on 21 April 1509, promised wonders. In his young days, Henry was a handsome giant with a predilection for athletics; he hunted and shot, played tennis and wrestled, with the best of them. In addition he was intelligent, a capable musician, quite well-seen in theology, a patron of the arts and learning. Foreign ambassadors as well as his own subjects praised him to the skies. Parts of this chorus may be discounted as the sort of exercise in Ciceronian Latin of which the age was fond, and as the kind of adulation which a king-conscious generation offered to a youthful monarch as a matter of course. But scepticism can be taken too far. Undoubtedly Henry was an impressive figure; he remained one throughout a long reign even in later days when muscle had turned to fat. Undoubtedly, too, his mental powers were considerable. At eighteen his character was yet forming, and precisely what his abilities were can only be decided when his life's work has been considered. There is no doubt, however, that many men both high and low, both commonplace and exceptional, expected great things. A month after his father's death, Henry fulfilled his dying wish by marrying Catherine of Aragon, six years older than himself. The scene seemed set for a happy and prosperous reign.

The very fact of Henry's peaceful accession was a triumph for his father's policy; the blood of both the Roses had at last mingled in one unquestioned claimant to the throne. The change of kings made little immediate difference in affairs, for the government continued to be dominated by the previous reign. Henry VII's chief councillors composed Henry VIII's first council: no one else was yet available. To two men the change proved fatal. Both Henry and his council wished to add some concrete foundation to the popularity which so far rested largely on hopes. A gesture proved easy to find. Hatred of Henry VII's policy concentrated on his 'fiscal judges', Empson and Dudley; their sacrifice would cleanse the dead king's name and earn the new king golden opinions. A proclamation asked all who would to come and charge the late king's servants with unjust extortion; many came. Since, however, the intended victims could prove that they had only acted under instructions, it became necessary to arraign them on an entirely fictitious charge of treason. Empson and Dudley went to the scaffold, predecessors of many in this blood-stained reign. The whole story is highly instructive and has been too little regarded. The fact that Empson and Dudley were thrown to the wolves is not significant in itself; it was an obvious way of cementing popularity. But the method employed deserves attention. A fictitious charge of treason brought against two loyal servants marked a notable break with the conciliatory practices of Henry VII who had used that dubious weapon only once— against the earl of Warwick who, however innocent, represented a real threat to the dynasty. Under Henry VIII many were to be caught in that trap. That the reign should have started in this fashion makes it difficult to agree with the view that Henry VIII began as a strong, even wilful, man of sound character who deteriorated through the exercise of power into a suspicious and bloodthirsty autocrat. From the first, he was utterly sure of himself as only a man born to the purple can be, passionately devoted to his own interests and inclinations, unscrupulous but careful of legal form, and clever. Moreover, as this business shows, he was good at picking up the ideas of others. The newcomer to the throne, though he could of himself think of killing two innocent men as a way to quick popularity, cannot possibly have thought of the expedient adopted in face of their inviolability on the real charge. Whoever suggested the treason trial of Empson and Dudley had much to answer for when Henry remembered the lesson on later occasions. The affair also displayed the king's inherent cruelty. This is something so strikingly different from his father's clemency that one is tempted to see here an inheritance from his grandfather, Edward IV, whom Henry VIII resembled physically and in more than one unfortunate aspect of his character.

At any rate, the trick worked. The first parliament of the reign (January 1510) readily endorsed the murders by an act of attainder and voted the supplies which a cessation of the late king's activities made doubly necessary. Therewith the reign was under way; it remained to exploit the momentum gained. Affairs were dominated by the war in Italy where the assault of the League of Cambrai on Venice, begun in 1508, had been rather too successful for its architect, Pope Julius II. French victories threatened to engulf the whole north of the peninsula, with dangerous consequences to the independence of the Holy See. Julius II therefore, reviving the papal policy of holding the balance even between the French in the north and the Spaniards in the south, succeeded in October 1511 in forming the Holy League with Spain and Venice against France. England's adherence was something of a foregone conclusion. There was the memory of Cambrai to wipe out, when England had been left in the cold. France was still the traditional enemy, and many, from the king downwards, were bitterly jealous of her successes. The king, indeed, was the decisive factor. A good papalist, he could not listen unmoved to appeals from Rome; an almost uxorious husband, he was exposed to the influence of Ferdinand of Aragon, since Catherine thought herself in duty bound to manage her husband in her father's interest. Everything was in favour of war, except the tradition of Henry VII, and that was crumbling even in the minds of councillors trained under him. The council was not united: Surrey, an old soldier, resented the priest-ridden peace policy of Warham (archbishop of Canterbury), Fox (bishop of Winchester), and Ruthal (bishop of Durham). The king was bent on war, his wife and father-in-law were egging him on, the treasury was full, the country willing, the pope calling; thus, some sixty years after England had last fought on the continent, Henry VIII went to war against France, in search of glory and for no genuine interests of his own or his nation's. The parliament summoned in February 1512 supplied the necessary grants and listened approvingly to propaganda against the kings of France and Scotland. From the first it was taken into account that the northern border would not remain quiet while the king of England disported himself on the continent.

The war so lightly entered into proved suitably confused, with fortunes as wavering as Henry's allies and results as puny as his reasons for fighting. 1512 produced an expedition to assist Ferdinand in Spain: an English army under the marquess of Dorset landed near Bayonne and occupied the attention of the French while the king of Aragon overran Navarre. The Spaniards made no secret of the fact that the English force was only a pawn in a Spanish game; the reconquest of Guienne, mooted once again, was never a serious possibility. Dorset's men were ill looked after;

dysentery and wine killed numbers, and the rest returned home, refusing to obey their feeble commander's orders. At sea, England at first did well, but attempts to direct action from a distance ended with Henry sending his navy and admiral (Sir Edward Howard) to disaster at Brest (April 1513). Failure and disgrace only spurred Henry to further action. Early in 1513 Ferdinand deserted his allies, but the pope, who unlike Spain had not yet obtained his ends, was eager to carry on. Henry VIII now determined to invade France in person and from the north. Having succeeded in postponing the expected Scottish intervention, for which the king of France was pressing, he crossed with a large army to Calais and from there undertook the siege of the little town of Thérouanne. A French relieving force was beaten off in the 'Battle of the Spurs' (August 1513), so called because of the French speed in reverse, a victory which yielded a fair harvest of important prisoners, including the great but aged Bayard. Thérouanne fell late in August, and Tournai was captured a month later. Leaving garrisons in these towns, Henry returned in triumph, only to find that much more substantial successes had been won during his absence on the Scottish border, by an army under the earl of Surrey. James IV declared war in July and crossed the border in August. After some minor successes he met the main English army, assembled with commendable speed and well led by the old earl, at Flodden Edge on 7 September. The Scottish army was rather the larger and its position exceedingly strong; but Surrey, assisted by James's lack of generalship, forced the Scots from their stronghold and into action on disadvantageous terms. Flodden was a major English triumph: among the 10,000 or more killed that the Scots lost were their king himself and many lords. The accession of a child (James V) whose mother and regent was Henry VIII's own sister Margaret, ended the danger from Scotland for most of Henry's reign.

The war was near its end. Julius II was dead, succeeded by Leo X who wanted peace; Ferdinand continued his game of joining alliances and then repudiating his word; both he and Maximilian were negotiating behind Henry's back. But Henry was not a Tudor for nothing. Early in 1514 he himself opened negotiations with France and, much to their surprise, stole a march on his treacherous allies. The treaty of July 1514 gave England possession of Tournai and a larger pension from France; it was sealed by the marriage of Henry's younger sister Mary to the elderly Louis XII of France. Henry's fury with his father-in-law vented itself in futile dreams of allying with France to drive Ferdinand from

Navarre and assert Catherine of Aragon's claims to Castile. But these were idle thoughts; the facts sufficed to satisfy both king and country. The war had been successful, graced by two major victories and an acquisition of territory, though the victories were petty compared with the battles in Italy, and Tournai proved nothing but a liability. England had asserted her right and power to play a leading part in European affairs; Henry had won some personal renown and learned—very rapidly—how to conduct himself in the treacherous diplomacy of the time which so largely consisted in switching allies at the right moment. But the outstanding result of the war was very different: it provided Henry with the first of the two great ministers who were to give purpose and importance to his reign.

2. WOLSEY'S RULE IN ENGLAND

Thomas Wolsey was born in about 1473, son of a butcher and cattle-dealer of Ipswich.[1] He showed early intellectual promise which he followed up in the traditional way, by going to Oxford and into the Church. Taking his B.A. at fifteen, he became a fellow and then bursar of Magdalen, leaving the college—it is said—when the authorities protested at his high-handed dealings with the college funds. He continued an ordinarily successful career as chaplain to Archbishop Deane of Canterbury and Sir Richard Nanfan, deputy at Calais; in 1507 the latter's death and recommendation transferred him to the service of Henry VII who at once discovered his new chaplain's diplomatic ability. The king's death nearly wrecked a promising start, but late in 1509 Henry VIII made Wolsey almoner and a member of the council. The coming of the war gave him his opportunity. Always careful, at this time, to remain near the king and so augment his influence, he took upon himself the better part of the enormous burden of work involved in raising, equipping, dispatching, and maintaining the 30,000 or so men that Henry took to France. His zeal and ability in administration, his outstanding powers of work, and his assertive self-confidence soon made him indispensable, and from 1512 onwards he rapidly ousted all other men from Henry's confidence. Soon the council of the early years vanished. Surrey—now, as the victor of Flodden, restored to the Howard dukedom of

---

[1] The snobbery of the sixteenth century insisted on Wolsey's low birth and made his father a common butcher; the snobbery of the nineteenth found this unpalatable and elevated old Wolsey to the status of a 'prosperous grazier'.

Norfolk—was too old to fight the upstart, and his son (who succeeded to the title in 1524) was as yet too young to do so. In 1515
Warham resigned the chancellorship and Wolsey stepped into his
shoes; in 1516 Fox retired from the privy seal to devote himself
to his episcopal duties at Winchester, and Wolsey obtained the
office for Thomas Ruthal, a faithful follower. From 1515 to 1529
Wolsey was not only the king's chief minister but virtually his only
one. Though Henry never surrendered ultimate control over
affairs, it was Wolsey who ruled. He devised the policy which
Henry endorsed, and he saw that it was carried out. Henry was
still only twenty-four years old in 1515; his tastes did not alter while
vigour remained, and he could never be induced to devote himself
consistently to business and affairs. As one of his secretaries put it,
he turned the pursuit of hunting into a martyrdom, often spending
all day on horseback with the few who could keep up with such
prowess; but when it came to the reading of dispatches or signing
of instructions, all sorts of excuses were snatched at, and exasperated secretaries often had to pursue him for days before things
got attended to. Wolsey owed his advancement to his ability to
take these tedious tasks from the royal shoulders; in consequence
the reality of power was his—until the king should choose to
assert himself.

Wolsey's rapid rise was marked by an equally rapid accumulation of preferments and offices. Dean of Lincoln in 1509, he added
several other deaneries by 1513, the bishopric of Tournai in that
year, and then—after a brief interlude as bishop of Lincoln—the
archbishopric of York in 1514. The next year he obtained a
cardinalate from Leo X and the chancellorship from Henry VIII.
The only office he thereafter added was that of papal legate *a
latere* (1518), which will be discussed hereafter; as far as possessions went, he acquired the abbey of St Albans and exchanged
subsidiary bishoprics in succession—Bath and Wells in 1518,
Durham in 1524, Winchester in 1529. These appointments were
taken for their revenues—St Albans was the richest abbey in
England and Winchester the wealthiest see—so as to enable him
to support his inordinate love of pomp and display. Wolsey was
arrogant by nature and unbelievably fond of showing off his estate,
so much so that he far eclipsed even the showiness of the Tudor
court and angered nobility and gentry by his intolerable pretensions. He built palaces, dressed and ate and drank lavishly,
surrounded himself with a huge household, and developed great
skill in adding to his income from extortions and bribes. With all
his high intelligence and valour, he was vain, shallow, and greedy.

For many years the king did not mind: Henry's devotion to the favourite or confidant of the moment was invariably complete, a fact in which lies much of the secret of his success. Where he trusted he trusted without reservations; when trust ceased, it ceased at a blow. Wolsey's self-glorification only once took a turn which deserves some respect. In 1525 he began to build two colleges at Ipswich and Oxford: even here he aimed characteristically high, for he was deliberately copying the royal foundations of Eton and King's College, Cambridge. The Ipswich school was abandoned at his fall, but Cardinal College at Oxford was refounded by Henry VIII as Christ Church. It is comforting to think that that college continues to remember Wolsey rather than the king as its true benefactor.

Though he was an able administrator, Wolsey displayed surprisingly little interest in the details of the administrative machine. It was, on the whole, running well under the impetus given by Henry VII's revival of household activity, and the cardinal found it unnecessary to tamper with it. Sir John Heron held the crucial office of treasurer of the chamber until his death in 1524; he was succeeded by two experienced civil servants in Sir Henry Wyatt (1524-8) and Sir Brian Tuke (1528-45). The only change which Wolsey made arose directly out of Henry VIII's refusal to work hard at the business of government. The supervision of the 'chamber system of finance' had been in the hands of the king in person and such individuals as he entrusted with the task; now a more formal arrangement became necessary. Successive acts of parliament therefore appointed two general surveyors of crown lands who were to administer the revenues from these properties and to audit other revenue accounts. The system was still based on 'household' ideas inasmuch as the general surveyors did not preside over a proper department of state; their office existed only from one parliament to another, a new act being required in each case to continue it. Such changes as there were in the rest of the administration only reflected Wolsey's all-powerful position. Thus he controlled the royal seals, either directly or through his nominees; he caused difficulties by taking the great seal abroad with him on his diplomatic missions, and on at least one occasion improperly retained the signet which should have been with the principal secretary. Most important of all, he virtually destroyed the inner ring of the council by concentrating its powers in himself; councillors rarely knew what went on until the cardinal deigned to inform them, and—if Sir Thomas More is to be believed—the king himself was at times in a like state of ignorance.

The history of the council under Wolsey is the history of the star chamber where the cardinal presided, holding his court among the admiring sycophants before whom he displayed his talents. The king meanwhile was accompanied by his boon-companions, his fellow wrestlers and card players and dicers; though at times he complained at being left without a sufficiency of councillors, Wolsey never relaxed his determined hold on his exclusive powers.

Wolsey contemplated administrative reforms: in 1519 he drew up, at Henry's instigation, plans which would have enabled the king to take an active share in government, and in 1526 the great Ordinance of Eltham projected a thorough overhaul of the king's household establishment as well as the consolidation of a small advisory council of leading ministers. But these plans remained plans; to have made them a reality would have destroyed the basis of Wolsey's unrivalled position. Though Henry might stir in an occasional access of zeal he always returned quickly enough to his harts and hounds, to his wife and his occasional mistresses, to his cards and dice, his music and dancing; for many years the cardinal knew how to handle this king who hid behind a bluff façade and frivolous preoccupations an inflexible will and a powerful if intermittent intelligence. During Wolsey's supremacy observers as a rule underestimated his dependence on the king and took him at his own exalted valuation; the insecurity of the cardinal's position was not seen till the test came. Still, it remains true that from 1515 to 1529 Wolsey and not Henry was the effective ruler of the country.

Wolsey's greatest weakness lay in the realm of finance. He knew how to spend money to the best purpose: except in his own affairs he was not extravagant, but he was a bad financier because he could neither make do with the existing revenue nor effectively increase it. He had little understanding of economic facts. His intervention in the anti-foreign riots in London on 'Evil May Day', 1517, when a crowd of apprentices tried to kill and plunder the rich alien merchants, was prompted by his dislike of disorder rather than by any appreciation of the great part played by foreigners in the economy of England. Wolsey never grasped the importance of trade or attempted to manage and exploit it. Worst of all, his autocratic temper would not let him manage parliaments; yet he expected them to supply the means for his dizzy foreign policy. In 1513 he secured a novel tax called a subsidy, a levy of 1s. in the £ on income from land and wages; this, because it was based on a realistic assessment, was to remain the chief direct tax

under the Tudors, though it soon lost that advantage. The next
parliament (1515) had to be dismissed before it made a grant
because Wolsey wished to stop its attacks on clerical privilege and
administration. When war broke out again in 1522, the coffers
were empty and emergency measures had to be taken. In 1522
Wolsey collected a forced loan from (it seems) the wealthy which
doubled the yield of the 1514 subsidy to bring in £200,000. In
1523 he at last again confronted a parliament from which he
demanded a tax of 4s. in the £; after a stormy and prolonged
session they granted 2s. and arranged for the levy to be spread over
several years. Wolsey got round this by his so-called 'anticipation':
holding out promise of certain reliefs, he ordered individuals to
pay their share at once. In 1524, when the cardinal tried to supplement the revenue by an arbitrary forced loan from all men owning
property in land and goods, a levy which he described as an
Amicable Grant, things came to a head. Collectors were still out
for the loan of 1522; other commissioners were trying to obtain
payment of the 1523 subsidy; and now a third lot of commissioners
added their exactions. There was no prospect of the loan-money
being repaid, though the subsidy of 1523 had been granted after
a promise that it would be used to redeem the previous year's
loans. The result might have been foreseen. Both the laity and the
clergy began by muttering and ended by violently resisting the
demands; in East Anglia and Kent there were signs of armed
rebellion—against Wolsey, not against the king—and there was no
hope at all of collecting a penny of the Amicable Grant. Only
Henry's personal intervention saved the situation: he ordered the
collection to cease and granted a general pardon to all who had
resisted, thus proving that his common sense and political instinct
could overcome even his high pride. For Henry hated giving in
under pressure, especially to his own subjects. It availed Wolsey
little that he pretended to have secured the remission of the grant
by his own intercession; people knew who had been behind the
demand, and for the first time Henry's confidence in his minister
was seriously shaken.

Wolsey's taxation made enemies of many whose hostility could
be dangerous. Another of his attempts to cope with economic
difficulties, commendable though it may have been, was equally
impolitic. He tried to solve the great problem of depopulation and
enclosures, the standard complaint of contemporary moralists and
amateur economists. The agrarian difficulties of the sixteenth
century were caused directly by the vast inflationary movement
known as the price rise which took effect soon after Henry VII's

death.[1] The amount of money in circulation increased, with the result that goods became dearer. Men living on fixed incomes were in difficulties, and landlords found it necessary to increase their incomes by various practices of which enclosure for sheep-farming (wool being a profitable crop) and the raising of rents and fines on entry (rack-renting) were the most hated. Contemporaries put it all down to greed and wickedness; the search for scapegoats is ever popular in times of distress. They painted a picture of vast areas stripped of their peasantry, turned into parks for the pleasure of nobility and gentry, and exploited as sheep-runs by lords who found the market for wool more attractive than the maintenance of a stable rural society. This picture continues to be accepted, though most of the bases for it have disappeared. It is quite true that economic pressure forced many gentlemen to obtain better returns from their lands, but it is also true that the inflation profited the primary producer—the small yeoman farmer or even peasant who had a surplus to sell on a rising market, and who could thus afford to pay a higher rent for his land even if he did not much like to do so. A little inexcusable imparking took place, but the whole amount of enclosure was astonishingly small—astonishingly, that is, if one has listened to the false prophets of the day. It has been calculated that some 2 or 3 per cent. of the affected counties (mostly in the Midlands) was enclosed before 1525, and much of this enclosure—often the work of small farmers and yeomen—was designed for better farming and not for pasture at all. The main corn-growing areas remained untouched until the eighteenth century.

That there was a problem cannot and need not be denied. There was an increase in vagrancy, that is in rural unemployment, though here, too, the fact that Tudor governments tried to do something about an evil which earlier governments had ignored has served to distort the picture. There was a certain 'decay of ploughs': here and there the fusing of holdings was replacing several hovels by one homestead. Distinct from this, some towns had decayed—for instance Coventry whose industries had fallen on evil days. There was an increase in sheep-farming, but it really amounted to little more than a return to the great wool-days of the twelfth and thirteenth centuries. Since then the area under sheep had declined; now it increased again; there is every reason to suppose that the increase left the acreage of good arable land virtually undiminished. There was some raising of rents and fines, for the reasons already mentioned, and it naturally caused some

[1] For a full discussion of the price rise see below, Ch. IX.

hardship. How difficult it is to understand the truth is illustrated by the fact that some writers will speak of the decay of the yeoman at this time and others of his golden days. The agrarian revolution laid the foundations of the characteristic structure of the English countryside (landlord, tenant farmer, landless labourer) and destroyed the true land-holding peasant. But the categories developed according to circumstance and individual fate: some yeomen bettered themselves and some fell by the wayside, some gentlemen prospered and some decayed, by no means all peasants were depressed. No class rose or fell as a class; a man's fate depended on whether he succeeded in sharing the advantages which the inflation offered to the enterprising and lucky, or joined those whom rising prices and static or declining incomes were pauperising. Individual greed and stupidity might aggravate the difficulties on occasion; they certainly did not cause them.

The problem was simple at heart. After nearly two centuries of stable or declining prices, and a stable or declining population, both prices and population were now rising. Why the population rose we do not know (population changes are commonly mysterious), nor can we give figures of the increase; but that it rose is plain from many signs and symptoms. Interacting upon each other, these forces, not understood at all at the time and in any case uncontrollable, produced the familiar evils of the sixteenth-century countryside. No industries existed to absorb the surplus of money and men; the result was inflation and unemployment. It struck people with special force because the fifteenth century had been a time of depression and static conditions, thus assisting the notion that economic life in the past had always been stable. They did not know the real reasons for the change, but they saw some of the symptoms (such as enclosing and rack-renting) and argued that these must be the causes of a transformation which—since they believed in the past and held no brief for progress—they thought to be necessarily evil. Thus from the reign of Henry VII onwards, legislation was passed prohibiting enclosure and compelling the upkeep of houses and ploughs in accordance with the conditions of a vanishing age. The laws would have been futile at the best of times because they treated superficial aspects of a profound change; they were rendered merely silly by having to be enforced by the very men—the gentry as justices of the peace— whom inflation was forcing to exploit their assets or go under. Wolsey, eager to champion the poor and humble against the rich who refused to recognise him as one of themselves, determined to make the law effective. In 1517, 1518, and 1526, he appointed commissions to enquire into enclosures made since their prohibition in 1488. The returns showed a good deal of petty and a little major enclosing, but—as we have said—when properly studied they also reveal the essential falseness of the contemporary view. However, Wolsey proceeded to a spasmodic destruction of illegal enclosures; hedges were pulled down here and there, and some open fields restored. It did nothing to relieve the economic problem—naturally not, since it did not tackle that problem. The only result was to enrage the landed gentry still further against the upstart minister, while enclosing went on because, in fact, it did good to more people than it harmed. But Wolsey had succeeded in adding to his enemies.

At home, then, despite his abilities and display, Wolsey proved a singularly ill-advised minister who ruined the finances, exasperated those people whose support was essential to the monarchy, and could not translate his boundless energy into anything profitable to the commonwealth. The one exception to this sad tale lies in his judicial activities. Wolsey gloried in the majesty of a judge, and though he had no legal training that we know of he possessed a remarkable natural ability for the task. His office of lord chancellor gave him a wide sweep of judicial competence, and there are signs, though it is difficult to be sure, that he did much to establish the regular court of chancery. He certainly increased the amount of business transacted there, speeded up decisions, and enforced them by the weight of the authority he derived from his general position: he may be said to have put on a solid basis the system of equity jurisdiction which came first to supplement, then to rival, and finally to accompany the common law. Wolsey did not found the court or its principles of justice: the fifteenth century did that. Nor was he the man who classified these principles and saved them from the accidents of an individual chancellor's whim: that was not to be done until the seventeenth century. But since equity, like the common law, was to grow out of case-law— judges' decisions, that is—the fourteen years of case-law which Wolsey made and on which he impressed the features of a strong and penetrating mind were to have great influence on equity as it ultimately developed. The great chancellors-judges of the sixteenth century—Wolsey, More, Audley, Nicholas Bacon, and Ellesmere—defined and developed the principles on which the seventeenth century erected a coherent system of law.

Chancery was a court of civil jurisdiction: it handled matters of property, contract, trusts, wills, and the like, and since its decisions

still depended on the chancellor's private sense of justice the law
here made owed a good deal to the Roman law which was then
sweeping the board in the other countries of Western Europe.[1]
Things were different in the other of Wolsey's courts, the one that
may be called the chancellor's court for criminal cases. This was
star chamber. Sir Thomas Smith, professor of civil law at Cambridge, diplomatist, and principal secretary to Queen Elizabeth—
a man who knew what he was talking about—said in his book on
English government, written in 1565, that star chamber, though
it began long before, 'took great augmentation and authority'
under Wolsey, so much so that some even then thought him to be
the inventor of that court. As has already been said, the star
chamber originally derived its judicial authority from the fact that
it was the king's council meeting to adjudicate upon petitions; to
the end of its days, its official title remained 'the lords of the council
in the star chamber at Westminster'. Wolsey revived this judicial
activity which appears to have been languishing since Henry VII's
death, monopolised its authority, and vastly increased its business.
He used it, as Henry VII had done, to suppress the riots and disturbances raised by men who thought themselves above the law
and whom he taught, as he put it, 'the law of star chamber'. By
this he meant not a different kind of law but the powers of enforcement (of statutes, proclamations, and the common law) which the
authority of king and council gave to star chamber. To jurisdiction
in riots and violent disputes, he added perjury, libel, and forgery.
These the medieval common law left to the Church courts which
were by now quite incapable of making their decisions effective. It
was easy for a prince of the Church to do what no layman could
have done and transfer these matters to an efficient secular court.
He also punished contempt of court, wherever committed, and
continued to deal with false juries; thus he enlarged star chamber's
capacity to supervise the whole enforcement of the law. His main
achievement was to turn star chamber from a tribunal of state into
a court used freely by the king's subjects in the settlement of their
affairs; it was under Wolsey that it became (what it remained until
its abolition) a part of the regular system of law-administration in

[1] The theory once prevailed, and is still to be found, that in the early
sixteenth century the English common law was in danger of being
superseded by the Roman or civil law which is more amenable to
authoritarian interpretation; this view has, however, been disproved
(cf. W. S. Holdsworth, *History of English Law*, iv. 217-83, and below,
p. 169). Chancery was saved from Romanisation by the fact that Wolsey's
successors, from Sir Thomas More onwards, were as a rule common
lawyers.

England. Probably we must not yet speak of a court of star chamber as a separate institution,[1] but Wolsey's work there certainly prepared the ground for just such a development. He left the distinction between the council in star chamber and the court of star chamber in so shadowy a state that modern scholars have been much confused.

Not content with so wide and effective an application of conciliar jurisdiction, Wolsey attempted further to draw all legal business within his orbit; if the common law was ever in danger it was during the cardinal's ascendancy, though the danger was never very serious. That protean institution, the court of requests for poor men's causes, revived together with the council's activity in star chamber; it became subject to Wolsey's machinations when the chancellor tried to extend his powers by commissions. In 1518 he established four conciliar committees to do what was in fact requests' work: they heard poor men's suits concerning civil disputes. Of these four only the committee in the White Hall survived into the 1530s; this became the court of requests proper. Throughout his ascendancy, Wolsey issued commissions to hear individual cases, a common conciliar practice which, however, in Wolsey's generous hands seriously encroached on the business of the common-law courts. In 1524-5 he attempted a general delegation by commission. Cases in the north and in the marches of Wales were committed to the councils there; fresh commissions to individuals issued to relieve pressure at the centre; even the council of the duchy of Lancaster was to be employed more fully in general litigation. The truth was that Wolsey had overreached himself. He had encouraged people to bring their suits to him, and he had found them respond only too readily. There is a familiar story that he announced his willingness to give justice to poor men and then had to change his mind in disgust when he discovered that he was being imposed upon with a flood of unjust claims. True or not, the tale reflects the position: Wolsey had to give up trying to concentrate all justice in his person, as he would have liked to do. He virtually admitted defeat when in 1528 he ordered all minor matters brought before star chamber to be heard on assize; the common law could not be dispensed with.

However, though according to his habit Wolsey cherished plans beyond his or any man's capacity, he did much good and praiseworthy work in his judicial employments, and it was work that endured. He put the court of chancery on a solid foundation and made the fortunes of star chamber; he endeavoured, with

[1] Cf. below, p. 184.

much success, to enforce the law on people who thought themselves free of it; and he gave good justice to all men, many of them
weak and poor, who brought their suits before him. The common
lawyers, of course, hated him as a rival, and he gained no popularity with the nobles and gentlemen whom he humbled before
the law, but it seems that with the poor and the generality this part
of his work gained him some credit. It was unfortunate, from his
point of view, that the friends thus made were generally weak and
without influence, while those he added to his enemies were
powerful and dangerous.

3. WOLSEY AND THE CHURCH

As chancellor, Wolsey dominated the state; in the Church he
ruled as cardinal and legate. Wolsey's ambitions always reached
for the highest goal, and throughout his life he never lost hope of
one day being pope. That hope had no reality outside his own
mind: the circumstances of European and Italian politics rendered
the election of an Englishman quite out of the question. Failure to
reach the heights left Wolsey with only the smaller field of England
in which to exercise his power and his love of autocracy, but what
he lost in scope he made up for in intensity. The first thing to
understand about the English Church in the middle ages is that it
never existed. There was no one authority in ecclesiastical affairs
co-terminous with the king's in secular affairs. Instead, there were
only two provinces of the Universal Church—the provinces of
Canterbury and York. Each was quite independent of the other;
each had its own organisation and its own convocation; the only
link between them was their common allegiance and subjection to
the papacy at Rome. Naturally, this rigid division could not in
practice be maintained in face of a secular organisation which
comprehended both provinces. That of Canterbury was much
larger and its archbishop the senior of the two; some aspects of
their relations with each other were determined by common
allegiance and subjection to the crown in temporal matters. The
situation was complex and unresolved, giving rise to much bicker-
ing and rivalry between the two archbishops. Some ecclesiastical
bodies in England—especially many monasteries—were exempt
from all episcopal and archiepiscopal authority and came directly
under Rome. No priest, of whatever rank, could claim to be in
charge of all the clergy in England—except the pope whose
authority was distant and foreign. On the other hand, the Church,
with its hierarchical organisation, offered a better chance to an

autocrat than did the state with its parliaments and franchises; Wolsey, who delighted in personal power, could hardly be expected to forego it in a sphere to which his profession drew him as strongly as his tastes drew him to secular politics.

It would have been something to have obtained the highest ecclesiastical honour in England, but here fate was against him. When Cardinal Bainbridge died at Rome in 1514—of poison, it was said, but then every cardinal's death was at this time followed by that rumour—Wolsey immediately obtained his see of York and a year later the cardinalate. But the road to Canterbury was blocked by Warham who, though born about 1450 and therefore due to die in an age when sixty years were a respectable limit to a man's life, in the end outlived Wolsey. But for this accident it is likely that Wolsey would have added Canterbury to York and thus created an unprecedented unification of the English Church by means of existing offices. Instead he was forced to resort to methods which involved him in objectionable innovation, conflict with the English clergy, uncalled-for dependence on papal authority, and ultimately the king's deadly displeasure. He decided to have himself made a permanent papal legate *a latere*. Papal legates had always been of two kinds. Every archbishop was a *legatus natus*, exercising certain aspects of his authority by grant from Rome. In addition, the pope could send envoys with specific powers on separate occasions; these *legati a latere* might be no more than ambassadors, or they might be sent with a commission superseding for a time all other ecclesiastical authority in the region affected. Wolsey turned the occasional expedient into regular practice and used an office ordinarily confined to genuine envoys from Rome to make himself the permanently resident ruler of the Church in England. His powers were circumscribed by the bulls granting them, and he was always, from the first grant of the legacy in 1518, appealing for renewals and extensions; but the limitations proved theoretical only, for pressure at Rome secured a steady enlargement of scope and, in 1524, a grant for life. His legateship made Wolsey what no one had ever been before: the ecclesiastical ruler of the two provinces of the Church which between them covered the realm of England.

The ostensible purpose behind his demands was his desire to reform the Church. Church reform was very much in the air at this time; many, both churchmen and laymen, admitted that there were things in the conduct of individual priests and the state of the monasteries that needed attention. Wolsey himself was very free with pronouncements and promises on that score. Unfortunately, however, it would have been difficult to find a better example of most of the glaring abuses in the Church than the cardinal himself. He exemplified pluralism at its worst: he always held at least one other bishopric in addition to York, and—most improperly of all— he, a secular priest, was abbot of St Albans. No one could have excelled him in non-residence: he never visited the seats of any of his sees, and until his fall he never attempted to deal with their affairs. As for simony, his income from improper bribes and patronage was large and notorious. No priest was richer or displayed the fact more proudly. Celibacy sat lightly on the man who had probably several daughters and certainly one son whom he promoted rapidly to some valuable benefices in his extreme youth (nepotism and the ordination of minors). This was the would-be reformer of clerical morals and affairs. His plans were considerable. He wished to dissolve decayed monasteries and to found new bishoprics which were badly needed; he wished to throw his whole power and energy into a campaign for the reform of abuses. Out of these dreams came nothing but the dissolution of a few small houses whose property he employed in the founding of his colleges. We need not think that he never meant to do the things he so freely talked about, but apart from his personal unsuitability there was also the fact that Wolsey never knew how to confine himself to the possible. He tried to do the work of ten men and not surprisingly failed. Foreign affairs and star chamber came first; Church reform very definitely last.

In any case, he had in mind a more clearly defined purpose for his legateship. It enabled him to exercise a supreme authority over the Church in England, and this he intended to exploit. With vigour and success he superseded the powers of others—abbots, bishops, archbishops, and convocation. His agents carried out visitations of some small monasteries, reported unfavourably, and dissolved them—altogether an admirable training for the later wholesale destruction which was to be managed by Thomas Cromwell, Wolsey's chief instrument in these matters. His attack on the liberties and independence of the episcopal bench went much further still. He permitted long vacancies on the deaths of bishops, reserving the profits to himself. He encouraged the appointment of foreigners who never visited their titular sees or took care of their charges; Wolsey then paid them a fixed stipend and administered the temporalities to his own advantage. When he fell, five English bishoprics were in foreign hands, and the effective number of bishops was thus seriously reduced. Over those that remained, the cardinal-legate exercised almost despotic powers. He interfered in the administration of sees. He drew cases from episcopal courts to his own legatine court, thus reducing the bishops to cyphers. He compelled some bishops to enter into contracts by which they made over part of their revenues to him. Even Canterbury fell before the onslaught. As early as 1519, Warham had occasion to complain of interference by Wolsey's commissioners, and a long drawn out quarrel over Canterbury's traditional rights in matters of probate ended in the legate's victory. It was proper and usual for a legate *a latere* to supersede a *legatus natus* (which Warham was), but Wolsey's legacy was unprecedented in being permanent, and his claim therefore threatened to extinguish all lawful episcopal jurisdiction except his own. Nor can he be said to have acted in the interests of reform or good practice. His sense of justice and delight in legal matters may have resulted in occasional advantages to litigants, but his greed was more to the fore. Especially obnoxious were the heavy exactions he made on probate of wills, the more so since these affected the laity. But the clergy, too, had no love for the all-powerful cardinal. Though he ought to have been their natural protector and representative, he seemed more like a destroyer; eager as he was to concentrate power over the Church in his own hand, he overrode all other authority and made himself more enemies. Never had the Church been so little able to order its own affairs. The two provincial convocations ceased to meet, except at parliament time when they were treated even more haughtily and mulcted more heavily than their secular counterpart. Wolsey's legatine council, ostensibly designed to represent the English Church, was a fictitious body which never met. He simply took all power to himself and governed as a despot.

The consequences of this energetic but misguided policy were seen at Wolsey's fall. The cardinal, prince of the Church though he was and equipped with the most far-reaching powers for reform, did only two things for the Church. He lessened its allegiance to Rome and weakened it past hope of recovery. Wolsey's legatine powers were papal; the hatred excited by their exercise reflected on the pope. An authority which was tolerable in a pope too weak in his own troubles and at so great a distance to make it felt became quite insupportable when wielded by the restless, interfering, forceful, and tactless cardinal. Wolsey's activities left many clergy, especially in the higher ranks, with the feeling that if subjection to Rome involved such interference with established rights and such heavy and constant demands for money there was little to be said for it. When the attack on the Church came after Wolsey's

fall, resistance was in part weakened by the thought that the king's
rule could not be worse—must indeed be lighter—than papal rule
as exemplified by the pope's legate. By the time the Church realised
its mistake the matter was beyond remedy. Furthermore, by
accumulating the Church's powers and jurisdiction in himself,
Wolsey bound the fate of the Roman Church in England to the
fate of Rome's legate; the legate's fall dragged down the legate's
superior. Lastly, a bench of bishops weakened in numbers and
authority, united only in hatred of Wolsey but kept by him from
all corporate action for some twelve years, was in no condition to
lead opposition to the king's demands.[1] In one way and another,
therefore, Wolsey dug the grave of the institution from which he
derived his own greatest glory. Creditably enough, he did not try
to build up support among the clergy in face of the hostility which
he excited among the nobility and gentry, but it was surely over-
weening folly that insisted on adding the bishops to his most
virulent enemies.

4. WOLSEY'S FOREIGN POLICY

It may be thought that the picture painted here is getting a
little too dark. After all, Wolsey was a man of great mental powers,
enormous application and assiduity in business, a wide grasp and
firm intentions. Yet, with the exception of his judicial activities,
nothing has so far been found in his work that can be called
successful or deserves praise on other grounds; indeed, all his
doings were attended by folly, arrogance, false aims, and final
failure. However, it still remains to discuss that part of his work
for which he is primarily remembered: his foreign policy. We
must therefore go back to the beginning of his career as chief
minister and take up the tale where we left it, at the victorious
conclusion of the French war in 1514. For fifteen years Wolsey
occupied himself with the details and the greater conception of
diplomacy, but there has been much doubt about his purpose. At
one time it was usual to credit him with the invention of the so-
called balance of power. However, as has been pointed out repeatedly, the policy which tries to prevent any one power from
becoming too great by forming alliances with its potential enemies
is too obvious to be 'invented' by any statesman; moreover, it is

---

[1] It is a curious and significant fact that among the clergy whose opposition Wolsey had to combat there were some who later offered equally
strong resistance to the crown, as for instance Bishop Fisher and Rowland
Phillips, vicar of Croydon.

plain that Wolsey did not always pursue it, often allying himself
with the stronger power. Bishop Creighton thought he was inspired by the highest patriotism—that he wished to dominate Europe
in the interests of England and give England the leadership on the
European stage. It is difficult to see why one should praise a goal
which was not only not achieved but at the time was manifestly
impossible of achievement; but then Creighton, influenced by his
(the late Victorian) age, seems to have thought of Wolsey as an
earlier and better Bismarck. A. F. Pollard, whose assessment is
not only the most recent but also the coolest and best supported,
concluded that Wolsey's main principle in foreign policy was to
serve the interests of the papacy whose great servant he was and
to which he always hoped to succeed. Wolsey was not an anachro-
nistic English patriot, but the true late-medieval Churchman,
deriving his glory from Rome and creditably enough convinced
that Rome had a claim on his services.

In 1514, the French war ended with a treaty which marked a
notable victory for England. But on the last day of that year,
Louis XII died, and with him died the marriage alliance which
had given reality to the treaty. Henry and Wolsey immediately
planned to give the widow to the new French king, Francis I, but
the 'French Queen' (as she was known till her death in 1533) put a
spoke in that wheel by secretly marrying Charles Brandon, duke
of Suffolk, Henry's personal friend and her own previous choice
before she had been forced into the French match. For a time the
young couple were in danger of death from Henry's fury, but in
the end the king was content with exacting money. Wolsey always
claimed that his intercession had saved Suffolk, but there is nothing
except his unreliable word to support this, and Henry may well
have felt merciful towards his favourite sister and his special
friend. In any case, no prospect of Mary Tudor's hand could have
stopped Francis I from a course of action that was highly dis-
pleasing to England. He was young, active, vigorously athletic,
and vainglorious—that is, he had all the qualities of the young
Henry VIII himself; the king of England soon felt violently jealous
of this younger man who supplanted him in the adulation of men.
His own temper, if not the interest of his country, drove Francis
to renew the Italian wars, and so he set about pacifying his northern
border while engaged in the south. A treaty with the young
Archduke Charles of Burgundy removed all threat from that
quarter; as for England, Francis was not content with renewing
his predecessor's treaty of alliance but made sure by sending the
Scottish claimant, the duke of Albany, to stir up trouble in

England's northern neighbour. Albany was fully successful: he overthrew the government of the regent, Henry's sister Margaret, who fled to England with her second husband, the earl of Angus, and Henry—breathing fire—thought seriously of restoring her by force of arms. In the meantime, Francis crossed the Alps and won the great victory of Marignano against the Swiss and Milanese (September 1515); at one stroke all the north of Italy was French again and Rome itself under the French shadow.

Marignano annoyed Henry intensely: it wiped out the memories of his own petty triumphs and displayed Francis as Europe's first knight and conqueror. But there was little England could do about it. The country had not yet recovered from the earlier war, and the parliament of 1515 would vote only enough supplies to make up for the fact that the previous grants had never been collected in full. Yet there was an even more compelling reason for intervention than Henry's jealousy of Francis and his resentment at events in Scotland. Marignano and its consequences threatened to turn the papacy into a French chaplaincy, and Wolsey—with his eye ever fixed upon attaining the see of Rome himself—could not permit a situation which destroyed his hopes. Leo X himself, wishing to be free of French predominance, played the papal game of restoring the balance of power in Italy; on this occasion Wolsey's policy of following the papacy and preserving it intact for himself led him to fight for the European balance. The means he adopted were feeble: unable to start a war, the cardinal tried to use the Swiss and the Emperor Maximilian by paying them secret subsidies. This policy, for which Wolsey took all the credit and which, it seems, led to the retirement from the council of Warham and Fox, proved a failure when Maximilian took the money but no action. Wolsey then tried to build up an alliance against France, with Rome, Venice, Spain, and the Empire. Here fate intervened, for in January 1516 Ferdinand died, and the concert of Europe began to look very different. Of the men who had directed affairs in the 1490's only Maximilian remained, and he was old and ever ineffectual.

Ferdinand was succeeded by the Archduke Charles, then in his Flemish dominions but aware that he would have to visit Spain in person to assure his inheritance. Since for the moment neither he nor Francis wanted trouble, they had no difficulty in coming to terms at Noyon (1516). Francis renounced his claim to Naples, while Charles promised to restore Navarre and marry the infant princess of France. Wolsey tried hard to prevent Maximilian from acceding to this treaty, throwing further good money after the bad already wasted on the insatiable emperor, but in 1517 Maximilian joined his grandson in the French alliance, with a comment that remains worth quoting although it is so well known. 'Mon fils,' said the veteran of a dozen betrayals, 'vous allez tromper les Français, et moi je vais tromper les Anglais.' It was an adequate summing-up of the situation. Wolsey's policy had failed all along the line. France was secure in Italy, Noyon seemed to make certain that the balance there between her and Spain would stay stable, the pope himself was tired of wars and negotiations, England had been treated with scarcely concealed contempt.

A dozen years later this sort of failure was to cost Wolsey the king's favour, but in 1517 he had another chance. Charles had no sooner got safely to Spain than he began to feel his way towards breaking the treaty. It became obvious to Francis that the amity with Spain would not endure, and he was only too glad to seek an alliance of which Wolsey, like Leo X, held out hopes. Albany, who had incautiously returned to France, was detained there as a friendly gesture towards England. But Charles, too, had cause to woo England who thus, so recently ignored and isolated, found herself the object of solicitations from both France and Spain. The negotiations were prolonged; but in October 1518 Wolsey celebrated his great triumph in the treaty of London, a compact of universal Christian peace in which the pope, the emperor, Spain, France, and England bound themselves in common action against the Turk. Throughout Wolsey had taken every opportunity to display his master's power and his own glory. The papal envoy, Cardinal Campeggio, was kept waiting for months at Calais, until Wolsey received his own commission as legate *a latere*, and the summer and autumn were full of feasting and display. But there was some cause for congratulation: in the material sphere, the tiresome conquest of Tournai was given up in return for large annual payments to the king and to Wolsey himself;[1] in the matter of prestige, Wolsey made London the centre of Europe, his king its foremost prince, and himself its arbiter.

However, gorgeous though it all appeared, it was but illusion with nothing solid behind it. The conference had hardly broken up before yet another diplomatic edifice crumbled into nothing. In October 1518 something like a concert of Europe was engineered by Wolsey; in January 1519, the death of the emperor Maximilian was enough to shatter these dreams and entirely recast the state-system of Europe. The election, on which Francis I spent vast

---

[1] By a separate treaty with France, concluded a few days after the treaty of London.

sums in bootless bribes while even Henry VIII toyed for a time
with the idea of standing, resulted in the elevation of the obvious
candidate, Charles of Spain and Burgundy, grandson of the late
emperor, and hereafter the emperor Charles V. The conflict
between Habsburg and Valois now stood out stark and unencum-
bered by other considerations. France, apparently weaker and
encircled but—as events were to prove—fully a match for her
rival, faced the vast but heterogeneous and troubled empire of
Charles. While there had been more counters to move about,
Wolsey could play the game of exercising influence from outside;
after 1519 England was really out of her class in this contest of
heavyweights. Unfortunately for himself, Wolsey failed to realise
how circumstances had changed: his own skill and delight in
diplomatic manœuvres, his attachment to Rome and persistent
hope of becoming pope, and the vanity which prevented him from
understanding the true state of affairs kept England in the running.
Vital tasks at home were neglected: Irish pacification, administrative reform, financial recovery were all planned in 1519, and all
had to be shelved until the cardinal had time to spare from foreign
affairs—which in the end proved to be never. Trade was interrupted and the country unsettled by the wars and rumours of wars
in which Wolsey's activities resulted. Most telling of all, even in
the narrow field of foreign affairs itself there is nothing to record
but failure. From the triumph of 1518, Wolsey's influence in
Europe declined steadily; bolstered at first by reputation and by
the needs of Charles V, it collapsed ruinously after 1525.

From 1519 onwards all diplomacy was governed by the impending struggle between Francis I and Charles V. While the Turks
advanced into Europe, conquering Rhodes (1522) and Hungary
(1526), and threatening Vienna (1529), eyes in the West remained
fixed on the battlefields of Italy and Northern France. This is no
place to enter into the reasons for the conflict; suffice it to say that
everybody expected it, and that it came in 1520 when French
satellites attacked Spanish territory. Both sides had cause to wish
England friendly or at least neutral, and as usual it was the
imperial interest which stood the better chance. Partly there was
the ancient hostility to France and the commercial link with
Flanders, partly the policy of a pope (Leo X) who continued to
resent the French ascendancy in Northern Italy, partly Wolsey's
hopes of being elected pope with imperial support as soon as the
declining Leo should die. But before the Anglo-Spanish alliance
could be renewed and bear fruit, there were some displays to get
through. In 1518 Henry and Francis had arranged to meet, and in

the summer of 1520 the arrangement took effect in the joustings and festivities of the famous pageantry of the Field of Cloth of Gold, held near Calais but in French territory. The sovereigns' amity was troubled not only by unexorcisable suspicions, but also by the fact that Charles V had previously paid a visit to England, to make sure that the meeting should not result in hostility to himself; as soon as the Field dispersed, Henry and Charles met once more on Burgundian soil. In July 1521, Wolsey arranged a conference at Calais, to arbitrate between France and Spain, but this sounded better than it was. Though the very appearance of acting as umpire gratified Wolsey deeply, he was in fact already committed to the imperial cause, and late in the year a treaty of alliance and for common war against France was signed with Charles V. Soon after, Leo X died, but neither then nor two years later on the occasion of another vacancy did Wolsey achieve his great ambition. His very energy, his comparative youth, his English birth and allegiance, made him an impossible candidate to the largely Italian cardinals; and whatever Charles V might promise in the worthy cause of tricking Wolsey, he had at his disposal more convenient candidates for the papal throne.

Thus in 1522 England stood committed to a war in which her interests were not involved, while her ally intended to use her for his own concerns only. Trouble immediately appeared on the northern border. Albany, once again unleashed upon Scotland, renewed the attack; prevailed upon to observe a truce when no defence of the marches was possible, he let slip his opportunity through sheer ineptitude. In 1524 he sailed for France, never to trouble Scotland or England more, but the English escape was due entirely to Albany's incompetence and the skill of Lord Dacre, warden of the west march. It owed nothing to Henry or Wolsey who had left the north unprotected in their rash concentration on war in France. As for this war, the activities of the earl of Surrey, who ravaged Normandy and Picardy in a campaign in 1522 without retaining a foot of land on his return to Calais, and a futile expedition by Suffolk in 1523 which was supposed to be part of a general assault from all sides, amounted to the whole English contribution. There was no enthusiasm in the country, as there had been ten years earlier, the more so because this time there was no inherited treasure to spend and the government attempted to extract heavy taxation. Wolsey's expedients in these years have already been discussed. The parliament of 1523 sat for over four months—a very long spell indeed—and spent nearly all that time in refusing Wolsey's demands—despite all that the

Speaker, Sir Thomas More, could do, despite an ill-judged personal intervention on the cardinal's part, and despite the ordinarily attractive prospect of a French war and reconquest. The commons' stubbornness induced Wolsey unfairly to curse the day he had jockeyed More into the speakership, and next year to attempt the expedient of the Amicable Grant with its dire consequences. The war was paying impressive dividends. Apart from the customary protestations of poverty the commons even dared attack the general purpose of Wolsey's policy. A speech reliably ascribed to Thomas Cromwell, which may or may not have been delivered, passed the whole policy of French war and domestic neglect under a reasoned and—with all its courteous language—devastating review. This, together with Cromwell's own report that in this parliament the commons discussed among other things peace and war and the reform of the realm, is good proof that in the reign of Henry VIII the lower house freely debated things which later governments tried to withhold from it.

The war conferred thus neither glory nor material advantage upon England, and it threatened the king with a resistance from his subjects not seen since Henry VII defeated Lambert Simnel. The murmurs of 1523 were a roar in 1524, and Henry's calling off of the Amicable Grant left him without means to play his part in the alliance. It was reserved to the year 1525 to show up Wolsey's false foreign policy in the field of foreign affairs itself. In February that year, imperial arms won the overwhelming victory of Pavia: the French army was destroyed, the French king taken prisoner, and Italy—and, it might seem, all Europe—passed under the ascendancy of Charles V. In the long run Charles's victory destroyed Wolsey's policy and ultimately Wolsey himself. At first, indeed, the cardinal saw no reason why England should not profit greatly from her ally's triumph: he suggested an immediate invasion of France, and Henry VIII seems to have dreamt of reviving his claims to the French crown. However, despite his victory, Charles—short of money with which to pay even the army of Pavia—was in no position for such enterprises; he remembered Wolsey's dubious dealing after the failure of the projected invasions of 1523 and felt no duty to cut his partner in on his gains. Turning away from the northern theatre he concentrated on Italy, while Wolsey for his part began seriously to contemplate the advantages of coming to terms with France. There ensued something like a diplomatic revolution. In August 1525 Wolsey concluded a treaty with France who was forced to buy peace by greatly increasing the pensions she paid to both Henry and the cardinal; further negotiations resulted in the treaty of Cognac (May 1526) in which England, France, and several Italian states agreed to oppose Charles's dominance in the peninsula.

It is on this change of front that Wolsey's reputation as protector of the balance of power chiefly rests; up to then he had commonly supported Spain and the emperor, even when they were manifestly stronger. But in 1526, too, he was not especially concerned with attempting to redress the balance upset by Pavia. In part he followed self-interest: the imperial alliance lost much of its attraction when it failed to give Wolsey the papacy and to yield the pensions which could always be obtained from France. The rebuff which his plans received in 1525 played a powerful part: there was much personal animosity between Wolsey and the emperor. Certainly he had first tried to tilt the balance still further against France; it was Charles's refusal or inability to comply that changed the cardinal's mind. Probably the most powerful inducement, however, was the example of the pope. Clement VII wanted peace on two counts: he, alone of all the rulers, remembered the Turkish menace, and he more than anyone else dreaded the predominance of one power in Italy. Clement's advice and guidance led to the League of Cognac, and Wolsey once again showed himself a consistent follower of the papacy. Though in throwing over the emperor and embracing the cause of defeated France he may in fact have acted in agreement with some principle of preventing the ascendancy of one great power, there is no sign that this consideration weighed with him. Personal grievances, particular causes, and the diplomacy of Rome were instrumental in producing the new alignment. From England's point of view it was disastrous, as might be expected from a policy shaped to the needs and interests of an Italian power. The country's attitude to foreign affairs was dominated by two factors, one emotional—hatred of France—and one realistic—the imperial alliance protecting the vital cloth trade with Spain and the Low Countries. Wolsey was soon to discover how lamentably he had blundered. The League of Cognac achieved nothing; so far from moderating his policy in Italy, Charles V was driven further in 1527 when his mutinous armies, eager for pay, loot, and—some say—Lutheranism, seized and sacked Rome itself. The event burst upon Europe with devastating effect: that Rome should be treated like any conquered city was shattering enough, but the special extent and savagery of the sack made a lasting impression.

The balance of power was now properly upset, and the old fears of the papacy were at last realised. Clement VII, a prisoner in imperial hands, lost control of the destinies of Italy and of the fortunes of the Church everywhere. Wolsey had three good reasons for trying to rescue the pope. The league of 1526 bound him to an anti-imperial policy; he genuinely and passionately resented the fate of the papacy from which he derived his most cherished powers; and—most pressing of all—things had happened at home which made it essential that Clement should be delivered out of Charles V's hands as quickly as possible. In 1527, the king's private and matrimonial life had reached a crisis; the next six years were dominated by his desire to divorce his first wife, Catherine of Aragon. Catherine was the emperor's aunt, and the pope alone was competent to pronounce the marriage void: it was most unfortunate for Henry, tragic for Wolsey, and fatal to the papacy in England that events in Italy had produced conditions which made a straightforward solution of Henry's troubles impossible. Thus Wolsey threw himself into the rescue of the pope. He failed to find support for a desperate plan to establish a deputy-papacy under himself on French soil during Clement's captivity. Only four cardinals obeyed his call, and Charles permitted Clement to escape to Orvieto, a move which continued his virtual subjection to the emperor without justifying action based on the view that he was a prisoner. Nothing but war remained, and this Wolsey declared in January 1528. It was a useless step: the country refused to fight, and threats against the cardinal mingled with complaints of interrupted trade. Nor did it avail Wolsey's personal position that he arranged a local truce which allowed the cloth trade to continue while the sovereigns were at war. For a time, French successes in Italy bolstered up Wolsey's hopes, but Charles's victory at Landriano (in June 1529) settled the question. Clement VII, in whose interest Wolsey had gone to war, resigned himself to the inevitable and came to terms with the emperor, and in August 1529 the final blow fell. Without consulting or informing Wolsey, France and Spain signed the peace of Cambrai which left Charles dominant in Italy and England isolated.

Wolsey took his fate hard. He refused to believe the news of Cambrai, for he knew well enough what it meant for him; he could not think that Europe should have acted without its arbiter. He had spent two desperate years trying to get Henry his divorce; his own fate, as he was fully aware, depended entirely on his being able to do so. Reluctantly and wondering, but still—after so many years and apparent successes—relying on him, the king had followed his minister's manœuvres. Wolsey's promised success depended on the French alliance and the ultimate defeat of the emperor; it depended on the impossibility of agreement between France and Spain. Cambrai shattered the dream, and—since the parties to the peace completely ignored the cardinal and his high opinion of his place in their counsels—it shattered it in a specially brutal manner. Two months after the complete failure of his foreign policy Wolsey had fallen from his high power. It is time to turn to the circumstances which tied his personal fate so closely to the rivalries of France and Spain.

Chapter V

THE KING'S GREAT MATTER

I. THE ORIGINS OF THE DIVORCE

WHEN Henry VIII, a few months after his accession, married Catherine of Aragon, he married his brother's widow: in the momentous story of Henry's first divorce this is almost the only statement one can make without fear of contradiction from some quarter. Catherine's previous marriage had put her into a prohibited degree of relationship with her second husband, and the contracting parties had therefore obtained a dispensation from Pope Julius II. Since this original dispensation was so badly phrased as to leave room for much doubt, Julius allegedly satisfied further questions from Spain with an additional letter or brief in which he resolved the doubtful points. The dispensation was not nearly so matter of course as is sometimes assumed; it was a difficult point of theology and canon law whether the pope could in fact dispense in this particular case. For the authority of Holy Writ was involved: Henry's marriage contravened Leviticus xx. 21, which verse declared that a man who marries his brother's widow shall be childless.[1] It is, however, likely that the papal dispensation would never have been questioned but for the events that followed.

The marriage seems to have been a happy one in the early years, but a sad blight rested upon its children. One after another they were still-born or died within a few days of birth; the queen had several miscarriages; and by 1525, when all hope of further issue had to be given up (Catherine was by then forty and there had been no pregnancy for seven years), Henry's sole heir was a girl, Mary, born in 1516. The Tudor stock was always unhealthy and childbed invariably dangerous in the sixteenth century; but it is not surprising that an amateur theologian and fervent formal Christian like Henry VIII should have remembered the curse in Leviticus. Nor did the doubts arise suddenly. Henry had registered

[1] On an unbiased interpretation the verse appears rather to refer to a man's adultery with his sister-in-law; the verse really applicable to Henry's case is Deuteronomy xxv. 5 which orders a man to marry his brother's widow if she is childless. However, the canonical prohibition against a man so marrying rests on Leviticus (though the Jewish law adheres to Deuteronomy), and Henry therefore had a case in canon law.

a politic protest as early as 1505 when his father wanted to retain a chance of repudiating the marriage; this had never been altogether forgotten. Catherine was the visible sign of the Anglo-Spanish alliance with which her personal fortunes were always bound up. In the later years of Henry VII she had a very miserable time indeed while her father and father-in-law haggled over her second marriage, and in 1514, when Henry VIII fell out with Ferdinand, he vented his anger on his wife, good husband to her though he commonly was. As early as this, rumours began to circulate that the king was thinking of divorcing the queen.[1] These rumours came to nothing, but as the years passed two things combined to revive the king's early doubts about the validity of his marriage. One was the interest of the realm—the danger of a disputed succession; the other Henry's own concupiscence—his falling in love with Anne Boleyn. Which of the two played the greater part in settling his determination is a fascinating problem, often debated, but really insoluble. Nor, in the last resort, does it greatly matter, except that with the divorce, and the Reformation that ensued upon it, we enter a field where 400 years after the event historians' passions are still far from spent.[2]

Fear of succession troubles was ingrained in sixteenth-century England: nation as well as statesmen never forgot the history of the wars of the Roses. How this question affected Henry VII's foreign policy has already been seen. Now it came to plague his

[1] This is the place to dispose of one point. We are often told that no divorce was involved since no such thing exists in canon law, and that one should speak of nullity—for what Henry always claimed was that his marriage had been unlawful and therefore void from the first. That is a perfectly accurate description of the law, but the matter was called a divorce by contemporaries simply because they could declare a marriage fully dissolved only if it had never properly taken place, and—provided the implications are understood—it is quite proper to retain the shorter and traditional term.

[2] It is as well to know where to find the more reputable versions of the different points of view. The Roman Catholic point of view appears moderately in John Lingard's History of England (1819-30), with a great deal of partisanship and error in F. A. Gasquet's Henry VIII and the Monasteries (1888) and The Eve of the Reformation (1900), and judiciously in P. Hughes' The Reformation in England (1950). High Anglicanism finds expression in R. W. Dixon's History of the Church of England (1878-1902) and briefly in J. Gairdner's English Church in the Sixteenth Century (1902). The Protestant interpretation in its extreme form is still best read in J. A. Froude's History of England (1862-70); more temperately Protestant is A. F. Pollard's Henry VIII (1902). It is fair to say that no full-scale review of the evidence has ever been made by anyone free from evident religious bias, nor has there been a modern appraisal (in the last fifty years) except Dr Hughes'.

son: it looked as though the safety of the Tudor throne, and with it the tranquillity of the country, depended on the life of one girl. These uncertainties accounted, in 1521, for the execution of Edmund Stafford, duke of Buckingham, on a dubious charge of treason; it was probably Buckingham's descent from Edward III's youngest son and his arrogance in displaying the fact, rather than Wolsey's hatred of the disdainful duke, that led to his death. The same fears also promoted to public place Henry's illegitimate son, Henry Fitzroy (born in 1519), who in 1525 was made duke of Richmond and given offices which recalled his father's early distinctions. When the divorce got under way there were even suggestions from Rome that Richmond should marry his half-sister Mary and thus clarify the succession; but Henry—always rather a simple man in matters of morality—drew the line at that.

This policy, which could hope to put a Tudor bastard on the English throne, indicates how desperate the position looked to the king. Even if Mary survived (and who could be sure of that?) it would only mean the accession of a female sovereign, for which undesirable event the sole dubious precedent lay in the unsuccessful attempt to seize the throne by Henry I's daughter Matilda (in the twelfth century). That had meant civil war; there was little hope of better things when men still alive had assisted in wars for the crown, and when a queen regnant was bound to raise a whole crop of questions connected both with her right and power to rule, and with her own subsequent marriage. As we shall see, Mary's reign later bore out all these fears; we find them less comprehensible only because we know in how daring a manner Elizabeth I disproved them. Considering solely the interests of his dynasty and his nation, Henry VIII had reason to wish to end a marriage from which no further issue could be expected. But the problem did not appear in such straightforward terms either to the king himself or to onlookers then or since. Some time between 1525 and 1527 Henry fell violently in love with one of the ladies at court, Anne, daughter of the courtier and minister Sir Thomas Boleyn and sister to one of Henry's earlier mistresses. His infatuation is fully attested by the famous love-letters which he laboriously wrote in his own hand; it is also a little difficult to understand, both from her portraits and from contemporary descriptions. Historians, who like to rationalise, speak learnedly and a little absurdly of Anne's French ways (she was brought up at the dissolute court of France) and her skilful use of the great eyes which seem to have been her chief attraction. But perhaps there is little mystery in the passion for a lively girl of a man of thirty-five whose wife had grown old

and ugly with confinements and disappointments and was moreover displaying a growing addiction to Spanish piety.

Be that as it may, Henry determined to win Anne, and the shock
which this first appearance of his inflexible will must have occasioned may well be imagined when it is remembered that most
people then thought the king a mere cypher behind the overpowering cardinal—a mistake into which Wolsey himself fell at
times, to his destruction. It is alleged that Anne played her royal
lover skilfully, for she wanted the crown and not the status of a
mistress. Perhaps she did: certainly the allegations of enemies
that Henry overcame her resistance as early as 1529 deserve no
credit. But the decisive point was that nothing short of marriage
would do for the king who wanted a legitimate heir to the throne.
Thus by the beginning of 1527 the stage was set. Old doubts reinforced by the deaths of his children led Henry to question the
validity of his marriage; the problem of the succession intervened
to represent the matter as urgent; and Anne Boleyn was there to
inflame a naturally imperious temper to volcanic heat. It all fused
in the king's conscientious scruples. For Henry did not argue the
matter out: he was convinced in his conscience that his marriage
to Catherine had been a great sin. Henry's conscience is, indeed,
the clue to the whole affair. Extreme and uncompromising egoist
that he was, he possessed to perfection that most dangerous
weapon—a complete conviction of his own rightness. When Henry
told the cardinal, the pope, and the world that his conscience was
violently troubled by the illegality of his marriage he was not being
hypocritical. He did not, in his heart, admit that he wished to see
the succession settled or to get him a new and more attractive wife,
but he genuinely knew that his life with Catherine was a sin.
Therein lay his strength: it was this unshakable conviction into
which all the arguments of policy and passion had been transformed by the forces of his self-centred nature that carried him
through the setbacks of six tiresome years, through the break with
Rome and the creation of a new polity, through the vast and profound revolution which grew out of Catherine's childlessness and
Anne's winning ways.

Of course, the view that these personal and accidental factors
were really behind the Reformation has found little favour with
the writers of history who rightly argue that things of such
magnitude do not happen in so superficial a manner. The part
played by Henry's personal ends can only be understood against
the state of affairs upon which his fierce determination impinged.
Henry's passionate will can explain why the king drove the country

along the path of war with Rome; it cannot explain his success or how he came to take the country with him. For it is most certainly true that he could not simply force the nation to his will; for one thing, he lacked all physical means of coercion. He had to have, at best, their enthusiastic support, or at worst their ready acquiescence. In order to understand the singular and rapid success of Henry VIII's political Reformation we must look at the condition and reputation of the Church and papacy in England.

2. STATE AND CHURCH IN ENGLAND

One ought not to generalise about whole nations, but if one thing can be said of the English people early in the sixteenth century it is that they thought little of priests. They were not alone in this: popular opinion all over Western Europe, though it preserved some respect for the Church as an institution, often treated its members with ribaldry. The literature of the later middle ages is full of stories which rely for their point on the peccadilloes of the priesthood; the hero of one discreditable adventure after another turns out to be a monk or a clerk in secular orders. In a way, this does no more than reflect the natural feelings of men who, being sinners themselves, love to see self-professed virtue stray from the path of righteousness: a priest's gluttony, greed, or lust was funnier and more deserving of notice than a layman's because it conflicted so much more with his professional claims and status, not because it was necessarily more common or notorious. But people cannot laugh at or abuse their spiritual pastors for generations without losing all respect for them. There was thus much of that feeling which is generally summarised in the word anti-clericalism. The higher clergy were disliked because they were wealthy and ostentatious; Wolsey provided a suitable epitome of this alleged trait. The lesser clergy—parish priests and unbeneficed men—earned contempt and dislike by rapacity and pretensions with which their intellectual equipment, material means, and private morality too rarely kept pace. Monks and nuns, hidden away in convents which—like all unfamiliar territory—were peopled by ignorance and lascivious imagination with all the abominations possible, gathered about them a reputation which was to make the most extravagant accusations credible and their overthrow easy.

Apart from reprobation of real or supposed immorality, there were more potent interests at work to turn the laity against the clergy. One was the latter's wealth, concentrated in the hands of the larger monasteries, the bishops, and some prosperous incumbents. The Church held probably about one third of all land in England, and the incomes of great abbeys like Glastonbury or St Albans, and of bishoprics like Winchester and Durham, exceeded the revenues of the greatest temporal lords. These lands the laity had for some time coveted, the more so since in the depression of the fifteenth century many monasteries had leased out their demesne lands to a local gentleman who thereafter wished to convert his leasehold into direct tenure by expropriating his landlords. If the lands of the Church were ill-administered, the argument ran that they could be put to better use in lay hands; if— as was now too rarely the case—they were efficiently exploited, the cries against rapacious and wicked lords were loud. Before the dissolution of the monasteries, many complaints were recorded of sharp practices with which the next generation charged the monks' successors in the lands; the growing difficulties and the glamour of the past quickly gave the dispossessed monks a reputation for exceptional fair-dealing which historians are still trying to dispel. The simple truth is that the Church, and especially the monasteries, were in the intolerable position of owning great wealth but having lost the respect and devotion which permitted and encouraged the accumulation. Instead they were surrounded by a laity which resented their wealth and in addition thought it could make better use of it.

People also objected to the exactions of the Church and to its courts. Tithe was a standing grievance. The payments due upon the probate of wills, and more particularly the mortuary payments demanded even of the poorest before a body could be buried in consecrated ground, had roused a vast and sullen resentment which only awaited a chance to show itself. But the chief grievance concerned the courts of the Church. Side by side with royal and baronial jurisdiction, England also harboured a great system of courts held by bishops, their officials, and archdeacons. To these not only the clergy itself but also the laity were subject in matters technically affecting their spiritual welfare. All testamentary and matrimonial causes fell under this head, as well as straightforward breaches of the moral law and heresy—itself a very wide term. Moreover, these courts enforced the financial demands of the Church. Thus large numbers of laymen came into contact with a jurisdiction which was particularly rapacious in fees, unreliable and dilatory in decision, and corrupt in procedure. It was alleged that frivolous charges were common, that citations from one diocese into another were resorted to for purposes of chicanery, that bribes were taken, that excommunication was applied for no reason at all, even that ecclesiastical lawyers (proctors) laid false information themselves in order to augment their business.[1] Of all the clergy, the archdeacon in his court and the summoner travelling around the country to serve summons on often innocent people were probably the most hated. When all the necessary reservations are made, it still remains beyond dispute that the Church courts, having ceased to serve a useful purpose, were an intolerable burden; their rapid decline after the Reformation demonstrated their essential superfluity well enough.

All in all, men were tired of being ruled or badgered by priests—that is what one means by speaking of the secular temper of the times. From the villager who did not see why the parson should castigate him for doing as he himself did, to the duke of Suffolk who smote the table with a great oath and cried that times were merry in England before there were cardinals, the laity wished to humble, dispossess, and discipline the clergy. Anti-clericalism may not have been general or equally strong everywhere, though it is difficult to avoid the conclusion that the clergy as such rarely commanded respect and obedience. But it was strongest in the south, and particularly in London—that is, in the most populous and politically most influential part of the country. There was nothing new in it either. Since the fourteenth century, at least, the gentry and merchants, and especially the citizens of London, had repeatedly expressed their dislike of clerical wealth and jurisdiction; plans to confiscate the one and curb the other were canvassed repeatedly during the 150 years preceding the Reformation—though not by the government. In his own day, Henry VIII witnessed an outburst which displayed the real feeling on the subject. In 1514, the bishop of London, Richard Fitzjames, arrested a prosperous London merchant, Richard Hunne, on a charge of heresy, and in December Hunne was found hanged in the bishop's prison. According to his supporters, his arrest had nothing to do with any suspicions of Lollardy but was meant to punish him for refusing to pay a mortuary fee and threatening to bring an action of præmunire against the priest who demanded it.[2] Fitzjames hoped to dispose of the issue by trying, sentencing, and burning Hunne's dead body for heresy, alleging that he had committed suicide; but a coroner's jury returned a verdict of murder against the jailer and the bishop's chancellor Horsey, a

---

[1] Especially in the 'Commons' Supplication against the Ordinaries' (1532), a document which embodied the genuine grievances of the laity.

[2] For præmunire cf. below, p. 109.

clerk in orders. The case caused an uproar and had political reper-
cussions in parliament and before the king which shall be discussed
in a moment. Its most striking immediate effect was to unleash the
anti-clerical temper of the city to such a degree that Fitzjames
begged the king not to let Horsey come to trial, for—he said—any
London jury would convict him, were he as innocent as Abel; in
the end, Horsey got off with a fine and removal from London. Sir
Thomas More wrote a very effective piece of polemic on the side
of the ecclesiastical authorities, but a recent investigation has left
little doubt that Hunne was murdered.[1] Hunne's personal fate was
less significant than the temper it revealed. Both London and the
king were to remember Hunne when there came cause to attack
the Church.

Such were the feelings in a nation which, though formally pious,
had little esteem for its clergy; but was the Church really in so
deplorable a condition? The answer to that question does not
affect the other issue: people thought the Church corrupt, whether
it was so or not, and their opinion is a factor in the history of the
Reformation. In great part they spoke truly. The Church was full
of weaknesses and abuses; reforms had been talked about for a
very long time. The parish clergy were often ill-educated and
ignorant, unable to understand and sometimes even to read the
Latin of the services; often, too, they were wretchedly poor.
Coming from the same class as their flocks, they could rarely
command the respect which a better education or a little higher
standard of living would have produced. The higher clergy
were wealthy and worldly and resented by their own inferiors;
many of them practised those abuses against which pope
after pope, and council after council, had issued their edicts.
There was plenty of pluralism (the holding of more than one
benefice) and consequent non-residence which left many men without the consolations of religion; there were simony and nepotism;
there were lapses from morality, ranging from money-grubbing to
persistent incontinence. Monastic institutions were in a decline: of
the roughly 800 religious houses in England few had more than
twenty-five inmates, while the average of the 600 lesser houses was
four to five. The monastic ideal was dying when masses for the
dead could not be said for lack of men to take the vows. Here and
there one can find genuine scandals: visitation records of pre-
Reformation days show that accusations of vice, ill-discipline, and
scandalous quarrels were not based on invention, though they also
show that the allegedly general was often only exceptional. The

[1] A. Ogle, *The Tragedy of the Lollard Tower* (1949).

monasteries' real canker was worldliness. Abbots and priors lived
the life of the rural gentry with whom they consorted, administering
their estates, hunting, dining, and occasionally drinking. Too
often monks took the vows before they were old enough to understand their meaning; naturally they might later find it impossible
to forsake the world. Most of these men were decent folk and
harmless, but they had no claim to the religious devotion of the
commonalty and no justification for the wealth which past fervour
had showered upon their predecessors. That these and other abuses
existed was no secret; the best spirits of the age—among them
men who were to die for the old religion and the papacy—clamoured insistently for reform. But the Church as a whole was content to ignore the coming day of retribution. The pope acted the
Italian prince; the English bishops busied themselves with the
king's affairs; the great cardinal put Church reform at the bottom
of his long list of preoccupations. When Wolsey, with all his special
powers and exceptional energy, failed to make the slightest advance
towards genuine reform, it was settled that the Church could not
put its house in order and that the state would have to do it instead.

The state had a special reason for interference: in the consolidation of royal power which Henry VII had fostered, the privileges of
the Church remained virtually untouched. Yet these privileges
and liberties hindered the full development of national kingship.
To start with, they interfered with the restoration of order. Benefit
of clergy, the outcome of Henry II's failure to defeat Becket,
protected any man in orders against the consequences of his first
crime: only after he had been deprived of his orders for a felony
did he become subject to the king's courts. The rights of clerical
sanctuary provided refuge for criminals, though they were thereafter forced either to surrender themselves to the law or abjure the
realm. Neither privilege, in fact, was as serious an infringement
on the king's powers as seems still to be thought, and both were in
process of being whittled away before ever Henry VIII attacked
the Church. An act of 1491 ordered convicted clerks to be burned
in the hand, so that they should not escape the punishment for
further crimes through the ignorance of the judges; another of
1512 restricted the privilege to clerks in major orders, thus
removing its worst anomaly which had protected numbers of
rogues who could claim brief acquaintance with the Church or the
universities. In 1515, however, the problem suddenly rose from
the ashes when Richard Kidderminster, abbot of Winchcombe,
preached a sermon at St Paul's Cross in which he attacked the act
of 1512 from the text 'Touch not Mine Anointed'. He was only

interpreting a recent papal renewal of the claim, but, coming as he did into the middle of Hunne's case where a clerk was threatened with secular prosecution, he provoked an uproar. The laity in parliament petitioned the king, and Henry arranged for a disputation between Kidderminster and Henry Standish, a friar and well-known preacher. The royal theologian himself presided. Standish, putting the case for relative independence from papal decrees, had the better of the argument, only to see himself attacked and threatened with a heresy trial by convocation. Parliament exploded; the king summoned Standish and his accusers before the judges and himself; and the whole clergy in convocation were adjudged to have rendered themselves liable to the dread penalties of præmunire by appealing to a foreign jurisdiction in denial of the king's. 'Kings of England,' said Henry, 'have never had any superior but God alone.' These words, spoken as early as 1516, must be remembered. Wolsey, who had to ask pardon for the clergy, secured the rapid dissolution of this hotly anti-clerical parliament, but the lesson was not forgotten by the one man who mattered. Henry now knew from his judges that the law declared such reliance on Rome punishable by imprisonment at pleasure and forfeiture of goods. Benefit of clergy, won in the pope's triumph over Henry II, played a strange part in Henry VIII's rescinding of that triumph.

Sanctuary represented a different problem, largely because its ecclesiastical character was somewhat fortuitous. Truly ecclesiastical sanctuaries existed in every church and churchyard, but these mattered little in comparison with the great liberties, especially in the north, where the king's writ did not run. Due to a number of historical accidents, those that survived were mostly in the hands of the Church, as the archbishop of York's liberties at Ripon and Beverley, or the whole county palatine of Durham. In these places criminals found a refuge for life, provided they never left the sanctuary. Throughout the fifteenth century the judges had done their best to limit the privilege, and under Henry VII and Henry VIII parliamentary legislation carried on the good work on a somewhat larger scale. However, sanctuary was not fully abolished until various acts of the years 1530-40 destroyed it in one place after another, subjecting all monastic liberties, the county of Durham, and finally all England to the king's law.

Benefit of clergy and sanctuary were only aspects of the real difficulty posed by the Church—the problem of its dual allegiance. The clergy owed obedience and loyalty to the king, for they were Englishmen dwelling in his peace, holding their lands from him, and possessed of property and rights protected by his courts. They also owed loyalty and obedience to the pope, the supreme and absolute monarch in the Universal Church. Such double allegiance involved much difficult delimiting of spheres and much burdensome double taxation. Ordinarily, when king and pope were at peace, the Church was the real sufferer, for both these powerful potentates then combined in exploiting it. In England, king and pope had been working in harmony for a century and more before Henry VIII came to the throne. Earlier there had been trouble—the struggle over investitures between Henry I and Anselm, the bitter war over criminous clerks and clerical jurisdiction between Henry II and Thomas Becket, the decisive intervention of Innocent III in the affairs of John. The fourteenth century looked likely to bring matters to a head. With the defeat of Boniface VIII, with the 'Babylonish captivity' at Avignon, and finally with the papal schism when one pope at Rome and another at Avignon demanded the obedience of distracted and disgusted Christendom (1377), the stock of the papacy slumped badly. Throughout the reign of Edward III it was closely associated with the national enemy, France, and therefore liable to attack by the growing national fervour of which the Hundred Years' War was both expression and nurse. Typically enough, the quarrel took the highly practical form of a conflict over property rights in the issue of 'provisors'. Objection was taken to the papal habit (nourished by poverty) of 'providing' incumbents for benefices, especially bishoprics, all over Europe, a habit which was crystallising into a doctrine of the pope as the universal patron. In the course of the fourteenth century the English parliament passed successive statutes known as acts of provisors and of præmunire which protected the property of English patrons of benefices, prohibited papal interference with these rights, and punished those who either sought out or published papal bulls affecting them. The legislation culminated in the statute of 1393 which had a much more restricted scope than was once thought: it was not a general code against papal intervention in the affairs of the English Church, but a limited and practical summary of earlier legislation designed to protect the temporal rights of the laity (and especially the king) in appointments and advowsons.[1]

The legislation, significant as an expression of views hostile to

[1] W. T. Waugh, 'The Great Statute of Præmunire', *English Historical Review*, 1922; see also C. Davies, 'The Statute of Provisors of 1351', *History*, 1953. Advowsons—rights of presentation to benefices—were in England subject to the secular courts.

the papacy among the propertied classes represented in parliament, produced the writ of *præmunire facias* under which proceedings for infringements of these laws were to be taken, and the large penalties—forfeiture of property and imprisonment at the discretion of king and council—which were their sanction. The real significance of præmunire, as the whole complex of laws limiting papal encroachments on the king's 'crown and regality' came to be called, lay in its vagueness and dark threats. Largely because the Lancastrian kings needed papal support, and because the papacy of the schism was too weak to counterattack, the laws of the fourteenth century remained virtually dead. In the fifteenth century there were no more orthodox and papalist country and monarchy than those of England. The laity stood protected against the pope by laws which needed no application for the simple reason that popes were careful not to infringe them, and the kings down to Henry VIII—equally secure in their regal rights—had no difficulty in remaining on good terms with Rome. The victim of this happy harmony among its masters was, as usual, the English Church which paid heavy taxes to both king and pope and learned to dread the demands of their absolute sovereign at Rome even more than those of their limited sovereign in England. This long period of co-operation between crown and papacy culminated in Wolsey's legateship. Wolsey combined the powers of both king and pope, and—being an active autocrat as well as near at hand—brought home to the Church what papal powers could mean. At the same time, he revived the laity's dislike of a foreign potentate's pretensions. Few Englishmen had any objection to the pope's spiritual supremacy, and many rather enjoyed the discomfiture of the Church at the hands of its own champion, but none in an age when temporal nationalism first became a fully realised doctrine wanted to see an Italian prince interfere in their affairs. The duke of Norfolk summed it all up in answer to Wolsey's lament at his fall that his legacy was gone 'wherein stood all my high honour'. 'A straw for your legacy,' was the duke's reply, 'I never esteemed your honour the higher for that.' But, he added, he had reverenced Wolsey as archbishop of York and cardinal whose estate 'surmounteth any duke within this realm'. Where the pope was concerned, the anti-clerical passions which denounced the pretensions of the priesthood found an ally in nationalist prejudice and national interest.

However, in England none of these feelings were translated into religious opposition to Church or pope. Almost to a man, the English people, high or low, were content with orthodoxy. The stress so commonly laid in discussions of the Reformation's pre-history on intellectual or doctrinal disputes misleads entirely. This was, in any case, not a religious age, in the sense that men followed their faith rather than their material ambitions, as on the whole they were to do a century later. Nor was the Reformation of this reign greatly concerned with doctrinal changes. The peculiarly political and jurisdictional preoccupations of the English Refor-mation arose from the fact that it was made from above, by the government, but it could have been made in no other way in a nation which abhorred heresy and prided itself on its orthodoxy. The continental Reformation took its origin in the religious revolt of individual prophets, only to fall in its second stage into the hands of secular governments; in England, the government led the way, and it was only the political changes carried out which made possible and even necessary the subsequent religious transforma-tion. It is a fact, however difficult to grasp, that an England which showed no deference to priests and much dislike of the papacy yet stood firmly by the mass; active anti-clericalism and doctrinal orthodoxy were somehow combined. At the same time it is worth noting at once that the success of the attack on the papacy brought in its train a swelling attack on orthodoxy: conservatism in doctrine and ritual seems to have lacked any deep roots. In part, the English were orthodox because they had had earlier experience of heresy. The Wycliffite and Lollard movements of the fourteenth century produced a violent reaction; because of them England had a law for burning heretics. No one now doubts that Lollardy played no part in the Reformation. Here and there it survived, mostly among the poorer artisans; in some places the Lollard bible was still read, and views were held which represented the last and crudest sim-plifications of Wycliffe's difficult scholastic arguments on the nature of the priesthood or the sacrament of the altar.[1] But these poor men of Cotswold villages and London shops had nothing to do with the movement which got under way when Henry VIII broke with Rome.

In the 1520s a different form of heresy began to appear, and the bishops, in trying to deal with it, often confused the two. The universities, especially Cambridge, began to respond to Luther's teaching on the continent. The official attitude found expression in the book *Assertio Septem Sacramentorum* which appeared over the name of Henry VIII in 1521 and won him the title of Defender of the Faith from a grateful pope. It is now commonly admitted that the book is not so learned as to preclude

[1] Cf. K. B. McFarlane, *John Wycliffe* (1953).

Henry's authorship, though he certainly had assistance from Bishop Fisher and Sir Thomas More. But among the younger generation of university dons, Lutheran views were received with much delight, and in the meetings of a discussion group dubbed 'Little Germany' in the White Horse Tavern at Cambridge one source of English protestantism has rightly been discerned. The leading English heretic was William Tyndale who fled abroad in 1524 to translate the Bible and conduct a vigorous pamphlet war with Thomas More, before he was betrayed to the imperial authorities and burned in 1536. England, too, saw some burnings. Wolsey, cardinal though he was, proved true to his secular temper by displaying much tolerance, though even he could not stomach heretical teaching at the universities. He was particularly unfortunate in that he inadvertently infected Oxford when he staffed his new college there with Cambridge men some of whom held Lutheran views. When Thomas More succeeded Wolsey as chancellor, and such bishops as Nix of Norwich and Longland of Lincoln (in whose dioceses the danger of heresy was greatest) could at last act on their own, a minor wave of persecutions followed; More's record in the matter is rather that of the convinced and high-minded sixteenth-century believer that he was, than that of the nineteenth-century moderate liberal he is so often made out to be. John Foxe found material here for his martyrs. They were men like Little Bilney—Thomas Bilney, who was orthodox on the pope and on the mass and most things, but died because he relapsed after recanting his views on saints and image worship—or John Frith who shared Tyndale's extremer views. As individuals they were harmless enough—sincere men of very limited influence; but in view of what had happened in Germany the Church could not afford to overlook even small-time heretics. These first rumblings of attack played no part in bringing about the Reformation; but for the political revolution they would have been stamped out.

Nor was the Reformation in England a result of the so-called intellectual Renaissance. That the fourteenth and fifteenth centuries saw a revival of classical learning spread from Italy to the rest of Europe is certainly true, though few historians today would regard it as the profound break with the past which it was once held to be. It effected a general shift of emphasis, the more marked because it coincided with a general decline in piety and deference to the Church. Which was cause and which effect is not a proper question; there was mutual interaction. Out of it grew humanism, a phenomenon of the schools like other medieval trends of thought;

in part, at least, it represented a revolt against a curriculum dominated by such outstanding teachers of an earlier generation as
William Ockham and Duns Scotus, even as they had superseded
their predecessors. Such sweeps of fashion are familiar in universities, and to universities and learned men the movement was
throughout confined. Like all scholastic doctrine humanism appealed to authority, but the authority on which it relied was that
of pre-Christian pagan writers rather than that of the writers of the
Church. This dependence on authority, so natural to the age,
prevented an appeal to independent reasoning; humanism did
not mark the triumph of the individual mind over some collective
system. Medieval schoolmen were on the whole more subtle and
penetrating than their humanist successors; where they differed
was not in powers or independence of thought but in preconceived
notions and relevant subjects. The humanists' devotion to the
classics opened whole new fields for study, and the high critical
standards of the best ancient authors (whom they admired)
supplied them with new and effective weapons against their
professional opponents. In their own sphere, the humanists were
as uncritical and credulous as any medieval believer in miracles
and authority; the typical humanist, to take an example, would
base his knowledge of a plant or an animal on Pliny, even if his
own eyes could convince him that Pliny had erred. Men of genius
like Leonardo da Vinci or Copernicus did not belong to the
humanist movement proper. This was not the age of science but
the great age of alchemy and astrology, an age of odd superstitions
replacing a lost faith. Only in dealing with the assumptions and
beliefs of their opponents—of those *obscuri viri* whom the great
Erasmus satirised—were the humanists armed with well-tempered
and sharp critical weapons from the armoury of Greece and
Rome.

In England, humanism never acquired the pagan tinge of the
Italian prototype. Its prophet was Erasmus of Rotterdam, a man
of great learning, sharp insight, a satirical humour, and valetu-
dinarian habits, who produced an edition of the text of the
New Testament from the original Greek which corrected the
Vulgate in places so as to undermine the scriptural authority of
the priesthood and the papacy. Erasmus' work influenced
heresiarchs like Luther and Tyndale, but Erasmus himself,
though quarrelling with monks and friars and the 'old learning' in
general (as a good university controversialist was bound to do),
always remained orthodox and free from suspicion. In this his
English associates followed him. Men like John Colet, dean of St

Paul's and the founder of St Paul's School, William Grocyn and
Thomas Lineacre—Greek scholars both and the latter an eminent
physician—and Thomas More were eager to apply the new learning
to England in order to refresh the Church and its doctrine. It was
an age of much intellectual activity. Young men questioned the
syllabus of the universities; colleges were founded to promote
new studies and old; royal and noble amateurs took much interest
in the arts and sciences.[1] Henry VIII himself liked to have brilliant
young men about; of a large number of exceedingly clever and
highly trained humanists the brightest star was Thomas More
whose *Utopia*—describing an imaginary commonwealth—is
rightly regarded as the outstanding product of the early English
humanism, before the Reformation came to turn that carefree
playing with ideas into a sombre and serious business. More made
a career in government service, rising ultimately (1529-32) to the
office of lord chancellor, but his fame rests rather on his personality, his wit and genius, and his sacrificial death. In the history of
English thought—indeed, of European thought—he is a figure of
note; in the political history of his country, fate determined that
his part should be small.

There was thus a good deal of 'new learning' in England, but it
was not heretical. Colet and More, the churchman and the layman,
wanted reform in a Church whose abuses More only started to
deny when they were attacked by the Lutheran partisans whom he
combated, but they stayed orthodox. No humanist of note joined
the ranks of the protestants; on the contrary, in More and Fisher
they supplied the leading martyrs of the papalist party. In the next
generation, indeed, the potential link between new learning and
protestantism was more evident: such men as Cranmer or, on a
lower plane, the propagandists employed by Thomas Cromwell
came under the influence of the new ideas in religion while at the
university. But once again the essential relationship is the other
way round: the new learning no more than Lutheran doctrine
could work upon the English Reformation until the crown had led
the way in the political and jurisdictional break of the 1530s. To
see in those poor stirrings of protestantism which Little Bilney and
his like represented, or in the humanistic new learning of Erasmus'
friends and followers, anything that could cause or lead to the

[1] Thus Cardinal's College was founded by Wolsey. Christ's and St
John's Colleges at Cambridge owed their foundation to John Fisher's
influence with Lady Margaret Beaufort, Henry VIII's grandmother.
The patron of English humanism was William Blount, Lord Mountjoy,
a friend of Henry VIII.

Reformation in England is vastly to overrate the place of intellectuals in the sixteenth century, and vastly to misjudge the character of the revolution that actually took place.

Thus when Henry VIII began his attack on the papacy, he had in his favour the strong dislike of the clergy and of foreign interference in English affairs which animated certainly the politically effective part of the nation and was represented in parliament. He did not by an exercise of superhuman power and coercion drag a faithful people from the fold; rather he at last unleashed those passions which for years only the government's frown had been able to stem. Attacks on the Church, on its way of life and its great wealth (rumoured to be even greater than it was) were some 150 years old at least; and so was dislike of papal 'usurpations' and encroachments. But despite statutes of provisors and præmunire, the crown had stood good ally to Rome; the antipapal legislation remained a dead letter, and England's medieval history culminated in a royal minister who was also papal legate and who adapted his country's foreign policy to the needs of the pope. Until Henry fixed his desire upon Anne Boleyn, and Clement VII, to his despair, found himself a prisoner of Charles V, there was nothing to disturb the harmony of king and pope; and until their alliance was broken all the latent feelings which Henry VIII was to harness remained powerless. That is the place which the divorce occupies. It did not alone cause the Reformation; it did not even, if we like, play any large part in bringing about a movement which rested on national feeling and the scandal of a corrupt Church; but without it there would still have been no Reformation because the powerful intercession of the crown would have been against it and not for it.

It is, then, easy enough to see why Henry's war on the pope was accepted so readily by his people—though we shall see later that there was some opposition—and there is no need to postulate despotic action which anyhow would have been beyond Henry's means. It must still, however, be explained how the opponent came to be so weak as to make Henry's task relatively easy. He had to coerce the Church into obedience to himself, and to force the papacy either to give in to him or to withdraw from England. Not that he saw it in that light: as shall be shown, he had no idea of the outcome and no plan for the future when he first set out to get his divorce. All he knew was his will and desire which his conscience had turned into right and justice, and all he wanted was to achieve these. The pope, a weak man at other times but now rendered obstinate by his greater fear of Charles V and by his reluctance to endorse what amounted to a denial of the papal power to dispense, was no suitable opponent for the determined Tudor king whose physical resources were so much larger. Any danger that threatened from secular princes taking up the cause of Rome was removed by the unstable relations between France and the emperor which kept both at peace with England—though only the event was to prove right a calculation which the peace of Cambrai of August 1529 rendered unlikely. Indeed, one of the most striking things about Henry VIII's break with Rome was the ease with which it was accomplished: all the imposing façade of papal power and imperial displeasure vanished like the mirage it was once the king could take Thomas Cromwell's advice and act boldly.

As for the Church in England itself, much ingenuity has been spent on the question why it gave way so readily; yet the answer is not really so hard to find. As has already been said, the fall of Wolsey left it in a specially weakened state. Battered and badgered by the cardinal-legate, the bishops were the less willing or able to resist the demands of the king; disorganised and superseded as their administration had been during Wolsey's ascendancy, they could not hope to marshal opposition when attacked by the laity with the crown's connivance. The king alone had stood between the Church and its lay enemies; now that protector cheered on the hunt. In any case, the bishops were almost all king's men; their past predisposed them honestly to obey his will. Warham, of Canterbury, had made a conventional career, rising to the chancellorship from which Wolsey dislodged him in 1515. Longland of Lincoln was king's confessor before his promotion, Stokesley of London almoner and ambassador; both these men hated innovations in religion, but they obeyed the king against the pope. Not all had mortgaged their conscience: Standish of St Asaph, who had preached high royalist doctrine in 1516, took up Catherine's cause in 1527—but he was to consecrate Cranmer. There were exceptions, like Fisher of Rochester who had never had anything to do with politics; there was Tunstall of Durham who, while he avoided all action that might get him into trouble, yet did not surrender his independence and integrity to the habits of an old official of the crown. But the custom by which for over a century the way to the bench had lain through the king's service and good grace made of the leaders and guardians of the Church active or retired ministers of the crown rather than prelates obeying their spiritual head. Perhaps the bishops deserve a less lukewarm defence. The pope's spiritual headship was indeed unquestioned dogma, but the relations

between Church and state and papal authority in the temporal
sphere were much less certain than later definition has made them.
In the fifteenth century the popes had fought a long battle against a
constitutional movement in the Church which tried to replace
monarchical by representative government—the conciliar movement; and though in the end the pope won hands down, the fact
that Henry kept appealing from the pope to a General Council of
the Church gave him a case in the eyes of men who, especially
after their recent experience of Wolsey, were not over-ardent
papalists. Altogether, as the legal and philosophical arguments of
the time show, there was much to be said on the king's side, at
least until 1533, even by those who did not hold with his later
activities; it is unfair to condemn the English bishops, king-trained
as they were, for not taking up a position which only events
clarified, and which was never really as simple as the partisans of
either side would make it. In addition, as we shall see, the government were careful to ensure obedience by skilful pressure.

3. THE PROGRESS OF THE DIVORCE TO WOLSEY'S FALL

All of this lay yet in the future when Henry VIII, in the spring
of 1527, decided that he was living in sin with his wife, and that
the marriage ought to be annulled. Who or what finally brought
him to that view is not certain. The king himself put it about that
the Bishop of Tarbes, on embassy from France, had cast doubts
upon Mary's legitimacy and therefore on her usefulness in a
dynastic marriage. Catherine, and Spain with her, believed
Wolsey to be the origin of it all, but in this she was certainly
mistaken. Though the cardinal did not like the queen and had
fallen out with Charles V, he had nothing to gain from a plan
which aimed at putting the Boleyns in the saddle; Anne herself
had personal reasons for hating him, and her family represented
very strongly that anti-clerical gentry of whom we have spoken.
No one now believes that the Boleyns were Lutherans, but they
and their party unquestionably approved of Luther's attack on
the Church and of the secularisation of Church property. As the
niece of the duke of Norfolk, Anne also commanded the powerful
Howard interest, unshakably hostile to Wolsey. In all probability,
there is no reason for depriving Henry himself of the credit, such
as it is, for turning upon his innocent wife. In the whole sordid
tale, Catherine stands out as the one person wronged but not
wronging; no one has ever had anything but pity for her, victim
as she was of a movement she could neither understand nor

approve, and of a husband who could only dislike when he ceased
to love. The people, especially of London, seem to have expressed
a preference for her, but in these questions of popular attitude and
reaction to Henry's doings the evidence is very shaky. Most of it
comes from the reports of hostile observers, especially the imperial
ambassador Eustace Chapuys who in those years used his office
to plot for Catherine; his reports must be treated with the greatest
care. Some men were charged with speaking vilely of Anne; but
men who praised Anne and abused Catherine (if any there were)
would not, of course, have got into trouble and therefore into the
record. In general, much caution is needed in assessing a public
opinion which undoubtedly mattered, especially if it appeared in
parliament, but of which far too little is known.

The actual history of the divorce is extremely complicated and
confused, full of twists and turns which it would be pointless to
follow. At first, Henry thought he could get his divorce from the
pope, the only proper authority, as others had done before him;
the matrimonial adventures of his sister Margaret and his friend
Suffolk, both of whom had been freed from inconvenient commitments by a compliant papacy, provided recent precedents, and,
after all, the pope owed both king and cardinal a burden of
gratitude. It all began with a secret collusive action in May 1527
when Wolsey summoned Henry before his legatine court to explain
why he was living in sin with his brother's widow. He intended to
establish a *prima facie* case for declaring the marriage invalid which
would then be confirmed by the pope. But the apparently unexpected indignation with which Catherine received the news first
arrested the easy progress of the matter; and when, late in May, the
imperialist troops sacked Rome and took the pope prisoner the
situation changed entirely. Wolsey, well aware that all his power
depended on the successful accomplishment of Henry's desires,
now proved full of invention, but at all points Clement VII,
horrified at the quandary into which he had been put, was a match
for him. In 1527, the cardinal proposed to act with the assistance
of the Church without Rome—*capto papa*—a plan which was
wrecked first by the failure of the French cardinals to back him up
and then by the politic 'liberation' of Clement in December. In
1528, therefore, Wolsey concentrated on getting a sufficient commission from the pope which would enable him to dissolve the
marriage and free Henry in all respects for re-marriage. The king
insisted throughout on the safest dispensation that could be got:
there must never be a shadow of doubt on his second marriage and
the issue he hoped it would produce, and therefore full papal

EET

authority was necessary. He had thus no use for Clement's desperate suggestion that Henry should get himself divorced in England and in any way he liked, or even commit bigamy, as long as the papacy was not involved. Wolsey wanted a decretal commission virtually empowering him to declare the marriage void; instead the pope at last (April 1528) granted a commission to try the case as though it had not already been tried and settled in Henry's own mind. This public commission was made out to Wolsey and Cardinal Campeggio, bishop of Salisbury and protector of England at the papal curia. Further pressure, however, together with the French successes in Italy early in 1528, induced Clement to add a secret decretal commission which he entrusted to Campeggio with private instructions not to use it. By October, when Campeggio at last reached England, the situation in Italy had been completely reversed by the imperialist triumph at Genoa which once more persuaded the pope that his way lay with Charles V.

Campeggio now played a masterly game of delays and procrastinations, designed to keep Henry quiet without committing the pope. Wolsey, who understood better that the king was only being driven into anger and unpredictable action, was desperate but powerless; the signs were multiplying that his supremacy had nearly reached its end. At least one of the embassies dispatched to Rome had gone without his knowledge.[1] Early in 1528 he seriously displeased his master by persisting in his advocacy of an unsuitable candidate for the office of abbess of Wilton nunnery; Henry was beginning to speak sharply to 'his cardinal'. For the moment, the king still relied on him, but Wolsey knew that one failure would be enough. Well might he lament to Clement VII: the pope's hesitations, he wrote, were ruining the cardinal, and with the cardinal would fall the Church. But much as Clement desired to oblige the defender of the faith, much as he dreaded the spread of schism in the north, nothing could overcome the near presence and definite views of the emperor or the pope's primary interest in Italian affairs. So Campeggio dallied, suggesting various ways out (as that Catherine should retire to a nunnery), all of which were blocked by the queen's determination to have right done to her. The delays encouraged ribald rumours about these supposedly secret matters, till Henry found it advisable to hold a meeting of courtiers and city dignitaries at Bridewell Palace in November 1528 to announce to them his scruples of conscience and fears for the succession. It may be doubted whether this convinced those

[1] Knight in 1527; on the other hand, Gardiner and Foxe who extorted the legatine commission in 1528 were Wolsey's own agents.

of the people who—according to the chronicler—said that the king wanted another wife and therefore had summoned the legate to divorce him, or reassured the women who generally were on Catherine's side against Anne.

Even Campeggio's ingenuity could not have manufactured delay out of nothing, but in October 1528 the legate heard of a document whose importance to the case made a trial impossible until it had been thoroughly discussed. This was Julius II's brief of 1503 to Isabella of Spain in which he allegedly resolved the doubts raised by his dispensation for Catharine's second marriage; the Spaniards now announced its opportune discovery. Since the whole English argument depended on the insufficiency of the dispensation, the brief—if genuine—would have left them without a case, except to deny outright the pope's power to dispense, an extreme step they were reluctant to take; they naturally claimed it to be a forgery, and it is a fact that its authenticity has never been satisfactorily established. The English would not admit the brief until they had seen and studied it; the Spaniards would not entrust the precious document to men interested in its disappearance; one more deadlock was added to those already existing. But now Wolsey realised that the trial must open, for while his envoys failed to persuade the pope of the need to support Henry, the emperor was urging Clement to revoke the case to Rome[1]—and he seemed likely to succeed. Should Henry find himself summoned to Rome to answer for his marriage, his boundless wrath would be worth seeing; it would also sweep Wolsey into oblivion. Thus, on 31 March 1529, the court at last opened at Blackfriars. The proceedings dragged on; the queen made a deep impression by her impassioned pleas and steadfast bearing; Henry endeavoured to prove that her marriage to Arthur had been consummated, which she denied. The whole unsavoury business continued until 23 July when—a decision being confidently expected—Campeggio sprang his concealed mine: he announced that, since the court was part of the Roman consistory, it would have to keep the terms kept at Rome, and that it thus stood adjourned through the hot Italian summer until 1 October. It never met again: this desperate step, to which Wolsey had assented because he could see no good coming out of a decision, ended the matter as far as Henry was concerned. A day earlier Wolsey had heard that Clement had given in to Charles and revoked the case to Rome; a week later the peace of Cambrai, concluded without his knowledge, put paid to a last hope

[1] I.e. to order its trial at Rome instead of in the court of the legates commissioned in 1528.

that the Italian wars might take another turn, Clement be set free, and Wolsey's policy triumph.

This concluded the first stage of the divorce—the attempt to achieve it by co-operation with Rome. The second stage followed almost at once: Henry, still convinced that only the pope could legally free him from Catherine, now determined to exercise pressure at Rome. For three years he battered away with threats and hints of dire things to come. But before he felt free to attack he had to rid himself of the man who had failed him. Once the king had made up his mind, Wolsey's fall was headlong. When on 9 August writs went out for a parliament—in itself a threat to Wolsey—the cardinal was deprived of the control which his office of chancellor gave him. The king refused to see him or join him at his manor of the More, and the subtle barometer of courtierdom reacted quickly. Where all the councillors had thronged to hear the cardinal in the star chamber, leaving the king deserted, the opposite was now true: when the term opened in October, Wolsey found himself alone. On 9 October the blow fell: the attorney-general indicted him for præmunire in the king's bench. But the king would not ruin him entirely; he was saved by the memories of fifteen years and the possibility that he might yet again be useful. On the 18th he surrendered the great seal. On the 22nd he confessed his guilt in writing (for technically he was guilty) and was sentenced to the penalties of the statute. The bill of attainder brought against him in the parliament that met on 3 November was his special enemies' doing and not the king's; it therefore need not surprise us that it was thrown out.

Wolsey fell because he could not serve the man who had made him. His dependence on the papacy had only lost him the one favour that mattered; he had no prop but the king. All men of influence hated him—and women too, for he always thought that Anne Boleyn was instrumental in his overthrow. The pope, for whom he had waged many a diplomatic battle and real war, made no move to save him. By accepting the legatine commission from which so much of his power stemmed, and thus exercising a foreign authority to the detriment of the king's regality, Wolsey laid himself open to the charge of præmunire. That Henry had of course endorsed Wolsey's legateship mattered nothing. Papal power in England was already exercised only at the king's discretion. This must be remembered when it is said that Henry learned from Wolsey the possibility of combining all secular and ecclesiastical authority in one man: it seems rather that Henry was always fully persuaded that he was supreme and unchallengeable in England.

The king's mind was not of the kind that works out such matters in theory and then transforms them into action. As he saw it, he had such power that no man should gainsay it; but he had no idea how to apply that power to the problem in hand, or that it could be developed into a revolutionary theory of the state. All he did in the next three years showed that. If he learned anything from Wolsey it was the need to have the agreement of parliament, the folly of an over-enterprising foreign policy, and an enhanced opinion of his own sagacity. In the deeper aspects of statesmanship Henry learned nothing from Wolsey because the king was not a good pupil at any time, and because the cardinal had nothing to teach.

For Wolsey turned out to be the most disappointing man who ever held great power in England and used it for so long with skill and high intelligence. He survived for a year after his fall. Saved from imprisonment by Henry's unwonted mercy, restored to part of his preferments and property, he determined to devote himself to his archbishopric of York which he had never yet visited. But the pull of the great world proved too strong. He moved north slowly, casting longing glances over his shoulder; he continued to excite hostile comment by his lavish living; finally he involved himself in plots which his enemies turned against him. In November 1530 the council had him arrested and conveyed to London; he knew what was in store. By easy stages the ailing man reached Leicester; there, met by the captain of the king's guard, he died on the 24th. His fall had been tremendous, for he had risen to tremendous heights, and only pity will be excited by that famous death-bed in Leicester Abbey. But the historian must also ask what Wolsey had really achieved. His foreign policy, often brilliant and never negligible, had resulted in the isolation of England, the enmity of both Spain and France, and the king's failure to get his divorce; it had been based on a false estimate of English power and directed consistently to ends in which England had little interest. The administration, badly in need of reform, was on the contrary more confused than before; the reserves of treasure were gone, prosperity was declining, trade neglected. The Church, his special charge, Wolsey left in an unprecedented state of weakness, facing a most untempered storm in a freshly shorn condition. Only in the law he had done things that bore fruit, and much though he liked the work of a judge he would surely have been dissatisfied with a verdict that allowed him but this piece of success. And yet it is hard to see what else one can say. Embodying in himself the link with Rome and the height of the medieval polity, he pulled them

down in his fall; his death marks the close of the old order with
as much definition as any man's fate ever marks the fate of
nations.

4. YEARS WITHOUT A POLICY, 1529-32

The government which replaced Wolsey did not make his mistakes, but it neither had his successes or brilliance. It was a stopgap
without either brilliance or success, composed of second-rate men.
The chancellorship went to Thomas More whom one can certainly
not describe as second-rate; but More took office only on condition that he would not be involved in the divorce to which he was
immovably opposed. Since the divorce naturally dominated the
events of those years, the king's promise meant that he deprived
himself of the services of far and away the ablest minister left after
Wolsey's fall. More concentrated on some useful work in the court
of chancery where he began the tradition of great common lawyers
and laymen who, building on the foundations laid by the ecclesiastical chancellors of the middle ages, acclimatised this potentially
alien court to the common law. As for the rest, he was rather
more questionably active in searching out heretics and writing
polemical works against Tyndale. The government was really in
the hands—under Henry—of the triumvirate of Norfolk,
Suffolk, and Wiltshire. The duke of Suffolk, an admirable sports-
man, had no ability whatsoever in affairs; the duke of Norfolk,[1]
a good soldier and competent administrator, never displayed
sufficient originality of mind to rank as a statesman; the earl of
Wiltshire, father of Anne Boleyn, owed his rise to noble rank to
his daughter's place in the king's affections, though he too made
a good enough agent of others. These were not the men to succeed
where Wolsey had failed. For three years after August 1529 the
conduct of government really depended on the king; in its unco-
ordinated vigour, piecemeal attack on problems, and essential
bankruptcy in ideas it displayed Henry's mind to perfection.

When Henry decided that co-operation with Rome must be
replaced by hostile pressure on Rome, he realised that to this end
he had to have allies in England. The summoning of a parliament
for 3 November 1529 was a very significant step. No parliament
had met since 1523, and none had met since Wolsey rose to power
without causing trouble to the government. In falling back on
parliament, Henry therefore showed that he understood the nation
he governed. He remembered the anti-clerical temper of 1515 and

[1] The third duke, son of the victor of Flodden (see above, p. 75).

saw that it could be turned to advantage against the independence of the Church. We may take it from what followed that Henry had two lines of attack in mind when he assumed the direction of affairs himself: he wished to reduce the Church to absolute obedience to himself, so as to prevent their natural allegiance to the papacy from weakening his case, and he wished to use parliamentary anti-clericalism to make the pope's fear of what might happen in England greater than his fear of what Charles V might do. Since Charles was near at hand and England far away, this policy was from the first without hope of success.

The parliament which met in November 1529 was no more packed than any other of Henry's parliaments. That is to say, it naturally contained a number of royal councillors and servants, for these usually had some standing in their own localities and—being in politics anyway—also some interest in being elected. The government presumably exercised such influence as it had in elections (not a great deal), and in other elections private patronage was undoubtedly at work. Contemporary statements about a packed or servile house of commons are exaggerations, often prompted by hostility to Henry's policy. The house was representative of the men of the middle sort, gentry and merchants and lawyers, on whose faithful support Tudor government depended and who were particularly hostile to the pretensions and exactions of the Church. The lords, of whom about half were bishops and abbots while many of the rest owed their elevation to the Tudor kings, were immediately less important: opposition was not to be feared from the lay peers, and the presence of the spiritual lords made the house as a body less useful in attacks on the Church. It was therefore in the commons that the critical events took place. Henry gave them full liberty to discuss what they would, and they replied by putting forward bills against abuses in the Church. Three of these—those limiting the fees taken for probate and mortuaries, and one against pluralism and non-residence—passed into statutes; another document, which attacked in the form of a petition the activities of the Church courts, remained in the hands of Thomas Cromwell, then a private member, when the session ended. It is quite certain that these measures of the first session were taken on the commons' own initiative: they attacked evils of great interest to themselves and of none to the king, and the documentary evidence is conclusive. Henry's decision to let loose the hatred of the Church which Wolsey had greatly augmented paid full dividends; the activities of the commons frightened the bishops and proved useful as propaganda material at Rome where

Henry's representatives were careful to point out the danger to the Church. The king would readily call off his dogs if only the pope agreed to his just demands: the point was taken, but the little finger of Charles V seemed thicker than Henry's thigh.

After six weeks the parliament was prorogued (16 December 1529), not to meet again until January 1531; plague and policy prevented an earlier recall, but meanwhile the king was not idle. He increased his diplomatic pressure at Rome, using an intellectual weapon which he found congenial. Following the advice tendered in August 1529 by Thomas Cranmer, an obscure Cambridge divine, Henry's agents spent the better part of 1530 gathering opinions from the universities of Europe in favour of the king's point of view on the canonical problem of his marriage. Oxford, Cambridge, and the French universities not unnaturally supported a view hostile to Spain; but even the great North Italian universities of Bologna, Padua, and Ferrara voted for the king. The rest of Italy and Spain, as well as Germany, decided for the other side. It was a typical piece of work: expensive in time and treasure, for bribery played its part, it could do no good. These opinions were to be used at Rome together with the threat of calling a General Council of the Church which would act if the pope did not. Faced by the hint of another conciliar movement even the weak Clement proved strong, though in any case no prince or Church in Europe was sincerely interested in reviving these ancient controversies; it took the Church forty years to assemble a council under papal guidance to deal with protestantism. The opinions of learned divines, too, could have no effect in a struggle in which power counted much more than argument. That Henry genuinely thought he could batter in the iron gates of Rome with such feeble weapons is evidence both of his failure to understand the situation and of his inability to find his own way out of the maze.

He proved rather more successful in the other part of his policy, for he managed to stifle opposition from his own clergy. The weapon employed was that used to destroy Wolsey, the statute of præmunire. From the summer of 1530 a number of bishops and leading clerics found themselves accused in the court of king's bench of having broken the statute by obeying Wolsey's legatine authority; it does not surprise to find that the men so attacked were connected with the queen's party, including for instance Bishops Fisher, Clerk, and Standish who had been her counsel at the legatine trial.[1] Significantly enough, these victims of Henry had

---

[1] I owe the information on these proceedings to Mr J. J. Scarisbrick.

also been Wolsey's victims; their alleged offence consisted in agree-
ing to pay part of their revenues to Wolsey as legate, an agreement
which the cardinal had extorted by threats of the very same præmunire which their compliance was now judged to have fallen foul
of. However, before these individual thrusts took effect, the
government decided to extend the operation to the whole clergy,
purposing both to cow and to amerce a body whose essential loyalty
was beginning to weaken after the parliamentary attacks of 1529.
In December 1530 the whole clergy were indicted of præmunire
on the sweeping grounds that they had unlawfully exercised
their spiritual jurisdiction.[1] Everyone understood the meaning of
the threat; rather than forfeit its corporate property, the Church
surrendered. In February 1531 the two convocations bought a
royal pardon for their 'offence' by paying £100,000 and £18,000
respectively. Not content with this, Henry also demanded that
they recognise him as their supreme head; after much opposition
the aged Warham of Canterbury proposed an alternative title—
'singular protector, only and supreme lord, and as far as the law
of Christ allows even supreme head'—and took the ensuing silence
for consent. What meaning the title of supreme head had at this
time is far from clear. Since it involved spiritual as well as temporal supremacy only the pope was in strict law supreme head of
the Church; this accounts for the opposition. Henry himself
explained the words away and showed no sign, for two years, of
understanding their implications; it is very likely indeed that it
meant no more to him than the claim he had made in 1516 (when
he had no quarrel with the pope) that the kings of England never
had any superiors on earth. He simply wished to assert his control
over the Church and remind it that its duty lay with him rather
than the pope; as yet he had no thought of replacing the pope
altogether. This conclusion is supported by his acceptance of the
modifying clause which really invalidated the claim. In the canon
law—the law of Christ—the king could not be supreme head of the
Church in the technical sense, whatever his practical power might
be. At the time, the heavy fine imposed was much more important
than the nominal surrender, and more significant still was the fact
that the parliament, in its session early in 1531, was asked to
register the pardon in an act. Henry again indicated that he would
rely on the temporality and its anti-clericalism, and he underlined
this when he consented to a free pardon for the laity who had also

[1] As Mr Scarisbrick has shown, in work as yet unpublished, the
common view that the charge was obedience to Wolsey's illegal authority
rests on a mistake.

technically offended against præmunire by using the Church courts. Otherwise the session was barren of political interest.

Indeed, the year 1531 served to show up the weakness of the royal policy. Determined to render his second marriage as safe as papacy and canon law could make it, Henry persisted at Rome several years after that road had proved to be firmly blocked; his patience and the endurance of his love for Anne Boleyn are both a great deal more evident than his supposed sagacity and political skill. Clement VII forbade re-marriage in 1531, and though Spain could not as yet persuade him to declare the first marriage fully valid he also refused to release Henry. Catherine would not solve the problem by either giving in or dying. The king has even been praised for forbearing to poison her, though it is not likely that he ever thought of doing so, for Henry had a superstitious dread of poison in general; in any case, with all his faults he was not an assassin, and his conscience always required due forms of law in his murders. As 1531 drew to a close, the king's mental bankruptcy became increasingly apparent. Now and again he had hinted at Rome that England could at a pinch do without the pope, but that he had no plan ready for such desperate expedients was plain after his long frustrations. What he was after was probably the kind of concordat by which Francis I had in 1516 acquired very wide powers over the Church in France; but Francis had then merely exploited his position after Marignano and been negotiating from overwhelming strength. Henry, thundering from England, could not hope to achieve similar results. His ministers were broken reeds, without ideas to offer or sufficient skill even to take the burden of government from Henry's shoulders; as early as 1530 he had talked pointedly of recalling Wolsey. But Wolsey was dead, and these Norfolks and Wiltshires, Gardiners and Suffolks, had no answer to the royal perplexities. It was at this point that Henry discovered among his lesser councillors a man who knew exactly how the problem could be solved, and who was an even better administrator than Wolsey. In December 1531, Thomas Cromwell was promoted to the inner ring of the council, and the Tudor revolution was about to begin.

Chapter VI

THOMAS CROMWELL AND THE BREAK WITH ROME

1. THE NEW MINISTER

THOMAS CROMWELL was born about the year 1485 at Putney where his father had a small business as a smith and fuller; of his youth very little is known. He seems to have pursued a most adventurous and unorthodox career which took him abroad as a soldier of fortune in the Italian wars; later he became a merchant with interests and connections on the Antwerp market and somehow got enough learning in the common law to set up as an attorney. He himself told Cranmer that he had been quite a ruffian in his early days, and there survive a number of unreliable stories which only agree in showing that he knocked about Europe in surprising fashion. No doubt it was in these years that he acquired not only an understanding of men and the world, but also an outlook remarkably free from the prejudices of his time and country, and a wide knowledge of languages. He had a reputation for pleasant conversation and wit, for never forgetting old friends and benefactors, and for being a good master to his servants and protector to his clients. His naturally powerful intellect was developed by his unusual history into the most successfully radical instrument at any man's disposal in the sixteenth century; as a statesman he displayed cool indifference in destroying the old and perspicacious dexterity in constructing afresh. His temper was secular, sympathetic to the prevailing anti-clericalism of the time; dislike of the priesthood may have been magnified into contempt for the papacy by what he saw in Italy. But he appears to have been virtually devoid of passion, even in his anti-clericalism: he did not hate priests as such, or as purveyors of bad religion, but simply objected to them as obstacles to his plans. Cromwell seems to have been incapable of merely negative opinions; everything he did was designed to achieve some positive end, some lasting result. His qualities made him the most remarkable revolutionary in English history—a man who knew precisely where he was going and who nearly always achieved the end he had in view. Though he was ruthless in affairs, he lacked cruelty; seeing little purpose in mercy, he yet had no trace of vindictiveness. Like all politicians of the age he took bribes and presents, but the wealth he accumulated he also spent: ostentation was as foreign to his nature as the pride which values the appearance of power above its reality.

However, he was essentially a cold man, and many who—curiously enough—find it easy to forgive Henry VIII his cruelties and murders because they were carried out in hot blood have nothing but execration for the man who killed for a purpose only and as rarely as possible, but who showed no weakness—attractive or otherwise—once he had decided on a course of action. The men of his day knew him as the all-powerful minister and held him responsible for everything done; he took then, and has since taken, the blame for the unpopular actions without the credit for the rest. Though he had many personal friends and political adherents, his enemies—who comprised all the victims of his devastating policy—were more numerous and more influential. In the last resort, Cromwell, like Wolsey, rested his power on the king's support only. Such popularity as attended him in life did not survive in history. The protestant martyrologist, John Foxe, made him his hero, but in the end Cromwell's fame collapsed in face of the reaction against the Reformation and of the renewed adulation of Henry VIII. The sentimental eighteenth century went maudlin over the ruins of the monasteries, and the Oxford Movement completed what 'sensibility' began. Desire to exculpate Henry VIII increased the burden of contumely heaped upon his minister.[1] By now, general opinion has accepted Thomas Cromwell as a 'Machiavellian', though it is doubtful if he ever read Machiavelli and certain that he did not learn his statecraft from any book; as the cruel, sly, and greedy servant of an imperious master, the wicked though clever destroyer of a civilisation, the unscrupulous builder of a despotism which justly destroyed him in the end.[2] Little of this is true, and even the truth has been distorted by exaggeration. Yet we must endeavour to understand Cromwell's character and aims aright, for in the last analysis it was he who

---

[1] The serious attack on Cromwell began with S. R. Maitland's *The Reformation in England* (1849), a formidable indictment of 'protestant' history, John Foxe, and the sixteenth-century iconoclasts. Moreover, the leading writers on the period in the last hundred years on the Protestant side (J. A. Froude and A. F. Pollard) were both admirers of Henry VIII and played down the importance of the king's advisers.

[2] The modern picture of Cromwell is derived from the attack made on him by his enemy, Cardinal Pole; though Pole was certainly an honest man, he was also a polemical writer in the medieval tradition which believed in heaping abuse, and he had personal reasons for hating Cromwell and his work which disqualify him as an impartial witness.

founded the modern constitutional monarchy in England and organised the sovereign national state.

Cromwell's travels ended round about 1512 when he appeared once more in England, engaged in legal and commercial affairs. By 1520 he had entered the service of Wolsey whose solicitor and general man of business he became; in this work, and especially in the dissolution of the monasteries used to found the colleges at Ipswich and Oxford, he earned much dislike. In Wolsey's entourage he rose to a leading position, but his patron's fall threatened to end his career. Unlike, for instance, Stephen Gardiner (who was to be his leading opponent), Cromwell did not desert the fallen cardinal; he continued to work for him. In this there was much loyalty but also some calculation, for he used Wolsey's affairs to bring himself to Henry's notice, and he knew that with the king a reputation for faithfulness would be worth having. However, he had to struggle hard before he rose to eminence. In November 1529, he managed to enter parliament pledged to support the king's policy, though he did not owe his seat to official patronage. He played a leading part in the anti-clerical debates of the first session and was rewarded soon afterwards by being taken into the king's service; towards the end of 1530 he was sworn of the council, and a year later he belonged to the inner ring. Throughout he displayed his astounding administrative ability, working his way up through the duties of a civil servant to the king's confidence. It was not until April 1532 that he obtained an office—that of master of the king's jewels. To this he added others: clerk of the hanaper (1532), chancellor of the exchequer (1533), principal secretary and master of the rolls (1534), and finally lord privy seal (1536). These offices he used to acquire wide and precise control of the administration; even at the height of his power he always supervised minutely every detail of government. What gave him power, of course, was not any office but the king's confidence, and this he first secured in the year 1532 when he came forward to cut the knot which none of Henry's other advisers could untie. Cromwell's suggestion for a way out of the king's difficulties had about it a kind of tremendous simplicity. He offered to make a reality out of Henry's vague claims to supremacy by evicting the pope from England. To the king this meant a chance of getting his divorce, and a chance of wealth; to Cromwell it meant the chance of reconstructing the body politic.

2. THE ROYAL SUPREMACY

Cromwell's advice was apparently too overwhelming to be fully accepted at once; nevertheless the parliamentary session of 1532 made it plain that a new temper had taken hold of the government. The uncertainties and futilities of the last three years were to give way to a definite plan and purpose. In this session both the English Church and the papacy were for the first time attacked with real weapons instead of with threats, and the measures used to do this are indisputably linked with Cromwell. In 1531 the Church had been compelled to acknowledge a so far meaningless title and agree to a heavy fine (much of which was never paid); in 1532, the constitutional independence of the Church was overthrown. The instrument employed for this was that petition against Church courts of which Cromwell had taken charge in 1529. As he revised it, a document originally representative of the genuine grievances of the commons concentrated on the one issue in it which affected the crown—the fact that the laws of the Church did not depend on royal sanction. The petition known as 'the Commons' Supplication against the Ordinaries' was introduced into a house exasperated by the king's demands for their assent to a bill strengthening his feudal rights; naturally, the commons took it up with relief and soon convinced themselves that they were debating their own proposals—as in a manner they were.

On 18 March the Supplication was presented to the king. It asserted the commons' orthodoxy, stressed their dislike of the Church's independent legislation, and recited at length many complaints against the practices of the ecclesiastical courts. Henry accepted it graciously and passed it to convocation who drew up a long and not ineffective answer, largely inspired by Gardiner. Henry, however, expressed himself dissatisfied with the answer and suggested to the commons that they might react likewise. Pressure thus having been kept up, the scene was set for the king's demands put before convocation on 10 May: the clergy were to enact no canons and ordinances without the king's licence, the existing canon law was to be examined by a commission of thirty-two men (half of them lay) whom the king would appoint, and the laws approved by them were to receive the king's assent. To impress convocation with the need for surrender, Henry next day summoned another commons' deputation and informed them that he had discovered the clergy to be but half his subjects since they took an oath to the pope; he asked the commons to consider what might be done. Rather than leave their fate and the fate of the canon law in the hands of parliament, convocation on the 15th surrendered them into the hands of the king by accepting his demands in a document known as 'the Submission of the Clergy'. The threat of parliament did more than the threat of præmunire, because there was now a minister in power who knew how to translate generalised assertions into severe practice. In 1531 the clergy had called Henry their supreme head (with vital reservations); in 1532 they accepted the king in the pope's place as their supreme legislator (without any reservations). From that point the English Church ceased to be a potential obstacle in the progress of the breach with Rome.

At the same time, the first direct attack on Rome itself was made. As the discussion in the commons of the government's bill concerning feudal rights made way for the Supplication, the lords began to consider the bill of annates. Annates were the payments made by the bishops to the pope on succession to their sees, rated at one third of a year's income; they had been a long-standing grievance in the whole Western Church. The bill proposed to abolish them on the ground that these payments involved a heavy loss to the nation; it also provided for the consecration of bishops-elect by English authority if the pope were to retaliate by refusing bulls of consecration. The bill thus contained a double-pronged attack: it removed the chief papal source of revenue from England, and it virtually destroyed one of the essential aspects of the pope's spiritual headship. However, the time for extremes had not yet come; Henry still hesitated to throw the pope out altogether; and so Cromwell drafted a clause which became famous. By it the operation of the act was held up until the king should confirm it by letters patent; in the meantime, he was to see what negotiations could do. From a double-edged sword, the first act of annates became a mere diplomatic counter: Henry told the pope that he had had the clause inserted so as to be able to stop the parliament's vigorous attack. In fact, parliament expressed its doubts. In both houses the bill led to a division, an unusual step especially in the commons; the king thought it advisable to be present on both occasions, though there is no reason to think that improper influence was exercised. The ostensible beneficiaries—the bishops and abbots—voted against it to a man; one may suspect that they were expressing their feelings over the progress of the Supplication rather than giving vent to their eagerness to pay taxes to Rome. The opposition in the commons is usually ascribed to the clause which delegated parliament's legislative authority to royal letters patent; there is no evidence for this, and it is at least as likely that the fears of reprisals (such as the stopping of the Flanders trade) which came out a year later were already at work. This interpretation certainly fits this house of commons much better than one which would make it jealous of its legislative powers in the best seventeenth-century manner.

Though fears in parliament and the king's desire to continue with his diplomatic pressure at Rome halted the attack in 1532, the signs were clear. The day after Henry received the clergy's Submission, Sir Thomas More resigned the chancellorship and retired into private life; at last he realised that his attempt to serve the king in everything except the one thing that mattered was putting him in an impossible position. He was succeeded by Sir Thomas Audley, an ally of Cromwell's and lately speaker of the commons. Cromwell himself spent 1532 consolidating his hold over the king and preparing for the real attack. In September, he accompanied Henry to his meeting with Francis at Boulogne, a meeting intended to confirm the Anglo-French amity upon which the foreign policy of these years rested. Francis was more than willing to support Henry at Rome against his own imperial enemy, but he quite failed to realise that the king, and especially the new minister, were beginning to think of more than a concordat with the pope. When Cromwell's policy developed in full the French interest turned against him. It is the mark of Cromwell's ability that he managed to combine a pro-Spanish foreign policy in the interests of English trade with the destruction of everything that Spain wanted to see preserved in England.

1532 declared the new policy; 1533 saw it put through. On 25 January Henry secretly married Anne Boleyn. The matter had become urgent: about this time it must have become certain that she was with child—that child Elizabeth who was to be born early in September—and the expected heir had to be legitimate. But the events of the next session had been planned before this; indeed, it is likely that the sudden pregnancy, after six years of delays, was the result rather than (as is commonly assumed) the cause of the policy embodied in the great statute passed, with an ease that surprised many, early in March 1533. This was the act in restraint of appeals to Rome which made possible the settlement of the divorce in England, as Cromwell had recommended. In August 1532 Archbishop Warham died; in January 1533, Henry appointed Cranmer to the see—Gardiner, who had been angling for it, was in disgrace after his opposition over the Submission of the Clergy—and secured him the papal bulls of consecration by means of the diplomatic threat contained in the conditional act of annates. All this time, and before Anne's pregnancy called for rapid action the act of appeals was drafting in Cromwell's hands; it proved a difficult document to compose and underwent many changes in a lengthy course of preparation. As finally enacted, it prohibited appeals in testamentary and matrimonial causes from the archbishops' courts to Rome. Thus enabled, Cranmer—the canonically appointed archbishop who was to lead the English Church away from Rome and into protestantism— opened his court at Dunstable and on 23 May delivered sentence. The marriage with Catherine was declared void, that with Anne true; the long business of the divorce was over. On 1 June Anne was crowned queen.

Henry had got his will, but what really mattered was the instrument of success, the great act of appeals, Cromwell's master-piece in statute-making. The enactment confined itself to a practical issue; in effect, it extended the provisions of Richard II's statute of præmunire to appeals lodged at Rome. This was no new grievance: English courts had suffered, and the papal court had profited, from a practice which removed cases to Rome at the instance of one of the contending parties. Money left the realm, justice was delayed, a foreign jurisdiction exercised wide influence on English affairs. The immediate purpose of the prohibition was to enable an English court to free Henry for re-marriage: there had been a plan to pass an act for this specific purpose only, but Cromwell succeeded in getting a general statute which put all ecclesiastical jurisdiction in the king's control. The act of appeals was thus important enough as the most decisive single step towards Cromwell's goal—the expulsion of the papacy—but its famous preamble held even greater significance. This declared that 'this realm of England is an empire . . . governed by one Supreme Head and King', quoting in support the testimony of 'divers sundry old authentic histories and chronicles'. Basing itself on uncertain traditions, the act enunciated new doctrine: it stated as accepted facts that the king was supreme head and the realm a sovereign state free from all foreign authority. The full meaning of these assertions—which amounted to a fully fledged theory of the state— will be discussed in the next chapter. Cromwell's conservative revolution, a revolution resting on strict constitutionalism and dubious historical claims, was therewith really accomplished; it only remained to work out its detailed application. In that impor-tant work the enacting clauses of the statute of appeals played themselves a major part by defining the operation of the supremacy in the sphere of jurisdiction as the Submission had defined it in the sphere of legislation. When the annates act was put into force (July 1533), the pope had been deprived of all effective temporal authority in England.

For the rest, the year 1533 saw the fading away of the earlier conflicts, about to be subsumed in the total rejection of the papacy. The divorce—*fons et origo* though hardly any longer the main issue—was, as we have seen, settled by Cranmer, Henry's special archbishop. Cranmer's rise had been rapid. A Cambridge don of reforming tendencies (partly at least because he was given to matrimony), he had come to Henry's notice when he suggested to Gardiner that the theological opinions of the universities might be worth collecting. For twenty years after his sudden elevation to the primacy he was to play a leading part in the story of the English Reformation which in some ways is a fair reflection of his painful and sincere search for spiritual truth. He suited Henry, for he was somewhat unworldly and a change from the political prelates and ambitious laymen who surrounded the king; his gentle, scholarly temper and convinced adherence to the supremacy of the crown—obedience to which he held to be enjoined by the divine law—made him an agreeable leader of the new Church. He and Cromwell presided over the beginnings of the Church of England, and both have had many hard words for their pains; but while Cromwell continues to be maligned, Cranmer's good name has been saved by historians with more sympathy for scholarly hesitation and sincere doubts than for ruthless statesmanship and the truly secular temper.[1] In the Dunstable judgment Cranmer did as he was told, though he also believed the divorce to be just. In reply, the pope excommunicated Henry in July, holding the sentence over till September; Henry in turn confirmed the act of annates and in November lodged an appeal from the pope to a General Council of the Church. This annoyed Francis I who told Gardiner that while he was studying to win the pope the English as fast studied to lose him. Clearly he still failed to understand what was happening. These were but motions to be gone through; Cromwell—and Henry, under his influence—had no intention of winning the pope. The appeal to a general council was useful for propaganda purposes—in December the king's council decided so to employ it—but the reality lay in the preamble of the statute of appeals. The English government wound up its negotiations with the pope and prepared the measures which would put the implications of that preamble into operation.

---

[1] A. F. Pollard, *Thomas Cranmer and the English Reformation* (1905); C. H. Smyth, *Cranmer and the Reformation under Edward VI* (1926).

The work was done in the two parliamentary sessions of 1534. In the first (January to March) a further act of annates confirmed in full statutory manner the prohibition of these payments to Rome and laid down the procedure for the election of bishops and abbots. Election now became purely formal, the chapters and monasteries being bound by nominations given in the royal licence to elect.[1] The act against the payment of a small annual tax known as Peter's Pence cut off another source of papal revenue; it also transferred the granting of dispensations and licences from Rome to Canterbury, thus removing one further juridical link between the pope and England. The act for the submission of the clergy embodied in a statute the 1532 surrender of convocation and changed the course of appeals in ecclesiastical causes as laid down in the statute of appeals. There, the archiepiscopal courts had had the last word; now appeals were authorised from them to commissions appointed under the great seal, that is to the king in chancery. Thus the Church lost jurisdictional independence to the secular courts. Lastly, the first act for the succession registered the invalidity of the first and validity of the second marriage, drawing the logical conclusion that therefore Mary was illegitimate and the crown must descend to the children of Henry and Anne. More important than this declaration, precedents for which can be found in the reigns of Henry IV and Henry VII, was the clause which made it high treason 'maliciously' to deny or attack the second marriage 'in writing, print, deed, or act', while similar denial in words only was made misprision of treason, a milder offence which carried with it imprisonment and loss of property instead of the death penalty. The act proposed to bind the whole nation by a general oath to observe it; this, not specified in the statute but devised soon after, was intended as a political test of obedience to the new order and of adherence to the royal supremacy in the Church.

The session of November-December 1534 added, first of all, the act of supremacy. It is a short act, containing little of practical import, but it put Henry's full claim on the statute book. It did not make the king supreme head but acknowledged that he 'justly and rightfully is and ought to be Supreme Head of the Church of England', going on to enact that he shall be so 'taken, accepted, and regarded'. Further, it conferred authority to carry

---

[1] Such interference had been habitual for a long time: the act, by making it statutory, gave it a worse odour in the nostrils of the independent churchmen of today but did not, in fact, alter the contemporary position at all.

out visitations proper to the spiritual power, an indication that the later attack on the monasteries was already decided upon. Another statute showed how hollow had been the pretence that payments to Rome were forbidden as too burdensome to the Church: it ordered the payment of first fruits and tenths to the crown. First fruits meant the payment of one year's income by the new incumbent of any benefice, from episcopal sees to parish vicarages, and tenths an annual levy of one tenth the annual value of every benefice (that is, a ten per cent. income tax); in the event, the Church paid vastly more to the king than it had ever paid to Rome, even as the royal supremacy was in every way nearer home and more troublesome than the pope's had been. At this stage, at least, the Reformation was not the victory of the national Church over an alien domination, as its later champions have too readily imagined, but the victory of the state over the Church in any form. Lastly, the treason act of this session recited a number of treasons, mostly closer definitions of old ones, but it added calling the king or queen heretic or schismatic—which things were presumably being said. Moreover, it extended treason from intent expressed in deeds to intent expressed in words (maliciously). On this much ink has been wasted. Treason by words could be a terrible weapon in the hands of a government dominated by the determined Cromwell and the vengeful Henry, but it was not a new weapon. Throughout the fifteenth century, the judges had been forced by the insufficiency of the treason law of 1352 to 'construct' treasons—that is, to adjudge matters ostensibly outside the statute as falling within it—and words had been so interpreted. The act of 1534 embodied in parliamentary legislation a principle already developed by the common law. Of course, in these years of revolution when opposition had to be stamped out every extension or confirmation of treasons was so much further equipment for the government. But the picture so often drawn of a rule of terror based on a vast network of spies, of innocent men convicted for harmless words twisted against them, is not to be supported by the evidence and must be discarded.

These acts of 1534 completed the work of setting up the royal supremacy in the Church and of destroying the pope's power in England. In January 1535 Henry added the title 'Supreme Head of the Church of England' to his style. A final summary was published in the act of 1536, 'against the papal authority'; this was a good deal ruder to the 'bishop of Rome' but did not deprive him of anything further or add anything to the king's competence. It could not have done so: the work of transferring the papal powers

to the crown, begun in the act of appeals, was completed by the
enactments of 1534.

3. THE OPPOSITION

The revolution was carried out with the consent of parliament,
given readily enough except when fears of papal retaliation
through the cloth trade had to be reasoned away. Such fears
delayed the first act of annates and the act of appeals; having twice
been proved wrong, they did not recur. Some burgesses showed
that they preferred Catherine to Anne, and some lords talked
wildly to Chapuys of the support that Charles V would receive if
he were to invade England; but though the ambassador—wishing
to believe—was taken in, his master was not, and nothing ever
came of it. The commons proved themselves capable of opposition
by freely resisting demands for money and financial assertions of
the prerogative, but that there was any real feeling against the
king's ecclesiastical policy is denied by the smooth progress of
events and cannot be deduced from the deluded hopes of enemies
or from a later remark (1537) that the act of appeals passed only
because members did not like to displease Cromwell. A little
hesitancy there was in parliament, and some opposition—most of
it hidden or sullen—outside it. Certainly the government equipped
itself with formidable legal weapons against doubters and resisters,
but—considering that we are dealing with a revolution—the
astonishing thing is that there were so few victims. The reason is
plain: this revolution was made and led by the government with the
consent of the politically conscious and active classes, and with an
almost finicky attention to constitutional propriety. Opposition was
confined to those few whose objections rested on principle or
conscience, and who moreover rated their consciences higher than
anything else. The English Reformation under Henry VIII
produced, one might say, no victims and only martyrs. Since
among these martyrs there were also some of the most attractive
personalities of the day, much attention has always been given to
the opposition and its downfall, but the most impressive thing about
it is its exiguous size. After the careful repression of the bishops and
the Church in 1531-2, only the adherents of the so-called Nun of
Kent (including Bishop Fisher), Sir Thomas More, and a few
monks felt strongly enough to call into action the treason legislation
passed to protect the revolution.

The fatal train was lit by Elizabeth Barton, a poor servant-girl
afflicted with epilepsy and visions, who from about 1525 began to

attract attention by her trances and prophecies. She was taken up by Dr Edward Bocking, a monk of Canterbury, and acquired a reputation for holiness throughout the county, being named the Holy Maid or Nun of Kent. Unfortunately for himself and his protégée, Bocking, who stage-managed her ravings, conceived the notion of using the Nun against the king's policy. She began to prophesy against the second marriage, alleging that the king would not survive for six months after putting away Catherine, and she actually forced her way into the royal presence to admonish Henry on his way of life. This was dangerous stuff to put about, especially as the Nun had many adherents among the simple folk of Kent (a shire notoriously volatile) and was in touch with the papal representatives. It is hardly to be wondered at that the government could not ignore her activities. She and the accomplices in her tragic farce were arrested and made to confess their impostures publicly in November 1533; in the February session of parliament that followed they were attainted; and in April the deluded woman was executed together with four of the men who had thought to use her for political ends. One's pity must be reserved for Elizabeth Barton; Dr Bocking and friends deserved their fate, and the government cannot be blamed for taking action against such treasonable talk.

But the talk was not yet treasonable in statute law, and this necessitated process by attainder in addition to a trial. Henry intended to use this attainder to attack more illustrious opponents of the divorce: the names of Fisher and More were included, though they were accused only of misprision of the Nun's treason by having kept silent about her doings. Fisher had played an equivocal part: as bishop of Rochester he was in a position to deal with the Nun, and as an eminently sane and learned man (of the famous new learning, too) he should have known better than listen to her with reverence. But listen he did. Perhaps he simply proved how wrong it is to equate humanism with scepticism and a critical attitude to the past; perhaps he allowed his dislike of the divorce to get the better of his judgment. He was lucky, at this time, to get away with a fine of £300. Thomas More, on the other hand, had always judged the Nun rightly, going so far as to call her 'the wicked woman of Canterbury'; his inclusion in the bill was indefensible and shows how Henry's liking for his ex-chancellor had turned to virulent hatred. The bill encountered strong opposition in the lords, but it took much entreaty on the part of his councillors to persuade Henry into leaving More's name out of the bill. More himself remarked that this was but deferring the issue.

The king, now growing ever more intolerant of opposition from his own subjects (parliament always excepted), was determined to pursue both Fisher and More to the death.

His chance came in April 1534 when commissioners began to administer the oath to the act of succession. The oath demanded adherence not only to the succession as laid down in parliament, but also condemnation of the first marriage and an implied denial of the papal supremacy. While Fisher and More were prepared to swear to the first—reluctantly, but after all it was a fact—they would not compromise their consciences to do the second. The resistance of these two well-known leaders of conservative opinion was felt to be deplorable, even though nearly all men, clergy as well as laity, took the full oath readily enough. Both Cranmer and Cromwell tried hard to save More from Henry and himself, but the differences were fundamental. Both men were lodged in the Tower for refusing the oath, until the treason act passed later in 1534 made possible a further attack. More, in particular, defended himself brilliantly in a trial scene as famous almost as that of Socrates, but by dint of declaring that the inclusion of 'maliciously' in the act was invalid, and by accepting the perjured evidence of Sir Richard Rich, the solicitor-general, who deposed to having tricked More into speaking treason, the judges commissioned for the trial felt able to convict him. Fisher, whom the new pope (Paul III) had very injudiciously elevated to the cardinalate in May 1535, was executed in June; More suffered in July; and Henry had demonstrated both his implacable cruelty and his determination to suppress opposition. Two months earlier five clerics, among them three Carthusians of the London Charterhouse, suffered similarly for the same reason, after unspeakable ill-treatment which failed to break their spirits; three more Carthusians followed More to the scaffold.

These executions, and especially those of More and Fisher, have always been considered the worst blot on Henry's record, and rightly so. The king must bear the responsibility. It was he who pressed for extreme measures throughout; baulked of his revenge in the attainder of Elizabeth Barton, he did not rest thereafter until his victims were dead. Cromwell seems to have had a real liking for More whose integrity, personal charm, gentle determination, and miserable fate make him the most attractive figure of the early sixteenth century (not a difficult achievement); for Fisher, his sympathy was less. In any case, Cromwell probably realised the folly of a policy which made martyrs of these well-known men. The brief sharp terror was successful in the short run, but it has

since lain heavily in the balance against Henry VIII. Two things,
however, must be noted. The country reacted as Henry had
reckoned: Edward Hall, the chronicler, a lawyer and member of
parliament, spoke for his important section of society when he
thought Fisher 'wonderfully deceived' and reproved More
solemnly for his excessive levity which could jest even on the
scaffold. The victims died without exciting much sympathy in an
England given over to loyalty and anti-papalism, though later
generations have rehabilitated and even canonised them. The
other point is that both Fisher and More were, in fact, dangerous
to the government; in a measure, their condemnation was justifiable even though their trials were rigged and the law was twisted.
Fisher had been in treasonable correspondence with the emperor's
ambassador for some years, though the government were not
aware of it; and More, in the fine speech he made after sentence
had been passed, expressed his unshakable allegiance to the papal
supremacy. These honourable men stood in the way of a revolution; it is tragic but not surprising that they had to be removed,
even if the law could get at them only by chicanery. But no one
need condone the determined blood-lust displayed by the king who
resented opposition to his own will where Cromwell applied the
dangerous but not indefensible principle of reason of state.

The case of the Carthusians was different. They suffered for the
same reason and deserve even more sympathy because they were
not, in fact, anything like as dangerous; also they were treated
very badly indeed while More was handled with comparative
gentleness. Torturous imprisonment instead of reasoned persuasion was applied to break them, but they did not break. Throughout
one feels that this resistance from monks only angered everyone:
no one had any patience with monks. The royal supremacy was
achieved and opposition to it wiped out; it was time to consolidate
the position by putting the supremacy to practical use. Cromwell
turned his attention to the monasteries of England where the last
centres of resistance might be suspected to be, and where there
lay the wealth which the laity desired.

4. THE DISSOLUTION OF THE MONASTERIES

The attack on the monasteries has usually been regarded as the
most important part of the great upheavals of the 1530s; but
though it was unquestionably spectacular and had some consequences of note, it does not really merit the central position
commonly allocated to it. In some ways it was almost the least

revolutionary part of the revolution, for attacks on clerical property and piece-meal dissolutions had taken place at intervals over the centuries, whereas the royal supremacy differed altogether from whatever powers the king might previously have exercised over the clergy. The monastic institutions of England had always been in rather a special case, many of them enjoying independence from the bishops and answering for their conduct only to visitors appointed by the pope or by the superior of their own order. They were less national than the secular clergy and owed a special duty to Rome. It is not too much to say that throughout the middle ages regular orders of various kinds—monks as well as friars—had formed the papal vanguard; in the Jesuit order, they were to do so again in the sixteenth century. True, few monasteries or orders displayed any resistance to the royal supremacy, most of them taking the oath readily enough; but what resistance there was came largely from the orders. The six small houses of Observants (strict Franciscan friars) suffered dissolution in 1534 for their opposition, even though they had been Henry VII's favourite order; and apart from More and Fisher, the martyrs of 1535 were men who had taken the vows. The government could be pleased at the ease with which even the traditional papal strongholds had succumbed, but they could not risk a monastic revival in favour of the pope.

The orders collapsed so readily before the assault because monasticism in England was on its last legs. Riddled by worldliness and deadened by routine, the institution had lost all or nearly all meaning; the ideal was as near extinct as no matter, and the practice not such as to encourage sincere men. Sir Thomas More found it more congenial to wear his hairshirt outside a formal order. Intellectually, only the friars retained any vigour; for that reason they supplied so many leaders of the Reformation. An Austin friar led the way in Germany when Luther 'hopped from his habit', and in England, too, the leading heretic and preacher of the 1530s (Tyndale being exiled) was a friar of that order, Dr Robert Barnes. The laity had no respect left for monasticism, and quite a number of the monks themselves were interested only in getting out of vows they had taken before they were old enough to understand their meaning. Nor did the monasteries play a useful part in the community. Old notions of the kindly monks as gentle landlords have been disproved; where they administered their own estates they were quite as keen on making the most of things as laymen, and indeed it would have been dereliction of duty if an abbot or prior had neglected the welfare of his house. In any case, most monastic estates were by this time leased to local yeomen or gentlemen. Monastic charity and hospitality, too, played little part in sixteenth-century England: it has been calculated that the monks gave rather less than five per cent. of their net income to charitable purposes, and—except in the desolate north—the abbeys were no longer needed as places of refuge and refreshment. The people who used them as inns were not so much poor way-farers (as sentimental writers think) but more commonly the great —men and women connected through patronage or honorary office with the abbeys, like the duchess of Suffolk who often visited Butley Priory in Suffolk to be entertained with dinner and a fox hunt. The monasteries' sole remaining purpose was also their original one. They still stood for a spiritual ideal (though too often their practice denied it), and they still prayed for the souls of the dead. But few men now included in their wills those bequests for prayers which in earlier centuries had testified to the real need served by monastic institutions. Their spiritual value cannot be assessed by the historian, outside whose competence this matter is; what he can say is that contemporaries had largely ceased to care about it, and that the monks themselves were often too few to carry out these duties.

Monasticism was, then, in such decline that its end might have come spontaneously, but the real reason for the attack on it lay elsewhere. It was the property of the orders that men desired— the lay lords and gentlemen as much as the government. Schemes of secularisation were of long standing: the whole property of the Church—between one fifth and one third of all land in England— had been under spasmodic attack for some two centuries. Plans were mooted to transfer all the lands to lay hands and pay bishops and incumbents a fixed stipend, but this was too vast a task to contemplate seriously. From an early date the government realised that it could bind the gentry and nobility to the new order by bribing them with lands which any reversal of policy would force them to restore. But Cromwell had a more urgent reason still for sequestrating the monasteries. The crown's finances were far from healthy. Cromwell inherited a financial problem from Wolsey who had not managed to keep the revenue on a level with his expenditure, and the exigencies of the years when the royal supremacy was established aggravated the situation. Regular revenue was dropping because of a decline in the wool customs; this reflected an increase in the amount of wool exported as cloth (which paid less duty than raw wool) and therefore an encouraging trend in English trade, but was nevertheless awkward for the government's finances. The years 1533-4 saw a determined effort to put England's defences in order against the possibility of an attack from Spain; affairs in Ireland, to be discussed hereafter, demanded heavy expenditure; and the French pension, which Wolsey had found so useful, was surrendered in 1534 as part of the diplomacy which tried to maintain friendship with France to balance the danger from Charles V. It was patently impossible to ask much from parliament at a time when its harmonious co-operation was desired in the expulsion of the pope. Cromwell succeeded in getting supplies in 1534, but they amounted to less than £200,000 payable over four years; he needed an increase in the regular revenue. For a time he made do with revivals of Henry VII's practices: distraint of knighthood appeared again, and he exploited the chance of mulcting the clergy collectively or individually in fines imposed for real or imaginary offences. The feudal rights of the crown came to the fore in the long battle for the statute of uses, not passed until 1536; this was intended to follow up Henry VII's recovery of prerogative rights by preserving the king's just claims upon a tenant's death from infringements by means of legal fictions and evasions. But all this, useful though it was, amounted to no more than temporary expedient and failed to solve the lasting problem of a static revenue in an age of rising costs.

Thus Cromwell turned to the Church. In 1534 he transferred to the crown the payment of first fruits and tenths, calculated as likely to yield an average annual income of about £40,000. There was to be a realistic assessment, and in January 1535 commissions issued for the valuation of all ecclesiastical property in England. The stupendous task was done within some six months, and it was done thoroughly and well; its product, the tax-book known as the *Valor Ecclesiasticus*, has been carefully tested by modern historians and found astonishingly good. The achievement spoke well for the administrative capacity of Tudor governments and the skill of the minister and his agents. Equipped with this detailed and complete knowledge of what there was to be had, Cromwell could proceed to the real attack. He had had it in mind for some time, and he had precedents to guide him: he himself had been trained by Wolsey's dissolutions in the technical details of the task. First one had to discover an official pretext: this was to be found in the monasteries' corruption and decay, established by means of the traditional ecclesiastical weapon of a visitation. The act of supremacy, which included a clause authorising the king as supreme head to visit all institutions of the Church in order to search out and correct abuses, superseded at will the disciplinary powers of the bishops and brought within the royal survey all houses hitherto free from control in England. In January 1535, Thomas Cromwell, appointed vicar-general by the supreme head, began to dispatch a group of visitors to gather evidence. These men have been the object of violent attack, even as they themselves violently and unfairly attacked the institutions they visited. Admittedly, they were hardly prepossessing characters, and they knew that they were expected to turn in damaging details. Dr Richard Layton, a cleric of salacious tastes, Dr Thomas Legh, an arrogant young man with a 'satraplike countenance' (as one of his colleagues put it), John ap Rice, a man of servility, Dr John London, a persecutor born: no one need admire these and their like. But the visitation, hostile though it was, followed precedent in everything, even in the speed of its work and the extremity of its conclusions. The only difference was in the ultimate outcome. The visitors brought questionnaires of the traditional type and imposed the sort of injunctions to obey the rules which bishops had time and again and with increasing weariness put to their charges; but Layton and Legh knew that they were to enforce the rules as to residence, asceticism, clean living, and obedience with all the rigour possible, so as to encourage monks to opt for a dispensation from their vows and the end of monasticism.

The whirlwind went through the country, sweeping up many discontented brethren, finding plenty of scandals (though hardly more than earlier visitors had done, so that one need not suspect fabrication), and providing much ammunition for the attack. Medieval propaganda relied on denigration; that is, it assembled every charge, silly or heinous, and flung everything—regardless of truth—at the accused. Cromwell's government acted likewise against the monasteries, not so much because these were so utterly corrupt—though by high-lighting the wicked the truth could be made to appear quite bad enough—as because they wished to prepare the ground for the dissolution. The visitation of 1535 was never intended to mend but always to end; it was an hypocritical weapon. Equally hypocritical was the pretence in the bill introduced into the parliament of February 1536 that only the lesser houses were corrupt; the bigger ones served religion, maintained discipline, and knew no vice. It appeared from the bill that the line between virtue and depravity followed with curious fidelity the line which divided £200 a year from incomes larger than this: realising well that he could not carry out the whole dissolution at one stroke, Cromwell first attacked only the smaller monasteries.

Another statute set up the court of the augmentations of the king's revenue which was to administer the transfer of their lands to the crown. The court started work at once. Throughout 1536 its officers went the rounds of the monasteries affected, dissolved the institutions, took surveys of the lands, made inventories of lead, gold, silver, and precious stones found, and disposed of the monks either by sending them to a bigger house of their own order or—if they wished to leave the religious life—by paying them pensions or finding them vicarages and benefices. The dissolution violently destroyed centuries-old communities and wiped out ancient landmarks; but it was carried through not only with efficiency but also with unexpected humanity and with a regard for property rights which, though typical of the age, is a little ludicrous in the midst of the great expropriation. Thus debts incurred by the monasteries were taken over by the government and paid, and the personal goods of monks were guaranteed to them.

In the midst of the dissolution a sudden storm of opposition took the government by surprise; for a time it looked likely to threaten not only Cromwell's policy but even perhaps Henry's throne. This was the northern rising, also known as the pilgrimage of grace, which convulsed Lincolnshire, Yorkshire, and finally all the north in the last three months of 1536. The movement was complex. The north had never yet been properly settled; conservative and dominated by old feudal allegiances, it resented the interference of the central government which was increasing under Cromwell. The gentry and nobility objected to successive attacks on 'liberties' and hated the statute of uses with its augmentation of royal rights. The influential Percy interest was discontented because of the downfall of the sixth earl of Northumberland who had wasted his substance and attempted to govern the north as the king's lieutenant in opposition to the king's interests. As always, there was an agrarian element in the unrest: cries were heard against enclosures and raised rents. The collection of the subsidy of 1534 and the enforcement of legislation for the better manufacture of cloth stirred up additional trouble among the well-to-do of the West Riding. The final impetus was given by religion. The attack on the old religion had barely begun, yet already it smacked of far too much heresy to the northern people, and the dissolution of the monasteries—of which Lincolnshire and Yorkshire were particularly full—proved the last straw. Resentment at the various commissioners who went round assessing for the subsidy, dissolving and pulling down abbeys, and administering to conservative parish priests the heterodox Injunctions of 1536 no be discussed later), was exacerbated by wild rumours: it was said, among other things, that many parish churches would also be put down, that the king would have all the gold in the country, that no one would be allowed to eat white bread, pigs, and capons without a licence. All this only shows how profoundly disturbed the north was. Trouble, signs of which multiplied during September, broke out at Louth in Lincolnshire on 1 October with a riot which soon spread further; in a few days the whole county rose, the gentry followed willy-nilly, Cromwell's commissioners were taken and manhandled. The rebels demanded that no more abbeys be suppressed, that Cromwell be handed over to the people, and that the heretical bishops (especially Cranmer) be dismissed. All through they declared themselves loyal to the crown; perhaps the most remarkable thing about the whole rising was the confidence of these deluded men that the king was on their side and they on his.

Although the rebels occupied Lincoln in force and the king's representative—the duke of Suffolk—had not a fortieth of their army, the Lincolnshire rising collapsed abruptly on 19 October when the king haughtily refused to listen to the demands of men under arms against his authority. But in the meantime more serious trouble began further north. Yorkshire was up, and here there appeared a leader in the person of Robert Aske, a country gentleman and lawyer. To Aske the rising was religious; it was he who popularised the banner with the five wounds of Christ and spoke of a pilgrimage. His followers took York where he set up in state, issued ordinances for the government of the north and received the adherence of great men like the archbishop (Edward Lee) and Lord Darcy. By the 24th he had 30,000 armed men at Doncaster, while the king's commanders had nothing. Suffolk was stuck in Lincolnshire which could not as yet be safely left without a royal army; Shrewsbury had rashly advanced too far with too few men and was useless; and Henry's ablest general, the duke of Norfolk (rapidly recalled from the retirement into which Cromwell had shunted him) was as yet collecting a force. On 27 October he met Aske at Doncaster Bridge and, unable to take action, agreed to communicate the rebels' demands to the king. He told Henry that he had no intention of keeping his promises; indeed, his conduct at this time does not suggest—as has been suspected—that he was secretly encouraging the rising in order to get rid of Cromwell. Instead he temporised, tricking Aske into disastrous delays. In any case, the rebel leader found it impossible to lead his followers south; they wished to stay near their homes, and there was no response to their appeals anywhere south of the Trent where the country remained firmly loyal. Furious at having to treat with rebels, Henry yet played his part well: he delivered an interim answer which kept the door open, while Norfolk rapidly increased his army. On 2 December Aske gathered a 'great council' at Pontefract to draw up the pilgrims' final terms; these repeated the earlier demands for an end to the dissolution, for the repeal of the statute of uses, and for the dismissal and punishment of Cromwell and his supporters, but added also the restoration of the papal jurisdiction and the liberties of the Church. In addition, Aske demanded a reformed parliament free from royal interference; this is remarkable enough as a recognition of the place held by parliament, though it differs little from past complaints on that score back to the reign of Richard II and reflects rather northern resentment at the activities of the Reformation parliament than that parliament's corruption and subservience, which it has been taken to prove.

However, the crisis was nearly over, for Aske had waited too long and trusted too well. Neither Norfolk nor Henry thought themselves bound by promises made to rebellious subjects. The duke met Aske again at Doncaster on 6 December; Norfolk promised vaguely to adhere to some of the demands and offered a full and free pardon. Thereupon Aske ended the pilgrimage. He declared himself the king's faithful subject and with great difficulty prevailed upon his followers to disperse. The king had won, seemingly at the cost of surrendering to the pilgrims on essential points, but he could bide his time. The unrest was not ended by Aske's resignation at Doncaster; throughout January and February 1537 there were minor riots and upheavals which were used to free the king from his promise and to exact his vengeance. In the first half of 1537, Norfolk, as Henry's lieutenant in the north, summarily executed men all over the northern provinces, distributing the hangings so as to impress all parts with the terror of the king's power. The leaders of the late rising were separately executed, including Lord Darcy, an old servant of the crown, and Aske who died at York after a travesty of a trial and despite promise of pardon. Altogether some 220 to 250 people suffered, not many by the standards of contemporary Europe but a sufficiently fearsome retribution. Moreover, it was made possible only by a wholesale breaking of promises. Yet, when all was done, the pilgrimage stood out for the futile, misdirected, and ill-considered venture it was. The grievances of the commons and especially the religious enthusiasm of some (Aske in particular) deserve respect and sympathy, but much of the spirit of the rising was sordid, self-seeking, and particularist. The pilgrimage achieved nothing. The one major protest against Cromwell's revolution and seemingly dangerous for a time, it was always confined to the backward and barbarous north. The tranquillity of the south demonstrated that Henry and Cromwell had the majority of their people behind them. Even the factions among leading politicians, profound though they appear, proved to be only superficial when Norfolk prevented the success of a movement designed to destroy his rival. Loyalty and obedience to the king, the guardian of peace and order and the symbol of the state, dominated everything. Even the rebels used the language of loyalty, though in the circumstances their protestations sounded odd. Five months of trouble resulted only in the reorganisation of the north, which will engage our attention later, and in a vigorous renewal of Cromwell's revolution both in the progress of the dissolution and in the seeking out and suppression of further malcontents in the next few years.

The rising had involved many monks—naturally enough, for they had most to gain by it. A number of abbots and priors lost their lives because they had participated in the Pilgrimage, though others, and many lesser brethren, were pardoned. But the executions of the abbots of Kirkstead, of Whalley and Jervaux, and of the ex-abbot of Fountains (March to May 1537) led the way in the attack on the bigger monasteries. Their suppression had always been intended, despite the kind words used about them in the act of 1536; now the collapse of the rising—their last hope—encouraged the greater houses to surrender themselves and their property into the king's hands. Furness, in Lancashire, led off early in 1537, and many others followed. In 1538, Cromwell's commissioners began another visitation of the abbeys yet standing, offering a prepared form of surrender which was commonly signed without protest. Action reinforced threats: apart from a general attack on the old religion which produced in 1538 a first burst of image-breaking and the suppression of relics, Cromwell took care to remind recalcitrant monks of the government's power by obtaining the conviction and execution of the abbot of Woburn for attacking the supremacy. The parliament which met in April 1539 passed an act securing to the crown all property that had come to it or would yet come by surrender or dissolution; in the autumn, the three great abbeys of Glastonbury, Colchester, and Reading were dissolved after their abbots had been hanged for treasons they probably contemplated but had barely yet committed; and when Waltham surrendered in March 1540 the monasteries were gone. In 1539 the friaries had been similarly absorbed, and in 1540

Cromwell added the preceptories (or branch establishments) of the Order of St John of Jerusalem. Therewith the vast secularisation was complete; monasticism had ended, and the crown and the laity had acquired a great mass of lands whose disposal was to have far-reaching effects on the social structure of England. The dissolution increased the revenue of the crown by well over £100,000 a year, roughly the total royal income at the beginning of Cromwell's ministry.

The wider effects of the dissolution belong to the story of economic change;[1] what were the immediate results? Much undoubtedly was destroyed. A whole form of religion was gone; England could not be protestant while the monasteries stood, and unquestionably—whatever the intention of Henry VIII—protestantism was brought nearer by the dissolution. There was destruction of buildings, works of art, and libraries, lamentable enough but neither complete nor without its compensations; many of England's finest buildings today—the great houses—would not exist but for the dissolution. The dissolution hardly aggravated the problem of poor relief: neither had the monasteries played a great part in supplying it, nor did the number of paupers much increase. The old pictures of exiled monks wandering about the roads of England to die in ditches were wildly inaccurate. The monks received pensions which were generally adequate and lavish for the late abbots and priors, though nuns and friars, whose houses were mostly poorer, did less well and often badly. But both monks and friars were as quickly as possible placed in livings, unless they preferred to be rid of their vows and take to a secular life. Some of the many servants employed in the monastic establishments no doubt went to swell the ranks of the poor, but many took service with the new owners who still had to till the lands and maintain their establishments.

The really surprising thing is not that there was some dislocation—even at times a good deal of it—but that the dissolution passed off so easily. Within a few years the monks were but memories, and as memories they soon acquired a glamorous reputation for holiness and kindliness which in their decline they had done little to earn. The effect of the great secularisation on the land market—the leases and sales—is a different matter. It had never been intended that the crown should keep all the lands, and from 1538 onwards Cromwell began to organise a judicious disposal. The men who carried out the dissolution—the vicar-general himself, the lord chancellor, and the officers of the court

[1] Below, Ch. IX.

of augmentations—were well rewarded with gifts, as were some courtiers. But others had to buy lands or take up leases on terms advantageous to the crown; certainly until Cromwell's fall there was no question of squandering the wealth with which he had equipped the king. In the Church itself the dissolution produced one commendable change. In 1540, Henry was at last able to carry out a plan of Wolsey's by establishing six new episcopal sees;[1] these were badly needed, for Lincoln and Lichfield were much too big to be properly administered. The dissolution destroyed the last possible refuge of papalism, enriched the crown, and anchored the new order firmly in the self-interest of the land-owning classes who purchased the estates. It did all this with the thoroughness and amazing ease (despite the pilgrimage of grace) which characterised all Cromwell's achievements.

5. FOREIGN POLICY AND RELIGION, 1536-40

The dissolution of the monasteries was far from being the only business to occupy the government in the years 1536-40. The break with Rome demanded the greatest care in relations with other countries; the correspondence of Chapuys is full of references to malcontents ready to rise if only the emperor will invade England, and though the ambassador was unquestionably prone to daydreams it cannot be doubted that Henry VIII took an enormous risk in the 1530s. Real action from the champions of the pope and Queen Catherine would, to say the least, have been most embarrassing to a country undergoing a revolution, however well-conducted and peaceful this was. On the other hand, the English war with Rome could hardly hope to go forward without some attention to other men elsewhere who were assailing the same target for very different reasons. Henry VIII himself wished to hold his nation to that orthodoxy of the catholic faith which he and they valued so much: he never saw any difficulty in remaining a good catholic without the pope and never envisaged the spread of protestantism which the break with Rome encouraged. From the first the few reformers in England raised joyful voices at the supreme head's doings, even though they equally miscalculated in thinking that Henry's anti-papalism would mean the speedy establishment of their own doctrines. The appointment to Canterbury of Cranmer, not so far a well-known protestant but known to have leanings that way, foreshadowed great changes; the

[1] Oxford, Chester, Gloucester, Bristol, and Peterborough endured; Westminster was abolished in 1550.

religious Reformation in England owed a great deal to Henry's strange whim in picking on this man as his primate and his stranger fidelity in supporting him against his enemies for fifteen years. Cromwell's position is more dubious. It is now fashionable to suppose that he had no religion at all, but that is as demonstrably wrong as the old notion that he was an inspired protestant. In a careless moment he once told some Lutheran envoys that he was on the whole of their opinion, but that 'as the world now stood he would believe even as his master the king believed'. This seems reasonable enough. He did not propose to push through a form of religion, or to die for it, in which he (as secular a man as has existed in a pre-scientific age) had at best a lukewarm interest; but to his logical mind the religion of all those who opposed the pope ought to be the same, that is to say, protestant in some fashion.[1] He held this the more strongly because throughout his ministry he overestimated the danger from abroad and therefore overvalued an alliance with foreign Lutherans or native reformers. After 1536, the question was no longer the defence of the royal supremacy against attack, but the growing faction strife between those who wished to establish a reformed Church and those who wished to keep the Church catholic. This struggle, in which diplomacy and religion were intricately entwined, is the story of the years 1536-58.

While Cromwell was establishing the king as supreme head, he had to rely on the alliance with France inherited from Wolsey's last years. This proved relatively easy until late in 1533 when Francis I, at last understanding where things were tending in England, began to waver. In consequence other feelers were put out. In 1533 Cromwell tentatively opened fruitless negotiations with the Lutheran princes of Germany; in 1534, Henry himself, forsaking the determined neutrality which he normally favoured after witnessing the collapse of Wolsey's policy of alliances, involved himself in the affairs of protestant Lübeck, a Baltic town which was trying to prevent the imperial nominee from ascending the vacant throne of Denmark. Nothing came of all this except ephemeral trouble; Charles V was hindered from succouring his aunt (whose treatment grew worse after 1533) not by English skill but by his commitments in the Mediterranean and his troubles in Germany. In 1535 things began to look black. France showed signs of turning from the understanding with England to friendship with Spain: the spectre of a union of the catholic powers

---

[1] I personally consider that his religion was rather more sincere than that, though it never interfered with his politics; but this is a point that cannot be developed here.

against schismatic England, which was to haunt Cromwell to his
death, seemed for a time very real. Immediately, negotiations with
the German Lutherans were resumed, though still to no purpose;
this time it was hoped to get not only a political alliance but also
the services of great reformers like Melanchthon. Melanchthon
stayed at home, but Cromwell took advantage of some episcopal
vacancies to promote well-known English protestants. In 1535
Hugh Latimer succeeded to Worcester and Nicholas Shaxton to
Salisbury; these and others were the heretical bishops whose dismissal the pilgrims of grace demanded a year later. Cromwell
clearly wished to face attack with Henry as the leader of a reformed
country, but it is much less certain whether the king was with him
in this. Henry seems to have understood the essential safety of
England's isolated position. Cromwell was always much too
inclined to practise the directness and thoroughness of his methods
in the field of foreign affairs which required delays, waiting, and
opportunism; he was temperamentally a worse foreign minister
than the king.

Not only did the danger pass in 1535; the next year seemed to
bring promise of complete success and a chance of getting Europe
to accept the new England without engaging on either side in the
increasing religious split. In January 1536 Catherine died, to the
king's open and indecent (if understandable) rejoicing; and in
May Anne Boleyn perished on the scaffold. Her fate had been
creeping upon her for some time. Henry's passion, steadfast
enough through six years of frustration, does not appear to have
long survived its fulfilment, and in the great matter of the succession Anne proved a disappointment. The child born in September
1533 was a girl, named Elizabeth, and thereafter the dreary tale of
miscarriages was resumed. Henry, like the gentleman he was,
showed his disappointment openly and reminded his queen of her
origin and his ability to humble her again. The story of her overthrow is confused. The king's conscience again came conveniently
into play; there was a new candidate for queenly honours in Jane
Seymour, a lady of the court; Anne's last safeguard died with
Catherine during whose life the second marriage could not be
repudiated without implying the validity of the first. Cromwell,
whose alliance with the Boleyns had always been one of convenience only, decided the more readily to sever it because he was
anxious to restore the Anglo-Spanish alliance and to break with
the French understanding of which the Boleyns and Howards had
been the protagonists. In April a secret commission was appointed
to find evidence against Anne, and in May she was accused of

manifold adultery, one of her alleged lovers being her own brother. That some of the charges—which included conspiracy to kill the king—were wild is certain; whether there was any truth in them at all has never been settled. At any rate, Anne and five men were put to death by due process of law because the king wished to marry again. Of all the victims of Henry VIII, Anne Boleyn—light-hearted and light-headed instrument of revolution—has had almost no sympathy; yet by her death and the manner of it she deserves it. Henry had now so far discarded scruple that to get his way he was prepared to appear as a cuckold and a victim of witchcraft. Anne died on 19 May; on the 17th Cranmer declared her marriage void, and on the 30th Henry married Jane Seymour.

These events cleared the deck. With Catherine and Anne both out of the way, England stood much better internationally, the more so as relations between Spain and France worsened noticeably during 1536. Henry was determined to continue in isolated neutrality, confident—rightly confident—that he was safe; Cromwell, on the other hand, fearing danger from abroad and even more perhaps the activities of the Francophile faction at home (led by his enemies Norfolk and Gardiner), attempted in vain to restore the alliance with the emperor. On one occasion he got into serious trouble with the king for acting precipitately. At the same time the religious problem grew pressing. The break with Rome had left the Church in a very uncertain state; some definition of the faith to be observed was urgently required, for the country was being set by the ears by wild teaching and revolutionary preaching. The pope gone, many thought the time had come for a full religious reform, but neither the king (who remained attached to the old faith) nor Cromwell and Cranmer (moderates in Church reform) were prepared to go as far as the extremists whose voices were loudest. In July 1536 the government issued the first formulary of the Church of England, the Ten Articles, a compromise between the old and the new. On the sacraments of the altar, penance, and baptism, and on good works, the Articles were orthodox; but they deemed no other sacraments necessary, and on the vexed problems of prayers to saints and prayers for the dead they cautiously advanced towards the Lutheran view that these were of no value. The document rested, of course, on the authority of the supreme head, not on that of convocation or parliament, and in August Cromwell, as the supreme head's deputy or vice-gerent in spirituals (a title bestowed some time before January 1536) issued Injunctions making the Articles binding upon the clergy. The Injunctions also taught priests their business and ordered a bible in English to be placed in every parish church. The translation was already in hand, though not until 1539 were the first official bibles supplied—Matthew's Bible, as it is called, a compilation drawing on the work of two leading English protestants, William Tyndale and Miles Coverdale. But while there were signs of cautious reform, continental hopes, nourished by negotiations in 1535-6, that England would adopt the Lutheran faith were disappointed with the appearance in 1537 of a primer (or book of faith and instruction) called *The Institution of a Christian Man* or 'The Bishops' Book'. This 'found again' the four 'lost' sacraments of 1536 and generally defended catholic orthodoxy against innovation.

The reasons for these vacillations are partly to be found in the international situation. Late in 1536 war broke out between Charles V and Francis I, freeing Henry from all need to serve any interests but his own; and the king was as anti-Lutheran as ever. The 'Bishops' Book' may also reflect second thoughts after the pilgrimage of grace had demonstrated the great strength of conservative opinion in religion. Altogether, 1537 was a year of marking time and clearing up after the northern rising and the first act for dissolving the monasteries. Even Cromwell forbore to push his two schemes of alliance—a political and commercial understanding with Spain, and a religious rapprochement with the German League of Schmalkalden. In October, Henry at last had a son— Edward—and though his birth cost his mother's life, it seemed as if Heaven was blessing all the supreme head's enterprises. But not for long: 1538 saw the beginning of a crisis which first swept Cromwell away, outlived Henry and two of his children, and was only settled with great difficulty by Elizabeth. The struggle between the old religion and the new was joined in earnest, with the usual intricate interplay of foreign affairs and doctrinal reform. The vague factions crystallised: Norfolk and Gardiner assumed the virtual leadership of conservatism against the radicals led by Cromwell and Cranmer. For nearly two years Henry carefully felt his way between them before falling in with the orthodoxy with which his own sympathies lay; so far from directing this storm, he was determined to put his weight in the scales only after he knew where majority opinion tended.

The crisis really began late in 1537 with better relations between France and Spain which led to the peace of Nice in the summer of 1538. All Cromwell's fears revived, as his energetic activity throughout the year in restoring England's military defences proves clearly enough. Splendid isolation did not seem enough now, and the approach to Germany was resumed with vigour. From May to October 1538 German ambassadors tried to come to an agreement with Cromwell and Cranmer, but Henry's reluctance both to commit himself to a political alliance and to commit the country, whose temper was far from radical, to protestantism prevented a treaty. In his Injunctions of September 1538 the vicegerent renewed the war on 'popish and superstitious' practices: throughout the year, centres of pilgrimage were attacked, ancient wonderworking images were exposed as frauds and destroyed, even Becket's shrine at Canterbury was demolished and despoiled. The crown gained much treasure in gold and jewels, but the chief reason was religious: it was all part of the radical party's programme during its first brief ascendancy.

At the same time Cromwell proceeded against disaffection. The protagonist of the papal project to reconquer England was Reginald Pole, a kinsman of Henry VIII and a cardinal since 1536. Pole's activities provoked an attack on his family in England—who were also the last remnant of the old Yorkist faction. In August 1538, the Poles (Reginald's brothers Geoffrey, pardoned after he had supplied evidence against the rest, and Lord Montague, and his mother, the aged countess of Salisbury), as well as the marquess of Exeter (Henry Courtenay) and Sir Edward Neville, were arrested; in December all except the countess, who survived until 1541, were executed. The attack on them arose directly out of treasonable activities in defence of the pope and the old faith in which they had been engaged; but it also completed the dynastic policy of the first two Tudors by removing their last potential rivals. This second aim does not appear to have been deliberate; rather were the victims themselves induced to pit themselves against Henry's policy by their dynastic ambitions as much as by their religion. The onslaught caused an uproar abroad and much fear among the nobility at home who saw in it proof of Cromwell's contemptuous attitude to their order (a debatable point). The real leaders of the opposition to him—Gardiner and Norfolk, whom with misplaced generosity he spared from all attack—decided that only his death could make them safe. As 1538 closed and 1539 opened, the situation worsened. Attempts to reform the French alliance were rebuffed by Francis who would not let Henry find a wife among his subjects; the alternative—marriage with the duchess of Milan to secure the friendship of Spain—also collapsed when Spain and France renewed their amity in January 1539. Cardinal Pole went on a mission to these two countries in order to win support for a campaign to execute the bull of deprivation of

1535. This, calling upon all Christians to destroy Henry VIII, was put into effect late in 1538. All through 1539 Pole travelled over Europe, achieving nothing, narrowly escaping assassination, and keeping Cromwell apprehensive. Henry seems by this time to have believed himself invulnerable, and though such arrogant egotism deserved a worse reward he was proved right in his conviction that there was no danger to be feared from abroad which England could not weather on her own.

Cromwell thought differently, especially after a clash over religion which occupied most of the time of the parliament that sat from April to June 1539. His Injunctions of the previous year, which had attacked images and pilgrimages, ordered the reading of the English bible, and incidentally inaugurated the keeping of parish registers, marked an advance in radical reform. The reaction was not long in coming. By early 1539 it became clear that the country was being riven in two by a religious controversy which the supreme head would have to settle. Henry ordered the convocations, which met concurrently with parliament, to consider the matter, and after much debate conservative orthodoxy prevailed. The king waited upon the outcome rather than interfered to determine it:[1] the radicals were in a minority even among the bishops, and Cromwell and Cranmer gave way when they saw the trend of things. Even so Cromwell had a bad two months before he could recapture control from Norfolk and Gardiner who came very near to unseating him. The decision on religion was given force by a parliamentary statute appointing penalties for transgressors against the six articles agreed upon—the act of six articles. These articles embodied full catholic doctrine: they asserted transubstantiation, the need for auricular confession, the sanctity of monastic vows, communion under one kind only, the justness of private masses, and the illegality of clerical marriage. The act might have been a decisive weapon against the reformers had it ever been employed very widely, but while Cromwell lived it slept, and it was never fully operative. The radicals, with few exceptions (Latimer and Shaxton resigned their sees), accepted the verdict of king and parliament and awaited a better future. The importance of the act has been overestimated by both sides; it did not even signal the overthrow of Cromwell who recovered most of his strength by July.

However, the rough handling of these months and the continued danger from abroad now betrayed Cromwell into action fatal to

[1] This is not to deny that in the course of the discussions he proved himself interested and very knowledgeable in theology.

himself. A second Lutheran embassy had departed in May with even less satisfaction gained than the first; but there still remained the projected treaty with the duke of Cleves, no Lutheran himself but allied to Lutherans. To this alliance Henry showed himself inclined in March 1539 when even he began to have his doubts about England's isolation in Europe. Cleves, astride the lower Rhine, was a thorn in the emperor's side and a useful ally to have while Pole seemed likely to stir up a crusade against England. The situation changed in the course of the year, especially when the arrival in June of a French ambassador to England suggested hopes of ending the Franco-Spanish friendship. Nevertheless, Cromwell determined to force the king to his side, and in October he dragooned Henry into a marriage alliance with Anne of Cleves. Holbein, who painted a flattering portrait of Henry's fourth bride which deceived both king and minister, bears an ironical share of the responsibility for Cromwell's downfall. In January 1540 Anne came over; Henry, meeting her, was shocked by her plainness and bad manners; but, as he said, there was no cure—he had to put his neck in the yoke. From 6 January 1540, when the marriage was celebrated, Cromwell's position was in danger; though his mistakes were not beyond remedy, he had forced the king into a distasteful policy and an even more distasteful marriage both of which could most easily be discarded by getting rid of Cromwell.

The conservative faction now gathered its strength. In February, Norfolk went on embassy to France and, from a court conditioned to hate Cromwell by Gardiner's long residence there, brought back a virtual promise of friendship if only the vicegerent were removed. Late in March, Gardiner recovered his seat in the privy council by an attack on the Lutheran Dr Barnes, an overconfident and self-assertive reformer whose extravagances brought upon him the king's displeasure. Barnes was Cromwell's protégé, and though Cromwell was careful not to involve himself in the affair he could not but be displeased at Gardiner's success. Rumours of coming changes flew about the capital. When parliament reassembled in April Cromwell displayed his accustomed skill and leading position in steering through a subsidy bill and the confiscation of the lands of the Order of St John. On 17 April he was given fresh honours, being made earl of Essex and great chamberlain of England. But while he was busy at Westminster in parliament and council, his enemies gained the upper hand at Greenwich where the court was. Norfolk, taught nothing by the fate of his niece Anne Boleyn, succeeded in interesting the king in the charms of another niece, Katharine Howard, and so Henry's demand for a third annulment of a marriage was added to all the other problems. In the second half of May Cromwell counterattacked, at last seeking out his real enemies among the bishops; but though he seized Richard Sampson of Chichester and got evidence against unnamed others, it was too late. Even early in June Henry still trusted the man who had removed two queens from his path to bring off yet a third miracle, but Cromwell could not remove Anne of Cleves if it meant putting the Howards in the saddle. Thus, in stroke and counterstroke, the drama was played out. On 23 May Sampson was arrested and the conservatives felt their heads loose on their shoulders; on 10 June, the captain of the guard arrested Cromwell in the council chamber. By convincing Henry at the last that his vicegerent was an heretic and favourer of heretics, the Norfolk-Gardiner faction won the day. Cromwell was never heard in his own defence, being condemned for treason and heresy—and guilty of neither—by an act of attainder without trial, a procedure he is alleged to have invented for the countess of Salisbury (who, incidentally, was kept alive while he remained in power). After lingering in the Tower until his testimony should have enabled his grateful master to obtain a divorce from Anne of Cleves, he was executed on 23 July. On the scaffold he said that he died in the catholic faith.

Cromwell's fall and manner of death have provided much material for moralising. He had more enemies than friends: the nobles hated the upstart, the clergy the man who had disciplined them, the bishops the vicegerent, the conservatives the radical. Many had suffered in his eight years of power, and the hatred engendered rested on him; indeed, though the cruelty and vengefulness which there were must be laid at the king's door, Cromwell must bear his share of the heavy burden. A man of great mind and enormous ability, he had little gentleness and no mercy once his purpose was fixed. He was well fitted to carry out a revolution, and if—like most revolutionaries—he did not die in his bed, that is a matter neither for wonder nor for rejoicing. Nor must one's abhorrence of some of the means used blind one to the achievement. Cromwell lived in a violent age, but he used violence only when he thought it indispensable, and his habit of striking terror at the first and then easing up probably prevented the much worse bloodshed which commonly results from a procrastinating and vacillating policy in disturbed times. Unlike Henry, he preferred opponents to survive if they but ceased to trouble him; he would have liked to save More. Unlike Norfolk and Gardiner, he did not pursue personal vendettas in the guise of political campaigns. Among the men of that day he stands out not only by his ability, nor even by his undoubted ruthlessness, but by the singleminded purpose to which he put both ability and ruthlessness. In eight years he engineered one of the few successful revolutions in English history, and he achieved this without upsetting the body politic. The end does not indeed justify the means, but at least it explains and to some extent excuses it. When all is said and done, the fact remains that Cromwell's work endured and proved not only important but also beneficial. We must pity the victims, most of whom hardly knew what they were resisting; but we must also judge fairly the man who, directly or indirectly, caused their deaths. His own was to less purpose than theirs and did incalculable harm to the country and state he had served.

Chapter VII

THE TUDOR REVOLUTION: EMPIRE AND COMMONWEALTH

I. SOVEREIGNTY

THE changes described in the last chapter were so many and far-reaching that we have had no opportunity yet to investigate their real significance. They were revolutionary, if that term may be applied to any changes which profoundly affect the constitution and government of a state even when they do not involve the systematic and entire destruction of what there was before. The Tudor revolution grew from roots which can be traced well back in time, and it was peculiarly unrevolutionary in appearance because its makers insisted on the utmost show of legality and constitutional propriety. For everything they did, they claimed the authority of ancient prescription, and in everything they did they adhered to the forms of the old law. This made the revolution most conservative to look at, and out of this arose both its enduring permanency and its ready acceptance; but none of it makes it any less of a revolution. When Thomas Cromwell died, the state and kingship of England were very different from what they had been at the fall of Wolsey, the difference lying less in the real power exercised by the king—this depended largely on personality and circumstance, not on the forms of government—than in the potential power released by the establishment of national sovereignty. A revolutionary era commonly produces vast upheavals and immediate profound differences, only to see the old state of affairs creep back after a time: the faster men proceed at the start, the sooner they lose their momentum and the less securely they build. The revolution of the 1530s, on the other hand, proceeded by safe stages, never outrunning its own strength or breaking its lifeline with the past; as a result there was never anything like a successful reaction.

The essential ingredient of the Tudor revolution was the concept of national sovereignty. The philosophy underlying Cromwell's work was summarised brilliantly in his preamble to the act of appeals (1533), the operative clause of which reads as follows:

This realm of England is an Empire, and so hath been accepted in the world, governed by one Supreme Head and King having the dignity and royal estate of the imperial Crown of the same, unto whom a body politic, compact of all sorts and degrees of people divided in terms and by names of Spirituality and Temporalty, be bounden and owe to bear next to God a natural and humble obedience.

The critical term is 'empire'. Kings of England had before this claimed to be emperors—the title occurs in Anglo-Saxon times and was taken by Edward I, Richard II, and Henry V—but the meaning here is different. Those earlier 'emperors' had so called themselves because they ruled, or claimed to rule, more than one kingdom, as Edward I claimed Scotland and Henry V France.[1] In the act of appeals, on the other hand, England by herself is described as an empire, and it is clear both from the passage cited and from what follows that the word here denoted a political unit, a self-governing state free from (as they put it) 'the authority of any foreign potentates'. We call this sort of thing a sovereign national state. The introduction of the term into the controversy can be brought home to Cromwell, but it had been used in that sense before. In the fourteenth century some exponents of the Roman law concluded that any state which did not acknowledge a superior was an empire (*imperium*); Cromwell, who has been falsely accused of wishing to introduce the Roman law in England, nevertheless may possibly have encountered the notion during his travels. He seems also to have been familiar with the parallel thought, on the subject, of Marsiglio of Padua who in the same century defended the authority of the medieval empire against the papal claim to 'fullness of power' (*plenitudo potestatis*). Since England was engaged in shedding papal power, the assertions of anti-papal authority made in preceding centuries obviously came in useful. The English attack on Rome therefore rested on the ancient claim that *imperium*—lay authority—derives as much from God as does the pope's authority, elaborated into an important theory of the state by the addition of Marsiglio's and the civilians' conclusion that *imperium* exists wherever a body politic governs itself without superior on earth.

The statute thus enunciated this doctrine: England is an independent state, sovereign within its territorial limits. It is governed by a ruler who is both supreme head in matters spiritual and king in matters temporal, and who possesses by grant divine ('by the goodness and sufferance of Almighty God') 'plenary, whole, and entire power, preeminence, authority, prerogative, and

---

[1] Richard II's use of the term is markedly like the Tudor use; much that that king thought and did anticipated Tudor ideas and practices.

jurisdiction to render and yield justice' to all people and subjects resident within the realm. This ruler is one part of the empire, or—as we should say—one part of the constitution; the other is a 'body politic' or nation composed of clergy and laity, each —the act goes on to show—authorised to administer justice under the king within its own spiritual or temporal sphere, without interference from outside the realm. The special preoccupations of an act concerned with prohibiting appeals from courts within the realm to courts outside the realm naturally put the stress in the preamble on such points of jurisdiction, but behind these particulars there stands the general theory of a sovereign state composed of those who live within the realm of England and owe exclusive allegiance to the holder of its 'imperial' crown who is also supreme head of its Church. It is this supremacy in the Church which, being quite new, stands out as apparently the chief characteristic of the revolution. But this is so only because the principle of national sovereignty was established in a struggle with the ecclesiastical authority of Rome; it is at least possible to imagine a state of affairs where the temporal authority of the English crown might have had to be defended against foreign encroachment while the king's control of the Church was not questioned, and where the stress would have been on kingship rather than supreme headship. The principle, which is much more important than the particular application, is the same: absence of outside authority or, to say it again, national sovereignty.

2. CHURCH OF ENGLAND

The royal supremacy over the Church virtually replaced the pope in England by the king. Papal power had been defined as of two kinds: *potestas jurisdictionis*, or rule of the Church's temporal sphere, and *potestas ordinis*, or the spiritual functions which the pope shared with any bishop. The former was transferred entirely into the king's hands with his acquisition of the rights to administer the Church, to tax it, to appoint its dignitaries and officials, to control its laws and to supervise its courts. The second Henry VIII never claimed, for he never claimed to be a priest: he never pretended that he could say mass or ordain priests. But he claimed the highest jurisdictional authority in the Church: he controlled legislation and administration, and by virtue of his headship he could and did determine doctrine and ritual. As supreme head, Henry VIII acquired all the administrative episcopal powers of the papacy and none of the sacerdotal ones: he was as much of a bishop as a man can be who is no priest. The appointment of Cromwell as vicar-general is good proof of this episcopal character of the supremacy: the title was one bestowed on the deputies of bishops and on no one else. If it is remembered that Henry VIII's supremacy meant episcopal but not sacerdotal rights and functions, its difficulties are more easily resolved.

These rights Henry claimed to hold by ancient prescription and grant from God: kings had always held powers which the papacy had then usurped. There has been much stress on the significance of the coronation oath, the anointing at the coronation, the power to touch for the king's evil, all of which seem to show the king as a quasi-sacerdotal person, but the full meaning of the Henrician position is often missed. Those points were part of that medieval line of thought which saw in the king—*rex et sacerdos*—a ruler who, deriving his powers from God, had certain spiritual (though, despite the term *sacerdos*, no priestly) functions and faculties. Henry VIII came to fulfil the doctrine of 'True Monarchy' which ultimately went back to Constantine the Great and his position in the Church; the frequent references to that emperor in the writings of the English Reformation demonstrate how conscious the descent was. What made these assertions of kingly powers so striking was the earlier failure of the doctrine of True Monarchy before the onslaught of the papalist doctrine which had certainly triumphed in England: in the writings of the early sixteenth century there is no trace that would suggest doubts about the papal supremacy. The rights and wrongs of it may be argued for ever. Certainly, kings of England had never exercised the episcopal functions of a *rex et sacerdos*; when they had interfered in the appointments of bishops and had taxed the clergy they had done so as temporal rulers, not as being bishops themselves. The doctrine of True Monarchy was developed for the benefit of German emperors and French kings; it was a curious accident that brought about its fulfilment by a king of England. The significance of these derivations is obvious. For one thing they explain how Henry VIII could persuade himself that he had rights in spiritual matters and how he—a layman—came to be accepted so readily as holding those rights. For another, they gave the respectability of ancient arguments to the revolution, once again displaying that careful traditionalism that distinguished these upheavals. But most significant is the fact that really these theories did not matter greatly. Though king, bishops, and propagandists might fill volumes with proofs and precedents from Constantine downwards, the strength of the storm lay not in this backward-looking justification and revival of a moribund doctrine, but in the forward-looking assertion of secular sovereignty.

Attempts have been made to link the supremacy with the legislative authority of parliament; it is still usual to assert that Henry's supremacy was a parliamentary one. But this was certainly not the way that Henry VIII and Cromwell saw it. According to the official doctrine, the royal supremacy was divinely ordained: it rested on direct grant from God. By virtue of his kingship, the king was automatically also vicar of Christ on earth, as far as his territorial dominions extended. The supremacy was personal, vested in the king by no earthly authority, and exercised by him without reference to any earthly authority. The king as supreme head not only issued injunctions for the doctrine and government of the Church (as the Ten and Thirteen Articles of 1536 and 1538); he was even able, by his own unaided power, to transfer all his spiritual authority to a deputy when by commission he appointed Cromwell vicegerent in spirituals. In that capacity, Cromwell not only carried out the visitatorial powers of the supreme head, as he had done as vicar-general (acting for his bishop like any vicar-general), but exercised all the king's spiritual functions (including, for instance, the determination of dogma) by delegation. Neither parliament nor convocation played any part in these manifestations of the supremacy. The supremacy was taken from the monarchical papacy, and it remained monarchical, even despotic. In the Church, the king, as supreme head, was an absolute ruler, the more so as there existed no single assembly of the English Church. The convocations of Canterbury and York were neither in theory nor in practice a limitation on the king's spiritual headship.

That these were revolutionary changes is perfectly obvious, though from that day to this attempts have been made to prove that the post-Reformation Church was identical with the pre-Reformation Church, attempts which incidentally involve a playing down of the king's share in Church government and religious regulation that is possibly very proper for the twentieth century but highly improper for the sixteenth. This is no place to enter into that controversy, but it must be stated briefly that the Henrician Reformation and the creation of the royal supremacy turned the Church *in* England (the archiepiscopal provinces of the Universal Church lying in the realm of England) into the Church *of* England. This does not affect the issue of the apostolic succession and canonical derivation of the English episcopate, preserved when Clement VII granted Cranmer's bulls in January 1533, nor the question of the English Church's claim to be catholic, but it does assert that the Henrician Reformation amounted to a schism. The act of supremacy of 1534 begged the question with the calm assurance characteristic of Cromwell's beautifully drafted preambles when it spoke of the 'Church of England called *Anglicana Ecclesia*'; this after all, need mean no more than English Church and ought rightly to be translated (before 1533) as 'the Church in England'. The act of appeals admitted as much when it mentioned 'that part of the body politic called the Spirituality, now being usually called the English Church'; the term *Anglicana Ecclesia* meant all the clergy (or spiritualty) in England, and not—as it did after the Reformation—a separate ecclesiastical institution called the Church of England. From 1533 or 1534 such an institution may be discerned and must be admitted: in Church affairs, where it began, the revolution of the 1530s is most obvious. The establishment of the royal supremacy and the creation of the Church of England are fundamental breaks with the past, giving the English Church a new unity, a new organisation, new authorities under God, though not as yet a new doctrine. It was a jurisdictional revolution in the Church, not a religious revolution.

3. PARLIAMENT

As has been said, the establishment of national sovereignty produced a new kind of political community with new potentialities and new duties. The precise character of that sovereignty and who it was that exercised it must now engage attention, the more so as the prevailing interpretation is demonstrably wrong. It is generally said that Henry, and especially Cromwell, planned to erect a despotism in the state to match the despotism of the royal supremacy in the Church. This they did not do; indeed, basing themselves on the past, on constitutional propriety, and on the law, they could not do it. It becomes necessary to investigate the place of parliament in the royal supremacy.

That the supremacy was parliamentary, depending either for its first authority or for its exercise on parliament, has already been denied; yet all through the 1530s every important step was embodied in statutes made by king, lords, and commons—for it must be remembered that the king was and is as much a part of parliament as are the commons. The accepted interpretation of this use of statute is distinguished by a kind of enthusiastic vagueness sometimes deviating into rhapsody.[1] It argues that Henry VIII's

[1] Especially in A. F. Pollard's *Henry VIII* and *Factors in Modern History*, the standard accounts of the view here combated.

turning to parliament proved his supreme political genius; that his deliberate decision to take the nation 'into partnership' was the most momentous step in the rise of parliament; that parliament, and especially the commons, were asked to endorse matters by enactment in order to make acceptance of the changes easier and advertise the unquestioned unity of king and people. It claims both much too much and, in some respects, rather too little. This becomes clear when we ask what parliament actually did and distinguish between the preambles and the enactments of statutes. Parliament 'does' only what is set out in the enactment. The preamble may explain and justify; it may—as in the act of appeals —outline a whole political philosophy, or—as in the act of supremacy—accept as given vast novel assertions; but it can never record what parliament has done. In the political legislation of the 1530s the form is quite plain: the preamble of the statute declares as fact some aspect of the Cromwellian revolution (as that England is an empire, or that the king rightly is supreme head), while the enactment draws administrative conclusions from this fact (that therefore appeals outside the realms must be forbidden, or that therefore the king ought to have certain taxes and how they are to be collected) and appoints penalties for transgressors. The acts of this time are declaratory in that they set out in their preambles as already in existence what the government really wishes the nation to accept; their preambles are propaganda. The acts are also administrative orders, laying down procedure and practices. But above all the acts are penal: they decree punishments. Parliamentary statute cannot create the supremacy which is conceived of as derived from God, but it alone can make the supremacy enforceable at law, in the law courts. Until parliament has decreed that certain activities (such as the denial of the supremacy or the seeking out of appeals at Rome) are criminal and carry appointed penalties, there is no way in which the supremacy can be enforced on the country, especially on the laity: the king has no means of forcible and extra-legal coercion, and only statute can add felonies and treasons, involving loss of life or member, to the body of law. This disposes of the notion sometimes encountered that Henry could have established his supremacy by proclamation: had he wished to do so he would have had to give to proclamations powers they had never had.

Parliament thus legalised the Reformation, not in the vague sense of giving the consent of the realm to what was done, but in the severely practical sense of making possible the prosecution at law of those who opposed the royal policy. The place of parliament in the Tudor revolution is both less and more than has been alleged. It is less because the supremacy did not depend for its existence on parliament but on divine appointment. It is more because parliament was not an agency of government propaganda but an essential element in the establishment of the whole revolution and its protection in law. Henry and Cromwell had to employ parliament and statute if they wished to make their revolution legally enforceable; no time need be wasted on admiring their penetration in choosing parliament as a partner because in fact they never had any choice. What does deserve praise and study is the skill with which these two men employed the means to hand in their tremendous task.

But the matter goes further than that. The Reformation statutes demonstrate that the political sovereignty created in the 1530s was to be a parliamentary one. There was no thought—no possibility— of a purely royal despotism. The highest authority in the land was recognised to lie in that assembly of king, lords, and commons whose decrees (by name of statute) commanded complete and universal obedience and could deal with any matter on earth, including even spiritual concerns hitherto reserved to spiritual authority. The Tudor revolution established the supremacy and omnicompetence of statute. That statute was the highest way in which the state (the laity) could pronounce law had been acknowledged since the reign of Edward III; but that there was no sphere of life closed to it—that it could do what it wished—was demonstrated only in the 1530s when statute extended to new fields. It is likely that few so far realised all this to the full; perhaps there were only two men who genuinely grasped the import of events. Thomas Cromwell certainly knew what he was doing; his immense labours in drafting the acts of the time and his great care in parliamentary management show him well aware of the supreme importance of statute and parliament in the revolution. The other man was Thomas More who declared that he could not obey an act of parliament when it went contrary to the law of Christendom. In this More represented the conception of a universal Christian law to which man-made law must conform, as well as the persistent fears of all thoughtful men at putting absolute legislative sovereignty in the hands of any human body. But however right More may have been in abstract philosophy and as a member of a Christian community, as a subject of King Henry VIII and his laws he was utterly wrong. When Cromwell, the first statesman to understand the potentialities of statute, used it to enforce great revolutionary changes through the courts of law, he demonstrated that in law and on earth there is nothing that an act of parliament cannot do. Of course, this truth was not at once put in so clear-cut a fashion; it took centuries of talk about the law divine and the law natural, with which the law made by man was supposed to be consonant, before men would admit in all its starkness the simple theory of Thomas Cromwell. To this day one may meet with attempts to discover some sort of morally binding restraint on the powers of parliament. But in the modern state there are, in fact, no limitations on the supremacy and competence of statute: parliament may forbear doing certain things because it is too sensible or too frightened to attempt them, but there is no one who can dispute its authority.

The Tudor revolution thus not only created national sovereignty; it also acknowledged the supremacy of statute on which the modern English state rests. That means that it established the sovereignty of the king in parliament, otherwise known as constitutional or limited monarchy. Whatever may have been the case before Cromwell's work—whatever Wolsey may have stood for—there was no Tudor despotism after it. Wittingly or not—and the present writer has no doubt that it was done wittingly—Cromwell established the reformed state as a limited monarchy and not as a despotism. He gave the king great power—power over the Church, power of the purse because for a time he was wealthy—and Henry VIII was at all times a formidable ruler whom it was difficult to limit; but the polity which Cromwell wanted rested not on the supremacy of the king, but on the supremacy of the king in parliament. Of course this was not totally new; all medieval development stood behind this flowering of parliamentary monarchy. But the Reformation freed the sovereign body of England not only from the authority of foreign potentates but also from the limitations of the laws divine and natural: from now on parliaments made laws. Because men's thoughts can take generations to catch up with reality, the 'declaratory' concept of law-making—pretending a discovery rather than a creation—survived for a time; in truth, however, the Reformation had shown once and for all that parliament, the king in parliament, exercised untrammelled powers of true legislation. The essential characteristic of medieval government was that it discovered the law and then administered it, while modern government first makes and then administers laws; thus the 1530s mark quite definitely the end of the medieval constitution and the beginning of the modern.

Though the rule of Henry VIII was strong, ruthless, at times very arbitrary, it could not be despotic because it always rested on the law—the law which was made by parliament and administered by the courts. The common law of England may nearly have suffered eclipse during Wolsey's rule, but, in contrast to his predecessor, Cromwell practised a policy of deference to it. He may have learned the idea of empire from the Roman law, and he may have wished at times to use its more autocratic weapons (as Gardiner alleged he did); but if we go by what was actually done, the triumph of the common law is manifest. Indeed, it was Cromwell's administration that saved the medieval common law, as it saved the medieval parliament, and used both in the service of the modern state. The use of parliament meant enforcement through the courts of the common law to whom the statutes of the 1530s opened up a great and important new field. Cromwell himself was a common lawyer, as were his chief assistants, especially Lord Chancellor Audley. At the same time, the judges' attitude to parliament changed. It is noticeable that from the 1530s onwards they began to obey statute in a way they had never done before. In the fifteenth century they had often merely taken statute as the basis for argument: as the crown's legal advisers they had themselves often 'made' acts of parliament and felt competent to interpret them—at times almost out of existence. A more rigid adherence to the letter of the act now became apparent, leading up to the modern principle that judicial interpretation means the strict application of the act, not an arbitrary explanation roughly within its limits.

Even where means of extra-parliamentary action existed and were lawful, the prevailing deference to statute comes out. Cromwell's whole attitude was consistent: he believed in statute above all else and would proceed nowhere without its sanction. His natural reaction to any problem of government was to draft a bill; in this he was so 'modern' that only the nineteenth century fully returned to his lavish law-making. In 1535 it was desired to stop the export of coin from the realm; Cromwell at once insisted on discovering a relevant statute, though he was glad to hear from the judges that, failing a statute, the king could in such a matter proceed by proclamation. The judges were perfectly correct: a government must be able to put out orders about immediate economic needs or temporary policies without having to await the meeting of an occasional body like the sixteenth-century parliament. Yet Cromwell remained unsatisfied, and four years later he introduced an act designed to give general legal sanction to royal proclamations. The act of proclamations (1539) was once wrongly considered the height of Henry's despotism. It ordered that proclamations (of the traditional type, unable to impose the death penalty or forfeiture of goods) should be obeyed 'as though they were made by act of parliament' and appointed machinery for their enforcement. There was never any intention of replacing statute by proclamation or of legislating without the consent of parliament; no one intended to wipe out the vital differences in standing and sanctity between the two. The act was simply meant to resolve such doubts as Cromwell himself had felt about the legality of any proclamation not grounded upon statute. Its practical significance lay in the clauses for its enforcement. Almost certainly Cromwell intended originally to let the common-law courts enforce proclamations (as they enforced statutes—this may well be the meaning of the phrase quoted above); opposition in the lords forced him instead to accept a council nominated in the act which proved quite incapable of doing the work. The statute was not employed for despotic purposes and its repeal in 1547 made no difference to the legality of royal proclamations: superfluous as a basis for proclamations, it is proof of Cromwell's veneration for statutory authority and therefore for parliament, not of any attempt to do without parliament and govern by proclamation.

The supremacy of statute meant the sovereignty of the king in parliament, and this raised difficult practical problems. If laws are to be made only by the consent of three partners—king, lords and commons—then agreement between them must somehow be secured or government will become impossible. This again was scarcely a new problem, for parliamentary legislation—the thing if not the name—had existed for some two centuries; but the constitutional revolution of the 1530s—the new stress laid on sovereignty and the newly expanded use of parliament—made it both more pressing and more constant. On the whole, Henry VIII and Cromwell had comparatively little difficulty, especially since on the main issue of the Church the royal policy represented very fairly the feelings and desires of the majority of those who sat in the parliament. The lords were a 'safe' house; with their Tudor lay peers and their cowed spiritual peers, few of them felt able to offer opposition. The commons were both able and willing to oppose. No full study of the parliaments of this reign has yet been made, but we know roughly that the members of the lower house were on the whole less independent than they were to become later, though there can be no question of subservience or intimidation. Many were servants of the king, forming a kind of government party in embryo around the privy councillors who sat in the commons. Numbers of substantial gentlemen sat for boroughs, instead of the local burgesses whose duty it ostensibly was to represent their towns and who in general had less independence of mind than knights and gentlemen; but this 'invasion of the gentry'—already well under way—had not yet produced the kind of commons familiar from the reign of Elizabeth onwards in which the gentry called the tune. Moreover, in this age when the property of the Church was under attack, the gentry's interest coincided with the government's. When they felt like it, the commons of the 1530s stood up to the crown readily enough; money grants were never easily obtained, and the bill of uses, designed to protect the king's feudal rights against the very people who sat in the house, took five long years to get through. Henry VIII allowed opposition in parliament; with all his imperious arrogance, he had little of the true tyrant's temper which will not listen to objections, and his councillors as well as his commons could generally speak frankly to him even when they advised against his desires. He permitted full freedom of speech in the first two sessions of the 1529-36 parliament because he knew that he would thus obtain ammunition for his attack at Rome; he never tried to prevent members even from defending Catherine or desiring him to take her back. Only on one occasion did a member of parliament get into serious trouble in those years. This was an advanced protestant from Calais who in 1539 was sequestered by the shocked house of commons itself for putting forward his extreme views on religion. Strode's Case of 1512 had established freedom of speech in parliament as far as the complaints of private persons were concerned;[1] the wider issue of freedom from interference by the crown did not arise in this reign because Henry avoided all attacks on such liberty. Both his genuine feelings and his diplomatic skill came out in the words he addressed to parliament in 1543 when he declared his pride in the fact 'that we at no time stand so highly in our estate royal as in the time of parliament'.

He could afford these sentiments the more readily because of the natural community of interests between him and his parliaments, but also because subtler means of management existed than frontal assault. The Speaker had for long been a royal nominee, despite the appearance of a free election by the commons, and the Speakers of the reign were all crown servants, like Sir Thomas

---

[1] Richard Strode was imprisoned for proposing some bills to regulate tin-mining and interfering with the stannary courts; the commons secured his release and enacted that no member should be sued in a court of law for anything said or done in parliament.

More (1523), Sir Thomas Audley (1529-32), Sir Humphrey Wingfield (1533-6), Sir Nicholas Hare (1539-40)—all common lawyers and king's legal counsel. The Speaker's control over the business of the house made him a useful instrument of royal influence. Similar tasks were performed by privy councillors sitting in the commons; it was Cromwell who first exploited the position of a government minister in the house in the manner which was to become typical in the reign of Elizabeth. Apart from managing matters by speech and answer, Cromwell also took up aspects of government management of whose previous existence there is so little evidence that one may say he virtually initiated them. He bestowed great care on a legislative programme; dozens of draft acts with his corrections all over them and many notes among his memoranda testify to the labour involved in putting before the house a series of well-designed measures. In 1529 and 1531 parliament largely discussed bills introduced by members of the house of commons, like those acts mending abuses in the Church which heralded the whole attack; but from 1532 onwards the houses mostly debated the bills produced by the government. Such a government legislative programme was something new, for the simple reason that no one had ever dreamt of establishing a complex of fundamental changes by means of acts of parliament. The new practice, soon to become normal and revived as normal after the interruptions of the seventeenth century, put upon government a heavy task of parliamentary management. Attendance in the house, organisation of opinion there, and the preparation of measures were important aspects of the art of management which Cromwell developed and in great part almost certainly invented.

His name is linked with another side of parliamentary history that was to play a great part in the centuries of the 'unreformed' house of commons. He was the first man to pay systematic attention to the composition of the house and to attempt to influence it in favour of the government. He saw to bye-elections, made necessary by the unprecedented length of time for which the Reformation parliament sat; he used royal influence, and the influence of loyal noblemen and crown officials, to secure favourable returns at general elections; he wrote letters to local authorities moving them to elect men agreeable to the crown. It will not do to speak of packing. Elections were not then 'free' in our sense (that is, limited to a choice between the nominees of official parties), nor were they to be so until the reforms of the nineteenth century. Free elections and the secret ballot reflect accurately the social structure of a democracy, but the England of the Tudors, Stuarts, and Hanoverians was characterised by the social dominance of the gentry and nobility (under the crown), and its parliamentary system did right to reflect that very different structure. Few constituencies returned members without listening to the orders of a borough patron or deferring to the wishes of the great shire families. Cromwell merely tried to organise these isolated examples of influence by making them all serve the interests of the crown. He did not 'pack' the house with nominees but employed the local powers of dukes and earls and knights to secure the return of men he wished to see elected, a practice continued by parliamentary managers down, at least, to 1867. In one case—the Canterbury election of 1536—he ordered the city to rescind their choice and return the two men previously named by the king; nothing is known of the circumstances which provoked so peremptory an order, and in any case one must not generalise from one instance. In 1539 Cromwell mobilised all the electoral resources of the crown and secured what he himself called a tractable parliament; but he did so by the use of perfectly proper influence—his own, or the king's, or the duke of Norfolk's, and so forth—and in a manner fully approved of by his age and by succeeding centuries.[1] Now that the commons had become an indispensable partner—even if not an always existing partner—in the sovereign nation state governed by the king in parliament, it was necessary to ensure harmony in the mixed sovereign; Cromwell first employed the methods used to achieve this in the centuries of the monarchical parliamentary state which endured from the Tudor revolution to the democratic revolution of the nineteenth century.

It is obvious, therefore, that in the history of parliament, too, the 1530s are of vital significance. Its importance increased, its procedure developed, its use by the king grew into a working alliance in which the crown was at this time much the more evidently powerful partner. The structure of the institution also developed. The house of commons had been a 'house'—an organised body—since the fourteenth century; from this time it was invariably a house of parliament, and any idea that a body meeting without the commons could be called a parliament was at an end. We hear for the first time of the use of committees, that remarkable expedient which was to turn the house from an assembly of critics into an efficient instrument of government. The seven years of the Reformation parliament, followed by two more elections in three

---

[1] Nor (as has been alleged) was he trying to get a parliament in his own interest; it was of course tractable to the king.

years, provided an invaluable training in co-operation, experience, political and personal friendship, even—as Pollard has shown—in the growth of a political class based on intermarriage. The house of commons never forgot those years, or the importance of the work on which it had been engaged. In 1543 the house acted directly to secure the release of a member (George Ferrers) imprisoned at a private suit and punished the officers of the City of London for contempt; thus began the long struggle of the commons for control over their own privileges and for the powers of a court in ordering their own affairs. For the lords, too, the period was one of consolidation into modern form: from being the parliament itself (as the great council of magnates) they now quite definitely turned into one of the houses of parliament. With this went many complicated developments in the law of peerage and blue blood, and a growing definition which deprived the crown of the right to summon whom it would, making the writ a matter of hereditary right. The act of 1539, 'for the precedence of the lords in the parliament chamber', marked an important step. The great council of magnates assembling around a core of professional councillors (judges, officers of the chancery, and so on) became a body consisting only of peers of the realm; the professionals lost first their voice in the house of lords and ultimately also the right to sit there.

Thus the second notable revolution of the 1530s is the establishment of the sovereignty of the king in parliament, and the effect this had on the three partners. Parliament's growth in importance had nothing to do with its making the king supreme head, for it did no such thing; but the working out of the royal supremacy produced the supreme statute and provided parliament with a novel eminence in the state. The crown grew in real power despite the constitutional limits placed upon it. That realisation was behind Henry VIII's pride in his place in parliament. By admitting the alliance of the nation represented in parliament, the Tudors made the powers of government—the powers of the king— so much more effective that the crown itself, whether the personal crown of the Tudors or the crown in commission of our day, can do much more than even the strongest medieval kings had dreamt of. Commons and lords developed into precise institutions, part of one sovereign body. Of the two, the lords, the more important socially, also retained for the time being greater political weight. This was especially proved during the reign of Edward VI. The commons experienced a few short and rather spurious years of

primacy, at first (1529-31) because they were the natural mouth-
piece of anti-clericalism, but then simply because Cromwell sat
there. In 1536, Cromwell was made a baron just before parliament
met, with a special provision that he was to retain his place in the
lower house for the session, so that he might steer through the
measures he had prepared for it. In 1539, when he sat in the lords,
all the important bills were introduced there first, whereas in
1532-6 they had been introduced in the commons. For the history
of the English parliament, and therefore of constitutional monarchy in England, it was of great importance that Henry VIII had
an admirable political sense and knew how to work together with a
representative institution. He deserves the more credit for this
because he had not been brought up to it either by his father or by
Wolsey. But it was even more important that he chose for his
leading adviser at this time a man who had deliberately made a
career in parliament, entering it in 1529 with the express determination to rise to power through it; a man who could see the potentialities of the institution and who knew how to exploit them; a
man who realised what statute could do and how the statute-
making body could be harnessed to the needs of a constitutional
revolution. So far from attempting to build a despotism in
England, Thomas Cromwell was that country's first parliamentary
statesman.

4. CONSOLIDATION OF TERRITORY

If England was to be an empire 'governed by one Supreme Head
and King', the pope's was not the only authority that stood in the
way. The work of attacking franchises and semi-independent
rights within the borders of the realm itself, which had gone
forward since the days of Henry VII at least, was as yet unfinished.
Cromwell resumed it with vigour and—typically—with a more
systematic approach. In place of the piecemeal suppression of such
franchises as caused trouble (like the Tynedale liberties abolished
by Parliament in 1504), he wished to put forward a general statement of policy. This he achieved in the act of 1536, entitled 'for
recontinuing certain liberties and franchises heretofore taken from
the crown'. Despite this title the act was really meant to do away
with all those franchises that prevented an effective dissemination
of royal authority. The preamble, in Cromwell's usual style, stated
a grievance in succinct and, for once, historically accurate terms:

Where divers of the most ancient prerogatives and authorities of justice appertaining to the imperial crown of this realm have been severed and taken away from the same by sundry gifts of the king's most noble progenitors . . . to the great diminution and detriment of the royal estate of the same and to the hinderance and great delay of justice . . .

The act reserved all pardons for treasons and felonies to the crown, laid down that judges and justices of all kinds anywhere in the realm (including counties palatine, Wales, and the marches thereof) could be appointed only by the king, provided that writs in counties palatine were to run in the king's name, and in general extended the operation of the royal justice and shire administration to all England. Though a few minor exceptions were made, in effect all franchisal rights of any consequence were destroyed: for the first time, the whole realm, without qualification, became subject to government from Westminster. In particular this ended the independence of the county of Durham which alone of all the great palatinates had escaped absorption into the Tudor crown lands.

The act played a part in the unrest which led to the pilgrimage of grace; in turn, the collapse of the rising gave the government a chance of effectively suppressing the liberties of the northern counties. The death of the earl of Northumberland put all his lands into the king's hand to whom they were mortgaged; Norfolk's executions broke the spirit of resistance; finally, in the summer of 1537, Cromwell devised a new council of the north, a permanent body dominated by royal officials and controlled from the centre which was to govern the five northern counties, suppress independence, and bring the north into line with the more advanced south. This permanent bureaucratic council, replacing the temporary and personal councils which had fitfully governed the north since Edward IV's day, achieved its aim; despite the rising of 1569, it may be said that the medieval history of the north came to an end in 1537 when its separatism fell before the centralisation of the modern state imposed by Henry VIII and Cromwell.

In Wales, too, Cromwell's policy of consolidation was thoroughly successful. He began in 1534 by securing the appointment of his friend Rowland Lee, bishop of Coventry and Lichfield, as president of the council in the marches; for the next six years, Lee concentrated all his notable energies on the task of reducing both the marches and Wales itself to order. Statutes were passed to equip him with better weapons. An act of 1534 transferred the trial of

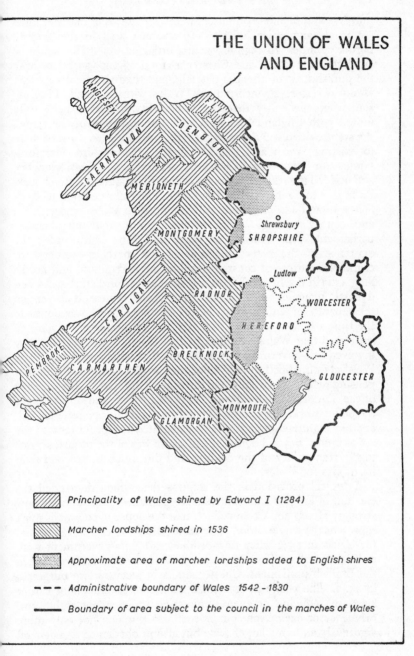

THE UNION OF WALES AND ENGLAND

ANGLESEY

CAERNARVON

DENBIGH

FLINT

MERIONETH

MONTGOMERY

Shrewsbury

SHROPSHIRE

Ludlow

CARDIGAN

RADNOR

WORCESTER

HEREFORD

PEMBROKE

CARMARTHEN

BRECKNOCK

GLOUCESTER

MONMOUTH

GLAMORGAN

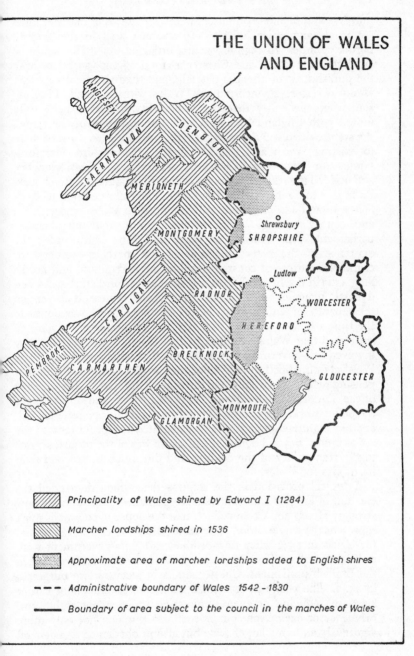 Principality of Wales shired by Edward I (1284)

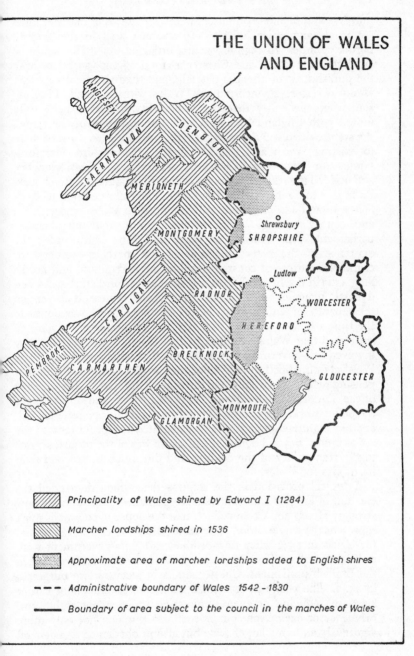 Marcher lordships shired in 1536

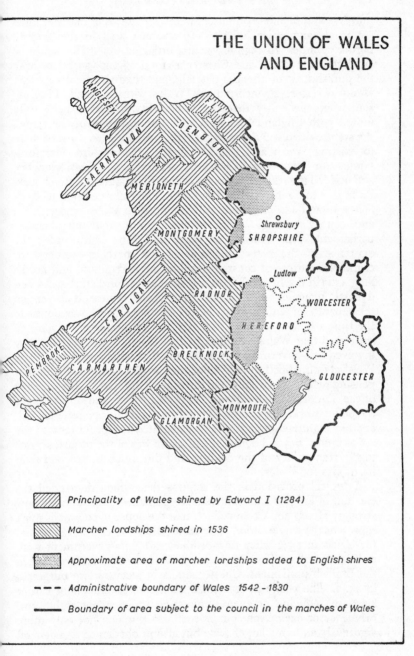 Approximate area of marcher lordships added to English shires

– – – Administrative boundary of Wales 1542 - 1830

——— Boundary of area subject to the council in the marches of Wales

murders and felonies committed in the territories of marcher lords
—virtual sanctuaries hitherto—to sessions held in the English
border counties. In 1536 it was first ordained that J.Ps. should be
appointed for Wales and Chester as for England, so as to make
the punishment of offences possible, and then the great act of 27
Henry VIII, c. 26 incorporated Wales with England. Pleading
somewhat speciously that the principality had ever been fully
united with England 'as a very member and joint of the same',
the statute dissolved the marcher lordships, annexed some of them
to existing Welsh and English counties (Shropshire, Hereford,
Gloucester, Glamorgan, Carmarthen, Pembroke, and Merioneth),
and divided the rest into five new counties (Monmouth, Brecknock,
Radnor, Montgomery, and Denbigh). The full operation of English laws and administration was extended to Wales whose shires
and county boroughs were to send twenty-four members to
parliament. This 'shiring' of Wales and Monmouth ended the
existence of the petty kingdoms of the marches—refuges for
criminals, sources of constant trouble and corruption, and not so
long ago (in the fifteenth century) the centres of disturbances and
dynastic struggles which engulfed the whole country. It also ended
the separate organisation of the principality. There was doubt at
the time whether Cromwell's policy was not premature; even Lee
suggested that Wales was not ripe for these changes because they
involved self-government by J.Ps., an office which he thought few
Welshmen qualified to hold since they would be incapable of dis-
pensing justice impartially. On the other hand, the Welsh ancestry
of the Tudors provided Henry VIII with enough loyalty to make
the policy workable; Cromwell persisted, and in 1543, after his fall,
another statute summarised and elaborated the provisions of the
act of union. Beyond doubt, the measure was of the utmost service
to the tranquillity of the country and did much more good than
harm also for Wales.

A typical provision in the act was that which demanded the
election of knights and burgesses for parliament; it indicates how
strongly Henry and Cromwell felt that the house of commons must
represent the whole nation. The same policy was therefore adopted
for Calais in 1536 when new ordinances for its government were
ratified by statute; from 1536 to 1558 two burgesses sat for Calais in
the English parliament. Chester similarly received two burgesses
in 1543. The whole policy rested on the achievements of earlier
kings in reducing or even suppressing independent rights and
privileges of exemption, but now it was pursued not only more
vigorously and on a larger scale but also in obedience to a general

principle. Cromwell (or Henry—but Henry had not stirred until Cromwell was his chief minister) wished to turn the empire of England into a properly consolidated state, governed throughout by the king in council and subject to the legislative sovereignty of the king in parliament. This ended the kingdoms within the kingdom typical of the middle ages and made possible full national government. It is no denigration of the achievement of Henry VIII and Cromwell to recall that they started with the advantage of an unusually centralised medieval state where the king already held more real power than anywhere else in Western Europe.

In the history of Tudor relations with Scotland and Ireland the 1530s marked an interlude of comparative success. Scotland offered few problems at this time. It had to be kept quiet so as not to interfere with the delicate progress of the English Reformation. This was achieved easily enough as long as England remained on good terms with France, and when the French friendship wore very thin Henry kept his nephew James V at peace by refusing to take notice of such provocations as James's successive marriages to two French princesses, despite his uncle's preference for others. Cromwell had recommended peace with Scotland as long ago as 1523, and he practised it successfully in a period when no troubles arose to jeopardise it. Ireland, on the other hand, demanded attention. Since the departure thence in 1521 of the earl of Surrey, it had again reverted to the rule of local lords—Butlers at first and later Geraldines—with but the slenderest link of allegiance to England. Wolsey had neither time nor money to spare for Ireland; he attempted to control it by putting the Geraldine earl of Kildare in the Tower as a surety for the good behaviour of lesser Geraldines whom he appointed vice-deputies. Disorders continuing, Kildare was released in 1529, but the duke of Richmond became nominal lord lieutenant and the actual ruler of the country was the deputy, Sir William Skeffyngton, master of the ordnance and therefore nicknamed the gunner. Skeffyngton, an able soldier and conscientious official, was starved of the means to persuade the Geraldines and Butlers to peace, and in 1532 Kildare recovered the office of deputy. He used it in the accustomed fashion to pursue his feud with the Butlers and add to the disorders of the wild and unhappy country.

The beginning of the break with Rome made the question urgent; England could not afford a hostile Ireland where a papal counterattack might find a ready foothold. In 1533, complaints from Ireland led to Kildare's fall; he returned to the Tower where he died of natural causes in 1534. Even before this his son Thomas Fitzgerald, deceived by a rumour that his father had been executed, renounced his allegiance and called upon the pope and Charles V to assist him. But only the Geraldine faction rose, the towns held out, no help came from abroad, and the revolt collapsed before Skeffyngton's forces when 'the gunner' returned to Ireland in 1535. The final defeat was accomplished by Lord Leonard Grey who in January 1536 succeeded as deputy on Skeffyngton's death. Thomas Fitzgerald was promised his life on surrender, but five of his uncles were later arrested by treachery, and all six were ultimately executed in 1537. Therewith the Geraldine faction was destroyed, and Grey proceeded to enforce Cromwell's anti-papal policy on Ireland. How far Ireland remained attached to Rome simply because the break with Rome came from England will always remain in dispute. Grey was superficially successful, though his methods involved him in a quarrel with the Butlers ending in 1541 in his own execution—ostensibly for treason but really for failure. Before this, in December 1540, Henry adopted the title of king of Ireland. However, Ireland was far from pacified or reconciled, and the progress of the religious Reformation was to render futile all hopes of a genuine settlement.

5. ADMINISTRATIVE REFORMS

Cromwell was an administrator of genius. He could work harder at more details than seems quite believable; even in a century that boasted of Wolsey and Burghley, his ability and many-sidedness stand out. But it is more important still that he was also a natural reformer of administration. His temper was bureaucratic: he liked to organise and loved to record. Of this his devotion to statute is striking proof. It was well that he should do these things by preference, for the new state he was building demanded reform of precisely this kind. Cromwell took over a government dominated by that revival of household methods which had been Henry VII's great achievement. But the polity which Cromwell envisaged and largely achieved needed national government. Both household and national governments were of course the king's governments. But household methods meant that the king stood actively at the centre of things; they demanded a great deal of personal effort from the holder of the crown and relied on his immediate entourage for the driving power behind the machinery. National bureaucratic methods, on the other hand, while they still depended—in that age of monarchy—on the existence and power of the king, were freed from the personal activity of either king or entourage. The older system always broke down when there was no active or powerful king, or at least some deputy like Wolsey to play the king's part. Thus government collapsed in the fifteenth century, and it also declined very markedly after Henry VII's death. Such institutions as the council in star chamber or the general surveyors of crown lands appear to have been almost dormant for two or three years until stimulated into new life by Wolsey. The extrusion of the household from national affairs and its replacement by a series of bureaucratically organised institutions largely removed that danger and gave to modern government an air of permanency and independence from the accidents of politics. Cromwell was quite capable of copying Wolsey and governing in a highly personal fashion. Thus he himself acted as an informal treasurer for public money from 1532 to 1536 simply because he wished to have ready access to cash in the affairs of government. There are other examples of high-handed and irregular action, explicable only as manifestations of his commanding personal position. But in addition he spent much time and thought on reorganising the machinery of administration.

The financial system which Cromwell took over centred upon the general surveyors of crown lands and the treasurer of the chamber. Since he could not make sufficient use of an organisation so directly dependent on the crown, he tried to reduce the importance of the chamber and turn the general surveyors into a proper, but restricted, department of state. He began to deprive the chamber of revenue, much to the sorrow of its treasurer, Sir Brian Tuke, who was himself a civil servant of ability and responsible for much of the increasing bureaucratic organisation of his department. Soon Cromwell had to set up new agencies of finance as the additions he made to the revenue came to complicate the problem. The acquisition of the clerical first fruits and tenths in 1534 could have been handled by the chamber, as was originally intended, but Cromwell instead appointed a personal servant of his own, John Gostwick, as treasurer for this money, using him very much as his personal paymaster in affairs of state. The monastic lands raised much greater administrative difficulties which were solved by the erection of a separate and self-contained institution capable of acting both as a court (since litigation over the lands was bound to arise) and as a revenue department. It was modelled on the duchy of Lancaster whose simple accounting methods it copied. It seems that in about 1535 Cromwell decided on this policy of revenue courts, planning to allot the royal income properly to various departments whose reserves would be drawn upon indiscriminately by the government (himself) as need arose.[1] In 1535, an act of parliament made the general surveyors permanent —they had hitherto existed from one parliament to the next only— and deprived them of all chance of new revenues. Though it was not until 1542, after Cromwell's fall, that they were incorporated in a fully organised court, it is certain that Cromwell had meant them to develop in that way. In 1540 an act drafted by Cromwell but not passed until after his fall added the court of wards;[2] and a few weeks later the treasurer of first fruits also became treasurer of a proper court, a step which Cromwell had been reluctant to take because of the needs of his personal government.

The financial administration as reformed by Cromwell or under his immediate influence therefore consisted of six courts or departments of state, each fully organised with its own specialised officials, equipped with seals and habitat, and responsible for a particular kind of revenue. The exchequer administered the ancient revenues and especially the customs and parliamentary taxation; the duchy of Lancaster the body of lands belonging to it; the court of general surveyors the crown lands collected by Henry VII and Wolsey; the court of augmentations the monastic lands; the court of first fruits and tenths the revenue contributed by the Church; and the court of wards and liveries the feudal income of the crown. The system did not work with the admirable precision which this description suggests: nothing in the sixteenth century did. But such an organisation was the ideal aimed at, and it gave to the finances a management which did not involve either the excessive formality of the old exchequer or the excessive informality of the chamber system. Its drawback was the multiplication of departments whose sole unifying agent was Cromwell himself; his fall raised difficulties necessitating further reforms which, however, followed his principle of relying on bureaucratic institutions.

In the secretarial departments, too, Cromwell broke with tradition by relegating the royal seals to a secondary place and elevating the king's principal secretary to the position of chief executive and co-ordinating minister. Cromwell acquired the office in April 1534 and used it to make himself the master of the administrative machine. He set the example which the great Elizabethan secretaries were to follow. Wolsey was the last man who headed the

[1] These courts were statutory, since they were set up by acts of parliament, and not prerogative, as they are always being called.

[2] Turned into the court of wards and liveries in 1542 by the addition of the surveyor of liveries.

administration as chancellor; Cromwell's choice of the secretaryship foreshadowed the future. In his hands the office acquired
control over everything: revenue and finance, home and foreign
affairs, defence and religion—a hundred different tasks. He
virtually took the secretary out of the household and made him
an officer of state capable of standing side by side with the earlier
executive ministers, such as the treasurer and controller of the
household.[1] The change was described in an act of 1539 which
included the secretary among the great officers of the realm. In
April 1540 Cromwell surrendered the office for reasons both
administrative and political; he was succeeded by two of his staff,
Thomas Wriothesley and Ralph Sadler, who divided it between
them. This division, designed to enable both Henry and Cromwell
to dispose of the constant services of a secretary, was to endure,
though for a time one secretaryship might occasionally be left
vacant. In some ways, Cromwell's exploitation of the secretaryship
was his chief contribution to English administration; the secretary
of state has always been the executive mainstay of modern government. At the same time, Cromwell deliberately assisted the for-
malisation of all three royal seals. The privy seal lost its old place
as the administrative centre and clearing-house of government
orders; its functions were taken over by Cromwell himself as
secretary and lord privy seal, acting through his own signed letters
rather than by instruments under any seal. Both privy seal and
signet were reduced to mainly formal functions which made their
survival for another 300 years something of a triumph for official
conservatism.

Lastly Cromwell saw to the organisation of the central government itself when, round about 1534-6, he transformed the inner
ring of the king's council into a proper institution known as the
privy council. The inner ring of important councillors, virtually
dissolved while Wolsey ruled, came to the fore again after Wolsey's
fall. So far from attempting to suppress it as his predecessor had
done, Cromwell applied his usual bureaucratic methods to it.
Building on the plans outlined in the 1526 Eltham Ordinance, he
drew together the king's nineteen leading councillors as a separate
board, provided them with a clerk, and continued to use them in
the business of government. Admittedly, he also kept them firmly
under his thumb, preparing their agenda and directing their
deliberations: in this he instituted the normal relations between

[1] These were really already nominal titles; their holders exercised few
functions in the household but acted as ministers without portfolio in
council and government.

Tudor privy councils and Tudor principal secretaries. Admittedly, too, his personal standing prevented the complete emergence of the privy council which only in August 1540, soon after Cromwell's death, met to appoint an active clerk and inaugurate its register. But it was Cromwell who created the typical governing board of Tudor and early Stuart times, which in turn was to produce the modern cabinet. This reform resulted in the first institutional split in the king's council, so that for a few years we hear of 'ordinary' councillors—councillors who are not members of the privy council. By the reign of Elizabeth, however, the privy council was the sole survivor of the old council, except for the court of star chamber (itself largely composed of privy councillors) which achieved institutional separation as a result of the setting up of this small, tightly organised, and efficient conciliar board.

This brief summary of a very difficult and complicated subject should have proved the assertion that Thomas Cromwell reformed administration by replacing medieval household methods by modern national and bureaucratic methods. Of course, he did not create from nothing, but though he invariably and necessarily built up on what there was before him, he altered the very concepts and basic nature of things. His administrative reforms—many and enduring as they were—provided the machinery for governing the new state he had started to construct. In this as in everything he proved himself capable both of long views and of the detailed application: here too he displayed to the full a constructive statesmanship the like of which is seldom found.

6. PATERNALISM

So far we have considered the 'imperial crown' of England and what happened when Cromwell persuaded Henry to establish national and parliamentary sovereignty. But there were two sides to the constitution. The act of appeals spoke of the king and the body politic owing him obedience; more clearly, Henry himself defined the notion in 1543 when he spoke of the parliament 'wherein we as head and you as members are conjoined and knit together into one body politic'. The reformed polity rested on an organic view of the state. That is to say, it conceived of crown and subjects as living in natural harmony and mutual dependence. This indeed was good traditional doctrine, theorised about only a few years earlier by Edmund Dudley in his *Tree of Commonwealth* (1509) and practised, for instance, by Henry VII; however, Cromwell's administration both witnessed a renewed vigour in the practice and a closer definition in the theory because the Tudor revolution naturally raised all sorts of problems. The doctrine of the body politic knit together demanded obedience and assistance from the governed and put upon the government the duty of looking after the welfare of its subjects. It was once thought that this represented typically medieval doctrine with which the *laissez faire* principles that dominated the state from 1660 to 1906 could be usefully contrasted; more recent development has shown that attitudes to the state which regard it either as a natural protector or an unholy but necessary evil may alternate without regard to the categories of historical development. In fact, the Tudor revolution produced a much more effective example of the paternal state than anything the middle ages knew—something so effective that only the twentieth century has come to eclipse it. The sixteenth century called this sort of thing 'commonwealth' or 'common weal'. The term is almost as frequent in statements emanating from Cromwell's circle as is the word empire itself, and together these two—national sovereignty and paternalism—make up Cromwell's philosophy of the state which matters so much because he actually impressed it upon the realm and government of England. Commonwealth was to become the watchword of a group of social reformers in the 1540s; these 'commonwealth-men' had their predecessors in the 1530s among men working and thinking about the welfare of the community and putting their trust in Thomas Cromwell. The whole important subject has been little studied so far, and all one can do is to suggest a few points and stress the more obvious aspects of Cromwell's social policy.[1]

The group of commonwealth enthusiasts contained men well known as well as obscure, both men connected with the government and private individuals. Many of them were printers, a trade much given to pamphleteering in a century when the best way to get published was to own your own press and the best way to supply your press was to write your own material. Thus John Rastell, at first connected with the circle of Sir Thomas More but later with that of Cromwell, or William Marshall and Thomas Gibson, employed by Cromwell, were all printers who wrote on social and political questions. Others stuck to pamphleteering and took service under Cromwell, the great patron of political theorists; in this circle of men employed as propagandists and also sometimes

[1] The only relevant study is W. G. Zeeveld, *Foundations of Tudor Policy* (Harvard 1948) which discusses the political thought of some lesser writers. There is nothing on the social and economic investigations of the group.

as planning staff the names Thomas Starkey, Richard Morison, and Richard Taverner are the best known. The first two had been with Reginald Pole at Padua, which shows how closely progressive thought on the Romanist side was allied to its counterpart across the schism. Starkey was probably the abler theorist but Morison the more fertile pamphleteer; neither of them was an original thinker of note, though both could put into words the ideas of their patron and serve the ends of propaganda. They put forward interesting theories on the supremacy, on the state, and on social equality which indicate what Cromwell had in mind. They are more obscure but probably much more significant than the conservative defenders of the supremacy, such as Bishop Gardiner (*De Vera Obedientia*, 1535) or Bishop Edward Foxe (*De Vera Differentia Regiae Potestatis et Ecclesiae*, 1534). Gardiner and Foxe wrote to a brief they but partially subscribed to; they wrote in Latin; and they wrote scholastic and theological argument. The radicals, on the other hand, ordinarily wrote in English, discussed burning questions of the hour with a specific purpose (for which reason there is no point in quoting titles of their works),[1] and employed practical arguments. They were political and social reformers concerned with realities. When the whole question comes to be properly studied, it will at last be seen how the second generation of humanists supplied writers and propagandists for a theory of the state first developed and applied by the exceedingly practical Cromwell.

Of a different significance are the critics, men less closely tied up with the government and commonly more interested in economic and social problems than political. Here the outstanding name is Clement Armstrong, a London merchant (like so many of the active minds of the age) who wrote a number of treatises on questions of trade. (The identification of the authors of these commonly anonymous manuscript tracts presents often insuperable difficulties). More than anyone else, he anticipated the specific preoccupations of the later commonwealth-men. Hugh Latimer, bishop of Worcester and a violent (and unreliable) critic of religious and social complaisance, was also already active; he was to be the nominal leader of the movement in the 1540s. Gibson, already mentioned, may have been the man who produced a scheme for

---

[1] An exception should perhaps be made for Starkey's *Dialogue between Pole and Lupset* which has been much praised for its ideas on state and society; but Starkey never published the work which was first printed in 1871, and his contemporary importance really rested on the occasional pieces analysed by Mr Zeeveld.

erecting a standing army in which are included some criticisms of the dissolution of the monasteries—lack of alms and hospitality— which strongly remind one of Latimer's views in the next decade. There were critics among the lawyers, too, like the over-publicised Christopher St German who wrote some interesting treatises in which he investigated the royal supremacy from the point of view of the common lawyer and found it good, or the anonymous author of a draft act of parliament designed to establish an efficient police force in England under a committee known as 'Conservators of the Common Weal'. As the Henrician Reformation released a spate of theological speculation, so the concomitant revolution in the state produced an outburst of writings on political, social, and economic problems which was to swell from that day into an immense flood of printed stuff, most of it worthless and unread- able, which reached its height in the civil commotions of the seventeenth century. Men's minds were stirred up, and the printing press—so recently invented—stood ready to serve them. At the head of this stream we must put not a work like More's *Utopia* (1517), which is on its own both in literary merit and in irrelevance, but the propaganda put out to explain and justify Cromwell's revolution—the national constitutional monarchy and its duty to its subjects.

There was indeed much for pamphleteers and critics to write about, and the interesting thing is that most of the problems were economic. It is usual to call the age materialist, and certainly it displayed a quite modern preoccupation with the questions involved in getting a living. But very largely this was so because no thoughtful man could doubt that there was something seriously wrong with the daily life of the nation. Poverty seemed on the increase, trade was in difficulties, the sheep—it was thought— were driving the men from the land. As has already been pointed out, the early Tudors faced a problem arising out of increases in population and the amount of money circulating—a problem of unemployment and inflation. In the 1530s there was the additional difficulty that political factors made it impossible to satisfy the common people's desire for an end to enclosing without anta- gonising the gentry whose support in parliament was indispen- sable. Cromwell took a few steps against enclosures: an act of 1539 made possible a more effective prosecution of those who enriched themselves from depopulations, while other legislation attempted to prevent the commercial exploitation of land. The dissolution of the monasteries actually had little effect on rural life: enclosing and rack-renting, the two chief grievances, were not practised only by men who bought monastic estates. Nor did it make much difference to the already swollen ranks of the vagrant poor, though it rendered agrarian society unusually fluid through the sales and re-sales of land which did not really cease until about 1660.[1] Yet since it was thought that the dissolution had altered or even created the problem, and since people's views influence their actions, the resentment built up led to the pilgrimage of grace, and this in turn preserved even among adherents of the Reformation like Latimer a false picture of the causes of distress and of the excellence of monastic estate-management.

The outstanding social problem of the day was that of the poor, and during Cromwell's ministry an important step was taken towards its solution. The poor law of 1536 represents the one positive achievement of the commonwealth movement in the 1530s. In Tudor England, unemployment took the form of vagrancy. Those who could not find work at home took to the roads, at first no doubt because they hoped to be luckier elsewhere, but some of them soon because they began to prefer vagabondage and begging. The country was full—or comparatively full—of men, women, and children, moving from place to place, maintaining themselves by begging and living on charity, often organised into bands which were capable of terrorising isolated farmsteads or small villages. Many of them, especially those that drifted to London, were professional criminals. It is only necessary to recall the nursery rhyme which tells of the beggars coming to town to understand the light in which contemporaries were compelled to see the problem. The core of the begging bands were no doubt honest husbandmen fallen on bad days, but they were joined by many rogues, like the rufflers or swaggering vagabonds, often discharged soldiers from wars abroad or armed retainers whom royal policy had thrown out of work. There were, in fact, two kinds of poor—those capable of work but either unable or unwilling to find it (sturdy beggars), and those too old or sick to work (the impotent poor). It took the government quite some time to grasp this essential difference; the first reaction—as against the unfortunate gipsies then beginning a career of misery in England—was to hate and to punish and to wipe out by force. Whipping and branding seemed the only answer in an age which regarded suffering with indifference and idleness among the lower orders as wicked. How many such poor and vagrants there were it is quite impossible to say. The 'hundreds of thousands' sometimes so

[1] Monastic, episcopal, noble, and crown lands all came up for sale in stages, producing a fluid land market for some 120 years.

rashly alleged are certainly nonsense; we are dealing with a total
population of less than three millions. If there were 20-30,000
workless the problem was quite big enough.[1]

Solutions and remedies were tried as early as the reign of
Richard II, but all the acts down to 1531 did little except provide
punishment for vagrants and order them to return to their homes,
there to support themselves by begging. Charity remained private,
and therefore insufficient. The act of 1531 for the first time made a
clearer distinction between those able to work and those unable; it
ordered the former to be whipped and the latter to beg under
licences. The justices of the peace were coming to be used
as the general executive agents of local administration; the
poor act of 1501 had specifically saddled them with the punishment of beggars, and in 1531 they were given charge of
the impotent poor permitted to beg. But the statute made no provision for the work which the sturdy beggars were to do, and the
system of licences was excessively clumsy and impossible to control. Moreover, the spread of reformed ideas with their contemptuous attitude to good works was making respectable the general
turning away from charity; it came to be held that all begging was
bad and should be prevented. Of necessity, therefore, the state had
to accept the responsibility for the failures and victims of society,
and the admission and elaboration of this important principle mark
the development of the effective poor law from 1536 to the great
Elizabethan codifications in 1597 and 1601. In the autumn of 1535
Cromwell commissioned one of his assistants (probably William
Marshall) to draft a poor law. Marshall produced a magnificently
comprehensive scheme which displayed a real knowledge of the
varied causes of pauperism and introduced three principles on
which the poor law rested until its revision by the Utilitarians in
1834: work must be found for the unemployed that are able to
labour, begging is wrong and the helpless must be a charge on the
community, the unit responsible shall be the parish supervised by
the justices of the peace. Marshall planned rather too well. He
provided a general scheme of public works to absorb the unemployed, and a hierarchy of officials both local and national to
administer both this and local relief. In the year designed for the
dissolution of the monasteries, the government could not face
such a task, and Cromwell contented himself instead with an
enfeebled version of part of Marshall's draft. But though the

[1] It was incidentally a problem common to all Western Europe in the
sixteenth century, not—as one might think from some statements—
confined to a specifically brutal, capitalist, and anti-monastic England.

scheme of labour and even the parish overseers were dropped—so that little remained except some assertions of principle and policy —the act of 1536 still embodied the essential ideas on which the later poor law was to rest. Especially it still made the parish responsible for collecting alms, employing the fit, and relieving the needy. It was the real, though so far ineffective, beginning of that main achievement of Tudor paternalism, the Elizabethan poor law, and it arose out of the ideas of men who served Thomas Cromwell.

Cromwell himself was more interested and successful in the active encouragement of English trade. Himself once a trader with interests in the chief centre of English exports—Antwerp—and closely connected with the Merchants Adventurers of London, the great trading company which controlled the cloth export from London to Antwerp on which England's commercial prosperity largely depended, he was both inclined and qualified to do his best for trade. In this respect he initiated little that was new, but picked up the threads from Henry VII who had helped trade by commercial treaties, by encouraging alien merchants in order to increase the volume of trade, and by navigation acts designed to protect English shipping. Wolsey, on the other hand, showed himself both ignorant and careless of the intricacies of English commercial relations. The war of 1528 was rendered silly by the need to maintain friendly relations with the Netherlands while trying to fight their ruler, the emperor Charles V; even so, Wolsey bequeathed a legacy of bad blood. The danger grew more serious in the years 1529-32 when the emperor's desire to humble Henry VIII and the Brabanters' ambition to alter the reasonable terms of the existing treaties in their own favour co-operated in a general attack on England's monopoly of the cloth supply. The negotiations were protracted by the Netherlanders' chicanery, and not until Cromwell took over the direction of affairs in 1533 was the assault beaten off. Thereafter the trade continued in a flourishing condition despite the hostility between emperor and king; it cannot be doubted that Cromwell's often expressed preference for a Spanish alliance and an end to dallyings with France derived from his care for the English export trade.

It appears, however, that he had much more far-reaching plans, designed to enable England to exploit fully her favourable position as the chief supplier of unfinished cloth. Why should Antwerp be the centre of a trade which depended much more on English sellers than on Flemish buyers? The events of 1528-33 had shown how dangerous the English dependence on a foreign mart could be, and the years 1538-9, once more threatening attacks from abroad, drove the point home. There were thus good negative as well as positive reasons for attracting trade from Antwerp to London: England would profit from becoming the centre instead of the periphery of the whole trade, foreign merchants would be encouraged to resort to her in greater numbers, and at the same time the trade could be freed from the political pressure which was always to be feared while English merchants depended on a staple in Antwerp. These ends Cromwell hoped to gain by two measures. In 1539, a proclamation reduced the customs paid by merchants strangers to those payable by English merchants; in 1540, a great navigation act—amounting to a general code for English shipping and the sea-borne trade—confined the privileges of the proclamation to foreign merchants exporting English cloth in English ships. The effects were instantaneous. Foreigners flocked to England, the cloth export by merchants strangers rose at once without affecting the volume exported by Englishmen, and the navy and merchant marine derived all the benefits which a monopoly of the carrying trade could bestow. The effectiveness of Cromwell's policy is best illustrated by the violent reaction it provoked in the Netherlands where protests soon developed into an energetic attempt to get these measures rescinded. Cromwell's fall removed the one man of sufficient skill to carry through the attack on the Antwerp staple, and after two years of inept negotiations Henry VIII had to admit defeat—the first defeat in trade matters which an English government had suffered since 1485. It is an adequate comment on the abilities of Henry VIII when left to himself.

In one respect Cromwell's commercial policy was open to question. It concentrated on the interests of the Merchants Adventurers of London and thus encouraged their growing monopoly; Cromwell did nothing to arrest the decline of the once flourishing trades with Italy and Spain which had been mostly in the hands of the south-coast ports, especially Southampton. It was in the 1530s that the direct trade with Venice nearly ceased with the ending of the annual fleets which had been wont to sail up the Channel, and that the break with Rome terminated the prosperity of English merchants settled in Spain. The future seemed to lie with the Antwerp trade—easier, cheaper, safer, and larger than any other possible export trade—and here the Merchants Adventurers held a monopoly because the age believed in organising commerce in companies, and because these companies demanded a monopoly if they were to take all the risks. We shall have more to say about trading companies; here we may note that the events of the 1530s greatly assisted the development by which English trade put nearly all its eggs into the Antwerp basket. The obvious dangers of such a policy were shown up later when the Antwerp trade collapsed, but Cromwell at any rate had intended to prevent such troubles by transferring the mart and staple for cloth to London. That would have made the English cloth trade quite safe, secure in its hold over supply and selling at home to all comers; it was, once again, unfortunate that Cromwell's fall led to an abandonment of Cromwell's plans.

Chapter VIII

THE CRISIS OF THE TUDORS, 1540-58

I. THE LAST YEARS OF HENRY VIII

THOMAS CROMWELL'S fall marked something of a period in Tudor history. By depriving himself of his outstanding servant, Henry VIII destroyed the efficiency and the purpose of his government. For eighteen years—first under an ailing old man, then under a child, and finally under a woman—Tudor rule was tested to the utmost. That it survived at all was a tribute to the work of Henry VII, to the depth of king-worship and obedience to established authority which Henry VIII's terrifying personality had riveted upon an England anxious to avoid disorder, and also to the administrative reforms of Thomas Cromwell which up to a point made continued government possible even when the crown failed to play its part. But while Tudor rule survived, to be resuscitated by Elizabeth and her more than competent ministers, it underwent such vicissitudes in those years —was so rarely animated by a steady or intelligent purpose—that the total achievement would fill barely a page. The years served a purpose: passions played themselves out in the clashing of extremes which, having had their turn, retained the less strength to trouble the government of Elizabeth; but such an argument savours of the ancient heresy that all things work to the best of all possible ends and that success crowns the work. It also under-estimates the degree to which the free play of passions, mostly religious, under Edward VI and Mary encouraged the growth of divisions which beset England in the second half of the century. It is impossible to say what would have happened but for the relaxation of good government between 1540 and 1558. The keynote of those eighteen years of somewhat purposeless turmoil is found in the development of the doctrinal changes which Henry VIII's constitutional revolution had set in motion despite his will. It is a story of the conflict of two extremes in religion alternately getting the upper hand, with a complicating admixture of inter-national troubles and diversified by a gigantic economic crisis. This last deserves, and shall have, a chapter to itself.

Of all Henry VIII's follies none cost his country dearer than his illusion that he was an old and experienced king who knew his business and needed no one to do it for him. Cromwell had no successor, partly no doubt because the privy council after 1540 contained no one of his stamp or Wolsey's, but partly because the king thought a successor unnecessary. The council was from the first divided into two parties. The orthodox or conservative section naturally held the ascendancy immediately after Cromwell's fall. Its leaders were Thomas Howard, duke of Norfolk, a second-rate man skilled only in surviving adversity, and Stephen Gardiner, bishop of Winchester, a political ecclesiastic of great ability who was throughout handicapped by being a churchman and by an arrogance, masquerading as the patriotic Englishman's plain speech, which caused mistrust. Nevertheless, with Henry married to Norfolk's niece Katharine Howard (August 1540) and Cromwell dead, this party could feel secure. The radicals included on their right wing—the extremists, quite out of favour, did not count at this time—the archbishop, Thomas Cranmer, and Edward Seymour, earl of Hertford, whose influence owed much to the fact that he was the uncle of Henry's sole legitimate heir. Cranmer's hold on the king's friendship seems never to have weakened; it is either sign or cause of the curious fact that in his last years, and after the triumph in 1539-40 of religious conservatism, Henry moved away from the orthodoxy of his life's devotion to occupy a kind of middle position not dissimilar to that advocated by Cromwell in the 1530s.

The catholic success of 1540 was not complete. In August Henry signalled his neutrality between the parties by burning three reformers as heretics and executing three conservatives as papalist traitors, all on the same day. Cromwell was gone, but none of his side followed him to the scaffold; and Cranmer retained his crucial position at Canterbury. The Six Articles were still only patchily enforced. For a time, no further move was made towards establishing the true faith of the English Church; no parliament met until 1542 by which time the situation had changed again. In April 1541, memories of the pilgrimage of grace produced a desperate plot in Yorkshire to restore the old religion and overthrow what was felt to be Henry's tyranny; it was a plot of discontented men, restive under the even but heavy hand of the council of the North, which deserves little sympathy. The conspirators were betrayed and many executed; in their wake they dragged the old countess of Salisbury, in the Tower since 1539 and now beheaded as a warning to catholics, and Lord Leonard Grey, recently deputy in Ireland, who probably fell victim to his aristocratic connections rather than his alleged treasonable dealings with the Geraldines. Perhaps, however, this ominous clearance of the Tower had to do more with the king's plans for war than with the abortive Yorkshire conspiracy.

If the revival of catholic conspiracies undermined the standing of the orthodox party, the fall of Katharine Howard was a more serious blow still. In November 1541 the council obtained evidence that the queen had been unchaste before her marriage, and there were strong suspicions that her misbehaviour had not ended there. Henry was shattered by the discovery. After the political marriages with Jane Seymour and Anne of Cleves, he had re-discovered his youth with the lively and frivolous Katharine; indeed, he had given a somewhat ludicrous display which was yet touching in its happiness. But the queen was unquestionably very generous with her favours; at a court not especially noted for licentiousness (as courts went) she seems to have behaved with singular disregard for both morals and circumspection. Thus she was attainted by parliament—for treason!—and went to the scaffold in February 1542. With her she pulled down the Norfolk faction and really ended all chance of a full reaction in the sense favoured by Gardiner. The duke himself escaped by joining in his niece's condemnation, but his influence was pretty well gone. When Henry married once more, in June 1543, he chose Katharine Parr, herself a widow, who proved capable of dealing with the ever viler temper of an egoist soured thoroughly by ill health and by what he conceived to be his unmerited tribulations. Henry's last queen, who apparently had protestant sympathies, managed on the whole to keep out of politics, so that she survived her husband. She was a mild and moderately sensible woman much given to matrimony, but she scarcely merits the somewhat sanctimonious praise bestowed on her by the reformers and often echoed since.

In more than one way Henry demonstrated that he had recaptured the ardour of youth. Secure now in his triumphant establishment of the royal supremacy at home, free from the anxiety of ten years when foreign intervention was always threatening, he once again looked round for a way of displaying his greatness. In the summer of 1541, the amity of France and Spain which had driven Cromwell into the disastrous Cleves alliance cracked with a resounding report when the Spanish governor of Milan murdered two French envoys passing through his territory. With war imminent, England found herself the object of overtures from both sides. This suited Henry very well. Though he had avoided continental involvements while the situation created by the break with Rome made it desirable, he had always continued to harbour the ambitions which had led him into the wars of his younger days. Hostility to France and the hope of conquering Scotland still dominated his unoriginal mind. Scotland, indeed, could be said to be a danger, ruled as she was by a French and papalist faction led by the militant and immoral Cardinal Beaton. Diplomacy was tried first; Sir Ralph Sadler, one of Cromwell's young men, went north in 1540 to wean James V from his French associations and break Beaton's power. He was so far from successful that conditions on the border deteriorated, until in August 1542 an English raiding party was wiped out at Hadden Rig. In October 1542 Norfolk invaded Scotland, in order to compel acceptance of terms which would have made the northern kingdom England's satellite; the expedition achieved nothing and ended in an ignominious withdrawal. In November, James launched his counterattack. The better part of his forces, riven by internal dissensions, was met by a greatly inferior English army in the marshes of Solway Moss and destroyed in a rout. The English lost seven men killed and the Scots twenty, but hundreds more, including many nobles, surrendered. The news killed James V. His realm was left in the hands of the French party acting for the infant Mary, herself the daughter of James's second and French wife.

In the spring of 1543 Henry thus had a magnificent chance of achieving his ends in Scotland. He used the prisoners taken at Solway Moss to form the nucleus of an English party in Scotland; he encouraged a reaction there which overthrew Beaton and put the near-protestant earl of Arran temporarily in power; in July he forced upon the Scots the treaty of Greenwich which arranged for a peace to be cemented by the marriage of Mary Stuart to the prince of Wales. However, Henry's arrogance defeated itself. The spectre of English domination revived Scottish nationalism at its fiercest; Beaton escaped from imprisonment and re-established the French and catholic ascendancy; and Henry had to resume military action. But the activities of the earl of Hertford, who burnt Edinburgh and laid waste much country, only made the English party and policy more unacceptable. Even the murder of Beaton in 1546 did not alter the position; though the English party, protected by English naval strength, held Edinburgh Castle until after Henry VIII's death, the king's policy proved a failure. So far from achieving his great aim of subordinating Scotland to England by a marriage alliance, he only ensured the triumph of the French faction: the French might be unpopular, but the English were hated and much nearer.

In any case, with characteristic over-confidence, Henry had entered another war in 1543. Something might be said for the

Scottish enterprise which had an intelligent purpose behind it,
though the execution of the design can earn little praise; but the
only justification (such as it is) that can be found for the ultimatum
which Henry delivered to France in 1543 is that he thought the
Scottish war at an end. For two years imperial diplomacy had
been trying to draw England into the continental war, while
France had endeavoured to keep her out of it. In the end, traditional alignments combined disastrously with Henry's old desire
to display his power in Europe. In actual achievement, the war
proved modest but far from disgraceful. A small force of Englishmen, dispatched in 1543 to assist the imperial armies in Flanders,
impressed knowledgeable observers on both sides. The real effort
came in the following year when some 40,000 men invaded France
from Calais in a move intended to combine with a Spanish thrust
towards Paris. Henry would not be prevented from accompanying
his army, though his old,[1] unwieldy, and diseased body had to be
carried in a litter. The conduct of the campaign was in the hands
of other old men, the dukes of Norfolk and Suffolk, who had first
displayed their military skill thirty years earlier. In the event, the
great army, too slow and cumbersome to sweep the undefended
province of Picardy, was content with the rapid conquest of
Boulogne. After this the alliance of Henry and Charles, each of
whom wanted different things from the French, broke up, and
Charles made peace. England would have joined in, but Henry's
determination to keep Boulogne prevented agreement. The war,
dragging on, now concentrated on the French effort to recapture
the town from the sea, so that the only actions of note were naval
engagements in the Channel. In the course of these operations the
French actually rowed their galleys up the Solent, but the most
serious English loss—that of the *Mary Rose*—occurred when the
ship turned turtle in making a sharp turn with gunports open, and
the only real result of it all was to enhance the reputation of the
lord admiral, Sir John Dudley, Viscount Lisle. Like Hertford in
Scotland a commander of the younger generation, he demonstrated that England would not always have to rely on her Suffolks
and Norfolks.

Peace was finally concluded at Ardres in June 1546, largely
because neither side saw much hope of decisive success. France
once again promised to pay sizable pensions, and England was to
retain Boulogne until 1554 when France would buy the town back.
Henry could imagine that he had waged another successful war, but
the gain was infinitesimal and the loss, especially to the crown,

[1] At fifty-four Henry was in fact an old man.

terrible. The wars had been astonishingly expensive, costing altogether well over £2,000,000—perhaps ten times as much as the first French war of the reign. The reasons are obvious now: the price rise of the period had driven up costs, a factor for which the government failed to allow, and in the absence of an efficient minister the administration of the war was wasteful and corrupt. To cover these costs Henry had recourse to several expedients. The years 1540-7 saw an unprecedented burden of taxation, some £650,000 being obtained in this way. In addition, forced loans and even illegal benevolences appeared again on the scene. It is a sign of Henry's increased power and of the hold he had over his nation that parliament voted subsidies, and the rich 'lent' sums which they knew would never be repaid, without any of the troubles which similar demands had caused in 1522-4. For the crown thus to pillage its subjects might have been politically dangerous, but it did little harm to a country which could well afford to pay. The same cannot be said for Henry's other methods of raising money. He sold crown lands, especially—though not exclusively—the property taken from the monasteries. The sales made before Cromwell fell had been few and carefully controlled. But from 1542 onwards vast quantities of crown lands were alienated, bringing some £800,000 into the court of augmentations. On the whole the crown still obtained fair value, though it is significant that it also began to sell the rights and rents originally reserved on the lands sold: all capital was being realised. The real trouble was that the money so obtained did no good; it was all poured into the war. Thus Henry VIII impoverished the crown only so recently enriched by Cromwell's financial policy, and he further burdened it by contracting great loans on the Antwerp money market, often at high interest (14 per cent., and never less than 10 per cent.), leaving some £75,000 in debts. Most disastrous of all, however, was the debasement of the coinage. By recoining the available bullion with more alloy, the mint increased the face-value of its output without spending more precious metal; in effect this meant an income of about £360,000 in Henry's last three years. But the result was to ruin England's coinage and destroy confidence in it; in exchange for immediate gain to himself, swallowed up by the insatiable war, Henry damaged the economic life of the country so seriously that even twenty years of varied efforts could barely retrieve the situation.[1] The sum total of Henry's last years of direct personal rule was therefore to undo the good work of his father

[1] The details of the debasement and its effect on prices are discussed in the next chapter.

and of Thomas Cromwell. In order to pursue his futile and ill-conducted wars, the king destroyed the financial independence of the crown and undermined the prosperity of his country.

While the king pursued dreams of imperial conquest in the north and effective intervention on the continent, he still had to deal with the problem of religious unity at home. The crisis of 1538-40 resulted in the fall of Cromwell and the temporary ascendancy of the conservative party; orthodoxy, which Henry favoured, triumphed in the act of six articles. But Cromwell's fall did not destroy the reforming party, and the conservatives suffered a setback in the fate of Katharine Howard. The king continued to display that genius for cautious and opportunist adaptability, disguised as strong-minded decisiveness, which had already brought him far. Despite high words, he did not encourage the persecution of heretics which some of the bishops wanted.[1] The English Bible survived Cromwell's end, and Cranmer showed no inclination to return to strict orthodoxy. However, 1543—with its alliance with Spain—saw the balance once again turn to conservative views. The king was seriously perturbed by the manifold blasphemy reported from all over the country: God's Word was bandied about in taverns and ale-houses, and the scurrility which was always near the surface of medieval piety broke through in disconcerting fashion. The remedy adopted is most significant of the age. An act of 1543 limited the right of reading the bible to clerics, noblemen, gentry, and substantial merchants; women below gentle rank, servants, apprentices, and base people were forbidden to read what it was alleged they simply could not understand aright. Hierarchical paternalism—both contempt for the lower orders and fatherly care for their welfare—was here neatly and unquestioningly expressed by a government which—and this is typical too—thought it could do the impossible by legislative enactment. The act also promised a definition of doctrine, and this was achieved in the *Necessary Doctrine and Erudition for any Christian Man*, published in 1543. The book was the work of the bishops but the king had greatly influenced it; it deserves its name of the 'King's Book'. It came down entirely on the side of traditional orthodoxy, merely replacing the papal supremacy by the king's; those traces of

[1] The outstanding example of the sporadic persecution going on in Henry's last years was the torture, trial, and burning of Anne Askew, a gentlewoman who went to the stake for her denial of transubstantiation in July 1546. Attempts made to implicate others—especially Cranmer and Katharine Parr—led nowhere.

Lutheranism which had penetrated into the 'Bishops' Book' of 1537 had quite disappeared.

Gardiner and his party now thought their time come. The only obstacle to a firm stand on catholic doctrine seemed to be the suspected heretic at Canterbury. But once again they had mis-judged their master. Henry had by now acquired a thorough dislike of episcopal pretensions very much at variance with his earlier attitude to Wolsey, and he never trusted Gardiner who, despite his modern defenders, can hardly be interpreted as anything but an overbearing and over-subtle schemer. It is probable that Henry's attachment to Cranmer, so strong despite their not inconsiderable differences in matters of theology, derived largely from Cranmer's refusal to engage in politics. At any rate, the catholic party three times between 1543 and 1545 devised plans for charging the archbishop with heretical opinions, and each time they were foiled by Henry's personal intervention. Secure in the king's protection, Cranmer busied himself along lines which might easily have lost it: he composed liturgical books which he was later to combine into the Book of Common Prayer. However, unable to get either con-vocation or the king to accept his own strong views against many ceremonies, he had to be content with the English litany of 1545. Henry determinedly stuck to a middle way which Cranmer was rapidly leaving behind.

In his famous address to parliament in December 1545, the king once more stated his own position. Making an impassioned plea for charity, the fierce and intolerant old man, who one way and another had shed so much blood, denounced the stiffness of both extremes—the intolerance of the old religion and the unquiet and disturbing curiosity of the new—and deplored their mutual recrim-inations. He wanted moderate orthodoxy: the old religion with some of those late-medieval excrescences in image-worship, pilgrimages, and ceremonies pruned away. But in a way it was already too late to hope for the maintenance of this compromise. A new generation was growing up; in court and council the divi-sion between conservatives and innovators came to coincide largely with the division between the older men and the younger. Hertford and Lisle, whose reputations were eclipsing those of the old dukes (Suffolk died in 1545), both favoured protestantism and were known to do so. For some reason which has never been satisfac-torily explained, Henry permitted his son and heir to be brought up by reformist tutors; Edward VI was to be a bigoted protestant. Late in 1546 a temporary catholic ascendency in the council made way before the influence of Hertford and Lisle, returned from the wars; Gardiner, refusing to exchange some lands with the king, fell quite out of favour.

Worst of all for the conservatives, the reign did not close without another political upheaval, and this time the victims were the Howards, the secular mainstay of the orthodox party. Henry VIII had never lost the sense that his throne was somewhat insecure; throughout the reign, dynastic worries accounted for more illustrious victims than any other preoccupation. Buckingham, the Poles and Courtenays, the countess of Salisbury—whatever their immediate offence, connection with the White Rose was common to them all. Now the duke of Norfolk's brilliant young son, Henry earl of Surrey, thought fit to remember his own descent from Edward I and to display the arms of Edward the Confessor. Surrey himself probably leant nearer to protestantism than to orthodoxy, but the trouble did not arise over religion. At heart, everything turned on the personal rivalries and jealousies among the men who were getting ready to seize the inheritance of the dying king. The Howards had many enemies, and Surrey's indiscretion offered a ready handle. In December 1546 father and son were arrested; in January 1547 Surrey was executed for treason in displaying the royal arms; on the 27th the old duke was condemned to suffer likewise because he had concealed his son's offence. That night King Henry died and Norfolk escaped the scaffold; but the power of his house was broken, and as a child ascended the throne the protestant party looked to have it all its own way.

Henry VIII retained the reins of power to the very end; despite his physical decay there was no dotage. In his last months he concentrated on one thing only—the safe and peaceful succession of his son. He had long provided for the accession of a minor; an act of 1536 had authorised a king to revise all legislation passed during his minority, and the succession act of 1543—after settling the crown on Edward, Mary, and Elizabeth in that order—had reserved to the king the right of altering the succession by testament. In his will, Henry first repeated the terms of the act as far as his own children went; failing their heirs—a possibility which no one thought likely though in the end it came about—he then excluded the heirs of his sister Margaret (the Stuart line) and gave the crown to the heirs of his other sister Mary (the line of Suffolk). Determined to prevent trouble after his death, he had to decide between the parties and factions which for so long he had kept in strict subjection. The developments of the last two years of his reign—the rise of Hertford and Lisle, the fall at the critical time of the catholic protagonists—as well as a preference for laymen

who could be better trusted than ecclesiastics to keep the royal
supremacy intact, determined that his decision should advance the
party of reform. In the end, Henry proved true to the two outstanding features of his reign—his own skilful opportunism and the
triumph of the secular state—even though it meant the surrender
of a lifetime's religious opinions.

Fifty-seven years old, King Henry VIII died on 27 January
1547, his hand in Cranmer's, convinced as he had always been of
his own righteousness. The nation, informed three days later by
Lord Chancellor Wriothesley (in tears), was stunned and frightened of the future. The follies of the last seven years made sure
that the next reign would be burdened with an evil inheritance,
but the earlier work of Henry VIII and his great ministers had not
been done in vain.

2. EDWARD VI AND THE REVIVAL OF FACTION

The death of Henry VIII left the crown in the hands of a child
nine years old. Since the Tudor constitution, like the medieval
constitution whose development it was, required the presence of
an effective king, this virtual lapse of the crown posed enormously
difficult problems of government. In theory, of course, and also in
his own opinion, Edward VI was a real king: his surviving diary
and other papers show this boy adopting almost his formidable
father's tone in his supposed dealings with ministers and events.
In fact, as one might suppose, Edward played no part in his reign;
his so-called opinions were those of his advisers, and his so-called
acts were his endorsements of accomplished fact. Yet, since he was
king and the nation pathetically worshipped all wearers of the
crown, he could not be ignored and had to be persuaded, so that
his character and views mattered a little. They were neither
attractive nor promising. Edward was naturally haughty and arrogant, like all the Tudors; also like all his family, he had a marked
intellectual ability which an appalling schooling had turned into a
precocious passion for protestant theology. The king was a cold-
hearted prig, a fact which not even the pathos of his miserable
death can make one forget. Self-righteous, inclined to cruelty, and
—need we wonder at it?—easily swayed by cunning men, he
exercised such little influence as he possessed in favour of disastrous policies and disastrous politicians. Unable by reason of his
years to support the kingly pretensions to which he was heir, he
reduced the king-worship of the early sixteenth century to
absurdity and broke the spell which Henry VIII had cast over the

nation. The crown was never quite the same after Henry VIII died.

Of more real importance, especially in 1547, were those who actually ruled—the privy council. Henry VIII had tried to prevent friction by appointing a council for his son from which the extremists on the catholic side—Bishops Gardiner and Bonner—were absent, and to prevent the ascendancy of one man by laying down that all the council were equal. But the council at once broke Henry's last will by appointing the earl of Hertford, Edward's uncle, protector of the realm and duke of Somerset.[1] Somerset had secured Edward's person and the support of both the protestants and the civil servants in the council; his only possible rival was Lisle, now earl of Warwick; and that there needed a regent was not really in doubt. The man so chosen is one of the enigmas of a century whose personalities as a rule fall readily enough into obvious categories. Personally ambitious and rather haughty in manner, he was also liberal in ideas and generous in practice. An excellent and successful general in the field, he proved visionary, short-sighted, and incompetent in politics. Beyond question he was a man of ideals: as Sir William Paget, who originally supported and even stage-managed him, once wrote to him in despair, it was nothing but liberty with him. He sympathised with the poor and helpless, but to so little purpose that his sympathy in the end cost them dearer than other men's indifference. Always willing to make enemies among the powerful, and specially skilful in alienating the council who resented his assumption of a power above their own station, he deprived himself of any chance of putting through his ambitious programme of religious and social reform. Somerset is an attractive figure, with his frequent gentleness and relative unselfishness, especially in an age when the greed and unbridled self-seeking of others make him appear unique; but when all is said, he yet remains the type of the ignorant idealist, applying the wrong remedies to troubles wrongly diagnosed, who is the very worst man to be in charge of a state. As Pollard (who admired him) said, 'he took his office seriously and himself too seriously'; he was simply not up to managing the inheritance of Henry VIII.

That inheritance was admittedly a pretty burden. Henry left a heavy debt, a debased coinage, a shaken administrative system, and an example in spoiling the Church which the self-made men who filled court and council were eager to follow and enlarge upon.

---

[1] Paget, the secretary of state, produced a list of promotions which he said Henry VIII had intended to make. All the leading councillors moved up a step in the peerage: probably these were their rewards for acquiescing in Somerset's protectorate.

He left an unsettled doctrine and a nation divided in religion. He left an uneasy truce with France and a flaming war in Scotland. All these problems Somerset tackled in his two years' ascendancy. First he freed himself of all restraint when he removed the last notable catholic from the council by securing the fall of Lord Chancellor Wriothesley on a somewhat curious charge of exceeding his competence. That left a council of protestants and pliable indifferents. The protector then turned to the one task for which he was fitted, the war with Scotland. Here, too, his aims were visionary: he dreamt of a peaceful fusion of the two countries in one 'empire' of Great Britain. But though he wanted consent he saw no way of getting it except by war, especially as the Scots persisted in believing that the marriage between Edward VI and Mary Stuart, arranged by the treaty of Greenwich, would simply put their country into an English pocket. So Somerset crossed the border in September 1547 and won the bloody battle of Pinkie, retiring thereafter in the belief that the retention of a few strongholds and the sending of protestant missionaries would gradually win the Scots over. Pinkie, never followed up, marked the end of the Henrician policy in Scotland. In 1548, Mary Queen of Scots was sent to France and the ground prepared for her own personal tragedy as well as the long rule of the French at Edinburgh.

In the meantime, the burning question of the day was advancing towards a solution. Somerset had at once ended all persecution of protestants, and England now became for a few years the Mecca of continental reformers. Those that came were mostly of the Zwinglian persuasion—John à Lasco from Poland, Peter Martyr from Italy, Francis Dryander from Spain, Martin Bucer from Strassburg, and others. Their influence was to turn Cranmer more and more away from the moderate reforms of the Lutherans who refused his invitation to come over, but his own moderation always prevented the Church from fully embracing Zwingli's doctrines. Controversy centred largely on the nature of the eucharist, the sacrament of the altar, and with it on the quarrel between the mass and the communion service. The theological background to all the events of this period must be remembered even though space forbids a full exposition of it. Cranmer stood characteristically between the extremes, though precisely where is still a matter for some dispute. Somerset advanced the protestant cause he had at heart at first by allowing the Henrician legislation to lie dormant, and then by repealing it in the parliament which met in November 1547. Most of the treason and heresy laws of the last (and earlier) reigns, including the act of six articles, were repealed, together

with the proclamations act of 1539 and the act which permitted
Edward VI to repudiate all legislation passed during his minority.
Unquestionably these measures were, and were intended to be, a
manifesto of freedom, and Somerset invariably earns much praise
for a liberalism commonly described as far in advance of his time.
That phrase itself implies a censure, and his own fellow-councillors
thought ill of these repeals. A policy which retains some strong
weapons to check disorder but applies them with restraint deserves
respect: this had virtually been the policy of Henry VIII from
1534 onwards. But a wholesale abrogation of such weapons at a
time when a country ordinarily turbulent enough was about to be
thrown into further confusion by the proposed religious changes
was idealist folly—even criminal negligence.

The other measure of 1547 which merits attention was the act
dissolving the chantries, the many small foundations for religious,
charitable, and educational purposes which abounded in medieval
England. This step had originally been planned by an act of 1545,
but the death of Henry VIII interrupted the proceedings which
Somerset now resumed with energy. In theory, the dissolution was
justified by the new hostility to the doctrine of purgatory and to
masses for the dead, the chief religious purpose of the chantries;
in fact it was simply another stage in the secularisation of Church
property. The lands and goods went to fill part of the large hole
in the royal coffers, and then as rapidly passed out again by sale
and grant to the eager purchasers who had already absorbed so
much monastic property. Somerset himself profited notably. Some
was used to found grammar schools: the old legend of Edward VI as
the patron of schooling is now dead, though the newer legend of the
great system of education available in the old chantry schools still
awaits overthrow. The attack on the chantries involved an attack
on some gild property in the towns which caused difficulty in and
out of parliament, but on the whole the measure passed easily enough.

The chantries act and some others which almost incidentally
introduced communion under both kinds and the appointment of
bishops by royal letters patent indicated the way things were going.
Even before, Cranmer had stirred up trouble by publishing *Homilies*
contrary to the King's Book and *Injunctions* based on those of
1538, all of which Gardiner attacked as unconstitutional to such
good purpose that he was for a time confined to the Fleet. The year
1548 saw the flood swell. The continental mentors continued to
arrive and to spread their doctrines, especially at the universities.
The protector and council issued orders and literature of a reforming
kind. In June Gardiner was sent to the Tower for his public

opposition, remaining there throughout the rest of the reign. The removal of Henry's restrictive legislation let loose a flood of preaching, teaching, and disputation, often of a scandalous and scurrilous character, but much of it also profound and searching. The new protestantism had the support of some of the clergy and bishops, especially Cranmer; Somerset and a few other councillors adhered to it; there may have been some real enthusiasm in London; but it seems never to have penetrated to the nation at large. Unlike the anti-clericalism of the previous reign, it struck no deep roots; its safest support came from those gentry and nobility who, disliking or ignoring its doctrines, yet felt themselves bound by their secular interests in monastic and chantry lands to oppose a conservatism which, by seeking the leadership of the Princess Mary and talking of the absent Cardinal Pole, threatened a return of the papal supremacy.

The first stage of the doctrinal Reformation culminated in the Prayer Book of 1549, enforced by a mild act of uniformity. The book represented a compromise intended to persuade catholics to accept it; the concessions made to them, especially in the matter of ceremonial, greatly disappointed Cranmer's Zwinglian friends. It was so darkly worded that Gardiner and Cranmer had no difficulty in interpreting it very differently; Gardiner virtually killed it by giving it an orthodox catholic reading which finally convinced the reformers that it was worthless. In its hesitant advance towards protestantism, in the mild measures taken for its enforcement, and in its general ineffectiveness, it well represented the policy of Somerset's government—laudably moderate in intent but also deplorably futile in execution.

Even so, the first Prayer Book was to cause trouble enough. The year 1549 was one of crisis in which religion formed one of the chief issues. The other was economic distress, especially agrarian grievances. Throughout the 1540s prices rose rapidly and poverty mounted. Enclosure for pasture revived as wool boomed; in particular, there were many encroachments on commons.[1] Even so, however, enclosure and its worst product, depopulation (the disappearance of whole villages as the sheep took over), were not so much the real cause of the dearness and destitution as the cause advanced by a number of reformers who composed what was called the commonwealth party.[2] They were mostly clerics—

[1] The 'agrarian revolution' will be discussed more fully in the next chapter.
[2] From their catchword, commonwealth or common weal. For their forerunners see above, p. 185.

moralising preachers like Hugh Latimer and Thomas Lever, skilful pamphleteers like Robert Crowley—but their expert was a civil servant, John Hales of Coventry, who may have been the author of the movement's literary monument, the *Discourse of the Common Weal of this Realm of England*. They believed that enclosures were at the root of the trouble, and that enclosures were simply the work of greedy money-grubbing landlords; and they convinced the lord protector. In 1547 Hales attempted to secure the passage of three bills dealing with enclosure and, more sensibly, with tenants' rights, but the house of commons, dominated by the lords of manors who were themselves driven on by economic necessity, would have none of such things. It showed its true temper by enacting the most savage of the century's poor laws by which vagrants were rendered liable to slavery. Baulked by parliament, Somerset turned to the weapons of conciliar government: in 1548 he condemned enclosures once again by proclamation and appointed commissions to investigate and enforce the laws against the practice. The only commission which seems to have taken action was that of which Hales was the moving spirit, but it dealt with the main enclosing counties—the Midlands from Leicestershire down to Buckinghamshire—and authorised the destruction of many enclosures, among them a park recently made by the earl of Warwick. When, in the year after, a great rising took place, the interests which Hales and Somerset had offended charged them with inciting the commons to riot and rebellion; but in truth, hedges fell and ditches were filled in all over England at different times throughout these and earlier years. Enclosure riots—protests on a small scale by individual villages or even only a few peasants —were frequent; what happened in 1549 was only the culmination of this sporadic and spontaneous movement.

Nevertheless, the commission of 1548 played an unwitting part in stirring up trouble. Somerset's deeds, and even more his words, created the impression that 'the good duke' would assist the poor against the local gentry, and the Norfolk rising of 1549—known from its leader as Ket's rebellion—was a definite attempt to enlist support from the centre against the ruling class of a county which was particularly ill-administered by its traditional magistrates. The rising seemed formidable: Ket at one time had some 16,000 men under arms on Mousehold Heath outside Norwich, controlled that city, and governed his territory and followers in an alarmingly independent manner. Early fears that the rising might by inspired by catholics eager to put the Princess Mary (who lived in the county) on the throne proved groundless; Ket's rebellion was the only major agrarian disturbance of the period with a protestant bias. But it came on top of an upsurge in Cornwall which was caused by the new Prayer Book: the insurgents wanted the old faith as well as the pope, pointing out that a service in English was as incomprehensible to them as one in Latin without even the merit of familiarity. The Cornishmen allowed themselves to be absorbed by a fruitless siege of Exeter, and Ket failed to seize his advantage because he was concerned only with Norfolk. The risings were suppressed with great violence, not by Somerset whose generous and muddled mind prevented him from taking action either way, but by the outraged representatives of the gentry. Russell and Herbert pacified the West, Warwick destroyed Ket; and by the autumn of 1549 England was once again at peace.

However different in their origins and aims, the troubles showed up the protector's failure to govern. His position had already been weakened by the execution for treason of his brother, the wayward Lord Admiral Thomas Seymour, for which justifiable act of stoicism he was much blamed; nor did it help that the French were besieging Boulogne with every appearance of an early success. Somerset did not deserve all the blame heaped upon him, and historians who have seen the cause of his fall in the self-interest of the great landlords opposing him and the specific ambitions of Warwick have seized upon the heart of the matter; yet there are things to be said on the other side. Somerset had talked much of liberty but had produced disorder; he had acted with the best intentions but without any sign of administrative ability or political sense; he had attempted to fill a position reserved to the crowned and anointed king, thus alienating his fellow-councillors whose feelings and ideas he persistently ignored. When the crisis came, he found friends among the poor and power-less; all men of standing were against him. This speaks well for his heart, no doubt, but his championship did the poor the less service because he had concentrated all the strong against them. In October 1549 he was arrested by a group of councillors supposed to favour catholicism, but by February 1550 his real rival, the earl of Warwick, got rid of the conservatives and released Somerset from the Tower, attempting for nearly two years to achieve co-operation on his own terms. He never took the title of protector, preferring to govern through his domination of the council and the young king over whom he acquired the ascendancy of an indulgent older man playing at grown-ups with a child. But Warwick wanted full power, and Somerset's popularity stood in his way. After preparing the ground in 1550, the earl attacked in 1551. He and his followers acquired new honours—Warwick became duke of Northumberland; the king was introduced into the council to work against his uncle; and in October Somerset was arrested on a frivolous charge of treason. In the following February, among impressive scenes of popular sorrow, he suffered under the axe. The story of these faction struggles need not be rehearsed in detail. Their occurrence, indeed, and their virulence are highly significant, for they demonstrate the decay of good royal government in Edward VI's minority; it is also important to note how long it took Northumberland to get rid of his rival, since in the end he proved to have left himself insufficient time to consolidate his triumph.

Thus Somerset, noble-minded and generous, but also ambitious, high-handed, and incompetent, made way for a man for whom no one has ever had a good word. Northumberland, son of that Edmund Dudley whom Henry VIII had executed in his early days, was the second of the young soldiers who came to the fore in the renewal of war after Cromwell's fall. A reputation then made was enhanced somewhat easily in the rout of Ket's half-armed followers at Dussindale in 1549. Unquestionably Northumberland was exceedingly ambitious of power and very greedy. He represented, at its worst, the type of man who was speculating in monastic property and the exploitation of land, and the businesslike landowning gentry looked to him to save them from Somerset's predilection for the peasants. The manner in which Northumberland and his followers grasped honours and lands from the powerless hands of a boy king demonstrates to the full that the evils of factious magnate rule were reviving under this upstart nobility. Their attitude to economic problems, embodied in legislation in 1553, was straightforward: they confirmed their own gains at the expense of the king and refused to be tied in any way in the use of their property. But in some ways Northumberland's rule marked an improvement on Somerset's. He recognised the evils of a debased coinage and did something to tackle them, and he undertook a thorough review of the dilapidated administration of the country. The financial reforms which the new lord treasurer, the marquess of Winchester,[1] carried through in 1554, and which provided the basis for sound finance in the reign of Elizabeth, were begun by Northumberland's government at the very time when we are

[1] Sir William Paulet (1485?-1572), successively Lord St John, earl of Wiltshire, and marquess of Winchester, was probably the outstanding example of the Tudor civil servant in high places who avoided the complications of politics. His life and work want studying. He himself accounted for his survival through four reigns by saying that he was sprung from the willow and not the oak.

commonly told that government was at its worst. They are no credit to Mary who merely permitted measures to develop which her brother's death had interrupted. It looks very much as though Northumberland had to cope with an administration allowed to rot by Henry VIII and Somerset, and as though he attempted genuine remedies, hampered as he admittedly was by his own and his party's selfish greed. Where Somerset was attractive as a man but disastrous as a ruler, Northumberland displayed every unpleasant personal characteristic but seems to have shown skill and penetration in public affairs. It is difficult to say who did more harm to the country they were supposed to govern.

However, Edward VI's reign is associated not only with the near-collapse of the Tudor system, but also with the progress of the protestant Reformation; and here Northumberland's part is even less easy to understand. In the end he affirmed that he had always been a catholic, and when he first attacked Somerset the conservative faction had hoped great things from him. Yet in between he directed a headlong advance towards full protestantism, overthrowing the compromise of 1549 and encouraging extremes in iconoclasm and doctrine which went even further than the settlement of 1552 which he sponsored. Very probably the reason must be sought not in any convictions he may have had, but in the designs which he and his like had on the property of the Church. Any retreat from the position of 1549 might have involved them in demands for the restoration of lands already acquired—the lands of monasteries and chantries; and if they wanted more, they had to turn to episcopal lands which the spread of protestant doctrine and the weak position of protestant bishops were, in fact, to deposit in their laps. Every bishop of the old persuasion deprived of his see meant a protestant successor whom the dominant party would only appoint after they had wrung material concessions from him. Henry VIII had pointed the way and Somerset had followed; but it was in these years of Northumberland's ascendancy that the Church was really ruined as the wealth of the bishops began to follow that of monasteries and chantries into lay hands.

Early in 1550 the reformers gained control of the council and set to to promote greater changes than any yet accomplished. More continental experts arrived, and Cranmer was swayed by Bucer and the Zwinglians. The catholic bishops fell in numbers: Gardiner, so far from being released from the Tower, was deprived of his see for his opposition (February 1551), and others of his persuasion followed. The appointments in 1550 of Nicholas Ridley at London and John Hooper at Gloucester greatly

reinforced the extremer party. In Hooper the government came
up against the first genuine representative of that puritanism which
was to cause so much trouble later on. He had all the hallmarks:
blazing sincerity, intolerable obstinacy, devotion to small points,
bad manners, and utter confidence in his own judgment and
conscience. Characteristically he had been in exile under Henry
VIII, imbibing the pure Swiss doctrine and returning eager to
establish it. An exasperated council and an uneasy Cranmer
struggled with him over the question of priestly vestments, until
Ridley persuaded him to compromise. 1550-1 witnessed a
general attack. A new Ordinal (February 1550) simplified the
rites of ordination and abolished minor orders; later embodied
in the revised prayer book, it marked the change from catholic
priest to protestant minister. In 1551, a controversy between
Gardiner (sending his thunderbolts from the Tower) and Cranmer
raised the central question of all, the sacrament of the altar.
Cranmer rejected transubstantiation but accepted the real presence
in a spiritual though not a corporeal sense; he held that the communion service was more than the mere commemorative act of the
Zwinglians but that, unlike the mass, it contained no element of
sacrifice. This satisfied the reformers to whom Latimer, hitherto
a conservative in doctrine though a radical in policy, now adhered.
Celibacy and priestly marriage, always a ticklish point, assumed
importance in 1551 because of the appointment of John Ponet to
Winchester and Robert Holgate to York, both of whom were
rumoured to be married to wives with first husbands yet living.
The story, which was true of Ponet but not of Holgate, did much
to embarrass the reformed party and to weaken the standing of
the Church at a time when it needed strength and good repute to
resist the secularisers. In accordance with the Prayer Book of 1549
altars were replaced by communion tables, especially by Ridley in
London; this caused irreverence on the one hand and unease on
the other. There was, however, little enough opposition to the
innovations. The Edwardian Reformation was superficial—
imposed on a reluctant or indifferent people by a few ardent
spirits and the politicians—but twenty-five years of royal control
following upon a century and a half of obedience to papal direction
had accustomed the nation to accept authority. One who did resist
was the Princess Mary whom the council tried in vain to deprive of
the mass.

It was not until after the fall of Somerset, when the last
moderating influence had gone from the council, that the final step
was taken. The 1549 Prayer Book had from the first been attacked

by the protestants who abominated its attempts to compromise with the old religion; like most compromises in violently disturbed ages, it only succeeded in falling foul of everybody. Bucer, the most learned of the foreign divines, wrote a long commentary whose criticisms are fully reflected in the later revision, while John à Lasco set to work on Cranmer himself, claiming afterwards that he had persuaded him to Zwinglianism. Cranmer certainly moved further towards the Swiss position in these years, but it would seem more correct to accuse him of an eclectic mind which adopted parts of several systems; from its first archbishop the Anglican Church inherited not only a beautiful liturgy and a readiness to obey civil authority, but also a doctrine half-way between the extremes. The revised Prayer Book, published after much consultation in 1552 and enforced by an act of uniformity which appointed penalties for failure to use it as well as for positive attacks upon it, marked the arrival of the English Church at protestantism. The various 'popish' remnants in doctrine, gestures, and vestments, which had still attached to the communion service, were dropped, and even Hooper could be satisfied that the mass was abolished in England. One hurdle remained: the book demanded kneeling at the communion, and the extreme reformers had to be placated by the insertion of the so-called Black Rubric which stated that the practice denoted only respect for and not adoration of the sacrament. In 1553 Cranmer produced a statement of faith for the English Church in his Forty-two Articles which represented a compromise between the Lutheran and Calvinist (or Zwinglian?) creeds without attempting to accommodate the catholic faith except where the branches of Christianity did not, in any case, differ. The Prayer Book of 1552, the Ordinal of 1550 which it took over, the act of uniformity which made the Prayer Book the only legal form of worship, and the Forty-two Articles binding upon all Englishmen, clerical and lay—these between them comprehended the protestant Reformation in England. Matters had changed rapidly in the five years and few months since Henry VIII had died, an orthodox catholic still except for his break with the papacy; they had moved even faster in the two and a half years since Somerset's fall. Gardiner and the Henricians seemed utterly overthrown; the sees of England were filled by upstart protestants; there was rejoicing at Geneva and Zürich, and Cranmer was revolving further plans for uniting the dangerously divided protestant Churches.

In fact, the moves had been too rapid. The whole English Reformation depended on the life of Edward VI, and so did—

what mattered more to the man in charge—the ascendancy of Northumberland. Edward was probably the most ardent lay protestant in England; he was certainly the only complete adherent of the duke who had succeeded in making enemies of all men by his greed and arrogance. His party was held together by self-interest only; he had one only as long as he commanded wealth and patronage. In 1552, Edward's health, never good, took a turn for the worse; measles and smallpox attacked a frame constitutionally consumptive; and in the spring of 1553 the king contracted a cold which brought him to his death. Northumberland was faced by a sudden crisis. If Edward died his sister Mary would succeed him under the terms of the act of 1543 and of her father's will. Her accession would mean the end of the Reformation in England and as certainly the end of the duke who had tied his career to advanced protestantism. Out of this dilemma grew Northumberland's desperate and doomed attempt to pervert the succession in his favour. He persuaded Edward to set aside the will of Henry VIII, to declare both his sisters bastards and therefore incapable of inheriting the crown, and to bestow the succession upon the daughter of the duke of Suffolk, Lady Jane Grey, descended from Edward's aunt Mary and married to Northumberland's son Guildford Dudley. The council was coerced into supporting the plot which would leave Northumberland the real ruler of England as father-in-law to a helpless young queen. No attempt was made to abrogate the succession acts of 1536 and 1543, but in the event legal points mattered nothing. Failure was assured when the council failed to get possession of Mary's person: warned in time (oddly enough by Northumberland's younger son Robert), she fled into Norfolk, the stronghold—despite its protestant feelings—of the catholic Howards.

Edward died on July 6th; four days later Queen Jane was proclaimed in London, but Queen Mary was proclaimed in Norfolk. Much against his will, Northumberland set out to overcome her by armed force, only to find the country up in her favour and his troops melting away. Deprived of his strong hand the council ratted; in the end Suffolk himself told his daughter that she had ceased to be queen and proclaimed Mary on Tower Hill. The news reached Northumberland at Cambridge. Hoping to save his life he threw up his cap in the market place for Queen Mary. No sudden plots could take the crown from the Tudors where the passionate loyalty of the nation desired it to be: Mary's triumphant success owed everything to her being King Henry's daughter and very little to her catholic faith. This she quite failed to understand—

HƗT

with dire results. But in the meantime all was rejoicing as she rode into London, acclaimed by the multitude which had pelted the captive Northumberland on his way to the Tower where he was soon joined by the rest of his party, including Lady Jane Grey, the innocent victim of his ambition.

3. MARY AND THE FAILURE OF REACTION

The reign of Mary Tudor lasted only five years, but it left an indelible impression. Positive achievements there were none: Pollard declared that sterility was its conclusive note, and this is a verdict with which the dispassionate observer must agree. Even the financial and administrative recovery, which has been noted,[1] owed nothing to the queen or her policy; planned in the previous reign, it was the work of Winchester who played no part in Marian politics. The decline of good government was accentuated by Mary's preference for a large council of nearly fifty members and her encouragement of cliques and cabals, not to mention the influence of Charles V's ambassador Simon Renard and of Mary's husband, Philip of Spain. For the first time in English history, a queen regnant occupied the throne, an event which on this occasion only served to prove right the fears which had gripped Henry VIII in the 1520s. After the rule of factions in the reign of a child, the accession of the wrong kind of queen nearly completed the ruin of dynasty and country. Yet Mary herself is often regarded as the most attractive of the Tudors. She was personally gentle and inclined to mercy, though her history—the vicious attack on her mother, her own bastardisation, the treatment of her religion and her person by her father and brother—ought to have turned her into a fearsome instrument of hatred and vengeance. She was also sensible and generous—altogether of a better character than was common in her family. But all her good qualities went for nought because she lacked the essentials. Two things dominated her mind —her religion and her Spanish descent. In the place of the Tudor secular temper, cool political sense, and firm identification with England and the English, she put a passionate devotion to the catholic religion and to Rome, absence of political guile, and pride in being Spanish. The result cannot surprise. Welcomed by the nation as a Tudor and a relief from the ambitions of selfish politicians and the extravagances of reforming divines, she died only five years later execrated by nearly all. Her life was one of almost unrelieved tragedy, but the pity which this naturally excites

[1] E.g. F. C. Dietz, *English Government Finance, 1485-1558.*

must not obscure the obstinate wrong-headedness of her rule.

Mary's own single ambition was to restore England to the papal obedience, to save—as she saw it—her country from mortal sin. This overriding issue was complicated—both advanced and retarded—by problems of foreign policy. Since Henry VIII's death England had played little part on the continent. In 1550 Northumberland gave up Boulogne whose neglect he had made one of the charges against Somerset. The emperor had been busy in Germany and in Lorraine where the French king (Henry II) had been making conquests; for once the Rhine, and not the Channel seaboard, had been the scene of the Habsburg-Valois struggle. But in 1553 the war between Spain and France had reached stalemate, and both sides began to look for additional strength. The accession of Mary, the emperor's cousin, seemed to promise a revival of that alliance between England and the Burgundian House which Henry VII had made the basis of English diplomacy, and which rested firmly on a common interest in the cloth trade between England and the Netherlands. Mary had been, as it were, the seal of that alliance, and even Henry VIII's behaviour to his Spanish wife had not destroyed it. Charles V now saw a chance of giving it still greater solidity. The question of Mary's marriage loomed large from the first. A few there were who thought that this woman of thirty-seven would do well to avoid trouble by not marrying at all; these included Cardinal Pole who was himself mentioned as a possible husband. (He was as yet but in deacon's orders, and a papal dispensation could have been secured.) But Mary herself was clear that she would marry a Spaniard and no one else, and Charles V decided upon his son and heir, Philip, at the time archduke of Burgundy. The marriage would add England to the Habsburg dominions; successful marriages had built these up so amazingly in the previous half-century that the idea seemed sensible enough and France had cause to fear it. London became the centre of a diplomatic battle between the great European powers in which England played barely the part of a pawn. To make matters more difficult still, few members of the council favoured Mary's own choice of a Spaniard for husband; Gardiner especially, released from the Tower to become lord chancellor and (at last) chief minister, sturdily opposed a policy which would reduce England to a Spanish colony. But the English candidate, Edward Courtenay, earl of Devonshire, was a weakling and a poltroon: the Spanish match seemed likely to come off.

Thus the reign started with every promise of trouble. A new set of councillors replaced those of Northumberland; the Henricians, led by Gardiner and Paget, were back in power. The queen's determination to spare bloodshed meant that only three men died on the scaffold for Northumberland's conspiracy, the duke himself vainly endeavouring to save his life by embracing the catholic religion. His recantation was the first move in a distressing game of chess. In its determination to reverse the Reformation and restore the papal power, the government sought to produce as many apostates from protestantism as it could because by lowering the reputation of that faith one could most quickly reduce the numbers of its followers; meanwhile the other side triumphantly chalked up each death of a steadfast believer on the principle—borne out by results—that the Church is fructified by the blood of its martyrs. Northumberland's death opened the score for the catholics and lost many recent converts to protestantism.

However, for the time being, the queen could do no more than rescue catholic councillors, deprive heretic bishops, and arrest Cranmer for treason. This eager daughter of Rome, this unswerving adherent of the papal supremacy in the Church, found herself inevitably saddled with the title of supreme head and compelled to resort to parliament in order to reverse her father's and brother's doings. Suggestions that she might restore the realm to Rome without parliamentary sanction were quashed by, among others, Gardiner. There were technical legal reasons for this, but a very practical problem existed also in the lands taken from the Church and absorbed by the laity since 1536. These Mary wished to recover, but she and everybody knew this to be impossible; any attempt to declare the Henrician and Edwardian legislation null and void—which, since it contravened canon law, Mary adjudged it to be—without giving parliament a chance to safeguard the interest of the new owners would lead to rebellion. It is most striking how everybody around the queen all the time smelled or feared uprisings; Mary herself, her ministers, Renard, and the French ambassador Noailles moved in an almost palpable fog of violent political disorder which in part was real but in large part only existed in their apprehensions. About the Church lands, however, they were right. The Reformation sat as yet lightly on most Englishman's minds, but the nobility, gentry, and yeomanry who had invested in those lands were not prepared to disgorge them, and their self-interest saved protestantism in England. It may also be noticed that the vigorous dislike of priests and priestly rule had not abated since 1529.

The first parliament of the reign met in October 1553 in an atmosphere disturbed by forthcoming events. Neither house made any bones about repealing the Edwardian act of uniformity, thus restoring the religious situation of the end of Henry VIII's reign— with this difference that, the heresy laws repealed by Somerset not being re-enacted, the state did not yet assist in the enforcement of catholic orthodoxy which Mary and Gardiner wished to put in train. It was also made plain to the queen that she could abandon all hope of returning the Church lands to their late owners and therefore of restoring the monasteries. Worse still, the commons sent a deputation to protest against the proposed marriage with Philip, a move which demonstrated that the relaxation of discipline since 1547 and the freedom enjoyed in Edward's reign had given the lower house a good conceit of itself. Mary expressed her angry displeasure and hurried into the match; it was concluded by proxy in October 1553. This brought discontent to a head in various plots secretly assisted by Noailles who still hoped to prevent England from acceding to the side of Spain. Only one of these conspiracies came to anything, but it turned out to be serious. In January-February 1554 Sir Thomas Wyatt, son of the poet, roused the gentlemen of Kent and beset the capital itself with some 3,000 men. Stopped at London Bridge he crossed the Thames at Kingston and penetrated as far as Fleet Street, but the desultory and confused fighting petered out against the government's superior forces (marshalled by Northumberland's late supporters rather than by Mary's party proper), and Wyatt surrendered. His enterprise had been inspired both by protestant-ism (Kent had a tradition of heresy) and by nationalist resentment at the proposed foreign king; it was so serious because it was the only rising in Tudor times to take place in the neighbourhood of the seat of government itself. The fright which the council had had was reflected in its actions. Mary's desire for mercy was over-ruled both by her advisers and by Charles V. Wyatt and many of his followers died in London and in Kent; the innocent Jane Grey and her husband were executed; the Princess Elizabeth, on whose behalf Wyatt had allegedly risen, narrowly escaped a like fate, though she did not escape imprisonment in the Tower.

In the meantime Mary was no nearer her real aim—the restora-tion of the papacy—and she found it difficult to stomach the cautious advice of Charles V who cared little for the healing of the schism but did not want to send his son into a country possibly torn by religious war. A second parliament met in March 1554, only to prove more troublesome than the first. Gardiner attempted to revive the heresy laws and the act of six articles, but was defeated in the lords; the reaction against the Reformation and the persecution of protestants had to continue to wait. Trouble arose over attempts to give Philip the protection of the treason laws and other privileges, though Wyatt's rebellion made sure that the marriage treaty itself was accepted without opposition. Philip, the commons thought, should be Mary's husband and might even bear the name of king, but he was not to be a real king and above all he was not to retain the crown if he survived his middle-aged wife. All this opposition came perhaps less from the nation than from a party in the council led by Paget who in this parliament won a marked victory over the clerics under Gardiner; the state of a government so badly and so publicly divided needs no comment. In July 1554 Philip at last arrived, and the marriage was celebrated. Mary, who persuaded herself into deep and real love with her unprepossessing husband (who did not reciprocate), had a brief interlude of happiness; the country looked on and disapproved.

Their disapproval was strengthened by the first real signs of ecclesiastical reaction which ensued upon Mary's failure to restore the link with Rome in her second parliament. The government began to eject a large number of beneficed clergy, nearly always because they had taken wives; if these married clergy had once been monks or friars they were forced to put their wives away as well. This deliberate concentration on those who had broken their vows of celibacy was inspired by the queen herself. Altogether probably a quarter of the English clergy were ejected from their livings—some 2,000 or so; but the figure itself contains a hint that the authorities could not be as rigorous as their words pretended. There were not enough ordained priests acceptable to the catholic party to fill so many vacancies. Many, in fact, reappeared in other parishes where their earlier history was unknown. Deprived Essex clergy have been traced in Gloucestershire, and so forth, though the task of tracing them all is hopeless. In more rural areas neighbouring priests sometimes exchanged parishes, changing back again when the accession of Elizabeth brought another turn of the wheel. Nevertheless, many suffered because they had taken women in marriage, especially in London where the Reformation had made most progress.

Protestantism had ceased to be the religion of the land, many old ceremonies and practices were again used in the churches, mass especially was again being said. But, except for the repeal of the

Edwardian laws on uniformity, all this had been done by Mary's authority as supreme head: England had not returned to the Roman communion, and the devout queen could only do what she thought right by the exercise of a power she held to be wrong and usurped. It was time that the schism was healed. Two things stood in the way: the impossibility of recovering the Church lands, and the refusal of the chosen instrument to admit defeat on this issue. That instrument was Reginald Pole, cardinal and papal legate. His was an obvious choice—the only English cardinal, related to the queen, a persistent fighter for the papal supremacy against the English schism. It was, however, also an unfortunate choice in some ways, for Pole lacked all diplomatic and statesmanlike abilities. His temper agreed most unfortunately with that of Queen Mary: both were personally kind and inclined to mercy, both put principle far above expediency, both believed earnestly and immovably in the necessity of exterminating heresy by fire. Neither was a match for the children of this world among whom it soon appeared that there had to be numbered not only Gardiner, Paget, and the Henricians, but also Mary's husband and father-in-law, and even the pope himself. Fearful of what he might do, Charles V delayed Pole's journey to England until he had accepted the necessity of surrendering the Church lands; then at last, in November 1554, Cranmer's successor in the see of Canterbury landed at Dover, bringing with him the absolution of the realm and reconciliation with Rome. His arrival coincided with the meeting of yet another parliament (November 1554) whose elections had been influenced by the government with sufficient success to bring about some degree of co-operation. The old heresy laws were re-enacted and ferocious new treason laws passed (a weapon which no effective sixteenth-century government could avoid); more important still, parliament at last agreed to repeal all the anti-papal and anti-ecclesiastical legislation passed since 1529. Pole and Mary much regretted the necessity of seeking parliamentary repeal of acts which they held to be inherently void as contrary to the laws of God and Holy Church, but even the defenders of the medieval Church had to imply acceptance of the principle that statute stood above all other law in England. As far as enactments could kill it, the Reformation was dead and Henry VIII and Cromwell need never have laboured; by and large there was reason to suppose that the country, some irreconcilables apart, would accept the fact.

This hope, however, was never more than an illusion. England had so far little sympathy for protestantism on the Edwardian model, but the anti-clerical and anti-papal nationalism which Henry VIII had exploited continued as strong as ever. It now found reinforcement from the government's activities against heresy. The responsibility for the persecution and burnings which are the best-remembered thing about Mary's reign is easily attributed. The Spaniards, with Philip and Charles V to give a lead, were against it, for reasons of policy. Gardiner and Bonner (in whose diocese of London the majority of the victims were found) went at it with a will, the latter especially displaying a coarse liking for the task; neither can be exonerated from a charge which seems more serious to the twentieth century than to the sixteenth, but neither also was the originator of the policy. It was the queen and the cardinal who inspired it, believing that only so the souls of Englishmen could be saved from eternal damnation. The trials opened in January 1555, and before the reign was out nearly 300 men and women were burnt for their faith. Most of them were humble folk—shopkeepers, artisans, and the like; most of the leaders of the Edwardian Church had taken the opportunities offered to flee abroad, but Hooper, Ridley, Latimer, and Cranmer died in the flames. The last-named suffered much perturbation of spirit at the end, being torn between his religious convictions and his lifelong adherence to the principle of obeying the civil power. But when he came to die he rejoiced the reformed and disappointed the government by revoking all his recantations and facing the fire as steadfastly as the others had done. These martyrs, celebrated by John Foxe in his *Acts and Monuments*, deserve no doubt no more and no less sympathy than the victims of Henry VIII or Elizabeth, but their importance is vastly greater. Mary burned few as compared with continental practice, but for English conditions and traditions her activities were unprecedented and left an ineradicable memory. More than all the denunciations of Henry VIII, the fires of Smithfield and the like places all over southern England created an undying hatred of the pope and of Roman Catholicism which became one of the most marked characteristics of the English for some 350 years. This in itself is an adequate comment on the activities of these earnest and good and rather stupid fanatics, and an answer to those who would always judge people's place in history by their personal morals rather than by the work they did

Her efforts on behalf of the faith had to be Mary's sole consolation from the middle of 1555 onwards, for after the appearance of triumph in the Spanish match and the absolution of the realm everything went wrong. In September 1555 Philip departed to take over his inheritance in Spain; he left behind him a disconsolate woman looking eagerly and hysterically (and in vain) for signs of the child upon whom all her hopes now centred. The parliament of October 1555 proved obstreperous to a degree, resentful of the persecution, eager to throw off government control—it even proposed a bill to exclude from membership all office-holders under the crown—and unwilling to grant the supplies which had been the real cause of its assembly. In November Gardiner died. Much maligned in the past, too much praised today, he had played a prominent part in thirty-five years of public life without ever attaining to the power and influence he craved. Henry VIII distrusted him, Somerset and Northumberland feared him, Mary found him too English for her taste. Yet he had stood for a certain continuity and for a definite party of conservative patriots. He was very able, learned (especially in the canon and civil law), and energetic, but overbearing and violent in manner. His few years of office and influence (1553-5) were spent in attempts to restrain and divert the one of his sovereigns with whom in general he was most in sympathy. His life achieved little, for even the continuity of the Anglican Church with pre-Reformation days owes more to Cranmer than to Gardiner. His death, however, deprived the government of the one man able to combat the influence of Pole and of Spain.

The Spanish match and England's virtual absorption into the Habsburg empire had played relatively little part until 1556 because domestic issues had then predominated upon which Philip and his advisers exercised little influence. Despite their studiously good behaviour they were hateful to the simple and virulent nationalism of the English, the more so as the Spanish alliance coincided with a decline in the Netherlands cloth trade (though it did not cause it) and did not lead to better trade for the English seamen trying to break the Iberian monopoly of transoceanic trade. In 1556 the Spanish connection began to have positively harmful effects. Philip quarrelled with the pope, Paul IV (a man whose violence of temper amounted to madness) over Italian issues, and Mary had the dreadful experience of seeing her husband excommunicated by her spiritual father. Pole, too, fell under the pope's displeasure; he was deprived of his legacy and accused of heresy. Into these distractions there dropped the renewal of war between Spain and France in 1557. Philip briefly returned to England—of which, after all, he was still king—in order to press for military assistance; the queen felt it her duty to provide it, and her council, more mindful of the constant rumblings of disaffection and of the crown's financial straits, resisted in vain. In June 1557, England declared a war on France in which she had no concern, of which the country disapproved, and which was singularly ill-managed. Empty coffers and the inadequacy of parliamentary grants (January 1558) compelled recourse both in 1557 and 1558 to forced loans and other expedients both desperate and illegal. Spain used English assistance, for instance at the battle of Gravelines in July 1558; but she treated English interests with contempt. All the fears that the alliance would but make England a Spanish province proved justified. The chief blow fell in January 1558 when the French overran the ill-defended Calais in a week; the last remnant of England's medieval empire in France, a base held for over 200 years, was virtually thrown away. Probably Calais—expensive and useless—was better lost than kept, but neither the nation nor Mary saw it that way. The failure broke her spirit and destroyed the last vestige of loyalty to her.

As 1558 dragged on it became clear that the queen's days were numbered, and all thoughts turned to the successor. Elizabeth was very nearly holding court before her sister died. Mary's last year was as tragic as all her life had been. Still thinking that she might yet have the child that would perpetuate her work, she mistook the symptoms of her disease; surrounded by the ruins of all she had striven for—self-produced ruins at that—she died on 17 November 1558. Twelve hours later Cardinal Pole followed her. It was a fitting close. The catholic reaction was over, though no one yet knew what exactly the Church and the religion of England were to be. The situation looked grim indeed. Church and state had decayed since the day on which King Henry was quick and dead. Neither Edward VI nor Mary lacked some of the qualities necessary in a Tudor sovereign. They had courage and intelligence, and they enjoyed the advantages of the king-worship of the day. But the rule, successively, of an incompetent idealist, a reckless adventurer, and a devout and devoted Spaniard had well-nigh ruined the achievement of the first two Tudors. Disorder at the top was again threatening the stability of the realm. The work of restoration was to prove relatively easy, because the foundations were much more solid than the years 1547-58 would suggest; but the real saving of England lay simply in the fact that Edward died young and Mary ruled for only five years. Good government came back in the nick of time. As for Mary, all she had achieved was to destroy both the old religion and the Spanish alliance by making them the heart of her policy. Even before the Council of Trent put it beyond doubt, the Marian reaction demonstrated that an anti-papal Church preserving the doctrine and ritual of pre-Reformation days was an impossibility; while the Spanish match began to teach Englishmen to see in Spain rather than France the national enemy. The main lines of Elizabeth's reign were determined from the start by her sister's disastrous failure.

Chapter IX

ENGLAND DURING THE PRICE REVOLUTION

NOTE. Of all the categories of historical writing those dealing with changes in economic and social life are least easily accommodated to ordinary critical divisions. In this chapter I shall therefore try to describe the main facts of sixteenth-century economic history, although this will involve much reaching back and forward from the point attained. This attempt to set out in outline the chief points of Tudor economic history is necessary—to avoid it would leave the picture very incomplete—but it is also doomed to some sort of failure. All over England research is going forward of the only kind that can ultimately tell us the truth—research into the economic and social history of individual localities and especially counties—and the results make the generalisations so confidently put forward by both past and present historians look ever more dubious. Yet we must have generalisations. These studies demand and use statistics; but Tudor statistics are bound to remain patchy and therefore very dangerous. This chapter is certainly not going to avoid all the pitfalls. All one can do is to sketch the broad lines of economic and social change in a particularly restless century, as they appear to one writer who has consulted the authorities and, while gratefully accepting most of what they say, feels compelled to dissent respectfully on some vital matters. The outstanding economic event of the period was an unprecedented inflation; prices—especially those of food—rose rapidly and persistently; and these changes were reflected in much upheaval, great distress, but also much opportunity for improvement. Not all the changes to be discussed were due to the price rise, and in many cases the effects of inflation were complicated by other factors; but the heart of the story is that increasing 'dearth' or dearness which contemporaries viewed with such dismay and so little comprehension.

I. THE INFLATION

AS has already been mentioned, the static or falling price levels which persisted for something like 150 years before the accession of the Tudors gave way round about the beginning of the sixteenth century to a gradual increase. Between 1500 and 1540 prices rose by a half; they then more than doubled

in the next twenty years; thereafter the curve flattened, but by the
end of the century prices were about five and a half times what
they had been 100 years earlier.[1] Of course, this rise must not be
thought of as a straightforward advance along a consistently
climbing line. Occasional sharp lifts must still be ascribed to the
ancient causes of famine and dearth; there were bad harvests in
the 1530s and 1590s which produced perfectly natural sudden
increases in prices. At times prices might even drop again a little.
But despite local and temporary differences it is plain that they
were constantly on the upgrade, that better harvests after a famine
did not reduce the price of wheat to its former level, and that
contemporary accounts of hardships reveal a persistent though
uneven and not altogether calculable inflation.

The causes of the phenomenon were but little understood at the
time. It was usual to think of the price of goods as stable, an
opinion which the experiences of the later middle ages of course
supported, exception being made only for times of shortage. But
now men were faced with rising prices in an age of comparative
plenty and they naturally thought, as men will, that the greed of
unscrupulous individuals was responsible. Inexperience was reinforced by doctrine—the medieval doctrine of the 'just price'. This
declared that everything had its proper price corresponding to an
abstract value fixed by natural law and consisting of such components as the true value of the material, the labour, and the time
which went to the making of the product. This just price was
always and everywhere the same, except that a shortage, by
increasing the value of the material, could increase the value of
the total product. Since the age also supposed that the value of
money represented the intrinsic value of the metal (its just price,
as it were), it followed that prices were invariably stable unless men
improperly and even blasphemously interfered with the natural
order. Both doctrine, therefore, and the common desire of
bewildered men to find a scapegoat led people to suppose that the
price rise could be arrested if only the unlawful and selfish doings
of the few were prevented from afflicting the many. The result
may be seen in the numerous statutes against those who enclosed
lands or rigged the market by forestalling and regrating, that is by
buying goods cheaply on their way to market and holding them to
sell when prices rose. It was a long time before thinkers recognised
that an inflation which affected at least all Western Europe was
likely to arise from deeper and more general causes. Not until 1574

[1] See Sir John Clapham, *Concise Economic History of Great Britain*,
pp. 186-7.

did a French philosopher, Jean Bodin, at last relinquish entirely the doctrine of the just price by discovering what may be called the modern theory on prices. This is that prices represent the relationship between the goods available and the money available. If goods become scarce while purchasing power remains equal, prices will rise; this was the common experience of the middle ages in times of famine. Originally dearth and dearness meant the same thing. Bodin understood that the same result would come about if the amount of money in circulation increased while the supply of goods remained more or less stable; this in its turn has been the basic cause of most modern inflations resulting from the putting out of paper money. Bodin therefore argued that the sixteenth-century price rise was due in the main neither to the malpractices of greedy men, nor to shortages, but to a vast increase in minted bullion, and in this he was perfectly correct.

The amount of money in circulation can be increased by a number of factors. More coin may be available from freshly minted bullion, from hoarded treasure, or through debasement (making the existing bullion go further), and an increase in the amount of trade itself, by accelerating the circulation of money, may add to the effective amount of coin. The later middle ages had suffered from a chronic shortage of bullion which in fact hampered trade, though it also benefited it by encouraging the invention of credit instruments. The needs of merchants led in the late fifteenth century to a more energetic exploitation of the chief European silver mines in Germany and Bohemia. The beginnings of the price rise are commonly ascribed to this. Even at this date major changes in price levels could not be confined to one country; the organisation and operation of trade was sufficiently international to make sure that fluctuations in one place would soon show in another. This was particularly true of England whose commercial life was dominated by the export trade in raw wool and woollen cloth, changes in which affected all men from the king (much of whose revenue came from wool customs) and the big merchant exporters down to the primary producers, whether they were big sheep-ranchers like the Yorkshire monasteries or the least little peasant who sold the wool off the backs of his few animals. Thus England almost at once shared in the rising prices of Western Europe.

The first serious English inflation, however, in the reign of Henry VIII, was due to particular local causes. Henry's early wars and Wolsey's diplomacy by subsidy greatly increased government spending and in particular released the treasure laid up by Henry

VII. The worst effects resulted directly from the government's manipulation of the coinage. In 1526 Wolsey undertook a recoining in the course of which he increased the money in circulation by reducing the weight of silver coins—the first instance of a serious debasement since the Conquest. Wolsey's action had this to recommend it: that it merely brought English coins into line with continental money, thereby preventing the loss of silver which always takes place when one country's coinage is 'better' (richer in silver) than another's.[1] But unfortunately the example was remembered eighteen years later when Henry VIII, once more engaged in war, found himself desperately short of money. The series of debasements between 1544 and 1551 reduced English coins to an unexampled state of badness. They altered both in weight and in 'fineness' (the proportion in their alloy of precious metal to base) until the silver content of each coin was only about a sixth of what it had been under Henry VII. This meant, of course, that the available silver could be recoined at a much greater face value, so that the crown technically made an enormous profit— something like £500,000 in all. But it was only seen afterwards that the debasement was bound to drive up prices so disastrously that the advantages of the nominal increase of revenue were soon lost. Debasement achieves its worst effects when people treat money as possessing a real value. In the sixteenth century a shilling piece containing 90 per cent. of silver was thought of as worth about four times as much as a shilling piece containing 25 per cent.: Latimer, in one of his sermons, cried that he had almost mistaken this new 'pretty little shilling' for an old groat. Since, in consequence, sellers of goods would not accept the new coin as equal to the old, prices rose swiftly and appallingly. For once economists got on to the trouble quickly enough; by 1551 it was realised that prices could only be stabilised and confidence restored if the debased coin was called in and reminted with a proper silver content. Unfortunately the duke of Northumberland, planning to do this, made two mistakes; he decided to reap just once more the short-term advantages of debasement, and he announced the proposed improvement of the coinage four months in advance. Since he thus first made the problem much worse and then warned all men that they would lose most of the money they would take

[1] 'Bad money driving out good', a principle known as Gresham's Law. Its essence is that people will hoard good coin and spend bad, so that less and less good coin is used, with cumulative effects showing in lack of confidence and lack of readiness to accept bad coin. That is, prices will rise again.

before the recoinage, it cannot surprise that prices shot up again in the summer of 1551. However, Northumberland then began a stabilisation which Elizabeth completed, and by 1560 English coins had recovered a decent silver content and the confidence of the nation. These irresponsible manipulations had caused disastrous hardships to many, but at last it could seem that the bad period was over and that the price rise had been arrested.

But the price rise continued. It was much less violent than before; there were years of stability and even years of recession; but by and large prices still rose—by something over sixty per cent. in the reign of Elizabeth. The correct reason was stated by Bodin in his analysis of the phenomenon. The discovery of enormous new sources of silver and also gold in South and Central America added so vastly to Europe's total of coinage that the whole of the price rise has been—not unjustly—linked with this single cause. Quantities of gold and silver entered Europe from the first days of the Discoveries, and the finding in 1545 of what seemed an inexhaustible mine—a solid mountain of silver—at Potosi in Peru ensured a steady flow of precious metal to the old world. The effects were first felt by Spain since that country first imported and exported the American silver, but international trade quickly spread them around the rest of Western Europe. England felt them very early, partly because of a flourishing direct trade with Spain in the first quarter of the century, but largely because the English cloth trade concentrated on Antwerp which was also the financial centre of the Spanish Empire.

These, briefly and with some simplification, are the causes conventionally assigned to the price rise in Tudor England. There is some argument about them; some scholars feel less and less certain about the effects of American silver and more and more inclined to look for particular reasons here and there. In any case, inflation is the natural state of mankind. The times when prices have remained static are very few, and they were usually bad times. A little gentle inflation stimulates trade, encourages enterprise, and tends to increase national wealth. What was so serious about the Tudor price rise was its suddenness and violence, most marked in the years between 1547 and 1551 whose troubles were certainly due in the main to a foolish and selfish financial policy. The effects of that inflation were indeed wholly bad.

When a stable community is suddenly attacked by an impersonal economic movement of great violence and long endurance, when moreover the enemy is not really recognised or sought in the wrong quarter so that no valid remedies are applied, the effects are many and far-reaching. Taken in all, they amounted to a revolution. This remains true even though earlier views of the sixteenth century as one of pure revolution in economics and society are no longer tenable. This was not—as used to be supposed—the time when capitalism first arose, involving an economy based exclusively on money relationships, an industry centred on a primitive factory system, and the appearance of a so-called middle class. It is quite apparent by now that all these developments had a very respectable ancestry right back into the middle ages, and that on the other hand much sixteenth-century life remained nearly untouched by these supposedly modern features. But because existing tendencies towards change were enormously stimulated by the price rise, so that movements discernible before became indisputably visible, it is still possible to speak of a revolution, a great and often violent change in the fortunes and standing of individuals, and in the methods by which men earned their living. But the new never swept the old away even though it may have pushed it aside.

2. THE LAND

Sixteenth-century England was and remained a predominantly agrarian country. Nine-tenths of the people earned their living on the land, and the remaining tenth retained some connection with it. There were few entirely urban people, for even townsfolk still had their fields around the borough, and even workmen in the woollen and other industries continued to add to their livelihood by growing things in plots of land. London alone was a town in the modern sense, with a population perhaps twenty times that of the next town in the realm, Norwich.[1] Even the proud mercantile ports—the rising Bristol, the declining Southampton and Hull—or the so-called manufacturing centres—Norwich, Coventry (declining), Manchester (rising)—were at best country towns or, to our eyes, large villages. Thus the land ruled everything, for on and by it people lived, and the economic effects of the price rise on the land were far and away the greatest. The basic changes arose from this: the rise in prices compelled people to make more out of their lands if they could, and they would find this easiest if they could sell produce on the rising market. In other words, the price rise encouraged—even compelled—what is known as the commercial exploitation of land. The three main ways of achieving this were changes in agrarian organisation and land tenure, changes in

[1] London can be estimated very tentatively at about 300,000 in 1600.

the kind of product produced, and improvements in agricultural method.

Of these three—which incidentally are really always found in co-operation—the last is the most obvious and may be quickly disposed of. Better methods of husbandry engaged attention throughout the Tudor period. Books were written to instruct improving farmers how to go about it. Sir Anthony Fitzherbert, one of his Majesty's judges, published works on husbandry and surveying in 1523; the shrewd Thomas Tusser's *Five Hundred Points of Good Husbandry* went through five editions between 1557 and 1580. Other Elizabethan textbooks on the use of marl, the special problems of the newly introduced hops, and similar points indicate the strength of the desire for the better use of land and new inventions to exploit it. Gradually the horse replaced the ox before the plough and cart. But the advance was slow and far from general. Cumbersome and inefficient ploughing, harvesting methods which wasted much of the straw, and the persistence of the open field with its narrow strips prevented really large-scale innovations. Hops, for instance, as a new crop which required compact fields where a man could experiment, established themselves in Kent where fields had always been enclosed. But all reservations allowed for, it is a fact that many Tudor landlords, small and great, tried to improve the yield of their lands by becoming better farmers. The foundations were being laid for the scientific farming of the eighteenth century.

However, changes of this kind take their time, and Tudor landlords, pressed for money as their incomes dwindled, required more rapid returns. One way of achieving this was to concentrate on stock-rearing. One hears of cattle-ranching on a considerable scale in the hill country of the west. Almost a new profession arose with the graziers or owners of large herds, often themselves butchers and retailers as well, and frequently attacked for combining trades which gave them a monopolistic hold over meat supply. But more important and more famous than cattle are the sheep. As we shall see, the first half of the century in particular was a time of increasing demand for wool, and throughout a rising population[1] provided more mouths for mutton—London especially proved a ready market there. Sheep were easy to keep and to feed on England's extensive grasslands; they required little labour

---

[1] Population figures are largely guess-work, though the increase is a fact. Mr A. L. Rowse (*The England of Elizabeth*, p. 218) accepts 4½ million in 1558 and 5 million in 1603 as the nearest he can get to the truth; these estimates are higher by a million than most people would think safe.

since one shepherd, his boy, and his dog could look after a whole
flock; and they yielded immense returns. There was therefore an
increase in sheep-farming, even if the contemporary picture—in
Sir Thomas More's graphic but unreliable phrase—of the sheep
devouring the men must not be accepted too readily. But many
men—if they could—turned from an unprofitable arable economy
to pasture; large stretches of farmland in the Midlands went under
grass in the earlier part of the century, with the result that some
villages quite disappeared (the modest basis of fact for the
hysterical complaints of depopulation raised by contemporaries);
and in East Anglia the demands of the local textile industries even
called forth a type of grazier who, owning no land, ran his flocks
on commons and waste ground. England has a good deal of land
unsuitable for extensive and intensive arable farming but admirably suited for the sheep; a gentry and yeomanry desperate for an
increased income to set off increased costs turned naturally to this
way out, sometimes with bad effects on rural economy, but by and
large to the increase of the national wealth. There is really no
evidence that the rising population went without food, except in
years of bad harvests, though the fear that more sheep-farming
would destroy food-supply was ever present to Tudor statesmen;
throughout the century, England tended to export both grain and
meat. In the present state of knowledge it looks as though the
increase in pasture-farming started about the middle of the fifteenth
century, continued steadily—despite government measures to
arrest it—to a peak in the years 1540-55, and then declined, in
part because the sheep had conquered about as much land as they
could, and in part because the bottom dropped out of the wool-
market. There are signs that more sheep were reared for mutton
in Elizabeth's reign than in Henry VIII's.

These changes in the practice of farming, whether better husbandry or concentration on stock, could only be carried out
efficiently by profoundly altering the distribution of land among
the people. It is in this—the changes in land-tenure and the
structure of the countryside—that the real agricultural revolution
of the century lies. The new methods required consolidated
holdings and individualistic exploitation which were not available
under the medieval system of agriculture. Of course, the traditional
view of one general manner of farming the land in use all over
England in the middle ages—with open fields around the village
divided into strips allotted to the villagers who necessarily adjusted
themselves to a common plan—is no longer tenable: many parts of
the country had never known this so-called classical open-field

system. But the chief corn-growing area—the eastern Midlands from Leicestershire and Warwickshire down to Berkshire, as well as much of Yorkshire, Lincolnshire, East Anglia, and parts of the Home Counties—fell within the area of the open fields. It was here that the movement for enclosing mostly applied. 'Enclosure' is a very general term—and usually simply a term of abuse—which covers at least three distinct operations. There was the individual tenant, often of villein stock, who began to buy up strips adjoining his own, put a hedge round the field so created, and farmed land thus cut off from the open fields. The movement in that direction was strong in the fifteenth century, a time of peasant prosperity, and the whole practice of enclosing seems to have arisen first in this form of enclosure for better small-scale farming. Then there was the bigger man who somehow consolidated large stretches of open field—by evicting his tenants or by purchase—and put the land to pasture; this—depopulating enclosure—was the evil inveighed against by the preachers and pamphleteers and resisted by the government. This form of enclosure dominated the first half of the sixteenth century. Lastly, there was the enclosing of commons and wastes. Every medieval village, however it arranged its farming land, had a common—some stretch of ground usually under rough grass on which the villagers pastured their animals and geese, or with bits of timber which were also shared proportionately. It is not too much to say that a village deprived of its rights of commons could not survive, and the machinations of some lords of manors who successfully intrigued and bullied to get exclusive use of commons for their sheep were of all the forms of enclosure the most resented. In Ket's agrarian grievances they played the biggest part.

This, then, was enclosing, the great evil—so contemporaries claimed—of the first half of the Tudor century. The total area affected by one form of enclosure or another was not large, though it is hard to give figures; perhaps 30 per cent. of the arable in an enclosing county (Northants or Leicester, for instance), or some 3 or 4 per cent. of its whole area, would be a generous estimate. One need only remember the great enclosing movement of the eighteenth century to get things into proportion. Hedges were raised and ditches dug in the sixteenth century, now to mark off some strips of open field thrown together by a peasant on the make, then again to distinguish the sheep run, or (worse) the park, or the big arable farm of a greater landlord or leasehold tenant, or perhaps to prevent the villagers from driving their cattle on the common where a speculator grazed his sheep. But much the greater part of the open fields remained open for another two centuries. Yet the effect of the enclosure movement cannot fairly be measured by extent alone. Not only was it—or rather the outcry against it—a political factor of some magnitude, but it also embodied a very deep-going change in rural economy.

Once the activities of small tenants had shown the way, the chief source of land for enclosure was to be found on the manorial demesne. Originally, very nearly every manor possessed a demesne, or land reserved to the lord of the manor and not let out to tenants, whether free or bond. In the open-field area that demesne consisted of strips distributed among the tenants' strips; elsewhere it might be one consolidated home-farm. On it—in the 'pure' form of the manorial economy—the villeins had done the labour for which their lord recompensed them with their own bits of land. The total of the demesne—its lands, its rights of common and woods and meadows, its buildings, and the rights of rents or services attached to it—was naturally very much bigger than any other single holding in manor or village. By the fifteenth century lords of manors had gradually ceased to farm their own demesnes; many, particularly the greater lords who held many manors, found it best to let the demesne to rent on lease to some tenant who might quite possibly be the wealthiest local peasant. Monasteries often leased their demesnes to those same local gentlemen who later bought the lands at the dissolution. In this way the lords of manors got a steady income from fixed rents, while the tenant made what he could out of his leasehold. For him the temptation to enclose was considerable, especially because he held a block of land well worth throwing into a consolidated farm, and so enclosures for agricultural purposes extended further.

Upon this relatively stable society, where such changes as took place in the holding and exploitation of land were small and achieved by purchase and agreement, there impinged the price rise. All at once the life of a rentier ceased to suit the lord. What had been a handsome regular income became first barely adequate and soon much too little as prices and costs rose. These lords underwent the common experience of men living on fixed incomes in a time of inflation: they found it impossible to keep up their standard of living in a world in which everything grew dearer while their revenues remained the same. On the other hand, tenants holding lands on the old terms and selling produce on a rising market were very favourably placed. The price rise put money in the pockets of the actual producers but took if from those of whom the lands were held. Thus men who had hitherto been content to let their lands at fixed rents now tried to get more out of them. They could try to recover direct control of the farms and themselves pocket the profits which enterprising agriculture was yielding, or they could try to raise rents. The first expedient, where practicable, was closely bound up with the more energetic exploitation of land which has already been discussed. Gentlemen and yeomen turned from corn to wool and later in the century back again to corn; they endeavoured to increase the yield by enclosing and by such scientific farming as was known to them; they exploited any additional resources there might be by mining for coal and dabbling in industrial pursuits, if their lands offered a chance. Also they often endeavoured to add to their lands. The price revolution assisted enterprise and luck; a man who acquired capital, either in farming, or in trading, or in the law, or even in marriage or the exploitation of an office under the crown, would wish to buy land both because it alone gave social standing and because it was a sound economic investment. More land meant an additional source of income. Thus there was a large body of eager purchasers for any land on the market, ready to spend their accumulated capital, or if necessary to borrow on security from the growing class of men who were as yet moneylenders but would soon become bankers, or again to take advantage of the instalment system which the government operated on its land sales. Before these buyers there was spread the most fluid land market since the Conquest—the lands of monasteries and chantries, of traitors and felons, of the bishops and of the crown, and at times of the great aristocratic lords who in the reign of Elizabeth were selling either because they needed money or more often because they wished to consolidate their property around their most important manors and to dispose of those in distant counties. Between them, the great land market and the desire for land—the one the outcome of the crown's attack on the Church and its own later needs, the other of the price rise—caused a widespread redistribution of landed property. The social effects of this shall be discussed later.

The substitution of direct farming for letting to rent, and the acquisition of fresh property constituted two ways in which the hardpressed upper classes could make ends meet (or in which the successful could grow exceedingly rich). The more direct way was simply to raise the rents they got from their lands and to increase the fines charged when one tenant succeeded another. There were many complaints against rack-renting (as it was called), a grievance less spectacular but more widespread than that against enclosing. But in fact both the recovery of lands previously let out and the raising of rents came up against obstacles in the law. The economic life of the countryside was dominated as much by the legal problems involved in the possession of land and the relationship between lord and tenant, as by the purely economic questions of the use of land. Feudal law recognised only one owner of land—the king—from whom all land was held on varying terms. In practice, however, lands held by one of the free tenures—the tenure in knight's service of the nobleman or gentleman, or the socage tenure of the smaller freeholder—were pretty secure and barely distinguishable from true possession. They were subject to demands. The freeholder paid a rent, but this had been fixed long before and constituted a small and diminishing burden under the new conditions. Lands in knight's service bore the various feudal incidents which were much resented, but these after all only occurred exceptionally and not at the whim of the lord. The upper ranks of society could feel secure in their possession of lands which technically they only held in tenure, unless they undermined their security by extravagance or got involved in the pitfalls of Tudor politics, with confiscations and forfeitures waiting upon the false step. The real problem of security arose in the lower orders—among the manorial tenants of individual lords.[1] Leaseholders presented a simple case. Their contracts terminated at some fixed day—most Tudor leases were short—so that lords could revise the rents at intervals or, if they wished, could resume direct use of their lands. Before the sixteenth century, leasehold was largely confined to the manorial demesne; when it became difficult to live on rents, demesne lands were the first to be taken back by progressive lords. But the demands of the new agriculture—especially of sheep-farming—required larger units than those strips of demesne scattered among villagers' strips in the common fields; a lord who wished to enclose in the Midland area of the open field needed to acquire lands held from him by tenure and not upon lease. Hence the 'rack-renting' landlord came up against the tenants' rights of the peasantry.

Peasant is a general term which covers a variety of status, wealth, and security. The commutation of labour services for a money rent and the leasing out of the demesne had altered the condition of the peasantry a good deal before the end of the fifteenth century. Bondage itself, the low social status of the villein with few rights and tied to his village and manor, was disappearing;

[1] It may be as well to point out that 'lord' in the sense constantly used means only a man holding a manor and does not imply that he was noble or even necessarily gentle.

though a few cases are known in Tudor times, economic change and the hostility of the common law were to make all Englishmen free and equal before the law by the time that Elizabeth died. Land held originally in villeinage was now held in one of three basic ways. The tenant could be 'at will', that is, he held the land as long as his lord pleased and on his lord's terms. He might, on the other hand, be a customary tenant whose right was protected by the 'custom of the manor' enrolled in the manorial court roll, or, if he was lucky, he might possess a copy of the record and be a copyholder. At first the decisive difference between the copyholder and the merely customary tenant was that the former could defend his tenure in the king's court where his 'copy' was admitted as evidence, while the latter had no remedy outside the manorial court held by his own lord. But by the middle of the sixteenth century, manorial custom was generally enforced in the king's courts, and what mattered then was not the technical name of the tenure but the terms on which an individual peasant held his land. Ideally, a copyholder would have an 'estate of inheritance' with fine certain: that is, when he died his heir succeeded and the lord had no say either in the disposal of the land or the size of the fine. Such tenants were the lucky elite of the peasantry. But if the entry on the court roll (whether or not a copy had been granted to the tenant) provided for a life-interest only or for a fine arbitrary (at the will of the lord), that copyholder was no better off than a tenant-at-will: his heir had to pay what the lord asked or get out. The differences in manorial custom were so many and so large—and so doubtful—that they provided the basis for a vast deal of litigation, in chancery, requests, and also at common law, in which the peasants as often as not succeeded in asserting their rights. Thus lords soon began to dislike these tenures; throughout the reign of Elizabeth there was a movement to alter copyholds into leases. Pressure could be applied or agreement secured, for the tenant too might prefer the precision of a leasehold to the uncertainties of custom, and by the time that the first Stuart ascended the throne leasehold had replaced copyhold as the characteristic contract of the agrarian system.

When, therefore, need or greed—or both—compelled lords of manors to raise the rents and burdens by which their tenants retained their lands, they were faced by a problem so complex that only an account of individual fortunes would really describe it. The very fact that all freeholders and most copyholders and customary tenants could resist pressure concentrated the attack on the unfortunate tenants-at-will, in any case by and large the poorest section of the peasantry. There was bound to be pauperisation of some, just because others, legally and economically better off, were going ahead. Simple economic causes—the price rise and the needs of lords of manors—took effect through people of very varying character and temperament. Many lords, especially in the north, preserved the ancient society through pride and conservatism, even if it meant that they themselves remained at best backward and at worst poverty-stricken. The men who bought monastic lands sometimes did so as a speculation: they bought in order to make a profit—either by reselling or by direct exploitation—and they therefore naturally raised rents and enclosed to the destruction of the more helpless tenants. But the romantic indignation of so many writers is misplaced. The majority of the monastic lands went to the established gentry and yeomanry who added them to their own lands and treated them like the rest. Exploitation was neither new nor general. After the middle of the century rents rose very markedly, though whether they rose more slowly or faster than prices—whether in fact they were truly rack-rents—is still being debated. The movement on the land market must have assisted the break-up of rural society, but we must not ascribe the decline of the peasantry to the activities of the supposed villains who dabbled in buying and selling land. Complaints against enclosing and rack-renting were heard before the monasteries were dissolved. Furthermore, not only the agents but also the victims of change were various, in their different tenures and copyhold rights, in their different capacities and accidents of luck or fate.

Though generalised conclusions must be stated, they must not be thought of as more than guides to that true understanding which only the investigation of county after county can bring. The causes of the upheaval were the price rise, the demand for wool, the free market in land. Its phenomena were trade in land, enclosing for both agriculture and pasture, the raising of rents and entry-fines accompanied if need was by eviction, and the general application of the principles of leasehold. The results were the creation of a considerable class of landless men who either earned a living by working as day-labourers for wages, or (a few of them) went to the towns, or turned to vagabondage; the rise of the substantial farmer holding on lease; and an increase in the so-called capitalist attitude (by no means new) which treats land as a source of wealth rather than as the basis of political function and social degree. The changes affected only parts of the country and not even those wholesale. Yet their total outcome was prodigious. The sixteenth century began the destruction of the English peasantry (at least in the South) and laid the foundation for that characteristic structure of landlord, leasehold farmer, and landless labourer which has marked the English countryside from that day to this. Compared with this change, the innovations in the practice and organisation of farming itself, not inconsiderable though they were, pale into insignificance.

3. INDUSTRY AND TRADE

Until the Industrial Revolution of the eighteenth century, industry definitely took second place to commerce. The man who made things was commonly a small craftsman, either independent or in the employ of a big merchant; the man who sold things could reach the heights of wealth, power, and social standing. The big problem of earlier days was to sell products: markets were thought of as limited, and though such an idea has roused the hearty laughter of free traders, Manchester liberals, and other moderns, it was much nearer the truth than the books lead one to suppose. While populations remained small and poor, and while transport difficulties limited range, it was very difficult indeed to expand existing markets and add to the volume of trade. Consequently there was less interest in increasing production, whereas in modern times, with markets either unlimited or falsely thought of as limitless, this latter point has become the main concern of economists. However, English trade has always rested on a firm foundation of English industry—it has never specialised in merely importing from one direction and exporting in another, as the great Dutch traders were to do—and in the sixteenth century there took place a real widening of horizons with prospects of an expanding trade. Not only were there the new markets overseas, the newly discovered lands on the coasts of Africa and America, the end of the Venetian monopoly in the Near East; there was also a general shaking up of established trade routes and marts in Europe itself which offered chances for the enterprising. Furthermore, the closer definition of the national state and the cash needs of the government encouraged a policy of producing at home rather than importing from abroad. These various stimulants produced a notable increase in English industrial activity; new manufactures were introduced and old ones improved. It has almost become the fashion to speak of an industrial revolution in the sixteenth century, but that is to debase a very useful term. The changes, though considerable by comparison with the small amount of industry then in the country, were really on too small a scale to deserve such a resounding name.

The only two medieval industries pursued on a sufficiently large scale to require a major organisation were textiles and shipbuilding. (Building, which might have rivalled them, was in the hands of thousands of individual craftsmen.) Ships continued to be built in Tudor times near or in all the major ports; their number increased, though their size did not, and no change in method took place. In the clothing industry the chief developments to note are the introduction of new textiles and the adoption of a few pieces of machinery. The old staple products—woollens and worsteds—began to lose favour, partly because their export declined in the second half of the century and partly because fashion demanded finer and lighter cloths. Hence we find the so-called new draperies (bays and says) encouraged by the government; the use of cotton in fustian began in Lancashire (*c.* 1600); silk was attempted. Yet wool retained pride of place. England exported in the main unfinished or 'white' cloth—undyed and not treated to the point where the tailor would use it—to the industrial centres of Flanders and Brabant where the rough cloth was turned into the finest stuff in Europe. Of course, some cloth had always been finished in England for the home market, but the English finishers (even the elite among them, the dyers) were insufficiently skilled, and the Flemings refused to buy any but white cloth. Attempts to concentrate all cloth manufacture in England—to exploit industrially England's virtual monopoly of the raw material—thus proved only partially successful. The new inventions mattered little. Since at least the thirteenth century cloth had been fulled (beaten in water to felt the fibres) by water-driven mills; now there was added a gig-mill to raise the nap for shearing, a stocking-frame on which stockings could be knitted more rapidly than by hand, and the Dutch loom which made possible a sort of mass production of narrow goods like ribbons. All were resented by the workers as dangers to employment, and none amounted to more than a slight adjustment in one or two minor processes. More stockings were certainly produced and worn, and also more English-made ribbons, but this chief of England's industries was in the main remarkable for changing very little.

There was also virtually no change in organisation. As before, the yarn was spun in countless cottages and then woven into cloth by weavers on their hand-looms in their own houses. For a long time now, the industry had been dominated by capitalist clothiers —the putters-out—who supplied the yarn to the domestic weaver, took the finished product, and paid him wages. This early stage of capitalist organisation (the domestic system) seems to have conquered almost the whole field in the sixteenth century; cloth of whatever sort was produced in this manner—new draperies and old, woollens and worsteds and mixed, linens and cottons and silks. It used to be thought that some enterprising clothiers inaugurated the factory system by bringing their weavers under one roof, but even the factory of the celebrated Berkshire clothier, Jack of Newbury, has had doubts thrown on it. The industry was well past the truly domestic stage when a man's wife span for him the wool of his own sheep for him to weave; the clothiers, originally middlemen between weaver and merchant, had long established their firm hold on it. Bad times for them—and they were to be bad through most of Elizabeth's reign—meant unemployment for many, with complaints, even riots, and ineffective government interference to stimulate the trade which would set the looms going again. On the other hand, in those days before the building of textile mills, the various workers in the industry did not depend exclusively on wages. The domestic weaver usually had a patch of land; even this largest of all English industries, employing by far the biggest number of workers, did not involve the existence of a purely wage-earning class. To find that one must look to building, for since this occupation was both urban and migratory it offered none of the chances of independent side-lines which the cloth-worker still enjoyed.

Wool required capital, but the new industries developing in the century needed it even more. Mining, in particular, showed signs of remarkable life. Some coal had always been dug for use as fuel in the neighbourhood of the mine; now, with the decay of the great forests, coal was gradually replacing wood or charcoal as the main fuel in both domestic and industrial use. London imported some 15,000 tons a year in Elizabeth's reign—coal carried by colliers from the Newcastle fields and therefore dubbed sea-coal. Transport difficulties, however, restricted the spread of coal to the sea-board, and technical difficulties prevented its use in the industry which needed it most, iron smelting. The necessary process—the making of coke and its use in furnaces—was not invented till the beginning of the eighteenth century. But other industries used coal. The saltpans of Cheshire and the North-East needed much; one capitalist enterprise on the Wear, extracting salt from sea-water, employed some 300 men. Coal was used in the refining of sugar and the manufacture of glass, both processes introduced into the country in this century, and in soap-boiling which expanded enormously. Nor was coal the only product to be mined. Henry

VIII looked for gold in Wales, and some of the worn-out silver mines were investigated again by a government in need of cash. More particularly, however, the government concentrated on finding zinc-ore (calamine), a mineral vital to the manufacture of brass which in turn was needed for the new cannon. In the reign of Elizabeth, England began to export pieces of artillery to the continent. Saltpetre was sought and found for the making of gunpowder; alum for its use in the dyeing of cloth. The metal industries developed, though handicapped by the growing shortage of charcoal; rolling mills for the production of sheet metal and drawing mills for that of wire were built. The whole movement was still scattered, piecemeal, and confined to a small proportion of the population. But all these processes required equipment and therefore capital; their growth foreshadowed the growth of a genuine factory industry and provided both incentive and example for later expansion.

These major industries had one thing in common: they were not subject to the medieval gild organisation, either because they were new, or because they were pursued in the country. Gilds were associations of urban craftsmen, designed to protect their own interest by maintaining a local monopoly and (ostensibly) the customer's by maintaining a high standard of work. Many of them performed also social and religious functions; these suffered heavily from the legislation of Edward VI's reign which confiscated chantry and gild endowments made for 'superstitious' purposes. But on their economic side, too, as organisations of crafts and manufactures, the gilds declined in the sixteenth century. As early as the fourteenth, the various processes involved in cloth-making (though not the finishers), leaving the towns in search of the water power demanded by the new fulling mill, had emancipated themselves from gild regulations. Now with the rise of new crafts and with a growing disregard for the monopolies of gilds, the old organisations decayed. National legislation took the place of municipal legislation. Statutes dealing with the proper making of cloth or leather rendered superfluous the piecemeal enactments of gilds on which they very often rested. Thus the great statute of artificers of 1563, an industrial code which among other things wished to enforce a seven-years' apprenticeship in all trades including husbandry, was most effective when the local craftsmen's companies employed its assistance to enforce their own views on apprenticeship. The decline of the gilds was reflected in the tendency to amalgamate several widely different trades into one association; the Ludlow hammermen of 1511 controlled not only ironworkers but also masons, and the Hull goldsmiths' company included in 1598, among others, plumbers and basket-makers. Though the gilds survived for a long time they soon ceased to play a part in the structure of English industry; their last attempts to continue their control collapsed after 1660 when the state ceased to support their aspirations.

The organisation which prospered in the sixteenth century was the livery company, first seen in London whose twelve great companies, old and new, came to rule the city in this period. Companies of this sort, though nominally composed of certain trades (as the London mercers, fishmongers, goldsmiths, and so on), were less concerned with industrial and craft problems than with municipal politics; their members were the great men of the city, not its manufacturers, and they made their position as merchants.[1] Other towns soon copied the London example. Henry VIII, Elizabeth, and James I all chartered such companies who clamped a firm control on the affairs of their municipality. The expansion of industry and trade brought with it not a growing freedom for individual craftsmen and merchants, but an increasing complexity of monopolistic organisations which bought their privileges at heavy cost from an impoverished crown and recouped themselves by steering all possible profit towards their own members. These organisations fell into two groups. The so-called regulated companies were associations of individuals each working on his own with his own capital but licensed by his membership to pursue his trade and subject to the rules of his company. In industry gilds and their descendants, the great companies, represented this kind of organisation. By their side, the needs of an expansionist age raised companies based on joint-stock. The principle here was that several men put their capital into a common enterprise and either took it back with a share of the profits when the company wound up, or—if it carried on—drew a dividend (a share of the profits) proportionate to their investment. The advantages of this second kind of company were felt in affairs which required a considerable initial outlay of capital. They were more important in foreign trade, but industry could use them too, especially in the various mining experiments which required both the capital which only joint-stock could provide and the monopoly only to be got from a royal charter. Such were the Mines Royal Company and the Mineral and Battery Works, both incorporated in 1568 but developed from earlier

---

[1] Of the London 'Great Twelve' only the clothworkers were not mercantile, but many lesser craft-gilds continued a decreasingly influential existence.

enterprises in mining, the making of brass, and the casting of cannon.

There was thus plenty of life in English industry, so much so that one is in some danger of overrating the scale on which things happened. In economic growth the categories of reigns and political history are particularly meaningless, and the phenomena discussed really came to fruition under the early Stuarts. The sixteenth century merely laid foundations, even as the seventeenth only expanded these foundations upon which the genuine industrial revolution of the eighteenth was to build. Yet the growth of industry under the Tudors—the development of both old and new crafts, the expansion of coal and mineral mining, the elaboration of industrial organisation—is marked enough to require explanation. What stimulated all this? There was some profit inflation because prices rose faster than wages, so that the industrialists' costs lagged behind their increasing profits. This encouraged enterprise and the accumulation of capital for expansion. The profit inflation was not as great as was once supposed, and other things played their part, as for instance the new inventions, the greater purchasing power of the home market, England's freedom from internal war, and her ancient industrial traditions— though much greater traditions did not prevent the rapid decline in this period of the industries of Flanders, Germany, and Northern Italy. Mining developments owed much to the needs of gentlemen who had to exploit their lands in other ways than by farming. War stimulated especially the metal industries; the new brass manufactures depended on such factors as the government's need for artillery. The increasing population probably assisted the clothing industry whose periods of decline are attested only as far as exports are concerned, while we know nothing of its home market. Luxury trades in ribbons, silks, laces, and so forth received support from the growing ostentation of the upper classes trying to copy Italy and France and enabled to do so by the expansion of their own incomes as both agriculture and office-holding grew more and more profitable. All in all, the marked if limited expansion of the century resulted from as striking a mixture of causes as its own haphazard and varied character would lead one to believe. But among them the effects of the inflation, causing changes, forcing action, and rewarding efforts in all sorts of trades, must come first.

The story of trade is both more straightforward and much more important. The industrial changes already described in a manner reflect the vicissitudes of trade: the expansion of Elizabeth's reign, with its new industries and new organisations, in part resulted from the decline of the main export trade of the first half of the century. Admittedly, straightforward or not, the whole story cannot yet be told and may never in fact be fully known. In the first place, we know too little of internal trade; that is, we know that it took place, we suspect that it increased and that Elizabethan Englishmen bought more—were wealthier—than their Henrician fathers, but we can rarely measure it. The story is thus confined to goods exported and recorded in the various documents produced by the customs service. Here arises the second difficulty: except in London, there was a great deal of smuggling, often connived at or even encouraged by the customs officials, and the figures of exports which can be produced represent neither the total turnover of trade nor an accurate yardstick of industrial production, but merely the percentage of trade which paid its tribute to the royal coffers. The smuggling of this time concentrated not on the import of taxable luxury articles as it did in the classic age of smuggling literature, the eighteenth century; it concentrated on the free export of customable goods and of goods whose export was forbidden except under special licence from the crown—which licence had to be paid for. Thus foodstuffs—especially wheat and barley—were taken from the East Anglian ports to the continent; even in time of war the government could not stop the trade with France and Scotland. Coin and bullion, too, trickled through the leaky net of the customs controls, despite proclamations to the contrary. Sixteenth-century legislation must ever be regarded as evidence of intentions rather than as a policy rigidly carried out, and this is especially true of economic legislation and customs regulations. One can only hope—with some reason—that the proportion between legitimate and illicit trade remained much the same throughout, so that the known figures at least describe with some accuracy the trends and changes in English trade.

The chief English export was cloth; everything else—leather, hides, tin, lead, grain, coal, and later the new manufactures—came a long way behind. During the fifteenth century, cloth woven in England and exported mainly to the Netherlands to be there finished for re-export took over from the raw wool previously exported to the continental weaver. In the earlier sixteenth century the trade concentrated more and more on one channel—Antwerp. Flourishing trades with Italy and Spain decayed at this time as that great city rose to its commercial supremacy in the Habsburg empire and sat itself astride England's trade routes to the continental interior. Antwerp's monopoly called into being an English monopoly. To trade in the emperor's dominions, an English merchant needed a licence, and these imperially licensed 'merchant adventurers haunting Brabant' (that is, living and trading in Antwerp) soon captured most of the export of cloth—mainly of white cloth—from England. These Merchant Adventurers were based on London, being mostly freemen of the mercers' company, and they succeeded in the course of the first half of the century in destroying their English rivals at Southampton (once the centre of the trade with Italy and Spain) and Hull (which had traded directly with Scandinavia) by exploiting their monopoly of the easiest and cheapest route by which England's chief manufacture could be exported. The export of cloth from London increased about threefold between 1500 and 1550, a period of such mounting prosperity that trade could be freed far beyond the usual practices of the time. Restrictions on cloth export vanished, English merchants ceased to harry their German rivals of the Hanseatic League because there was trade enough for all, and the usury laws (which limited trading expansion and the investment of capital) collapsed until, in 1546, parliament admitted the propriety of taking interest upon loans. These fair conditions suffered occasionally from disruption by war, but, as we have already had occasion to point out, it was more usual for war and politics to accommodate themselves to the chief English and Flemish commercial interest. The cloth trade affected not only the Merchant Adventurers but also the clothiers who supplied the exporters, the weavers and spinsters in the clothier's employ, and everybody back to the man who owned and herded the sheep, the ultimate source of all this activity and wealth. Thus the alliance with the Habsburg rulers of the Netherlands—with the Emperor Charles V and therefore with Spain—rested on a mutual economic interest much stronger than the differences over Henry VIII's wives or religion.

This period of expanding trade was assisted, if not caused, by the price rise. In the 1520s direct trade with Spain brought generous profits as the wealth of America drove up prices there before the rest of Europe followed suit, so that English merchants could buy cheap at home and sell dear in Spain. Even when matters levelled out, England remained in a position of advantage. The flood of the price rise reached Antwerp before London—indeed, Antwerp was the chief means of extending the general rise beyond the Channel—so that the purchasing power of money always remained a little higher in England than on the continent. That meant that English merchants were persistently trading from a country of lower prices into one with higher—selling for more than they paid out—with results which encouraged them to develop the trade to the limit. Then, in the years 1550-2, artificial aids suddenly drove the cloth trade into an enormous and unhealthy increase. The debasement of the English coinage had its natural effect of stimulating exports because it lowered the exchange rate between London and Antwerp. Where £1 English was worth 32s. Flemish in 1522, it was worth 26s. 8d. in 1526 and only 13s. 4d. in 1551. In other words, an English merchant who bought a £1's worth of cloth in England and offered it for sale in Antwerp at what had been his usual profit seemed, to the purchaser, to be asking only half of what he had asked before. Naturally Antwerp rushed to buy, exports rose to amazing heights, and merchants welcomed the debasement. But in this they were alone. As has been seen, the debasement endangered the internal economy of England by destroying confidence in her coinage; it also ultimately ruined government finance, even though it began by aiding it in an unrepeatable manner. So unfavourable a rate of exchange closed the only way out when all possible profit had been made from land sales and recoinage—the raising of loans abroad. Natural causes (exchange rates tend to stabilise in time) and the desire of the government for sounder finance led to the activities of Northumberland and Elizabeth in restoring the coinage to some soundness and therefore the rate of exchange to near-normal. The agent employed by both Mary and Elizabeth to act for the government in Antwerp was Sir Thomas Gresham, a leading London merchant and financier who was to found the Royal Exchange. Gresham proved a skilful diplomatist who raised loans for his government at such unpropitious moments as the accession of Elizabeth, but his claim that he had restored the exchange and therefore solvency by his manipulations arose from a misunderstanding. The exchange rate recovered as the silver content of English coins recovered; for good English money the Antwerp exchangers would pay their 20s. or more of Flemish coin as they had done before the debasement.

The end of the disastrous inflation also ended the boom in the export trade. After 1552 the volume of cloth exported fell with a crash, and the third quarter of the century was full of slumps and depressions. The expansion of the half-century had led to an increase in sheep-farming and in the manufacture of cloth; now land had to revert to arable, and clothiers and weavers felt the pinch. Other causes assisted. The 'Spanish Fury' of 1576, which destroyed Antwerp, only sealed the steady decline which that vital

commercial centre underwent with the accession of Philip II in
1555. Charles V had always protected the interests of the Netherlands, even at the risk of tolerating heresy. His son was to ignore
this, the most prosperous and valuable part of his dominions,
preferring instead to rely on the unproductive and disastrous
wealth of America and to pursue a religious policy fatal to the
interests of Flanders. During the reign of Elizabeth, for reasons
which England could not affect, the simple steady trade of the first
half of the century came to an end. Wars, religion, and politics now
took precedence over commerce, at a time when the economic
conditions had in any case turned against further expansion. The
boom of the early 'fifties marked in effect the end of the Antwerp
trade and the happy conditions when the Merchant Adventurers
of London ran a hugely profitable business without having to
obtain a formal monopoly or fight off foreign rivals because there
was enough for everybody. The later 'fifties and the 'sixties were
a time of depression when trade stagnated and the government
was inundated with complaints from unemployed clothworkers.
Both the needs of the trade and the permanent Tudor fears of
unrest compelled the government to intervene at a time when the
merchants began to look to restriction and rigid monopolies for
their salvation. Trade had to do two things—to find new outlets if
it could, and to be more dog-in-the-manger about the old. The
reign of Elizabeth was an age of control and organisation, following
upon a period of virtual free trade.

The Merchant Adventurers naturally suffered most from the
difficulties which had arisen in the Netherlands trade. The closing
of their staple at Antwerp compelled them to find a new continental
depot; after many travellings and attempts to settle both on the
Elbe and the Ems, from where they could easily have exploited the
trade with Central Germany, they came to rest at Middelburgh in
the Northern Netherlands in 1598. But their great days were really
over.[1] Admittedly they seemed more powerful than ever and even
increased their own exports. But this they could only do by
driving all rivals from the field and monopolising the reduced
amount of cloth exported each year.[2] They obtained government

---

[1] Mr A. L. Rowse, in reverting to a traditional but dubious view of the
Merchant Adventurers, claims great things for them in the reign of
Elizabeth (*The England of Elizabeth*, pp. 116, 149-50). He is right to
warn us against judging the sixteenth century by the conditions of the
nineteenth, but his rather airy account ignores the facts as recited by
Unwin (cf. below, p. 248n.).

[2] In the last quarter of the century exports remained steadily about
20 per cent. below the high level reached in mid-century.

action against the German Hanse whose privileges were revoked in 1552, restored at Philip's request in 1554, and taken away by Elizabeth in 1558 after the Germans had broken off relations in high dudgeon. A long and fruitful association thus came to an end, but not until the usefulness of the German traders had nearly disappeared in the internal decay of their league and the decline of the English cloth trade. Worse still, the Merchant Adventurers limited the activities of their own members. They turned upon the so-called New Hanse within their ranks—provincial members admitted with reservations in 1497—and excluded them from the trade, while even the solid London core of the 'Old Hanse' was forced to adhere to a stint (or quota of exports) which prevented the company from promoting an expansion of the industry or acting (as it was once thought to have done) as the agent of a vigorous English penetration abroad. In 1564 the Merchant Adventurers at last obtained a royal charter granting them in effect a monopoly in the export to Europe of white cloth—the cloth with the readiest market—and thereafter they were content to maintain what they had won. Their monopoly did not remain unchallenged; especially towards the end of the reign, as the difficulties caused by the Spanish war began to diminish, numbers of 'free-traders' or 'interlopers'—merchants not of the company but trading in its territory—greatly annoyed the Adventurers who again and again pleaded for action with the government.

The Adventurers' monopoly was attacked both in their own day by interlopers and their representatives in parliament, and later by economic historians.[1] It has been shown that they failed to help the cloth industry to expand, and even to exploit to the full the potential it had displayed in the boom years. They did not promote the national interest but (understandably) those of some merchants whose profits they thought could only be maintained by limiting trade. Their own argument ran that markets were restricted: there was only so much trade to go round, and if they let others have a share they would go short themselves. Hence they set their faces against the German Hanse, their own New Hanse, and the interlopers. The idea that trade is naturally limited was anathema to Victorian freetraders, though perhaps it seems more convincing again now. In sixteenth-century conditions there was

[1] Especially George Unwin in his lectures on 'The Merchant Adventurers in the Reign of Elizabeth', *Studies in Economic History*, pp. 133ff. Although Unwin probably underrated the company's difficulties and failed to understand the position of the government, his work remains fundamental to the subject.

something to be said for it: populations stood still or rose only slowly, while their wealth almost certainly declined in the wars of religion which swept the continent for a hundred years after 1550; transport difficulties stood in the way of opening up new trade; conflicts and nationalist barriers everywhere were ruining the freedom of the later middle ages. Conditions were, in fact, comparable to those of the twentieth century rather than the nineteenth; then, as now, depressions led to trade restrictions and attempts at self-sufficiency. Hampered by the small number of potential purchasers and the relatively small area they could cover, the Merchant Adventurers had quite a good case, but they overdid it, as the interlopers proved. The only really sound argument for the company is that in the unquiet conditions of the time only a strongly organised body, with authority and reputation to back it, could establish a steady trade; this view supposes that the interlopers cashed in on the position created by their enemies. With this point the Adventurers themselves made most play, but proof is difficult if not impossible. On the whole, taking into account that all Europe practised trade by companies and in the form almost of international treaties, one gives the Adventurers the benefit of the doubt: they were necessary. Nevertheless, their monopoly did not advance trade or help the clothing industry.

The government, too, have received much blame for permitting and licensing the monopoly. Here the answer is simple. Burghley, in particular, was fully aware of the disadvantages, and during the depression which followed the virtual breach with Spain in 1586 he tried to help trade by freeing it; but the interests opposed to free trade were too strong. The government, pressed by Gresham, had in the first place made the monopoly possible—by the break with the Germans and the charter of 1564—simply because it needed the money which only the Adventurers were in a position to advance. After 1558, when new customs rates raised the value of the cloth custom, the government depended financially on the good will of the chief cloth exporters. The whole policy of granting monopolies—the trading companies, the farming out of various customs (especially on wines), ultimately the granting of manufacturing monopolies (for instance in leather)—followed simply from the crown's penury: monopolies were sold and the purchaser paid heavily. It did not help that many courtiers profited from the practice and encouraged it without special regard to the needs of the crown, but the queen herself and her chief minister acted under financial duress. Especially was this the case with the Merchant Adventurers who offered their loans and assistance in return for special privileges. The price rise, which badly injured the finances of the crown, thus assisted the tendency towards monopoly and restriction which dominated the economic policy of Elizabeth's government. It may be added that in part at least this policy resulted also from a desire to put things in a rigid order and system. Fluid expansion and changeability were not welcome to Elizabethan statesmen with their passion for degree and order. Cromwell and the profiteers of Henry VIII's time had a better appreciation of the advantages of change than the rigid queen and her conservative ministers.

The story of the new companies seeking to open up new trades is rather more cheerful. The Elizabethan age witnessed England's entry into transoceanic trade. The collapse of the traditional market released production for new markets and in fact compelled search for them; the discoveries of the previous half-century showed the way; the inflation supplied both the capital needed for investment and the hope of large profits which drew forth that capital. The real story of Elizabethan commercial and geographical enterprise centres round these new routes and new organisations.[1] They, too, have been attacked as monopolistic and restrictive, and once again an abstract case can be made out against them. But it is a worse case than that against the Adventurers, for new trade with such distant lands as Russia or the coast of Africa required an organisation to start it. This was proved especially in India where the trading company had to act virtually as a sovereign power commanding armed forces and conducting diplomatic negotiations. However, the Tudor period only saw the beginnings of the vast expansion. A number of projects were started, some as regulated companies modelled on the Merchant Adventurers (for instance the Eastland Company—1579—trading with the Baltic), some as joint-stock. The first joint-stock enterprises were organised only for one journey: Hawkins' slaving expeditions to Africa in 1562-7 and Drake's circumnavigation in 1577-80 were famous Elizabethan examples of an extension of the partnership principle of which instances can be found earlier. A number of people— merchants, seamen, courtiers, country gentlemen, even the queen —put up the capital needed, taking it back with a share of the profits at the end of the voyage. But in 1555 Sebastian Cabot and a group of London merchants founded the Muscovy Company, the first trading company whose joint-stock remained in use from voyage to voyage, and in the same year individual enterprises in Africa culminated in the foundation of the Guinea Company. In

[1] The maritime side of the matter is discussed below. Ch. XII.

1581 there was added the Levant Company which mainly subsisted on a very lucrative monopoly of the trade in currants, and in 1600 some merchants of this company obtained a charter for trading in East India—the beginning of the East India Company, the greatest of them all. Similar organisations were used in the early colonial enterprises, such as Raleigh's Virginian settlements from 1584 onwards. The companies often passed through difficulties: the Levant Company suffered so severely from the Spanish war that it had to reorganise itself by 1589 as a regulated company, a more rigid body with less risk but also less chance of expansion. Greater days awaited both the trading and the colonising companies under the Stuarts, but handsome and notable beginnings were made in the reign of Elizabeth when English traders found their affairs forcing them to follow the romantics overseas.

In trade and commerce, too, the sixteenth century was a restless period, an age of marked advances and disastrous depressions, but in general of improvements. Trade expanded—at first through the old continental markets and later through new markets in the opening world. The difficulties of the government and the selfishness of established merchants encouraged a restrictive policy whose worst effects were only avoided because it could never be rigorously enforced. The age was not—as some would have us believe—one of unhindered and lavish expansion. Indeed, to the Elizabethans themselves it seemed dark and distressful, with war and depression destroying England's commerce and wealth. In fact it laid sound foundations for later expansion in industry and trade. To the best of our knowledge national wealth increased markedly. In part this resulted from legitimate trade and in part from the piracy which made up for the ruin it caused to trade by importing stolen bullion; but the most solidly prosperous part of English life was its booming agriculture. Altogether, the price inflation, while it brought much hardship and many problems, also offered fine chances which did not go begging.

4. SOCIAL CHANGES

In his account of the government of England, written in the first half of Elizabeth's reign, Sir Thomas Smith listed the various classes of men.[1] He divided them into four groups—gentlemen, citizens and burgesses, yeomen artificers, and labourers. Among

[1] He probably borrowed the whole section from William Harrison's *Description of England* (cf. *De Republica Anglorum*, ed. Alston, pp. xvi seqq.).

gentlemen he included the king and the nobility, classifying the latter into greater (aristocracy) and lesser (knights). These, together with esquires (those entitled to bear arms), make up the gentlemen—'those whom their blood and race doth make noble and known'—and Smith thought that the English manner of 'making gentlemen so easily' was an advantage to the realm. Citizens and burgesses are the substantial inhabitants of the towns. As for the yeomen, Smith equated them with the 40s. freeholders who had the vote in county elections and served on juries; he grew quite enthusiastic over their sterling qualities and happy condition. The rest he admirably defined as 'the fourth sort of men which do not rule'—husbandmen and labourers, craftsmen and artificers, and even all merchants and copyholders without free land. The principle of his classification, however, is exceedingly artificial. It is not by wealth: many a merchant could rival the proudest gentleman in England, and many a copyholder had more land than the average freeholder. Freehold was relatively rare, and Smith's definition of the yeomanry is much too narrow. At the same time, his definition of the gentry appears to be too wide for modern opinion which (as we shall see) has tried to find a class distinction between noblemen and gentlemen. His ascription of nobility to the knighthood falsifies the picture completely, though it may have made it more comprehensible to the French public for which he orginally wrote. Smith's fourth class includes both substantial men and the very poorest. Up to a point his catalogue rests on birth, but since birth—even by this time villein birth—was not in England an obstacle to advancement or deterioration in status he had to admit the ease with which men became gentle. Fundamentally his criterion is tenure and the duties that go with it, a criterion of much less significance in the sixteenth century than in earlier days.

Smith's list is antiquarian; it takes insufficient notice of the fluidity of a social structure buffeted by the price rise. But it is a reasonable beginning for an understanding of the problem, and it should act as a warning against the modern tendency to impose a class structure on the sixteenth century. The whole concept of class belongs to an industrial and urban society; it should be altogether discarded for a society which indeed rested on degree and differences in status but knew no economic divisions rigid enough to be called classes. The Tudor age is not the age of the rise of the middle class, let alone the bourgeoisie, both meaningless terms in the context. The story is much more subtle and difficult than that, and the only distinctions which it is perhaps worth making are three: the prince, those sort of people that took their part in government (nobility, gentry, even yeomanry in the widest sense, but also the merchants and lawyers commonly indistinguishable from the gentlemen), and those who took no part. A brief section of this sort cannot hope to clarify the whole question of English social structure in the sixteenth century: we shall treat of the effects of the price rise on the crown, the gentry, and the poor.

Nothing perhaps shows up Sir Thomas Smith's conservatism so much as his inclusion of the prince among his gentlemen. There was good reason in past history and in etymology for so doing, but it was contemporary nonsense. The Tudors had raised the crown to a place of lonely eminence which even its possession by a child and a couple of women could not threaten for long. Despite many authoritative statements to the contrary, the sixteenth century managed quite well to distinguish between the crown and its holder. A visible embodiment of state and nationhood was of enormous political value—indeed, it still is—but that does not mean that men could not grasp the mystical entity of the crown as an almost religious symbol and think of it apart from the human being to whom they paid such semi-religious honours because he (or she) was clothed in the majesty of monarchy. We must remember that a religious age has less difficulty in dealing in abstracts than a scientific age, though it will also make a less clear distinction between the abstract and the concrete, the mystical and the personal. Tudor king-worship came at times perilously near to idolatry, but commonly it embodied rather a natural confusion between the specific and the general attributes of the crown—the person on the one hand, the emblem of nationality and statehood on the other. It need surprise us the less that an unrelenting devotion to monarchy could go hand in hand with a decline in the powers of the crown in the second half of the century. The cause of the decline was simple: the inflation depressed the royal income and increased the royal expenditure.
       During an inflation, as has already been pointed out, those who live on fixed incomes suffer because their revenues remain the same while everything they have to buy grows dearer. Of all people, the king (or queen) was most relentlessly pressed by that difficulty. The crown's finances had been established on a sound basis by Henry VII on the supposition that rents from lands were the best sort of income; these the price rise rendered progressively less valuable. Unlike other landlords the crown could not adapt itself: its lands were too vast and the income required too large to

make direct exploitation of land feasible, while the practices of rack-renting and raising fines could hardly be pushed to extremes by the official guardian of the poor. As it was, rents and fines rose on crown lands, but never sufficiently to compensate for the price rise. The other foundation of the royal finances, the customs, suffered from unavoidable maladministration: not until 1558 was a realistic tariff put on the chief English export (cloth), while smuggling and the peculations of officials away from the administrative centre reduced the value of this source. The government of Elizabeth therefore resorted to farming: at intervals some or even all the customs revenue was sold to courtiers and syndicates who for a lump sum bought the right to extract the customs for themselves. This at least ensured a steady income and cut down administrative costs, but it meant that the elasticity of the customs revenue—its chief advantage—tended to benefit the farmer and not the crown. Parliamentary taxation proved less expedient under Elizabeth than under her predecessors because the commons and the queen wished to pursue different policies: rather than face them often, Elizabeth did without subsidies.

There were other ways of augmenting revenue. Crown lands were sold, licences and offices granted for money, episcopal property came to the crown. Many expedients both sensible and undesirable were resorted to, but the only effective one was rigid economy, the much-maligned 'parsimony' of Elizabeth and Burghley. Contrary to Tudor habit, the queen—a woman fond of show and glitter—had to cut and pare because she was poor. For while skilful and desperate administration succeeded in raising the ordinary income of the crown to two or three times what it had been under Henry VIII, expenditure kept easily ahead of this. The price rise vastly increased the cost of keeping up the royal palaces and household, the armed forces, the diplomatic service; all the unavoidable expenses of government rose steadily till towards the end of Elizabeth's reign Burghley estimated them at £200,000 at least, twice as much as the whole revenue of the crown in 1530 which had been adequate for all purposes. When on top of that there came war with Spain and the constant drain of Ireland, all Burghley's measures failed. Elizabeth died £400,000 in debt, leaving also a legacy of trouble over the financial expedients of her last years. Financially shaken, the crown faced a body of men—call them gentry or what you will—who were cashing in on the price rise and thus able to back with power their political and religious disagreements with the government. As the inflation did its work, the great achievement of the earlier Tudors began to divide: the strength of the nation increased while that of the crown declined. The price rise was not the cause of the conflicts between the Stuarts and their parliaments, but by redistributing national income it made the struggle possible. In the reigns of Henry VII and Henry VIII the two parties (had they existed) would have been so ill matched that parliament would not have stood a chance. Throughout the reign of Elizabeth the balance was being redressed.

That brings us to a problem at present much in dispute—the so-called rise of the gentry. In 1941 Professor R. H. Tawney put forward a brilliantly argued theory that between 1540 and 1640 a class whom he called the gentry rose to economic supremacy by effectively exploiting their increasing lands, while what he called the aristocracy declined since it could not adjust its extravagant mode of life to a decreasing revenue. Mr L. Stone then elaborated the second part of the theory till it appeared that the Elizabethan aristocracy was altogether on the rocks. This ingenious piece of special pleading was so obviously at variance with the vigorous splendour of the great Elizabethan and Jacobean families that the whole theory became suspect, and Mr H. R. Trevor-Roper then devoted several articles to overthrowing the Tawney thesis. His own suggestion is that there was both decline and rise in the gentry: land alone proved unprofitable, so that only those who could obtain office and its bye-products improved their position. He therefore sees a conflict between office-holding gentry (court gentry) and country gentry, leading straight to the civil war of the seventeenth century.[1] The matter is far from ended yet, but several points are already quite clear. The idea of a declining aristocracy cannot be maintained, nor can that of the gentry rising as a class; apart from everything else, Professor Tawney's original version fails to explain the civil war which was not a war between crown and gentry but a war between sections of the gentry supporting either crown or parliament. But Mr Trevor-Roper's ideas cannot stand either in entirety: there is ample proof that many men both noble and gentle built up sizable fortunes from land

[1] The controversy may be studied in the following papers: R. H. Tawney, 'The Rise of the Gentry', *Econ. Hist. Review*, vol. ix (1941); L. Stone, 'Anatomy of the Elizabethan Aristocracy', *ibid.* vol. xviii (1948); H. R. Trevor-Roper, 'The Elizabethan Aristocracy. An Anatomy Anatomized', *ibid.*, 2nd Ser. vol. iii (1951); L. Stone, 'The Elizabethan Aristocracy: A Restatement', *ibid.*, vol. iv (1952); H. R. Trevor-Roper, *The Gentry, 1540-1640* (Econ. Hist. Soc., 1953); R. H. Tawney, 'The Rise of the Gentry: A Postscript', *Econ. Hist. Review*, 2nd Ser. vol. vii (1954).

alone and that office or court-life might bring disadvantages as easily as advantages.

There are several misconceptions to which this discussion has given rise—not perhaps among the participants but certainly among readers. For one, no distinction can be made between aristocracy and gentry; Sir Thomas Smith realised this better than the modern student labouring among the artificial creations of Marxism. The upper ranks of English society in the sixteenth century included men of noble title as well as those who had none, and traffic from one to the other was brisk, partly because the principle of primogeniture forced younger sons downwards into the ranks of commoners or 'gentry', and partly because the crown could push men upwards into gentle or noble condition. The Tudors made relatively few noblemen (though they made some), but they made very many gentlemen and esquires. Rather unconvincing attempts have been made to find in the reign of Henry VIII a tendency to give the nobility the structure of a closed caste; whether one agrees or not that such ideas were about, the fact remains that nothing of the sort was ever carried through. The essence of this upper structure of Tudor society was not class but status—or as they termed it, degree. What mattered was not the group but individual personal condition. A nobleman exacted higher respect and obedience than a gentleman, a knight more than an esquire—but if the knight became noble (as well he might) his place in society was that of his noble peers and his acquaintances adjusted themselves accordingly. The correspondence of any of the many Tudor statesmen who ran the gamut from low to high rank will bear this out. This is not to deny that noblemen of older vintage resented upstarts, or that many men developed pride of birth and blood; but the truth remains that society was constructed on lines not of class but of degree, and that a man's place depended entirely on his personal status in an intricate scale of ranks—a status which fate or his prince might alter—and not on a kind of fixed group or class to which he belonged once and for all.

More serious still is the fact that no common economic factors can be discovered to mark off class from class. If it is sometimes far from easy to distinguish classes in an industrial society, with its wage-earners and employers, the task becomes hopeless in the mostly rural society of the sixteenth century. Landowners are of all kinds, great and small, and both great and small include some that are going up, some that are falling, and no doubt some that are standing still. Indeed, the whole controversy has been able to develop only because the gentlemen of Tudor England were of so many kinds that accidental or deliberate selection can find proof for a number of theories. Professor Tawney is right in stressing the activities of improving landlords, of men who exploited the mineral resources and industrial possibilities of their lands, the advantages of the price rise to the enterprising; Mr Trevor-Roper is right in stressing the advantages of court life, the chances provided by wardships and monopolies, the difficulties of the 'mere' country gentlemen. But, in Tudor times at least, these are not mutually exclusive versions: they are parts of one picture. The plain economic facts—inflation and the need for an income rising as prices rose—were the same for all, but they impinged on a highly diverse society. Some men had exploitable lands, some had none. Some had court connections, others temperamentally hated London and Westminster. Some suffered from accidents and ill luck—sudden death, disease, incompetence, lack of sons; some were lucky and married heiresses or found coal or took the queen's eye. The story is really quite as individualistic as that. When the fate of all or nearly all families that claimed to be gentle—their number runs into thousands—has been studied, it may be possible to trace accurately what happened to the gentry as a whole; at present this cannot be done. The 'lucky dip' principle of historical investigation produces only a succession of discarded theories. But sometimes it is necessary to proceed in that way, and no harm is done provided no one is led to believe that the truth is yet known.

The third difficulty is probably the most serious and the least realised. It results from the impression given (perhaps unintentionally) by any theory which seems to treat the 'rise of the gentry' in the sixteenth century as a new phenomenon. The rise of a new class—a 'middle' class or whatever one wishes to call it—is one of those repetitive instruments of historical generalisation which are in danger of losing all meaning. Every other generation can provide examples of men lamenting the invasion of the higher ranks by new men from below, and the essential truth of that observation has been obscured by historians trying to see in it the rise of classes. There are theories of a rising middle class in the fourteenth, sixteenth, eighteenth, and nineteenth centuries—and of course we can see the thing happening again today. The truth is rather that at all times men try to better themselves by approximating to a social ideal. Those that succeed (always a minority of those that hope and try) come as new men into established ranks, but in a society as flexible as that of England they generally get established in a generation or two, just in time to bewail in their turn the arrival of others from below. Now the social ideal of Tudor

England was the landed gentleman, and those that could—having made money in trade or the legal profession or by adding acre to acre—pushed through into that position. But this is not peculiar to the sixteenth century. If—after all this belabouring of generalisations—a vaster generalisation still may be hazarded, it is this: from the decay of feudalism proper round about the year 1300 to the rise of an industrial and urban society round about the year 1850, the social ideal of England was that of the landed gentleman.[1] These five hundred years may be called the age of the gentry. During them the gentry, and the nobility growing out of it, dominated English society, giving it its standards, its structure, its purpose, and its way of life. What, therefore, could be more natural than that men on the make should constantly be refreshing and enlarging the ranks of that gentry?

But five hundred years are a long time during which trends and movements may change direction and momentum. They were the age of the gentry, but the gentry is essentially not so much a class as a form of existence always drawing in new men and discarding failures by the wayside, frequently changing in character as circumstances change. In those 500 years the sixteenth century was a critical period when the gentry changed most radically and achieved a novel power. It grew in numbers, in self-consciousness, in political and religious and commercial vigour; it also incidentally for the first time produced great poets. The reasons are many. The restoration of peace and order by the Tudors was an essential condition, as was the consolidation of the national state. Protestantism may have been a cause or a symptom, a point too vast to discuss here. But one obvious factor stands out. The gentry rested its existence on land, and the sixteenth century witnessed the biggest transfer of land since the Conquest. When the great monastic estates came on the market, to be supplemented by other lands of both lay and ecclesiastical owners, many men could either acquire land for the first time or add to what they had. The great inflation provided the capital and the desire for investment. Thus in the century after 1540 the gentry spread and grew as it profited from the effects of an economic revolution, even though some of the gentry were also destroyed by this same revolution. What was new was not the gentry as a rising class nor the gentry as an ideal, nor even the gentry as a power in the land; what was new was the number of gentlemen and their power relative to other sections of

[1] Need I add that these dates are to be taken as the merest general guides? There are places today where the gentry, refusing to acknowledge itself dead, persists in a rearguard action.

the community. The redistribution of property meant that the middle sort of people—those between the crown and the great magnates on the one hand, and the landless and small farmers on the other—came into their own.

Lastly, what of the poor? It has been shown that the price rise assisted a sorting out in the lower ranks of society, some men becoming prosperous and sometimes rising through yeoman status even into the gentry, and others declining into genuine poverty. Something has also been said about the problem of vagrancy. It is extremely difficult to be accurate in these questions, for it is of the essence of the poor that they do not appear in history. Now and again they made themselves felt, as in the agrarian disturbances of the century; quarter sessions dealt with vagrants and recorded the harrying of these outcasts of society; there is comment from reformers, and there is government legislation. These last two have combined to make the issue appear unduly big. The times were harsh for poor people, but then they always are. Undoubtedly the price rise increased pauperism. It helped to add to the number of landless men and, through sheep-farming, to the number of rural unemployed. The depression in the clothing industry after 1560 raised another problem of unemployment. None of the attempts made to deal with all these difficulties were very successful. Various piece-meal enactments for labour culminated in the great code of 1563, the statute of apprentices or artificers, a comprehensive enactment which attempted to fix the structure at the bottom of society in an earlier mould. Men were to stay both in the locality and the work into which they were born. This was to be achieved by strictly controlling the movement of labour, by enforcing apprenticeship in all existing crafts and even in agriculture, by preventing idleness, and by having justices of the peace fix wages. None of these ideas were new; the statute summed up a long history of economic legislation both local and national. It was no dead letter: its apprenticeship clauses were invoked in crafts and trades, though not in agriculture, and wage assessments were made frequently. In the textile industries, where wage-earners suffered from unemployment and exploitation by clothiers, minimum wages were often fixed; in agriculture, where small employers suffered from the shortage and demands of labour, maximum wages were the rule. Professor Tawney has suggested that the purpose of the statute was rather to protect the small men and the poor than to exploit the labourer in the interests of farmer and capitalists, but in the main it embodied a stern if paternal concept of society. The

statute seems to have done a little to preserve stability and maintain the supply of labour on the land, but it never achieved anything
like the complete stabilisation it was intended to secure—a hopeless
endeavour in that age of upheaval.

Stability and order were the government's chief concern; it was
for their sake that it turned its attention to the unemployed, the
vagrants and vagabonds. That their numbers have been quite
astonishingly exaggerated has already been shown; the statute of
apprentices offers further proof that the number of unemployed
was not large, for even on the land the supply of surplus labour
seems to have been so small that employers had to be stopped from
paying higher wages. This is not the sort of thing that happens
when many landless men press on a glutted labour market but can
only occur when labour can make its own terms. The real problem
of the poor was twofold. There were those who could not work and
those who would not work; so at least contemporaries saw it, and
there is really precious little evidence that those who wanted work
but could not find it ever made up a sizable proportion of the
wandering poor. After the beginnings of a considered poor law in
1536, various acts gradually elaborated a general system for providing charity, work, and punishments, a system which was
codified in the two great acts summing up the Elizabethan poor law
in 1597 and 1601. The duty of looking after the helpless, aged, and
sick devolved upon the parish; it was administered by parish
overseers and financed out of a compulsory rate levied upon house-
holders. The parish was also to provide work for the genuinely
unemployed by supplying stocks of hemp and similar material for
them to work on; the incorrigibles who (can we blame them?)
preferred the open road to beating hemp were punished by the
justices of the peace. As the century drew on, the worst dislocations
of the agrarian revolution began to wear off; new industries on the
one hand, organised crime on the other, absorbed most of the
workless poor; the problem became manageable, and the Elizabethan poor law proved satisfactory till the greater upheaval of the
late eighteenth century raised entirely new difficulties.

More might be said about the poor, especially if one concentrated either on the protests—More's *Utopia* (1517) or Roderick
Mors' *Complaynt* (1548) or Latimer's *Sermons* (1548 onwards)—
or on the works of that journalist of genius, Robert Greene, who
both recorded and invented the traditional Elizabethan rogue in
his pamphlets on their practices. But we must observe a proper
proportion. In the flourishing, reckless, enterprising, often

disastrous and often very grim ebb and flow of Elizabethan society there is much light and dark; it is not easy to write about the period without seeming to ignore either one or the other. Many prospered, many failed; inconceivable poverty co-existed with solid wealth and showy display. An age of unexpected and unexplained inflation can be many things: it can bring trouble and decay as well as opportunity and advancement. But it cannot be humdrum and stable. The excessive preoccupation of the Elizabethans with the order of the universe and the fixed degrees of men reflects less (as has been argued) the memory of the disturbed politics of the fifteenth century than an awareness of the instability of their own day when society was being dragged from its moorings by new ideas, new worlds, and—most basically of all—by new wealth and new poverty. On balance, however, the gains enormously outweighed the losses, though this no doubt was small consolation to the losers. In its economic life, as in so much else, Tudor England broke loose from the past and prepared amid great turmoil for the easier prosperity and the wider horizons of succeeding centuries.

Chapter X

THE ELIZABETHAN SETTLEMENT, 1558-68

I. THE SITUATION IN 1558

THE young woman of twenty-five who ascended the throne of England on 17 November 1558 presented a much more formidable figure than her devout and blundering half-sister. A naturally imperious, self-willed and selfish character in the best Tudor tradition had been schooled by a hard childhood and adolescence into patience and calculation; even her rages were usually controlled by her mind. Elizabeth's character was of steel, her courage utterly beyond question, her will and understanding of men quite as great as her grandfather's and father's. She was a natural-born queen as her sister had never been—the most masculine of all the female sovereigns of history. At the same time she nourished several supposedly feminine characteristics. She was persistently dilatory, changed her mind as often as chance offered, exasperated everybody by her refusal to come to decisions, and charmed them all back again by some transparent piece of graciousness. Determined never to marry—her reasons seem to have been both political and personal—she developed two unpleasingly old-maidish traits: a show of permanent youthfulness and desirability on the one hand, on the other venomous jealousy of younger women who found husbands. Her parsimony has already been explained as the careful housekeeping of a poor queen faced with ruinous expenses, and it is certainly true that she needed to save all she could. But however justified she was in husbanding her resources, the shifts and deceits and broken promises she often resorted to came perilously near to genuine miserliness. She was a great queen and never less than queen: sagacious, brave, tolerant where it was wise, and tenacious of her rights where tolerance would have been weakness. But she fell far short of that standard of angelic perfection—that inability ever to do wrong—which some would like to ascribe to her, explaining even her errors of taste and judgment as superlative examples of political skill. After 350 years, the old spell is still at work.

What really matters, of course, is Elizabeth's ability in politics—her standing as a queen rather than her pretty obvious failings as a woman. One great difficulty in arriving at a fair verdict lies in her

long association with her chief minister, Sir William Cecil, from
1571 Lord Burghley. The partnership began only three days after
the queen's accession with Cecil's appointment as principal
secretary; it was not dissolved till Burghley died in 1598, less than
five years before his mistress. The son of a Northamptonshire
gentleman who had risen to affluence as a courtier of Henry VIII,
Cecil first obtained office in 1550 as a follower of the Protector
Somerset. He showed much pliancy in the years that followed,
serving Northumberland despite that duke's attack on his patron,
and though he lost his place under Mary he preserved life and
liberty by judicious attendance at the mass, even as the Princess
Elizabeth did. The two had much in common. Both were by
nature secular, holding religion to be a matter of conscience which
need not interfere with affairs of state, though Elizabeth may have
gone further in this than Cecil who held to a moderate but consistent protestantism. Both were naturally cautious, disinclined to
stir up trouble by magnificent gestures, and careful of the limited
resources of a poor monarchy. Cecil's mind was eminently judicious; he could never have committed a rash act. But if in this he was
rather drabber than the brilliant queen, he could be brisk enough
when the situation seemed to demand it and was free from her
besetting sin of dilatoriness and her incurable fear of responsibility.
Indeed, he suffered much from her, not only the occasional taunts
and hard words with which all Tudor servants were familiar, but
also the more insidious pangs of seeing things go wrong because
the queen would not make up her mind. Whether queen or minister was responsible for the great successes of the reign is not at
present a question we can answer; those who should know come to
different conclusions, and there is no adequate study of Cecil. As
a team they were superb, matching caution for caution, diplomatic
finesse for administrative ability, and a marvellous capacity for keeping six balls in the air at once for an equal skill in keeping a dozen
strings from getting entangled. In experience they grew old
together. Of course, the queen ruled over all and Burghley was not
her only servant: others often influenced her decisions which
(when at last they came) were always her own. But except for
occasional divagations, the government of England was for forty
years in the hands of this partnership between queen and minister.
Neither, incidentally, had the qualities of ruthless imagination
leading to revolutionary action which had distinguished the 1530s.
It was well so. That work was done; now it needed consolidation
and development—the immensely important and difficult exploitation of achievements which eighteen years of bad government had

put in jeopardy. For this the wayward but ultimately sensible genius of the queen and the steady, hardworking, eminently sane genius of Cecil were exactly right.

The immediate problem confronting the government was that of religion. The death of Mary left England technically catholic and reunited to Rome, but whether this would last depended on the new queen. Twice changes in rulers had produced changes in religion; it was likely that this would be so again. As the daughter of Anne Boleyn—as the visible pledge of Henry VIII's break with Rome—Elizabeth seemed bound to forswear her sister's religion. Rome did not recognise her legitimacy, though that was a snag which a papal dispensation could remove; Paul IV, fierce hater of heresy though he was, professed himself ready to consider the point. However, Mary's reign had really destroyed what hold Rome yet retained on Englishmen: the country had shown clearly enough what it thought of a religion which reimposed papal rule and added the dominance of Spain. Whatever the gentry's ardour for the new faith, they valued their new lands and continued to dislike priesthood and popes. While England and Europe waited for a sign from Elizabeth, English nationalism cast its vote by giving the new queen a vociferous welcome which implied a convinced condemnation of the old. Though some fond minds in Rome and Madrid deceived themselves into false hopes, the pope's power in England was from the start unlikely to endure. The further question whether Elizabeth would restore Henry VIII's religion or Edward VI's was less easy to answer. The least known factor of all was her own religious faith. Perhaps—as we are now commonly told, usually by way of commendation—she had none; certainly she had no patience with the quarrels of doctrine and wished to keep the peace. She would not, as she said, make windows in men's souls; her concern was that men, whatever they believed, should obey her government. Her personal taste was hostile to the mass but in favour of the pomp and splendour of the old religion; she liked candles and ornaments and vestments, and in another age might have liked images. But the situation was much too complicated to permit an indulgence in a personal bent.

As had been the case ever since Henry VIII broke with Rome, international involvements set the stage. England was still technically at war with France and allied to Spain, though the peace negotiations were nearing conclusion, despite English reluctance to give up Calais. In Scotland, the regent Mary of Guise ruled for her young daughter who was both queen of Scots and dauphiness of France. The ancient friendship between France and Scotland thus looked like turning into a personal union which would put England squarely between the jaws of a nutcracker—the deplorable outcome of Henry VIII's overhasty and overbearing attempt to dominate Scotland from London. Against this threat England's only protection seemed to lie in a continuance of the Spanish amity, and a genuine alliance with Philip II could hardly be combined with anything but catholicism at home. Again, if Spain and France came to terms the two leading catholic countries would be free to turn their combined strength on any heretic power: England might find herself alone against both her old ally and her old foe. Either way, the state of Europe counselled caution; a less astute and daring diplomat than Elizabeth might even have thought it compelled her to accept her sister's religion. Since, however, her own and her people's wishes definitely prevented a continued submission to the papacy, she rightly decided that she could only save herself by preserving Philip's benevolent neutrality while at the same time drifting away from Rome.

Such a course not only demanded uncommon diplomatic skill but also implied that the settlement of religion could not be too rapid or too radical. But here Elizabeth came up against the pressure of organised protestant opinion. On the news of Mary's death, a stream of exiles began to flow back with ever increasing speed, bringing with them very definite ideas about the establishment of religion. Definite these ideas were, but unanimous they were not, and in this lay the queen's chance of victory. Protestantism benefited by its martyrs, but if all its adherents had followed Cranmer's and Ridley's example it would have remained little but a memory. Many ardent protestant divines, and a few equally ardent laymen, fled therefore to various reformed communities on the continent as soon as Pole brought back Rome and the stake, rightly saving themselves against the day of triumph. Free from the relative moderation which a half-hostile England and a sense of responsibility to the government had previously induced, these English protestants were soon among the most extreme of their faith. As extremists will, they fell out amongst themselves. The quarrels centred on Frankfort where John Knox, lately King Edward's chaplain, tried to establish a Calvinist community but was defeated in the end by Richard Cox whose faction adhered to the specifically English system of the second Edwardian Prayer Book. Knox returned to Geneva with a band of extremists. There were other exile groups, but the Frankfort and Geneva sections— Coxians and Knoxians—were the ones that mattered. Both supported a religion 'purified' of all the works of Rome and therefore acquired the name of puritans, but the latter wanted the complete Calvinist system with the Geneva 'discipline' (or order of Church government and service) which put power over the laity in the hands of the ministers. The Coxians were the first to return to England, together with such moderate protestants as Edmund Grindal who had spent his exile in Strassburg, the late Martin Bucer's stronghold. The Geneva group found the queen hostile from the start: Knox, a Scotsman, was never allowed to stay in England again. Elizabeth objected to them partly because of Knox's unfortunate *First Blast of the Trumpet against the Monstrous Regiment of Women*, a violent attack on female sovereigns directed against Mary Tudor and Mary of Guise which proved a stumbling-block in the way of agreement with the equally female but much more protestant Elizabeth. In general, too, the Genevan ideals went counter to her ideas of a hierarchical and state-controlled Church.

However, if Knoxians were insufferable, Coxians were none too agreeable. Alliance with them closed the road to a restoration of the Henrician Church—a Church catholic in doctrine but divided from Rome. It meant upsetting the many to whom the old faith was still the most congenial, even if they had no wish to see the pope back. Yet despite Elizabeth's own sympathy with this point of view, the alliance could not be avoided. Where was she to find her bishops? Unlike her father she could not take the existing episcopate with her on the road away from Rome. Thirty years of strife and increasing protestantism had taught the Marian bishops the folly and indecency of yet another change of front, and with remarkable solidarity they all but one refused to accept the new state of things. Of the twenty-six sees—ten, including Canterbury, were conveniently vacant by death—Elizabeth had to fill twenty-five; she simply had to accept clergy of an Anglican or more definitely protestant hue. While she could set her face against the extreme puritans from Geneva, she could not do without the moderate puritans from Frankfort; some purification—some move towards Edwardian protestantism at least—was unavoidable.

What really tied Elizabeth's hands, however, was a phenomenon full of portent for the future. Puritanism in the clergy one might cope with; puritanism in the laity was another matter altogether. For the first time since 1529, the government found itself following instead of leading the nation as represented in parliament. From Elizabeth's very first parliament onwards, the puritan faction commanded a formidable support in the commons. A group of Marian exiles, including Sir Francis Knollys (himself a privy councillor) and Sir Anthony Cooke (father-in-law to two other privy councillors), co-operated with puritan divines outside the house in pressing for a protestant settlement. Such pressure in parliament was a serious matter. Parliament had played an important part in the Henrician Reformation: it had not erected the royal supremacy but it had enforced it. In consequence, the very existence of the supremacy—the structure of the Church— came to be bound up with statute. Edward VI's parliaments had really enacted the Prayer Books, not merely appointed penalties for refusal to use them; the 1552 act of uniformity spoke of 'a very goodly order set forth by authority of parliament'. The distinction which Henry VIII and Cromwell had so carefully made between preamble and enactment vanished as Somerset and Northumberland blithely permitted phrasing which implied that the royal supremacy was to be exercised in and with parliament only. Mary found that she could not restore catholicism and repair the break with Rome without parliamentary enactment; worse, she could not even divest herself of that shirt of Nessus, the Supremacy title itself, until parliament had spoken. In the violent changes of religion which agitated England between 1547 and 1558, parliament established a claim to participation which would have horrified Henry VIII and was to drive Elizabeth to distraction. She tried hard to preserve the original notion that the government of the Church was for the sovereign alone, while statute must be used to create penalties for offences against the order established by the crown, but the pass had been sold before she came to the throne.

Parliament's invasion of the sphere of Church government became a danger only as the crown lost the initiative. Elizabeth wished to adhere to her settlement, but even in this settlement—as we shall see—she had to go further than she intended because of puritan pressure in the commons. The puritans were far from satisfied, and the reign resounded with the battles waged by their dynamism in the commons against the static policy of the queen. This ominous alliance between advanced religion and the house of commons depended for its success on the constitutional growth of the house itself. If the puritans there were to make their views felt they had to be able to express them freely and without fear of the consequences. Thus the struggle seemed to turn on the privileges of parliament, especially those which guaranteed freedom from arrest and freedom of speech. By 1558 the house of commons had secured recognition of certain powers over its own members which gave it a corporate and effective existence; in this development of the house as a 'court' lay the foundation of its modern greatness. An act of 1515 transferred to the house itself the right to license absentees which the crown had hitherto exercised. Ferrers' Case (1543), when the commons by their own authority punished some city officers of London who had arrested a member, established their right of direct action and the sufficiency as warrant of their serjeant's mace. The crucial right of free speech has a more difficult and doubtful history. Medieval Speakers had petitioned for free speech for themselves—the right, that is, to inform the king of what had been discussed and agreed in the commons, without prejudice to themselves. The first reliable instance of the genuine privilege—the right of members to speak freely in the house—seems to date from Sir Thomas More's Speakership in 1523; it is supposed, with some probability, that More was himself responsible for this important advance in the claims of parliament.

By 1558 the request was regularly included in the Speaker's petition at the beginning of each parliament: it had become matter of form. But its precise meaning was still unsettled. Henry VIII adhered to a policy of persuasion, refusing to punish members' words even when they plainly attacked his plans or invaded his prerogative. However, leading parliament as he did he could afford to let a little opposition have its way; Elizabeth, trying to maintain a much-attacked *status quo*, felt unable to be as tolerant. She also displayed a more self-conscious awareness of her dignity and rights, and a more imperious contempt for the opinions of those presumptuous men who would teach her her business. The fact that crown and commons came to pursue divergent policies in religion, the most touchy matter of all, made certain that freedom of speech would become a battleground. The queen defined her concept of it most clearly towards the end of the reign, in the lord keeper's speech of 1593 in which it was said that 'to say yea or no to bills, God forbid that any man should be restrained or afraid to answer to his best liking, with some short declaration of his reasons therein, and therein to have a free voice.' Members were free to speak about all matters submitted to them, provided they preserved decorum and avoided license. There was much to be said for this view on grounds of precedent, and it was far from ungenerous. As a corollary Elizabeth refused the house the right to discuss her 'prerogative' without permission, for which limitation again precedent and the law were on her side; but in this prerogative she included ecclesiastical matters and matters affecting her person, as her marriage and the problem of the succession. In other words, she put precisely those things out of bounds which the opposition wished to discuss. They retaliated with a wider notion of freedom of speech, culminating in the theory of Peter Wentworth that the house had the right freely to discuss all matters affecting the common weal and to introduce legislation concerned with it. Such complete freedom of speech could not be reconciled with the queen's politic desire to keep 'mysteries of state' in her own hand; the quarrel was fundamental and insoluble.

Such, then, was the position in 1558. Elizabeth had to settle the Church and religion before she did anything else. Her own inclination and the international situation rendered it dangerous not only to establish a genuinely protestant Church, but even to restore Henry VIII's system. The situation in the country worked the other way. If she broke with Rome, as she meant to do, she would have to accept an alliance with protestant Churchmen: Henrician anglo-catholicism was out of the question. Moreover, she had to work through and with parliament if the settlement was to be constitutional and enforceable, and parliament was now a much less manageable ally. A house of commons accustomed by thirty years' work to participate—even, it seemed, to authorise— in high matters of state and growingly conscious of its rights, privileges, and powers, was dominated from the start by a minority of puritans who knew what they wanted. It must have appeared to the queen and Cecil that every solution must fail. The history of the previous two reigns offered no encouragement. How the government, stepping delicately and with a purpose, threaded its way through these troubles, how its actions were affected by pressure from both sides, and how its achievement was preserved both by its own skill and the folly of its enemies—all this must now be told.

2. THE CHURCH OF ENGLAND RESTORED

Elizabeth's claim to the throne was not a bad one, resting as it did on act of parliament (1543) and Henry VIII's will. If statute had once declared her a bastard, Mary's fate had been the same. London received her with joy and acclamation. But others there were who felt differently. The hint from Rome that her mother's irregular marriage might yet be put right also implied that until this was done she could not properly inherit the crown. Mary Stuart stood in the wings to take over as the catholic candidate. Philip II, through his envoy de Feria, an arrogant and stiffnecked fool, tried to claim all credit for Elizabeth's peaceful accession; he was firmly convinced that the new queen would have to depend on Spain as the old queen had done, and for some months he planned to marry Elizabeth himself. On the other hand, there were murmurings at the failure to remove the Marian bishops by prerogative action; though Elizabeth picked Cecil for her chief councillor she made no clean sweep of Mary's council; caution and circumspection, in any case her favourite attitude, were the necessary order of the day. To begin with she succeeded in allowing all men to believe what they wished while she kept herself free to act. Pope Paul IV, badgered by Spain, professed to believe it possible that she would yet prove faithful to Rome; Philip II persuaded himself readily into the same opinion because he wished to continue his sway in England; her catholic subjects saw with relief that she was no second Northumberland. But protestants knew better and hoped more eagerly. Her title was made to end in a mysterious etcetera: she was queen of England, France, and Ireland, she was defender of the faith, 'etc.' Thus she neither called herself supreme head nor clearly relinquished that critical name.[1] Each man might make of it what he would. This game could not be played for long. The queen would have to attend divine service, and then some of the matter at least would become plain. Nothing Elizabeth did was ever plain, and she invariably succeeded in talking herself out of even the most definite action, but hints soon appeared. On Christmas Day 1558 Bishop Oglethorpe of Carlisle, saying mass in the royal chapel, was ordered to refrain from elevating the host for the adoration to which reformers so strenuously objected; he refused, and the queen walked out before that point in the service. As a result she had great difficulty in finding a bishop to crown her, but in the end Oglethorpe again obliged. Elizabeth took every opportunity on this 15 January 1559 for a little significant playacting. She received the English Bible with dramatised fervour; she again withdrew before the elevation of the host. As far as she might she had signalled her acceptance of some sort of reformed faith, while her carefully obscure talk kept Spain and Rome in wilful delusion.

The crisis approached with the meeting of parliament, called for 25 January. The queen's control over the lords was weaker than was usual in the sixteenth century because the sixteen Marian bishops and one Marian abbot proved solid against all the government's blandishments. Tunstall of Durham made his excuses on the score of age and Goldwell of St Asaph received no summons because he was actually being translated to Oxford at the time; but these and other absentees gave proxies to staunch conservatives,

---

[1] Mary had used the device for the opposite reason.

especially Nicholas Heath, archbishop of York, only just replaced as lord chancellor by Nicholas Bacon, Cecil's brother-in-
law.[1] The lay peers were mostly Mary's but they had been
Edward's before that; a few new creations rewarded friends of
Elizabeth's hard days but did not pack the house. The queen
indulged in none of the practices—creations, orders to stay absent
—which might have been used to secure an obedient house; she
was hardly safe enough to do so as yet. Nor were the commons
packed; there seems to have been less influence exercised on
elections than usual, as one would expect from a government that
had yet to find its feet. About a third of the members had sat in
Mary's last parliament (with which she had managed well enough)
and undoubtedly there were many good catholics; but there were
certainly also several exiles and other ardent protestants. Religion
was not the only subject before this parliament, but religion was
the issue that mattered. Several eager pamphleteers submitted
their ideas to Cecil and Elizabeth. One of these writing—the
'Device for the alteration of religion' — agrees so well with
the final outcome that it used to be considered the basis for the
government's action, but in fact Elizabeth favoured something
much more gradual and piecemeal than the immediate establishment of a protestant Church of England. Her ideas were in accord
rather with the exceedingly cautious advice given by Richard
Goodrich and Armigail Waad, a lawyer and an official. Divines
she never liked.[2]

On 25 January 1559 the parliament met. The convocation of
Canterbury sat at the same time; its only action was to assert the
full catholic position on the papal supremacy and on dogma, on
28 February. It played no part in the settlement, a fact which
caused much trouble in the nineteenth-century Church but need
not worry us here. The commons, on the other hand, showed
their anti-papal inclination from the start when they tried to
impugn Mary's legislation on the grounds that she had dispensed
with 'supreme head' in her title, and to force Elizabeth to expand
her etcetera into the full glory of Henry VIII's invention. These
were skirmishings. Issue was joined on 9 February when the
government introduced a supremacy bill in the commons which

[1] Bacon held the lesser dignity of keeper of the great seal. Elizabeth
was fond of this compromise which saved money and the need of a
peerage, both of which she disliked bestowing.
[2] The following account of events in Elizabeth's first parliament is
based on J. E. Neale's analysis in *Eng. Hist. Rev.*, 1950, and in *Elizabeth I
and her Parliaments 1559-1581*, pt. I. His interpretation has successfully
overthrown views of long standing.

embodied Elizabeth's original plan. It would have revived the Henrician legislation by repealing Mary's second statute of repeal, would have enforced Elizabeth's title of supreme head by an oath to be taken by all the clergy, and would furthermore have permitted communion under both kinds. Thus it would have returned to conditions as they were in 1547; Somerset had also proceeded gradually, first permitting protestant doctrine and only later establishing protestant worship by law. To start with, Elizabeth wanted neither a prayer book nor an act of uniformity. However, she was not permitted to get away with so little. Strenuous opposition in committee forced alterations into the bill which came back to the commons as the second supremacy bill on 21 February. It is probable that this made the penalties for refusing the oath harsher and revived the 1552 prayer book. There was no chance of the queen permitting such extremism on the part of the protestant commons, and the lords soon reduced the bill to its original form. Even so Heath protested against the title of supreme head, especially because a woman could in no circumstances be head of the Church. The commons (whose leaders were working in close contact with the returned clergy, especially Cox, Grindal, and Edwin Sandys) saw all hope of a protestant establishment fading in face of the queen's desire to remain uncommitted; in despair they rushed through a bill which would at least have granted toleration to anyone practising the religion of Edward VI's last year. They had no hope of getting this past the lords, let alone the queen, but intended to impress the government with the strength of protestant feeling.

Whether it was impressed by this move or not, the government had by this time realised that the issue would have to be faced. Easter was near (26 March), and it had been intended to dissolve parliament before then; the second supremacy bill was ready for the queen's assent on 22 March. At the last moment she changed her mind, took no action over the bill, and prorogued parliament till early April. She had received the news that peace was concluded at Cateau-Cambrésis between Spain, France, and England. This meant that the powers recognised her as queen: for the moment she was secure and could afford to come off the fence. The turmoil in parliament had decided on which side she would descend. During the recess consideration began of the form of religion to be enforced. On 31 March a discussion was staged in Westminster Hall between some Marian bishops and some protestant divines. It served no purpose except to reduce the votes of the spiritual peers in parliament: White of Winchester and Watson of Lincoln were sent to the Tower for speaking against the supremacy. Meanwhile the various parties set about the production of a prayer book. There was no formal revision by a committee of clergy early in the year, as used to be thought; instead, negotiations took place between the queen, Cecil, and the protestants. The queen wanted the first Edwardian Prayer Book, the divines and the commons were barely satisfied with the second. The Prayer Book of 1559 is a compromise in which the queen conceded most. She had to accept the 1552 book with slight modifications of which the chief were the dropping of the 'Black Rubric'[1] and the addition of an ornaments rubric which ordered the wearing of vestments as in 'the second year' of Edward VI (1548); interpretation of this last was to provoke a major conflict.

Before the book was agreed parliament had reassembled (3 April). On the 10th the government produced a third supremacy bill identical with the second except that it substituted for the title of supreme head of the Church that of 'supreme governor as well in all spiritual or ecclesiastical things or causes as temporal'. The widespread feeling against a female head had taken effect. In this form the bill was passed rapidly through the commons and more slowly through the lords. On the 18th the commons gave a first reading to the uniformity bill which authorised the agreed Prayer Book; within a few days it had passed both houses—the lords by a majority of only three with the spiritual peers solidly against it and several lay peers also opposing the government—and on 8 May Elizabeth, dissolving this momentous parliament, gave her assent. The Elizabethan settlement was made. It now consisted of an act of supremacy enforcing the renewed break with Rome and the queen's position as supreme governor of things temporal and spiritual, and an act of uniformity enforcing a protestantism not quite so clear-cut as that of 1552 but much more extreme than that of 1549. It is usual to call this settlement a compromise, and so it was—but not quite in the sense commonly supposed. Contemporaries did not think that the established Church rested halfway between the rival denominations: they thought this was a protestant Church. Episcopacy had not yet become an issue: even Knox accepted bishops. It was only the further development of puritanism (whose Coxian representatives were moderately content in 1559), as well as Elizabeth's diplomatic suggestions to a number of deliberately blind Spanish and French emissaries that her protestantism was after all quite like catholicism, that disguised the nature of the settlement. The compromise was between

[1] See above, p. 212.

the queen and her protestant subjects represented in parliament, and it involved greater concessions from her than from them. In this first round of the long parliamentary struggle over religion, the queen came off worst; the puritan minority displayed their characteristic tenacity and tactical skill; and England at once got a protestant Church despite Elizabeth's desire for a gradual exploration of the way.

The settlement involved two constitutional issues worthy of attention. In the first place, it assigned to parliament a place which it did not hold under Henry VIII but had acquired under Edward VI. The act of supremacy—like Henry's similar act—gave to the sovereign all such jurisdictions and powers 'as by any spiritual or ecclesiastical power or authority hath heretofore been . . . exercised' in the government of the clergy; but it further expressly participated in the use of such powers by authorising their delegation. The act of uniformity stood on the principle first accepted in 1549 that the recognised legal form of worship was not only enforced but actually authorised by statute. Neither Cromwell's vicariate-general or vicegerency, nor the settlement of doctrine by such royal instruments as the King's Book of 1543, was therefore possible under the new dispensation. When Elizabeth delegated her ecclesiastical powers to successive commissions, those commissions' doings could be challenged by reference to the act of 1559; this happened and caused much trouble. Similarly, the Prayer Book could not be altered without parliament, and parliament had a perfectly sound case for claiming a share in deciding the official ritual and doctrine: it had done so once at the queen's invitation, and it was difficult to prevent ardent men in the commons from supposing that it could do so again on their unofficial initiative. The statutory character of the settlement—which could not be avoided—and the phrasing of the act of uniformity ended the queen's exclusive control of Church and religion, whatever she might say.

Elizabeth's position was therefore weaker than her father's. It is now usual to allege that there was no difference between the supreme head and the supreme governor—that the latter name merely saved the consciences of catholics and of those who remembered the Pauline injunction against women in the Church, without lessening the queen's control of ecclesiastical government. Contemporaries said the same: the Spanish ambassador and Elizabeth's very protestant ambassador in France, Sir Nicholas Throckmorton, were agreed on this. Yet they were wrong. Though she had a harder task in fighting off the interference of puritans in clergy and laity, Elizabeth governed the Church in practice as firmly as Henry had done; but that was because hers was as formidable a character. There was an essential difference between head and governor. The first was, so to speak, himself an ecclesiastical person partaking (as we have seen) of episcopal characteristics; the second stood outside the clergy. Henry as supreme head was himself the highest ecclesiastical dignitary in the realm; his deputy, a lay vicegerent in spirituals, took precedence over archbishops in convocation. Elizabeth ruled the Church from outside, through her archbishops and commissioners. Unlike her father, Elizabeth was no pope in England, not only because she was a woman but also because no such quasi-ecclesiastical character appertained to the supreme governorship. While the queen lived it made little practical difference, but the change profoundly affected the position of her successors. The Elizabethan settlement created a Church protestant in doctrine, traditional in organisation, and subject not to a lay pope but to the queen-governor in parliament. Statute had triumphed in this field also, with the natural consequence that the difficulties inherent in a 'mixed sovereign' were bound to show in the most contentious sphere of all.

Parliament had spoken; now the country had to be brought into line—for the third time in a dozen years. The oath of supremacy was the test; not to take it meant deprivation. By January 1560 all the Marian bishops except Kitchen of Llandaff were deprived. Their solidarity and refusal to bow to circumstances deserve praise, nor could they know beforehand that Elizabeth would treat them with a leniency which they themselves had failed to show during their ascendancy. Most of them lived out their lives under a mild and private surveillance; even Bonner, whose death was widely demanded in revenge for his bloody doings, was only imprisoned a trifle more rigorously and lived to embarrass the government in 1567 with shrewd thrusts at the legality of the act of supremacy. There had been hopes of taking some of the bishops along. The venerable Tunstall was wooed by Cecil, but Tunstall was content to have held Durham for twenty-nine years; in any case he survived his deprivation by only a few weeks. Thus twenty-five sees had to be filled. Elizabeth was lucky to have a man to hand for Canterbury who fulfilled exactly her idea of an ecclesiastical commander-in-chief. This was Matthew Parker, a Cambridge don of moderately protestant opinions in the Cranmer tradition. A believer in authority and monarchy, opposed to all extremes and disorder, and one who devoted his intellectual abilities to history rather than theology, he was at the same time an admirably firm and dispassionate administrator. On 17 December 1559 he sat consecrated—canonically, because some Edwardian bishops survived—in the late Cardinal Pole's place, and the Church of England had again a leader. The other sees were filled, some with bishops deprived in 1553, but more with those Marian exiles who had organised the puritan attack on the queen's ecclesiastical plans in parliament. Richard Cox took Ely, Edmund Grindal London, John Jewel Salisbury, Edwin Sandys Worcester, James Pilkington Durham, Robert Horne Winchester. These were the leaders of Frankfort and their allies. But Elizabeth had no choice: the new bishops stood high above the general level of the English clergy, and because of the Marians' firmness there were no other possible candidates. Episcopacy, administrative duties, and the experience of responsibility soon sobered down their puritanism, but some were to find it difficult to combine office with the memories of the past.

The lesser clergy gave little trouble. They had expressed their attachment to Rome, transubstantiation, and so forth under Bonner's guidance in convocation's protest early in 1559; a year later, as the bishops' visitors went about administering the oath, few only refused. The exact figures are in dispute: the most likely estimate reckons that some 240-300 beneficed clergy out of a total of about 8,000 were deprived in the years 1560-6. The government acted without rigour; evasion of the rules was for the moment winked at and the mass permitted to survive in remoter districts. This mercy was, of course, politic but none the less attractive for that; the type of writer who sneers at Elizabeth's moderation because it was calculated and praises Mary's intolerance because it rested on principle either cannot have much experience of persecution or feels sure that he would have been on the right side of the fiery divide. The settlement gradually took root in England. Men could not be sure but that another turn of the wheel might come any day; in the meantime, this moderate and moderately imposed system could be borne by nearly all. The threat to the re-established protestant Church came rather from abroad. The great triumph of Elizabeth's policy in her first few years was the elimination of the Scottish danger.

3. THE REFORMATION IN SCOTLAND

At Elizabeth's accession England was unbelievably weak. Her military strength had declined so disastrously that she entirely depended on the international situation for the minimum of national safety. Her finances were disorganised and her credit gone. Much was done in a single year to recover from this collapse for which Mary's reign must be held largely responsible: Cecil laboured successfully at the restoration of armed forces, the development of armament industries, and—with the assistance of Gresham in Antwerp—at the rebuilding of financial stability. Nevertheless, much continued to depend on factors outside English control, so that the first decade of the reign was filled with a bewildering complex of diplomatic negotiations both avowed and secret. The treaty of Cateau-Cambrésis (April 1559) confirmed Elizabeth's recognition by the continental powers, but it also ended for a time the rivalry of Spain and France on which England had for so long relied. Ultimately England was to be offered even better opportunities for fishing in troubled waters by the religious wars which destroyed French power for nearly half a century, and by the revolt of the Netherlands which fatally weakened Spain. It was the crowning irony of Elizabeth's reign that she, the champion of monarchy and avowed enemy of all who resisted authority, was to achieve her triumph in making England a great power by supporting rebellion in other princes' lands. She never liked doing it: a feeling of solidarity with all crowned heads remained a potent factor in her conduct of affairs. But, realist that she was, she always ultimately sacrificed it to the more obvious interests of her country.

The immediate result of Cateau-Cambrésis was the death of Henry II of France in the tournament which celebrated the peace. His successor, Francis II, fifteen years old, was husband of the seventeen-year old Mary Queen of Scots. Dominated by the great catholic family of Guise, he caused much apprehension in Spain. The duke of Guise and his brother, the cardinal of Lorraine, ruled France; their sister Mary governed Scotland as regent for her daughter; the Guises had thoughts of asserting their protégée's claims to the throne of England. The fear of a French empire stretching from Inverness to the Pyrenees kept Spain on England's side and prevented concerted catholic action against the heretic queen. Elizabeth and Cecil thought themselves reasonably safe from attack across the sea, but the northern border constituted a very imminent danger. Two things helped. In the first place, the French had outstayed their welcome in Scotland. Since 1550, when Northumberland abandoned the policy of Henry VIII, the regent, assisted by French troops and French officials, had ruled that country almost as a province of France. Scottish nationalism, which had frustrated Henry, now turned against the Guises. In

KET

this it found an ally in protestantism, for the Guises were the foremost champions of the Counter-Reformation. In December 1557 a number of Scottish lords, calling themselves the lords of the congregation, combined in an association which they named the Covenant. It might be only another of the traditional 'bands' formed by Scots nobles against their feeble monarchs, but it rested on religion and for a century was to be a powerful factor in Scottish politics.

Here was Elizabeth's chance. In May 1559 John Knox was permitted to return through England to Scotland, and wherever he went Rome fell before Geneva. A few months later the queen of England encouraged the Scottish opposition by smuggling out of France and sending north the Hamilton claimant to the Scottish throne, the earl of Arran, after first inspecting and rejecting this incipient lunatic as a candidate for her own hand. The lords of the congregation gathered their forces and attacked the French garrisons. These proved much too strong for the more numerous but untrained Scots, and by the end of 1559 it was clear that the revolt would collapse unless England did more than cheer on from the sidelines. Elizabeth, as always, was hard to persuade into action, but in the end she gave way in the face of the obvious Scottish need, the growing weakness of the Guises in France in face of Huguenot unrest, and the persuasion of Cecil, assisted by the one statesman thrown up by the Scottish lords, Maitland of Lethington. An English squadron under William Winter blockaded the Scottish East coast; an army under Lord Grey de Wilton joined the forces of the Covenant in besieging the French at Leith. Admirably led by the regent, the French resisted the amateurish assaults of Grey and the covenanters, but in June Mary of Guise died and Cecil arrived to see what could be done by negotiation. The result was the treaty of Edinburgh, concluded in July 1560, by which most French troops and all French influence were expelled from Scotland whose government passed into the hands of the lords of the congregation and the protestants—of Lethington and Knox. The Reformation was established, the threat removed; and for the first time in history an English army recrossed the border sped on its way by the cheers and gratitude of the Scottish nation. What centuries of arrogant claims to suzerainty had not been able to achieve was accomplished by community of religion and the reluctantly extorted assistance of the least arrogant English sovereign who ever interfered in Scotland.

Gloomy and hopeful prognostications that Elizabeth had let herself in for trouble were disappointed: France and Spain had been too preoccupied with matters nearer home to intervene—France with the growing divisions between religious parties, and Spain with troubles in the Mediterranean and Burgundian parts of her empire. Yet difficulties of another kind soon threatened. In December 1560 Francis II died, leaving his Stuart wife a mere queen-dowager at eighteen. For the moment the power of the Guises was broken, and her mother-in-law, Catherine de Médicis, had no intention of allowing this daughter of Mary of Guise any further part in French affairs. Reluctantly—for she loved France where she had spent most of her young life and dreaded the gloomy northern kingdom with its Calvinism—Mary turned to go back to Scotland and take up her crown. It remains impossible so to speak about Mary Queen of Scots that all are satisfied; she had to the utmost the Stuart ability of attaching men's loyalties to herself despite the most outrageous and the most foolish of deeds. Of her famous beauty her surviving portraits provide little evidence. She was passionate, wilful, intelligent, given to violent moods of exaltation and depression, and entirely without common sense—one might say, entirely without moral sense. It was too much to expect that this young woman, reminder of the recently overthrown French domination and ardently catholic, should bring peace to the land. Early fears that she would revive the French and catholic policy of her Guise mother were allayed by her readiness to accept the protestant party; Lethington and Lord James Stuart (soon to be earl of Murray) continued her chief ministers, John Knox preached at her in a tactless fashion which has needlessly distressed her sentimental partisans, and she took lessons in Calvinism from George Buchanan. Not religion but dynastic policy was her immediate concern: she wished to assert her claim to the English throne, inherited from Margaret Tudor, daughter of Henry VII who had married James IV of Scotland.

This half-French claimant north of the border drove Elizabeth into the most obvious diplomatic blunder of her reign when she drifted into assisting the Calvinist Huguenots in the first French war of religion, which broke out in 1562. It seemed a good idea to promote protestant revolt in the country which still constituted the gravest threat to her security; it seemed an even better idea to link this help with a revival of claims to Calais and other French territory. Whether Elizabeth herself favoured this extravagance, so much at variance with the moderation displayed in Scotland, is not known: it was bound to be a popular move. In effect it ensured failure. The English did little to affect the war but they occupied Le Havre, and when, after the assassination of the duke of Guise,

Catherine succeeded in opening negotiations for peace, the terms upon which Elizabeth had helped rapidly cemented an alliance between the French parties. Huguenots and catholics combined against the English at Le Havre and expelled them after a gallant defence ill-supported from home. In 1563 Elizabeth replaced her ambassador in France, the violently anti-catholic Throckmorton, by that elderly moderate Sir Thomas Smith who at once entered upon the negotiations which in the end led to England shifting her continental alliance from Spain to France. Her experiences confirmed Elizabeth in her dislike of continental commitments, especially on behalf of Huguenots; the campaign also ended for all time the English ambitions for continental conquest.

The problem of Mary remained. She had to marry: it was expected of every queen, and while Elizabeth showed how the question could stay unanswered, Mary was not likely to remain celibate for long. A plan to give her Philip's degenerate son, Don Carlos, for husband was foiled by England and France together for fear of spreading Spanish influence to Scotland. Elizabeth offered Lord Robert Dudley, created earl of Leicester for the occasion, whom rumour credited with being her own lover; the Scots considered this an insult—which it was. But in 1564 the man was found in Henry Lord Darnley, son of the earl of Lennox and grandson, by her second marriage, of Mary Stuart's own Tudor grandmother. To this vague link with the Tudors Darnley added birth on English soil which, by English law, enabled him to inherit in England, as Mary could not; thus their marriage, following upon Mary's ready falling in love with the tall, handsome man whose contemptible character was not yet known, greatly strengthened the Stuart claim to the English throne. Elizabeth had opposed it and was furious at Mary's defiance; nor did she much welcome the birth of a son, James, in 1566. It was a fateful business. In the short run it destroyed Mary; in the long run it put the Stuarts on the English throne and destroyed the Tudor state. Immediately, however, it reinforced the clamour in England for the queen to marry and settle the succession, for how could protestant England contemplate without horror an heir to the throne who was not only a foreign potentate but also a catholic?

4. MARRIAGE AND SUCCESSION

When Elizabeth came to the throne it was taken for granted that she would soon marry and produce an heir. The need was generally recognised both among the people and in the council.

Yet the problem of where her choice should fall stared them all in the face, for they had just experienced the troubles to which a queen's marriage could lead. Mary Tudor's example was a manifestly bad one, so manifest indeed that one can only wonder at Philip II's effrontery in offering to take the younger sister on as well for the sake of keeping the kingdom. Elizabeth thankfully used his offer to keep him quiet during the critical first months and then turned it down (January 1559); his subsequent marriage to Elizabeth of Valois threatened a Franco-Spanish alliance, but that was an ever-present danger which never materialised. The difficulties which confronted the queen were enormous—bigger than her sister's just because her sister had shown the danger. In the circumstances it was perhaps as well that Elizabeth privately determined never to marry. But while she would not marry, she also would not say so; she had no intention of depriving herself and England of one of the best diplomatic counters available in that age of dynastic marriages. The courtships of Queen Elizabeth were the joke and the despair of her time; we shall only understand them aright if we remember that to her they were not only a substitute for the emotional life which, despite everything, she missed, but also a vital part in the game of international politics, and a part in which she excelled.

Whether she married or not, the succession was a separate problem. As things stood, easily the best claim rested with the Stuarts, and Mary Stuart was not only a catholic but married to the dauphin, soon King Francis II. The Suffolk line, which Henry VIII's will had preferred to the Stuarts, had had its try in the person of Lady Jane Grey; its surviving representative was another woman, Lady Catherine Grey. It is astonishing how everything turned on females, and it was unfortunate that it did, for women claimants meant husbands and difficulties with dynastic marriages. When Catherine Grey clandestinely married the earl of Hertford, son of the Protector Somerset (1561), she became the pawn of a protestant faction in the council (who feared Elizabeth's entanglement with Robert Dudley) and the object of vigorous dislike to the queen herself. The fact that she disliked both Mary Stuart and Catherine Grey played its part in Elizabeth's refusal to contemplate the determination of the succession. A third candidate existed in Henry Hastings, earl of Huntingdon, descended from the Poles; he too was offered as a protestant alternative to the queen of Scots, and he too would have made a plainly unsatisfactory king. The problem thus seemed virtually insoluble. If Elizabeth died the succession would be disputed between several equally impossible claimants; that dispute could only be avoided if the queen agreed to say who should succeed; yet the choice was such that one cannot blame her for not saying. In addition, of course, there was Elizabeth's steadfast and at times almost hysterical refusal even to consider the matter. Judging from some obscure hints dropped by her, her own experience as 'second person' (heir apparent) in Mary's reign had left her deeply reluctant either to saddle herself with a similar incubus or to impose on anyone else the strain of becoming the centre of intrigues against the reigning sovereign. Elizabeth's position is fully understandable; but so is that of her subjects who dreaded the disorders of a disputed, and abominated the probability of a catholic, succession. No one could know that Elizabeth would solve the problem by living long beyond the normal Tudor span.

Though she rebuked the commons in 1559 for presuming to ask her to marry, she proceeded to raise hopes in the years that followed. The earl of Arran was summoned, looked at, and discarded; Philip II's suggestion of a German Habsburg led to negotiations with the Archduke Charles, son of the emperor Ferdinand. A crisis came late in 1560. When Cecil returned from Edinburgh he found himself in disgrace and the queen entirely taken up with Robert Dudley, son of the duke of Northumberland, a handsome vigorous man with very little sense and a lawfully wedded wife. When the latter, Amy Robsart, died in circumstances suggesting murder, it was freely rumoured that Dudley had had her killed with Elizabeth's knowledge so as to clear the way for his marrying the queen. The story—true or not—was enough to make Elizabeth recover her balance, if indeed she had ever lost it. The intimacy with Dudley (soon after created earl of Leicester) simmered down into the ordinary relations of queen and favourite; Cecil recovered control; politics and responsibility had triumphed over a particularly unsuitable infatuation. The contrast with Mary Stuart's later goings-on is instructive. Elizabeth returned to her diplomatic courtships, Eric of Sweden—another incipient madman—being the latest candidate (1561). Then, in the autumn of 1562, Elizabeth fell very ill of the smallpox and nearly died; though she made a surprising recovery, the problem of the succession loomed enormously large when the second parliament of the reign met in January 1563.

There is again no evidence of particular influence being exercised in the elections for this parliament; several new boroughs sent members, being authorised to do so by their recent charters, but this reflected rather the desire of local patrons for representation in the commons than an attempt at packing. The result was as unfortunate as could be. The lords were now a reasonably safe house, for the Anglican bishops supported a government which their popish predecessors had opposed; but in the commons there was a body of some forty or fifty very active members, mostly with puritan sympathies, who dominated the less independent men and were not afraid even of taking issue with the privy councillors who represented the queen and government. The unofficial leader of this 'choir', as a contemporary called them, was Thomas Norton, the first of the great puritan parliament-men and the hero of the two sessions of this parliament. Other business, of course, occupied much time. This was the parliament which passed the great statute of artificers, already mentioned;[1] an important act for poor relief and an attack on the government's right of purveyance absorbed energies; religion and the fear of papists grew vocal. The chief issue was the succession, together with the queen's hoped-for marriage. A new and dangerous phenomenon made its appearance: the leaders of the opposition met privately before and during the session to concert their moves. The consequences were seen in the revolutionary and highly effective tactics employed against the queen—in all loyalty, of course. Elizabeth often denounced, at this time and later, the discussion of affairs of state in taverns and the like; in the same way her father had denounced talk of religion, also without being able to stop it.

Parliament assembled on 12 January 1563; on the 16th a member raised the subject of the succession. On the 26th it was proposed to petition the queen to marry and permit the nomination of a successor. The first part of this request clearly invaded the queen's private life and was therefore improper; the second, however, could be based on the precedents of Henry VIII's reign when parliament several times declared the succession, and even on precedents going back to Henry IV. On the other hand, such action had never been taken except on the initiative of the crown, and Elizabeth had a tolerable case in constitutional law for refusing to allow the matter to be treated in the house. Her real reasons were the political inadvisability and emotional impossibility of a definite statement. The commons on their side were driven by fear of the queen's death into ever more extreme and unrelenting pressure for an answer. Elizabeth received the commons' petition on the 28th and a parallel one from the lords on 1 February; hiding her anger, she promised an answer which she had no intention of giving. Gentle reminders failed to stir her, till on 10

[1] Above, p. 259.

April she came to close the session. Because she could not give a positive reply and would not risk a plain no, she prorogued parliament rather than dissolve it; the speech she made on the subject of the petition is in her best—that is, her most mystifying —vein. She said that the rumour of her determination never to marry was false: 'for though I can think it best for a private woman, yet do I strive with myself to think it not meet for a prince.' Then she turned to the succession, but her words, sonorous though they were, carried no meaning that anyone could get hold of. With this experience of their queen in a mood familiar to her councillors and more familiar still to foreign ambassadors, the commons had for the moment to be content.

Parliament stood prorogued for over three years, an interval during which stories of marriage continued while the succession remained unsettled and the queen of Scots tried to assert her claims. The Archduke Charles's desultory negotiations for Elizabeth's hand carried on until 1567; there was never much in it on either side. A pamphlet war between the supporters of the Suffolk (Grey) line and the Stuart claim exacerbated feelings and annoyed the queen extremely. If she hoped that time would render the 'choir' more amenable she was sadly astray, the more so as these energetic protestants represented a growing public opinion. Finally, in the autumn of 1566, shortage of money—the heritage of her Scottish and French policy—forced Elizabeth to recall parliament. The move was the more dangerous because she was asking for supplies in peacetime, an unpopular step in itself. The houses reassembled on 30 September, the commons having to elect a new Speaker since the old one had died during the recess; this led to a quite unprecedented clash as the opposition challenged the official nominee (Richard Onslow) who was elected by only twelve votes in a house of 152. The real shock came when the government introduced the subsidy bill. On 18 October a Mr Molyneux made his mark in history by proposing to make supply depend on the queen's favourable answer to the three-years-old petition about the succession. Despite all the councillors could do, the house agreed. The lords, asked to co-operate, sent a deputation to the queen which received the full blast of Elizabethan invective. The parliament could do as they pleased; their bills had no effect without her authority. But, surprisingly, the lords stood firm and joined the commons' manœuvre. Elizabeth, deserted by all and pressed on every side, was beside herself, so much so that she even confided her anger and distress to the Spanish ambassador, de Quadra. They would not have dared to treat her father thus, she said with much justification; and she worked off her fury at court where even Leicester discovered that a queen's favour could be withdrawn. But political sense soon overcame mere anger. On 5 November she anticipated further petitions by summoning representatives of both houses and speaking her mind. She would marry, but the time was 'not convenient' for talking of the succession. It was 'a strange thing that the foot should direct the head in so weighty a matter'. She angrily rebutted their fears: 'I care not for death, for all men are mortal.' Nor would she surrender to pressure. 'Though I be a woman, yet I have as good a courage, answerable to my place, as ever my father had. I am your anointed queen. I will never be constrained to do anything. I thank God I am endued with such qualities that if I were turned out of the realm in my petticoat, I were able to live in any place in Christendom.' When she had a mind to, Elizabeth could speak as plainly as anyone.

  Unfortunately her speech was watered down by Cecil in his report to the commons who, undeterred, revived the agitation. The queen's patience gave way and she took steps which immediately provoked a major constitutional row—the first of many which in the end led to the breach between the Stuarts and their parliaments. On 9 November she commanded the commons to cease discussion at once and content themselves with her promise to marry. After two days the reply came. Paul Wentworth, burgess for Buckingham, moved three questions to the house. First, was the queen's command 'a breach of the liberty of free speech of the house'? Secondly, was the authority of the privy councillors who had communicated the order sufficient to bind the house? Thirdly, if the command was proper and binding, what offence would it be for a member 'to err in declaring his opinion otherwise' (that is, flatly to contradict the queen)? The house listened approvingly; battle was joined; the specific issue of the succession had led to a wide break between the queen and the commons. Elizabeth repeated her order, with a hint that anyone who disagreed might be summoned to argue the matter before the privy council. She was sure of the lords again, but she underestimated the tenacious courage of the lower house. The commons composed an address which, though humble enough in tone, did not withdraw an inch. They thanked the queen for her promise to marry, stressed that a decision on the succession had only been postponed, and affirmed their right of free speech which they felt sure the queen had never meant to attack. The address was never presented. Elizabeth saw that she had gone too far. Rather than face a real conflict over the liberties of the house she surrendered: on 25 November she graciously revoked her commands. The commons were delighted, especially when she followed this up by stopping proceedings against a member, James Dalton, who had made a speech offensive to the Scottish ambassador and was being examined by the council. Now at last she hoped to get her supplies and, to hurry them up, she remitted one third of the money asked. Cheerful after all their troubles, the commons rapidly passed the bill. However, Norton's 'choir' were not to be caught so easily. As a last attempt to pin the queen down over the succession they proposed a preamble for the subsidy bill which registered the queen's promise to marry and decide her successor. It was a skilful but impudent move. Elizabeth's reaction practically scorched the paper on which she scribbled it: 'I know no reason why any my private answers to the realm should serve for prologue to a subsidies-book . . . if these fellows were well answered and paid with lawful coin, there would be fewer counterfeits among them.' The preamble of the act as passed is short and innocuous.

The memorable session was not yet over; further trouble arose over religion—which shall be dealt with in the next section—and the queen could not be rid of her unwelcome advisers until after Christmas. When she dissolved parliament she made, as usual, a masterly speech, rebuking the forwardness of the commons but also acknowledging their loyalty and good will. The tie between crown and parliament was far from broken, but it had been strained very severely. Elizabeth had had to try every expedient to combat the determined and skilful attack of the commons' leaders. She had used patience with persuasion, to no purpose; she had commanded in her most imperious manner, again without avail; finally she had surrendered, pocketed her pride, given up much needed money, and restored the commons to good humour. On the immediate issue she had won, for the succession was not decided and her marriage remained a promised mirage. But she had experienced a new thing—the opposition of the house of commons on a major matter of state, an opposition well led, well disciplined, and based on principle. Worst of all, she had provoked a quarrel over the privileges of the house. The succession would settle itself as time went on; free speech remained to trouble her and later kings. When Elizabeth had acquired more experience she displayed greater tactical skill: never again would she keep in being a house of commons which had proved as refractory as that of 1563, and in future her calculated and always successful surrenders would be timed better. However, while she could stall opposition on marriage and succession by promises and tactics, she could not put off the problem of the Church in or out of parliament.

5. THE SETTLEMENT SECURED

In 1559 the settlement of the Church seemed satisfactory enough; in 1560 doubts began to appear. There were many, bishops and lesser clergy and laity, who thought the act of uniformity but an interim measure; the queen, on the other hand, held that it embodied the complete system. In the general view of the age all subjects of the imperial crown of England were joined with the holder of that crown in one body politic whose secular aspect might be called state or (more commonly) Commonwealth, while its spiritual aspect was comprised in the Church. In such a body, religious nonconformity was naturally the same thing as political opposition and, in extreme cases, as treason. The issue is confused by the fact that the term Church continued to be used for the clergy only, but that was a loose use. The puritans, or precisians, were not a nonconformist body outside the Church (though in time such bodies arose), but a movement within the Church—comprising both clergy and laity—which desired to 'purify' the Church of popish remnants and render it more 'precise'—like heir ideal of the Early Church, or in effect like Geneva. The radical wing within the Church was a threat to Elizabeth's settlement which had proved its strength in 1559 by bringing the Church more rapidly to a protestant condition than she had hoped. She was therefore compelled to keep a wary eye on the other wing—the conservative, catholic, even Romanist wing. The England which she came to rule was predominently catholic; of this there can be no doubt. Yet by about 1570 the catholics—those that looked to Rome rather than Canterbury—had been reduced to a hard core of no more than 150,000, at which number they roughly remained for the rest of the reign.

The reason for this decline was twofold. On the one hand, the queen's government treated this large body of Englishmen with deliberate and calculated moderation in order not to drive them from the fold. On the other, the catholic powers of Europe, including the pope, who should have succoured the catholics in England, left them in the lurch for over ten years. In that time the catholic cause was lost in England. Philip II at first persisted in treating England as his subject protégé; a papal emissary (Parpaglia) dispatched in 1560 to invite Elizabeth to the Council of Trent was prevented by Philip from crossing the Channel on the ground that he was pro-French, a step which saved the queen much embarrassment. Even as it became plain that the Church of England had broken with Rome for good, both the king of Spain, in the interests of his policy, and the pope (the gentle Pius IV who succeeded the fierce Paul IV in 1559) under Spanish pressure continued in their conciliatory attitude. Pius IV sent another messenger to England in 1561, the abbot Martinengo; since Philip did not oblige by stopping him too, Elizabeth had to show her hand by forbidding him to enter the country. In consequence the pope joined France at Trent in pressing for Elizabeth's excommunication, but Spain and the Empire resisted on the grounds that the sentence would do more harm than good since no one could carry it out. Their attitude was sensible, but it prevented the English catholics from receiving a clear lead from Trent. Since they were given no official indication that Elizabeth was a heretic and her Church damnable, most of them saw no difficulty in compromising their consciences by attending Anglican services. When to this feebleness from abroad there was added the studied moderation of the government at home—refusing to enforce the oath of supremacy too rigidly, careful not to enquire after fines for recusancy (refusal to attend at church) in notoriously catholic districts like Lancashire—the winning over of the catholic majority proved easy. As usual the queen was milder than her council and her parliaments. In 1563, the obstreperous commons forced upon her an act which sharpened the penalties for catholics: to support Rome by word, writing, or deed was made punishable by præmunire, while a second refusal to take the oath was made treason. The queen countered by ordering Parker not to tender the oath a second time, despite the clear tenor of the statute. Skilfully handled by a queen who continued to use cross and candles in her chapel and to drop hints of a possible return to Rome before credulous ambassadors, deserted moreover by their friends abroad, and without priests of their own before 1575, most of the English catholics accepted the new state of things and became Anglicans.

This gentle treatment of catholics naturally exasperated those to whom all Romish things were of the devil. Since the most vigorous and intelligent of the Anglican clergy inclined to puritanism, the bishops, who had to reanimate a Church fallen into deplorable ways of idleness, ignorance, and corruption, were in a quandary. Those clergy who answered to the official standard of behaviour tended to be those who opposed the official policy. In 1562, Bishop Jewel published his *Apology*, the leading defence of the settlement for some thirty years; in it he opposed to the puritan demand for a 'pure' Church on the primitive pattern the argument that the English Church had been rebuilt in accordance both with Apostolic principles and with the best teaching of the Church's history. The controversy came into the open in 1563. In convocation, which met at the same time as parliament, the puritans tried to pass measures making the settlement more radical, but failed. The commons signalled their sympathy by opposing a bill designed to improve the navy because it involved a compulsory fast-day on Wednesdays (to encourage the fishing industry) which they held to be a popish practice. However, the bill passed and 'Cecil's Fast' became law. The positive achievement of 1563 was the passage through convocation of the Thirty-nine Articles, a definition of doctrine based on Cranmer's Forty-two and sufficiently indeterminate to conciliate catholics and exasperate puritans. Even so the queen would not have them enacted by parliament: her diplomacy demanded a free hand.

The French treaty of 1564 and the growing strength of the queen of Scots turned Elizabeth more catholic and drove her into action against the puritans. The occasion of this first overt quarrel was the ornaments rubric of the prayer book which had spoken of the vestments of the second year of Edward VI. It probably meant those of the Prayer Book of 1549 which included not only the surplice but the alb and cope as well. Puritan ministers, on the other hand, objected to all distinctive dress and wished to conduct their services in their plain 'Geneva' gowns. There was thus much failure to conform to the rule, and for some years Parker and the queen shut their eyes to it. But in 1564 Elizabeth ordered action, first against the masters of two Oxford colleges—the universities were the chief breeding grounds of puritanism—and then, in January 1565, a general enquiry into the prevailing laxity. In March 1566 Parker published his *Advertisements*—the queen's refusal to accept responsibility delayed them by two years—in which he laid down rules on costume and other matters connected with worship. The Vestiarian Controversy was joined. It expressed itself in pamphlet warfare and puritan appeals for support from abroad which were unsuccessful: the old high-priest of English nonconformity, Henry Bullinger at Zürich, counselled submission to authority, though Theodore Béza, Calvin's successor at Geneva, was rather more friendly. Parker kept the bishops in line and at their task, and by early 1567 the controversy was over; even London, the centre of puritanism and too gently administered by the sympathetic Grindal, had been compelled to conform. However, the residue was worse than the actual trouble, for the affair left a strong bitterness with many against the bishops. So far English puritanism had not been noticeably anti-episcopalian, but the necessary appearance of the bishops as agents of a policy dubbed popish, and as the agents of the queen with her cross and candles, made them objectionable in the eyes of the precise. Though one could not afford to attack the queen, one could attack the bishops whom the queen herself treated with scant courtesy. The unfortunate prelates, assailed by the puritans, despoiled by the supreme governor and her courtiers, and reviled by Elizabeth both for not acting quickly enough and for acting at all, were the real losers in the controversy.

Defeated in convocation and the pulpit, the puritans took the significant step of transferring their agitation to parliament. In 1566 the long wrangle over the succession and the subsidy delayed matters, but early in December no less than six unofficial bills were introduced, imposing various reforms in the quality and practices of the clergy. The commons dropped all except one which gave statutory authority to the articles of 1563. Elizabeth held firmly to the view that the administration of religion was for the supreme governor with the advice of the clergy in their convocations; parliament could participate only if requested to do so. The opposition in the commons insisted that the precedents of the past thirty-odd years justified parliament in taking the initiative as well. Both sides had a case, the queen's being rather the better as the constitution stood. The issue could not have been made plainer than it was in 1566: Elizabeth had no real objection to the substance of the commons' bill, but she would on no account permit them to discuss religious measures at all. A word of command stopped the bill in the lords; so the commons tried blackmail by holding up a government bill which renewed eleven uncontroversial but necessary acts of the last parliament.[1] Both sides stood firm: the government lost its eleven acts, but the commons lost their bill on religion.

That session of 1566 contained in it all the ingredients of the long struggle between crown and parliament: the fundamental issues (succession, religion), the skilful tactics on both sides, the financial weapon, the sudden concentration on constitutional points and the liberties of the house. Above all it demonstrated

---

[1] It was common for acts to be made valid until the end of the following parliament, so as to provide a chance for revision; that next parliament would then simply extend the operation of the laws.

the strength of an organised and well-led puritan opposition in the commons and foreshadowed the triumph of puritanism through parliament and the laity rather than through convocation and the clergy. The clergy, so much reduced in numbers since the Reformation had abolished monasticism and the minor orders below deacon, were never again to rule the roost in England; but even as the secular state triumphed it found itself involved in the resurgence of religious feeling which the Reformation produced. The plainly secular Elizabeth could not abide a preaching and mouthing laity, and she seems never to have understood that the strength and toughness of the opposition she encountered derived from the conscience and religion of puritan laymen. There was much wrong with puritanism—it was narrow, intent on inessentials, incapable of generosity or tolerance—but it gave religion a positive content and stiffened character as nothing else could. In the midst of that pushing, self-seeking, and bootlicking society it served a most necessary purpose.

6. THE FALL OF MARY QUEEN OF SCOTS

In 1567 it might seem as though the worst was over; Elizabeth could imagine that she had ridden out the storm. France was fast drifting into civil war, Spain began to be absorbed by rebellious subjects in the Netherlands, in Scotland the catholic claimant to the English throne was being rendered harmless. At home, catholicism was rapidly turning into allegiance to the Church of England and puritanism had been defeated; as for parliament, economy in money and better management of elections might deal with that. In fact, however, the real crisis of the reign was only just approaching. Three events of the next few months laid the foundation for much trouble. Late in 1567 Thomas Cartwright returned to Cambridge, soon to be Lady Margaret professor of divinity and to give English puritanism a new lease of life. In 1568, William Allen, an English exile ultimately to become a cardinal, founded at Douai in the Spanish Netherlands a seminary for the training of missionary priests to keep the faith alive in England. And also in 1568, Mary Stuart was driven from Scotland, to remain a danger and an embarrassment to Elizabeth for close on twenty years.

The Darnley marriage quickly turned out a mistake. That young man, twenty when he became king of Scots, combined in himself all the worst features of the Stuart character—stupidity, arrogance, moodiness, obstinacy, licentiousness, unreliability. Mary's genuine love for him barely survived the year, but it sufficed to infect her with his wilful pride; she altered her sensible policy of peace with the congregation and circumspection towards protestants. In 1565 the earl of Murray, leader of the protestant lords, was forced to flee abroad, and Mary began to display her attachment to catholicism and dislike of the restraint so far put upon her. But in that queen's life politics were ever intermingled with private affairs. Disgusted with her husband, alienated from the Scottish politicians, she began to put her trust in a private secretary, the Italian David Riccio, with whom her relations may have been innocent. Darnley, wild with jealousy, broke into the queen's chamber with a gang, dragged Riccio out, and murdered him (1565). Mary was then with child, the later King James. She determined to be avenged. Dissembling sufficiently to extract from the idiot to whom she was married the details of the affair, she drove out his accomplices and welcomed back Murray. But when the year 1566 proved clearly that Darnley's one remaining usefulness—his help in asserting the Stuart claim to the English throne—was not likely to be great in view of the English parliament's attitude to the succession, his fate was sealed. He fell ill towards the end of the year; in February 1567 his devoted wife conveyed him to the house of Kirk o' Field near Edinburgh and left him there to be murdered and his body blown up with the house by a conspiracy of Scottish lords led by the wildest of them all, James Bothwell. Her complicity in the plot has never been proved or disproved; that she wished Darnley dead and suspected he might not return from Kirk o' Field is the least one must say.

In any case, it was her utterly mad behaviour after the murder that mattered. She allowed herself to be taken by Bothwell to Dunbar where they lived together until he was divorced and they could be married (by protestant rites) in May. This was the end of Mary Queen of Scots. Catholic Europe stood horrified and refused her countenance and assistance. The Scots went further. A murderous and adulterous queen, tainted moreover with the wrong sort of religion, was more than they could stomach. She who has had so many ardent defenders since her death had none to succour her at this critical point in her life, and whatever excuses one might make for the woman none can be made for the queen. Incidentally, her taste and sense must also be impugned, for she married both the imbecile and vicious Darnley and the wild, dissolute, and untrustworthy Bothwell for love. All the Scots factions combined against her. In June she was imprisoned at Loch Leven where she was forced to abdicate in her child's favour and to nominate Murray as regent. Bothwell, true to form, deserted her, fleeing to Denmark. But Mary's spirit was unbroken. Refusing to renounce her third husband, she managed to escape from Loch Leven in May 1568. Her attempt to recover the crown ended in the skirmish of Langside; she fled to England to appeal to Elizabeth for help against those whom she termed rebels.

It is often said that the move showed her open and trusting nature, while the consequences display the dark meanness of Elizabeth. In fact, Mary had nothing else left—Spain and France were still too shaken by her earlier exploits to be friendly—and Elizabeth was put in the most difficult position imaginable. Her deep-seated reverence for royalty inclined her to the side of a sister queen, the more so as Mary had for the time ceased to be a danger. To restore Mary she would have to overthrow her own best friends in Scotland; if she did not assist, she would give ready offence in the rest of monarchical Europe. Small wonder that even her resources of duplicity and procrastination were taxed to the limit. She kept Mary at Carlisle, under the discreet surveillance of that staunch puritan, Sir Francis Knollys, though even he seems to have fallen under the spell of that impossible woman. Elizabeth then proceeded to give vague promises to Mary and to encourage Murray to suppress Mary's partisans in Scotland. What was she to do with the refugee? She could not return her to power in Scotland without ruining the English cause there; she could not let her go to France, as Mary suggested, without reviving the situation of 1560; she could not keep her in England without providing a centre for any disaffection going. Perhaps the second course would have been best, but it would have involved a known risk which she was not prepared to take.

Thus the business dragged on in devious negotiations and spurious promises. In the end Elizabeth offered to hear both sides: the Scottish lords led by Murray were to produce their proofs of murder and adultery against Mary who was to defend herself and give proof of rebellion, not indeed in a formal trial but in a general examination of the case. Commissioners for all three parties— Mary, Murray, and Elizabeth—met first at York and then at Westminster (October-January 1568-9). Murray and Lethington produced the famous 'Casket' letters, documents allegedly found after Mary's flight which proved her to have been Bothwell's mistress and involved in the plot against Darnley even before Kirk o' Field. Whether these letters were genuine or forgeries has become the subject of almost a special branch of historical science; Mary's partisans have of course refused to admit them, but the truth is that they alter matters very little. On no grounds can Mary be absolved of completely reckless and foolish behaviour, and if she was not actually immoral she did her best to appear so. She sacrificed her place, her country, and herself to an exceedingly unprepossessing passion. At Westminster she refused to answer Murray, and Elizabeth in the end declared that no case had been made out against the Scottish lords while that against Mary lacked completeness. It was a damning enough verdict. Murray returned to Scotland as regent; Mary, long since brought south from Carlisle, began her long years in English prison-castles; and Elizabeth had saved the budding unity between the two parts of Great Britain.

She had weathered this particular trouble well enough, but only at the cost of saddling herself with an appalling burden. The queen of Scots had been a nuisance to Elizabeth in Scotland; she was a permanent and lively danger in England. There was always the possibility that she might escape and head a catholic conspiracy; she became the centre, usually innocent, of plot after plot; she caused trouble between Elizabeth and her parliaments. Too fearful of the Stuart claim to send Mary packing, too scrupulous of the divinity inherent in royalty and too averse to bloodshed to countenance either open execution or secret murder, Elizabeth lived for nineteen years under the shadow of her prisoner.

Chapter XI

THE GROWING CONFLICT, 1568-85

FROM the arrival of Mary Stuart in 1568 to the outbreak of war in 1585, England passed through a phase in which international complications played a greater part than ever before. Elizabeth was trying to preserve peace and her freedom of action in a tumultuous situation and without the positive strength which would have enabled her to stand aloof in safety. Her own inability to take a decision and adhere to it, and the growing split in the council between a peace-faction favouring agreement with Spain (Burghley, Sussex, and Crofts) and a war-faction seeking a protestant alliance with Dutch rebels and French Huguenots and moderates (Walsingham, Leicester, and Bedford) weakened the purposes of English policy. Spain was held back from decisive action by difficulties in the Netherlands, while France was kept divided and therefore ineffective by religious and political factions. Scotland, whose unstable politics maintained a Marian party against the successive regents for James VI who necessarily looked to England, added a further complication. A new aggressive policy from Rome and a new ardent protestantism in England raised problems both religious and constitutional at home, while far away from the turmoil, but playing their part in it, English seamen began the great expansion overseas. Elizabeth, Philip, and Catherine de Médicis were all opposed to war but prepared to work against one another behind the scenes in a manner which would have precipitated war at almost any other period of history. These seventeen years are therefore filled with a mass of negotiations, changes of front, agreements made and broken, secret and barely traceable doings, through which it is difficult to thread one's way. In the end, a clear enough situation emerged. England grew stronger as Spain grew weaker; their old friendship vanished as Spain became the champion not only of catholicism but also of Mary Stuart; and the old enmity with France was replaced by a partial though uneasy reconciliation secure enough in France's distracted state to prevent at all times the dreaded catholic alliance against England. When at last war came, in 1585, Elizabeth, Burghley, and Walsingham had brought their country to such strength and into so favourable a position that England could take on and defeat the greatest power of the day.

I. THE END OF THE SPANISH AMITY

From the marriage of Prince Arthur with Catherine of Aragon (1501) to the marriage of Queen Mary with Philip of Spain (1554), the Spanish alliance was the guiding star of English foreign policy. Often endangered and at times apparently dissolved, it had yet recovered time and again under the double stimulus of the cloth trade and French hostility. Not even Elizabeth's deliberate attack on Spanish susceptibilities from 1558 onwards provoked Philip into active enmity; on the contrary, mindful of the Channel route to the Netherlands and yet hopeful of recovering England for the Church and Spain by peaceful means, he played a leading part in shielding her from the consequences of the renewed schism. Nevertheless, throughout the 1560s, events were undermining the amity which had endured so long. Both sides were guilty of acts which in easier conditions and with sovereigns less bent on peace would unquestionably have resulted in war. Elizabeth permitted her subjects to volunteer assistance to the disaffected Netherlands, received the thousands of refugees who fled from the energetic restoration of order by the duke of Alva's 'council of blood', and sheltered the pirates who infested the Channel. Philip, on the other hand, offered secret assistance to the English catholics and permitted the Inquisition to ill-treat protestant Englishmen in the prisons of the New World and of Seville. The Spanish embassy in London became the centre of plots against the government under the egregious de Quadra, ambassador from 1559 to 1566, and—after the tenure of the discreet Guzman de Silva (1566-8)—under the meddling Guerau de Spes (1568-73) who did his successful best to ruin Anglo-Spanish relations. Even the commercial link with the Netherlands weakened as the revolt there gathered force. Under pressure from the Merchant Adventurers, Cecil promoted an attack on Flemish privileges which in 1563-4 led to a temporary interruption of the trade. Calvinist riots in 1566 and Alva's terror in 1567-8 began the ruin of the Flemish economy which was completed by the destruction of Antwerp in the Spanish 'Fury' of 1576. Overshadowing all other disagreements, however, were the English incursions into Spain's cherished monopoly in the New World, culminating for the time being in the treacherous attack on Hawkins and Drake at San Juan de Ulua (September 1568); news of this event had a direct influence on events in Europe.[1]

The arrival of Mary in England opened a new chapter in

[1] For the full story of English maritime expansion see Ch. XII.

relations with Spain. It ended the danger of a vast Guise empire which had kept Philip to his English policy, and it offered an opportunity for a catholic crusade against the heretic queen, the Jezebel of the North. In his endeavour to restore Spanish power in the Netherlands, Alva had run up against the unquestionable if unofficial intervention of England on the rebels' side, and he hoped to use the Spanish Netherlands as a spring-board for a counter-attack. Overt hostile action came first from England: in December 1568, the queen confiscated a large shipment of bullion despatched by Philip's Genoese bankers for the payment of Alva's troops. The ships, which had been driven into English harbours by fear of Huguenot pirates, offered a splendid opportunity for avenging San Juan de Ulua. When she discovered that the treasure would not be Philip's property until it was delivered to Alva, Elizabeth promptly borrowed it herself from the Genoese and thus forestalled all Spanish protests. Alva nevertheless replied with an embargo on all trade with England and seized English goods; Cecil in turn imposed heavy penalties and seized all Spanish property. In this game Alva was the loser by a margin, but both sides soon had reason to regret it. It was, however, highly significant of the true power and position of the two contestants that England's apparently irresponsible act led to nothing more than a five years' interruption in the Flanders trade.

Unwilling to risk war, Spain had to rest satisfied with fomenting and supporting English discontent which came to a head in the three years' crisis of 1569-72. De Spes, in touch with Mary Stuart and with a set of disgruntled noblemen led by the duke of Norfolk and the earl of Arundel, wrote wildly optimistic letters to Alva in which he demanded assistance for plot after plot whose folly and lack of substance were more sensibly assessed by that great soldier. The Norfolk faction had several grievances of which the main seems to have been hatred of the upstart Cecil. Through Roberto Ridolfi, a Florentine merchant settled in England, they approached de Spes early in 1569 with suggestions for the overthrow of Cecil, the subjugation of Elizabeth to their will, the restoration of catholicism, and the proclamation of Mary as heir to the throne. Unconvinced by de Spes' imaginative description of masses of English catholics only waiting for liberation, Alva refused to move until the conspirators could show some concrete result; the plot collapsed. Norfolk, the only duke in England and very conscious of the difference between his pretensions and his position, was a vain and feeble man, too ready to enter into secret machinations and equally ready to desert them in a panic. He hoped to marry Mary himself, but though the council was not opposed the queen put a stop to the idea. The duke fled to his Norfolk estates, intending to rise in conjunction with the earls of Northumberland and Westmoreland who had grievances of their own. Then, in September 1569, he was summoned to London and his courage left him; he tamely surrendered to the government and sent a soothing message north.

There, however, events were in the hands of more resolute men. The north had not forgotten the pilgrimage of grace, though it seems to have forgotten the outcome of that brave enterprise. Since Cromwell's death, the border country had tended more and more to fall back into magnate hands; Sussex, as president of the council of the north, found himself almost unsupported when the crisis came. The word of a Percy, a Neville, or a Dacre still counted for much more than the word of a Tudor. At this time the heads of these houses had special grievances whose character may be illustrated by the fact that Northumberland especially resented his loss of a valuable copper mine to the queen. Religion played little part in the disaffection, though it supplied a useful cloak. It would appear that the earls' plans for a rising had almost been put by even before Norfolk's arrest, but when Elizabeth then summoned Northumberland and Westmorland to London fear revived the movement. The earls called out their followers, entered Durham Cathedral where they said mass and tore up the English Prayer Book and Bible, and marched south with their demands. Catholicism was to be restored, Cecil brought to trial, Norfolk freed, and Mary (restored to Scotland) recognised heir to the English throne. Their attempt to liberate Mary was frustrated when the government rapidly removed their prisoner from Tutbury. Before the gathering forces of the queen the rebel host melted away; the leaders escaped into the Scottish borders. A belated rising by Leonard Dacre was destroyed by Lord Hunsdon. The north was swept by the queen's vengeance: some 800 men, all of little account, suffered death. Though the rising of the earls seemed a serious matter at the time, it really ended feudalism in the north. Exile, executions, and confiscations broke it, and under its new president, the puritan earl of Huntingdon, the reconstituted council of the north set about its task of wiping out the line of the Trent which since the Norman Conquest had divided England into two markedly different halves.

The government's victory had in part been eased by Alva's refusal to accept the rebels' offer of Hartlepool as a port of entry, but more important still had been the support given to Elizabeth by Murray, the Scottish regent. It will be as well to anticipate a little in order to explain how this northern 'postern gate' of Scotland, as Walsingham called it, came to be secured in the next few years. Murray was assassinated in January 1570, in the middle of the northern troubles, and there seemed a danger of the Marian party gaining the upper hand. However, with English support, successive regents—first Lennox, then Mar, and finally Morton—maintained the Anglophil protestant rule which Elizabeth desired, so that by February 1573 Mary's supporters had shrunk to a small force holding Edinburgh Castle. This happy development saved Elizabeth from a bad stain on her reputation because it rendered unnecessary a plan for handing Mary over to Mar who was to have her executed; before Mar's scruples (and Morton's after him—Mar died in October 1572) could be overcome, the dispersal of Mary's faction ended the civil war in Scotland. An English force was needed to compel the surrender of the Edinburgh garrison, but once this was achieved in May 1573 Scotland ceased to be a threat. Morton's interests were closely linked with England, and though Elizabeth's parsimony made it impossible to bind the Scots nobles firmly to the English interest by the only means they acknowledged—frequent bribes—the 'postern gate' was now in reasonably friendly hands.

The failure of the northern rebellion was a bad blow to Guerau de Spes whose activities in the matter had already attracted the attention of the English government. Reluctant as Cecil was to break with Spain, even he had to acknowledge the unlikelihood of enduring peace. It therefore became necessary for England to prepare for the worst by seeking better relations with France. Since the treaty of 1564, civil war in France had prevented true amity between the catholic Valois and the protestant Tudor. A chance of better things came in 1570 when the peace of St Germain ended the third war of religion and freed Elizabeth from the—to her—unpleasant necessity of supporting the Huguenots, rebels as they were but after all protestants and enemies to Spain, against their lawful king. Charles IX now called the Huguenot leader, the Admiral Coligny, into his council, while Catherine de Médicis began to listen favourably to the suggestion from England that Elizabeth might find her long desired husband in Catherine's second son, the duke of Anjou. In 1570 Francis Walsingham entered upon his long and distinguished career when he was dispatched to France to conduct the negotiations for an alliance and marriage. Since both Elizabeth and Catherine were pastmasters in procrastination, reversals of policy, and dark ways, the negotiations dragged on interminably. Elizabeth for a time maintained the pretence of wanting to marry Anjou, but ended the matter when it suited her by refusing any concessions in religious matters to this most bigoted of the Valois. Walsingham, greatly discouraged, nevertheless continued the negotiations for an alliance, and his endeavours resulted at last in the treaty of Blois (April 1572) by which the two countries bound themselves to mutual defensive assistance. The treaty, soon rendered nearly valueless by events, was nevertheless something of an achievement. At a critical time it removed all danger of a general continental alliance against England to carry out the bull of excommunication and deprivation which the pope had issued in 1570.[1]

The Anjou courtship had served to keep France friendly at a time when Cecil was wrestling with the most serious threat arising out of the northern rebellion and Spanish animosity. This was the so-called Ridolfi plot. Ridolfi—one of those business men who long to manipulate the strings of state affairs—had had a hand in the abortive plotting of 1569, and he took the opportunity of Norfolk's release from the Tower (August 1570) to renew his machinations. Travelling to and fro between England and the continent, he spun a somewhat unsubstantial web round a projected rising which was to get rid of Elizabeth and put Mary, married to Norfolk, on the throne of England. Mary, the bishop of Ross (her agent in France), Philip, the pope, and Norfolk were all involved; Alva alone remained sceptical. Cecil soon received information from such divers places as Scotland and Tuscany, and by September 1571 all the details had been secured by threats and torture. Nearly every conspirator—the queen of Scots leading —hastened to throw the onus on someone else. Norfolk was re-arrested, tried for treason, and sentenced to death (January 1572), but Elizabeth's reluctance to execute England's premier nobleman preserved his life for some months. However, in May 1572 parliament took a hand. The country was deeply stirred by the revelations of treason and danger to the queen, and the puritan faction did not hesitate to point out that none of this would have occurred but for the existence of Mary Stuart, herself heavily implicated. The demand was raised for her death as well as for the carrying out of the sentence on Norfolk. In the prolonged debates that followed, these partisans of Elizabeth soon found themselves gravely at odds with the object of their solicitude. But though the queen resisted even at the risk of another clash with the commons, she had to accept a compromise in the end. Mary

[1] See below, p. 303.

she saved, but Norfolk went to the block in June, victim of his weak vanity and irresolute ambition rather than of more positive and more dangerous qualities.

The crisis thus passed away in the summer of 1572, except that trade with the Netherlands was still at a standstill. The queen's enemies at home were down, her friends in Scotland were improving their position, France had signed a treaty, even Spain seemed ready for peace. In March 1572, ostensibly to conciliate Philip, Elizabeth ordered the closing of English ports to the Dutch 'sea-beggars'. Their leader, La Marck, Orange's admiral in theory and pure pirate in practice, thereupon descended upon the port of Brill. Its capture gave the rebels their first foothold on Spanish territory and immediately provoked a widespread revolt in the northern Netherlands. Town after town threw off the Spanish rule, until four of the thirteen provinces stood united under William of Orange. The revolt of the Netherlands was to provide the chief problem of international politics for the next sixteen years, as well as Elizabeth's best chance of fighting Philip by proxy. It does not seem likely—despite argument and some dubious evidence to the contrary—that she intended any such consequences when she expelled La Marck, but the result was bound to be pleasing though often perplexing.

However, the immediate outcome was to weaken the new alliance with France. In pursuance of Coligny's Huguenot policy, and cheered on by Walsingham, Charles IX encouraged a Huguenot raid into the Spanish Netherlands which was cut to pieces by Alva in July 1572. A violent revulsion at once took place. In order to save himself from war with Spain, Charles deserted Coligny, fell back upon the Guises, and permitted the carrying out of his mother's violent plans which culminated in the massacre of St Bartholomew in August. Walsingham was distraught and England horrified. The plaudits of the catholic world, from the pope downwards, confirmed the worst fears of Englishmen: this was the sort of thing they could expect if Rome and Mary Stuart triumphed. The massacre renewed the religious wars in France and revived Elizabeth's difficulties: she could not afford either to abrogate the treaty of Blois or to desert the Huguenots on whose aid she relied to keep France away from Spain. She did the customary thing by secretly assisting La Rochelle while publicly remaining neutral. Time eased the situation, though the massacre was never forgotten. In 1573, Charles IX made peace after failing to capture La Rochelle and resumed friendly relations with England. As usual, these were expressed in a courtship: the suitor now was the duke of Alençon the youngest of Catherine's sons. For the moment little came of this because Alençon involved himself in domestic intrigues and landed in prison (1574), but the suit was to be resumed later and afford Europe years of incredulous amusement. Also in 1574 Charles IX died; his brother Henry III (late the duke of Anjou) was expected to give rein to his known fanatical catholicism, but in the end, after much trouble and further secret assistance from England to the Huguenots, he confirmed Blois and received the Garter (April 1575). If less of an ally than had seemed likely in 1572, France was yet no enemy, and new internal disruptions were to prolong her inability to intervene in European affairs.

With Spain, too, Elizabeth now came to terms. One of the hopes of Blois had failed to bear fruit. It had been planned to transfer the centre of the cloth export from Antwerp to France, but French jealousy of English merchants and the lack of Antwerp's facilities prevented the trade from expanding. With the clothiers' lamentations at their 'lack of vent'—their inability to find a market—dinning in his ears, Burghley was eager to restore normal traffic. Alva had been ready for some time, but the plots encouraged by de Spes (who was expelled in 1572) had delayed matters. Finally Burghley, opposed to Leicester's French policy, recovered his ascendancy in the council with the news of the massacre and promoted better relations with Spain. The resumption of traffic was followed by a general settlement of the rival claims arising out of the confiscations of 1568-9 in the treaty of Bristol (August 1574), and by an agreement with Alva's successor Requesens be which the Spaniards expelled the English refugees from thy Netherlands and Elizabeth closed her harbours to Dutch rebels and forbade Englishmen to assist them in any way (March 1575). It was not to be a lasting agreement, but it once again postponed the conflict which men like Walsingham thought to be not only inevitable but even desirable. Spain needed a respite to deal with the Netherlands; as for England, she could well do with more years of preparation if the panic of July-October 1570 is anything to go by. In those months the double passage up and down Channel of a Spanish convoy escorting Philip's bride to Spain caused the calling out of the fleet and the musters at an expense which—in view of Elizabeth's feelings on that point—measures the depth of the scare. More particularly, Elizabeth and her government wanted a rest from involvements abroad because they needed time and a free hand to guard the Church at home against attacks from both sides.

2. THE CATHOLIC THREAT

The various scares and plots of the years 1569-72 have so far been viewed as accidental to a general problem of foreign policy, but they were this largely because they arose out of the first positive reaction from Rome to the English schism. This was the bull *Regnans in Excelsis*, proclaiming Elizabeth's excommunication and deposition, which Pope Pius V issued in February 1570. In many ways it was an unfortunate document. It was incorrect in canon law, inasmuch as it failed to give Elizabeth a chance to defend herself and pronounced the deposition at once instead of letting a year pass after excommunication; the explanation that Elizabeth was only a 'pretended' queen was made nonsense of by the recognition she had received from Rome between 1559 and 1570. The bull displayed a painful ignorance of English affairs, denouncing Elizabeth for taking a title (supreme head) which she had been careful to avoid. The pope published it without reference to Spain, thus depriving himself of the only champion remotely capable of executing it; Philip was greatly annoyed both at the bull and at the discourtesy to himself. Pius V, an austere and passionate Dominican, acted from conviction rather than sense. Political considerations did not enter his head: he did what he thought his duty against the heretic queen, but he did it with a precipitancy and neglect of proper form which gave men a chance of evading the issues he had raised. In the event Elizabeth had little difficulty in representing the pope as the aggressor, a view still held by reputable historians. Yet the truth is that Rome had valiantly ignored a series of blatant defiances and concealed attacks: for over ten years catholicism had been outlawed in England, and though the government were careful to mitigate the rigour of the law in its execution it is impossible not to admit that Rome had a real grievance and had at first shown much misguided patience. The rash, ill-conceived, and far-reaching step of February 1570 reversed the position.

The bull declared Elizabeth excommunicate, called upon all faithful sons of the Church to remove her, and absolved Englishmen from their oath of allegiance. It therefore contained a threat to the queen's position which was quite decisive if the pope found anyone to carry it out. This explains the fears of that summer of 1570 when a Spanish armament sailed down the Channel: it was thought, with some reason, that Philip had come to put the bull into effect. It explains the activities of Ridolfi, the plots of de Spes, the hopes of Mary and the fears of Cecil. It explains Walsingham's desire for a protestant alliance to forestall the dreaded association of Guisard France with Habsburg Spain and Burgundy which must destroy England. It explains Elizabeth's reaction to the massacre of St Bartholomew which was generally thought to be the first step in a concerted catholic action against all protestant countries. In reality the situation was nothing like as dangerous. Philip had always had his doubts about the possibility of carrying out a sentence of excommunication and deprivation; he had stopped Pius IV from passing one in the early 1560s and he was rendered no readier to act as the papacy's secular sword by Pius V's single-handed proceedings. France, whether under the direction of Coligny or Guise or Catherine de Médicis, was too distracted and too persistently distrustful of Spain to become an effective partner in a crusade. In effect, the bull fell flat. When the great attack at last came, in 1588, it was barely remembered and played a very minor part. As far as rousing Christendom against the defiant heretic was concerned, Pius V had flung his bolt in vain.

But the bull had its effects—in England. It involved the English catholics in a dreadful dilemma by ending the long years of compromise. The pope's claim to be able to absolve subjects from their allegiance struck at the core of the national state. A man was now virtually compelled to choose between his country and his religion, a choice which, of course, was at the heart of the whole struggle between Reformation and Counter-Reformation. Adherence to the queen meant denial of the bull and the papacy; obedience to Rome meant rejection of Elizabeth and active or passive treason. Most Englishmen, even those who still cherished the old faith, chose the side of the state, seizing eagerly on the technical shortcomings of the bull to save their consciences or taking the step over to the national Church. The government, however, could not afford to wait upon the event. All those who acknowledged the authority of Rome in any particular were now potentially hostile to the state and would have to be dealt with accordingly. The bull ended the period of temporising and the queen's hope of gradually making the Anglican Church comprehensive. From 1570 onwards the number of English catholics altered little, for those who stayed with Rome now chose deliberately. The stragglers, the compromisers, the many who had contrived to think little about it, dropped off.

But if the pope had hoped to rouse the mass of the nation against a heretic and excommunicate queen, he was quickly disappointed. At Rome, and up to a point also in Spain, English affairs were seen through the eyes of the catholic refugees most of whom had fled the country before 1567-8 when the dangers created by Mary Stuart and the Spanish quarrel induced the government to intensify its control over disaffected subjects. Assisted by the fantastic miscalculations of men like de Spes and Ridolfi, these exiles spread the impression abroad that England was ready to revolt and only waiting for a clear call. Instead the nation expressed its passionate revulsion against a hostile power which threatened to break the bonds between ruler and ruled. The bull's clauses shocked a nationalist and king-worshipping generation; from it dates the instinctive English reaction which equates popery with subtle and poisonous treason. The feeling found expression in the parliament of 1571. Led by the puritans, recovering under the Roman stimulus from their earlier defeats, the commons demanded legislation more vigorous than the queen would allow, though the council were on the commons' side rather than hers. An act was passed making it treason to introduce or publish any papal bulls in England, but only the queen's opposition prevented further statutes which, by vastly increasing fines for recusancy and compelling attendance once a year at the Anglican communion, would have rendered the lot of English catholics desperate. Another act deprived of their property all those who had fled abroad and failed to return within a year. The law of treason was reinforced by a third act which included in the offence any affirmation that Elizabeth was not queen or was a heretic and schismatic; the opposition wished specifically to deprive the Stuarts of the succession but failed. The uncovering of the Ridolfi plot added fuel to the flames in the next parliament, but Elizabeth continued to stand out against parliamentary interference.

The queen had shown her attitude: she still refused to admit the conflict to be inevitable. She would punish all those who actively threatened her and her realm, but she would not force her loyal subjects into a choice which might lead many of them into an opposition they did not desire. This policy might have been successful but for one thing: the English catholics were at last about to receive succour and spiritual guidance from abroad through the missions of catholic priests which from 1575 added so romantic—but also so important—an element to the great jurisdictional quarrel. In 1568 William Allen founded his college at Douai in the Netherlands for the training of priests to go and maintain the faith in heretic England. The seminary flourished with the influx of young and ardent students from England and under the guidance of a man who, though clumsy in politics, was a great

teacher. After Requesens had been forced to expel the exiles they
settled down at Rheims whence their most lasting achievement—
an English translation of the Vulgate—derives its name of the
Rheims Bible. In 1579, another college was founded at Rome; it
soon came under the sway of the Jesuit order and produced, by a
most carefully planned and rigorous course of training, a succession
of men longing for martyrdom at the hands of the heretic government. Other colleges grew up later in Spain. The whole movement
was a testimony to the vigour of English catholicism and to the
efficiency of Allen's and the Jesuits' single-minded training. The
Douai and Rheims priests first landed in 1575 and rapidly established contact with catholic families eager for the ministrations of
which they had been deprived since 1559, but it was after the
arrival of the Jesuits from 1580 onwards that the missions achieved
their great successes. They made few converts: the numbers of
English catholics did not increase. But they arrested their decline
and ended the government's hopes of destroying popery and
drawing all Englishmen into the English Church. By their vigorous
opposition to all compromise, their denunciation of the lax practices of semi-conformity which had grown up in the priest-less
years, the missionaries consolidated the catholic minority into a
body able to survive persecution and erected a firm barrier
between the Churches of Rome and Canterbury.

The missionaries' first task was a spiritual one, and they and
their later defenders claimed that they confined themselves to it.
Elizabeth and her government naturally saw it differently. Popish
priests were popish as well as priests: they were bound to support
the policy of the bull—which was treason. It is certain now that
the English government's natural suspicions—that the priests acted
as political agents stirring up disaffection—were unjustified. Their
instructions ordered them not to meddle in politics, to avoid talk
against the queen, and not to permit such talk. The missions were
not supposed to carry out the bull. Nevertheless, they could not
avoid the subject. If they were asked point-blank by their flock how
a man was to reconcile his duty to God and his loyalty to the queen
they could only evade the question—a difficult thing to do which
might lose them influence—or admit the necessity of pursuing the
overthrow of Elizabeth. The problem was a very real one, and the
first Jesuit missionaries, Robert Parsons and Edmund Campion,
raised it at Rome before their departure for England (1580).
Gregory XIII, Pius V's successor, replied that the bull was not
binding on catholics until it could be executed; thus obedience to
the state in power was not to lead to spiritual censures despite the

clear tenor of the bull. This sophistry provoked much scorn and subsequent heartburning, but it did save the English catholics from an intolerable position (into which, of course, they had first been pitchforked by Rome) and the priests from having to pronounce on political issues. It also made more difficult the task of the government in repelling the missions.

Throughout the 1570s and 1580s the persecution of catholics—'mass-priests' and their aiders and abettors—went on with growing vigour. Before 1580 priests could be charged with having brought in the bull and therefore with having committed treason under the act of 1571; the first martyr of the missions, Cuthbert Mayne, suffered for this in 1577. Few of those who landed in the creeks and on the deserted foreshores of southern, eastern, and western England escaped the government for long; the protestant zeal of magistrates and the self-interest of informers saw to that. The missionaries came to glory in martyrdom, and the English government—after vain attempts to moderate the rigour of the law—obliged. Elizabeth always claimed that no one was persecuted in England for his religion: the trials of catholic priests were always for treason. It was a sound enough argument on the surface, but specious withal; for the priests did not in fact commit treason except inasmuch as they were priests, and therefore, though Englishmen, emissaries of a foreign power. After Gregory XIII's decision on the bull it was no longer so easy to try them under the act of 1571, and the usual charge became one of conspiring against the queen, which was thought proved if the accused could be shown to have come from Rome or Rheims. At a time when the threat of foreign invasion seemed always about, when the presence in the realm of Mary Stuart encouraged frequent plots endangering both the life of the queen and the safety of the state, the government could act in no other way. But it had to twist the law to do it, and the men it caught were the victims of political issues in which, deliberately but of course unavailingly, they endeavoured not to engage. Edmund Campion, the most saintly and most attractive of all the Jesuit missionaries, was executed in 1581 for treason committed by simple adherence to the queen's enemies (under the basic treason law of 1352); although he had done nothing except preach the faith, he had clearly adhered to the pope who was pursuing an active war against England. Parsons, a much abler and more dangerous but also much more dubious character, escaped to carry on the war from Rome and Spain by pamphlets and intrigues. An act of 1581 heavily increased the fines for recusancy to £20 and made it treason to convert and be converted to Rome.

The last provision was designed to catch the missionaries now that the bull had dropped out of the argument; it preserved the political character of the persecution by expressly equating conversion with withdrawal of allegiance. Some 250 men died altogether in the reign for the catholic faith—or for treason, according to the point of view—and of them over fifty died in prison. The numbers are very small by sixteenth-century standards and no other contemporary government bothered to keep inveterate opponents alive in permanent imprisonment, as did that of Elizabeth when it created a special depository of priests at Wisbech in Norfolk. This was part of the policy which tried to make the recusants a profit to the state by touching their pockets rather than martyrs by seeking their deaths: it, too, was at most moderately successful in protecting the realm against Rome. Enough died, and more suffered torture and barbarous treatment in the course of the persecution, to remind us that we are dealing with a life-and-death struggle in which many very ugly weapons were freely employed by both sides.

A few attempts were made by the papacy itself to give effect to the bull by direct action. In 1572 the ardent and unpolitical Pius V was succeeded by Gregory XIII, as determined to extinguish heresy and recover the Western world for Rome but less troubled by moral scruples about the means employed. He was always hatching plots, planning action, driving others to take up the sword for Rome, but he displayed no ability to develop a single effective scheme. Rashness and foolish optimism characterised all his doings, and his impulsiveness—as in his 'explanation' of the bull in 1580—destroyed much of the moral basis on which the papacy might have acted. He saw the value of the Jesuit missions and encouraged them, but he wanted more immediate and more warlike results as well. The powers having shown themselves unready or unable to carry the crusade into Elizabeth's country, the pope himself undertook the fitting out of expeditions to carry out the *empresa*—the enterprise against England—of which papal and Spanish documents are full. He got his chance through the condition of Ireland where Elizabeth's policy of continuing the subjection of the country had roused savage opposition led by James Fitzmaurice, a Geraldine of the unruly province of Munster. Failing to secure Spanish help, Fitzmaurice went to Rome, and in 1578 an expedition was despatched by Gregory. Its leader, Sir Thomas Stukeley, one of the most extraordinary figures of the day, was an English renegade who had led a brilliant and adventurous military career all over Europe. He had had a hand in Irish troubles before this, had fought at Lepanto, had won and lost the confidence of Philip II. Gregory, sanguine and eager as usual, fell under Stukeley's spell, but the adventurer promptly diverted the papal armament to assist Portugal in Morocco (where he died at Alcazar) and the expedition came to nought. In 1579, however, Fitzmaurice himself, accompanied by the propagandist Nicholas Sanders as legate, landed with a scratch force at Smerwick in Ireland. For some time it looked as though a successful revolt might be raised, though Fitzmaurice was soon killed; Spanish reinforcements arrived in 1580, and Sanders was turning Irish hostility to England into zeal for the Church. But late in the year the English deputy (Grey de Wilton) captured Smerwick, putting to death as pirates the Spanish troops who had held it—for Philip had disowned them. That was the end of the last independent action by the papacy. Grey's savagery at Smerwick was justified by the law and standards of the time, though it was far from commonly copied: it shows starkly the state of mind into which these religious wars were driving all nations.

The hopes of Rome thus once again concentrated on Spain on the one hand and on the missions on the other. Spain was tardy, and the devoted priests were suffering terrible losses: Rome's hopes did not stand very high in the early 1580s. The priests are the more to be pitied because in fact they were pursuing a hopeless quest. They never touched more than a minority of Englishmen, and of that minority few only would in the last resort put their faith before their country. Throughout those years the international situation was growing darker and the name of Spain more obnoxious to Englishmen. When the crisis came the country stood united behind Elizabeth: the first thirty years of her reign, by preserving the peace and by judiciously mingling severe repression with prudent blindness to evasions, gave back to England a solid unity which she had not known since Henry VIII broke with Rome. To English catholics the failure of the Armada was only a sign that Spain was not God's chosen instrument, a point which they had long suspected. The catholic attack preserved the catholic faith in England, but it failed to shake the protestant state and in fact assisted, by reaction, in the growth of a more ardent and uncompromising protestantism.

3. THE GREAT AGE OF ELIZABETHAN PURITANISM

As has been seen, the Vestiarian Controversy ended in the technical defeat of the puritan opposition, but the real losers were the bishops and with them discipline in the Church. After 1568 the

LET

queen's preoccupation with the catholic threat gave the puritans a breathing space, while their denunciation of popish ways and their attacks on popish remains in the Church of England attracted to their side those who thought the protestant settlement in danger. For a time, the extreme wing of the Church seemed to represent all that was best and most principled in it; the moderates seemed too lukewarm, too tarred with the brush of Rome. Thus the movement for purifying the Church revived, and more and more voices were raised against the shortcomings of pluralist, worldly, and unlearned clergy. In their struggle the ecclesiastical radicals found allies in the press and in parliament; until the imposition of a stricter censorship in 1586 puritan pamphlets and manifestoes flooded the country, and every meeting of parliament offered an opportunity for airing puritan views and putting forward puritan bills for Church reform. The council was either indifferent or downright friendly: Leicester and Walsingham both favoured puritanism, the former probably because it demanded the war with Rome in which he hoped to distinguish himself. Sir Francis Knollys and Sir Walter Mildmay, privy councillors and regular government representatives in the commons, were of the same colour. The queen continued to abominate puritanism, an attitude in which she probably represented the views of the inarticulate majority of the people rather than those of the educated and politically active minority. In these years between the bull and the Armada puritanism had its ups and downs, but in the end it was shown to have lost the battle for control of the Church and to have won a substantial and highly significant following in the lay gentry. Kept out of the higher ranks of the Church and driven from official place, the puritan ministers found refuge in the chaplaincies and rectories which puritan gentlemen or municipalities like the city of London bestowed on them.

The most significant development in puritanism was its closer definition. It had hitherto been a somewhat amorphous movement, gaining cohesion from a general opposition to things thought popish, and it had therefore expressed itself in quarrelling over such inessentials as vestments and church ornaments. For another dozen years there were many both clergy and lay who thought that the Church needed reform and wished to alter some of its practices, but who stopped short of adopting the full Calvinist theology and constitution. By the side of this moderate puritanism there grew up after 1568 a definitely presbyterian movement—a movement, that is, which wished to reform the Church by abolishing bishops and putting in their place the Genevan system of government by ministers and elected elders, through a hierarchy of synods ranging upwards from local congregational bodies to a national assembly. The English prophets of this movement were Thomas Cartwright and Walter Travers, and its organisers were the young London ministers John Field and Thomas Wilcox. Cartwright, a Cambridge don of great influence in his circle, was appointed Lady Margaret professor of divinity in 1569. He devoted his courses to a general attack on the constitution of the English Church, fell out with John Whitgift, the master of his college (Trinity), and went into exile at Geneva. Refreshed by draughts from the fountain-head he returned just in time to join Field and Travers in the preliminary manoeuvres before the session of 1572. These culminated in the publication of the *First Admonition to the Parliament* (June 1572) which attacked the state of the Church and asked parliament to introduce the Genevan model of discipline and government as the only one properly based on Scriptural authority. A shrewd and passionate appeal, it led to a prolonged pamphlet warfare, with Whitgift's *Answer*, Cartwright's *Reply*, and a *Second Admonition*. The presses on which this puritan propaganda was printed were secret, but so far the government's censorship could not prevent a liberal output of hostile writings. Direct methods proved more effective: Cartwright was once more driven from England in 1573, and Travers followed him a year later. They continued to put out numerous pamphlets and books defending the presbyterian system and attacking episcopacy; of these, the most significant was Travers's *De Disciplina Ecclesiastica*, a detailed exposition of presbyterianism with its organisation of ministers, deacons, and ruling elders, which remained the text-book of English presbyterians. Edmund Dering, the most outspoken preacher of his time who had not hesitated to accuse the queen to her face of permitting the abuses with which he charged the clergy and the patrons of livings, died in 1576; Field and Wilcox confined themselves to parish duties; the vigorous leadership of extreme puritanism was dispersed.

The movement then entered a new phase. Militancy, nourished by the catholic plots of 1569-72, had failed to carry the Church by storm; now moderate means, well disguised as merely moral reform, were to attempt the conversion of the Church from within to a quasi-presbyterian condition. The chance offered because in 1575 Matthew Parker died, after sixteen years of honest and diligent labour in the service of a queen who had done her best to render his task of establishing uniformity difficult by her delays and her failure to back him up. The obvious successor, Cox of Ely, was married and therefore anathema to the queen; the choice fell in 1576 on Grindal of York, a man who since his Strassburg days under Queen Mary had displayed a consistently mild temper and a readiness to approve of the reforming ideas of puritans. It was a serious mistake to make and one that surprises, for Elizabeth rarely picked the wrong man. Grindal was at once confronted with a development among certain of the clergy which went by the name of 'prophesyings'. These were regular meetings to expound the Scriptures with discussions on the expositions offered. Round them there might grow up, as there did at Northampton, a virtually puritan cell within the Church, supported by the lay magistrates and spreading Calvinist teaching among clergy and laity alike. To Grindal, the movement seemed innocuous and even meritorious, for it certainly helped to bring learning and skill in preaching to a clergy who were in general notoriously deficient in both. The archbishop wished to encourage the spread of such spontaneous reform; the queen who, with much justification, suspected the seeds of a presbyterian organisation ordered him to prohibit prophesyings. He refused, respectfully but definitely, and in June 1577 he was suspended from the exercise of his authority. To have publicly removed him would have caused a scandal which the Church could not afford; in the event Canterbury remained virtually vacant till Grindal died in 1583, on the point of at last resigning. In the meantime, disorder reigned. Some bishops, especially John Aylmer of London, the centre of puritanism, did something to enforce conformity, but others encouraged the prophesyings. The council continued to give support to moderate puritanism behind the queen's back, while Elizabeth insisted on not being involved actively at all despite her strong opinions on the subject.

The dangers of weakness were shown in the rise of a further division with the growth of separatism, a movement affecting individual congregations who wished to elect their own ministers and pursue their own way to salvation without any superior authority. There had been such bodies in the London of the 1560s; in 1581, a more serious deviation occurred at Norwich under Robert Browne and Robert Harrison. Browne, a preacher and pamphleteer of great ability, had hopes of converting the whole Church to congregationalist ideas but had to be content with leading a separatist movement. Here the authorities did not hesitate, for neither Anglicans nor presbyterians had any sympathy with splinter groups. The Brownists were driven to take refuge at Middelburgh in Holland (1582) where the inherent instability of such organisations soon produced quarrels. Excommunicated by his own Church and badly disillusioned, Browne retired into a country parish in England where he spent forty-two conforming years (1591-1633) to live down his revolutionary past. But his example survived his retirement. Brownists were soon rivalled by Barrowists, the followers of Henry Barrow of London who actively organised separatist groups from his prison where he spent seven years before he was hanged in 1594 for sedition. Separatist groups were to have a great future, to dominate puritanism in the next century, and—as Independents—to win the civil war and set up their own government in England, but under Elizabeth their influence and importance were small.

In any case, the government turned to a more energetic repression of nonconformity from about 1580 onwards. In that year the various ecclesiastical commissions, established at intervals since 1559 to seek out and destroy failure to conform to the official Church and worship, were consolidated into the regular court of the high commission for ecclesiastical causes. In 1583, Whitgift succeeded Grindal at Canterbury. An uncompromising opponent of puritanism since his Cambridge quarrels with Cartwright, he was just the man for the queen's purpose. Unlike Parker he does not seem to have been greatly troubled by Elizabeth's evasions and refusals to commit herself, but went ahead, using the high commission to destroy the puritan organisation. Out of the prophesyings had grown what is known as the 'classical movement', that is an unofficial but effective organisation of 'classes' upon which a further organisation of provincial and national synods was to be erected. The Dedham classis began it in about 1582. The movement threatened at one time to engulf the lower clergy, but it began to break up from within as some classes showed themselves less presbyterian than others. Field, the movement's organiser and real inspiration, died in 1588, and the general synods of that year and of 1589 proved to be agreed only in their desire for an ill-defined presbyterian model. When it came to action there was a split between those who wanted to attack the bishops and those who were content to resist passively. The extremists did the movement little good, especially when the publication of the violent and scurrilous, but clever and amusing, 'Martin Marprelate' tracts (1588-9), attacking the bishops, provoked the active anger of the queen. Leicester died in 1588 and Walsingham in 1590, and with them passed away the puritan party in the council. The defeat of the Armada also played its part by robbing puritanism of its specifically patriotic appeal: it ceased to profit from its out-and-out opposition to catholicism when the whole country was at war with catholic Spain. Furthermore, the established Church was now, after some thirty years' existence, at last acquiring a firmer hold on the country. Exploiting all these factors, Whitgift, ably assisted by Richard Bancroft who acted as detective-in-chief to the high commission, steadily continued his work of routing out and suppressing nonconformity. In 1571 three articles had been devised as tests for conformity—acknowledgement of the royal supremacy, the 1559 prayer book, and the Thirty-nine Articles. In the interval, many clergy had evaded the duty of subscribing to these, but Whitgift now revived and applied them consistently in examinations before the high commission. By the end of the period under review Elizabethan puritanism was past its peak. It had failed to capture the Church, first by the attack of militant presbyterianism, then by alliance with Grindal and through the peaceful means of prophesyings; the classis was dead or conforming; and the movement had entered upon a decline which made it, after its failure to exploit James I's accession, a permanent minority opposition outside the Church.

There its strength lay in the laity, especially the gentry and the city of London. Outmanœuvred and defeated in the Church, it found a refuge in parliament. Even in these middle years of the reign, when the commons were on the whole amenable, a minority of puritan members continued the struggle by bills for Church reform and pleas for a purer clergy. The growing Spanish menace assisted them: they represented the genuine fears of Spanish and popish influence at court which found nourishment in the queen's enigmatic policy. The opposition which had grown up round constitutional issues in the 1560s continued into the 1570s and after. The spark was fanned into flame by the arrival of the greatest of the Elizabethan 'parliament-men', Peter Wentworth.

4. THE CONSTITUTIONAL QUESTION

With such stalwarts as Thomas Norton, Walter Strickland, and William Fleetwood, the precedent-hunting recorder of London, surviving from earlier parliaments, and with Peter Wentworth sitting for the first time in 1571, the puritan faction continued strong. But there is a difference about the opposition. The frequent protests that no disloyalty is intended to the queen now truly represent the curious double feeling of these ardent parliament-men: their fear for the future of the country and their passionate

devotion to the crown. Even Wentworth, a constant thorn in
Elizabeth's side, a contentious and often unreasonable obstacle in
the path of smooth government, in all his violent attacks on the
queen's policy never intended any attack on the queen's person.
As he put it on one occasion:

> I will never confess it to be a fault to love the queen's majesty,
> while I live; neither will I be sorry for giving her majesty warning to
> avoid her dangers, while the breath is in my belly.

Elizabeth rightly thought herself as fit to notice danger as this
puritan gentleman from Northamptonshire whose blunt but
eloquent speeches and constant readiness to see offences against
the rights of parliament both greatly helped to develop the doctrine
of free speech and greatly hindered the discharge of parliamentary
business. To the queen he was nothing but a nuisance; while
appreciating his stand on principle and admiring so uncompro-
misingly consistent a career, we should also remember the fact that
in the policy he advocated Wentworth was almost invariably
wrong and often captious. This goes for the whole tribe of parliamentary puritans. One may understand their fears as they looked
round and saw Spain stronger, the protestant Dutch in sad straits,
the queen dallying with a French catholic suitor; but one can now
see that England was safer in Elizabeth's hands than she would
have been in those of Wentworth and his associates.

The earlier problem of the queen's marriage barely evoked an
echo after 1571. Elizabeth was soon into her forties, so that there
seemed the less point in asking her to marry. Even so, she was
once more provoked into a reference to the matter, in the speech
with which she closed the 1576 session. In it she again stressed her
natural inclination to the single state and her readiness to sacrifice
preference to the interests of the country. The long-drawn negotiations with Alençon seemed to bear her out and kept the commons
quiet. Of the succession, on the other hand, they could hardly
forbear to speak, with the queen of Scots in the country and plots
being uncovered (and many more suspected) all around her.
There was an outburst in the 1572 session, when parliament
demanded Mary's head in revenge for her part in the Ridolfi plot,
only to have to content itself with Norfolk's and a characteristic
evasion on Elizabeth's part. Refusing either to approve or to veto
a bill for the execution of Mary Stuart, she promised to adhere
faithfully to the courteous formula which normally masked the
royal veto: *la reine s'avisera*—the queen will think about it. This

aptly literal interpretation left the commons—and the council—baffled and preserved Mary's life for another fifteen years. In 1584 parliament hastened to embody in an act the spontaneous association formed the year before whose members were sworn to protect the queen and to avenge her death by the punishment of anyone who had shared in its guilt. This, a reaction to the assassination of William of Orange, was designed to prevent the succession of Mary, but no positive statement depriving her or settling the succession in any way could be got in the face of Elizabeth's continued refusal to touch the matter. Thus these delicate topics, not forgotten but passing out of mind, gave place to other issues. By and large, all the conflicts of these years fall into one of two constitutional categories—those concerned with the privilege of freedom of speech and its application, and those illustrating the growing and growingly touchy selfconsciousness of the house.[1]

In 1571, after some preliminary manœuvres, Walter Strickland introduced a bill for the reform of the prayer book. For this—as she saw it—plain invasion of her prerogative, the queen had him called before the council and forbidden to attend the house. This raised a storm: despite the efforts of the privy councillors present, members protested against this unexplained semi-arrest of one of their number and raised the question of privilege. Warned of the excitement, the queen realised her mistake, and before matters could go further Strickland was permitted to return to his place. It was a tactful and timely withdrawal which tacitly acknowledged the commons' freedom from any sort of arrest during a session; but the bill was dropped and Elizabeth had preserved her prerogative and protected her Church.

However, there was one in the house now who remembered such things and pondered them during and between sessions, wrestling in the best puritan fashion with his soul and invariably coming up (as puritans were and are liable to do) with some unpleasant but necessary duty in which clearly he delighted. Peter Wentworth did little in this first parliament in which he sat, but that little was significant. The point which struck him was the frequent mention of the queen's displeasure—rumours went about that the queen had said such and such, while in turn the queen herself received garbled rumours from the house. He unburdened himself of all this in a violent attack on Sir Humphrey Gilbert, the explorer, himself a member, who had made a speech needlessly flattering to

[1] The following parliaments sat in this period: 1571, 1572 (prorogued to 1576 and again to 1581), 1584-5, 1586-7.

the sovereign and hinting at improper channels of information. Wentworth recurred to the point in the next parliament, in 1572, when Mr Snagge complained that a speech of his had been twisted into an attack on the lords. Wentworth enthusiastically followed the lead, and the Speaker, Robert Bell, who as a private member had suffered similarly in the previous parliament, lent his support. The grievance, such as it was, had some body in it. It was one of the unacknowledged duties of privy councillors in the house to keep the queen informed of what went on there, and their fellow-councillors in the lords naturally shared in the information. In the process, no doubt, many a rash word might be inconveniently preserved, and the queen's reaction, as conveyed in hints and rumours, might act as a serious limitation on members' liberty to speak their minds. In 1572 the matter blew over, after a vigorous debate and protests to the lords, but with Wentworth it rankled.

When the house reassembled in 1576, Wentworth immediately opened a prepared oration on freedom of speech which he had composed as much as three years earlier. It is one of the great classics of parliamentary oratory. Taking as his text the words 'sweet indeed is the name of liberty and the thing itself a value beyond all inestimable treasure', he complained of seeing free speech infringed in the two sessions during which he had attended parliament. He argued that the commons were in duty bound freely to discuss all matters affecting God's honour and everything 'commodious, profitable, or in any way beneficial for the prince or state'—that is, those points of ecclesiastical legislation and affairs of state which Elizabeth determinedly reserved for the prerogative. Else the parliament were no parliament. There were two things very hurtful to its privilege. One was the sort of rumour which said that 'the queen's majesty liketh not of such a matter; whosoever preferreth it, she will be much offended with him' or alternatively that she would resent opposition to a matter she liked. The other was that messages came to the house, ordering or inhibiting some action. 'I would to God, Mr Speaker, that these two were buried in hell: I mean rumours and messages.' He elaborated these points at length, indulging in so much of his own desired freedom of speech that the house sat aghast. 'Certain it is . . . that none is without fault: no, not our noble queen. Since, then, her majesty has committed great faults . . .' Such language was unheard of.

Wentworth was stopped in mid-career, and the house considered what to do with him. In the end they committed him to the

serjeant-at-arms and had him interrogated by a powerful committee. In this examination Wentworth—it is his report alone that
we have—acquitted himself nobly, defending his attacks on the
queen's policy and his rude references to Mary Stuart as well as
his remarks about rumours. The house was deeply disturbed.
Wentworth had clearly gone too far, and they were both angry at
his attack on one who had already become an idol and apprehensive
of what she might do. Realising that she could for once trust the
commons to do all that was needful, Elizabeth kept out of the
affair. Wentworth was committed to the Tower by the house itself;
there he spent four unrepentant weeks—his first but by no means
his last sojourn there. He had been presumptuously rude by the
standards of the time, but no more so than puritans thought it
right to be; that other puritan, Sir Francis Walsingham, frequently
lectured the queen as frankly—though not, of course, as publicly—
which may account for her dislike of him. But Wentworth had
raised a genuine point of principle, and his fate showed that there
was something in it. The commons would not be really free in
their speech while the crown exercised subtle influence through
'rumours and messages'. That without some such contact affairs
of state might resolve themselves into an intolerable series of
unexpected conflicts is plain and was to be lamentably proved by
the Stuarts. The problem of how to provide free speech for those
who thought it their duty to oppose, without ruining the co-
operation of crown and parliament on which English government
rested, was yet far from solved.

   In 1581 Wentworth kept fairly quiet, and the problems that
arose were minor ones. As if to illustrate his brother's point, Paul
Wentworth moved for a general fast; Elizabeth took this to be
an encroachment on her control of ecclesiastical affairs and forced
the commons to apologise humbly for letting the matter go forward.
Thomas Norton had a last fling in trying to make even fiercer the
fierce recusancy act of that year. Before the next parliament met, he
died (1584) after nearly twenty-five years in the commons. A ready
debater, skilful tactician, and strongly-principled puritan, he more
than anyone had nursed and shaped the parliamentary opposition
of the reign. His reward was a general fame as 'Master Norton the
parliament-man', though it is only recently, after being for long
overshadowed by the more assertive and dramatic Wentworth,
that he has come into his own again.[1]

   In 1584-5 Wentworth did not sit, but the parliament of 1586-7

[1] Norton is the real hero of Professor Neale's *Elizabeth I and her
Parliaments 1559-81*.

saw him revive the agitation for free speech. He got his opportunity when Anthony Cope introduced his 'bill and book'—a bill for the repeal of the prayer book and its replacement by the puritan book of discipline and worship which he offered instead. It was an impudent move, but one which found the house in sympathy in that desperate year before the queen of Scots was dead and while a Spanish descent on England seemed only too likely. The queen ordered the Speaker to render up both book and bill, which he did. Thereupon Wentworth submitted ten articles which he wished the Speaker to put to the house for its resolution. In them he asked whether parliament was not necessary for the existence of the state as the only maker and abrogator of laws, and whether free speech was not granted by law since parliament could not operate without it. He went on to attack his old targets. It was injurious to the order and liberties of the house for messages to be carried to and fro; the house would be failing in its duty if it permitted such messages and rumours; anyone who infringed the liberties of the house was to be regarded as an enemy to God, the prince, and the state. The language of this remarkable document reads astonishingly like the pronouncements of Stuart parliaments; Wentworth was rapidly travelling towards an opposition so intransigent —and so puritanically biblical in expression—that his place as the forerunner of such men as Eliot or Pym becomes unmistakable. The Speaker showed the paper to a privy councillor, and in consequence Wentworth spent another spell in the Tower. This time the council—that is the queen—committed him. Others followed, including Cope, but it seems that they were arrested for their activities in improperly concerting a parliamentary campaign before the session opened rather than for anything they did in the house. The ten articles were Wentworth's last word on privilege. In his attempts to get past Elizabeth's obstructionist tactics to a reform of religion he had been driven into an unprecedently complete doctrine of free speech. Though for a time he seemed defeated, his example was not forgotten when crown and commons began to clash without the shock-absorbing interposition of an essential loyalty to the wearer of the crown.

While the struggle for freedom of speech centred on—indeed, emanated from—the heroic and craggy figure of Peter Wentworth, the signs of the commons' growing self-consciousness centred on the egregious, ill-tempered, and rather petty Arthur Hall. Hall attracted attention when he spoke in favour of Norfolk and Mary Stuart in 1572: from first to last he was always out of tune with the feeling of the house, though despite this ill-timed if honourable

320 THE GROWING CONFLICT, 1568-85

championship he was no catholic himself.[1] Round him there revolved a storm in the session of 1576 which is known as Smalley's Case. It arose in a private quarrel of Hall's which ended in one of his servants, Edward Smalley, being sued for debt. Smalley got himself arrested during the session in order to secure his release on grounds of privilege and thus baulk the debt. When Hall moved for his servant's release, the house ordered the serjeant-at-arms to fetch Smalley from prison, but the serjeant objected that the correct thing to do was to obtain a writ of privilege from chancery. Here the matter stuck, for chancery refused to issue a writ, on the sufficient grounds that a man once arrested for debt and then released could not be proceeded against thereafter—the very reason, of course, for which Smalley had sought arrest in the first place. Oddly enough the house did not use Ferrers' Case as a precedent for freeing Smalley;[2] one may suspect that Hall's unpopularity made them reluctant to find a way out. In the end, however, the serjeant was ordered to bring Smalley to the bar of the house. The rest of the story concerns the attempts of the commons to defeat Hall's and Smalley's conspiracy by forcing payment of the debt: arbitration having failed they went so far as to send Smalley (freed from his original arrest) to the Tower, but Hall, furious at being shown up, would not allow his servant to pay until his wife saved him from himself by settling the affair behind his back. Out of this unsavoury business there arose a further precedent for the right of the commons to secure a release from arrest by warrant of the mace—that is, by order of the house—without the intervention of chancery—that is, the crown.

Hall continued to brood over his injuries and, unfortunately for himself, vented his spleen in two pamphlets in which he not only published the proceedings of the house—a serious offence in itself—but attacked the pretensions of the commons to ancient powers and privileges. Describing them as a 'new person in the Trinity' of crown, lords, and commons, he rightly denied the false history by which the Elizabethan parliamentarians were creating for their institution prescriptive rights and powers, perhaps the most significant sign of the new spirit in parliament and a portent of the future. That Hall was right is beyond doubt, but his sound

[1] Another member who defended Mary was a conservative married to a catholic, Francis Alford. The existence of such men and their liberty to express their views should warn us to remember that the puritans never composed more than a minority—a loud and influential minority—of the house, and that the Elizabethan commons were a varied crowd, very different from the regimented supporters of party we are accustomed to.

[2] See above, p. 174.

history only added to the wrath to come. In the next session (1581) he was arrested, sentenced to fine and imprisonment, and expelled the house. He submitted with an ill grace, and the queen spared him the fine and the six months in the Tower, but though he was re-elected in 1584 he did not take his seat for fear of reviving the agitation against himself. Choleric and sulky though he was, he deserves some pity as the first victim of the commons' use of privilege to protect their exalted opinion of themselves. In the course of his troubles he had helped inadvertently to increase their powers by confirming that the house could release by its own mere order prisoners who claimed privilege, could expel members and by implication exercise exclusive control over them, and could inflict punishments in the manner of a court. They claimed to do these things by ancient privilege; in fact these powers, if not unprecedented, were of such recent origin that only the story of Arthur Hall really marked their establishment.

The commons' assertiveness also came out in several clashes with the lords, a rather ominous development. There existed machinery for the settling of such disputes: joint committees of both houses had met on occasion since 1529 to discuss difficulties. The queen naturally used the lords' readiness to support her in order to weaken the commons' chances of thwarting her, and from 1572, when Burghley sat in the upper house, the chief architect of legislation could no longer control at first hand the discussions in the less amenable house. Since bills were often introduced in that house which contained the councillor concerned with them, the commons were on occasion presented with a controversial bill already discussed and passed by the lords, a procedure they resented. Thus they objected to two bills in 1576, and minor quarrels recurred at other times. None of it was very serious— conciliation prevailed—but it was significant enough of a new temper in the lower house. Beyond question, the commons, resentful of anything that savoured of dictation by lords, council, or queen, had become a factor to be reckoned with. Even in these years when she had at last found a parliament (1572-81) which was so far from obstreperous as to make its retention for nine years agreeable, Elizabeth could never relax her vigilance. Her and her councillors' skill in management was constantly called for, and she employed all her arts, from threats and persuasions to the appearance of gracious surrender.

The strength of the commons lay in the fact that they represented accurately the uneasiness, even fear, of protestant England in face of foreign threats and—as it seemed and often was—

domestic irresolution. England was far from puritan, but it was becoming more definitely protestant, and in this movement the extremists naturally took the lead. When men fear an enemy they prefer to follow those who denounce that enemy most strongly rather than those who chart a middle course. These events at home—action against catholics, the struggle with the puritan clergy, disputes in parliament—took place against the background of a darkening international situation.

5. ALENÇON AND THE NETHERLANDS

We left the realm at peace in 1575: agreements had been concluded with both Spain and France, and Scotland was in the safely Anglophil hands of the regent Morton. But the centre of disturbance remained untouched. Since the beginning of the revolt in the Spanish Netherlands (1572) the prince of Orange had maintained his hold on the provinces of Holland and Zeeland and his stubborn resistance to the forces of Alva's successor, Don Luis de Requesens. Though willing to stay on good terms with Spain—in 1575 she even expelled Dutch refugees from England—Elizabeth could not avoid involvement in the affairs of the Channel seaboard, the less so because, if she refused to assist, Orange was ready to turn to France. And French control of the Netherlands was, if anything, more intolerable than Spanish because it could not be limited by a return to the relative independence which the Netherlands had enjoyed under Charles V and which Elizabeth tried to secure for them under Philip II. Thus, despite the treaty of Blois and France's abandonment of Mary Stuart, France also remained a danger-spot. There the tripartite division into the Guise faction of ardent catholics intent on alliance with Spain, the Huguenot section determined to secure religious toleration and co-operate with the protestant powers, and the court of Henry III dominated by his mother Catherine who was trying to play off the factions, preserved a general instability which made France an incalculable element. In the late 1570s, the Huguenots, disorganised after the massacre of 1572 and the loss of their leaders, began to revive under Henry of Navarre and to find a successor to Coligny's ambitions, though not to his ability, in Catherine's youngest son, Francis duke of Alençon and Anjou.[1] The French court party were eager to be rid

---

[1] Alençon succeeded to the dukedom of Anjou on his brother's acceptance of the Polish crown in 1574, but it is usual to avoid confusion by referring to him throughout under his earlier title, a practice which shall be followed here.

of Alençon and he wished to carve a kingdom for himself: his restless activities in 1578-84 provide the thread which runs through Elizabeth's policy in those years.

In 1575-6 the queen was so much opposed to renewing trouble for herself by assisting the Dutch that, early in 1576, the two countries were even involved in a minor commercial and naval war. But the situation was changed by the death of Requesens and the wild excesses of his unpaid soldiers who devastated the Netherlands in the summer of 1576. After the sack of Antwerp, Orange's arguments at last prevailed with the southern provinces, and in November the Netherlands were reunited in the Pacification of Ghent. The arrival of a new Spanish governor, Don John of Austria, threatened to lead to further trouble, but in February 1577 Don John, by the so-called Perpetual Edict, accepted the Pacification on the terms offered by the States General. These included the removal of all Spanish troops. Don John complied, but with a heavy heart. One of the foremost soldiers of his day— the victor of the great battle of Lepanto against the Turks (1571)— this natural son of Charles V had not come north to act as figure- head for a parcel of commercial and industrial provinces. In fact, he was planning, with Philip's approval, to restore order in the Netherlands and then carry out the much heralded *empresa* against England. Elizabeth had done much to forward the Perpetual Edict, but in July 1577, when Don John recovered his freedom of action by a military *coup d'état*, she was forced back on Orange. The prince alone had not joined in the rejoicings of February, and now that his suspicions were proved correct he more than ever seemed the only hope of the distracted provinces. In turn, his only hope seemed to be Elizabeth, as reluctant as ever to enter the war. The queen pursued a futile policy, spending good money on the leader of a mercenary army, Duke John Casimir of the Palatinate, whom at intervals she had subsidised to assist both Huguenots and Dutch but who never achieved anything. She also negotiated direct with Spain, a move which seemed to promise success when diplomatic relations were resumed in 1578. However, the new Spanish ambassador, Bernardino de Mendoza, was a foolishly arrogant and blustering man, sent less to represent his country than to organise the moves against Elizabeth.

Negotiations failed to arrest the progress of Don John in 1578: Orange was once again confined to his northern fastness and his plight was desperate. Since Elizabeth would not help, he turned to Alençon. The duke re-entered European politics in 1578 with an offer, received with suspicion and reluctance, to take charge of the

Dutch revolt; at the same time, in order both to advance his own ambitions and to conciliate English opposition, he resumed his courtship of Elizabeth which had died a quiet death in 1576. The second Alençon courtship was Elizabeth's last fling in this field, and it was the most ardent, most tricky, and—to all appearance—most serious of all her amorous manœuvres in the interests of diplomacy. She was forty-five, but Burghley argued that she might easily and without danger yet have children, and she herself may have been making a last attempt to secure a normal family life for herself. Thus Alençon's suit, encouraged by his mother and brother, prospered. In October 1578 Don John died suddenly and with him, it seemed, died the Spanish project for the conquest of northern Europe. Alençon became protector of the Netherlands by a treaty with the States General, but his enjoyment of his position was limited by the arrival of another Spanish governor, Alexander Farnese of Parma, far and away the ablest general and diplomatist in Philip's employ. The short storm of Don John's meteoric career was over; there began the slow but more certain reconquest by Parma and the ill-concerted opposition offered to his steady advance by Orange, Alençon, and Elizabeth.

From all points of view it seemed best that the last two should link forces and do so by marriage. Early in 1579 Alençon sent his friend, Jean de Simier, to plead his cause with the queen, and there followed scenes of public affection which seemed indecorous even to that age. Elizabeth showed herself her father's daughter by abandoning affairs of state in favour of a round of amusements mixed with dalliance. She excelled at the game and Simier was her match: undoubtedly there was no more in it than a high-spirited delight in her own skill. But it served Alençon's turn. Elizabeth added the two to her menagerie of pet names: Simier became her ape and Alençon—a short, slightly misshapen figure with a pock-marked face—her frog. In August 1579 he arrived in person—secretly, but it was a well divulged secret. When he left after three weeks of ardent wooing, the marriage seemed very near. The country took alarm: few wanted a French prince. A puritan gentleman, John Stubbs, with the honest but ill-considered vigour of his kind, published an attack on the match for which he and the printer lost their right hands. The scene has become famous: the silent multitude, sullenly hostile to the queen's angry revenge, Stubbs shouting his 'God save the Queen' before fainting, the printer's cry that he had left there the hand of a true Englishman. Enmeshed in the toils of the Alençon courtship, Elizabeth was in danger of

losing touch with her people. It is easy to understand and to pity
her. Her greatness lay in that she recovered her senses before it
was too late. She quarrelled with her council in a series of tempera-
mental scenes in October 1579, but a few weeks after Alençon
left the marriage was really dead: no one any longer seriously
wanted it.

At this point circumstances revived it, but now it was much
more a diplomatic manœuvre and much less a serious affair of
Elizabeth's heart. In 1580 there arose the problem of the Portuguese
succession. The king of Portugal, a cardinal-archbishop, died in
that year, and the claimant with not only the best right but also
far and away the greatest power to enforce it was Philip of Spain.
He quickly overran the country, thus combining the two largest
empires of the day and conjuring up a spectre of overwhelming
Spanish power. In consequence the anti-Spanish countries took up
the cause of a native Portuguese claimant, Don Antonio. Elizabeth
toyed with the idea of sending Drake to the Azores, where Antonio
had retained a foothold, but she wanted French assistance which
was delayed until she dropped the plan. In 1582 the French tried
by themselves, only to be heavily defeated in the naval battle of
Terceira. Unable to exploit the Portuguese succession in her
endeavour to involve Spain in sufficient distraction to prevent
a descent on England, Elizabeth was forced to assist Alençon in the
Netherlands and thus to revive the game of his courtship. She
hoped to win success in her Dutch policy by using him as an agent
and without spending either blood or treasure herself. He re-
visited England in November 1581 and to all appearance Elizabeth
was as enamoured of him as ever. She publicly kissed him and
proclaimed her desire to marry him. Behind the scenes, however,
things stood rather differently. Alençon was wanted in the Netherlands where Parma's success in bringing the southern provinces
under Spanish control endangered the whole war of liberation;
instead he dallied for three months and was then finally persuaded
with difficulty to return to his place in the country whose sovereignty he had accepted in 1580. The marriage project was over,
despite mutual protestations to the contrary; the party of Leicester
and Walsingham, who had consistently opposed it as dangerous to
the protestant alliance they hoped for, had triumphed. In 1582
Alençon proved his utter incapacity in a series of disastrous encounters with Parma and even more disastrous quarrels with the States
General; his part in the Dutch revolt was virtually ended by
January 1583, although he survived until May 1584. His death
affected Elizabeth deeply; she had all the rather facile emotion of

her age and family, but her sorrow was never prolonged or so sincere as to cloud her judgment.

Elizabeth's dealings with the Netherlands were constantly bedevilled by her refusal to sink money in that country without such securities as the ports of Flushing or Brill which the Dutch were equally determined to keep out of foreign hands. But her attitude will be the more readily condoned—exasperating though it was both to Orange and the English war party—when it is remembered that the queen was virtually fighting on three fronts: or rather, was desperately involved on three fronts in an effort to avoid fighting. Relations with Spain, superficially normal, were threatened by the distant exploits of Drake and his fellows, and more by England's involvement with the Dutch; it seemed in 1580-1 that the great attack of Pope Gregory XIII would be carried on Spanish wings. In reality Philip still hesitated quite as much as did Elizabeth to take an irrevocable step, but like her he was ready to do all he might to undermine English power by secret means. After all, there was always Mary Stuart, still alive, still a centre of plots, still an obvious candidate for the English throne if only the *empresa* succeeded. To Rome the cautious attitude of Spain suggested the need of readier allies, especially after the failure of the Irish expedition. Thus after 1580 there was added to the trouble centre in the Netherlands the so-called Lennox-Guise plot, a revival of the earlier alliance between France and Scotland against England. Into it the Spanish threat was also woven, as well as the ambitions of Mary Stuart. The story began in Scotland.

Here the friendly government of Morton ended abruptly in 1578 when the regent, after several ups and downs, had to resign and James VI, at the age of twelve, became nominally king in person. Next year there arrived from France Esmé Stuart, sieur d'Aubigny, soon created earl of Lennox, who with the assistance of Captain James Stewart (later earl of Arran) won his way to the control of king and kingdom. Morton was arrested late in 1580 and executed, despite vigorous English protests, next year. Lennox and Arran were now supreme, and they represented the French interest. Lennox was in fact in close touch with the French League, a catholic association dominated by the duke of Guise and determined to destroy protestantism in alliance with Spain. He hoped to restore Scotland to the Roman Church and Mary to her throne. English relations with France, always endangered by Elizabeth's persistent secret support of Huguenot ambitions, were not improved by Walsingham's embassy of July 1581; charged to negotiate a treaty of alliance and the Alençon marriage, he was prevented from achieving either by Elizabeth's rapid changes of mind. His failure increased the League's influence at court. With Lennox well established, the plot got under way. Two Scottish Jesuits arrived in 1581, full of illusions about the support which an invasion from the north would receive in England; Guise prepared to attack from the south. But the machinations were well known in England where Walsingham's intelligence service—often overrated in both size and perspicacity—for once did all that was required of it. Nevertheless, it was the internal feuds of Scotland that ruined the plot. In August 1582, some protestant lords abducted James in the Raid of Ruthven and drove Lennox and Arran from the country. Elizabeth joyfully seized the occasion to seek a close alliance which would restore English supremacy at Edinburgh. The English diplomats found James much readier to abandon his mother than they had expected; this somewhat precocious and selfish young man was only interested in securing his own throne in Scotland and succession in England. From 1583, sixteen years old, he played a real part in the rapidly changing faction strife of Scotland. The Ruthven party lost control in June 1583 and Arran returned; Walsingham himself, sent north, failed to achieve much beyond annoying James whose self-confidence did not take kindly to the elderly statesman's lectures; then England found an ally in an intriguer even more skilful than Arran. This was the Master of Gray with whose help the French party was finally destroyed in October 1585. Arran was exiled; James, who had tried to use French influence in order to blackmail Elizabeth into nominating him her successor, gave in; and the treaty of Berwick (July 1586) ended at last all threats from the north and the ancient disunion in the island.

It came none too soon, for other things were in train. When the Ruthven raid put a stop to Lennox's plans, the Guise interest, in alliance with Spain, the pope, and Mary Stuart decided to attack direct across the Channel. The plans were long maturing. Walsingham knew that something was up but for a long time, blinded by the Scottish troubles, failed to track the right game. In 1583, however, he almost accidentally stumbled over an unsuspected link in the conspiratorial chain. This was Francis Throckmorton, an English catholic, who acted as intermediary between Mary and the Spanish ambassador, Mendoza. At once, all the secretary's resources were switched from the innocent French ambassador to the guilty Spanish envoy. Torture made Throckmorton reveal all he knew, and the plot was broken. Mary, whose part is understandable but was nevertheless very real and dangerous, once again escaped the consequences of her action, while those whom religion, chivalry, or self-interest involved in her affairs suffered as usual. In January 1584 Mendoza was called before the council, informed that his part in all these doings was fully known, and told to leave the country within a fortnight. He exploded in a rage and eased his gall with an outburst of threats, but he left in disgrace—the second Spanish ambassador of the reign to be expelled from England for plotting against the queen to whom he was accredited. The exceeding latitude which the time allowed to diplomats and governments in working against each other while nominal peace reigned can only be understood if it is remembered that we are dealing with a conflict of ideologies in an age in which international law had barely begun. The rules governing relations between sovereign states were even more obscure and less tested than they are today.

Mendoza's expulsion brought war very close. In the Netherlands Spain was advancing under the able leadership of Parma, and the events of 1584 at last compelled Elizabeth to come into the open. In May Alençon died, leaving the headship of the rebellious provinces empty; in June a much worse calamity befell the Dutch cause when, after several attempts, an assassin at last managed to kill William of Orange. The deed found much praise in catholic countries, then the home of the doctrine of tyrannicide —and among tyrants heretic rulers stood high—even as it shocked England into horror and probably exaggerated fears. The result was the bond of association formed to protect the queen and avenge her if need arose, to which parliament gave its blessing in 1585. The long-drawn period of unquiet peace was nearly over; all those twists of diplomacy, secret assistance and open avowals, plots and conspiracies and treacheries, in which both sides had indulged, were at last to be subsumed in real war. Elizabeth, who hated the folly and waste of war, could not for ever resist the determination of Rome and its allies to have her down and the determination of her people to defend the protestant religion. Least doctrinaire of rulers and averse in temper and thought to the bigotry of either side, she was yet doomed to lead a war of religion.

Not that religion alone caused the war. In Europe the power politics of Spain, France, and England had played round the Channel coast and the Netherlands, and had exploited the internal dissensions of France and Scotland. To Elizabeth and to most of her contemporaries those seemed the stages that mattered. But the story is very incomplete without an investigation of what was going on across far oceans where England and Spain clashed—distantly but with reverberating effects on the narrow scene in Europe—in the first great colonial and naval struggle of modern times.

Chapter XII

SEAPOWER

IT was in the sixteenth century that the seeds were sown which were to grow into English seapower and the British empire. The discovery of America turned the Atlantic from the edge of the world into a busy traffic centre; command of the sea routes superseded control of overland roads in deciding the fate of nations; the distant island off the north-western corner of the Eurasian landmass automatically acquired immense possibilities. Medieval England had had her seamen: an island must have shipping. But such part as the kings of England had played in wider affairs had depended on their continental possessions and ambitions, and on the military prowess of their land-based armies. Under the Tudors the ancient military traditions—the memories of Crécy and Agincourt—were being replaced by a new national folklore of sea-heroes. The military past was a long time a-dying: its memories dominated the wars of Henry VIII and frustrated under Elizabeth the revolutionary notions of the new naval school of strategists. Nowadays, when the Elizabethan age seems to be obviously dominated by its Drakes and Hawkinses, when the defeat of the Armada overshadows all other warlike events of the time, when attention so readily concentrates on the distant exploits of explorers, colonists, traders, privateers, and pirates—nowadays it is necessary to remind oneself at every step that these men stood only at the opening of an era. Their mistakes, their irresolutions, their frequent folly and vicious selfishness cannot otherwise be understood, nor can due praise be given to their remarkable achievements. The traditions of maritime England, of England's navy and England's empire, go back no further than the Tudor century. They began hesitantly in the reign of Henry VII and received but partial advancement under Henry VIII; it was not until the second half of the period that a real start was made.

I. THE ROAD TO ASIA: FROM CABOT TO FITCH

Whatever the various motives that led to the wonderful movement known as the early explorations—and thirst for knowledge, the desire to convert the heathen, and military ambitions all played their part—the driving force was supplied by trade and the search for wealth. Although the Portuguese had for some time been carrying on a brisk trade with the west coast of Africa—Upper Guinea and Benin Bay—the story really began when various men determined to investigate the possibility of direct commercial relations with the sources of silks and spices and other goods in South Asia. It is alleged that Henry VII might have had the honour of employing Columbus who spent a long time looking for a government to finance his enterprise; but even if the king had been at liberty in 1490 to listen to the Genoese visionary, it does not follow that England lost what Spain gained. If Columbus had sailed from Bristol in 1490, as John Cabot did seven years later, he would have reached the inhospitable shores of Nova Scotia (as Cabot did), and not the promising islands of the Caribbean: the winds would have seen to that. In considering these early voyages we must rid our minds entirely of the knowledge that there lie between the western shore of Europe and the eastern shore of Asia two great oceans and a huge continent. What may be called the western school of navigators supposed that the route to the west would reach China and the Spice islands—known from a curious amalgam of accurate information, garbled reports, and pure legend—more quickly than the Portuguese were progressing in their laborious search for the southern end of Africa. Columbus died in the belief that he had found some barbaric islands only ust off the coast of civilized Asia, and when John Cabot, a Genoese seaman settled in Bristol since 1490, offered his services to Henry VII he promised a route straight to Cipango (Japan) from which, by laying a south-westerly course, he would reach Cathay (China).

In March 1496 Henry responded by granting a charter to a syndicate of Bristol merchants, headed by Cabot and his sons, permitting them to sail east, north, or west to discover lands so far not known to Christians. By this time the step had been taken which was to render all maritime enterprise politically dangerous. In 1493 Pope Alexander VI, himself of Spanish descent, issued a bull which divided the discoveries between Spain and Portugal along the line of the meridian passing through the Azores.[1] The bull spoke of lands 'west and south' of this meridian, which is nonsense, and the best interpretation—adhered to, for instance, by Philip of Spain as long as he was king of England—reserved only lands west of the meridian, and south of the parallel, of the Azores. Henry's grant was thus careful to prevent any incursion

[1] The precise details were worked out by the two powers in the treaty of Tordesillas in 1494.

into pre-empted territory by excluding exploration southwards and by prohibiting Cabot from landing on soil already visited by European seamen. Cabot sailed in May 1497, reaching land to the westward which he called the new-found land, and which was probably Nova Scotia. Of course, he was convinced that he had found Asia, and the trend of the coastline confirmed his notion that by following it he would strike Cathay with all its riches. In 1498 he set out again, never to return. There are indications that he got some way south in his coasting, sufficient to alarm the Spaniards: he may, in view of the savage lands he passed, have realised that he was nowhere near China. But his death, Henry's preoccupations in England, and an international situation which made it inadvisable to fall foul of Spain, for a time ended the official enterprise. England had got off to a good start in exploring but none at all in trading, and so the matter virtually dropped. In 1501 and 1502 licences were granted to groups of Bristol merchants who continued to interest themselves in discovering new markets, but little is known of activities which do not seem to have produced much profit. The only result of these early voyages was to establish the great Newfoundland cod fisheries, found by Cabot; from that time onwards they were visited regularly by fleets from England and France.

Meanwhile the Spaniards had realised that Columbus' discoveries were not in Asia; by 1500 the existence of the new continent was known. This did not kill the hopes of finding a westerly route to Asia, the less so because the Portuguese had established by now a monopoly of the eastern route—Vasco da Gama reached India in 1498 and all Europe knew it a year later—which was so enormously profitable that it encouraged everyone to try to break it. The way east was blocked by the papal bull, the Portuguese forces, and most convincingly of all by Portugal's carefully guarded exclusive knowledge of the charts. In the west there lay a landmass whose breadth was unknown until Balboa saw the Pacific in 1513, but which it was thought might be outflanked. Here was the origin of that famous and disastrous chimera, the north-west passage, which was to bedevil the history of voyages almost to the end of the seventeenth century. Its first prophet was John Cabot's son Sebastian, a navigator of ability and boundless faith in himself, equipped with a conveniently selective memory and a gift for telling the tale. He made his first attempt under Bristol auspices in 1509; when he failed and found enthusiasm on the wane in England, he left to make a career in Spain.

For some forty years after this England took little part in the movement. While Cortez and Pizarro proved that Columbus' discoveries had led Spain to vaster power and wealth—as it seemed —than she could ever have obtained if he had really found a route to Asia, England stood aloof. Committed to the Spanish alliance, she could not afford to interlope, especially after the break with Rome which made every additional provocation mere folly. Her statesmen had other matters to think of. Most important of all, the merchants of England who had taken the lead in the 1490s found in these years that the flourishing cloth trade absorbed about all their energies. A booming trade in Europe left little inclination to risk capital in dubious enterprises. In 1521, when Henry VIII tried to form a national company for exploration, it was the opposition and lethargy of the London commercial community which frustrated the project. They had had recent experiences of such follies when a group of lawyers and men about town, led by John Rastell (Thomas More's brother-in-law), had fitted out an expedition for America, only to come to grief in Ireland. At Bristol, the memory of Cabot's last voyage and the petering out of the subsequent trading ventures seems to have sufficed.

England at large cared little for explorations, and even individuals, whether statesmen or traders, who might have been interested, failed to share in the spirit which in the 1520s was driving Spanish power across Central and Southern America. A few men's imaginations caught a little of the flame: More's *Utopia* reflects an intelligent man's interest in this astonishing widening of the horizon, and Rastell used his own experience in a play—*A New Interlude of the Four Elements* (1519)—to popularise knowledge of the new continent. But the only Englishmen who really knew what was going on were those who traded and often settled in Spain. Many did so in those halcyon days when Spain and England were allied and before the religious schism destroyed the easy terms on which they lived with their Spanish neighbours and the Spanish government. Quite a colony of them existed near Seville, the centre of the Indies trade in which they shared. One of them, Robert Thorne, was the first significant English propagandist for overseas expansion. In 1525 Ferdinand Magellan discovered the straits to the south of America and a possible western route to the Spice Islands. Political circumstances and the difficulties of the voyage persuaded the emperor to forego this new addition to his dominions and to offer it for sale. The English ambassador in Spain consulted Thorne who replied with a pamphlet, *A Declaration of the Indies*, in which he spoke of hitherto undiscovered islands in the Pacific, rich in spices, pearls, and gold, and suggested that the shortest route to them from England was by way of the North Pole. England's position, he argued, indicated that God meant her to build an empire by using that road. Like many men then and later, Thorne underestimated the arctic ice: all calculations were based on the ice-free conditions of north-west Europe which, of course, are due to the gulf stream. He died in 1532, back in England and disappointed of his hopes. Few would enterprise into distant seas and in the teeth of Spanish disapproval, at this time when the Flanders trade was going well and Spain must not be provoked. An exception was William Hawkins, of Plymouth, who in the 1530s initiated a profitable trade in dyestuffs with the coast of Brazil; if others there were they have left no trace.

The initial impetus given by the voyages of Henry VII's time thus seemed to have died when it was revived in the middle of the century by the trade slump of the 1550s and the ambitions of the energetic and enterprising speculators who had already exhausted the possibilities of the land market. The duke of Northumberland, commonly (and rightly) belaboured by historians, here appears as the guardian angel of the maritime movement: after his time it never relapsed again. In 1548 Sebastian Cabot returned to England, after thirty-five years of profitable and honourable service under the Spanish crown, and from 1551 we can trace the remarkable career of John Dee, the power behind the scenes of early English exploration. Astrologer, necromancer, mathematician, and geographer, Dee was that mixture of genuine scientist and credulous charlatan so typical of the sixteenth century. But apart from his more dubious activities, he entered heart and soul into the movement for expansion. He became the prophet of the north-east passage and later of the fabled southern continent—the great Terra Australis Incognita supposed to lie to the south of the Pacific Ocean and to stretch from Cape Horn to the East Indian islands. It was the best opinion of the time that such a continent must exist to counterbalance the northern land masses and prevent the earth from toppling over. The new—rather belated—interest of England in the discoveries was shown by the inception of propaganda literature. In 1553 and 1555 Richard Eden published translations of continental works which he entitled *Treatise of the New India* and *Decades of the New World or West India*. There began now that fruitful co-operation of merchants, sailors, and moneyed gentry (including members of court and council) which was to lead to such splendid results in the days of Drake. In the first place the older but petty beginnings of direct trade with Africa were exploited. In 1551 and 1552 Thomas Wyndham led expeditions to the Barbary coast—the Atlantic coast of Morocco—and in 1553 he went right down the Guinea coast into Benin Bay. He himself died on his last voyage, but the survivors brought back so much gold that London went into raptures, and another and even more profitable venture was undertaken next year by John Lok. The Portuguese protests, allowed by Mary's government under Philip's influences, were ignored after 1558 on the grounds that the holding of a few forts on a coast a thousand miles long did not constitute effective occupation, and the Guinea merchants continued to bring in their gold and ivory.

The real goal, however, was still distant Asia, especially the Spice Islands (the Moluccas). The southern route round Africa being closed, and that round South America being both difficult and in Spanish hands, there remained the northern latitudes where, as Thorne had pointed out, England started with a special advantage. Cabot favoured the north-west passage round North America: it was supposed that once the channel was found the coast would trend south-westwards and lead straight to China. Dee thought well of the north-east passage, holding (falsely) that no part of Asia reached higher than the North Cape of Norway: once this was turned travellers would have an easy passage in icefree waters to the eastern extremities of Asia. In 1552 Northumberland formed a large joint-stock company to carry out Dee's plan, and an expedition sailed next year under the leadership of Sir Hugh Willoughby and Richard Chancellor. Cabot had contributed the experience of a seafaring life, Dee the theoretical knowledge of the geographers, and some 200 capitalists, led by the duke himself, the necessary money. The journey was only half successful. Willoughby, held up by storms, died with all his crew when he tried to winter on the coast of Lapland, but Chancellor entered the White Sea, found the village of Archangel, and established contact with the distant Czar of Moscow. He returned in 1554 with stories of the court of Ivan the Terrible and with the promise of a lucrative trade. In 1555 the Muscovy Company was formed to exploit these beginnings. Although further voyages by Chancellor and Stephen Borough ended in disaster—Chancellor failed to return in 1557—so that the north-east passage remained undiscovered, the accidental by-product of a new cloth trade straight into Central Russia remained to bring profit to merchants, training to seamen, hope to explorers, and assistance to the government in their struggle to break the Hanse's monopoly in the

Baltic whose shipping stores of timber, cordage, and pitch now began to assume the importance they were to have for some two centuries.

In the 1560s interest switched to a new theatre of operations— the Caribbean—which shall be dealt with in the next section. A more or less regular trade now existed with Muscovy and the Guinea coast; the Newfoundland fisheries grew yearly in value; England's maritime interests were firmly established, and more and more men, especially from the west coast ports of Plymouth and Bristol, were seeking wealth and adventure across the seas. The route to Asia, not yet found, remained to tease men's ingenuity. In 1566 Sir Humphrey Gilbert wrote his famous *Discourse for a Discovery for a New Passage to Cathay* which, with its mixture of sense and nonsense, remained the stand-by of north-western explorers. Dee preached his faith in the Southern Continent whose spectre was to haunt geographers until James Cook finally disproved its existence in the eighteenth century. In 1574 a Devon syndicate led by Sir Richard Grenville laid plans for an enterprise through the Straits of Magellan and for the Terra Australis, but that was the year in which Burghley was trying to make peace with Spain and the project was forbidden by the government. There ensued a tug-of-war between the advocates of the north-west passage and those of the Straits. Since to go north was to keep out of Spanish preserves, Burghley favoured that route, and despite the opposition of the Muscovy Company (who feared for their monopoly) an expedition commanded by Martin Frobisher sailed in 1576. He discovered a strait which he named after himself and which he claimed was the passage, though he had barely entered it: it was, in fact, a narrow and longish inlet. He also brought back some curious ore which sanguine hope and some highly peculiar assaying immediately declared to be gold-bearing. The outcome was a magnificent bubble: speculation in the mythical gold of the arctic wastes ran high, and Frobisher was dispatched on two more voyages in 1577 and 1578 to explore his strait and bring more ore. The moving spirit behind all this was Michael Lok, half visionary and half speculator, who was completely ruined by the collapse of the bubble; for, not surprisingly, no more gold was found. Frobisher discovered Hudson's Strait and entered Hudson's Bay whose shore, trending to the south-west, seemed to confirm that here was the northern shore of North America. But other enterprises and war distracted both government and investors; the Bay remained unexplored till the next century; the passage remained still a hope; and Frobisher, a rough, cantankerous, and at this time a needy man, conceived a lasting grudge at the neglect of his discoveries and the popular acclamation of Drake. The southern project, kept alive by Grenville, later fell into Drake's hands, so that Grenville was another who cherished resentment against this most famous of the great Elizabethan seamen.

One last Elizabethan attempt to find the north-west passage may be recorded here. In 1585 a small expedition sailed from Dartmouth under the command of John Davis, a seaman of that port. He had the backing of Sir Humphrey Gilbert's brother Adrian who had secured the patent, of William Sanderson, merchant of London, who supplied the money, and of Raleigh and Walsingham who represented the court interest. In three voyages (1585-7) Davis achieved remarkable things for geographical discovery, but nothing of commercial value. Together with the Armada threat of 1588 this explains why his efforts were not followed up. He was in many ways one of the most attractive of the Elizabethan explorers —eminently competent, a genuine scientific investigator, untainted by those touches of money-grubbing and piracy which hang around the others. As a single-minded discoverer he excelled them all. He established that Greenland is separate from America, sailed high into Baffin's Bay, and alone of all sixteenth-century seekers for the passage avoided the false turnings (Hudson's Straits, Frobisher's Straits, Cumberland Sound). The way he pointed was much later to prove the right one, though contrary to expectations the passage was ultimately found in latitudes too northerly to make it a practicable highway to Asia.

The west failing, the east beckoned once more. In 1580 the Muscovy Company, assisted by William Borough and John Dee, despatched a fleet to the north-east under Arthur Pett and Charles Jackman. Their purpose was to seek the passage to China, trade in cloth, and probably also to make contact with Drake, then in the Pacific. Ice, as always, stopped them. More profitable was the resumption of trade with the Levant: it is one of the curiosities of English naval history that the Caribbean and the Arctic were familiar to English seamen before they really got to know the Mediterranean. In 1581 the Turkey Company was incorporated, the title being later changed to Levant Company. And in 1583 John Newbery and Ralph Fitch made their memorable journey overland to India. They reached Portuguese Goa and, with difficulties, were permitted to trade; they visited the court of the Great Mogul, Akbar; they then parted, Newbery planning to return through Persia while Fitch headed east. Newbery vanished without trace, but Fitch travelled through Bengal, Burma, Siam,

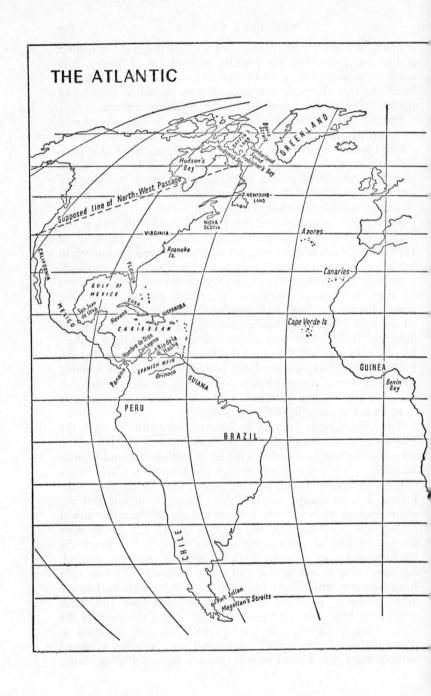

THE ATLANTIC

GREENLAND

Davis Strait

BAFFIN LAND

Cumberland Sound

Hudson's Bay

Hudson's Straits Frobisher's Bay

Supposed line of North-West Passage

NEWFOUND-LAND

Azores

VIRGINIA

NOVA SCOTIA

Roanoke Is.

CALIFORNIA

FLORIDA

Canaries

MEXICO

GULF OF MEXICO

CUBA

San Juan de Ulua

HISPANIOLA

Havana

CARIBBEAN

Cape Verde Is

Nombre de Dios

Cartagena

Rio de La Hacha

Panama

SPANISH MAIN

GUINEA

Orinoco

GUIANA

Benin Bay

PERU

BRAZIL

CHILE

Port Julian

Magellan's Straits

and the Malayan sultanates, to return in 1591 with the most remarkable traveller's tales of any in that age so full of wonders. Out of his journey was to grow the English East India Company and all that followed from it. As Chancellor secured trading privileges by treaty from Ivan the Terrible, so Fitch came to some sort of agreement with Akbar, or said he did; trade with settled countries always took the form of diplomatic negotiations. By now, English interests were spreading round the globe, but legitimate trade with the East and voyages of discovery were the smaller part of English maritime enterprise. Immediate returns were much larger from semi-piratical expeditions, or from the more respectable but barely more legal participation in the trade with the Spanish empire in the west.

2. THE CARIBBEAN: HAWKINS AND DRAKE

Of all the great discoveries, those of Spain were by far the most fabulous and profitable. By the middle of the sixteenth century the crown of Castile had established and organised a great empire in America, comprising Mexico, Peru, and Chile, and centring upon the islands and the mainland of the Caribbean. Here it preserved a jealous and rigid monopoly. No foreigner was allowed to settle or trade in the Spanish colonies without a royal licence which was rarely granted. All goods shipped to the Indies had to be registered at Seville, the seat of the central authority for the colonies (the Council of the Indies). Local officials, from viceroys downwards, could not act without direct orders from a government 3,000 miles—or anything from two or five months—distant. A notable part of the Spanish crown revenue consisted of the bullion mined in America and transported to Europe by two regular annual fleets: the *flota* which sailed by way of the Azores to San Juan de Ulua on the Gulf of Mexico to bring back the Mexican treasure, and the *galleones* which similarly reached Nombre de Dios on the Isthmus of Panama to collect that from Peru. These two great convoys and the many ships carrying contributions toward the collecting centres powerfully attracted men interested in a little piratical wealth. On the other hand, the insufficiencies of Spanish merchant shipping deprived the colonists of many badly needed commodities—above all of slaves to work their plantations—and rendered them willing to trade with anyone who could supply their wants in spite of the home government's vigorous and unswerving policy. In the middle of the century, the Spanish empire—immensely wealthy, too vast and too rapidly grown for efficient administration, and very ill protected—was ripe for exploitation by outsiders.

Though Robert Reneger of Southampton captured a treasure ship as early as 1545, it was French seamen from the Atlantic ports who first put the matter to the test. Spain and France were intermittently at war from 1521 to 1559, during which time French sails became a dreaded sight in the scattered Spanish settlements. Many of the privateers were Calvinists who both inflicted and suffered horrible things in the dominions of his Catholic Majesty. English maritime relations with Spain deteriorated after the break with Rome led to attacks on the English merchants in Andalusia. War in the 1540s added English privateers to French and gave a chance to men like Reneger. The Spanish ascendancy of 1553-8 delayed matters, but the beginnings of the conflict have been traced to the reign of Henry VIII. The treaty of Cateau Cambrésis (1559), which ended the Habsburg-Valois struggle in Europe, explicitly exempted the region beyond 'the lines'—the meridian of the Canaries and the tropic of Cancer—from its operation; it established the principle that diplomacy did not control the oceans. The wars of religion encouraged privateering by French, Dutch, and English in European waters. And the diplomatic situation was changing: the government of Elizabeth and Cecil, while reluctant to provoke Spain, saw much less cause to pander to her than Mary's had done and was ready to shut both eyes to West Indian enterprise if only it were not involved. Throughout the century hundreds of unrecorded sailings took place from the ports and creeks of the south and west coasts. Many a man sought to make his fortune in the fabled lands of the west, and many a ship left England never to return. Many others no doubt came back, some with wealth and some without, but only the greater enterprises and those which by chance left a record in the English admiralty court or the Spanish and Mexican Inquisitions have found their way into history.

Out of this confused situation grew the voyages of John Hawkins, one of the founding-fathers of England's naval tradition. The son of William Hawkins of Plymouth who had traded with Brazil in the 1530s, he was a man of commanding presence and intellect, of outstanding abilities as a seaman, administrator, fighter and diplomat, and endowed with such charm that even his opponents in the Spanish colonies could only remark ruefully that once you let Hawkins talk to you you would end up by doing his will. In the early 1560s, inspired by the French example and by his own wide contacts with both Spaniards and English at Seville and in the Canaries, he conceived a plan for peacefully invading the Spanish monopoly. Although he lacked a licence he had some reason to hope for favourable treatment: his queen was allied to the king of Spain, quite a few Englishmen were still trading from Seville to the New World, and he proposed to offer essential goods. His plan required capital which he gathered by moving his head-quarters to London and forming a syndicate in that city where maritime enterprise was at last attracting speculators. Even his first company included men like Sir William Winter and Benjamin Gonson (whose daughter he married), both officials of the queen's navy. In October 1562 Hawkins set out for West Africa where he bought slaves from the native rulers—by fair means, though the local Portuguese officials, to hide their complicity, later pretended that he had used superior force. He then crossed with the trade winds to the West Indies. On this occasion he landed on the island of Hispaniola (Haiti) where he tactfully overcame official reluc-tance and did a roaring trade. Two of his vessels were confiscated when he sent them into Spanish ports, and despite his best efforts he never secured compensation; that he did send them there indicates that he was not trying to act clandestinely.

Even with these losses his voyage showed sufficient profit to encourage both him and his backers to persist. The second voyage (1564) was a much grander affair. The shareholders included not only Cecil, Leicester, and the lord admiral, but even the queen who contributed a naval vessel, the famous *Jesus of Lubeck*, a high-charged, impressive, and wellnigh unseaworthy ship. It was a gift in the true Elizabethan manner, though admittedly the queen could hardly risk her best ships in so speculative a cause. At any rate, Hawkins was now in her service: his voyage had official standing. It seems clear that both the queen and the captain hoped to make these voyages regular by offering to police the Carib-bean against pirates in return for trading privileges. But these hopes foundered on Spain's intransigeance and her recovery of control in the West Indies after a general reorganisation in the 1560s and 1570s. As far as trade went, Hawkins was even more successful in his second voyage. He followed the same route and practice as on the first occasion, except that he made for the

¹ It may still be necessary to defend Hawkins because he went in for slaving at a time when few thought negroes human. Moreover, the men he sold in the West Indies were slaves in Africa before he bought them and may have been saved from worse treatment by their tranship-ment into an area where they represented valuable property. By the standards of age Hawkins, who valued seamen's lives and cared for his men, was exceptionally humane.

Spanish Main—the north coast of South America—instead of the islands. After the usual collusive display of intimidation, designed to save the faces of the Spanish officials, he filled his holds and sailed for Havana, which (lacking both map and pilot) he missed, and Florida where he called on a French colony a few weeks before its destruction by the Spaniards. He took in fish in Newfoundland and returned to Plymouth, paying a profit of 60 per cent. on the shares of the company.

Hawkins' second voyage established his route and his methods, but it was really the end of a very promising venture. Relations between England and Spain were deteriorating. Hawkins' scrupulous behaviour availed little when the officials with whom he had dealt covered their disobedience by blackening his character with accusations of piracy, murderous bombardment, and heresy, and when other English seamen were preying on Spanish shipping in European waters. Instead of accepting Hawkins' notion of peaceful and mutually profitable relations, Philip II launched vigorous protests at London and got down to mending the gaps in his imperial defences. Throughout 1565 energetic measures were in train to stiffen the backs of Spain's imperial agents and prevent the colonists from breaking the strict trading laws, so that John Lovell, who followed in Hawkins' footsteps in 1566, found the ports closed against him. Unable to emulate his model's diplomatic skill, he returned empty-handed from a voyage worth recording only because it served to introduce Francis Drake to the Caribbean. Drake, born about 1540 and therefore Hawkins' junior by some eight years, was an altogether different man. Of west country stock, he was raised at Chatham where his father was chaplain in the dockyard, and learned his seamanship in the wild and pirate-infested Channel. He surpassed Hawkins as a commander in war and in controlled if reckless-seeming enterprise, but lacked the older man's polish and diplomatic skill. Passionately protestant and given to preaching the gospel to his shipmates, he approached the Spanish empire from the first as a crusader against popish wickedness and Spanish arrogance rather than as a merchant bent on his peaceful pursuits.

In 1567 Hawkins equipped his third fleet, and this time Drake accompanied him, ultimately commanding the small *Judith* of fifty tons. It was the biggest enterprise yet, and the queen again held shares, but things went badly from the start. The Portuguese were watching the Guinea coast more carefully and Hawkins had to get his slaves by war: he assisted a negro king in the capture of a stronghold and took those for slaves whom his allies spared. When he reached the Main he found the Spaniards ready to resist him, so that he had to force his trade upon them. The officials, beaten off by a display rather than the use of force, stood aloof, and some trade took place. Then, as Hawkins turned to set course for England, disaster struck him. A hurricane so damaged the ancient *Jesus* that she would either have had to be abandoned or repaired in harbour. To his credit, Hawkins determined on the latter course: she was, he said, the queen's ship, and he would think it shame not to try to save her. His attitude was the more remarkable as he stood to lose by it. By the terms of the contract the queen would suffer the loss if any of her ships sank at sea, while those returned had to be repaired at the expense of the whole syndicate of which Hawkins was a leading shareholder. The storm left Hawkins only with the hope of putting into San Juan de Ulua where the treasure fleet from Spain was expected—that is, with the prospect of helplessly facing a much superior force. He did his best: he took possession of a fortified sandbank which commanded the harbour, and when the Spanish fleet appeared agreed to let them enter only on condition that he retained his hold on that vital point. The fleet was carrying the new viceroy of New Spain who deeply resented this heretic corsair making conditions to him on the threshold of his dominion; from the first it was intended to break the agreement. A treacherous attack led to confused and bitter fighting from which Hawkins came off with the loss of all his ships except the *Minion* and Drake in the *Judith*. In the morning the *Judith* was gone; she arrived in England a few days before Hawkins, but nothing at all is known of her journey or the reasons for Drake's desertion. Hawkins never reproached him for it. He himself made a terrible voyage home. The *Minion* carried at first more than twice her proper complement of men, so that some hundred demanded to be put on shore where they fell into the hands of the Inquisition; the remainder, very short of food, sailed on, but only fifteen out of over a hundred reached Plymouth.

San Juan de Ulua marked a turning point. The treachery—beyond question it was that, though of course Hawkins had no right by Spanish law to be in the Caribbean at all—was not forgotten for generations. It ended all possibility of peaceful trade with the Spanish empire and ushered in open attacks on Spanish cities and treasure ships. Hawkins' seagoing days were over after his tragic third voyage, for Burghley employed him to reconstruct the navy. The hero of the new phase was Drake, now about to launch out on twenty years of daring and continuously successful enterprise which made his name a terror to Spain and a by-word in England. He may have visited the Caribbean in 1570 and was certainly there in 1571, gathering booty from coastwise shipping and information for his projected attack on Nombre de Dios and the *galleones*. English relations with Spain were bad at this time when the effects of the quarrel with Alva and the mutual trade embargo still lingered, and it is possible (as had been argued) that Drake's expedition of 1572 represented an underhand but official policy of the queen's. It certainly represented Drake's vengeance for San Juan and his desire to be at the popish enemy. With two ships, seventy-five men, and a carefully prepared plan of attack he set sail from Plymouth in May 1572. He made for a harbour in Panama which he had chosen the previous year, hoping in vain to keep it secret from Spain. There he built three pinnaces from components brought from England and coasted up towards Nombre de Dios. The attack on this place, a town of some size, by his seventy men was completely successful, but a tropical storm held up the invaders, and in the end they drew off without treasure when Drake, wounded in the leg, collapsed from loss of blood. However, the enterprise was far from over. After some months spent in sweeping along the Main, looting and terrorising the local shipping, Drake heard news of a treasure train about to cross the Isthmus from Panama. Allying himself with the Cimaroons, a mixed tribe of runaway negro slaves and Indians who roamed the inaccessible interior of this narrowest part of America, Drake laid two ambushes of which the second, almost under the eyes of Nombre de Dios, succeeded. Thus he returned, carrying some £40,000 worth of Spanish silver and having left his mark on the Spanish colonies (and on history). By modern standards, his action was that of a pirate, but by the standards of the time it was that of a patriot taking advantage of the distinction between European and American conditions. It is now commonly alleged that the activities of Drake and his imitators, so far from bringing wealth into the country, harmed England by ruining her trade with Spain and the Spanish dependencies. But Anglo-Spanish relations were bad before ever the seadogs set out, and Anglo-Spanish trade was in the doldrums before the middle of the century. The government at least welcomed these much needed draughts of ready cash.

When Drake reached England with his booty in 1573 he found the government trying to restore good relations with Spain and realised that this was no time to advertise his doings. He therefore vanished from view: his track is lost for about two years at the end of which he reappeared in Ireland (1575). But the news spread among the west country seamen, and several expeditions attempted to emulate his achievements. Some are recorded, more are doubtless forgotten. The most famous of them was John Oxenham's disastrous voyage of 1576. Oxenham had been with Drake in 1572-3 and had then worked out a grandiose plan for capturing temporary control of the Isthmus: he wanted to attack the unarmed Spanish shipping in the Pacific and then retreat at leisure to the Caribbean shore. Taking only fifty men and relying on the alliance already made with the Cimaroons, Oxenham carried out the first part of his plan. But while he crossed the Isthmus and collected his treasure, the Spaniards found and destroyed his ships and prepared to capture him on his retreat. Oxenham behaved very differently from Hawkins and Drake, going out of his way to display a crude protestantism and showing himself carelessly over-confident. In the end he was surprised, lost most of his men and all his gains, and fell into the hands of the Inquisition who hanged him at Lima. Some of his men died with him, while others went into slavery in Spanish galleys. The stories of the treatment meted out to English protestants and interlopers by the Spaniards stirred up an enduring passion in England. The Spanish courts, and especially the Inquisition of Mexico, acted with perfect though merciless justice according to their lights and laws, by which the English were strictly pirates as well as heretics; but the cruelties and extravagances of the Spanish administration cannot be explained away and were severe even by the not very exacting English standards of the time. It was memories of this sort that induced Grey to massacre the Spaniards at Smerwick: there was little tolerance or gentleness to be found anywhere, though Hawkins always avoided illegality and fighting if he could, and Drake invariably treated his prisoners with courtesy and mercy.

Oxenham's failure ended the project of the Isthmus, the more so as the Spanish authorities now virtually exterminated the Cimaroons. But the vulnerability of the Pacific coast had been shown up: there could be no stopping the men who wanted to get at this easy target. The leading scheme was that put forward by Grenville: to pass through the Straits of Magellan, raid the west coast, and come back through the north-west passage the eastern end of which Frobisher claimed to have found. Its western opening was thought to be about the fortieth parallel of latitude. To this Dee added his desire for the discovery of Terra Australis. The possibility of following Magellan's route to the Moluccas was also considered. Drake learned of these schemes in Ireland from Thomas Doughty, a dabbler in the science of the day and an adventurer whom the event proved to be but an indifferent seaman and explorer. Thus when the government took up the idea in 1577, forming a powerful syndicate with the queen again contributing her share, Drake's reputation and his relations with Burghley caused him to be chosen for the command in preference to Grenville. The expedition set sail in November 1577, with three ships and with Doughty sharing the lead with Drake. To begin with, things did not go too well. The men had believed that they were making for Alexandria, and when Drake sailed to Cape Verde and then, turning west, got becalmed in the hitherto unfamiliar doldrums, the muttering began. From the first Doughty was an impossible subordinate and a bad colleague, and when the ships at last reached Port Julian, just north of the Straits of Magellan, Drake had to try him for mutiny and execute him. He rightly held that command had to be absolutely in one man's hands if these enterprises were to succeed, but it was a long time before the practice of appointing a council of commanders in naval expeditions finally disappeared. Having established control, Drake attempted the passage and covered its 300 miles in the remarkably short time of sixteen days. No sooner, however, had his fleet reached the Pacific than they were met by appalling weather from the north which for months prevented them from making any headway. In the course of this time Drake lost his other two vessels, remaining alone with the *Golden Hind* which was at one point driven so far south that he may have sighted Cape Horn. If geographers had not been so convinced of the existence of the southern continent, Drake's observations ought to have destroyed the notion, but, though some began to doubt, with many the conviction remained.

At last in November 1578 the gales abated and Drake sailed north. The whole vast and unprotected Spanish empire lay open before him. His single ship's guns could destroy anything the Spaniards could put against him, a notable early example of the rôle of gun-power in naval warfare. Thus he raided up and down, till in the end he struck lucky with the capture of a great carrack, the *Cacafuego* and her cargo of silver (March 1579). The exploit secured the financial success of the voyage, and Drake proceeded to carry out his other instructions.[1] Sailing north along the coast of California he made a hurried search for the passage to the Atlantic, taking the opportunity to claim possession of California by the name of New Albion. He got well above latitude forty before

[1] It appears from his own statements that the order to attack the Spanish empire was endorsed by Elizabeth herself but kept secret from Burghley.

deciding that the geographers were once more wrong and turning west for the islands of Asia. After an easy passage he reached the Moluccas in July 1579. Here he bought three tons of the precious cloves and made a so-called trading treaty with the sultan of Ternate who hoped to use the English against the Portuguese. The passage out of the rock-infested and uncharted archipelago nearly proved fatal to the *Golden Hind*—she struck a submerged rock and the cloves as well as some guns had to be jettisoned—but after that the rest was easy. Sailing round the Cape of Good Hope, up to Sierra Leone, and from there along a familiar trade route, Drake reached Plymouth in September 1580. His famous first question— was the queen alive—reflected not only his patriotic loyalty but also his wish to know whether his fantastic doings would be recognised or disavowed. He had completed the second circum- navigation of the globe—the first by an Englishman—and easily the most notable achievement of Elizabethan maritime enterprise.

While Drake was on his three years' journey the protests had been coming in thick and fast, but by this time Elizabeth was less careful of Spanish susceptibilities. In any case, Drake's exploits had made him a national hero whom she could not disavow, let alone punish, without risking a serious storm in the country. Nor did she wish to do any such thing. In April 1581 she visited Dept- ford and there, on the deck of the *Golden Hind*, by way of publicly proclaiming her approval of his work and her acceptance of the profit, she had him knighted by Alençon's ambassador—so as to commit the French to the same policy. But while England resounded with the news, and while men were dreaming of a new age of commercial prosperity—with easy profits off the west coast of America and lucrative trade with the Moluccas—the truth is that Drake's return marked the end of the heroic, the carefree, stage of Elizabethan maritime endeavour. In 1581 it was hoped to employ him to capture the Azores for Don Antonio of Portugal and establish a base across the path of the Spanish treasure fleets: nothing came of this, and the defeat of a similar French attempt at Terceira sobered everybody. Spain was not as decrepit as the fire-eaters had thought. A company formed to exploit Drake's treaty with Ternate sent a well-found fleet east, but memories of Drake's exploits stirred up trouble on board: the crews, eager to find more *Cacafuegos*, demanded to be taken west through the straits, and the proud expedition returned with nothing but loss. There were other lesser voyages. Spanish reorganisation was making the Caribbean anything but a pleasant hunting-ground, the Straits of

Magellan were very rarely passed as easily as by Drake,[1] and the approaching danger of war compelled the government to keep the best seamen of England close at hand. The scene narrowed down from the wonderful prospects opened by Hawkins and Drake to the immediate problem of defence against Spain.

3. PROPAGANDA AND COLONISATION

Vigorous as the maritime movement of the early Elizabethan age was, two aspects of it foreshadowed achievement rather than accomplished it: writings on the explorations and attempts at settlement. Stories of fabulous lands rich in gold, silver, ivory, spices, and pearls, as well as wonders for the curious and adventure for the restless, were now gaining a growing audience in England. The works of Thorne, Eden, and Gilbert, and the activities of John Dee have already been mentioned, but there is no harm in stressing them once again—especially the last, for without his constant output of mathematical and navigational memorials, of geographical speculation, of map-making and studies of instruments, the whole great movement would never have developed. A lesser man of the same ilk was Richard Hakluyt the Elder, a lawyer whose informed interest in trade and navigation resulted in learned and sensible memoranda which greatly assisted, for instance, the work of the north-eastern explorers. Altogether, the second half of the century witnessed an astonishing output of geographical literature, some of it original but most of it translated from the works of Italian, Spanish, Flemish, and German writers, mathematicians, and map-makers. The libraries of learned men as well as gentlemen's houses were filling with works on the new science of cosmography.

The greatest of Elizabethan propagandists did not write until the 1580s. This was Richard Hakluyt the Younger, cousin of the elder Hakluyt (1552?-1616). A clerk in holy orders, he received his initiation into geographical enthusiasm from his cousin and then proceeded to study and teach the subject at Oxford, before diplomatic employment—he was chaplain to the embassy in France—widened his view, introduced him to yet more continental learning, and suggested to him the lines on which he was to work. Inspired more by scientific interest but not unmindful of the commercial

---

[1] The prevailing westerly winds made the Straits a very difficult proposition, while the Cape Horn route suffered from the additional disadvantage of not supplying the penguins with which the ships commonly replenished their stores of provisions.

preoccupations which moved the elder Richard, the younger found his real vocation in collecting and publishing the adventures of others. In his first collection—*Divers Voyages touching the Discovery of America* (1582)—he gathered material both English and foreign on the early discoveries. *A Discourse of Western Planting* followed in 1584, one of a number of pamphlets connected with the colonising movement. But Hakluyt established his lasting fame with the volumes of his *Principle Navigations, Voyages, and Discoveries of the English Nation*, first published in 1589 and greatly enlarged in 1598-1600. It was Hakluyt's aim to counter the taunt that the English had done nothing to deserve a share of the world's discoveries, and to record for posterity the exploits of the great navigators of his day. Usually he collected his stories at first hand, and many of them are in fact preserved in the very words of the actors. Thus the only record we have of Hawkins' last voyage is his own rather terse report, happily preserved by Hakluyt. With such material, and writing Tudor prose at its best, Hakluyt could hardly go wrong.

Perhaps the most interesting of Hakluyt's tracts discussed, as has been indicated, the desirability of English settlement in America. While merchants and seamen of merchant descent (or less) supported the movement for an expanding trade and encouraged or carried out the attack on Spanish treasure, the movement for colonisation was in the hands of the gentry, and in particular of a small group of Devon gentlemen—Sir Humphrey Gilbert, his half-brother Sir Walter Raleigh, and their cousin Sir Richard Grenville. These three had had strikingly similar careers. Educated at the universities and inns of court, in the best manner of the Elizabethan gentry training for their tasks of local government, they had taken part at various times in the constant Irish warfare which proved so remarkable a nursery of soldiers, adventurers, and colonisers.[1] From the late 1570s the ideas of propagandists began to take effect. Of all North America, Englishmen were well acquainted only with the Newfoundland fishing banks, and these they knew only during the summer. Ignorant of the effects of the gulf stream, they thought reasonably enough that a coast which stretched down to Mediterranean latitudes should provide plenty of good land and fine conditions for European settlement. Unemployment and vagabondage at home provided a spur. The idea got about that England was overpopulated and, it was thought, could no longer feed or employ her people. Just how serious the situation was is not known—though certainly

[1] Ireland really belonged to the sphere of foreign countries which Elizabethan statesmen wished to colonise. See below, pp. 389f.

contemporaries exaggerated wildly—but the middle of Elizabeth's reign probably saw population at a height, before the return of plague and bad harvests, and the effects of war, once more put a brake on expansion in the 1590s. But colonies would do more than draw off the surplus. American settlements (as Spain had shown) were sources of wealth, or (as France had tried to show) might be a standing threat on the flank of the Spanish treasure route; one would find precious metal, it was thought, in any part of the New World; some held that another isthmus existed in the neighbourhood of Virginia which ought to be occupied as a stage on the road to Asia, in preference to the bootless search for the north-west passage. Above all else, of course, it was the example of the colonising powers which excited the rampant nationalism of the age to demand equal exertion and performance.

In 1578, Anthony Parkhurst, who had made a thorough study of Newfoundland, wrote two reports in which he advocated a settlement there: a permanent station would help the fishing industry, there were iron and copper waiting to be mined, the forests could provide naval stores, and—he argued—the climate was mild enough to grow crops on the English pattern. Gilbert, who had thought of colonies as early as 1572, took the matter up. In 1578 he got a royal patent authorising the settlement of North America, but difficulties in finding men and money, as well as his own inclination to do a little raiding à la Drake first, held up operations until 1582. Associated with him were the inevitable Dee, Sir Philip Sidney, and a catholic gentleman, Sir George Peckham, who hoped to found a refuge for his co-religionists. Queen and court gave their support; the elder Hakluyt wrote notes and the younger offered his *Divers Voyages* (dedicated to Sidney); hopes ran high. But only very formidable men—men like Drake and Hawkins—could handle the wild, lawless, and gold-hungry adventurers who alone would be persuaded to make up the crews and part of the higher ranks of these expeditions. Gilbert, a man of spirit with the wide if somewhat unstable interests usual among the Elizabethans, lacked the essential qualities of leadership and the power to drive discordant elements in harness. He lost his largest ship two days out of Plymouth: her captain simply turned back. Even so, the fleet reached Newfoundland, formally took possession of St John, and then explored southwards. But when the ships carrying the prospective colonists were wrecked off this uncharted coast, there was nothing left but to return. In his enthusiasm Gilbert had put every penny he possessed into the venture; had he returned he would have been both bankrupt and discredited. Fate proved kinder. He made the passage back in the tiny *Squirrel* of ten tons and was lost in a storm off the Azores, having won himself lasting renown with those famous words of stoicism—'we are as near to heaven by sea as by land'. Even the lesser of these Elizabethan adventures were truly heroic at heart.

Gilbert's mantle fell upon Raleigh, an altogether more important figure. A brilliant fighting soldier but only moderate in command, one of the masters of English prose, an accomplished dilettante in poetry and science, warrior and courtier and man of intellect, he epitomised the Elizabethan ideal—even down to his tragic death after worldly success. By 1583 he had made his fortune and marred his life by gaining the favour of the queen who showered him with wealth and advantages but deprived him of all chance of active enterprise. All he could do was to put his enthusiasm, knowledge, and wealth behind the voyages of others. In 1584 he obtained a new grant for a projected settlement to the south of Gilbert's site and dispatched a fleet under Philip Amadas and Arthur Barlow. It followed the usual route to the Caribbean but then struck north. Amadas made his landfall in the islands off the North Carolina coast, established contact with the Indians who in their awe were uncommonly friendly, and spent a few highly idyllic weeks of pleasant intercourse on Roanoke Island. Confident that they had found an earthly paradise, the expedition returned, bringing with them two Indians; Raleigh, playing the courtier, named the colony Virginia in the queen's honour. Though Elizabeth was naturally pleased and flattered, she never put anything into these ventures. A voyage of trade and looting, with a promise of immediate rich reward was one thing; these visionary, expensive, and profitless schemes of settlement were quite another. Undoubtedly, placed as she was in Europe, she could do no other.

Raleigh despatched his second expedition to consolidate the discoveries of the first in 1585. The command was entrusted to Sir Richard Grenville, so far better known as a soldier than as a sailor, but one who had already displayed vision and interest in those South Sea plans of 1573-5 from which Drake had in the end profited. Grenville was a man to whom the habit of command came easily, but he lacked Hawkins' humanity to his men and Drake's inspiration, so that he never recorded achievements worthy of his abilities. He put the colonists ashore on Roanoke under their governor Ralph Lane who unfortunately had none of the qualities necessary to a pioneer. The most striking thing about all those early settlements is the overconfidence of the adventurers: it was all thought much easier than it turned out to be. Of course, the

Spanish conquest of mighty empires by a handful of men and in a
few years gave the wrong impression. The first Virginian colonists
were not settlers but soldiers: they expected to live the life of a
garrison supplied by the local natives and an annual fleet from
home. Unfortunately the Indians, who during Amadas' summer visit
had been so lavish, themselves had little enough and nothing to
spare at other seasons. They also lost their awe and respect for the
white visitors when they found them to be but mortal and moreover
permanent neighbours. Lane could do nothing to establish a
colony on a sound footing, and when Grenville failed to appear
in April 1586 the settlers began to talk of going. A little later
Drake arrived at the colony from his last raid in the Caribbean.
In his most generous manner he offered a ship and supplies to tide
them over till the relief arrived, but a storm endangered his ships
in Roanoke's unsafe anchorage while the colonists debated among
themselves, and in the end they accepted a passage home. Only a
few days afterwards Grenville reached the deserted colony. He left
a token force of fifteen to preserve the English claims; none of
these men were ever seen again.

The first attempt to colonise Virginia thus ended in disaster and
with Raleigh too impoverished to contemplate further activity. He
leased his rights to a London syndicate who in 1587 despatched a
new body of men under John White to re-settle Roanoke Island.
The plans were sounder—it was intended to distribute land and
encourage genuine settlement—but the execution was worse.
White was forced to return for supplies, leaving the colonists under
uncertain and divided leadership. Then came the years 1588-9
when all English shipping concentrated on the Spanish war, and it
was not until 1591 that White managed to return. He found the
colony abandoned, but it looked as though the men had gone
peaceably into the interior, whereas Grenville's fifteen had certainly been killed in a fight with the Indians. White's men, eager to
seek for treasure, would not permit him to investigate, and Raleigh,
tired by this time of the whole project, had other things in mind.
Thus the mystery of the second Virginia colony was never solved.
The sole outcome of all the high hopes, manifold hardships, and
considerable expense was an abandoned stockade on an island off
the unknown continent. Or so it seemed: in fact the memory of
that beginning was never lost, and Lane brought home knowledge
of the great Chesapeake Bay round which the ultimate settlement
of Virginia was to grow up. Gilbert, Grenville, and Raleigh, with
all their failures, and Dee and Hakluyt with all their miscalculations,
remain the founders of the British empire.

4. THE NAVY

The voyages into distant countries trained a new breed of seamen and laid the foundations of England's maritime ascendancy. In time of war, merchant ships as well as private vessels built to be able to give battle composed the bulk of the nation's fighting force at sea, but they were collected around a nucleus of royal ships. The king's navy is said to date from the time of Alfred, but its history was discontinuous until the Tudors constructed ships, trained and employed officers, and set up shore installations. Henry VII, finding the Lancastrian navy dispersed, built a few ships, two of them at least—the *Regent* and the *Sovereign*—of real value. It may be noted that even before the Reformation English ships, unlike those of Spain, did not bear the names of saints: the common opinion which sees in this the influence of protestantism appears to be mistaken. These modest beginnings, designed rather to protect England from invasion than to provide a weapon for aggressive war, were continued on a much more impressive scale by the second Tudor. Whatever his shortcomings as an administrator, it appears that Henry VIII put much energy and considerable knowledge into the building of a fleet. As soon as he came to the throne, the problem of military strength occupied him: he wanted a navy which could hold the Channel and blockade the enemy while he invaded France. There were two periods of intensive naval building in his reign. By 1515 he had created an effective fleet containing as well such unwieldy monstrosities as the famous *Great Harry* or *Henry Grace à Dieu* of 1,500 tons, the pride of king and country alike but purely a prestige vessel which never saw action. Then again, in the later 1530s, when the threat of invasion from the continent grew serious, Henry and Cromwell rebuilt the navy on more efficient lines. It was this fleet that fought the naval actions of the 1542-6 war, a war marked by an unusual bustle of naval engagements because both the contending kings had paid much attention to their ships. At Henry's death the navy consisted of some fifty-three seaworthy ships, a considerable number of them of larger size.

The typical ship of the time was the carrack or high-built ship, very short in proportion to her beam and with a pronounced tumble-home above the waterline to carry the huge forecastles and poops, several stories high, which provided the accommodation for her fighting crew. For naval actions continued to be based on the tactics of laying-to and boarding; each ship carried a considerable number of soldiers who did the actual fighting once the sailors—

inferior creatures that they were—had transported them to the scene of action. Assaults of this sort profited from high towers which enabled archers and handgun-men to fire down upon the enemy. Until Henry VIII's reforms, ships' artillery consisted of very many (200-300) small calibre guns which fired chain and canister to sweep the opposing decks; there was no attempt to sink the enemy, and before the reign of Elizabeth the Tudor navy lost only one capital ship at sea—the *Mary Rose* which sank turning into the wind and not because of enemy action. Henry is credited with the invention of the heavy-calibre broadside. It is true that he believed in big guns placed in the castles and the waist of these high-charged ships, but there is in fact no sign that naval tactics had yet changed. In home waters, close to ports and supplies, the carrack with her very large complement could serve a purpose; but she was unfit to take to the oceans where her clumsy build, topheaviness, and problems of provisioning were shown up. The Spaniards had already abandoned her in favour of the more sea-worthy galleon—longer in proportion to her beam, with a low poop and no raised forecastle—but until the 1570s English naval construction, based on Mediterranean models, generally lagged behind that of Spain and France.

Henry's reign was more successful in producing a better supply and repair organisation for the navy. Portsmouth and Dover being exposed to French raids (and the latter repeatedly silted up), Henry founded dockyards in the Thames (at Woolwich and Deptford) for the building and laying up of his cherished fleet. A series of experiments resulted in 1546 in the creation of the navy board, consisting of the treasurer of the navy, controller of the navy, surveyor of ships, master of the ordnance, and clerk of the ships, which under the lord admiral was to administer the royal navy until later Stuart times. Henry's fleet was not so magnificent as he thought, but he had assisted at the laying of sure foundations. Under his immediate successors his achievement was endangered by the general decay which overtook the administration. Pecula-tion and neglect between them ruined Henry's proud battle-fleet: by 1558 its strength had declined from fifty-three to twenty-four, and in tonnage from 11,000 to 7,000. What was worse, many of the ships that remained were so badly decayed that they had ceased to be seaworthy. Wooden ships demanded regular overhauls to test for dry rot and check the caulking, while hempen rope immersed in water had a short life and ships' riggings needed constant attention. Although Northumberland had first-hand experience of naval fighting—he was Henry VIII's last and best admiral—and

attempted to arrest the decline, Elizabeth inherited a fleet which
as near as made no difference had ceased to exist. Northumberland's only achievement was the building of Chatham dockyard in
the safe reaches of the Medway: here was to be the nerve-centre
of the Elizabethan navy.

During the first twenty years of her reign Elizabeth—or rather
Burghley—could do little for the navy except attempt piecemeal
improvement. The end of the French danger removed the most
pressing need, and financial difficulties dictated a policy of dangerous parsimony. During this time the navy board was dominated by
Sir William Winter, surveyor of ships and master of ordnance,
while its nominal head was Benjamin Gonson, Hawkins' father-
in-law. The Winters were a family of sea-captains and merchants,
and Sir William had earned a just reputation for competence in
both respects. But the whole naval administration suffered from
the bane of Elizabethan government—minor peculation. The work
got done—things were not as bad as under Edward VI and Mary—
but it got done too expensively, and since the money available
was limited not much got done. Burghley knew too little of the
technicalities to stop practices by which the queen's timber was
sold back to her or used for Winter's own vessels, cordage and
pitch and other stores were charged more highly than they should
have been, and queen's ships were employed for the navy board's
private profit. When the *Revenge* was built in 1575 she cost the
queen £4,000, though the true cost had been nearer £2,200.
Aware that things were not as they ought to be, Burghley was
helpless until he found in John Hawkins a professional adviser.
After 1569 Hawkins left seagoing to others: under pressure from
queen and treasurer he turned his skill to the reconstruction of the
navy. It was he above all who enabled the English fleet to face and
defeat the Armada.

In a way this was itself ironical, for Hawkins saw little purpose
in concentrating on Channel defence. He wanted to base English
strategy on the treasure routes. His experience had shown him that
Spain could be kept helpless if the supply of American silver was
cut off: on this revenue, some ten per cent. of his total, Philip II
relied for the maintenance of his fleet and armies. Hawkins therefore proposed to cut the routes, either in the Caribbean or at the
Azores, and for this he needed an ocean-going fleet. The *Jesus*
stuck in his memory as an awful warning. In the place of out-of-
date carracks he wished to put improved galleons; instead of the
traditional floating castles he wanted to build fast-sailing and
manœuvrable fighting ships which would rely on seamanship and

fire-power. He owed his survival at San Juan de Ulua to the better gunnery of his ships: even in confined waters the broadside had proved more effective than boarding tactics. Hawkins' ideas met with violent opposition from the navy board whose members had had no experience of war outside the narrow seas, but Burghley trusted Hawkins. The *Revenge* was the first ship to be built to Hawkins' plans, and she was Drake's favourite among all the queen's ships, the one he picked as his flagship during the Armada campaign. But in order to build more ships like her Hawkins had to break the navy board; he had to obtain money and he could get it only by saving from the existing allocation, for there was no hope of more. Thus he convinced Burghley of Winter's corruption, was appointed treasurer of the navy in 1578, and next year took over the running of it for a lump sum, under the terms of a contract known as the 'first bargain'. He had promised an annual saving of £4,000, and he very nearly achieved it. Labouring under great difficulties, and hampered by the hostility of his colleagues who (since they held by patent for life) could not be removed from the board, Hawkins thoroughly reformed the administration of navy and dockyards. A 'second bargain' in 1585 gave him dictatorial powers which he used for a programme of new building. The outcome of it was that in 1587, when he laid down his office, the queen's navy consisted of twenty-three ships and eighteen ocean-going pinnaces,[1] all of them eminently seaworthy and representing a formidable fighting force. Among them was the great *Ark Royal* which the queen had bought from Raleigh and which was the last word in naval construction. Hawkins reduced the proportion of men to tonnage, with happy results. He wanted cleanliness and air on board to avoid disease, and he knew that an overmanned ship, short of supplies, was only a nuisance to an ocean-going fleet; but again he had to fight traditions grounded on Channel fighting with its near-by supply bases. He even succeeded in getting naval pay raised, so as to attract a better type of man; knowing what Elizabeth was, one may think this his highest achievement. And he had done it single-handed, against his colleagues though supported by Burghley. In the end, however, the famous Hawkins charm produced a lasting reconciliation with the Winter party. Rebuilt, renewed, and ready, the queen's navy was waiting at its anchorages in 1587, while rumours and threats of invasion were flying up from the south.

[1] Pinnaces were small oared vessels with a sail, very necessary for dispatch-carrying and the investigation of unfamiliar shores.

Chapter XIII

WAR, 1585-1603

I. ENGLAND AT WAR

FROM the moment of Elizabeth's accession, war was always impending. For twenty-seven years the queen managed to postpone its outbreak, but during the last eighteen years of the reign England was continually at war. Not indeed that moments of rest and something like peace did not intervene in this long period: like all the wars of the time this one too was very desultory, brief vigorous campaigns alternating with long-drawn sieges and months of stagnant inactivity, while armies rested and typhoid and dysentery did more efficiently what the enemies' weapons could not accomplish. Yet at all times during those eighteen years the drain on men and money went on inexorably. England was really engaged on four fronts. Defence of the realm came first: even after the defeat of Spain's greatest effort (as it proved) in 1588, the danger of invasion remained ever present, and repeated alarms—both true and false—underlined the necessity for constant vigilance, especially in the sea lanes. The war at sea went on without ceasing, a story of privateers and search for contraband in neutral shipping broken only by the occasional big expedition and more sizable action. Further, England was engaged on the continent of Europe. From 1585 to the end of the reign, Elizabeth maintained an expeditionary force in the Netherlands as well as garrisons in the towns of Flushing and Brill—the 'cautionary towns'—which were ceded by the Dutch into temporary English keeping as a guarantee of good faith and as safe ports of entry for English reinforcements. Ostend and Bergen, also garrisoned by English troops but outposts against the enemy rather than rearguard towns, completed a quartet of fortified places that over the years came almost to look like English colonies. In addition, English expeditions sailed to the support of Henry IV of France between 1589 and 1596. Fourthly and lastly, the biggest battlefield of all lay in Ireland, a danger spot from the beginning of the reign and nearly fatal to Elizabeth's policy after 1595 when rebellion there joined hands with the national enemy.

The effort required by such a war was naturally prodigious, and the results obtained were really very slight in proportion. After the repulse of Spain's attack in 1588 England never again won a decisive battle, though she continued to score successes in minor actions and an occasional exploit. On the whole the war lacked clear purpose or incisive action, but in this it merely conformed to sixteenth-century type. Nevertheless, much criticism has been levelled at the queen and her ministers. Elizabeth, it is alleged, was constitutionally incapable of conducting a war: she displayed qualities of indecision, procrastination, variability of mind, and cheeseparing parsimony which went far to ensure the failure of the various enterprises attempted. She prevented the effective use of England's resources, held up her admirals when they wished to sail, restrained them with foolishly rigorous and ill-considered instructions, and left the continental forces in the lurch when the timely despatch of reinforcements could have crowned great efforts with success. One school of commentators has concentrated on the alleged mistake of frittering away England's strength in continental expeditions, to the detriment of the war at sea where lay—as later history was to show—her best chance of triumph. The naval strategy had its exponents at the time, especially in Sir John Hawkins. In 1579 he recommended the despatch of a squadron to catch the plate fleet in the Azores and raid the Caribbean; in 1584 he proposed to cripple Spain by sweeping her shores in support of Don Antonio, the Portuguese claimant; in 1589 he submitted a grand strategical concept relying on a permanent force maintained by relays in the Azores, to cut for ever the flow of treasure which enabled Spain to make war. Though less articulate, Drake also supported a policy of concentrating on Spain's supply lines by means of sea-going squadrons. Much of this was at times attempted: the accusation against the queen is that too often she neglected this side of the war, insisted (with a landsman's failure to understand sea warfare) on keeping the navy in home stations to protect the Channel, and wasted time on continental actions. There is some truth in this comprehensive indictment. Elizabeth was often impossibly dilatory and wayward; as she grew older, her old tricks of indecision became an unbreakable habit. She hated war and was usually ready to seek her ends by other means, and neither she nor Burghley —unrepentant civilians—ever fully grasped the realities of military action. But the accusers miss their mark: the government did much better than alleged, and often the soldiers and sailors bore the guilt for failure. This will appear from an examination of the difficulties faced by England in those long years of war.[1]

In the first place, there is the problem of manpower: where did England get the men to fight her wars? As European populations went, the country ranked low: her 3,500,000 (at a rough estimate) represented perhaps a quarter of the French nation, less than half that of Spain, and stood even below the numbers of the United Provinces (the rebellious Netherlands). She had no standing army. The old feudal levy had proved its futility, though Henry VIII, for instance, still tried to fight his wars by summoning the leading nobility and gentry with their tenants and retainers. Financial difficulties as well as national considerations forbade the hiring of mercenaries, the expedient which had helped Henry VII to establish his throne. There remained volunteers, an uncertain and fluctuating source of supply, and the county militia, reorganised by statute in Mary's last year. All Englishmen between the ages of sixteen and sixty were liable to muster once a year for a review of the forces available, a check on equipment, and training. But exceptions were readily made; those of the militia that promised best—the 'trained bands'—were kept at home to defend the realm; and the armies overseas could be recruited only from the untrained men. In strict law the militia could not be compelled to serve overseas, though the government solved the legal problem by ignoring it and came down heavily on murmurings in the 1590s when the burden of the war began to tell. When men were needed, the usual practice was to send special commissioners to the shire musters to take what they required; these might be experienced officers like Sir John Norris who went recruiting in 1589, or more commonly the lords lieutenants of the counties. Thus in driblets reckoned by hundreds the total force was gradually assembled at the ports of embarkation. The numbers available were not large: in 1591 it was calculated that the whole amounted to some 104,000 men of whom only 42,000 were both trained and equipped —and these, of course, had to await the Spaniard at home. Yet out of such unpromising circumstances the government produced, according to the best estimates, some 20,000 men for France (of whom barely half returned), rather more than that for the Netherlands, perhaps 25,000 for Ireland, and new levies for the three great naval expeditions of 1589, 1596, and 1597 to a total of 17,000.

---

[1] For hostile views of Elizabeth's conduct of the war see e.g. E. P. Cheyney, *History of England from the Defeat of the Armada to the Death of Elizabeth*, and J. Corbett, *Drake and the Tudor Navy*. A useful corrective is applied, e.g. in J. E. Neale's *Queen Elizabeth*.

The armies so collected were far from satisfactory. Over the years, no doubt, the survivors turned into veterans: the performances of English detachments under such men as Sir John Norris in Brittany, Sir Roger Williams in Normandy, or Sir Francis Vere in the Netherlands were perfectly creditable. But they started as raw recruits, pressed men who did their best to desert on the march to the ports, or during the long waits while transport was assembled, or even abroad. As pressure mounted, it became more and more necessary to recruit criminals, prisoners, and vagabonds; the best military material from among the yeomen, ploughmen, and farmers was wanted to till the soil. Problems of supply, victualling, arming, and pay continued throughout the war, though experience gradually improved the services. Thus the council produced a ration organisation in the Netherlands after 1588, with regular contractors and warehouses, which was copied in Ireland in 1598. The ration scales were generous and varied, but the food often rotted before it reached the soldiers. Supplies of ordnance, powder, match, balls, armour, and so forth came partly from the ordnance office in the Tower and partly from county arsenals; here, too, organisation improved, though the practice of charging powder and match upon a soldier's pay (partly to prevent wastage) naturally led to a somewhat unwarlike reluctance to fire muskets at all. The men were supplied with winter and summer uniforms; here contractors had a field-day in the supply of ill-fitting and unserviceable shoes, cloaks, stockings, and so on. Most of these difficulties were to recur in all wars down to modern times; what is remarkable is that the Elizabethan privy council, starting from scratch and ever hampered by lack of money, yet produced some order out of complete chaos, and in the end sent English soldiers into action better equipped and fed than was usual even among the military powers of the continent.

Only one problem proved quite intractable. Corruption in the army itself could not be stamped out. It centred mostly on the captains of companies, responsible for allocating supplies and pay to their men, who with the assistance of the company clerks took their improper share of everything that passed through their hands. The common practice of returning more men on strength than actually existed produced the concession known as 'dead pays': for every ninety men under his command the captain drew a hundred men's pay, the difference being his perquisite. Even this did not satisfy the greed of these men, and illegal dead pays continued to appear on the returns. The overwhelming impression is of a government trying its best in the face of the criminal irresponsibility, negligence, self-seeking, and lack of public spirit of nearly all the men on the spot, from generals to privates.

These armies—and navies too, where conditions of life were of course even worse—were not, on the whole, led by any great commanders. Almost of necessity, the small and scattered English army never produced generals to compare with the best the continent could show—men like Alexander of Parma, Maurice of Nassau, or even Henry IV of France—though as the wars went on many English commanders became very competent warriors of the second rank. In one form of war the English acquired genuine mastery: that was the guerilla warfare of the Irish bogs and forests where they were held at bay, off and on, for forty years. Here men like Sir Henry Sidney and Lord Mountjoy displayed remarkable abilities as colonial conquerors. Mountjoy may be the exception to the rule: he succeeded even against trained Spanish infantry, though they were rather out of their element at the time.[1] At sea, the early years of the war saw the decline and passing away of a great generation of admirals. Grenville died in 1591, Frobisher in 1594, Drake and Hawkins—shadows of their real selves—in 1595; and though many hardy and skilful sailors still set out from Plymouth and Bristol and London, those heroes found only lesser (though still at times notable) successors in such men as Howard of Effingham, Lord Thomas Howard, or Sir Walter Raleigh. Worst of all in its effects on the war was the flashing career of the young earl of Essex, despite all his zeal and gallantry; this will appear in the course of the story. Almost all the actions of the war were marked by unbelievable courage, reckless enterprise despite all odds, fierce fighting, and too little skill in the higher reaches of military science.

With such men, such armies, and such physical difficulties in supply and transport, it ought to be evident that discussions of strategy cannot be based on the possibilities of a technically more advanced age. Sixteenth-century navies, for instance, always found it hard to keep at sea for more than two months. Victualling and watering were insoluble problems, for the large number of men required to work the sails of the day kept crews big. All operations away from home waters involved almost insuperable risks, as the Spaniards learned in 1588 and the English in 1589. The consequent need for a land base in hostile country led to much inevitable dissipation of time and energy in preliminary operations. Those careful plans that we hear so much about do not even seem to have taken sufficient account of the ordinary difficulties of navigation.

[1] See below, p. 393.

The ships of the time were seaworthy enough in the sense that they could outride most storms, but their primitive rig meant that they could not sail very close to the wind or at all into it. The various expeditions were held up in English harbours at least as much by the prevailing winds from the south-west as by the queen's changes of mind; and in a gale the only thing to do was to run before the wind. Bad weather thus invariably scattered a fleet, and a ship caught on a lee shore was lost for certain. None of the naval forces sent out by either side ever came back in a body; there was only one Armada simply because three others sent in the 1590s were driven back by storms before they got into English latitudes. All this helps to indicate how unusually difficult such actions as Hawkins advocated really were: both he and Drake drew on experience gained with small compact forces against very shaky defences and tended to overrate the skill of the English and the weakness of Spain. It is not even clear that either they or later writers were correct in ignoring the problem of Channel defence which the queen insisted upon. Since that day the best defence of English shores has often lain in attacks elsewhere, but in 1588 the English were nearly caught defenceless, and in 1597 only storms prevented a major Spanish descent while the English fleet was still straggling back from the Azores.

Above all else it was lack of money that limited England's effectiveness in the war. As always, war fantastically increased government expenditure, the more so because it was in this period that England came into line with continental practice by abandoning the long-bow and equipping her infantry with muskets, calivers (light handguns), and pikes. Precisely how much the war swallowed up it is hard to say since different documents give different amounts for the same items; figures can only be tentative. A soldier's pay was 8d. a day; the cost of raising a horseman with his equipment rose from £25 to £30; one winter uniform in Ireland cost £3 14s. 4d. For the 7,600 men sent to the Netherlands in 1585 the queen contracted to pay £126,000 a year, and this proved too low an estimate; something over £2,000,000 was spent there before Elizabeth died. The small expedition to Brittany, with reinforcements, absorbed about £280,000. The mobilisation for the Armada more than doubled the ordinary outlay on the navy, and the two expeditions to Cadiz and the Azores (1596-7) were calculated to have cost some £170,000. As for Ireland, Robert Cecil alleged in 1599—before the biggest campaign there—that £4,300,000 had been spent on it since 1588; but even on a lower estimate less influenced by desire to extract supplies, the Tyrone rebellion alone (1596-1601) accounted for little short of £2,000,000. These are staggering sums for sixteenth-century conditions. When Elizabeth died the Dutch owed her debts of nearly £800,000 (of which about half was in the end paid to James I), while Henry IV's debts were nearly £300,000 of which he never repaid more than a quarter. All this throws a flood of light on Burghley's desperate economies and on Elizabeth's care of her resources and her frequent complaints that she was pouring away her treasure to no purpose. In those years Spain defaulted with such regularity that the matter became a joke, while Elizabeth never went bankrupt; but the struggle for survival left a heavy burden of debt to the next reign.

After all, the ordinary revenue of the crown amounted to only £200,000 a year, augmented in the war years by rigorous exploitation to £300,000. Out of this the ordinary government of the realm and the expenses of court and household had to be covered. None the less, Burghley had built up by 1585 a reserve of £300,000 which served to support the war down to the Armada year. Thereafter the government were of necessity back to the hand-to-mouth existence of Henry VIII and his immediate successors. Elizabeth showed no hesitation to call parliament to aid her: every one of the six war-parliaments (1585, 1587, 1589, 1593, 1597, 1601) was asked for subsidies, and every one granted them, on the whole with surprising readiness. Members grumbled after 1593, and the taxpayers made even more noise, but there was no serious or lasting opposition. In those sixteen years the queen obtained about £2,000,000 in direct and extraordinary taxation, and even this unprecedented burden, which—since the assessment did not reflect national wealth at all accurately—was borne with some difficulty, came nowhere near to meeting the cost. Ready cash was always short, for taxes took their time coming in. Everything was tried. The government extracted more from the customs, mainly by returning to farming; it sold crown lands, thus once again impoverishing the crown in the long run; rents and recusancy fines were exploited more stringently; forced loans and benevolences were revived. But none of this sufficed, and Elizabeth was forced to borrow on interest, to skimp the war, and to conduct it by the curious expedient of joint-stock companies financed partly by herself and partly by private persons. Small wonder that she thought more of the possible profit when her ships sailed for Lisbon or Cadiz, than of the military problems involved; small wonder that a loss on such an expedition, which at the least was expected to pay for itself, was more than she would put up with.

The queen, Burghley, and after his death in 1598 Robert Cecil and Lord Buckhurst, did wonders; the country paid more, and more readily, than it had ever done; but even so shortage of money dogged every step. The war laid the foundation for that shaky financial position which the Stuarts, who made it worse without a war, were to find the biggest obstacle to autocratic government.

In truth, England entered the conflict without being in the least ready for it, Hawkins' navy always excepted. Not for 150 years had the country fought a major war, and things had changed beyond recognition since the days of Joan of Arc. England's economy was not organised for war; she had neither an efficient armed force nor experienced leaders; dangers threatened in too many places at once. All that England had were numbers of eager, brave, foolhardy men willing to fight, as well as many willing to plunder, and more reluctant conscripts whom war occasionally turned into good soldiers; she had a queen and council, inexperienced indeed in such matters, but willing and—as the event proved —well able to learn; and she had the advantage of a fierce protestant spirit among her best men which drove them into the breach at Cadiz, across the oceans, and into the bloody skirmishes round Ostend and Brest with more passion than mere discipline or the desire for booty would ever account for. As it is, those sixteen years nearly turned the English into a military people—militant they had always been. When Elizabeth died the treasury might indeed be empty, but she had an army and a navy which, despite many failures and too few decisive successes, could look back upon performances which by the standards of the time were creditable. As for the queen, she never ceased to think the war a calamity or to hope for its cessation; and of course she was right.

2. THE BEGINNING OF THE WAR, AND THE END OF MARY STUART

The assassination of William of Orange (June 1584) ended the queen's hopes of continuing her policy of peace. The earlier death of Alençon and the besotted incapacity of Henry III of France meant that she could no longer use French intervention to maintain Dutch resistance to Spain. Throughout 1584 and 1585 the prince of Parma was carrying all before him in the Netherlands; in August 1585, the great city of Antwerp, left without succour, fell into Spanish hands, and the Dutch cause stood at its lowest. Moreover, in January 1585 the Guise faction formed an alliance with Spain and raised rebellion against their king; by June the Catholic League dominated France. If Spain was to be held at bay and protestantism was to be saved, England would have to take an open part in the war. The decision proved difficult and the negotiations dragged on. Relations with Spain had been bad since the expulsion of Mendoza, but many—including Burghley—still hoped to be able to come to terms with her. However, in May 1585 Philip ordered the seizure of all English ships in Spanish harbours, thus ending the opposition of English merchants to a step which would destroy their trade with Spain, and the fall of Antwerp clinched matters. In August 1585 Elizabeth concluded a treaty of alliance with the Dutch States General by which she promised to maintain an army in the Netherlands at her own cost until the end of the war, while the Dutch handed over Flushing and Brill. The queen refused the sovereignty of the Netherlands, vacant since Alençon's death, but accepted the title of protector. After further delays, due largely to financial difficulties or the queen's parsimony—according as one sees it—Leicester sailed in December with some 7,600 men and a showy retinue. Though it remained undeclared, war with Spain was a fact.

Leicester's campaigns in the Netherlands proved both disastrous and humiliating. At this time England was in no position to wage successful war on land, and Leicester himself, now in his fifties, displayed little except arrogance, quarrelsomeness, and incompetence. A figure-head was needed, but this figure-head wished to act. The queen had strictly forbidden any arrangement which might suggest an English administration in the Netherlands: she was an ally, not a ruler. Yet the first thing Leicester did was to accept the title of governor. Elizabeth's fury nearly finished him and the whole enterprise; only the impossibility of deserting the Dutch so soon prevented his recall. The cost of the expedition was reckoned not far short of half the crown's annual revenue, yet Leicester wasted his supplies, arbitrarily increased officers' wages (including his own), and did nothing to stop the rampant peculation. Instead he complained of the government's parsimony, an unjustified charge which was to stick for 350 years.[1] The actual campaign of 1586 produced no positive results except some individual deeds of valour of which Sir Philip Sidney's death after the battle of Zutphen is the best remembered. Leicester quarrelled with his own best captains and his Dutch allies; in November 1586 he returned to England; the war, so eagerly begun by the English fire-eaters and so well received by the hardpressed Dutch threatened to end in mutual hostility, with ignominy for the former and disaster for the latter.

[1] It was proved groundless by J. E. Neale in *Eng. Hist. Rev.* (1930).

While the continental engagements yielded neither glory nor profit, English feats at sea amazed all Europe and raised Sir Francis Drake to the status of a legendary figure. The Spanish seizure of English property in May 1585 provoked a counter-stroke which was originally and officially intended to secure compensation, but was turned into a general attack on Spain's American empire. As early as 1579 Hawkins had suggested the despatch of a small mobile squadron to intercept the treasure fleet in the Azores and then to raid the Caribbean: in his opinion no harbour or shipping there need escape pillage and destruction. It was in effect to carry out this plan that Drake sailed in September 1585. He had with him nearly thirty ships and a force of over 2,000, both mariners and soldiers; the expedition was equipped by a joint-stock of £6,000 to which the queen contributed £1,000; he had official backing and instructions. Leaving Plymouth in great haste, for fear of countermanding orders from the queen, with watercasks half-filled and victuals taken on all anyhow, Drake made for Vigo. Here, on Spanish soil, he completed the fitting out of his fleet; although he did only very little material damage to Spain, Philip's prestige suffered a heavy blow, and since financial credit depended on prestige Drake's visit affected Spain's power to make war. He missed both the plate fleets of 1585, touched at the Cape Verde Islands where the fleet picked up a virulent fever, and made for the West Indies where his exploits were daring and eminently successful. In brilliant amphibious actions, he captured and sacked San Domingo, the capital of Cuba, and Carthagena, the capital of the Main. Losses by fever forced him to break off the enterprise sooner than intended, and he took insufficient booty to pay a profit, but if as piracy the voyage was a failure it did great things as an act of war. The Spanish West Indies were crippled—short of ships and guns—and Philip, forced to restore them and to pay a higher interest on his Italian loans, had to divert precious resources from the Netherlands where they could be ill spared. Parma's troops remained unpaid and therefore inactive: Drake in the Caribbean had done more than Leicester in Zeeland to ease the pressure on the Dutch.

The success of 1586 was not followed up, a fact for which Drake's financial failure and the needs of the Netherlands are quite enough to account. At the same time, Elizabeth and some of her councillors, continued to look for the possibility of peace. Throughout these years contact with Spain was maintained in devious ways, and the queen was ever ready to seize any chance of ending the war. That that chance never came was probably due to Philip.

As the king of Spain grew older he changed from a politician to a fanatic: the cause of the Church began to dominate all his plans. With Parma successful in the Netherlands and the League keeping France pro-Spanish, he was moreover free at last to turn his full power on that island whose protestant queen had thwarted him for thirty years. England seemed to have been behind every move against the Habsburg ascendancy since the abdication of Charles V, and although such a view underestimated the normal hostility of France it accurately interpreted the situation in the 1580s. Peace was out of the question. Elizabeth cannot be blamed because at this stage she did not concentrate on wiping out Spanish sea-power and obtaining a stranglehold on the treasure routes. England was on the defensive: the tone was set by Spain, immeasurably the stronger power, as it seemed to all men at the time.

However, before we turn to the great Spanish assault, we must follow up the story of one disturbing element in the first half of Elizabeth's reign. The imprisoned queen of Scots was drawing near to her tragic fate. Ever since Elizabeth saved her, in 1571-2, from the consequences of the Ridolfi plot and the nation's wrath, Mary had been a potential danger and an active centre of conspiracy. Until 1585 she was kept in Sheffield Castle, guarded by the earl of Shrewsbury and inflicted with the earl's formidable wife, Bess of Hardwick. But her imprisonment, though close, had been honourable; she was treated as a queen and permitted free contact with the outer world. The treaty of Berwick ended the plotting which centred on Scotland, but from France her relatives, the Guises, continued to buoy up her hopes. However, the discovery of the Throckmorton plot, the assassination of William of Orange, the parliamentary association to protect the queen, all combined to bring matters to a head. In January 1585 Mary was transferred to Tutbury Castle into the custody of Sir Amyas Paulet, a stern puritan who treated her as an immoral and dangerous woman, and not as a queen. Almost immediately another plot was uncovered, or as some would have it, manufactured. A Dr William Parry was executed in March for conspiring against Elizabeth. Parry was a thorough scoundrel who had escaped hanging for burglary by entering Walsingham's secret service. He even got back into favour and respectability sufficiently to sit in the parliament of 1584. But he either involved himself with Mary's partisans abroad, or else was sacrificed by Walsingham who employed him as an *agent provocateur*. In any case, he deserved hanging more than most of the political victims of the reign. One result was that Walsingham was induced to pay closer attention to the English catholic refugees in France and so to come upon the track of the Babington conspiracy which terminated the life of Mary Stuart.

That there were men plotting to free Mary and kill Elizabeth was certain, but Walsingham wanted proof of Mary's complicity since he was convinced that the danger could only end if the rival queen were dead. To that purpose he so arranged matters that ever since men have been found to say that he invented the plot for which Mary was executed. The truth is that Mary was guilty, but Walsingham tricked her into giving herself away. In December 1585 he had her transferred to Chartley Manor, and there, with the assistance of Paulet and a renegade catholic, persuaded her that she had found a safe way to communicate with France. In reality, every letter to and fro passed through the secretary's hands. By the middle of 1586 the new conspiracy was taking shape in the mind of Anthony Babington, a young man of more devotion than sense, and by July Mary was in Walsingham's toils. Babington wrote her a full account of the plot—which involved the assassination of Elizabeth—and asked her approval. There is both drama and disgust in the scene that followed, with Walsingham and his agents tensed in their wait for Mary's answer. It was delayed and all seemed lost; at last it came, and the queen of Scots was seen to have given her approval to everything. It was the end. By September the conspirators were executed—to the joy of the populace— and in October a special commission tried Mary and found her guilty. Guilty she was, but Elizabeth felt no more inclined now than earlier to exact the penalty. A fellow queen whose links with France made her execution a serious international matter—all Elizabeth's humane and political instincts rose up against the action. But the nation and the council were determined. Once more parliament, pressing for Mary's death, was put off with an 'answer answerless', but on 1 February 1587 Elizabeth yielded and signed the warrant. She would not let it go; she tried to get Paulet to act in secret which that narrow but upright man refused angrily; then the council, acting without her knowledge, despatched the warrant. On the 7th Mary mounted the scaffold in Fotheringay Castle and welcomed martyrdom, expiating her sins and also creating a legend and a continued attachment which no other death could have produced. Elizabeth was distraught. Her rage overtopped all previous experiences of that awesome natural phenomenon. All the council were in disgrace: there was talk of prosecuting them for murder. William Davison, the second secretary of state who had let the warrant out of his keeping, was

THE WAR WITH SPAIN

ENGLAND

London
Chatham
Dover
Plymouth
Brille
Flushing
Ostend
Antwerp
Bergen-op-Zoom
Zutphen
Calais
Gravelines
NETHERLANDS
Dieppe
Rouen
Brest
Crozon
BRITTANY
NORMANDY
Paris
FRANCE
Course of the Armada
Ferrol
Corunna
Santander
San Sebastian
Madrid
SPAIN
PORTUGAL
Lisbon
Sagres
Seville
Cadiz

fined heavily and committed to the Tower. But the wrath passed. Burghley, Leicester, and the rest returned to favour; Davison, the scapegoat, was released, his fine remitted, and though he relinquished his appointment he continued to draw his fee.

Elizabeth's anger and sorrow (temporarily real though they were) and the royal funeral accorded to Mary could not disguise the facts to anyone. Scotland burst out in a fury, but James VI soon subordinated his moderate feelings as a son to his passionate interest in the English succession; the danger of war in the north melted away rapidly. France, where the storm was even greater, proved harder to appease: the death of Mary cemented the alliance of the League with Spain. Yet all in all, the practical effects abroad were negligible, especially since Spain had been determined on attack long before the execution. In England a heavy burden seemed lifted. The traitors within the gate were frustrate, the queen—symbol of national survival—safe at last. When her anger abated, Elizabeth came to see that the council's disobedience had cut a knot which there had been no way of untying. If she suspected that later ages, more distant from the problem and therefore better able to take the wrong view, might condemn her for the death of the unfortunate queen of Scots, one hopes she did not let it trouble her. Whatever the moralists and the romantics may say, it is difficult to see what else could have been done about a proven danger to the state, properly and lawfully convicted of a capital crime. From the moment that Mary took refuge in England she created a situation which could not be resolved in a way that was both sensible and moral. And yet—the martyrdom of the queen of Scots remains to stain the record of Elizabeth's reign.

3. THE ENTERPRISE OF ENGLAND

In Spain the death of Mary Stuart acted both as a stimulant and a relief. It seems probable that Philip had made up his mind to settle with England as early as the middle of 1585; he knew well that there could be no hope of the great catholic triumph until Elizabeth was dethroned. The English assistance to the Netherlands, however ineffective Leicester may have been, proved that the Netherlands would not be reduced to obedience until England had fallen. Thus while Elizabeth continued her diplomacy of alternate negotiations and demonstrations of strength—all designed to bring the adversary to a pacific state of mind—Philip began to prepare for the invasion of England. In 1585 he offered himself to Pope Sixtus V as the sword of the Church, provided the

Church put up the money. Sixtus, outstanding among the Counter-Reformation popes, remained sceptical. Unlike the northern protestants with their fevered imaginations, he knew enough about Philip and Spain's religious policy to doubt the king's devotion to the catholic cause. What was more, he had a healthy respect for England whose growing power he divined and admired. When Drake set Europe talking of his exploits, the pope, oddly enough, was among his leading admirers, and it was not only an Italian delight at seeing the haughty Spaniard humbled. Sixtus suspected Philip's intentions because he thought that the catholic king was more interested in succeeding to the throne of England than in fighting the battles of the Church, in which conclusion he seems to have been right. In February 1587, when Mary's fate was sealed, Philip declared that James of Scotland, as a heretic, could not inherit, and that therefore he would assert his own rights.[1] Thus Mary's removal meant that Philip could enjoy both the practical advantages of an enterprise undertaken in his own interest and the asset of a good cause represented by his anger against the adulterous, illegitimate, heretic regicide who had usurped the English crown.

The preparations proceeded apace. Late in 1586 the pope gave a cautious blessing and an even more qualified financial assistance. In the meantime, the admiral, the marquess of Santa Cruz, busied himself in getting together the great fleet which was to bring England to her knees. His own plan, which envisaged a direct sea-borne invasion, had to be abandoned because Philip could not afford the enormous expense it involved; instead it was decided to send a fleet which would win command of the English Channel and so ensure the safe transport of 3,000 veterans under Parma from the Netherlands to England. Throughout 1586 and 1587 the west coast ports of the Iberian peninsula were full of vessels being got ready for the enterprise, and stores were collected from all parts of the Spanish dominions in the Mediterranean. It was now that Drake's Caribbean raid of 1585-6 took effect by making it harder for Philip to raise the necessary loans; also, Spain depended for naval stores on the Baltic, the route whither was blocked by Dutch and English squadrons. Nevertheless, the English government, kept abreast of developments by Walsingham's foreign intelligence, knew soon enough that it was facing a formidable threat and made counter-preparations. The musters were brought up to date and the militia trained; measures against catholic priests

[1] He had a species of hereditary claim and also alleged that Mary Tudor had willed the realm to him.

were intensified and a strenuous watch was kept. Late in 1586, while Hawkins was at sea intending to raid Spain, he was kept by the queen plying up and down the Channel; there was a rumour-induced panic which soon passed over. In June 1587, after long negotiations, Elizabeth reluctantly agreed to send Leicester back to the Netherlands; she neither wanted to renew the war nor deprive herself of the earl's company, but treaty obligations and the pressure of a united council, most of them anxious to see Leicester out of England, secured his return to the post of duty. He was, if anything, less successful than on his first visit: he failed to save Sluys from Parma, quarrelled with everybody both Dutch and English, and was recalled in November 1587, leaving the Netherlands and the English forces there in a pretty confusion.

The heavy drain and the failures of the Dutch war explain sufficiently why Elizabeth wished to open negotiations with Parma, but the threat from Spain could not be overlooked. The naval experts had long clamoured to be allowed to take counter-measures, and in April 1587 Drake had his way. Sailing with a strong fleet to tackle any Spanish armament (if one were on its way to England) and to cut up the treasure convoys, but also to 'distress the ships within the havens' themselves, he reached Cadiz on the 19th and went straight in before the Spaniards knew what was upon them. In a brilliant action he destroyed some thirty ships. Then he captured the fort and anchorage of Sagres near Cape Vincent from where for nearly two months he preyed on the ships carrying supplies for the Armada. A challenge to Santa Cruz to come out and fight having been sensibly declined, Drake took his disintegrating force—disease, lack of victual, and indifferent discipline doing their accustomed work—to the Azores where he captured a great carrack and secured a financial profit for the expedition which had been equipped by the usual joint-stock company. The material loss to Spain was great—many ships destroyed, naval stores burned, supplies taken away—but worse still was the blow to Philip's reputation and credit inflicted by an English squadron based on Spanish territory itself. Nevertheless the king remained undaunted. The preparations were resumed, and, since Elizabeth either would or could not try again, the sailing of the Armada was delayed by only one year. Even so England gained much when Santa Cruz died in February 1588, for Philip had no other experienced seaman to serve him.

Thus the initiative returned to Spain, though this proved no advantage to her. In May 1588 the lord admiral, Lord Howard of Effingham, a competent officer who displayed unusual skill in making the great sea-dogs work amicably under his command, took over, with nearly all the fleet, at Plymouth. Both he and his chief advisers—Drake, Hawkins, Frobisher—wished to sail to Spain and attack, especially when it became known that the Armada, having sailed in March, had been driven by storms into Corunna. The queen and council have usually been blamed because in their ignorance of sea-fighting they kept the fleet at home for fear that the Spaniards might slip past it and attack a defenceless England; Corbett even thought that Howard had to be driven by Drake into more seamanlike action. But it is now realised that all the commanders were for attacking, and that they were probably wrong in this: off Spain the English ships would have been in the position in which the Armada was soon to be. Drake's exploit of 1587 offers little guidance—though no doubt it influenced him at the time—because the Spanish defences had since then been greatly strengthened and because a Spanish fleet was now actually on the high seas. As it was, the weather defeated Howard's three attempts to reach Spain in May and June. The same winds which drove him back into Plymouth brought the Armada north. On 19th July it sighted the Lizard. The news caught the English imprisoned by a contrary wind in Plymouth harbour, but while the Armada shortened sail to take up its predetermined formation the English beat out of Plymouth Sound and in the night of the 20th sailed across the Spanish fleet to win the weather gauge.

The two fleets were in every way better matched than used to be supposed. On both sides there were rather less than fifty effective fighting ships with some eighty others. The Spaniards were unhandier and taller, with a much heavier short-range armament and burdened with an army intended both to fight at sea and to join Parma's forces for the invasion. The English ships —Hawkins' navy supported by some warlike merchantmen of the Turkey Company—sailed much better and were more skilfully handled, but against this the Armada put its tight line-abreast formation (its 'crescent moon') which nullified the new English tactics of line-ahead sailing with the concentration of superior fire-power on individual ships. In gunnery the English had the advantage of more and better long-range guns and better trained gunners, though the Spaniards had learned much in this respect; neither side carried sufficient ammunition. In the outcome the English were surprised by the tough resistance encountered which differed greatly from what the corsairs were accustomed to find in the Caribbean: it is too easily forgotten that Spain was still the foremost military power in Europe who could not help but be formidable when she concentrated her resources, skill, and discipline on one particular task. The greatest handicap imposed on the Armada's commander, the reluctant duke of Medina Sidonia, was strategic rather than tactical. His orders forbade him to capture a harbour in England: he was to make for the Netherlands to join with Parma. But Parma, too, could offer the Armada no safe anchorage: the only port suitable for the manœuvre which Philip had in mind was Flushing, and that was in English hands.

The Spanish progress up-Channel developed into a nine days' running battle, with the English ships sailing rings round the ponderous Armada but unable to make any noticeable impression on its militarily tight formation. This was maintained by sailing at a speed of barely three knots, which in turn enhanced the advantages of English manœuvrability. There was a good deal of rather piecemeal fighting with two bigger engagements off Portland Bill and the Isle of Wight when the English knowledge of the tides enabled them to bring the Armada to action on disadvantageous terms. But although the Armada lost two ships and suffered much superficial damage, it was still an almost undiminished fighting force when it arrived off Calais on 27th July. Both sides had used up much more powder and shot than they could afford, but the Spaniards—far from home, friends, and supplies—suffered worse. It was the enforced recourse to Calais sands which was to finish the Armada; the fatal error which had overlooked the necessity for a proper anchorage prepared the way for the English victory. On the 27th Howard dropped anchor a mile offshore. There he was joined by Seymour's squadron which had been blockading Parma; now at last the lord admiral had the full strength of the fleet and parity with the Spaniards. On the night of the 28th, the English launched six fire-ships which were so well handled that the tight formation, which had defied the English long-range tactics, at last broke up. In a panic most of the Spaniards cut their cables and drifted away in the night. When morning came, all but Medina Sidonia's own ship with three or four more were seen to be scattered to the north-east. The battle which followed is known as that of Gravelines. Though the duke fought courageously, restoring something like a fleet in the course of several hours' vigorous bombardment, the Armada was virtually destroyed. Only four ships were lost, but the rest took a terrible battering from the English gunfire and lost thousands of men.

What the guns had begun the weather completed. A rain squall from the north-east ended the fight and threatened to drive the Spanish hulks on to the Flemish sands, until at the last moment the wind shifted back to the south-west. Before it the Armada took flight. There was no question of returning through the Channel, let alone of carrying out the junction with Parma who had long given up all hope of the plan's success. Medina Sidonia determined to make his way round the north of the British Isles. Though empty of ammunition, Howard followed as far as the Firth of Forth. Its final fate yet awaited the Armada. As it doubled the north of Scotland it met the Atlantic gales which threw the unseaworthy ships in scores upon rocks and headlands or sank them in mid-ocean. Some half struggled back to Spain in 1589; the fate of most of the rest was never known. All round the northern shores of Scotland and Ireland there lay the wrecks of the galleons and the bodies of the seamen and soldiers killed by the savage sea and (supposedly) by the yet more savage natives of those parts.

The disappearance of the Armada into the northern mists left everything uncertain. Rome and Spain rejoiced over false rumours of a great victory, before the truth turned all to sorrow and reviling. Philip alone received Medina Sidonia, disconsolate but blameless, with kindness and without reproaches. The commander had done his best—a good best. He was defeated by better ships, better seamanship, a needlessly rigid plan, and at the last the weather. That the storms rather than the English had destroyed the Armada was a legend fostered by the English themselves in an endeavour to claim the Almighty for their side. 'Afflavit Deus,' said Elizabeth's medal, 'et dissipati sunt': God blew and they were scattered. The queen expressed disappointment at the small number of ships taken, and neither she nor her advisers thought England safe—so much so that the defence force was mustered at Tilbury ten days after Gravelines. Lest this be thought the folly of landsmen who could not tell a victory at sea, it must be noted that the naval commanders were similarly disappointed. They grumbled at the shortage of powder. The first onslaught had been 'more coldly done than the service required', and to the end the Armada never sank before the English guns. Used to the small-scale actions of raids and piracy, Drake and his fellows under-estimated the powers of defence of which a large compact fleet was capable. Howard expressed all their awe and wonder when he wrote: 'All the world never saw such a force as theirs was.' What with all this surprise and shock, the English undervalued their own achievement. The plain fact was that the Armada reached Calais a fighting force, if slightly battered and growing seriously short of ammunition. After the fire-ships had given the English guns their chance, the scattered fleet which fled before the kindly

south-west wind was a collection of defenceless hulks, incapable
of doing any further harm. No doubt, if the English shortage of
powder could have been remedied, the guns might have anticipated
the work of the gales. But the victory was won at Gravelines, by
human agency. England's mood of sober rejoicing and thanks-
giving to God was a creditable one and reflected moreover the
knowledge that the defeat of the Armada did not end the war.
Indeed, in a measure it proved its beginning and the renewal of
Spanish power. Yet all this must not hide the fact that in the first
great naval battle of modern times the English navy won a victory
based on its superior skill and advanced tactics, as well as on the
qualities of the new-style fleet of seaworthy, handy ships fighting
long-range gun-actions rather than engaging at short range and
boarding the enemy.

4. THE WAR WITH SPAIN, 1589-1603

The defeat of the Armada seemed to open the way to some
decisive counter-stroke, though it may be said at once that this
view has been more popular with historians than it was with the
men who had to work out the details. They knew that Spain was
not on her knees and felt rather inclined to underrate the extent of
their victory. However, by December 1588 a plan had been formed.
A counter-armada was to sail, commanded by Drake as admiral
and Norris as general—each the leading man in his profession—
and designed to break Spain at one great blow. The enterprise
came to be known as the Portugal expedition, though Portugal was
not among its original objectives. It was a dismal failure, made
worse by the initial hopes and the enthusiasm which sent thousands
of volunteers to swell the ranks of the adventurers. That failure
has customarily been put entirely at the queen's door: after all,
how could military men of the calibre of Drake and Norris possibly
be responsible for such egregious errors? A recent review of the
evidence has altered the picture considerably.[1] The queen has
been accused of halfheartedness in support (so that the expedition
had to be fitted out by a joint-stock company instead of being a
properly financed national undertaking), of causing the fatal delay
in sailing from February to April 1589, of a parsimony which
despatched the fleet short of victuals, of instructions either uncertain or fatuous which compelled the commanders to waste time
on side issues. But the truth is that the queen had neither ships

[1] R. B. Wernham, 'Queen Elizabeth and the Portugal Expedition of
1589', *Eng. Hist. Rev.* (1951).

nor men nor money of her own to equip such a fleet, so that the
normal method of a partnership with private enterprise was inevitable; in any case, Drake and Norris, who had conceived the
whole notion, as well as other gentlemen and financiers wanted
their share of the expected profits. The delays were due to a
quarrel with the Dutch, arising out of the projected withdrawal
of seasoned troops from the Netherlands for the expedition; though
originally caused by Elizabeth's highhandedness, it was prolonged
beyond February by Willoughby, the English commander in the
Netherlands, who did not wish to lose so many of his best men.
Victuals were short because the commanders foolishly allowed
popular eagerness to swell the numbers of the fleet far beyond
the original estimate. But the crux of the matter was the purpose
of the voyage.

The Armada had been scattered but not wiped out, and early in
1589 some forty vessels had found refuge in the ports of the
Biscayan coast of Spain, especially Santander and San Sebastian.
The queen, preoccupied as always with the defence of England
rather than raids in distant waters, intended that these should be
destroyed before anything else was attempted. Against this, the
adventurers argued that those ports in the eastern end of the Bay
were impossible to sail back from; they would not endanger the
whole fleet by getting themselves caught in that pocket. They
therefore put forward a plan for Portugal, based on the claims of
Don Antonio with the exploitation of which Drake had toyed since
1581. Why should they not capture the Azores and Lisbon,
stimulate a national rising, and take all Portugal? Elizabeth and
Burghley had rather less faith in Antonio and a problematic
uprising, but even as Philip II never ceased to hope for a catholic
revolt against Elizabeth so Drake fell victim to the Portuguese
exile's deluded hopes. The excuse put forward against going to
Santander was but a cloak for his insistent ambitions to strike a
really big blow: the Spaniards themselves had no difficulty in
getting their ships round to Ferrol after refitting. Elizabeth was
right: the first objective should have been the elimination of the
Spanish fleet while it was yet helpless. However, as a mere shareholder she had to compromise: the final instructions ordered
Drake to attack the Biscay ports and then to capture an island in
the Azores, while they left the possibility of an attack on Lisbon
open.

Even so, the expedition did not obey orders. It got away in
April 1589, but instead of making for Santander it went to
Corunna which could just about be considered a Biscayan port and

which harboured one Armada galleon. Here the fleet delayed a vital fortnight, taking the town but failing before the citadel and, worst of all, failing to revictual thoroughly. Only incompetence, induced perhaps by a divided command and a mistaken confidence in Spanish weakness, can explain such behaviour. Early in May they set sail for Lisbon, completely ignoring instructions. On the way they were joined by the queen's favourite, the young earl of Essex, who had stolen away without leave to satisfy his thirst for adventure and had thus drawn upon the expedition Elizabeth's personal rancour. Lisbon was reached, but the delay at Corunna had given plenty of warning, and the attack itself was carried out very inefficiently. Combined naval and military operations are always difficult since they depend on experience and faultless timing; here Drake and Norris made things harder by losing contact with each other. All the gallantry in the world could not overcome bad strategy; the expected Portuguese rising entirely failed to happen; and by the end of the month there was nothing for it but to re-embark. Even the lucky capture of a large Hanse convoy, carrying contraband, which was used to return the sick and wounded to England, only marked a tiny break in the lowering clouds. The biggest cloud was gathering at court: the queen's letters denounced the expedition's doings and demanded the return of Essex. The fleet now began to disintegrate and its action lost purpose. A raid on Vigo was followed by a desultory invasion of the Azores, and by the end of June what was left of the great enterprise—they had lost many men though few ships—had straggled back to Plymouth. None of its aims had been achieved. Philip had suffered great annoyance and a little damage, but the ships of the late Armada were being got ready for action, Antonio remained an exile, no captures worth the telling had been made, and financially the whole affair was a total loss. Naturally Elizabeth made no secret of her thorough displeasure, and Drake and Norris remained for some years in a disgrace which it is hard, on the evidence, to suppose undeserved.

Unavoidable continental commitments now began to absorb all the resources of the crown. The war at sea continued, but for a time it remained in the hands of private persons, with an occasional queen's ship in the larger fleets. Throughout the war privateers of various kinds, equipped with royal letters of marque and commissions to prey on Spain, roamed the seas; the earl of Cumberland, for instance, had at least one such ship and usually many more at sea all the time. It appears that an average of from 100 to 200 privateering ventures set sail from England every year after 1585, bringing in prizes to an annual value of £150,000-£300,000. The main backers were merchants, especially the great men of the Barbary, Guinea, and Levant Companies. The weight of enterprise shifted from the west country to London and it acquired a much more thorough organisation. Though the regular trades, such as that in cloth, suffered by the war, imports of prize goods increased enormously, especially of sugar in which England came near to establishing a European monopoly. Shipbuilding boomed. Altogether, though the crown and perhaps the country made little out of it, the mercantile community seems to have enjoyed considerable profits from privateering.[1] The better-known voyages brought less gain. In 1590 and 1591 Frobisher, Hawkins, and Cumberland all had squadrons in the Azores on the look-out for treasure ships. No captures were made, mainly because Philip II had stopped the 1591 *flota* from sailing; although he thus greatly added to his own difficulties, he also robbed the English raiders of all profit. In 1591 the Spaniards had their one naval success of the war. A fleet from Ferrol—the ex-Armada vessels which Drake had omitted to destroy in 1589—sailed to the Azores to bring home the delayed plate fleet. At Flores it surprised a squadron commanded by Lord Thomas Howard which got away, except for the *Revenge* under Sir Richard Grenville. To this day it is uncertain whether Grenville's failure to escape was due to folly, braggadocio, or misfortune. The vessel's heroic day-long fight against the whole Spanish fleet has become legendary. When the *Revenge* surrendered, Grenville was dying and all the crew were dead or wounded. But glorious as the action was it was also probably unnecessary, and it really marked the triumph of the new Spanish convoy system which made both her empire and her treasure fleets much more difficult to attack. The only English success of the time was the taking of the great East India carrack, the *Madre de Dios*, in 1592. The ship was so ruthlessly and carelessly plundered on their own behalf by officers and men of the capturing squadron that her treasures in pearls, jewels and specie vanished beyond hope of recovery into private pockets; during the search the candles of the gold-crazed horde started fires no less than five times. The hull with its immensely valuable cargo (£800,000) was nearly left behind in the rush, and though the queen got a very fair return on her outlay she felt, with some justification, that indiscipline had

[1] These facts and conclusions (which go contrary to some received notions) are derived from the printed summary of an unprinted London thesis: K. R. Andrews,'Economic Aspects of Elizabethan Privateering', *Bulletin of the Institute of Historical Research* (1952).

robbed her of more. The *Madre de Dios* played the part for a new generation which the *Cacafuego* had played for their elders: hopes of another such capture kept the ships at sea.

In the meantime the real centre of affairs shifted to France. Here the assassination of Henry III in 1589, in revenge for his earlier murder of Henry of Guise, had brought to the throne Henry of Navarre who as a Huguenot was quite unacceptable to the powerful catholic League but on the other hand was a necessary and valuable ally to England. In his plight he appealed for assistance, and Elizabeth responded promptly. In part she was moved by fear of a common enemy, but she also hoped to revive English claims to a French town—preferably Calais—and her demands for a 'cautionary town' on the Dutch model were to lead to much tricky negotiating and bad blood between the allies. Henry IV needed English help, especially in money, but he wished to secure his own throne and rule a united France, not burden his reign with the ignominy of having given away French territory. In 1589 he got a loan of £20,000 and an English force under Willoughby which proved quite useful, though disease forced its withdrawal after three months. Henry's successes in 1590 (the battle of Ivry) brought about Parma's first invasion of France from the north, which in turn eased the pressure on England's other ally, the Dutch, ably assisted by an English army under Vere. While things thus looked brighter in Picardy, the situation was complicated in October 1590 by the invasion of Brittany by a Spanish force in alliance with the League. The Spaniards in Brittany called up visions of important Channel bases in enemy hands, and Elizabeth did not hesitate to despatch an expeditionary force under Norris (recalled from his disgrace) which spent little short of five years in generally rather indecisive fighting. Unsupported by the French, weakened by disease and the withdrawal of troops to other theatres, though also at times reinforced by new levies, Norris and the deputies he left in charge during his occasional absences at court at least prevented Spain from obtaining a foothold in Brittany.

In the same year (1591) another English force came to Henry's assistance in Normandy. Its leader was Robert Devereux, earl of Essex, at this time barely twenty-six years old. A tall handsome man gifted with great charm of manner but also the moody testiness of the spoiled child, he touched nothing that did not decay. He was a brilliant and able enough fighter, though incompetent in command, given to foolish gestures which earned him the contempt of the professionals and the acid tongue of Elizabeth. Thus he challenged the Spaniards to come out and fight off Lisbon in

1589, and in 1591 crossed 100 miles of enemy-held territory with
a splendid train to impress the glamour of his orange-tawny on
the shabby and warstained Henry IV. The ageing queen found it
difficult to refuse him things, but she also tried hard to instil
some discipline and order into a mind potentially great but never
trained to discretion, consistency, or sound judgment. One need
pay no attention to the stories which would turn her feelings for
this favourite—just of an age to have been the son she never had—
into a matter of disgusting elderly passion. In any case, Elizabeth
never forgot that she was queen, not even with Essex. No Tudor
would ever let a man grow great without reminding him that he
who could make could also break; but Essex, rash fool, thought
that his greatness lay in himself.

At this time he only wanted to share in the war, and he persuaded
Elizabeth to sanction an expedition to Normandy. She tried to get
Henry to promise Le Havre and Rouen, both in League hands, to
the English, but to no avail. In the end Essex went proudly,
allowed his army to rot away, joined in a fruitless siege of Rouen,
and returned in January 1592, to brave a more formidable foe in
Elizabeth's displeasure and sarcasm. Sir Roger Williams, a genuine
soldier, stayed behind at Dieppe until the end of the year. The war
in France and the Netherlands dragged on without decision, until
Henry IV yielded to long persuasions and changed his religion
(July 1593). With that the French opposition to him collapsed, but
the war against Spain continued and friendly relations with
England remained important. Though in fact all English troops
were withdrawn from French soil by February 1595, negotiations
for a closer alliance resulted in a treaty ratified in January 1597 to
which the Netherlands acceded. For years Walsingham (who died
in 1590) had dreamed of just such a protestant alliance against
Spain (and Rome); now that at last it had come one of the partners
had ceased to be protestant.

The continental war no sooner showed signs of letting up than
naval projects were revived. Late in 1594 Drake at last got back
into favour, and he and Hawkins joined hands once more. The
third great sailor of their generation was dead: in 1594 Frobisher
lost his life in a combined operation in Brittany when Norris
captured the fortress of Crozon from its Spanish defenders. Drake
and Hawkins planned another powerful raid into the Caribbean.
Though a minor descent on Cornwall by the Spaniards expelled
from Brittany (July 1595) and the outbreak of rebellion in Ireland
held up their departure, they sailed in August 1595 with a great
armament and a greater reputation. But the outcome was sad: a

sorry ending to two wonderful careers. Drake was now about
fifty-five and Hawkins in his sixties; thirty years had passed since
they first invaded the Spanish empire, and while things had
changed much they had only grown old and set in their ways.
It does not appear that they found it easy to work together, and
the whole voyage was a series of misfortunes. Their intention
was to capture a big treasure ship which was known to have had
to put into Porto Rico, and to raid the Main and attack the Isthmus.
All this was known long before they reached the West Indies, and
the new spirit of active defence which they encountered played
havoc with their memories of superior skill and easy conquest.
Hawkins fell ill and died at sea as the fleet neared Porto Rico; the
attack on the harbour there was beaten off with ease; raids along
the Main brought very little booty because the inhabitants had
been forewarned and had withdrawn with their valuables; and the
march across the Isthmus was prevented by superior Spanish
forces. Mortified by all these failures Drake fell a victim to dysentery and died at Porto Bello. Sir Thomas Baskerville buried him
at sea and brought the disconsolate fleet home. Thus ended the
lives and careers of the two greatest of Elizabethan seamen, but
these shadows at the latter end cannot dim the splendid achievements of their manhood.

The failure of the 1595 expedition did, however, mark the end
of large-scale enterprises into the West Indies, though individual
privateers continued to do well for themselves in those waters.
With the land war still languishing, the energies and greed of the
adventurers thus once more concentrated on the coast of Spain
and on the Azores. In 1596 Essex, Howard of Effingham (who was
to survive them all and to die, at eighty-eight, in 1624), and
Francis Vere combined to plan an invasion of Spain herself.
Somewhat reluctantly the queen gave her blessing—together with
instructions to Howard to prevent Essex from needlessly exposing
himself to danger. They were distracted for a time by a sudden
Spanish investment of Calais. Essex wished to relieve it, but the
queen would only act if Henry IV agreed to hand the place over to
her. In consequence Calais fell in April 1596, and Essex set sail
for Spain in June. The fleet was the best equipped in the war:
nearly 150 vessels, forty-eight of them warships, with 6,000 troops
on board, and led by Essex, Howard, Vere, and Raleigh. For once
the Elizabethan warriors proved capable of complete success.
Cadiz was taken in a brilliant combined land and sea action and
held for a fortnight during which time it was thoroughly plundered
and rather inefficiently burned. Though for a time Essex wished

to establish a permanent base, the queen's objections and the difficulties of supply forced him to depart on an ineffectual cruise for booty. The fleet returned in triumph but little the richer. Elizabeth, ever harder pressed, resented its failure to obtain financial profit, but the earl's reputation stood at its highest. Moreover, Philip had suffered a very serious blow indeed as well as the most complete of his frequent bankruptcies. The supremacy of the English at sea could not have been more convincingly proved, nor the essential inability of the Elizabethan navy, even at its most successful, to bring the war to a close.

Old though he was, the king of Spain reacted with vigour: indeed, the capture of Cadiz put some long-missed energy into him. Within a month or two he had launched a new armada which was to invade Ireland in support of the rebellion there. There was again something like panic in England, but the fleet had been equipped and despatched in too great a haste and storms off Cape Finisterre ended the threat. In turn, Elizabeth recognised the need of, and Essex pressed for, a repetition of the brilliant stroke of 1596. The earl had had to contend with the queen's displeasure for some time: she had tried to reduce the swollen head brought on by popular clamour by disciplining him a little and advancing his rivals, Robert Cecil and Raleigh. Early in 1597 Essex made his peace with these, and the queen also forgave him his sulks, so that the expedition of 1597 was commanded by the same quartet as that of 1596. Its fate, however, was very different. The queen wished it to attack the Spanish ships which had been scattered the year before and now lay at Ferrol and Corunna, and then to intercept the treasure fleet in the Azores. Storms drove the expedition back in July, but when it sailed in August it ignored Ferrol and made straight for the Islands. Here some rather disconnected raiding resulted in the capture of a few small islands, but sheer incompetence permitted the *flota* to pass through into the safety of Terceira. The oft-desired success had never been nearer, nor had Spain throughout the whole war a more narrow escape from a really decisive disaster. Instead the English fleet could only return disconsolate in October. It ran into north-east gales which, as usual, scattered it widely; but they also turned back another Spanish armada, for the ships so foolishly left to refit at Ferrol had set sail in autumn. At one time two fleets—one Spanish and one English, the former well-found and the latter distressed—were approaching England's undefended shore on converging lines.

The fright which this danger, when it was known, gave to queen and council, together with the failure of the Islands voyage, sufficed to end the age of great naval expeditions. Essex's reputation with the people—ready as ever to overlook incompetence when it was accompanied by generosity, display, and charm—continued high, but the queen was very angry, and the Islands voyage played its part in his ultimate downfall. In May 1598 Henry IV made peace with Spain at Vervins, somewhat against the terms of his treaty with England. In August Burghley, hoping for peace, died, and a few weeks later Philip II followed him. But peace remained to seek, for Essex and his like had little interest in it, nor could the Dutch yet lay down arms since Spain still refused to recognise their independence. Thus for the next five years small but veteran English forces under Vere continued to assist Maurice of Nassau in his gradually complete conquest of the Northern Netherlands. It was as well that the war with Spain made only small demands in those years, for Elizabeth could hardly have spared it much attention. In 1598 English fortunes in Ireland entered a phase of extreme danger.

5. THE CONQUEST OF IRELAND

Throughout the reign Ireland presented a military rather than a civil problem. We have seen how Henry VII could do little to clear the way to the establishment of royal authority, and how Henry VIII displayed energy there only during the short time of Cromwell's ascendancy.[1] Cromwell destroyed the power of the house of Kildare, and his nominee, Lord Leonard Grey, did much to overcome Irish resistance, but after 1540 the island once more drifted out of control. Henry exchanged the title of lord of Ireland for that of king (1540) and continued the old policy of anglicising the Irish chiefs by turning them into earls: to the Geraldine earls of Kildare and Desmond and the Butler earl of Ormonde, he added the Burke earl of Clanricard, the O'Brien earl of Thomond, and the O'Neill earl of Tyrone. In Mary's reign the Pale was extended by the creation of King's County and Queen's County out of tribal lands in Leix and Offaly, but these new shires were far from securely held when Elizabeth ascended the throne. English authority in Ireland had once again reached a very low ebb. The country was divided into English and Irish territory of which the former included only the enlarged Pale and the towns of the south and west (Waterford, Youghal, Cork, Limerick, and Galway).

[1] Above, pp. 30ff., 179f.

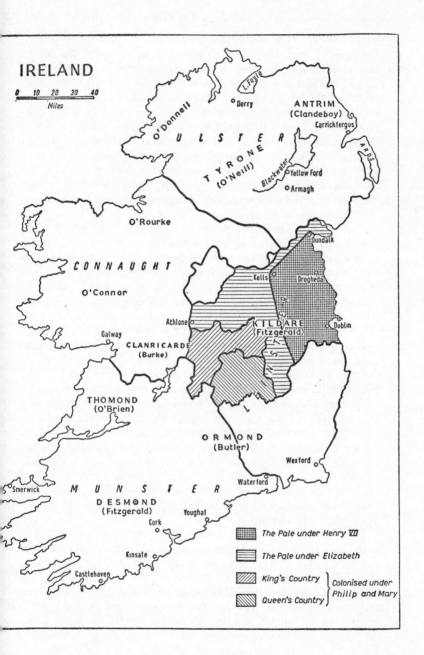

IRELAND

0 10 20 30 40
Miles

O'Donnell

Derry

ANTRIM
(Clandeboy)

Carrickfergus

U L S T E R

TYRONE
(O'Neill)

Blackwater   Yellow Ford

Armagh

ARDS

O'Rourke

Dundalk

C O N N A U G H T

Kells

Drogheda

O'Connor

Athlone

KILDARE
(Fitzgerald)

Dublin

Galway

CLANRICARDE
(Burke)

THOMOND
(O'Brien)

L

O R M O N D
(Butler)

Wexford

Waterford

Smerwick

M U N S T E R

DESMOND
(Fitzgerald)

Youghal

Cork

Kinsale

Castlehaven

The Pale under Henry VII

The Pale under Elizabeth

King's Country

Queen's Country

Colonised under
Philip and Mary

Irish Ireland consisted of the four provinces—Leinster, Munster, Connaught, and Ulster—in which the tribal authority of the chiefs, sometimes disguised as the palatine jurisdiction of nominal earls, exerted the only effective rule. Leinster, nearest the Pale, contained the lands of Kildare, but this branch of the great house of Fitzgerald gave no more trouble. The other magnate of the province was the head of the house of Butler, Thomas tenth earl of Ormond, the feudal ruler of Kilkenny and Tipperary (the latter part of Munster), who throughout the reign proved the queen's most loyal Irishman. An able commander who understood the needs of the country, ruthless in war but generous in peace, Ormond stood firm despite many disappointments at the hands of lords deputies who disliked all Irishmen; for his loyalty was grounded on a passionate devotion to Elizabeth of whose court the earl had been a shining ornament in his young days. Elizabeth repaid him with a firm trust and frequent kindness. Also in Leinster, County Wicklow—wooded, hilly, wild—was a standing threat of disaffection, much too near Dublin to be comfortable. In Munster, the O'Briens of Thomond preserved an intermittent attachment to the government, while the more powerful Geraldines of Desmond were one of the greatest dangers to English rule. Connaught was wild Irish, practically unaffected by the superficial anglicisation of south and east; Ulster was worse. Here lay the real centre of Irish resistance, pretty well inaccessible and held by tribes still virtually in the savagery of the bronze age. As far as they could control it, the houses of O'Donnell (Tyrconnel) and O'Neill (Tyrone, Fermanagh, Monaghan, and Armagh) divided the province between them; the situation was complicated by the settlement in Clandeboy (Antrim) of the Scottish Mac-Donalds, invaders from the Western Islands, who—at intervals refreshed by accessions from Scotland—provided an element of confusion as well as a source of mercenary soldiers (Redshanks) under such leaders as the enchantingly if improbably named Sorley Boy MacDonald.

The ordinary state of Ireland was war—cattle raids, the burning of the countryside, the murder of its people. Outside the Pale there was hardly ever anything like peace and order, and the tribes lived in conditions reminiscent of 'heroic' poetry and perhaps more familiar from the Scottish Highlands where a similar mode of life endured even longer. The protestant religion had no hold at all, but the old religion was also in decline: even in the eyes of a papal emissary, the savages of the north were only nominally Christians. To begin with, the resistance to the English was neither religious nor national; it was simply the struggle of one form of civilisation (if it deserved the name) against the superior power of another. That so far no really energetic attempt had been made to subdue these menaces to settled government was due in the main to English preoccupation elsewhere: it was easier to leave Ireland alone. But the Elizabethan break with Rome necessitated action. Ireland now became a possible landing-place for hostile forces, and in the end indeed a part of the Spanish war. In the process, the old religion gained a new vigour, partly as a counterblast to the English invader, partly because Rome was a potential ally in the struggle, but largely because of the devoted labours of a few missionaries. At the beginning of the reign Ireland was virtually ungoverned and heathen; by the end it was firmly under English control and Roman Catholic.

The first task confronting Elizabeth's government was that of conquest. Before anything could be done to give Ireland an effective civil administration or to establish the Elizabethan Church there, the power of the chiefs had to be broken in battle. As it turned out, this task occupied all the reign: final victory was won almost on the day of the queen's death. The country offered all the conditions for successful guerilla warfare. Broken by woods, hills, and bogs, it easily absorbed the elusive Irish who rarely stood to give battle but harassed the royal forces on the march and closed behind them again to wipe out the illusory successes of one army after another. Not until Tyrone created an Irish army in the 1590s could Irish levies ever confront with any hope of success even half-trained Englishmen, and even in Tyrone's day they were more commonly defeated than victorious. Bad discipline and inferior weapons were the chief reasons. But, on the other hand, the war could never be brought to an end. Pacifications never lasted. Time and again a rebellious chief 'came in' to make terms; time and again, obeying the rules of tribal life, he rebelled anew. Without the bases provided by the towns and the assistance of loyal Irishmen, the government forces would have been driven into the sea in the first ten years of the reign. But no single Irishman—not even Tyrone of whom this has been alleged—ever rose to the concept, much less the fact, of national resistance; at all times the ancient feuds and rivalries prevented unity and gave the English commanders their chance. With few exceptions, these last were able and energetic men, though often ruthless and savage in the murderous manner of Irish warfare. To the existing difficulties of the Irish landscape, the prevalence of malaria which killed thousands of soldiers, and the Irish character which kept the situation ever changing, the English sometimes added by folly and rashness, leading to defeats which roused the whole country, or by arrogance which lost them the support of men willing to be loyal. Worst of all, for a long time the government at home thought it could conquer Ireland on the cheap. Until 1596 the forces at the disposal of Irish viceroys were as a rule amazingly small—a few thousand, and at times less. Time and again one reads of forts garrisoned—and successfully held, for the Irish never learned about siege warfare —by twenty or thirty men. Elizabeth's chronic procrastination too often left the country without an effective governor at critical times, and her parsimony, however explicable, ultimately wasted much treasure and blood which more energetic action at the start might have saved. The government learned their lesson the hard way: in the last stages, in Essex's army and especially in that of Mountjoy, all the necessaries—troops, stores, organisation— were supplied with a ready and efficient hand. But by then the miserable country had lived through thirty-five years of war and devastation.

The story is a long one, full of fascinating details like the bottle of whiskey which assisted Mountjoy in his great victory at Kinsale;[1] but it cannot here be told in any way to do justice to an extended episode which, however small its scale, yet involved great national and international issues and much heroism. Out of the welter of skirmishes and raids, four main occasions stand out: the rebellion of Shane O'Neill (1559-66), the Fitzmaurice confederacy in Munster (1569-72), the Desmond rebellion (1579-83), and the great or Tyrone's rebellion (1594-1603).

The first trouble arose with predictable ease out of the attempt to convert the chief of the Clan O'Neill into the earl of Tyrone. In 1559 a succession quarrel broke out between the claimants by Irish and English law, and since the former—Shane O'Neill— was much the more forceful man he soon established himself. Three uneasy years during which the lord lieutenant, the earl of Sussex, tried to maintain the English nominee ended with a compromise in 1562: Shane was permitted to retain the reality of power as captain of Tyrone, while the young heir to the earldom— Hugh O'Neill—was taken to England to be educated at court. Of all Elizabeth's Irish opponents Shane was probably the most primitive—a true savage who has been described as 'a drunkard

---

[1] An Irish chief in Tyrone's army whose supply of whiskey had given out, sent to ask for more to Mountjoy's second-in-command, Sir George Carew, whom he had known in better days; during the proceedings Mountjoy discovered the enemy's intentions.

even by contemporary Ulster standards', but a formidable warrior. He next spent four years of horrible war and tyranny, winning control over all Ulster; by 1566 he was so far successful that he boasted himself greater than any earl, got in touch with Rome in the hope of finding allies against the English overlordship, and appealed for help to France. This compelled the new lord deputy, Sir Henry Sidney, to take action, and in one great march through Ulster with greatly inferior forces he destroyed the power of Shane. He was assisted in this by the hatred which the O'Neill had aroused in his triumphant but barbarous conquest. Shane's army was actually destroyed by Hugh O'Donnell, in revenge for the treatment earlier meted out to Tyrconnel, and Shane himself was killed by the Antrim Scots with whom he took refuge and who, after first welcoming him, later remembered his devastating attack on them a few years earlier. The O'Neill was a great man, as savages go, but his overthrow benefited most of all his own Irish neighbours. The chieftaincy of Tyrone passed to Tirlagh Luineach O'Neill, a man who through nearly thirty years of moderate ambitions and hard drinking proved the wisdom of a cunning policy and the preservative qualities of Irish whiskey. Though never quiet, and never conquered, Ulster ceased to be an active threat.

Soon after, trouble started in the south, in Munster. Here Desmond, whom Sidney called 'a man both void of judgment to govern and will to rule', tyrannised over some of the best land in Ireland to such a degree that murder and famine were the daily lot of the people. A feud with Ormond in Tipperary, and the conjoint activities of the younger Burkes in Connaught, as well as such other wolves as the MacCarthy More and O'Sullivan Beare in Kerry, kept the whole area in despair. Sidney took such action as his means permitted and removed Desmond to the Tower; he also set up presidents of Munster and Connaught to break the local power of the chiefs and had plans for anglicising both provinces. But in 1569, a Geraldine of more ability than the imprisoned earl of Desmond, James Fitzmaurice Fitzgerald, interrupted the lord deputy's plans by raising all Munster against him. Militarily his success was shortlived and the hoped-for assistance from the continent never came; Ormond and Humphrey Gilbert (knighted for his services) suppressed the rising, and Fitzmaurice submitted in 1572. Much trust was at this time put in projects of colonisation —'plantings'—of which one was attempted in Munster and Leinster (1568-70) by a group of west country gentlemen including Sir Richard Grenville; this came to little because of the determined resistance of all Irish leaders, of whatever allegiance. Two more promising ventures in Ulster—Thomas Smith's settlement in Ards (1572-3) and the earl of Essex's colony in Clandeboy—were wiped out by the MacDonalds some of whom Essex had quite needlessly massacred. The only outcome was a general state of desultory war, full of mutual brutality, in south-east Ulster and all over the west. In 1575 Sidney returned for a second spell of duty, and in an impressive progress through all Ireland proved his remarkable qualities of command: his was the true proconsular cast. When he left in 1578—no deputy stayed longer in that barbarous country than he could help—Ireland seemed almost on the road to peace and order; his policy of controlling the whole country by English presidents of provinces, and of turning Irish chieftains into landowners by accommodating their rights to English legal arrangements, was bearing fruit.

However, he had no sooner gone than another outbreak occurred, though it is some reflection of his achievement that this time there needed outside assistance. James Fitzmaurice, who had fled the country in 1575, had since been trying to gain help in those manœuvres at Rome and Madrid of which mention has already been made. The fate of Stukeley, the landing of papal forces, the death of Fitzmaurice, the slaughter at Smerwick, have been described.[1] But though the invasion failed, the response in Ireland was such as to involve the country once more in several years of war. The earl of Desmond, back in Ireland since 1573, gradually drifted into rebellion; Viscount Baltinglass rose in the Pale itself; the newly arrived deputy, Lord Grey de Wilton, incurred a needless defeat which fanned the flames. Happily for the English, Tirlagh O'Neill stayed quiet in Ulster. Grey and Ormond swept Munster with fire; Smerwick was taken (November 1580), Baltinglass driven abroad, and Desmond 'turned into a wood-kerne', the usual description of those forced to take to outlawry in the hills; but it was not until late in 1583 that Ormond, in charge during a vacancy of the deputyship, finally hunted the earl down. Desmond was killed in an inter-tribal affray, and with him really died the great house of Fitzgerald. His lands were confiscated and 'planted' by a syndicate of which Sir Walter Raleigh was the head; this 'Munster Plantation', a larger and more promising scheme than those that had preceded it, vanished in the conflagration of the Tyrone rebellion.

Ulster had been unnaturally quiet for a long time—a long time as peace went in Ireland—though of course minor depredations with their crop of attendant atrocities had occurred. But this

[1] Above, pp. 308f.

respite really hid the gathering of trouble. Old Tirlagh Luineach seemed at last to be declining, though he surprised everyone by lasting till 1595, and it became obvious that the next man to dominate Ulster would be Hugh O'Neill, earl of Tyrone. He returned to Ireland in 1585, ostensibly a good friend to the English but from the first ambitious to make himself free master of his territories—and more. Tyrone was a man of considerable abilities, a great organiser of troops who turned the irresponsible Irish forces into something like a disciplined standing army, and a subtle statesman who was ever ready to bide his time. In negotiations he repeatedly overreached his adversaries who would have sworn that Tyrone was loyal when Tyrone was plotting his deepest. But Tyrone lacked vigour; his exceptional, and by Irish standard unnatural, patience had its counterpart in a tendency to hesitate in a crisis. Because the earl rarely acted with open decision and continued at all times to protest his loyalty—he was invariably polite and deferential to the queen's authority against which he bore arms—it is difficult to assign a precise date to his rebellion. The situation deteriorated rapidly in Ulster in 1593 with the rise of Hugh Roe O'Donnell who dominated Tyrconnel. This chief, a young man of nineteen (Tyrone was already in his forties), bore a personal grievance against the English, to which he added religious fervour (which with Tyrone was but a pretence) and the ardent bellicosity of an Ulster clansman. More than Tyrone, he was a soldier and leader of men, but it was Tyrone who alone could turn a local rising into a coherent rebellion.

O'Donnell declared himself ready to fight to the death in 1593; two years later, after much shilly-shallying, frequent encounters and withdrawals, and several reverses for the English army, Tyrone came into the open. He disposed of a trained army of 6,000, to which Sir William Russell, deputy since 1594, could oppose perhaps 1,100. The government acted promptly, dispatching reinforcements under Sir John Norris who was given a special command in Ulster. This led to friction between Russell and Norris; Tyrone's guerilla tactics proved fully effective; and Norris came near to sinking his reputation in the Irish bogs. In May 1597 Lord Burgh replaced Russell, in December Norris died, a month later Burgh followed him. Affairs were in this unsatisfactory state when disaster struck. When a temporary truce ended in mid-1598, Ormond, once again temporarily in charge, stayed in Wicklow to protect Dublin and his own estates and sent Sir Henry Bagenal (an old personal enemy of Tyrone's) to relieve the Blackwater Fort which protected the Pale against invasion from Ulster. At the

Yellow Ford across the Callan brook, a tributary of the Blackwater, Bagenal ran into Tyrone and was utterly defeated, he
himself being killed with about 1,500 men (August 1598) It was
the biggest defeat—the only serious defeat—of English arms in all
the Irish wars, and it could have been avoided by more intelligence
on the spot. The worst of it was that for a time the government
had virtually no forces in Ireland: Dublin stood wide open, panic
reigned, everybody except Ormond disgraced themselves to the
queen's violent and well-expressed disgust. But Tyrone wasted
his chance. All along he had insisted that nothing could be
achieved without Spanish support, but the attempts of 1596 and
1597 to send a force to Ireland were, as has been seen, shattered by
the wind. The earl continued to wait rather than act.

Even so the Yellow Ford had serious consequences. All Munster
rose under a Geraldine offspring called the 'Sugane' (strawrope)
earl of Desmond, while Hugh Roe established himself in Connaught. Raleigh's plantation was washed away in blood. The
English hold on Ireland hung by a hair. The queen, whose failure
for eighteen months to appoint a successor to Burgh had done
something to bring about this state of affairs, now acted at last;
indeed, the government's behaviour for the next three years
deserves all praise for steadfast nerves, energy, and purpose. The
reason for the long delay was the earl of Essex who, wishing to
redeem himself after the Islands voyage and in any case unwilling
to let someone else earn the glory of settling Ireland, demanded
the post as of right. The queen hesitated. She did not want to risk
a man whose presence delighted her in that graveyard of men and
reputations; with her uncanny skill in judging ability even in those
she favoured, she seems to have doubted his fitness for the job;
above all, the post had become a matter of dispute among the court
factions, which obliged her to tread warily. Meanwhile Ireland
suffered. But at last she gave in: Essex arrived in Dublin in April
1599, with the largest and best equipped army yet sent there. He
missed his chances shamefully. Though he impressed everyone by
his bearing, his charm, and his personal courage, he failed more
abysmally than any of his less well-provided predecessors. Instead
of following the queen's instructions and tackling the root of the
trouble in Ulster, he went on an imposing but pointless progress
in Munster. Having achieved precisely nothing, he grew despondent and committed his crowning folly by entering into negotiations with Tyrone. That seasoned diplomat found Essex easy
meat: a truce was concluded which left him everything he had
and a breathing space in which to recruit his strength and await

the Spaniards. In the meantime Essex's splendid army wasted away in disease. The letters from court grew more acid; no one could boast in Elizabeth's hearing of what he would do and hope for compassion when he completely failed to live up to his high words. But Essex, increasingly suspicious and moody, alleged that the queen was listening to his detractors. So, in September 1599, he left his post without leave to rush travel-stained into the queen's presence at court and put his side of the case. It was the virtual end of him and his career, but that does not concern the present matter.

For the English cause in Ireland Essex's desertion was a blessing. The man who replaced him proved to be the man to do the job. Charles Blount, Lord Mountjoy was a general of the stamp of Wellington: thorough, tenacious, careful, and yet capable of that calculated rashness which wins battles. Though he suffered from indifferent health he displayed astonishing energy; contrary to all the practice of the time he even fought winter campaigns which vanquished the plan upon which Tyrone proceeded. Without the winter in which to sow their grain and raise their cattle, the Irish forces could not live off the land—that is, they could not live at all. While Sir George Carew settled Munster by weaning chief after chief away from rebellion, the lord deputy himself tackled Connaught and Ulster. Sir Henry Docwra was established in a new fort at Derry, near Lough Foyle; from here, assisted by disaffected O'Neills and O'Donnells, he soon subdued Tyrconnel and cut Ulster in two. By the end of 1600 the rebellion was virtually extinguished, the Sugane earl a fugitive (he was captured in May 1601), and Tyrone driven into the fastness of his own country. At that point the long-awaited Spanish aid arrived, too late now to alter the outcome but in time to prolong the struggle. In September 1601 a force of 4,000 trained infantry under de Aguila occupied the port of Kinsale on the south coast. Mountjoy reacted with typical vigour; in no time he had concentrated his and Carew's forces at Kinsale and invested that small and ill-protected town. By December the Irish forces had also arrived, free now to break out of Ulster, and Mountjoy at last saw his chance to bring them to battle. His army, between two fires, was in a bad way with disease and lack of supplies but quite undaunted, and the victory over a much more numerous enemy was won by great superiority in skill and dash. O'Donnell fled to Spain; Tyrone, his army shattered, reached temporary sanctuary among his own mountains. It was all over. De Aguila surrendered with the honours of war in January 1602; Carew, Docwra, and the rest mopped up what remained of rebels in the course of that year, and in March 1603 Tyrone gave himself up. His actual surrender took place after Elizabeth's death, but she knew of it before she died. He was ultimately pardoned and restored by James I, but fled to Rome in 1607 and died there in 1616.

The conquest of Ireland was complete, but the work of settlement could not begin until the reign of the first Stuart. The country had suffered dreadfully; Munster, the richest province, was twice burned completely, not to mention minor afflictions. Grey, Ormond, Sidney and others—but also O'Donnell, Tyrone, and many lesser chieftains—had time and again carried death and destruction from one end of the island to the other. Only the recuperative powers of a purely agrarian community in a naturally fertile country prevented the effects from lasting for years. The conquest was necessary. England could not permit the existence of this turbulent neighbour, only nominally subject to her and a standing invitation to her enemies. As for Ireland, only conquest by England gave her a chance of emerging from the prehistoric welter of tribal warfare, with its blood-feuds, raidings, and constant killings. It was England's triumph that made possible the growth of an Irish nation, even as it was the fact of conquest that really established the firm adherence of Ireland to the Church of Rome.

Chapter XIV

THE STRUCTURE OF THE AGE: CONSERVATISM

I. CONSERVATISM

THE question is sometimes raised whether the age of Elizabeth belonged to the middle ages or modern times. Some scholars, looking at the prevailing conceptions of nature and the universe, assert confidently that an age so blatantly 'pre-scientific' cannot be modern. Others, allowing their eyes to follow Drake and the rest across the uncharted oceans, or contemplating the activities of merchants and industrialists, make no doubt that the middle ages had been left behind. Did people think in terms of progress, the individual, and the power of man's reason? Or did they preach the fall from grace, the organic and orderly society, the ineluctability of sin? The answer is that they did a little of the first and a great deal of the second. Medieval notions, we are then told, continued strong in the Elizabethan age. If this means that the period, like every other, witnessed a mingling of the old and new, the thought is hardly worth expressing; if it is to imply that ideas to do with science, rationalism, individual claims, and progress are modern, while the middle ages thought only of religion, mysticism, the society, and the decline from a golden age, then the notion is plain nonsense. The labels medieval and modern cannot be usefully attached to ideas. But they may, with reservations, be attached to things, especially to institutions; and in that respect, the age of Elizabeth, coming after the revolution of the 1530s, was modern. All surviving limitations upon the national state notwithstanding, Elizabethan England looked much more like what was to come after than what came before.

As for the prevailing attitude of the period, it is more useful to enquire whether it was directed towards change or towards stability. The reign of Henry VIII provided violent changes in part at least because a revolutionary spirit was abroad. In contrast the age of Elizabeth stood for consolidation rather than invention, for preservation rather than revolution. That which was to be preserved was 'modern'—the national Church, the sovereign state, the bureaucratic organisation of government. Elizabeth herself was a conservative in the sense that she disliked and avoided change, and she represented a very strong feeling among her people. The chief concept of the age—often unconscious, never questioned—was that of order and degree. It came as easily to the Elizabethan to suppose that all things, man included, had their place in an eternally fixed scheme of things, and that there existed degrees among men, as it comes to the present day to think that there is neither order nor purpose in the universe, or that all men are equal. These last two propositions would have struck the sixteenth century not only as blasphemous but as manifestly absurd. The world which God had created had its settled laws, and in the great 'Chain of Being' every created thing, from the angels at the top to the animals and plants and metals at the bottom, had its assigned place. These ideas took a 'medieval' form: that is, they found expression in phrases and thoughts inherited from centuries of speculation and writing.[1] But that fact has no profounder meaning: ideas are rarely expressed in entirely new language, and conservative ideas never.

An age which insisted on degree could not think in radical terms or welcome the break-up of any established thing. The words of Shakespeare's Ulysses, often quoted, may yet be cited once again:

> Take but degree away, untune that string,
> And hark! what discord follows; each thing meets
> In mere oppugnancy: the bounded waters
> Should lift their bosom higher than the shores
> And make a sop of all this solid globe:
> Strength should be lord of imbecility,
> And the rude son should strike his father dead:
> Force should be right; or rather, right and wrong—
> Between whose endless jar justice resides—
> Should lose their names, and so should justice too.

Without degree, with the natural order of things disturbed, the moral order itself would dissolve. Sanctionless, right would fall before might. The statesmen of the age held this view with cold passion, and every means of propaganda was employed to preach order, obedience, and humble acquiescence in one's station. Cranmer's *Homily on Obedience* (1547)—an official sermon read in all churches—justified the existing political order as part of that universal order which the 'Chain of Being' exemplified. That the political order of 1547 was a very different thing from that of 1527 there was no need to admit: the Henrician revolutionaries always pretended to be preservers of the proper order. Afterwards,

[1] Cf. E. M. W. Tillyard, *The Elizabethan World Picture* (1943).

however, the new order was to be really preserved unaltered. The political common-place book of the Elizabethan period, the *Mirror for Magistrates* (first published in 1559 and frequently reprinted), a collection of tales about kings and others who came to a sticky end through offending against the universal order, preached both the supremacy of degree and the duty of obedience. Even evil rulers are for God to deal with, and not for man. Rebellion is the great political sin because it disturbs degree which is man's only right condition.

That such doctrines served a very practical need is obvious. An age of agrarian and political unrest was only just passing away; many of its feelers stretched right through the queen's reign. In such times the powers that be tend to inculcate the duty of obedience and wickedness of rebellion with a fervour born of self-interest. No doubt; but the matter went further. Even the rebels tended to be tarred with the same brush. Even the puritans, however much they might dislike the official hierarchy, did not question the queen's rule, the reality of degree, or the universal order of which both men and society must be reflections. If there were egalitarian ideas about, they spread among the lowly and have left no record. No matter whether men profited or suffered from the existing state of affairs, their minds were coloured by conservative preconceptions. It is impossible to define forty-five years so crowded with great men and great events in a phrase. Towards the end of the century, especially, speculation turned into different channels. Men said later that they had waited for the old queen's death before embarking on new enterprises; people can grow tired of a worthy and cautious conservatism. Such men as Raleigh and Bacon have been taken as prototypes of modern rationalism—and certainly Raleigh's *History of the World* and Bacon's *Novum Organum* seem to breathe a different spirit from the *Mirror of Magistrates*. Nevertheless, they were hardly rationalists, for they remained firmly within the religious mould of a far from pious age,[1] and influenced by the barely conscious general acceptance of the notion of order. If that was to be medieval then Newton was medieval whose greatest scientific discoveries were made in the desire to prove the rational order of God's universe; then men have never ceased to be medieval. In a sense this is

---

[1] 'The orthodox scheme of salvation is pervasive in the Elizabethan age,' is Dr Tillyard's comment. Before rationalism received the support of physical science, only religion could offer any sort of explanation of the universe and of life, and whether Elizabethans were pious or not, formally Christian or not, they thought in terms of a world made and ruled by God.

true; but what then is the value of so meaningless a definition?

Thus, exceptions and modifications allowed for, and in the knowledge that many may dissent, it can be said again that the reign of Elizabeth, especially when compared with that of Henry VIII, was a conservative rather than a radical period. This came out in its political thinking, the structure of its government, and the history of its Church.

2. THE CROWN AND SOVEREIGNTY

As has already been stressed, Tudor rule depended in the first place on a full, even fulsome, recognition of the prince as the visible embodiment of the state. Elizabeth maintained this tradition by carefully cultivating her own appeal as a queen and a woman, and by the splendour and ceremonial of her court. She entertained no small opinion of her place, and the words 'my prerogative' were frequently in her mouth. Compared with Henry VIII's calm assurance her attitude almost protested too much, but then she had to overcome the double handicap of a growingly vocal opposition and of her sex. About her capacity to govern opinions have differed greatly; perhaps one may say that no one can be consistently lucky for half a century unless there is more than luck in it. In many ways she was an unpleasant woman. Our age probably objects not at all to her coarseness, elementary sense of humour, or secular temper—all of which tended to distress the Victorians—but still dislikes her unfairness, occasional vindictiveness, frequent rages, and constant vacillation. Like her father she may not have been capable of an original thought, and like her grandfather she may have been a little too fond of treasure; but kings can be great without being great statesmen in their own right, and poor rulers ought to set a value on money. On the whole the light eclipses the shadow. She deserves admiration for her competence, good sense, lack of bigotry, and shrewdness. In any case, she was the queen; of her overwhelming personality, her unceasing personal activity, and her all-pervading presence there must be no doubt. Surrounded by a court as brilliant in show as in intellect, served with a ceremonial which set her permanently apart,[1] she

---

[1] Sir Thomas Smith noted, and foreign observers confirmed it with surprise, that no one spoke to the queen except on his knees, unless she deigned to raise him up. One of the minor problems of Elizabethan history is whether the queen could ever have had a hot meal. She dined in private (unlike her father), but the public ceremonial was still gone through, and she seems to have received the dishes at least half an hour after they had been carried in procession from the kitchen.

completely fulfilled the first duty of monarchy—to appear as the symbol of the nation and the sum of all earthly allegiance.

On the queen or those whom she might appoint depended the running of affairs. 'The prince,' said Sir Thomas Smith, 'is the life, the head, and the authority of all things that be done in the realm of England.' Administration in peace time as well as the needs of war and diplomacy were in his hands; he could act at need without reference to advisers or parliaments because he must be able to act at once and in secrecy for the safety of the realm; and he enjoyed certain financial benefits to equip him for his task. These special rights of the crown are its famous prerogatives among which Smith enumerated the making of peace and war, the appointment of the privy council, the administration of martial law, the minting of money, dispensations from the operation of the law (in the exercise of which prerogative 'equity requireth a moderation to be had'), the appointment of all chief officials in the realm, the administration of justice, and the collection of feudal dues of wardship and the like. The crown's prerogatives made sure that Tudor government, like medieval government before it and modern after it, should be the king's government.

But government is not identical with the state. The prince can be a symbol and even the ultimate source of all action, without thereby becoming identified with the state itself. This question of the nature of the state really raises the question of sovereignty, for the sovereign (in John Austin's classical definition) is that man or body of men whose every dictate is habitually obeyed by a given community. We are told that the medieval and modern states differ in this that the former is an association of all its parts (the famous 'body politic' metaphor) for a moral purpose, while the latter embodies a sovereign will (wherever it may be found) and serves the purposes of power.[1] It is a valuable distinction, though in practice a rather unreal one. Political bodies have always obeyed some will and depended on power, however much moral purposes may have been talked about; the differences lie, firstly, in the nature of the sovereign will and secondly in the absence of restraint which the discarding of the 'moral purpose' theory brings about. Once the facts of political life gained admission to the writings of the theorists—and here the sixteenth century, through Machiavelli and Bodin, achieved much—the new absence of theoretical limitations on the physical power of states and rulers encouraged a larger practical exploitation of forces which themselves were far from new. The modern state has been assisted by a description which

[1] E.g. W. S. Holdsworth, *History of English Law*, iv.196.

gives to it unrestricted and irresponsible sovereignty, and it has therefore been readier to act in a manner which at one time would have had to seek a cloak to satisfy the unquestioned belief in a moral purpose. It is at least doubtful whether that moral purpose really played a larger part in the middle ages than it does today.

The distinction is then unreal in practice, but its value lies in the fact that it summarises two different attitudes to the problem of political organisation. The question now is whether Tudor England believed in the allegedly medieval notion of the harmonious body politic or the allegedly modern notion of sovereignty. Scholars have inclined to treat these concepts as mutually exclusive because they have concentrated on the potential conflict between the law-giver and the subject. Yet another answer is possible. The principle of representation makes it possible to combine the idea of sovereignty with that of harmony. The attitude implicitly adopted by the Tudor revolution of the 1530s was this: the state is a harmonious unity of head and members, of king and subjects, which is quite independent of all outside authority; and this unity is represented in the parliament of the realm whose decrees therefore embody the common will and inevitably override all other orders as far as concerns the commonwealth. The supremacy of statute, divested in practice by Cromwell of all limitations, embodies botn a full doctrine of internal sovereignty and the 'medieval' notion of harmony, because it acknowledges the existence of a mixed sovereign comprehending within it by representation every individual and every individual will. It was one of the great moments in human history when the most centralised monarchy in Western Europe thus adapted the ideas of consent and representation to the demands of sovereignty.

But the concept of sovereignty, however implicit, did not persist into Elizabethan thought. The idea of parliament as representing the body politic became a commonplace. John Aylmer, later bishop of London, declared in 1559 that the government of England was a mixed monarchy 'the image whereof, and not the image but the thing in deed, is to be seen in the parliament house' with its three estates; in 1565 Sir Thomas Smith said that 'the highest and most absolute power of the realm of England consisteth in the parliament' because 'every Englishman is intended to be there present, either in person or by procuration and attorneys . . . from the prince . . . to the lowest person in England. And the consent of parliament is taken to be every man's consent'; in the 1590s Hooker employed very similar language, saying that the parliament was 'even the body of the whole realm', that it consisted of the king and all his subjects, and that from it depended 'the very essence of all government within this kingdom'. Practising statesmen recognised the omnicompetence of statute. Cromwell based his work on this interpretation; Burghley is reported to have remarked that 'he knew not what an act of parliament could not do in England'; Francis Bacon acknowledged that an act of parliament could not bind 'the supreme and absolute power' of future parliaments.

This deference to parliament ought to have resulted in the acceptance of a full doctrine of sovereignty—legislative supremacy— vested in king, lords, and commons. The reasons why Elizabethan theorists and politicians never took this final step were two, both of them essentially conservative. One was the old notion that no human sovereignty is possible—that there exists a law above man's will which regulates the behaviour of the universe and by which man-made law must be judged. In addition to this 'law of nature' the Elizabethan age inherited from centuries of speculation and practice the more humdrum fact of the law of England which defined the rights and place of every man, king or peasant. A sound doctrine of sovereignty was impossible until these two points had lost their force. In practice they were already dying: the Reformation, achieving unheard-of alterations through act of parliament, had, as has been seen, asserted an implicit doctrine of sovereignty. But men's thoughts had not yet caught up, and the law of nature—the traditional defence against an entirely man-ruled community—experienced a determined revival in the sixteenth century. In Henry VIII's reign, Christopher St German knew it, though he called it the law of reason; Hooker based his whole magnificent structure on the existence of a universal law giving unity and purpose to God's creation; and, late in the century, Edward Coke began to argue his narrow case which identified the law of nature or reason with the English common law and thus transmuted the inherent moral restraints on behaviour into the highly practical restraint of the positive law of the land.

This revival of natural law marked a conservative reaction against the makers of the Henrician Reformation which was assisted by the practice of the second half of the century. It has been rightly pointed out that a theory of parliamentary sovereignty was made no easier by the rarity of parliament's existence. Cromwell's belief in parliamentary sovereignty expressed itself in the fact that parliament met almost every year after his accession to power, and Henry VIII followed the precept down to his death. Elizabeth, on the other hand, called parliament only thirteen times in forty-five years; unlike Cromwell, she and her ministers were not so much concerned with the making of law as with its enforcement—with government rather than legislation. It is only when law-making becomes a reasonably regular expression of the state's functions that the problem of sovereignty enters politics at all; the decline of legislative pressure after 1559—though laws continued to be made, neither their number nor their importance can compare with those of the 1530s—revived a condition in which the state expressed itself mainly in administration. Elizabethan thinkers thus had the less reason to seek for the seat of sovereignty. Parliament continued to be seen as a high court—which it was—rather than as the legislative assembly which the Reformation had proved it to have become; it was a very honourable, even an important, part of the constitution, but it was hard to see in so intermittent an organisation a regular part of government.

Thus while the Tudor state in practice worked on the principle that statute was supreme—that parliament was sovereign—conservatism prevented a full realisation of what may be called the native theory of sovereignty. The man to free sovereignty from the trammels of natural law was Jean Bodin (1566), and he—arguing from French conditions—placed it in the hands of the prince alone. His monarchical theory spread in England after 1570, to encounter there not a rival, parliamentary (king-in-parliamentary) theory of sovereignty but a vacuum. Confronted with the idea of a king truly sovereign—a personal law-giver whose dictates are obeyed—English writers did not reply that in England sovereignty rested with a mixed body. They reacted in one of two ways. Either they used this imported notion to justify and exalt the autocratic tendencies which the strong kings of England had often displayed. Traces of such truly royalist doctrines appear in the writings of some, especially courtiers, but Elizabeth was not interested in theoretical claims and their full development had to await the coming of James I with his indefeasible divine right. Alternatively, being aware of the limitations on English kings—limitations which as lawyers they sought in the law rather than in a doctrine of representation—the theorists got into a muddle. Unable to see Bodin's sovereign either in the limited king of England or in the occasional sessions of the king-in-parliament, they tried instead to give to the English crown some sovereign and some not so sovereign attributes. Following a lead given already by Fortescue in the fifteenth century, they distinguished between an 'absolute' and an 'ordinary' prerogative, using absolute in the sense of discretionary. Since naturally they could not define limits to powers whose very essence was a vagueness depending on the demands of the moment, 'absolute' and 'ordinary' remained unresolved terms, reappearing in the next century in those murky discussions about emergency powers and the king's 'different persons' which tried to justify Stuart despotism.

In truth, these attempts to suit an imported concept of royal sovereignty to the facts of parliament's existence and the crown's subordination to the law mark the gradual breakdown of the Cromwellian polity which had ignored the idea of natural law and had given expression to the harmonious commonwealth in a sovereign king-in-parliament. The new theories really began to postulate an inherent conflict between monarch (sovereign?) and people; they defined royal power by trying to find its limits, either exalting it by itself or nibbling it away with 'safeguards'. The truer English doctrine exalted the power of government because it represented the joint will of an organic body politic.[1] With arguments of double nature and the like we approach the temporary collapse of the constitution which was to be the Stuarts' main achievement. In Elizabeth's parliaments, despite their loyalty, harmony was preserved with greater difficulties than in Henry VIII's, for interests once at one had begun to diverge. Confronted with the evidence of political squabbles and failing to see behind them the possibility of a mixed sovereign, the thinkers of the time either tended to miss the notion of sovereignty altogether or to revive the supremacy of natural law.

It is therefore hard to say that any well-developed doctrine of the state and the ruler was held in Elizabethan England. The queen, representing the crown, commanded loyalty, allegiance, devotion, even adulation. She herself clung to high views of her prerogative but avoided definition; on the other hand, though she may have stretched a point here and there, she never pretended that she was not a 'limited' monarch, dependent on parliament for taxes and laws and compelled to govern according to 'the law', not her will. The lawyers—Smith and his like—took over the theory of a constitutional monarchy from the previous century without ever grasping the full implications of mixed sovereignty. Those who, like Hooker, thought deepest also thought in terms of a divine order and a universal law which imposed a moral nature on the state and limited discussion of it as it really was. In practice everyone saw that of the parts of parliament the crown mattered much more than the lords and commons, so that discussions of power and sovereignty were sidetracked into attempts to define the position

[1] If the theory of 'safeguards' is Whig (as it is), that of the organic body politic is Tory. That makes Thomas Cromwell a Tory!

of the prerogative or to limit the supposed autocratic tendencies of the ruler. Few writers opposed the queen. In Mary's reign protestants like John Ponet (*Short Treatise of Politic Power*) and John Knox (*First Blast of the Trumpet against the Monstrous Regiment of Women*) had developed doctrines of justifiable resistance which in Ponet's remarkable book culminated in the right to kill tyrants. But though some catholic writers—especially Parsons —took up such themes in the next reign, English writers in general returned to the original protestant position of doing honour to 'the magistrate'—of obedience to secular authority. Ardent puritans were to find it difficult to 'tarry for the magistrate' when that magistrate was the immovable Elizabeth, but for most men political speculation began and ended with reliance on the safety of a strong crown in the hands of so competent a ruler.

Failure to define rights and prerogatives, and to delimit the spheres of what the crown could only do in parliament and what it could do by its 'absolute' power did not so much lay up trouble for the future as avoid, in the sound tradition of good government, the posing of insoluble problems. When political and religious difficulties, as well as private follies, put those questions squarely before the nation, the result was civil war. The weakness of the Tudor theorists lay not in their ignoring the concept of sovereignty but in their inability to develop the theme on a native basis by admitting the unrestricted sovereignty (not only the supremacy under the law) of the crown in parliament. Thus they permitted the conflict between improper and alien theories which wished to ascribe true sovereignty either to the king or to the commons alone. The practice of the Cromwellian constitution collapsed after 1603; it may be argued that its underlying theory remained obscure in the sixteenth century and did not come to be accepted more generally until Burke's revival of the organic body politic.

3. GOVERNMENT

This discussion of theories has not advanced an understanding of Elizabethan government which must rather be sought in the institutions of government themselves. The reign of Elizabeth was not one of reform but of exploitation and consolidation. After the vast but incomplete overhaul of the machinery which was part of Cromwell's amazing achievement, what was needed was a little development but in the main use; and these the great Elizabethan administrators provided.

Though the queen reigned, and though the queen may even

have ruled, it was the privy council that governed. Consolidated by Cromwell out of the vague 'inner ring', it made its first formal appearance in August 1540 when, in order to cope with the eclipse of its maker, it agreed to a more bureaucratic organisation by appointing a clerk and a minute-book. Thereafter this board of (originally) nineteen men underwent some vicissitudes which reflected the political upheavals of the times of crisis. From the first it was far from united because membership, being essential to participation in affairs, was, in that age of the Reformation, sought by and granted to men of very different religious views. Both Cranmer and Gardiner belonged to it in the 1540s. Henry VIII held the balance without difficulty, so that the ascendancy of one side or the other expressed itself not in the expulsion of the loser but in his temporary absence from the board. However, after the old king's death the faction leaders began to pack the council with their supporters and to remove their opponents from the council chamber to the Tower or, in extreme cases, to the block. The temporary ascendancy of the new nobility, aping their Lancastrian predecessors, was well displayed in a council of forty under Edward VI and forty-four under Mary. Many held no office: they joined the council to advance not the king's government but their patrons' or their own interests. A large council cannot govern: thus the privy council broke up into committees to which both Northumberland and Mary tried to give permanence. In the latter's reign Spanish influence worked for the creation of an inmost 'council of state' on continental lines; this would have destroyed the efficiency of the privy council itself and added to the irresponsibility of both councillors and crown. Elizabeth's accession ended these experiments which in truth marked only a decline of royal control over the government. Cecil took up where Cromwell left off—that was to be their relation throughout—and a small council of eighteen, at times reduced to twelve, was to govern England for forty-five years.

The Elizabethan privy council was a well-defined bureaucratic organisation. It had a staff of clerks which grew from one to four; it had ushers and messengers. Minutes were kept, though some meetings were so secret that the clerk was excluded from them and no record survives. It met at regular times and in regular places—regular but not fixed. Early in the reign, the council met on Tuesdays, Thursdays, and Saturdays, expecting to get its work done in the mornings; this left Wednesdays and Fridays free as star chamber days. But business increased, especially when the war was added to other concerns. In the last decade of the century hardly a day passed on which the council did not sit; even Sunday brought no respite. As for place, the council met wherever the queen was, which meant at one of the palaces she usually inhabited (White Hall, Windsor, Greenwich, Oatlands, Nonesuch), or in whatever mansion she might be putting up during her frequent progresses. Not indeed that all the council were always present: most of the routine business was handled by some four to six regular attendants. And most of the business was routine.

The privy council concerned itself quite simply with everything that went on in England, and it often dealt with these matters directly, though at other times it delegated them to a particular member (in the main, the principal secretary), a lesser official, or a different court. No mere summary can give an idea of the all-pervasive interests and influence of the council, but here is a list of the sort of things that came before it: war and peace, foreign affairs and diplomatic negotiations, military and naval matters, finance, religion and the Church, order and police duties, crown patronage in lands and offices, local government, private affairs, disputes, and suits for favour. The most vital concerns of the state rubbed shoulders with the petty troubles of individuals. On one typical day (5 September 1581) the council considered the catholic Lady Stonor's house arrest, trade with Spain, a minor land dispute in Guernsey, a poor man's complaint against the bishop of Hereford, various matters connected with recusants, the report that a man had spoken in favour of Edmund Campion, a land dispute between the earls of Northumberland and Bedford, a merchant's losses through Turkish pirates, Sir Peter Carew's debts, seven passports to foreign vessels released from embargo, and the provision of post horses for a messenger. Although there existed specific courts to attend to their wants, suitors continued to pester the privy council itself on the sound principle that one ought always to go as high as possible. Some judicial work the council necessarily retained: it could not afford to pass to a public court the interests of queen and state, whether they concerned the latest treasonable plot or the financial rights of the prerogative. Its own members, too, naturally exploited their position to advance their affairs through the authority of the council board. But at least one might discourage others from doing the same: hence repeated orders that 'the multitude of private suitors resorting daily to her majesty's privy council' should stop annoying their lordships and take their petty concerns to the courts properly appointed for the purpose. The repetition (1582, 1589, 1591) proves their futility. The courts of law and equity sat relatively rarely and grew more and more behindhand in their work; the structure of Tudor society compelled privy councillors to advance the interests of their clients and adherents; the interests of the age concentrated on litigation and pot-hunting; altogether it proved impossible to stop private suits from taking up the council's time and thus hindering it in its attempts 'to attend and proceed in such causes as do concern her majesty'.

The lords of the council resented these swarms of suitors the more because they were all men of importance, with affairs of state and affairs of their own absorbing quite enough time. The Elizabethan privy council always included a mixture of nobility and gentry who were also office holders—the great officers of the realm (lord chancellor, lord treasurer, lord privy seal, perhaps lord admiral and lord great chamberlain), the leading officers of the household (steward, chamberlain, treasurer, controller, master of the horse), the principal secretaries, and others—but also, especially at first, men of the same stamp who might hold no office. The judges had been excluded by Cromwell, and this valuable distinction between judicial and ordinary administration was maintained under Elizabeth. A curious case is presented by the bishops. Their presence was desirable in the middle of the religious Reformation when the council often discussed affairs of Church and faith, but with the accession of Elizabeth the clerical element disappeared from the council. This is usually thought to have been policy—the queen's deliberate assertion of the triumph of secular rule—but it may have been no more than an accident. Matthew Parker had no wish to take part in the government of the realm, while the other new bishops were, by and large, much too radical for Elizabeth's taste. When she got an archbishop in Whitgift whom she really liked she put him on the council (1586): it looks as though personal preference rather than policy brought about the exclusion of the bishops. It was assisted by the fact that the Church now definitely ceased to hold any of the offices of state: if in nothing else, the age was secular in reserving government to the laity.

All these councillors were technically equal and united in their desire to advise the queen and do their duty by the commonwealth; in practice they were neither. At nearly all times the council divided into parties and there was much personal rivalry. Unless a man sat on the council he could take no part in affairs: the Elizabethan system knew no place for the private favourite, the closet confidant. When the earl of Essex decided to transfer his ambitions to the scene of 'domestical greatness' he had to seek membership of the council (1593); by then he had been a special favourite of the queen's for six years without enjoying a voice in government. The two great struggles of the reign—between Burghley and Leicester, and later between Robert Cecil and Essex—are full of parallels: in each case a statesman opposed a courtier, in each case the fight had personal reasons behind it, in each case matters of public policy gave respectability to disagreement, in each case Elizabeth supported the man of sense against the man of charm. In that small and close-knit society rivalries often looked like family quarrels; at times they were nothing else. The two promising sons of lord keeper Nicholas Bacon, Anthony and Francis, originally belonged to the Cecil interest since Burghley was their uncle by marriage. But when the lord treasurer showed that his own son's career was nearest his heart they moved to the opposition, Francis especially hoping to become the intellect of the Essex faction. The purest example of the intellectual intriguer that the age supplies, he was a man of superlative gifts of the mind (though poetry was not among them), a great lawyer and potentially a great statesman, but also a singularly cold fish whose subtle calculations in politics were only matched by his lack of success. He did, of course, much better under James I.

The factions and rivalries dominated much of the inner history of the reign. A fuller account of them than is possible here would make Elizabethan politics more real, rather less heroic, and much more interesting. Not that everything depended on personal ambitions only. Walsingham's career provides an outstanding example of principles dividing the council. He began very much under the Burghley ægis; from Burghley he learned the scope of the secretaryship and the details of secret service and intelligence, all of which he was to bring to a fine point. But since the personal quarrel between Burghley and Leicester took the form of a contest between a moderate peace policy and a protestant war policy, Walsingham's passionate attachment to the protestant cause drove him into Leicester's camp. He was not even advancing his own interests: Elizabeth preferred Burghley's policy to Leicester's, and there is reason to think that by the later 1570s she even preferred the lord treasurer personally to the earl. Relations between Walsingham and his first patron, though of course disturbed by their disagreement over affairs, were never really hostile, and as soon as developments forced war upon the country they worked together again in perfect amity. But fanatics like Walsingham were rare at the queen's court: she saw to that, though she did not object to using his great abilities even if she disliked his temperament. Nor did she mind the existence of factions in the council. In that way dangerous personal cross-currents played themselves out away from her and a disunited council preserved her personal control. Her father, for much of his reign, had relied on a single great minister and had thus often ceased to be the determining factor in affairs; but she learned the lesson of his last years when the absence of such a minister and the existence of council factions gave greater freedom of action to the crown. The Elizabethan privy council was never a restraint on royal authority, and Elizabeth resembled rather Henry VII than Henry VIII in the practice of government—though when it suited her she could forcefully remind her hearers whose daughter she was.

The councillors were not equal because they included great men as well as lesser, and because the leaders of faction naturally loomed larger than the followers. More important for good government was that they did not all attend with equal zeal. The ordinary work was in fact done by a smaller group of executive ministers. Among these must be mentioned the treasurer and controller of the household whose titles represented sinecures; they were in effect ministers without portfolio available for any work that needed doing. That solid man, Sir Francis Knollys, cousin of the queen, supporter of puritanism, government spokesman in the house of commons, and one of the most regular attendants at the council board, held the office of treasurer of the household for a quarter of a century (1572-96). The executive agent was the principal secretary, as Cromwell had decided he should be. When Cromwell gave it up in 1540 the office lost somewhat in weight. The secretaries of the Tudor crisis either lacked the force and ability to be more than important civil servants, or else they left the office rapidly to seek higher promotion, as did Thomas Wriothesley (1540-4) who became chancellor, or William Paget (1543-52) who preferred the privy seal. It was William Cecil who resuscitated the Cromwellian secretaryship. In the fourteen years that he held it (1558-72) he once again made it the keystone of government. From this position it was not to decline, though the secretaries of the reign differed in standing and influence. At times only one was appointed, as when William Cecil, Walsingham, and Robert Cecil all preferred to avoid competition, and at other times—as after Walsingham's death (1590-6)—the queen kept the place vacant. But all in all, it was in the principal secretary that the activating force of Elizabethan government lay. He prepared the council's agenda and carried out the council's decisions;

in his hand met all the strands of domestic and foreign affairs.

Financial administration concentrated upon the lord treasurer. Here there had been certain changes since Cromwell's fall. The great reformer, as has been seen, had multiplied organised offices of state as need arose, so that when he fell in 1540 the management of the revenue was troublesome and expensive on account of the numbers of officials involved. The financial and administrative difficulties of the years 1540-58, aggravated by war, debasement, corruption, and inefficiency, produced further reforms which really embodied the Cromwellian system in one organisation independent of such accidents as his own death had been. The two men responsible were William Paulet, from 1550 marquess of Winchester, who had proved his great bureaucratic ability since 1526, and (probably) Sir Walter Mildmay, a somewhat humdrum but very sound civil servant whose fame rests on the foundation of Emmanuel College at Cambridge and the puritan sympathies which this act evinced, but ought to rest on the forty-four years of his labours in the courts of augmentations and the exchequer (1545-89). The lives of men like Paulet and Mildmay, spanning the reigns and devoted to the details of administration, explain the astonishing stability and marked success of Tudor government, behind the superficial disturbances of politics.[1]

The reforms which they carried out solved the problem by re-uniting most of the crown's finances under the exchequer. In 1547 the courts of general surveyors and augmentations were fused into a new court of augmentations which in effect administered all the Tudor crown lands except those of the duchy of Lancaster. In 1554, the courts of first fruits and augmentations were abolished, their business being transferred to the exchequer. The court of wards remained separate because it was a difficult organisation to subordinate to the exchequer, but also because its master was a friend of Queen Mary's; the duchy remained separate because of its own interests. Augmentations and first fruits did not, as is sometimes said, continue as separate departments in the exchequer, but they preserved some identity and the new work was done according to the better new methods. Even so the 1554 reforms marked a certain retracing of steps: Winchester's failure totally to conquer the conservatism of the civil service left the exchequer

[1] Other men similarly long in office were Sir Ralph Sadler, once Cromwell's secretary and active in finance, the secretariats, and diplomacy from 1533 to 1587; William Mill, clerk of the star chamber from 1572 to 1608; Nicholas Bacon whose legal career began in 1537 and ended in 1579; or of course Burghley himself, Elizabeth's guiding hand for most of the reign and an official for forty-eight years (1550-98).

with annoying relics of medieval practices which clogged efficiency until the court's abolition in 1833. Throughout the reign of Elizabeth pressure mounted for a further return to the old ways, but Winchester and Burghley resisted with sufficient success to prevent the administration deteriorating. No more structural reforms were made after 1554: here, too, the queen's reign was an age of consolidation not of alteration. The exception to this rule is to be found in the customs which the national administration was so incapable of exploiting that both ministers had to resort to farming.[1]

The chief effect of the 1554 reforms was to give to the lord treasurer, departmental head of the exchequer, almost complete control of the finances. The drawback of Winchester's failure to incorporate the court of wards was overcome by Burghley simply enough: he also held the mastership of that court (1561-96). This office, which administered the feudal rights of the crown, became the centre of speculation for courtiers and landed gentry desirous to profit from the wardships and lands which it had to sell; bribery by suitors made it also a centre of corruption, so that even the upright Burghley could not maintain really rigorous standards. Its mastership was a profitable office which, it was alleged (somewhat exaggeratedly), made Burghley wealthy; when Robert Cecil took over from his father, both corruption and the cheating of the crown for private profit increased. Administratively, the exchequer was now the only financial department that mattered. Winchester's reforms created the modern ascendancy of the lord treasurer and his chief assistant, the chancellor of the exchequer. In this reign, Winchester himself continued to administer the exchequer until his death in 1572, proving the while his training in the Cromwell school by further plans of reform which his successor abandoned in favour of stabilisation. Burghley held the treasurership from 1572 until 1598; his papers are full of the details of finance, as they are full of all the details of government. His successor, Thomas Sackville Lord Buckhurst (1599-1608), not a trained administrator, yet maintained the honourable traditions of Tudor treasurers. As Cromwell had begun and the Cecils continued the organisation of the secretary's office out of which grew the departments of the secretaries of state, so Burghley's private office

[1] The various expedients which culminated in the Great Farm of the customs in 1604 (cf. A. P. Newton in *Transactions of the Royal Historical Society*, 1918) are often praised; but it seems to me that by preferring an easy, if safe, return from the customs and leaving the enormous profits possible to the private farmers, they abdicated responsibility and failed to serve the financial interests of the crown.

laid the foundations for the department of state known as the treasury, which became fully established under the later Stuarts.

While the lord treasurer and the secretary thus embarked on careers of great promise, two other executive officers of the past dropped out of administration. The office of lord privy seal underwent a decline in this reign which reflected its future position as that of a ministry without portfolio. Throughout the period it was held for prestige and money by men who did the work of other real offices, in the main the secretaryship. The lord chancellor had by now quite gone over to his judicial functions, a point which introduces the subject of the courts. A very large number of these existed and not all can here be discussed. Thus the court of admiralty expanded with the business brought in by exploration, piracy, and war. The household court of the steward and marshal exercised its restricted jurisdiction over the 'verge' of the court—the area twelve miles each way from where the court happened to be. There were the courts christian, the courts of the Church, by no means yet dead. Many kinds of local courts flourished, whether franchisal (a few survived, as in Durham) or delegations from the centre (as the assizes), not to mention the declining sphere of the manorial courts and the growing sphere of quarter sessions. Locally one might find special courts, like the stannary courts of Cornwall, or the council courts of the north and the Welsh marches. Everywhere special commissions of magistrates were dealing with cases remitted to them to decide or merely to investigate and report upon. The important central courts were chancery, the conciliar courts of star chamber and requests, and the three courts of the common law. As has already been said, the earlier Tudors created a system in which common law and special (or prerogative) jurisdiction existed side by side; though in some ways they covered different things, they also overlapped a good deal.

Of the rivals to the common-law courts, the court of chancery was the oldest. Moreover, it had originally built up its jurisdiction by filling in the gaps of the common law: equity began and continued as a supplement rather than an enemy to the older law. Development was straightforward in the Tudor century. Wolsey represented the old type of chancellor who governed as chief minister, but also the new type who was first of all a judge. With Sir Thomas More (1529-32) there began the modern line of great lawyer-chancellors—chancellors bred to the common law who were to bring to the gradually crystallising principles of equity enough of the air of the inns of court to make a partnership possible. Thomas Audley (1532-44) and Richard Rich (1547-51) were of the same stamp, though neither such eminent lawyers nor such admirable men. Thomas Wriothesley (1544-7), a civil servant turned politician, and Thomas Goodrich (1551-3), a reforming bishop, marked irrelevant interludes. Mary's reign, on the other hand, produced bishop-chancellors who reverted to the medieval type in Stephen Gardiner (1553-5) and Nicholas Heath (1556-8). Here, too, the reign of Elizabeth declared itself on the modern side: all Elizabeth's chancellors were judges, and nearly all were trained lawyers. Nicholas Bacon (1558-79), the father of two brilliant sons but noteworthy in his own right, was succeeded by Sir Thomas Bromley (1579-87), probably the first chancellor to be known as nothing but a lawyer. More surprising was the appointment of Sir Christopher Hatton (1587-91) who had caught the queen's eye by his qualities as a courtier and a wit. However, he turned out a very sensible chancellor: he used his common sense where it sufficed, and where it did not he adjourned the case till he could have consulted the experts. His career proves that equity was still in the fluid stage, subject to the individual views of each chancellor. Sir John Puckering (1592-6) and Sir Thomas Egerton (1596-1617) revived the lawyers' hold on the office. In Egerton Elizabeth picked perhaps the greatest chancellor of the century, though only James I was to bestow the full title together with the barony of Ellesmere.[1] In his long tenure he went far towards defining the body of law known as equity by freeing it from the uncertainty and caprice which had beset it. More important still, he was to preside over chancery when its quarrel with the law courts was composed. Though chancery had at first interfered but little with the sphere of the common law, from Wolsey's time onwards its injunctions had taken away much business especially from the court of common pleas. The resentment of the common lawyers at this interference could do little till the revival and reforms of the later sixteenth century encouraged the common-law courts to take the offensive. The matter was not settled until the next reign when James I decided a quarrel between Chief Justice Coke and Lord Chancellor Ellesmere in the latter's favour. As far as chancery was concerned, the sixteenth century established it as a regular court, instituted its regular body of law, and enabled it to survive the attack of the common law to remain one of the courts of the realm until the reforms of the nineteenth century.

[1] Elizabeth preferred to appoint lord keepers of the great seal who could do all a chancellor's work without his great salary. This naturally assisted in the relative decline of the office. Bacon, Puckering, and Egerton were keepers.

The conciliar courts proper had a stormier career, although under the Tudors they seemed even more firmly founded. Both the court of requests and the court of star chamber originally were no more than specifically judicial sessions of the council or some councillors; both had a history of gradual growth, repeated starts, and occasional lapses under Henry VII and Wolsey; and for both the organisation of the privy council in the 1530s marked the beginning of permanent institutional existence. Requests, concerned with civil cases brought by 'poor men' and crown servants, administered a species of equity much like that of chancery but distinguished perhaps by a greater liking for the Roman law. Its advantages were cheapness and speed. In any case, the upheavals of the century—the agrarian changes and the rapid movement of land—provided plenty of work for two equitable courts. After 1536-40 the councillors who sat as judges in the court no longer belonged to the council proper, the privy council. In the reign of Edward VI the situation was stabilised by the creation of two permanent masters of requests, later, as pressure of business increased, augmented by two extraordinary (or unpaid) masters. The office was profitable in fees and pickings and one of the few rewards a doctor of civil law could hope for; the presidency of the admiralty court was the ultimate prize of his profession. Though conciliar in origin and in its own claims, the court lacked the prestige which the presence of privy councillors gave to star chamber, so that it fell an easy victim to the common law's counter-attack. In the 1590s common pleas began to inhibit requests from proceeding with cases brought there, and in 1599 the judges denied that this body of men sitting in the White Hall 'had power of jurisdiction' —that is, they deprived its actions of legal force. Nevertheless, simply because its work was still demanded by litigants, the court of requests continued to sit until the great rebellion; the only trouble was that if a defeated party cared to take the matter to the common law, the decision made by requests would prove unenforceable.

Star chamber has been a difficult problem to historians, but no purpose would here be served by entering into the tricky questions raised by it: one must be content with a brief and perhaps rather dogmatic statement.[1] It has already been shown that the court

[1] In this short discussion of star chamber I am relying in part on my own researches and in part—especially for the reign of Elizabeth—on the unprinted thesis by Miss E. Skelton [Mrs J. E. Neale] ('The Court of Star Chamber in the Reign of Elizabeth', London, 1930) which is the only satisfactory treatment of the subject in existence.

grew out of the immemorial jurisdiction of the king's council, especially in criminal matters. As far as is known it rested on no specific order, and certainly not on any statute. In the reign of Henry VII the council began to hold regular meetings in the council chamber of the palace of Westminster, which was known as the star chamber, to adjudicate upon petitions and especially to enforce the king's policy of restoring peace and order. A lapse in this work after Henry VII's death did not prevent its revival, on a vastly increased scale, by Wolsey. When in 1540 the new privy council rounded off its organisation by appointing a clerk and keeping records, the institutional differentiation between these two so-called offsprings of the council was complete. In fact there was only one offspring—the smaller council which at times composed the board known as the privy council and at times sat in the open and regular court known as the star chamber. They were two entirely separate institutions staffed by the same people (or nearly the same people) but with different officers attending upon each. Star chamber consisted of all the privy councillors but it could, and usually did, summon others: thus two of the judges, commonly the two chief justices, attended to provide knowledge of legal matters, though the privy councillors always remained the real judges in star chamber. The chancellor presided and dominated; in a very real sense, as chancery was his court of civil jurisdiction, so star chamber was his court of criminal jurisdiction. The court met on Wednesdays and Fridays during the sixteen weeks of the four law terms, and usually on the day after the end of each term. It was in every sense an ordinary court of the realm: public, with its fixed rules of procedure, a known body of law administered in it.

Nevertheless, traces of its conciliar origin continued to cling to it. The presence there of the queen's government—all or part of the council—gave to the court both a high standing and a somewhat unjudicial appearance. It was, said Coke, 'the most honourable court (our parliament excepted) that is in the Christian world, both in respect of the judges of the court and of their honourable proceeding according to their just jurisdiction and the ancient and just order of the court'. Star chamber dealt in the main with two matters—riots, and the enforcement of proclamations. On the interpretation that anything that might lead to a breach of the peace constituted a riot, the court had extended the first part of its competence to include conspiracy, fraud, perjury, subornation of perjury, forgery, threats, attacks on men in authority, waylaying, and challenges to duels—a generous field of criminal jurisdiction which covered many gaps in the common law and altogether provided even under Elizabeth still the best way of preserving the peace. Proclamations were enforced in star chamber because they were issued by the queen in council and therefore seemed naturally subject to the council sitting in judgment:[1] thus such matters as the censorship of the press, the control of building in London, or the temporary orders regulating trade and prices, came to be star chamber matters. But in all this the council acted as a court, and common views of the star chamber's 'continuing conciliar functions' arise from misunderstandings. The star chamber room was used by the privy council in public sessions: things not done on star chamber days—which includes the allegedly non-judicial actions—were not star chamber doings. Nor was star chamber employed in political matters by the Tudors; the state trials of the period were held before special commissioners of oyer and terminer, usually of course—since high matters of state were at issue—themselves leading councillors. Star chamber did not employ torture, as the privy council sometimes did in its investigations. But star chamber could impose unusual punishments more effective than those available to the common law: it could fine very heavily, imprison, whip and mutilate, or at need use weapons of ridicule like the pillory. It could not order the death penalty.

Two things only happened in the court of star chamber which were not straightforwardly judicial. It published orders which looked like proclamations, and its final session each term was at times used for a public address on the queen's policy. But those orders always arose out of a judicial decision in a case; they were in fact specially vigorous and solemnly pronounced precedents for future guidance, rather than the equivalent of legislation in council. The chancellor's or lord keeper's address at the end of term, to an assembly which often included justices of the peace as well as many officials, was given more regularly at the beginning of the reign when it was felt that these useful occasions might be improved by a little instruction to an as yet unsettled country; they tended to be dropped later as the need for them lessened. On the whole, it remains true that privy council and star chamber, comprising much the same membership, existed as two different organisations ('courts', as the sixteenth century would have said) from that day in August 1540 when the councillors at the board, and the same

---

[1] An attempt to transfer them to the common-law courts, made (it is conjectured) by Cromwell in 1539, was defeated in parliament, and the lapse of the mutilated act of proclamations in 1547 left the whole problem in a mess from which it was rescued by the action of the council in star chamber, irrespective of authority or right.

councillors in star chamber, found themselves recorded by different clerks in a different series of archives. The court of star chamber, however exceptional in its judges and solemn in its rather self-conscious authority, was still only a court like all the rest.

Chancery, requests, and star chamber employed a procedure greatly influenced by the civil law—especially in the use of written documents and witnesses, though they were in the English tradition by being open and by demanding verbal pleadings—but the law they administered was the law of England. At no time was there any question of the common law being superseded. But it needed expanding and amending; it had to be brought up-to-date and made more flexible. The work might be done by statutes enforceable both in the common-law courts and in star chamber; it might be done by equity, in chancery, requests, and later also in the exchequer; it might be done by proclamations enforced in star chamber, though these could produce only minor and commonly temporary changes; it might, finally, be done in the common law itself if it reformed its ways. This is a highly technical subject which it is unnecessary to enlarge upon here. Suffice it to say that from perhaps 1580 onwards the three courts of common law— king's bench, common pleas, and exchequer—began to revive in the hands of men who valued the old law and the old institutions but saw the need for change. The greatest of these was Sir Edward Coke, an unattractive but impressive character, who in his work as a judge and a writer recast and revivified the common law under the pretence of describing it. This revival produced, as has been said, a conflict with the newer courts in which chancery survived and requests succumbed; star chamber remained untouched in its majesty until the follies of Stuart kings and ministers destroyed the popularity of the most efficient and most impartial court of Tudor times.

Such then, in outline, was the central government of Elizabeth's day—a well-designed series of institutions presided over and co-ordinated by the small body of privy councillors, and given life and vigour by the even smaller group of great secretaries and treasurers who did the work of turning advice and direction into action. Nothing in it was new, but much of it was less old than some would have it; it was not medieval government, but the first phase of modern government, resting on principles and offices given a new twist in the 1530s and now in need of acquiring endurance through usage. This, as well as much hard labour, hard thought, skill and subtlety, Burghley, Walsingham, and the rest provided. If they lacked originality (as I think they did), it must also be said that originality can be overvalued, and that the startling outburst of originality associated with Thomas Cromwell gave his successors quite enough to do.

The same careful and inspired exploitation of what was given, rather than invention of new weapons, marked the diffusion of central authority through the realm. This is local government, another huge subject which can only be touched on here. The council kept its eye on the localities in various ways. Special commissions for enquiries, for the taking of witnesses' depositions, even for trials, were constantly going out under the great seal, in the same way as a steady stream of reports and informations made their way from local magistrates to the government. The unit not only of administration but also of social life was the shire on which Elizabethan government acquired a tight hold by developing to the full the office of lord lieutenant. Local noblemen had occassionally been commissioned, with that title, to organise the military forces of the shire in the reign of Henry VIII; under his successors the institution became regular, permanent, and extended to all counties. Too useful to be employed only about military duties, the lord lieutenant was entrusted also with the preservation of the peace and a generial supervision of his region by being put at the head of the magstrates. To equip him with judicial powers he was always included in the commission of tnal peace: in fact, he was as a rule made *custos rotulorum*, a nomihe office technically charged with the keeping of the records of the county justices, but in practice the title bestowed on the senior magistrate.

The justice of the peace, from the first the best weapon of Tudor rule, was exploited almost shamefully by Elizabethan administrators. To his original police duties the century added an ever expanding burden of administration and the enforcement of statutes. To take only two examples: the statute of apprentices (1563) made justices fix wages, while the poor laws of 1597 and 1601 entrusted them with the general and particular supervision of relief and welfare. The commission itself was revised in 1590 in a form which was to endure until 1875; thus the institution inherited from the past was insensibly transformed into something almost new. The commission increased to thirty or forty men in each shire, so that all those of the nobility and gentry who felt it their right to take a share in government could be accommodated. At the same time, to obviate the disadvantages which this influx of amateurs brought with it, the institution of the 'quorum' made

the justices capable of efficiently discharging their duties: some of
them were specified of whom (*quorum*) one at least had to be
present at all formal exercise of authority, and the men so named
were those with official or legal experience. The use of unpaid
justices in local administration had its advantages for an impecunious government. The council's hold over the justices was at the
same time hardly less secure than a salary could have made it.
No one had a right to be appointed to the commission: the queen
alone decided, and since to be dropped from it meant social death
the council could usually discipline a recalcitrant or negligent
justice. It failed where conscience or excessive self-interest
intervened, as in the standard case of the Lancashire justices who,
catholics themselves, would not enforce the recusancy laws, or in
the difficulties encountered with smugglers; but justices fixed
wages and protected the poor contrary to the alleged interest of
their so-called class and in accordance with express government
policy. Under the strict, active, and intelligent privy council of
Tudor times local government by local men was a success. It
exploited local knowledge and loyalties in the interests of the
state, a thing no centralised bureaucracy could hope to achieve,
and it provided a training in self-government which was in the end
to express itself in the self-reliance and skill of the parliamentary
opposition. The Tudors preferred to enlist the abilities of the
gentry even at the cost of foregoing a despotism they neither
needed nor wanted; but only great administrators and rulers could
make the system consistently successful.

The same conservatism is apparent in the remaining institutions
of local government which need concern this summary. For the
purpose of its welfare legislation—the relief of the poor, the provision of work for the unemployed, the care of the sick—the
Elizabethan poor law employed the parish. Two overseers of the
poor were appointed in each, to do all this and collect the poor-rate
which financed their work. This use of the parish and this careful
organisation were indeed in a sense new; the whole poor law, the
great achievement of the paternal state in action, was in practice
the product of the Elizabethan administration. But it borrowed
the parish from the old ecclesiastical organisation (if that is not
too strong a word) of charity, and it built up once again on ideas
which were first worked out, though not then put into practice,
in the 1530s.

The two councils which administered the outlying parts of the
realm were also taken over as reorganised by Cromwell. That of
the north did much good work under that honest puritan and able

man, the earl of Huntingdon, after the suppression of the 1569
rising, while that of Wales became little but a law court. Like the
privy council itself, these local councils acted both as conciliar
courts and as administrative boards. As has already been said, they
were not offshoots of the central council but parallel bodies which
received from Cromwell the institutional organisation which made
them such excellent instruments for the administration of disturbed regions. A third council, that of the west, established in
1538 to deal with Devon and Cornwall, disappeared about 1543,
its work done. The great success of these councils, modelled on
the central administration, in close touch with it, and as it were
extending its arm, appeared in the fact that by the end of the
century the ancient separateness of the Scottish border and the
Welsh marches had well-nigh vanished. Different still in some
ways of life and social structure, they were yet shire ground where
the queen's writ ran effectively.

A great deal has had to be left out in this survey of Elizabethan
government; in particular it has not been possible to show it at
work. Elizabethan government was good government; this was as
well because by any standards except those of the last fifty years
Elizabethan England was a much governed country. It needed to
be, not only because it was passing through upheavals of its own
but even more so because it had to cope with the legacy of the past
in bringing England into the new age of centralised national states
expanding overseas. Much of that legacy was good and was preserved—as the rule of law, the particular position of the English
crown, the place of parliament, the nation-state built up of local
and lesser units. But some of it was bad—the disorder, the disaffection, the particularism, the ascendancy of a fighting
aristocracy. The sorting had been done under Henry VII and
Henry VIII, and in particular by the revolutionary genius of
Tudor times, Thomas Cromwell; without the long labours, the
years of drudgery, the high and honest endeavour of the Elizabethans no amount of revolutionary genius would have sufficed.

4. THE CHURCH

In the reign of Elizabeth, the Church was still an organ of
government. It was now an instrument of the state which had
established its dominance under Henry VIII; since the supremacy
of 1559 was much less definitely ecclesiastical than that of 1534 it
may be argued that the Elizabethan Church admitted even more
completely to the primacy of the temporal power. This does not

mean that the age was indifferent to religion: on the contrary, an age whose thought and values were all animated by religious ideals saw no difficulty in according to the temporal power a quasi-religious deference. In theory, state and Church were one: to the queen, her councillors, and the majority of her people the Church of England coincided with the nation of England. The Church appeared as the spiritual manifestation and organisation of the state: as the queen governed in secular matters through councillors, judges, and the like, so she governed in ecclesiastical affairs through archbishops, bishops, and the rest of the clergy. That was the meaning of her title—'Supreme Governor . . . as well in all spiritual or ecclesiastical things or causes as temporal'. This straightforward theory did not in practice turn out so simple. The notion of one realm, one people, ruled over by one queen and ministered unto by two sets of officials in its secular and ecclesiastical affairs, implied beyond question that by Church was meant the body of all Christians. Yet by the side of this meaning, as old as the Christian religion itself, there had long stood another meaning—which during the middle ages had carried more weight—of the Church as the body of clergy, the mediators between man and God. The English clergy inherited from the past not only an aura of priesthood (which at different times has been differently regarded and stressed) but also the dislike and contempt which the late-medieval priesthood had inspired. The defeat of the papacy, the victory of an anti-clerical laity, reduced the clergy in circumstances without, however, removing all the scorn and distrust which the old clerical pretensions had produced.

Admittedly, it was difficult to feel enthusiastic about a clergy which included too many ignorant men of doubtful morals. The Elizabethan clergy were a mixed lot. They inherited from pre-Reformation times a burden of poor parishes served by men manifestly unfit in learning and behaviour, not to mention piety, to act as spiritual guides to their congregations; the situation was aggravated by secular raids on Church property, especially the inroads on bishops' lands made by Northumberland and Elizabeth; and their best men, most eager on bettering things, fell foul of the queen because they thought improvement possible only by following continental example. At the top the Church was not ill-served. Elizabeth's bishops, though neither so splendid nor so influential as her father's, included able scholars and administrators in men like Parker and Cox, Aylmer and Sandys. They also included men like Grindal—good but ineffective—and weak fools like Richard Cheyney who allowed Gloucester diocese to go to rack and ruin for twenty years. By and large, however, the Elizabethan episcopate displayed those qualities of mind which have become typical of the bench: sound learning, moderate zeal, honest conscientiousness, and a certain necessary pliability towards the secular authority. Whitgift, a hard vigorous man of few scruples when he saw his way clear, brought a different air with him: he swept along on the prophetic storms of conflict and persecution rather than on the gentle winds of indifference and accommodation which more correctly interpreted the queen's own attitude to the vexed question of uniformity in religion.

If the bishops did not lack worthy men, neither did the lesser clergy. There were saints like Richard Greenham, parson of Dry Drayton near Cambridge, a puritan whose fame was known to all England. Always in the first place a good shepherd to his flock, he spent all he had in time, energy, and money to bring the gospel to an unreceptive crowd of rustics. It was said of him that in his own parish he 'had pastures green but sheep full lean'. There were supporters of the establishment, like the great Richard Hooker, a man of so gentle and shy a temper that the vigour of his writings and the force of his opinions came as a great surprise; a scholar of unusual attainments and even more unusual charity in controversy, he also lived a life of genuine humility and example. But these were the fine flowers of their respective wings in the Church; the generality hardly came up to such standards. Not all were as bad as Thomas Powell, chancellor of the diocese of Gloucester for twenty years (1559-79), whose greed, corruption, and disgraceful private life brought the bishop's court, and with it all ecclesiastical authority, into utter contempt. Gloucester, like the other border dioceses, was probably worse than the average, but plenty of testimony survives of an unlearned, unpreaching, incontinent, and worldly clergy in all parts of the country. Most of this testimony comes from the compilations of puritans and has therefore been thought suspect; but after all, the puritan movement derived much of its strength from the inadequacy of the clergy whom it hoped to reform, and while those zealous men might at times exaggerate they certainly at most painted a dark enough picture in unrelieved black.

Yet this same clergy not only claimed spiritual authority but also continued to exercise a direct sway over the laity. The whole system of Church courts was still in existence, and they were still active—from the archbishop of Canterbury's appeal court of the Arches (sitting in St Mary-le-Bow in London) down through episcopal consistory courts to the judicial and visitatorial authority of archdeacons. Before the Reformation these courts had formed a second and all-pervasive system of jurisdiction by the side of the royal courts. They had indeed lost much since then, in particular much valuable jurisdiction over testamentary cases which the conciliar courts were taking to themselves;[1] but moral delinquencies and all matrimonial affairs as well as the enforcement of the clerical rights (such as the ever hated tithe) continued to be dealt with in the Church courts. Where they really declined was not in activity or business but in authority. The powers of the ecclesiastical judges rested upon spiritual penalties, especially the imposition of penances and excommunication. Both these were losing—in many places had lost—their terrors. The denial of purgatory and the spread of a Calvinist theology which firmly separated salvation from works removed the spiritual fears upon which such penalities had had to depend. More important still— for at no time did the majority of men take the thunders of the Church in quite such dread as the more sensitive spirits believe— was the new refusal of the state to support ecclesiastical censures with the more physical action of imprisonment and fine. To this must be added the growing abuse of the spiritual sanctions by the ecclesiastical courts themselves. Not all of them may have gone as far as Powell at Gloucester who generously commuted penances for money paid to himself, but it is doubtful whether the many penances imposed—public expressions of penitence, standing in a sheet, and so on—were often carried out, and it is certain that excommunication, often used for the merest trifles, was generally disregarded. As a result many culprits cited before the courts simply failed to appear, and ecclesiastical jurisdiction relaxed its ancient hold upon the laity.

Out of this general muddle which left a lay population still largely given to religious beliefs and observances without spiritual guidance, there grew the puritan movement and its quarrel with the official leadership of the Church. As has already been said, it is not easy to define puritanism. All its manifestations shared a desire to purify the Church in two respects: to stamp out abuses and thus render it fit to assume the moral leadership which was its due, and to remove the remaining traces of popish practice and traditions. The first of these aims was shared by all respectable and thinking clergy, and especially by the bishops; it was in the end to be accomplished without involving the march down the inviting but dangerous road to Geneva. To follow the example of the 'best

[1] Probate of wills was not removed from the ecclesiastical courts until 1857.

reformed Churches' became the ambition of men who saw their ideal of clerical life and spiritual authority embodied in the practice of Calvinism, but an unprejudiced observer must feel relief at their ultimate defeat.

Puritanism was not in the main a theological movement: it produced no original ideas in theology and almost no treatises on divinity. It borrowed these things from abroad, at first from the Zwinglians and later from Calvin and Béza. Its main characteristics have been analysed into four.[1] The first was a strong moral consciousness, a practical desire to counteract the chances offered to irresponsibility by the doctrine of predestination which in theory rendered a man's behaviour immaterial to his ultimate fate. In theory and practice, the puritan held firmly to an absolute moral standard. Among their best men this produced something like saintliness; among the not so great it could result in that inquisitorial and long-faced nosey-parkering which, unfairly perhaps, has come to be thought of as the hallmark of the puritan. It was secondly a movement which stressed at one and the same time the importance of the individual and the necessity of a social conscience—what Mr Knappen has called 'collectivist individualism'. In nothing else, perhaps, does the essential conservatism of English puritanism come out so well: at this time, at any rate, it preached and worked against anti-social selfishness and the self-assertive individual in a manner commoner among medieval friars and old-fashioned men like Latimer and Lever a generation earlier, than among the doctrines of the nonconformist commercialism of the future. Next, it was a zealous movement: it abominated compromise, gentle and perhaps devious advances to the desired end, and anything but absolute certainty of itself. Lastly, it was strongly clericalist, intent upon putting the clergy back in the saddle. Though not especially theological and always keen on solving the problems of this world, it kept the other-wordly end of salvation firmly in view and came at times near to a pride in priesthood which would have been very distressing to its sectarian offspring in the age of Oliver Cromwell.

None of these things necessarily brought puritanism into conflict with the established Church, except perhaps the zeal which rejected the time-serving, semi-secular policy of the queen and her bishops. When the possibility of an internal transformation of the Church ended with the appointment of Whitgift and the energetic persecution of the puritans (1583), there was precious

[1] M. M. Knappen, *Tudor Puritanism* (1939), the standard work on the subject where the whole problem may be found further discussed.

little between the sides. Both wanted an active clergy, a moral laity, a society harmonious rather than selfishly disintegrated. Both were zealous and uncompromising. Both were solidly Calvinist: not even Cartwright believed more firmly in predestination and the doctrine of the elect than did Whitgift himself.[1] The difference was political: it concerned rival views of the structure and government of the Church. Cartwright and his followers desired a presbyterian Church, resting upon a hierachy of individual congregations, provincial assemblies, and national synods, and administered by a democracy of ministers and an oligarchy of lay elders. Other puritans—the sectarians of Brownist and Barrowist allegiances—went so far as to deny the need for a general national Church. Against this the queen stood firm on the principle of an episcopal Church, with authority percolating from the top downwards—from the supreme governor, through archbishops and bishops, down to the parish clergy—and she found in the Calvinist Whitgift a staunch defender of this organisation which the other side dubbed popish.

This violent political disagreement rested ultimately on a deeper spiritual and intellectual conflict over the nature of authority. The puritans were above all else the people of the Book. What united all puritans was their belief in the Bible as the sole authority; what produced the many sects and divisions of puritanism was the varied interpretation to which the Bible may be subjected. Nothing matters so much in the history of the English Church and its derivatives as the English translation of the Bible. From William Tyndale (1525-31) and Miles Coverdale (1535-7), through the Great or Matthew's Bible which was officially sanctioned (1539), down to the wonderful achievement of the Authorised Version (1611), there was hammered out the chief—indeed the only—weapon of an exclusively English form of Christianity. To the puritan, everything—not only religion and theology, but also secular and ecclesiastical government as well as the rules of personal conduct and private life—was laid down in the Bible. He held that the Scriptures needed no interpreter, each man being able to understand them for himself, and that interpretation must be literal. Medieval scholasticism, inspired by St Augustine, had attempted to resolve the obvious contradictions contained in the

---

[1] Whitgift endorsed predestinarianism in the Lambeth Articles of 1595, but even then a contrary trend existed in the Church of England which was to culminate in the anti-Calvinist Arminianism of the next century. Richard Bancroft rather than Whitgift was the true forerunner of William Laud.

body of sacred writings partly by discovering different senses in difficult passages—ascribing to them figurative or allegorical meanings often the exact opposite of the literal meaning—and partly by recourse to the pronouncements of later authorities— the fathers, the early councils, the Church, the papacy. The true puritan would have none of this. Nevertheless, since he thus involved himself in serious difficulties, he was driven at times into attempts at interpretation and differentiation which conflicted with his basic belief in the universal and literal authority of the whole Bible. He might have recourse to a species of historical analysis, testing the Old Testament by reference to the New; he might fall back on later authority in order to reconstruct the early Church by working backwards; he might appeal to a different authority altogether by citing the example of 'the best reformed Churches'. But none of this altered his fundamental position. The only real authority was in the Bible where no one could find the episcopal structure of the Church: this was the abomination of Rome which must be purged away.

The puritan position had the advantage of simplicity and the strength that goes with it. The half-hearted objections of official defenders could be swept away every time with a demand to have the opponent's tenet proved from Scripture. Uncertain of itself, strongly influenced by continental protestantism of the same kind as that appealed to by the puritans, conscious of the political and uninspired nature of the settlement, the Church at first offered nothing to arrest the rapid advance of presbyterian puritanism. Especially the younger generation at the universities—in the main at Cambridge—took to the simple and authoritarian teaching of men like Cartwright with the readiness always displayed by certain young men to whom practical politics and compromise are anathema. Even so, the Anglican position was quite well defended in John Jewel's *Apology* (1562) which successfully justified the Church's renunciation of Rome but did not offer sufficient positive content for the Church of England's *via media*. Throughout the reign, many writings appeared which here and there managed to controvert the attacks of both catholic and puritan pamphleteers, but on the whole the presbyterians dominated the intellectual side of the English Church with their Calvinist theology and their insistence on Scriptural authority. It was not until the latter years of the queen's reign that puritanism as the leading movement within the Church fell on evil days. Its intellectual strength was undermined by Richard Hooker, while its organisation and practical resistance were destroyed by John Whitgift.

Hooker's greatest work, *The Laws of Ecclesiastical Polity*, appeared in stages—four books in 1593, the fifth in 1597, the remaining three after his death in 1600. Within its extended length there may be found a total view of the Church, the state, and the divine order of things which makes this obscure don and parish priest one of the great thinkers of the century and his book —the bye-product of a controversy—one of the important writings of political and religious thought. His insistence on natural law as the expression of God's world and his view of the state have already been touched upon. He derived much of his thought from predecessors like St Thomas Aquinas and Marsiglio of Padua; indeed, a notable part of Hooker's greatness is his learning and the way in which he applied tradition to the creation of something new—the doctrine of the protestant Church of England. For his theology proves him to have been a protestant; there is nothing, for instance, in his teaching on the sacraments with which any puritan could have found fault. But against the puritans' exclusive insistence on Scripture, Hooker put forward the claims of tradi- tion, authority, and the Church. He summarised his position in four 'propositions' in which he listed those rites and observances which may be justified even if they cannot be deduced from the Scriptures: 'such things as are apparently, or can be sufficiently proved, effectual and generally fit to set forward godliness . . . may be reverently thought of'; things whose fitness is not evident or easily proved may yet be rendered fit by tradition and the judgment of antiquity; innovation is proper because not 'all things could be of ancient continuance which are expedient and needful for the ordering of spiritual affairs', and 'the Church . . . hath always power . . . no less to ordain that which never was than to ratify what hath been before'; lastly, if necessity or common utility so require, the Church may dispense from ordinances otherwise profitable. Hooker thus gave back to the Church the authority to interpret and guide which puritanism denied it. He based his argument on such wide and cogent knowledge, so thoroughly informed by an all-pervading historical sense, that the book was immediately successful and remained the basis for every later justification of the Church of England. The 'judicious' Hooker— the adjective is John Locke's—had just the spirit and learning necessary for the justification of the *via media*, the one religious position of the sixteenth century that had within it the germ of toleration.

There was nothing judicious about Whitgift or his vigorous campaign to stamp out puritan divagation in the Church. The weapon employed was the court of high commission. It grew out of the commissions for the enforcement of the royal supremacy of which that granted to Cromwell as vicegerent in spirituals (1535) was the first. A body composed of bishops, privy councillors, civil and common lawyers, it was appointed and sat at intervals until 1580 when it was turned into a court. Its work had hitherto been mainly visitatorial—to seek out and punish failure to conform. Now it became judicial—cases were decided between party and party. In the manner familiar from the history of star chamber, the high commission court rapidly developed a regular body of judges, a regular procedure, and a regular province of jurisdiction. Its judges were in the main bishops and ecclesiastical lawyers. Unlike an ordinary ecclesiastical court it covered the whole realm and, because of the standing of its judges, it could make its decisions felt; thus it grew popular and attracted much business, mainly among clerical litigants. In 1583 Whitgift published his twenty-four articles which he desired to impose upon the clergy; since they prohibited 'prophesyings', reinforced the rules about clerical dress, demanded subscription to the Prayer Book and Parker's *Advertisements*, and supported the authority of bishops, they amounted to a declaration of war on puritanism. The high commission, so far simply an important Church court, now became the instrument with which Whitgift made his articles effective. Using the procedure of the *ex officio* oath, by which a man could be compelled to incriminate himself, he harried the puritans into submission, deprivation, or even death. His activities caused much anger. Burghley protested in a famous letter (and in exaggerated language) that these proceedings smacked too much of the popish Inquisition; the lawyers—always good allies to the puritans— assailed the legality of the court; there were attacks in parliament. But Whitgift, who knew he had the queen behind him, went on undeterred. By the end of the reign, puritanism as a movement in the Church was dead. Its synodal organisation had been destroyed, its propagandists silenced, its ministers made to conform to the episcopal standard. That the movement began at the same time to increase its formidable hold over influential parts of the laity was nothing to do with Whitgift. He could not prevent its future development, but he could and did prevent it from subverting the Church from within.

Thus when Elizabeth died, the Church stood strong and, to all appearance, secure. Founded as a political compromise—though never as purely a compromise or as purely political as its attackers then and later pretended—it had established itself in the faith and the affections of the majority. It had fought off assaults from catholics and puritans. It had developed its own doctrine and philosophy. Altogether it was an achievement of which the many who had contributed to it in various ways might well be proud—Parker, Grindal, and Whitgift, Jewel and Hooker, Burghley and the queen herself. Perhaps Elizabeth had been its most consistent defender, especially in the days, now distant, when the firebrands of puritanism and anti-popery seemed to carry all before them. To the queen as much as to anyone was due the eminently conservative character of the achievement. She had gone as far as she would in 1559, and she had really not moved forward from there. In any case, forward and backward are misleading terms. There is something to be said for holding that the most progressive, least conservative, religious movement of the age was the Church of Rome after the Council of Trent. All the English movements looked back: the idea of progress did not occur to them, and they could not believe in the perfectability of man. The Anglican based himself consciously on tradition of which he claimed to be the only true inheritor; the puritan went further back and sought his model in the dawn of Christianity. Neither side claimed to innovate even where they did, for authority—whether confined to the Bible or not—was the guiding star, not man's sovereign reason. Of course, the puritan movement demanded an advance away from 1559, but it was an advance dominated by backward-looking tenets. In religion, as in government, the age of Elizabeth tried hard to stand still, to consolidate, and to preserve the links with the past; and even its rebels were essentially as conservative as the things they rebelled against.

Chapter XV

THE STRUCTURE OF THE AGE: RENAISSANCE

FEW words today are more apt to rouse historical passions than the word Renaissance. It is therefore advisable to preface this chapter with a warning that the use of the term implies no claim that in the sixteenth century the influence of the classics and of Italian models produced, at a stroke, an outburst of the 'modern spirit'. At one time all art and literature, politics and international affairs, religion and morals, economics and philosophy and history were regarded as coming to the end of their medieval forms about 1500 and as turning out different and new under the influence of the Renaissance. That view is now as dead as it deserves to be, though its corpse, decked out in a semblance of life, may yet be met with in some books. However, the question is whether in rightly denying the Renaissance in politics and affairs, and in tracing with great learning the persistence of 'medieval' ideas and modes of thought, historians have not fallen into the error of opposing outright denial to an untenable outright assertion. The Master of Jesus College, Cambridge, who has himself done much to popularise the notion of the Elizabethan age as dominated by the intellectual temper of the past,[1] has recently reconsidered the question of a Renaissance in literature.[2] Though his arguments on this point carry less than perfect conviction, it is yet hard to escape his conclusion that in sixteenth-century England something happened in the arts that cannot be explained without the use of some such term as Renaissance. There are certain activities of mankind which, being of the mind and subject to fashion, do accommodate themselves to the intellectual categories discerned—or devised—by the observer. Whatever may be true of the mental climate of the period and the majority of men, the achievements in literature and the arts fulfilled a deliberate purpose. How far they derived from classical and Mediterranean models may become apparent as they are discussed; that there was a Renaissance in the strictest sense—a rebirth of English poetry in particular—the merest glance at the writings of the day will confirm beyond question.

[1] See above, p. 396 and n.
[2] E. M. W. Tillyard, *The English Renaissance—Fact or Fiction?* (1952).

1. INTELLECTUAL BACKGROUND

The basis of the revival was a movement in education to which the name humanism is commonly given. It has already been explained that humanism was not the coming of light after darkness; it was, however, a break with the over-formal, over-abstracted dialectics of the later middle ages. The inspiration came from such diverse sources as the Italian passion for the classics, Erasmus' intellectual attack on scholasticism, the introduction of Greek into England by William Grocyn (1446?-1519) and Thomas Lineacre (1460?-1524), and the religious doubts which drove people like Tyndale to the Greek text of the Bible. The ideal of education changed from the theological to the rhetorical, from the training of priests and scholars to the training of accomplished gentlemen serving the state. Cicero dominated sixteenth-century education —they were for ever citing 'Tully' for the example of his oratory and the wisdom of his *De Officiis*—until a reaction against verbosity towards the end of Elizabeth's reign replaced him by the models of the Jacobeans, Seneca and Tacitus. This Ciceronian tradition was far from dead through most of the middle ages; the movement was really new only in that it demanded intellectual attainments in the lay leaders of society. By combining classical learning with medieval knighthood it created the ideal of the gentleman, that powerful civilising influence of the next 400 years: of that ideal, Sir Philip Sidney, who fused knightly 'courtesy' with humanistic learning and the Elizabethan courtier's love of poetry, stands as the first English embodiment.

An early exposition of these aims (partly taken from Italy) occurs in Sir Thomas Elyot's *The Governour* (1531), a training-scheme for a ruling class. But the most influential figure in practice was Sir John Cheke (1514-57), the first professor of Greek at Cambridge, provost of King's College, secretary of state, and tutor to Edward VI whom he imbued with protestant beliefs. Cheke's personal standing as a scholar and a man of affairs saved the new learning from the contempt of practical men; his principles, which rested on a firm belief in the 'usefulness' of learning and its application to the service of the state, became standard theory. It was from Cheke that Roger Ascham (1515-68) traced his intellectual descent, and Ascham was not only the foremost Greek scholar of his day and tutor to two queens (Lady Jane Grey and Elizabeth), but also, as author of *The Scholemaster* (1570), the leading exponent of the theory of education. The book is full of sound advice on the practice of teaching—it deprecates the prevailing brutality of the schools and prefers the late-developing solid intelligence to flashy precocity—as well as some rather hysterical warnings against the atheistical and evil influence of Italy on visitors from the north. Another who came under Cheke's influence was Thomas Wilson (1525?-81) whose *Art of Rhetorique* (1553) describes the sort of training in ready speech and sharpened reason that humanists thought best. Scholarship, especially in Greek studies, rather declined later in the century (Whitgift had no Greek), but the education provided by schools and universities in the reign of Elizabeth was firmly based on the ideals developed earlier. Sir Humphrey Gilbert's *Queen Elizabeth's Academy* (1572), the first 'modernist' protest against the classical syllabus, describes an ideal school where modern languages, mathematics, law, and military exercises rival the study of Latin and Greek; but it did nothing to undermine the humanist method. The century imposed on English education that exclusive attention to the classics and the rhetorical treatment of language that did service down to very recent times. The consequent permeation of all thought with allusions to classical history and mythology was to produce a kind of *lingua franca* of poetry.

It ought perhaps to be pointed out that the secular ideal of education—the accomplished gentleman—did not stand alone. It was accompanied by the traditional professional training for the clergy in their various capacities. In the reign of Elizabeth the gentry invaded both the universities and the inns of court, not to become scholars and lawyers but to acquire the equipment and polish which contact with scholarship and law alone could give; but their invasion did not drive out those who went there for professional reasons. The universities remained always in part at least schools for experts and a road to employment. In this century they were doing well as new foundations increased their size and variety. The humanism of the earlier years produced, at Cambridge, Jesus College (1496), Christ's College (1505), and St John's College (1511), and at Oxford Brasenose College (1509), Corpus Christi College (1517), and Cardinal College (later Christ Church: 1525). The ambitions of lay founders added Magdalene (1542), Trinity (1546), and Emmanuel (1584) at Cambridge, and Jesus at Oxford (1571). Many of these foundations played a leading part in the Reformation: thus St John's was a breeding ground of early protestantism, it and Trinity produced Cartwright, and Emmanuel was founded as a puritan college. Gresham College (1596) in London, financed from the bequest of Sir Thomas Gresham, began the liberal and anti-classical tradition of the capital's academic training. Schools, too, made their appearance: the activities of that brutal but efficient teacher, Nicholas Udall, at Eton (1534-41) and Westminster (1554-6) were matched by those of his brilliant pupil Richard Mulcaster, first headmaster of Merchant Taylors (1561-86). Other new schools included Repton, Rugby, Uppingham, and Harrow, all founded between 1559 and 1590.

If this vigorous educational activity was one pillar of the intellectual revival, another must be sought in the development of printing. William Caxton (1422?-91), who began printing in England in 1476, also founded the tradition by which printers doubled their activities with authorship. The good work was carried on by his apprentice Wynkyn de Worde and by a succession of king's printers of whom Thomas Berthelet and Richard Grafton, under Henry VIII and Edward VI respectively, are the best known. Thereafter there was no holding the press. Licensed or unlicensed (like the secret presses that produced the Marprelate Tracts), it poured out a stream of books and pamphlets, created a book trade and the profession of publisher, and provided the ground for the first genuine literary movement. Much of the poetry of the age was not printed at the time—some even yet remains in manuscript—but a vast deal appeared in book form, stimulating demand and making possible mental contact and cross-fertilisation. It is a commonplace, but none the less true for that: though without the printing press there might still have been a revival in literature, it would not have been so fruitful and lavish and would certainly have been less rapid in producing perfection.

Another striking aspect of the age was its renewed interest in history. The great medieval tradition of historical writing declined in the fourteenth and fifteenth centuries into a series of undistinguished chronicles. The historic importance of the wars of the Roses, as well as foreign example, resulted in worthier attempts to write history proper. Polydore Vergil (1470-1555), an Italian who as papal collector was long resident in England, set a new standard with his *Anglica Historia*; employing the training of Italian humanism, he displayed an organising faculty and a critical acumen of which English history stood in much need. Of the native chroniclers of the earlier period, Edward Hall (*The Union of the Two Noble and Illustre Famelies of Lancastre and Yorke*, published in 1548) deserves special mention. He proved himself possessed of a vigorous personal style and genuine insight, transferred to the vernacular chronicle some of Vergil's literary quality, and was one chief source for the encyclopædic chronicle of Richard Holinshed (1578) on which the dramatists mainly relied. All these, and others like Richard Grafton (1568) and John Stow (1580), were eclipsed by William Camden, a genuine historian of great dramatic power whose *Annales Regnante Elizabetha* (1615)—though in Latin—are the highwater mark of Elizabethan historical studies. Modern biography began with Thomas More's *History of Richard III* (*c.* 1514), can claim a fine if homespun example in George Cavendish's *Life of Wolsey* (1557), and achieved a masterpiece in Francis Bacon's *Henry VII* (1622). The interest in history spread to local studies like Stow's *Survey of London* (1598), William Lambarde's *Perambulation of Kent* (1570), and Richard Carew's *Survey of Cornwall* (1602). General surveys of England, mixing historical and geographical knowledge, were produced by John Leland (*Itinerary*, *c.* 1540), William Harrison (*Description of England*, 1577), and especially by Camden in his monumental *Brittania* (1586). The catalogue could be extended beyond all patience, but even as it stands it may give some inkling of the enormous output of an age whose interests ranged from the Anglo-Saxon studies of Archbishop Parker and the foundation of a Society of Antiquaries before the end of the century to contemporary history chronicled in John Foxe's *Acts and Monuments*, popularly known as the *Book of Martyrs* (first edition in 1563).

There was much other serious writing. The main work of Francis Bacon belongs to the next century, but the *Essays* appeared first in 1597. They are a collection of philosophical and moral reflections, distinguished by flashes of thought and a severely elliptical style; the present writer has never been able to understand the praise showered both on their manner and matter. The geographical works of Dee and Hakluyt have already been noted; to them one may add the surveys with maps of which John Speed's *Theatre of the Empire of Great Britain* was the finest. Yet all this was only a part of the writing done—the lesser, and to contemporaries perhaps the less important, part. If this account concentrates on the secular literature of the age it is not because the output of theology was small: on the contrary. Religion and writings about religion loomed very large indeed, But, except for the occasional masterpiece like Hooker's, the literary quality and the intellectual interest are greater among the secular productions. In any case, these are significant of something new. Together with a number of treatises on hawking, archery (Ascham wrote a well-known one, the *Toxophilus*), husbandry, courtly life, and all the rest of it, they display a vigorous intellectual interest in matters rarely hitherto touched by literature. With creditable ease, the age accommodated a genuine feeling for spiritual things with an equally genuine devotion to the possibilities of secular life. No one can say how this fruitful turmoil was related to the outburst of great music and poetry. A view, still not uncommon, which seeks to explain Shakespeare and his fellows out of the intellectual zest of the age, tries too much. The activity in education, printing, and secular studies here described is not to be thought of as the cause of the artistic developments to which we must now turn. Rather is it an aspect of the same thing—the great increase, leading in the end to a unique manifestation, in the workings of the human mind and spirit which distinguish the sixteenth century in England.

2. THE FINE ARTS

The Tudor age delighted in colour and lavish display, as any portrait of—say—Henry VIII or Elizabeth makes plain. The lively brashness of an exuberant time often fell short of good taste, but its brightness and richness—even its bizarre touches—are signs of sprouting life. The moralists and legislators—the latter trying by sumptuary laws to limit the worst indulgence in silks, velvets, and jewellery to those who could afford them—fought a losing battle against the slashed doublets, wide ruffs, enormous (and very unsightly) breeches, massive chains and delicate feathers, the idiotically tall hats and high heels of the dandies who infested Elizabeth's court. The simpler fashions of the earlier reigns, even if often they went in for a sort of tough virility with their un-naturally broad shoulders and tight hose, are beyond question preferable. Women's fashions were rather less gorgeous, except in the hands of the very wealthy and especially the queen herself, but they were even more objectionable: the huge hooped skirts ren-dered movement difficult, while the tight bodices and deep stom-achers squeezed vital organs in a way not exceeded by the worst Victorian tight-lacing. But beautiful or not, sensible or not, all the clothes that mattered were designed to dazzle and overwhelm.

It is therefore a little astonishing to find that this taste for colour did not produce any great painting. Much Tudor painting seems to have disappeared; what there is is practically all portraits and the best of it by foreigners. Several important painters were brought to England by royal patronage, as for instance the Italian Vincent Volpe, the Flemings Hans Eworth and Antonio Moro, and the German Gerlach Flicke. The greatest painter to work in England in that century was Hans Holbein the younger, from Basle, whose splendid portraits—especially the series of drawings preserved at Windsor—have made the reign of Henry VIII the first age we fancy we know intimately. Holbein's work influenced others; despite the later impact of Italian, Flemish, and Spanish styles of portraiture, a trace of his purely linear style survived to the end of the century. Among a number of competent portraitists, he was the only artist of real genius, and the fact that he worked under Henry VIII has obscured the actual development from feeble beginnings early in the century to a genuine mastery of technique learned from abroad in the reign of Elizabeth. However, though there are many good portraits of the second half of the century, few succeeded in depicting character as Holbein's did. The later Elizabethan painters concentrated more and more on the careful description of detail—dress, jewellery, and the Renaissance accessories of the background—while contenting themselves with a linear suggestion of the features. This is particularly marked in pictures of the queen herself after 1584 when George Gower received a monopoly for royal portraits: most people are therefore liable to think of her as a stiff cone of brocade hung with pearls and surmounted by elaborately bejewelled red curls. Only in the field of miniature painting was there a native tradition. Growing out of the art of illuminating manuscripts and developed by the many craftsmen who 'limned' royal portraits in the initial letters of public documents, it reached astonishing heights of beauty in the work of Nicholas Hillyard and his slightly inferior successor Isaac Oliver. These artists combined a 'modern' technique of portraiture and mastery of perspective with the 'medieval' technique of illumination. Their colours in particular recall the vivid blues and golds of medieval manuscripts. By and large, the vogue for portraits represents less a genuine interest in the arts than a genuine interest in one's own face: the portrait painters—full-scale or miniature—did the work of the photographic studio.

More native traditions and more notable achievements may be recorded in building. Here the Reformation made an obvious difference: it ended the great era of church-building. The early Tudor period was the last age of Gothic—the age of late perpendicular. Opinions on this differ: some speak of decadence, arguing that the fretted stone-work which reduced the windowless wall-area to the least possible before the invention of steel-girders, the non-functional ribs of the fan-vaulting, the plentiful ornamentation (often heraldic), show that the purpose of the building had been lost sight of. It is true enough that a perpendicular chapel like that of King's College, Cambridge (the finest example of the style) creates less of a mystical gloom than does the solidity of thirteenth-century Early English, but it would be wrong to argue from this that it represents irreligion. The late perpendicular is sometimes mechanical and uninspired, but at its best it is a very high achievement in craftsmanship and architectural technique. The stained glass of the late fifteenth and early sixteenth century was the finest ever made.

Some of these early Tudor buildings, ecclesiastic and secular, owed much to foreign artists and workmen. The Italian sculptor Torregiano built Henry VII's tomb at Westminster, Wolsey employed Flemings at Hampton Court, Sir Richard Weston's typical early-Tudor palace at Sutton Place in Surrey was probably designed by another Italian, Trevisano. Nevertheless the domestic architecture of the period was strictly indigenous, owing little to foreign models. It marked the development of the rather cramped medieval castle, designed with at least one eye to defence, into the more comfortable palaces and manor houses of monarchy and gentry. The new inherited some points from the old. The central hall—once the sole public room—is a notable feature in them all; it still survives in college architecture. So is the quadrangle, developed as outhouses grew up around the hall and complete when these became additional dwelling-chambers. The great gate-houses with their crenellated turrets are a distinctive part of early-Tudor palace building; vestigial remains of embattled castles, they may be seen at Hampton Court, or at Queen's and St John's Colleges in Cambridge. The growing use of brick, the employment (for lesser houses) of half-timbered walls even where stone was found locally, the improvements in fire-places which appear in the sprouting of the famous Tudor chimney stacks (again very noticeable at Hampton Court), are other typical points. All over the country, palaces and manor houses were built; in the towns wattle-and-daub gave way to half-timbered buildings; a growing wealth and the needs of the new landowners after the Dissolution encouraged a vigorous activity. A few names may be cited: Henry VII's old palace at Sheen (Richmond) now covered up by Stuart alterations, Wolsey's Hampton Court, Henry VIII's St James's Palace, Haddon Hall in Derbyshire, Wollaton Hall in Nottinghamshire, Kirby Hall in Northamptonshire. And dozens more: many an Elizabethan manor house survives today as a farmhouse.

More remarkable, however, than painting and even architecture was the development of music. Of this nothing like enough can be said here, partly for lack of space, partly because the present writer can lay no claim to expert knowledge at all. The idea of all England as a nest of singing-birds, popular with writers of romantic history, may indeed be rather exaggerated—there are signs that it is coming under attack—but there is no doubt at all both of the extremely high level reached by the many great composers of the century and of the widespread interest in music shown by all classes and especially by the court, the centre of culture. Kings and queens, courtiers and poets, played and sang and many composed, especially Henry VIII whose efforts have, however, found little favour with the experts.[1] In music, too, one finds the familiar mixture of the traditional and the new. In particular, while much music continued to be written specifically for an ecclesiastical purpose—settings of services, and here the Reformation made almost no difference, especially because some leading composers were catholics—the reign of Elizabeth also witnessed the growth of a wonderful corpus of secular music, especially for voices. The great composers of the mid-century—Christopher Tye (1500?-73), Robert White (1530?-74), and especially Thomas Tallis (1505?-85) —produced church music of magnificent quality, but so far little worthwhile secular music was written. The change came with the introduction from Italy of the madrigal and the canzonetta, the pupils soon outstripping the teachers. Good opinion holds that Elizabethan part-song and solo-song reached the highest point possible in that field. Helped by the great poetry of the age, the composers achieved an unsurpassed marriage of music and words. Between 1588 and 1630 more than eighty collections of songs appeared in print, containing little short of 2,000 pieces, and others as beautiful remained in manuscript.

The great names here are John Wilbye (d. 1614), the supreme writer of madrigals, John Dowland (1563-1626) who wrote accompanied solo-songs, Thomas Campion (d. 1619), a poet who set his own verses, and Thomas Morley (1557-1602) who could do all kinds and was responsible, for instance, for 'Now is the month of maying'. Greater even than these in passionate intensity were two men whose fame rests mostly on their church music: Orlando Gibbons (1583-1625), the first composer of Anglican services, and the supreme master William Byrd (1543-1623) who must rank with the very highest, with Palestrina and Bach. In his long life Byrd produced a great deal of music. His attempts at secular songs are comparative failures; he seems to have needed the words of devotion, and especially of the services, to bring out his power of mystical thought and absorption in the remotest realm of musical language. There were others, barely less remarkable than those named. Not all madrigals are good, nor need one necessarily like

[1] E. Walker, *A History of Music in England* (1952), p. 45, describes the king, rather gratifyingly, as 'an eclectic of the feeblest kind'.

madrigals at all; but no one can resist Byrd's *Cantiones Sacrae*, Wilbye at his best, or Dowland's sad, sweet songs. In the reign of Elizabeth, England reached the highest concentration of musical genius in all her history and led Europe in this field.

3. LITERATURE

Any attempt to summarise here the work of the writers, poets, and dramatists who made of the sixteenth century one of the few really great periods of literature must obviously be hopeless. It was in language and its use that the English Renaissance mainly expressed itself. The visual arts played little part in it; music recorded astonishing achievements but for technical reasons remained a restricted expression of the age; in poetry, on the other hand, no more remarkable work has ever been done. Within the short space of some sixty years, and thanks to the labours of a few men of genius and many men of unusual talent, the English language shed the awkwardness and insufficiency which clung to it and became the flexible and all-competent instrument of an incomparable out-pouring. The greatest of all poets (perhaps in any language) was part of that band, but others beside Shakespeare added their efforts—more than can be listed here. Another difficulty is raised by the fact that the death of Queen Elizabeth marked a date of no importance in this story. There are differences between the Elizabethans and Jacobeans, but the significant years are really 1580-1630. Yet we cannot include here the whole reign of James I. As far as possible we shall therefore confine ourselves to work done before Elizabeth died and to men who were prominent before 1603, taking three subjects in turn—prose, lyrical poetry, and the drama.

Prose has always been later to reach perfection than poetry because poetic language is always the first to undergo the discipline of literary treatment. The age of Elizabeth is no exception. Some decent literary prose appeared under Henry VIII, though most of it was cumbersome and long-winded; under the influence of their Greek and Latin studies, Cheke and Ascham wrote a clear if rather pedestrian style; but when the literary men really got hold of prose they did terrible things to it. Dissatisfied with the plainness of daily speech and the artlessness of his predecessors, John Lyly, in his two romances *Euphues* (1579) and *Euphues his England* (1580), developed a style of his own which, by the name of Euphuism, became the model and bane of English writing. Its essence lay in a laborious display of rhetorical devices; Lyly was particularly fond of pointless but well-balanced antitheses, frequent alliteration, a prodigality of similes arranged in wearisome strings, and rhetorical questions. Sir Philip Sidney's *Arcadia* (*c.* 1580) suffers from much the same faults, though they are less glaring; oddly enough—in view of the large number of versified romances that ought to have been in prose—the episodic and often exalted *Arcadia* would be better all in rhyme than in a mixture of both. Unlike Lyly, Sidney (who after all was a minor genius) could turn out good prose within the limits of his convention, but too often he was guilty of conceits like the following description of a piece of sewing:

> The needle itself would have been loth to have gone fromward such a mistress but that it hoped to return thitherward very quickly again, the cloth looking with many eyes upon her and lovingly embracing the wounds she gave.

This stuff was popular for a time, but that it palled is evident both from the way in which Shakespeare later parodied it and from the career of Robert Greene (1560?-92), perhaps the first professional journalist, who always wrote in the fashion. Thus he produced a lesser *Euphues*, pastoral romances in the manner of Sidney, and—when realism grew in vogue—the splendid pamphlets, mostly of low life, on which his fame rests: *Notable Discovery of Cozenage, A Quaint Dispute between Velvet-Breeches and Cloth-Breeches*, and others (1590-2). Here the style has become racy, straightforward, and English. The main achievement of this greater freshness was Thomas Nash's *The Unfortunate Traveller* (1594), a picaresque novel full of humour and incident. Nevertheless, even at its best Elizabethan literary prose makes hard going and proves how much less universal prose is than verse.

The best prose of the day is probably found elsewhere—among the translators, among those who merely wished to convey their ideas without regard to the refinements of Latin and Italian example, in prose passages in plays, and in letters. The sixteenth century was a great age for translations; a list of the authors communicated to the English is some indication of the debt owed by this Renaissance to foreign inspiration. The Italians in particular made their appearance in strength: Boccaccio, Ariosto, Machiavelli's *Art of War*, the tales of Bandello, and others were all translated. In prose translations the restraint imposed by the original compelled the writer to drop the tasteless refinements and

adornments which beset English prose in its youth, with such
outstanding results as Lord Berners' *Froissart* (1523-5), Thomas
North's *Plutarch* (1579), and John Florio's *Montaigne* (1603).
Above all, of course, one must here mention the *Authorised
Version* of the Bible (1611), whose perfection, achieved by a
committee of rather dreary divines, is as good a proof of direct
inspiration as one can find. The needs of controversy exercised a
similarly salutary influence: those who wrote to convince could
not afford the graces and obscurities indulged in by those desiring
to amuse. Not that the vast pamphlet literature of the century was
always written in good English; much of it was unrhythmical,
crude, prolix, and tedious. But much also reached remarkable
heights. A useful study of the development of English prose
might trace the controversial style from the rather awkward
plainness of Thomas More to the accomplished ease of Hooker.
Take these two passages, one from More's *Apology* of 1528, the
other from Hooker's *Ecclesiastical Polity* of 1594:

> But yet for that I have myself seen and by credible folk have heard,
> like as ye say by our temporalty that we be as good and as honest
> as anywhere else, so dare I boldly say that the spiritualty of England,
> and especially that part in which ye find most fault, that is to wit that
> part which we commonly call the secular clergy, is in learning and
> honest living well able to match and (saving the comparisons be
> odious I would say further) far able to overmatch, number for num-
> ber, any nation christened.

This Doric, good of its kind, looks back to medieval writings; in
Hooker, on the other hand, we can hear the true English prose of
the centuries to come.

> He that goeth about to persuade a multitude that they are not so
> well governed as they ought to be shall never want attentive and
> favourable hearers, because they know the manifold defects where-
> unto every kind of regiment is subject; but the secret lets and diffi-
> culties, which in public proceedings are innumerable and inevitable,
> they have not ordinarily the judgment to consider.

Thus far had skill moved in the space of some sixty years.

The most interesting, characteristic, and vigorous prose is
found where there is least artifice. The common speech of the age,
as reported in law-suits and transformed by Shakespeare into a
species of poetry, reached a remarkable standard of succinct and
lively expressiveness: in that respect every succeeding century has

produced only progressive deterioration. The measured solemnity exemplified in a threat uttered in 1534, during a quarrel over the fixing of meat prices—'I will advise you not to meddle with the said weight of flesh, for if you do it shall be to your pain'— becomes, in the hands of the poet, the magnificent pathos of Mistress Quickly's threnody on Falstaff: 'Nay sure, he's not in hell; he's in Arthur's bosom if ever man went to Arthur's bosom', and the rest of it. And then there are the letters, to prove that few in the century could fail to write well when they had something to say and no need to clothe it in artificiality. Here is Thomas Cromwell, gravely rebuking Bishop Shaxton, one of his own party:

> My lord, you had showed yourself of much more patience—I will not say of much more prudency—if ye had contented yourself with their lawful appeal and my lawful injunctions and rather have sought fully to instruct me in the matter than thus to desire to conquer me by shrewd words, to vanquish me by sharp threaps [assertions] of Scripture which, as I know to be true, so I trust to God—as great clerk as ye be—ye allege them out of their place.

Queen Elizabeth, taking James VI to task for double-dealing:

> How may it be that you can suppose an honourable answer may be made me when all your doings gainsay your former vows? You deal not with one whose experience can take dross for good payments, nor one that easily will be beguiled.

And these two were hardly expert stylists, unlike Sir John Harington, that good Elizabethan, describing some goings on at a masque at James I's court in a manner which explains why Elizabeth once referred to him as 'that witty fellow, my godson':

> Now did appear, in rich dress, Hope, Faith, and Charity: Hope did essay to speak, but wine rendered her endeavours so feeble that she withdrew and hoped the king would excuse her brevity. Faith was then all alone, for I am certain she was not joined with good works, and left the court in a staggering condition. Charity came to the king's feet and seemed to cover the multitude of sins her sisters had committed . . .

In this field, as in every other aspect of prose, the century witnessed a marvellous growth of ease, rhythm, vocabulary, and general skill; one of the finest tools of human thought, instruction, and amusement was thus fashioned by the English Renaissance.

In poetry, the revival and change are very marked, and the part played by Italian (and French) models is unquestioned. As the century opened, the traditions of Chaucer were well-nigh dead. When historians of literature have to fall back on the tedious and clumsy Alexander Barclay, whose *Ship of Fools* (1509) imported from Germany a fashion in heavy-handed satire, English poetry was in a parlous state. Nor can much more be said for John Skelton (1460?-1529), not the last poet-laureate hardly to deserve the first part of his title, though his idiosyncratic doggerel breathed vigour, a crude humour, and—especially in his attacks on Wolsey (*Speke, Parrot* and *Why Come Ye Nat to Courte?*, 1522-3)—a genuine savagery. As he said himself:

> For though my rhyme be ragged,
> Tattered and jagged,
> Rudely rain-beaten,
> Rusty and moth-eaten,
> It hath in it some pith.

But the man who could think of commending a lady with the pedestrian lines

> How shall I report
> All the goodly sort
> Of her features clear
> That hath none earthly peer?

or another with these words—

> By St Mary, Lady,
> Your mammy and your daddy
> Brought forth a goodly babby,

was a very long way from true poetry. A revival was certainly called for.

It came late in Henry VIII's reign with two poets who formed the mainstay of a collection known as *Tottel's Miscellany* (1557)— Sir Thomas Wyatt (1503-42) and Henry Howard, earl of Surrey (1517-47). Their fame once rested on the fact that they introduced the sonnet into England, thereby both giving a new strictness and form to the sprawling genius of English poetry and laying the foundations for that mass of sonnet-cycles later in the century with which we must bear because to that fashion we owe Shake-speare's sonnets. If they had done nothing else the old view which ranked Surrey higher would have been justified: Wyatt's sonnets are clumsy, with an often atrocious misuse of English rhythm (once he scans harbour as an iambus, for instance), and altogether less accomplished. But Wyatt was the greater poet. Surrey's work —his conventional love lyric, his translations of Virgil and the Psalms—is meritorious, nice-sounding, unreal, and dull; Wyatt's lyrics are among the finest because they sprang from genuine feeling. The impressive thing about Wyatt is not his imitation of Petrarch—though he could produce a good sonnet like *The Hind* (his resignation of Anne Boleyn to the king, with the famous final couplet '*Noli me tangere* for Caesar's I am, and hard for to hold though I seem tame')—but his poetry in the English tradition, a tradition going back to the anonymous *Alison* (*c.* 1300). The man who could write

> And wilt thou leave me thus?
> Say nay, say nay, for shame!
> To save thee from the blame
> Of all my grief and grame.
> And wilt thou leave me thus?
> Say nay, say nay!

or

> What should I say,
> Since faith is dead
> And truth away
> From you is fled?
> Should I be led
> With doubleness?
> Nay, nay, mistress!

was a great poet in his own right. The themes and the atmosphere of Wyatt—the inconstancy of women, the corruption of courts and attractions of rural life, the vigorous melancholy—became poetic commonplaces and were worked to death; but with him they were real and personal.

Much of Wyatt's best work owed, to all appearance, nothing to foreign example; he was 'in the tradition'. So were all the great poets of the age. What is one to make of Sir Walter Raleigh, beyond doubt one of the most learned of men, deeply read in all Europe could offer, and the author of one of the best of Eliza-bethan sonnets ('Methought I saw the grave where Laura lay'), who could yet write that haunting ballad-type poem *Walsinghame?*

> As you came from the holy land
> Of Walsinghame,
> Met you not with my true love
> By the way as you came?
>
> How shall I know your true love,
> That have met many one
> As I went to the holy land,
> That have come, that have gone?
>
> . . . . .
>
> But love is a durable fire
> In the mind ever burning;
> Never sick, never old, never dead,
> From itself never turning.

It may be, as we are told, that he was here allegorically lamenting his lost court favour (though who can see it and what does it matter?) but in any case the mood and manner are the real thing, and the echoes are of folksong and Walter de la Mare! The 'Renaissance' did not produce an entirely new poetry, but gave to native genius new competence in expression, new vigour of thought, new metres (very important, this), a new language, and up to a point new subjects. There is no question of an Italianate poetry, but an invigorating stream came from the south. No rational explanation can fully account for the wonderful outburst of poetry that ensued after Wyatt and Surrey and has lasted, with interruptions, to the present day. But though one cannot explain, the fact of a rebirth is patent.

The impetus given by the authors printed by Tottel soon spent itself among the products of minor poets like Barnaby Googe (1540-94) and George Turberville (1540-1610). The best of that generation was Thomas Sackville, later Lord Buckhurst and earl of Dorset (1536-1608), who when he was about twenty wrote the very fine introduction to the *Mirror of Magistrates* and then abandoned poetry for politics and administration. He sounded a new note which was to find many to repeat it, a note of didactic solemnity expressed in sound metre and worthy language, the note (if one may say so) of Augustan poetry. Lines like these seem to find their nearest echo in Gray's *Elegy:*

> Here puled the babes, and here the maids unwed
> With folded hands their sorry chance bewailed,

Here wept the guiltless slain, and lovers dead
That slew themselves when nothing else availed;
A thousand sorts of sorrow here that wailed
 With sighs and tears, sobs, shrieks, and all yfere
 That oh, alas, it was a hell to hear.[1]

But despite Wyatt, Surrey, and Sackville, English poetry was once
again settling into a rut of imitation when the mould was burst
and made anew with the appearance of Spenser's *The Shepherd's
Calendar* (1579), Sidney's *Defence of Poesy* (1582-3), and Sidney's
sonnet-sequence *Astrophel and Stella* (1584, published 1591).

The place of Sir Philip Sidney (1554-86) and Edmund Spenser
(1552?-99) is assured, but the present writer finds it rather difficult
to do justice to them. Sidney's critical work—the first really fruitful
piece of literary criticism in the language—contains such misconceptions
as an attack on rhyme and an insistence on the classical
unities in drama; it is one of the best known ironies in English literature
that the great age of Elizabethan poetry which followed
immediately upon the book's publication triumphed by neglecting
most of its advice. But by taking poetry seriously and really thinking
about it Sidney did good work, and he saved it from such
futilities as the ideas of the Cambridge pedant Gabriel Harvey
who wanted to introduce the hexameter into English and nearly
stopped Spenser from writing his genuine poetry because it was
not classical in cast.[2]

Spenser's output consists in the main of *The Shepherd's Calendar*
(1579), a set of twelve eclogues or pastoral poems; the *Faerie
Queene* (1589 and 1596), a long allegorical poem written in the
'Spenserian' nine-line stanza; the satires *Mother Hubberd's Tale*
and *Colin Clout Come Home Again* (1595) in which he attacked
his enemies at court and the present state of poetry; and the
lyrical poetry of the *Amoretti, Epithalamion*, and *Prothalamion*
(1595-6). All his work is suffused by a high poetic spirit and displays
intense imagery and a superb mastery of words; the *Faerie
Queene* is in many ways the most highly charged of all English
poems, and it was this quality that prompted Keats to describe
Spenser as 'the poet's poet'. But even his greatest poem, rich and

[1] 'Yfere' means together. The last two lines are well outside Gray's
grasp.
[2] How wrong even sensible men could be when they followed the
classical fashion is shown by Roger Ascham's praise for the appalling
hexameters of Thomas Watson's translation of the *Odyssey*, beginning:

 All travellers do gladly report great praise of Ulysses,
 For that he knew many men's manners and saw many cities.

splendid as it is, is marred by a failure in purpose. Spenser himself intended it as a manual for the training of gentlemen, and his allegories are so badly mixed that at times it is hard to see whether his meaning is moral and didactic, or political and in praise of Gloriana, or both, or neither. Spenser also lacked humour—that is, he is usually elevated and invariably over-solemn—and was the first to try the invention of a poetic language based on archaisms, but all these faults are as nothing when he is at his best, as in the rapt and inspired lyric of his marriage poems. All his work, too long to quote, loses by extraction, but one may cite the refrain from *Prothalamion*—

> Against the bridal day, which is not long:
> Sweet Thames, run softly, till I end my song—

or a few lines from *Epithalamion:*

> Ah! my dear love, why do ye sleep thus long,
> When meeter were that you should now awake,
> T' await the coming of your joyous make
> And hearken to the bird's love-learned song,
> The dewy leaves among?

Sidney could not aspire to the same height of poetic passion, but he wrote much fine lyric verse, and his sonnets, influenced by Petrarch and Ronsard, provoked a flood of imitators. The 1590s are the years of the sonneteers, one and all copying the conceit of a mistress (nearly always imaginary) whose fickle love must be wooed though fulfilment is out of the question. Sidney's *Stella* found successors in Henry Constable's *Diana*, Samuel Daniel's *Delia*, Fulke Greville's *Caelica*, Thomas Lodge's *Phyllis*, Michael Drayton's Unknown of the *Ideas' Mirror*, and many others. Spenser wrote the *Amoretti* to his future wife; above all Shakespeare produced the 154 poems of the greatest sonnet cycle ever written. The value of this mass of poetry varied enormously. At their not uncommon worst, the sonneteers wrote mechanical stuff, full of conventional attitudes and unfelt borrowings. At their best they reached the heights of 'Farewell, thou art too dear for my possessing', 'When to the sessions of sweet silent thought', 'When I have seen by Time's fell hand defaced', 'Let me not to the marriage of true minds', and all the other masterpieces of concentrated thought and poetical perfection with which Shakespeare honoured the sonneteering fashion. Only one other is commonly thought worthy to rank with these—Drayton's 'Since there's no help, come let us kiss and part'.

Elizabethan poetry was not confined to sonnets, and this section may close with a brief consideration of two styles—the long narrative poem and the true song. Of the former Michael Drayton's (1563-1631) are the representative examples. In a long life, Drayton —with all his versatility—always adhered to the spirit of the late Elizabethan age and showed no sign of the revolution wrought by John Donne whom (though he started to write in the 1590s) we must here exclude, since he is essentially Jacobean and a man must make an end (to quote a much more recent poet). Drayton's long patriotic poem-chronicles—*The Barons' Wars, The Legend of Great Cromwell, Poly-Olbion*—contain some fine passages but also a terrible amount of sheer dross: versified prose which would have been more suitable, because more pithy and painless, if left in prose. At his best, however, as in the celebrated *Agincourt*, he produced a combination of noble thought and vigorous language which raised the patriotic poem to some height:

> Fair stood the wind for France
> As we our sails advance
> Nor now to prove our chance
>   Longer to tarry;
> But, putting to the main,
> At Caux, the mouth of Seine,
> With all his martial train,
>   Landed King Harry.

(Even here, the sixth line, though justified in the story, reminds one of Wordsworthian bathos.)

As for the songs, they were truly legion, and no bare idea even can be given of them. All the poets of the day wrote verse which was clearly meant to be sung and in many cases was published with music. Of the song-books, the most famous is *England's Helicon* (1600), containing contributions by Sidney, Spenser, Drayton, Greene, Lodge, Nicholas Breton, George Peele, Shakespeare, Sir Edward Dyer, Raleigh, Marlowe, and many others. Once again the secular lyric reached its height in Shakespeare's incidental songs in his plays:

> Under the greenwood tree
> Who loves to lie with me
> And turn his merry note
> Unto the sweet bird's throat,

Come hither, come hither, come hither!
  Here shall he see
  No enemy
But winter and rough weather.

Or, in another typical mood:

Come away, come away, death,
And in sad cypress let me be laid;
Fly away, fly away, breath;
I am slain by a fair cruel maid.
My shroud of white, stuck all with yew
  O prepare it!
My part of death, no one so true
  Did share it.

Technically, the interest of the songs lies in their extraordinary
variety and ingenuity of metre, in their vitality and sincerity, in a
tunefulness which almost never declines into mere prettiness, and
in the sheer verbal beauty of even the tritest. Apart from those
already mentioned, one name stands out—Thomas Campion, who
wrote both words and music for many lovely songs, lovely despite
his own preposterous objection to rhyme:

Rose-cheeked Laura, come;
Sing thou smoothly with thy beauty's
Silent music, either other
  Sweetly gracing.

On the other hand, the age produced little religious lyric, a form
which the next century was to bring to perfection. The only poet
always quoted in this context is the catholic martyr Robert South-
well (1561-95) whose work certainly shines with genuine ardour
but lacks the technical accomplishment of the secular poetry. He
seems to have escaped the influence of the great change made by
Sidney and Spenser, and his rather plain, sometimes awkward,
diction endows even the much-praised *Burning Babe* with a certain
pedestrian quality which is very different from the simplicity of
great poetry.

One could go on for ever. From about 1580 onwards, poet after
poet contributed work of imperishable beauty to this great age of
English poetry. It culminates in Shakespeare: no one else even
approaches his concentrated thought, his consistent beauty of
language, and especially his ability to use concrete imagery so as to

render real the passions and ideas which in others too often seem insincere because they are cast in conventional phrases. But if they were not all men of supreme genius, they all assisted in this rebirth of a literature.

Much the same is true of drama, except that here the achievement is even more astounding. There have been other ages of great lyric poetry, but—even including Periclean Athens?—never anything like the thirty years which produced the work of Marlowe, Shakespeare, Jonson, Dekker, Webster, and their lesser contemporaries. Moreover, while there was a real English tradition of poetry, however moribund, it is hard to discover anything in pre-Tudor times that deserves to rank as the ancestor of Tudor drama. The miracle plays and moralities (allegorical dialogues) of the middle ages, the mummings and disguisings that accompanied popular festivals, no doubt provided a certain tradition of acting and the staging of spectacles, but they are a very long way indeed from true drama. The early Tudor plays, such as they were, still were very close to these beginnings. In the main they are associated with a group centring on Thomas More's household: More himself, as a young man, seems to have had a fondness for acting and may even have composed a comedy. But these 'interludes'—like John Rastell's *Interlude of the Four Elements* (1519)—are little more than dramatic discussions in which personified abstractions —Vice and Virtue, Nature and Humanity, Experience and Ignorance—exchange views on given topics. John Heywood (1497-*c*. 1580) injected into this tedious art form some skilful writing and much really funny humour, in his *Play of the Weather*, *Play of Love*, *Witty and Witless*, and especially *The Four PP*, a discussion between a palmer, a pardoner, a potecary, and a pedlar. These plays are much closer to the literary dialogue exemplified in the *Discourse of the Common Weal* (1549), in which a knight, a merchant, a husbandman, and a doctor debate the state of the realm, than to true drama.

The inspiration which turned this somewhat barren tradition to new uses came from the classical past. Humanistic teaching stressed the practice of Latin speech, and several enlightened schoolmasters saw that the result could best be obtained by the acting of plays. Thus Mulcaster had his boys act even at court, and Udall himself wrote the first English comedy constructed on a classical pattern—*Ralph Roister Doister*, not uninfluenced by Plautus' *Miles Gloriosus*. Latin plays were specially written for performance at the universities, and the queen's visits to Cambridge

(1564) and Oxford (1566) stimulated eager activity on those lines. Cambridge can claim the first important rustic comedy, *Gammer Gurton's Needle* (*c.* 1560), which has the honour of having invented the traditional Mummerset speech of the English stage. At the Inns of Court, too, play-acting grew very popular after the middle of the century. Here the influence of Seneca's plays, marked in Sidney's *Defence of Poesy*, was paramount. The plays were full of dumb-shows and other effects borrowed from Italy; the two productions that deserve mention were *Supposes* (1566), a prose comedy adapted from Ariosto's *Gli Suppositi* by the prolific George Gascoigne, and the first blank-verse tragedy in English, *Gorboduc* (1561), a sanguinary chronicle from British prehistory. In this play two lawyers more familiar in other fields collaborated —Thomas Sackville and Thomas Norton; it causes no surprise to find that *Gorboduc* ends with a veiled but impassioned plea to the queen not to let the succession go unsettled!

But still true drama was to seek, and only developments after 1575 were to make it possible. Two lines must be followed: the growth of the court play and the development of the public stage. The first was mainly in the hands of John Lyly, whose Euphuistic novels had, in their dialogue, given promise of much dramatic ability. When he turned to comedy, Lyly produced a series of plays adapted to a fairly sophisticated taste in which he used a flexible prose. *Campaspe* (1584) is the best of a cycle based on classical mythology and history: it is the story of the rivalry for a captive girl's love between Alexander the Great and the painter Apelles. (The painter won.) The court grew very fond of plays; the office of revels developed into a theatrical company, and the lord chamberlain began his association with stage-licensing and censorship. Outside the court the movement was even more vigorous, with the growth of several companies of actors under noble patrons and the building of theatres. The earls of Leicester and Pembroke, the lord chamberlain and lord admiral, and others lent their names to famous players' companies. In 1576, James Burbage, father of the great actor Richard Burbage, built the *Theatre* in Shoreditch; the *Curtain* followed. Later the actors escaped the hostility of the City by crossing over to Bankside; there they erected the *Rose* (1587), the *Swan* (1594), and the *Globe* (1598). Conditions were ripening for the outburst of genuine dramatic writing. The theatres, players, and public existed; noble and even royal patronage smiled on the play; the example of ancient Romans and modern Italians had transformed the interlude.

The first man to take advantage of these conditions was Thomas Kyd (1558-95?) whose *Spanish Tragedy* (*c.* 1585) initiated a series of 'revenge' plays of which *Hamlet* was to be the acme. Kyd excelled in stagecraft and the construction of plots but lacked any vestige of poetry. The vogue caught on, and for several years plays turned on nothing but sudden death and the accumulation of corpses. When old stories of cruel wrongs and savage revenge gave out, one could use the stories of more recent murders, as in the anonymous *Arden of Feversham* (1592) and *A Warning to Fair Women* (1599). But more plentiful blood-letting mixed with the comforting moral was to be found in history: hence the chronicle play, so popular in the 1590s. Plays appeared on King John, on Henry V, on King Leir (as it is spelled there), all of which provided material for Shakespeare. The chronicle play could find material in recent history, as in *Thomas Lord Cromwell*, a straightforward 'dramatisation of the book' (Foxe's *Martyrs*), or the better-constructed *Sir Thomas More*. An entirely different element was added to these rather obvious examples of popular taste by the work of Christopher Marlowe (1564-93), the first great English poet to write for the stage. Like Kyd, Marlowe was a man of education who applied the teaching of the schools to dramatic work; unlike Kyd, he was weak on plot but strong on verse. The four great plays—*Tamburlaine the Great* (1590), *The Jew of Malta* (1589-90), *Edward II* (1591?), and *The Tragical History of Doctor Faustus* (1592)—are full of weaknesses in the story, absurd inconsistencies in character, and inadequate psychology; but they also contain the finest poetic writing of any English plays, outside Shakespeare. Marlowe took the halting blank-verse of his predecessors and gave it grandeur and fervent colour, now savage and now tender. But despite good opinion which reckons that his early death may have cut short the growth of one as great as Shakespeare, one may venture to suggest that Marlowe's verse is the weapon of the rhapsodist rather than the dramatist.

One other group must be mentioned—the so-called university wits. These men—especially Robert Greene, George Peele, and Thomas Nash—all came to London from Cambridge; they wrote plays (as well as other things) which are distinguished by a certain graceful ease, much wit, and experimentation with material; but they did not write very good drama and clearly belong to the second rank. Greene's well-known jealous remarks about Shakespeare illustrates the rivalry between the professionals of the London stage and these university wits, but neither his *Friar Bacon and Friar Bungay* (influenced by Marlowe's *Faustus*), nor

Peele's charming *Arraignment of Paris* and lively *Old Wives' Tale*, are major achievements.

Out of all this, and yet out of nowhere, came the genius of William Shakespeare, inexplicable but in no need of explanation. As he excelled his fellow sonneteers, as he wrote more consistently perfect songs than anyone else, so he stood high above all other playwrights. Of Shakespeare as of the *Authorised Version*, an amateur of literature cannot speak without simply repeating the encomium of ages, nor is there any need to discuss him at length when there are so many good books on him—and when he has written a better than any of these. The cycle of thirty-seven plays contains much hack-work, a good deal that is tedious or stop-gap or ranting, but all in all it represents the greatest achievement of both the poetic and the dramatic spirit in human history. Shakespeare surpassed all his contemporaries at their own specialities: his plots are much better constructed than Kyd's, his humour is profounder and funnier than Greene's, he was a much greater poet than Marlowe. In addition, he had what can only be described as the Shakespearian quality—a universality, embracing and understanding all men, mixed with a wonderful gift for the creation of character and a language so unique that in any collection of blank verse it stands out unmistakably. What he did with and to blank verse is nothing less than a miracle. He found it a rather stiff but impressive medium for dramatic verse; he left it so thoroughly exploited that after him no one could ever use it again in any form without danger of losing part of his individuality, a danger which perhaps only Milton overcame. The ending of *King John* is good enough verse and would have made the fortune of any other Elizabethan dramatist:

> This England never did nor never shall
> Lie at the proud foot of a conqueror
> But when it first did help to wound itself.
> Now these her princes are come home again,
> Come the three corners of the world in arms
> And we shall shock them. Nought shall make us rue
> If England to itself do rest but true.

But, with its regular beat, so deadening in the long run, this is lacklustre dullness by the side of Shakespeare's mature work—for instance the spiritual and poetic excitement of Lear's death:

> And my poor fool is hang'd! No, no, no life!
> Why should a dog, a horse, a rat, have life

And thou no breath at all? Thou'lt come no more,
Never, never, never, never, never!
Pray you, undo this button: thank you, sir.
Do you see this? Look on her, look, her lips,
Look there, look there!

Of all poets Shakespeare at his peak was the most sovereign, using his weapons at will and never at the mercy of his material in matter or manner. And of all poetic dramatists he was the only one in whom poetry and drama met in perfect marriage.

Shakespeare must be read or seen, and not talked about. He marks the height not only of Elizabethan drama but of all drama, and in a way he fittingly closes this chapter. But there were others who must not be omitted, though—like Shakespeare—they did their best work after 1603. Ben Jonson (1573-1637), more learned but less miraculous than Shakespeare, in his Elizabethan days almost revived the allegorical tradition with such plays as *Every Man in his Humour* (1598) and *Every Man out of his Humour* (1599), the 'humours' of traditional medicine standing for the embodied qualities of men. He did better work later in his satires (for instance *Volpone* and *The Alchemist*) and the realistic *Bartholomew Fair*. Thomas Dekker's (1570?-1641) *Shoemaker's Holiday* comes from the same stable. The rest—George Chapman, John Webster, Cyril Tourneur, Francis Beaumont and John Fletcher—are more completely Jacobean, and if that division is arbitrary it must still be obeyed here. The English Renaissance produced much magnificent poetry and many excellent plays. Even without Shakespeare it would have been an age of greatness; with him and because of him it moves into the realm of timeless magnificence, to be judged not by the standards of its own conventions but by the eternal criteria.

Chapter XVI

THE LAST YEARS

THE year 1588 has long been recognised as at most a stage in the military history of Elizabeth's reign, but in domestic events it continues to be thought of as a date of great significance. The view expressed by A. F. Pollard some forty years ago still holds the field: 'It opened a new chapter in the political and constitutional history of England. . . . The Tudor period is dissolving into the Stuart.' The dominant personalities passed from the stage—Leicester died in 1588, Walsingham in 1590, Burghley, a shadow of his old self, in 1598. The queen herself showed signs of her age, and in the end signs of the coming dissolution. The new men did not approach the stature of their predecessors. Robert Cecil may have matched his father in political skill and managerial dexterity, but he lacked both his profound sagacity and his unselfish honesty. The rest of the council were second-rate men. The great sea-dogs found only lesser epigones. Raleigh, who might have bridged the gap between the generations, was unpopular with the people who believed him to be an atheist and sorcerer; worse, he lost the queen's favour in 1592 when he was discovered to have seduced, and subsequently to have secretly married, one of her ladies-in-waiting—it is not clear which act Elizabeth thought the more heinous. As for Essex, he defies definition and stands apart. In the Church, Whitgift's stern Calvinism was growing old-fashioned before the sophisticated High Church tendencies of Lancelot Andrewes and Bancroft. What looked like a new spirit of restlessness and defiance appeared in parliament: control of the commons became more difficult, the government—and even the queen—were openly contemned, attacks were made on the prerogative. In 1604 the house told James I that they had held their fire before Elizabeth's death 'in regard to her sex and age which we had great cause to tender', and in expectation of 'freer times' under her successor. All this seems to support the view that the end of national danger in 1588 released the realm from the fears which alone had made it acquiesce in Tudor autocracy.

But this is not so. The Elizabethans did not realise that all danger had passed in 1588, any more than they could have thought of their period as 'dissolving into the Stuart'. While it is true enough that one must beware of marking too deep a break in 1603, it is wrong to treat the last years of Elizabeth as a kind of anticipation of what was to come; one must look at them for their own sake and not allow after-knowledge to exert its misleading fascination. The 1590s differed from earlier decades for perfectly plain and valid reasons. There was a war going on, demanding an unprecedented and crippling outlay of money. After the prosperous trading years of 1575-90, England now experienced a period of economic difficulties only very partially accounted for by the activities of pirates. The harvests of 1592-6 were very bad: such a run of disastrously wet summers had not occurred in living memory. Famine, or near-famine, brought with it a sudden rise in prices as well as the return of plague which had mercifully left England alone for most of the reign. War, plague, and economic distress produced social and administrative difficulties. The standing problem of vagrancy was aggravated by the bands of sick, wounded, discharged, and deserting soldiers, so that comprehensive legislation became necessary in 1597 and 1601. The needs of the national economy provoked, on the one hand, a more stringent application of controls which annoyed the gentry and the merchants, while on the other they showed up the inadequacies of Tudor government and led to complaints. It all boiled up in parliament—because parliament was the proper arena for the airing of grievances, and because the demands of war finance prevented Elizabeth from following her earlier policy of calling as few parliaments as possible. Even so, all except the last parliament were really less determined in their opposition than those of the 1560s had been, and the issues were really less fundamentally constitutional. Among those who departed the scene in these years was Peter Wentworth, and with him went the one man who could turn everything to constitutional profit.

More significant than the alleged foreshadowings of later troubles are the continuities with the past. Of course, as Elizabeth enters her sixties, as the familiar figures vanish, as men begin to think of the queen's successor, it is hard not to feel that an age is coming to an end. Yet except on the personal side, little was changing. The issues and problems of the reign—the Church and its adversaries, the constitutional questions, the voyages of exploration—dominated also these dying years of a great generation.

I. THE CHURCH'S ADVERSARIES

In the history of the Church of England, the 1590s were a time of consolidation and mounting triumph.[1] The internal enemy—puritanism—was subdued; the external enemy—catholicism—wasted its strength in private dissensions. The Marprelate attacks of 1589 succeeded only in rousing official anger to a pitch of grim determination and in alienating moderate opinion. Whitgift's work in the high commission has already been noted. The death of Field and Leicester in 1588 robbed the movement of its organiser and its leading patron. Cartwright survived, to know prison in 1590-2, to publish a last blast in his *Apology* of 1596, and to disappear into ineffectualness and semi-exile in Guernsey where he died in 1604. Even in parliament the puritan cause found fewer defenders and little support. In 1593 James Morrice, attorney of the court of wards and therefore a crown official, revived memories of Strickland and Cope by introducing two bills attacking ecclesiastical jurisdiction and especially the 'tyrannical' practices of the high commission. Although Sir Robert Cecil's reminder that Elizabeth would resent such an invasion of the prerogative met with little response, Speaker Coke was compelled to divulge the matter to the queen and bring back notice of her anger: he was charged, on his allegiance, to permit the reading of no bill concerning ecclesiastical causes. It seems that a command which in earlier days would have stung the puritan 'choir' into action moved no one in the house; Morrice underwent a spell in prison, and the last attempt by the Elizabethan commons to take the initiative about the Church fell by the wayside.

While the presbyterian movement thus entered upon a decline from which only Scottish support rescued it for a time during the civil war, the sectarian or separatist movements seemed to gain in strength. No one except themselves had any patience with these splinter groups: Cartwright was as opposed to them as was Bancroft, though he used rather less violent language and had no chance of emulating the bishop's violent deeds. The parliament that witnessed Morrice's failure also passed a vicious act against sectaries, though admittedly it toned it down from the even more devastating plans of the government. By this statute failure to conform was punished with imprisonment, to give the offender time to think it over; if he proved obstinate after three months he

[1] This fact, in such marked contrast with the troubles of the Church after 1603, is worth noting in connection with the theory that the period really anticipated Stuart times.

had to abjure the realm. Refusal to go into exile, or unlicensed return from it, meant death for felony. In the same year (1593) three leading sectaries suffered death—Henry Barrow and John Greenwood for seditious writings, and John Penry for treason. It may be that the executions were designed to create an impression. At any rate, the act did its work, and the London congregation which Barrow had organised moved to Amsterdam, as Browne's Norwich congregation had gone to Middelburgh some years earlier. Continuing to copy its predecessor, the group at Amsterdam soon fell prey to internal strife. But they were never dispersed entirely, nor did the survivors lose their fervour: it was from among them that the movement started which a generation later took the *Mayflower* to New England.

Thus puritanism in the Church, presbyterian and separatist, collapsed before the determined onslaught of the hierarchy, supported by the state. No one thought that it had been wiped out, and Bancroft came to hold that its hard core was irreconcilable and should be driven forth. However, while Elizabeth lived the theory at least of uniformity was preserved: she would have no two ecclesiastical bodies in one state. The government found it easier to adopt these energetic measures because they no longer required the aid of the zealots against the threat from Rome. The war with Spain not only confirmed the protestantism of the majority of Englishmen; it also discovered the patriotism of the catholic minority. To offset the attack on puritanism, another act of 1593 made a catholic's life truly unbearable: he was forbidden to move more than five miles from his residence, and inability to pay the heavy recusancy fines resulted in exile. Many catholics began to think of ways in which to convince the government of their essential loyalty and thus obtain relief. Even though Philip of Spain carried papal blessing, they had much difficulty in seeing in him God's chosen instrument. As early as 1590, a priest had publicly asked whether English catholics could lawfully defend the realm against Spain, and he had answered himself by saying that they could because Philip, being merely intent on his own ends, was no true defender of the faith. Not surprisingly, his doctrine met with no success at Rome, but it became clear that a split was developing. The moving spirit behind the Spanish attack were the Jesuits, especially Robert Parsons who had become Philip's adviser and propaganda expert on England. Between the Jesuits and the secular priests no love was lost, and when in 1594 Parsons published a pamphlet which, by pressing the claims of the Spanish Infanta before the Stuart claim to the English throne, seemed to confirm all the old suspicions of Habsburg ambition, the united front of English catholicism collapsed. The seculars rebelled against the Jesuits' ascendancy in the English college at Rome and among the imprisoned priests at Wisbech in Norfolk, and feelings ran very high.

In this unhappy situation the death of Cardinal Allen (1594) produced all the difficulties of a disputed succession. The pope had to appoint someone to rule the English catholic community: whom would he choose? Jesuit influence was so high at Rome that the outcome need not surprise, though it also displayed the Roman proclivity for compromise. The pope refused the seculars' request for a bishop elected from among their ranks, but appointed as archpriest one George Blackwell who was himself a secular, but a secular with a difference. He had pronounced leanings to the Jesuit ideal and the Jesuit habit of autocracy; to cap it all, he was instructed to follow the Jesuit lead. For six years the conflict raged as the seculars refused to accept the archpriest's authority. In the end, after many appeals, the court of Rome confirmed its original decision and left the secular clergy at the mercy of Jesuits and Spaniards, unless they could make their peace with the queen. The ensuing negotiations showed that the government, too, were far from united on the issue. Bancroft, for ecclesiastical reasons, and Cecil, on political grounds, hoped to bring about the submission of the catholics, but these would only agree to swear loyalty if freedom of worship were granted. Bancroft would have consented, but Elizabeth, mindful of the reaction this would have produced among the people, refused. Her attitude may have been intolerant, but how wise and necessary it was appears plainly enough from the unhappy history of James I and Charles I whose gentle treatment of catholicism did more than any other single thing to bring them into odium with their own subjects. No one at this time could afford to tolerate Rome in England without arousing suspicions of treason; Bancroft's attitude—he practised secret and unlawful toleration—shows how far the 'high' movement in the Church had gone thirty years before the heyday of William Laud.

The queen's statesmanlike obstinacy seemed to end the chance of splitting the catholic ranks by exploiting the archpriest controversy, but in fact it secured such a split without surrendering to catholic demands and by a typically Elizabethan manœuvre. In November 1602 a proclamation ordered all priests out of the country but permitted seculars to stay if they swore allegiance to the crown. Thirteen of them did, much to the government's satisfaction; they thus advertised the divisions within the catholic Church in England, branded the Jesuits as supporters of Spain rather than religion, and destroyed two legends—Spain's pose as a crusading power, and the idea that English catholics were waiting to welcome her armadas. Elizabeth did not survive this submission for long, but the signs were clear. Catholicism was rendered innocuous, even as puritanism had been driven out of the Church. What neither she nor the two parties could foresee was that the next dynasty would fall over backwards in trying to make up to catholicism for what it had suffered under Queen Elizabeth, thus provoking a vast revival of puritanism and making anti-popery the only sure-fire cry in a century of political strife.

2. THE CONSTITUTIONAL QUESTION AGAIN

The queen's difficulties with her parliaments also continued, though the older problems caused little stir at this time. As has been seen, Morrice's bills of 1593 were the only positive reminder of the old puritan tactics in parliament. Free speech did not again become an issue, but this was because its champion, Peter Wentworth, had discovered another outlet for his furious energies. He picked on the question of the succession, decently interred for some twenty years, but now—he thought—urgent again because the queen was growing old. Wentworth did not stand alone in thinking about the succession—it would be fair to say that few politicians thought of much else as the 1590s drew on—but only he dreamt of bringing it up in parliament. As early as 1587 he became convinced that unless the queen agreed to settle the succession on safely protestant lines, the danger of a catholic claimant would grow potent. He composed his *Pithy Exhortation to her Majesty for Establishing the Succession* in which, with his usual freedom of language, he urged the queen to regard the country's interest. Only an unaccustomed touch of caution, or failure to find a printer fool enough, prevented him from publishing the pamphlet. In 1591 his agitation got him into trouble with the council who rewarded his zeal with six months in prison. Baulked out of parliament, Wentworth returned to his proper sphere of action in 1593. But he discovered that his day was past. With much energy and ingenuity he did his best to organise a campaign on the succession issue; yet even Morrice, himself ready to brave the queen's anger on other matters, tried to dissuade him. Nearly thirty years had passed since Norton and his fellows had fought tooth and nail on this issue; if anything, the queen's age made

Wentworth's agitation more reasonable than theirs had been. But no cock crew. His scheming outside parliament during the session constituted a constitutional impropriety—faction making—and the outcome was his last imprisonment in the Tower. There he survived until 1597, undauntedly refusing to give the promise to cease his agitation which would have released him and still writing on the state. Seventy-three years old he died, undefeated and unvictorious, a crotchety nuisance but also a martryr in a cause which a subsequent generation was to understand better. His violence and rigidity had deprived him of real influence in parliament; not only privy councillors thought him a needless complication. But he had raised the issue of free speech to the high pinnacle of principle which it deserved; he had begun the deliberate organisation of opposition; and he had lived and died for his beliefs in a manner which makes him a fit forerunner of the seventeenth-century parliamentarians.

The real problem of the 1590s was money. War expenditure demanded a constant and unusually heavy burden of taxation.[1] In practice only the demands of 1593 roused serious opposition: the war was too obvious an emergency and too obviously expensive to make the levies anything but reasonable. But out of this problem of taxation and finance grew two serious constitutional quarrels which reflected the commons' self-confidence and the dangers inherent in the unsettled relations between the three parts of parliament. These quarrels were a conflict between the commons and the lords in 1593, and an attack on the prerogative in finance and the making of grants in 1597 and 1601.

In the parliament of 1593, the commons made heavy weather over the granting of supply, largely because they had granted unusually large subsidies four years earlier and were not yet used to the persistence of such needs in the long war. In the end they offered two subsidies, as in 1589. However, this seemed insufficient to the government who tried to use their unquestioned control of the lords to extract more. The upper house therefore asked for a conference at which Burghley, explaining some details of expenditure, declared that the lords would insist on giving three subsidies. This occasioned a vigorous debate on the question of privilege. Francis Bacon, in whom throughout this session the lawyer and statesman triumphed over the ambitious politician (partly at least because in attacking the subsidy he was attacking the Cecil interest), pointed out that the commons alone had the right to decide on the amount to be granted: the lords were to be warned

[1] For the details of the subsidies see above, p. 363.

off. It was therefore suggested that the commons should protect their privilege by themselves offering the three subsidies deemed necessary by Burghley. The ensuing debate was distinguished by the number of eminent men who took part in it and by the expression of bewilderingly diverse views on the country's ability to pay. In a speech which cost him the royal favour for six years, Bacon asserted that if the proposal went through the gentlemen would have to sell their plate and the farmers their brass pots; some others seemed to think that the country had never been so rich; others again suggested new, ingenious, and largely impracticable methods of taxation. In the end the grant passed—three subsidies to be paid within three years—but in this serious clash between the houses—the first in the century—the commons had successfully protected their right to initiate all money bills.

The attack on the prerogative, culminating in the very stormy session of 1601, arose out of the question of monopolies. Of course, the prerogative had been involved in all those debates about the Church, the succession, and the control of policy which had disturbed earlier parliaments; but it was only when its financial effects came under review that it succeeded in creating something like a unitedly resistant house of commons. One of the undoubted powers of the crown was to make grants for the regulation of trade, a power which in this period took the form of establishing monopoly rights by letters patent. The rights differed in kind. A man might be licensed to perform certain things notwithstanding (*non obstante*) statutory provisions to the contrary: thus he might be permitted to export goods otherwise forbidden or to evade the laws regulating the manufacture of cloth or leather. He might hold a grant entitling him to sell licences to others: in 1588 Raleigh obtained the privilege of licensing all taverns for thirty years. Or he might be permitted a monopoly in the manufacture and sale of certain articles, such as salt and sugar, or in the import of others—as Raleigh's famous monopoly of playing-cards.[1] Some of these monopolies did only the work of the modern patent laws— that is, they protected a legitimate interest in new inventions. But most of them were noxious. Those of the *non obstante* type raised the issue of the crown's control of legislation: could the prerogative

---

[1] Though he blushed for it on one occasion, Raleigh rather specialised in monopolies. A contemporary lampoon alleged that

'He seeks taxes in the tin,
He polls the poor to the skin,
Yet he swears 'tis no sin;
Lord for thy pity!'

dispense with a law at pleasure? In practice, Tudor statesmen employed the licensing system both to maintain control of economic life and to extract money, and when not carried to excess some such flexibility was essential if the rigid regulations were not to be disastrous or stultified. Worst, however, were the monopolies of the last kind. Granted as favours to courtiers and for payment to syndicates of capitalists, they were widely exploited at the expense of the public by raising prices. Their enforcement caused the greatest annoyance. The monopolist was commonly authorised to protect himself against interlopers by wide powers of search and punishment, and the resultant arrogant dealings and invasions of privacy led to much trouble. The queen liked monopolies because they enabled her to reward services and show favour at little cost to herself; more farseeing men like Burghley had often objected to them. In the depression of the 1590s they became a serious grievance, made especially intolerable because there was no redress in the courts.

Discussions started in the parliament of 1597 when it was proposed to petition the queen to abolish burdensome monopolies. Elizabeth, as usual, made a fair answer but had no intention of doing anything. This time that policy did not pay. Within four years she had to face another parliament. It opened with an inauspicious muddle: the better part of the commons, arriving at the parliament chamber for the opening of the session, found the door accidentally locked against them. Thereafter nothing would go right. The session was marked by a constant undercurrent of touchiness, jealousy, and discontent. Few would say 'God save your majesty' when Elizabeth passed through their crowded ranks after the Speaker's installation; members' servants created much noise and disturbance around St Stephen's Chapel; the two houses bickered; debates were frequently interrupted as unpopular speakers endeavoured to make themselves heard above the laughing, hawking (clearing of throats), and spitting with which the Elizabethan commons liked to express their disapproval. The Speaker and the privy councillors could hardly preserve a modicum of order and entirely failed to keep control of the proceedings: the house seems to have grown a little tired of Sir Robert Cecil's guidance and was not to be appeased by his overworked favourite opening in which, time and again, he declared that he had not really meant to intervene at all. Up to a point the impression of special turbulence in this parliament may be due to the fuller information available about it; but there can be no doubt that it was a troublesome session.

Monopolies provided the issue, and they were more than merely a convenient pretext. Without the exasperation produced by their abuse and the queen's transparent evasions, there is little reason to suppose that this parliament would have been more of a nuisance than any other. It had no sooner met than the subject was revived; this time, several members introduced bills against monopolies one of which was only twelve lines long but allegedly sweeping. The commons were trying to legislate about the prerogative; all the makings of a pretty show-down were assembling. Bacon, explaining that the queen's prerogative enabled her 'to set at liberty things restrained by statute law and otherwise' and to 'restrain things which be at liberty', warned the house that it was putting itself in the wrong and advocated established practice: 'the use hath ever been to humble ourselves unto her majesty, and by petition desire to have our grievances remedied, especially when the remedy toucheth her so nigh in point of prerogative.' The fact that a year or so before he had at last succeeded in putting his great gifts at the service of the crown ought not to obscure the truth of his view. The debate turned less on the proposed bills—apart from a few extremists, the commons were not really yet ready to flout the prerogative—than on the evils of monopolies. One member recited a list of over twenty commodities, many of them in common use, which were involved; this provoked young William Hakewill (who was to make a forceful speech against the Stuart prerogative in 1610) into the only half facetious suggestion that bread would next be added unless the house took action. Cecil magisterially rebuked members for behaving in a manner 'more fit for a grammar-school than a court of parliament', but his only positive suggestion was to wait till the committee already appointed should report to the house.

At this point, after days of debate, Elizabeth realised the danger. However autocratic in manner she might be, she knew better than to stand obstinately on her prerogative and refuse redress for justified grievances. Her master-stroke in parliamentary management did all the commons wanted yet saved the prerogative from the bills before the house and herself from either risking a serious quarrel or appearing to act under pressure. She professed herself much surprised and angered that grants she had made should have proved oppressive to the people and declared her intention immediately to review the situation and abolish all bad monopolies. A proclamation to that effect appeared at once: many monopolies were withdrawn and others put under the law by permitting people who had grievances to sue against them in the courts. This gracious and skilfully timed surrender immediately changed the whole temper of the house. They had been behaving like wayward children rather than determined politicians: the queen's concession turned all to smiles and acclamation. On 30 November 1601 Elizabeth received a large deputation from the commons who came to express their thanks; she answered them in the most famous oration of her reign—her 'golden speech' in which, like Prospero, she took farewell of her arts.

> Though God hath raised me high, yet this I count the glory of my crown, that I have reigned with your loves. . . . I was never so much enticed with the glorious name of a king or royal authority of a queen, as delighted that God hath made me his instrument to maintain his truth and glory and to defend his kingdom from peril, dishonour, tyranny, and oppression. . . . Though you have had and may have many mightier and wiser princes sitting on this seat, yet you never had nor shall have any that will love you better. . . . And I pray you, Mr Comptroller, Mr Secretary, and you of my council, that before the gentlemen depart into their counties you bring them all to kiss my hand.

The humility of this speech has provoked scepticism, but its measured clarity contrasts so strongly with Elizabeth's usual style that, patently, she must have been sincere. On this occasion, the last on which she was to address her people, she recorded the proud faith and humble gratitude of a ruler who, with all her faults, had been as well and as deservedly loved and served as any in history. With equal pride and humility she could look back on the long years of her own devoted service to her people. As the commons passed by to kiss the old woman's hand, the strength and glory of the Tudor state stood visibly embodied.

The difficulties experienced with these last parliaments might suggest that something had gone wrong in the matter of management. There is certainly no sign that the government tried harder either to secure a pliable house of commons or to weaken the commons' independence of action. But that was not due to any failure on the part of Elizabeth's councillors: rather it expresses the truth that management was at all times just that and nothing equivalent to control. Difficulties, grievances, conflicts could not be avoided—no one thought they could—but only minimised, adjusted, or in the last resort given way to. Elizabethan elections were largely free; that is, they were influenced by local powers only, such as the great families in the shires or the patrons and municipal authorities in the boroughs. Occasionally, the council tried to obtain the election of nominees. An early example of this occurred in 1553 when Mary's council sent out a circular letter with nominations attached in the hope of getting a parliament which would reverse the Reformation. More commonly these council circulars merely asked that men fit for the place be elected, and the two Elizabethan letters which went further—one of 1584 asking for members well-affected to the queen, and one of 1586 suggesting the re-election of the last parliament's knights and burgesses—had little effect. No one at this time tried deliberately to create a government party, though members sitting for the few crown boroughs and the rather more numerous seats controlled by councillors and courtiers formed a reliable unofficial body of support for the privy councillors in the house who represented the queen and managed policy. The powers of the Speaker—always a government nominee—and the authority of the councillors, as well as natural awe of the queen, generally kept things in order in the commons themselves; but in a house growingly developed in its procedure[1] and growingly aware of its opportunities for opposition, nothing could be done to maintain a really safe ascendancy. This was so from the start of the reign; the last parliaments do not mark a new spirit of independence but rather a change of subject and at most a growing feeling that the younger generation ought to have its say. The Stuarts failed to cope with their parliaments because they were less skilful and less adaptable than Elizabeth, not because their problems were more insoluble, or because they were confronted by a new kind of commons of which the first signs might conceivably be looked for in the four parliaments after 1588.

3. MORE NAVIGATIONS

Though the war occupied most of the ships and seamen of England, some of them continued to go further afield. Of course, whether they sailed into American and Asian waters or hung around the islands of the Azores, they were often preying on the enemy; but the greater voyages really carried on from the exploits of Drake, Hawkins, Frobisher and their like before 1588, so that they deserve separate treatment here. The journeys of the 1590s followed the tracks already marked out. Now that war had broken out and the susceptibilities of Spain did not have to be regarded any longer, the dangerous and futile attempts to reach Asia by a

[1] The very interesting and important subject of parliamentary procedure is too detailed to be treated here. It may be read up in J. E. Neale's *Elizabethan House of Commons*, chs. XIV-XXI.

northern route were abandoned in favour of following Drake into the South Seas. Asia—the Spice Islands in particular—continued to be the real target, with two ways there available: some went westward, as Drake had done, while others began to find the Portuguese route round Africa more promising. There was also another project on the American mainland, again in the hands of Raleigh.

Of those who went westward, Thomas Cavendish proved at first the most successful: in 1586-8 he became the second Englishman to circumnavigate the globe. His exploit reads like a copy of Drake's, with the spectacular success left out. He crossed the Atlantic from Sierra Leone to Brazil, sailed down the coast to the Straits, and after a seven week's passage entered the Pacific. Despite the capture of one rich prize coming from Manila with silks and spices, his raiding along the west coast brought little profit. An easy crossing of the South Seas and a prosperous voyage home led him to underestimate the difficulties, and when he sailed again, in 1591, he took too little care. On this occasion he was joined by John Davis. From the first, lack of preparation had the expedition in trouble—short of victuals and full of unrest. Cavendish, who seems to have suffered from the ungovernable temper that distinguished so many Elizabethans, quarrelled with his officers, took refuge on Davis's ship, then returned to his own. In the face of violent winds they failed to make the passage of the Straits, after which the ships parted company because Cavendish had not provided for so obvious a danger. He re-appeared in Brazil, trying to gain treasure by fighting; but he had to draw off empty-handed and died, only thirty-two years old, on the return voyage. In the meantime Davis, hampered by a half-mutinous crew, tried to find his commander in and out of the Straits; in the course of these sailings he performed such incredible feats as taking the vessel safely at night through rock-infested waters which he had memorised on a single previous passage. But in the end he had to return with a ship soon populated by little more than ghosts. His was another of those dreadful voyages which wind, weather, the sea, and scurvy made so common before the eighteenth century.

There was one more attempt to attack the Pacific coast of Spain's empire. The news of Cavendish's failure had not reached England before, in 1593, another small fleet set out under Richard Hawkins, old Sir John's son. They made the Pacific all right but found the Spanish defence so thoroughly reorganised that that safe hunting-ground had become a graveyard. Chased by better-equipped vessels built to exploit the light winds of those latitudes, Hawkins and his men avoided capture once but were in the end defeated and taken. Hawkins, treated with respect, was sent to Spain and did not see England again until 1602, long after his father and Drake had died at sea in their last disastrous invasion of the Caribbean, which has already been described.

The high old times of plundering a defenceless Spanish empire in the west were clearly over: only a sizable and well-found fleet could now hope to make an impression on the forces which the viceroys of Peru and Mexico could send out, and at this time— with so much to do near at home—there was no prospect of one going all that way. A little more promising, though at the time equally beset by shipwreck and disaster, the eastern route attracted the merchants of London. In 1591 the Levant Company equipped a fleet of three ships one of which, under John Lancaster, reached the Malacca Straits after touching at Zanzibar. As sickness struck, his crew forced him to abandon his intention of cruising around on the look-out for spice ships, and another expedition returned very bedraggled and with nothing but loss to report. However, the Levant merchants could afford an occasional financial disaster. Driven on by hopes of emulating the Dutch who were then rapidly pushing their trade into India, the London capitalists kept up the good work. In 1600, after a few more profitless voyages, the East India Company received its charter and dispatched a trading fleet commanded by Lancaster and guided by Davis. With its departure a new era began in English expansion. Trade—peaceful trade— was at last ousting privateering, raiding, and plain piracy as the first preoccupation of sailors and navigators. The story of that further expansion belongs to the Stuart century and cannot here be followed up.

One last Elizabethan enterprise remains—Raleigh's attempt to establish an English base off the Spanish Main and discover the legendary gold mines of Eldorado. The presence of much gold and the absence of any gold mines in Peru had early raised the question of the real source of this precious metal, and by the late sixteenth century Spanish explorers had narrowed its supposed site down to the inaccessible mountains of Guiana, stretching between the basins of the Orinoco and the Amazon. Raleigh's imagination was fired by what he heard and read, and when in 1592 his disgrace left him with nothing else to do he devoted himself to the project. In 1595 he sailed for Trinidad where he established a base. The only way into the mountains seemed to be up a tributary of the Orinoco, but all these were barred by formidable waterfalls where they precipitately descended from the range to the river basin. After four weeks of far from reckless enterprise Raleigh gave up, disgusted with the heat and dirt and worn out by hardships which were slight by the standards of the Spanish explorers. He was nearly forty-five: his life at court had not equipped him for this work; and, as always with Raleigh, the last obstinacy was lacking. Although he sent another fleet a little later to investigate the Guiana coast itself for access to the interior, the whole project must be added to the many which Raleigh took up in his generous enthusiasm but failed to carry through. This is quite apart from the fact, of course, that the country of Eldorado, its magnificent city of Manoa, and its gold-mines amounted to a myth.

The 1590s thus marked a decline in real maritime enterprise after the glowing achievements of the previous thirty years. In part this was because so much money and energy concentrated on sea-warfare—whether the small privateering expeditions or the great attacks on Cadiz and the Azores—and in part because the heroes were going out and finding only successors of a lesser stamp. But the chief reason lay deeper. English mariners and merchants were only beginning to grasp that their real future lay not in the search for rapid enrichment—the capture of treasure ships, the plundering of gold-exporting shores—but in the ordinary pursuit of a trade whose horizons had grown enormously in those hundred years. And while they sought profit at the expense of Spain, they found Spain growing stronger. The defeat of the Armada and Philip's failure in the Netherlands had indeed heralded the decline of Spain, but the greatest empire of the day could still give a good account of itself in defence. In the last analysis the rather sombre note which hangs over the naval story of the 1590s describes only the difficulties encountered by a somewhat slapdash and over-confident attacker in the face of a resistance whose competence was novel and surprising.

4. THE TRAGEDY OF ESSEX

Before the violent century closed it witnessed yet another violent incident. There was in England one whose arrogant pride, assurance of high place, hold over Elizabeth's affections, and complete command of popular favour made him a standing danger to the state. Essex—'a nature not to be ruled'—could not live as anything but the first of men. He looked down upon Elizabeth as an old woman jealously frustrating his greatness; he ever thought that others—especially Cecil and Raleigh—were plotting against his fortunes; the just retribution of his follies he ascribed to their burrowings. In the end these feelings turned to a pathological hatred. The pity of it was that Essex had it in him to be a great man; he had vision, generosity, courage, and vigour—as well as charm. But he lacked in character and ability; rash, unstable, ungovernable, and not very clever, he dug his own grave with persistent skill. Any Tudor except Elizabeth would have had his head much sooner and saved much trouble; she hoped that discipline and temporary setbacks would make another man of him. But with him her sure touch deserted her. His meteoric rise to fame, favour, and fortune, and the plaudits of a sycophantic entourage, gave Essex such a conceit of himself that the queen's repeated attempts to tighten the reins only exacerbated his recklessness. There was a famous scene, soon after his return from the Islands voyage, when he discourteously turned his back on her: she boxed his ears and told him to go and be hanged, whereupon in a blind passion he half-drew his sword. Essex completely misjudged the old lady: he had yet to learn that she was a statesman and a queen before she was a woman.

After Essex's unauthorised and mud-bespattered return from Ireland in September 1599 things took their fatal course. He was committed to the keeping of Sir Thomas Egerton; for six months he was closely imprisoned and for another six in easier confinement, before he regained a measure of liberty. All this time the evidence of his popularity accumulated. London was crowded with officers who had deserted from the Irish army to follow their leader—a dangerous crew, desperate for profit and advancement, absolutely reckless as to means. The people, especially of London, shouted for the earl and poured scorn on his rivals. Impecunious gentlemen, kept out of office and favour by the ascendancy of the Cecil faction (or so they thought)[1], rallied round Essex. The earl himself does not appear to have done any party-building at this time; eating his heart out in prison, full of the festering self-pity which brought on the last fatal outburst, he devoted his thoughts to his own fate and as far as he plotted plotted ineptly. Elizabeth wanted to bring him to public trial in the star chamber; very sensitive to his popular appeal which rivalled her own, she hoped

---

[1] After six years of power without office, Sir Robert Cecil was appointed to the vacant secretaryship in 1596. His character is only a mystery if his libellers are believed, for then his own actions and protestations clash with their picture of a Machiavellian near-devil. He was ambitious, able, clear-sighted, not over-scrupulous, and extremely hardworking—a suitable and typical Tudor minister, which Essex was not. His meagre personal appearance told against him with the queen, but she trusted his judgment and his loyalty, and she never made mistakes in such matters.

to recover sole possession of her subjects' affections by publicly exposing his guilt. But wiser counsels and Essex's humble submission spared him the public disgrace. In June 1600 he was brought before a commission sitting in private. He was charged on five main counts: desertion of his post, failure in Ireland, his making of knights and appointing Southampton as general of horse despite the queen's orders, the presumptuous tone of his letters, and his private interview with Tyrone. The commissioners, who were eager to spare him, persuaded him with some difficulty to forego his defence and throw himself on the queen's mercy. He was deprived of most of his offices, suspended from the privy council, and confined to Essex House (in the Strand). A promise of ultimate restoration to favour was not given but allowed to hang in the air.

Unfortunately for Essex, he had at last aroused the old Tudor distrust. Humble appeals availed nothing now. In September the queen failed to renew his monopoly of the import of sweet wines on which single pillar his tottering finances rested; despair grew on him. In private he expressed views of the queen, of Cecil, of the rest of his supposed detractors, which inflamed his followers and came near treason. He lost all sense of proportion and succumbed to the influence of the wild adventurers who surrounded him. Growing convinced that Cecil was plotting to put the Spanish Infanta on the throne after the queen's death, he entered into negotiations with James of Scotland and tried to get Mountjoy to bring over the Irish army to restore himself to power and secure the Stuart succession. Luckily for himself, Mountjoy (away from the influence of his mistress, Essex's sister Penelope Lady Rich) was too cautious for such folly, and Elizabeth ignored what came to her of the business in the knowledge that Ireland would purge him of treason and employ him usefully. At Essex House, however, the plots grew ever thicker and more absurd. Puerile schemes were evolved for seizing Essex's enemies and 'freeing' the queen. In February 1601 the council at last took notice and summoned him to attend; this lit the fuse. One evening some of his followers paid Shakespeare's company forty shillings to perform *Richard II* at the Globe—a play fraught with meaning for these hotheads who saw in their Essex another Henry Bolingbroke. When on 8th February four privy councillors, all rather his friends, came to Essex House in the queen's name, the earl arrested them and with a crowd of two hundred gentlemen, armed only with swords, issued forth to raise the city.

It was a mad and pointless thing and came to the end it deserved.

QET*

Crying, 'for the queen, for the queen! there is a plot against my life', Essex rode up Fleet Street, Ludgate Hill, and Cheapside. All who would listen were told how Raleigh, Cecil, and Cobham were aiming to murder him and were exhorted to come to the rescue of queen and Church. No one moved. Instead the Lord Mayor began to barricade Essex's following, while from court there came troops and heralds to proclaim him traitor. The aimless riot petered out. Essex began to lose all control, displaying something very like persecution mania; for fifteen minutes he held a city official's horse by the bridle while he poured out to the astonished man his grievances and imaginary injuries—'looking wildly up and down'. At last he let himself be pushed down to the river and returned to Essex House. Here he found that the man he had put in guard over his hostages had lost his nerve and let them go. It was over. In the late evening he came out with the earls of Southampton and Rutland to surrender; the whole band was soon under lock and key. After the events of the day the end could be in no doubt, and no satires about

> Little Cecil tripping up and down,
> He rules both court and crown,
> With his brother Burghley clown,
> In his great fox-furred gown.
> With the long proclamation
> He swore he saved the town.
> Is it not likely?[1]

or later laments such as the *Lamentable Ditty composed upon the death of Robert Lord Devereux, late Earl of Essex* ('Sweet England's pride is gone—welladay, welladay'), could alter the fact that Essex had firmly placed his head on the block when he rode into the Strand on 8 February. Within nine days he was brought to trial, Coke and his old follower Francis Bacon appearing against him, and the sentence was carried out as rapidly. Southampton, also found guilty, was spared sentence; Rutland escaped even trial but paid a heavy fine, as did many others. Only a few of Essex's lesser followers, among them those who had really stirred him up, suffered for their treason; as usual, the queen's vengeance was moderate.

[1] Thomas Lord Burghley, the old treasurer's somewhat boorish elder son, had led the troops that pushed Essex out of the city; the proclamation in question was that issued next day to declare the earl's treason. As for who saved the city, the satirist was right in implying that it did not need saving.

The significance of Essex's rising is too often explained in purely personal terms. Admittedly, it is a story of high ambitions and headlong fall, given even greater interest by the play between earl and queen. E. P. Cheyney thought Essex worth pity; he put everything down to Elizabeth's jealousy of his popularity.[1] If a wider significance is found at all, the rising is usually described as an example of belated feudalism. But in truth it was a far from belated example of bastard feudalism. Essex acted as an 'over-mighty subject', or more specifically as one of those leaders of affinities whose military power had been broken by Henry VII, but who continued to play their part in politics right down to the end of the eighteenth century. In effect he attempted to revive the military side of the social system which depended on clientage and the great 'connexion'—the grouping around a magnate of gentle-men and lesser men eager for advancement. There was nothing territorial about Essex's power: he was no feudal lord. But the charges against him (which Cheyney, for instance, thought absurdly insignificant) assume their real meaning if we remember the nature of bastard feudalism. Those Irish knights he had made amounted to a body of personal retainers; altogether, his behaviour in Ireland looked far more like a king-maker's than a crown servant's. There was plenty of discontent and disappointed ambition for him to fashion a party from: 'swordsmen, bold con-fident fellows, men of broken fortunes, discontented persons, and such as saucily use their tongues in railing against all men'. In that light the queen saw it, and the event so proved it. At the end of her reign Elizabeth had to turn once more to the original task of her house and suppress the overpowering ambitions of one individual who was creating a private following for himself. Unhappily for her, the individual was a man she would have liked to favour and cherish; happily for the state he was a man without political sense without patience, and afflicted by a mental instability which even expressed itself in bouts of nervous sickness. The career of Essex is a tragedy in the Shakespearian sense because potential greatness was wrecked by a flaw in the man himself.

5. THE END

The passing of the Essex storm left all in a strange quiet. Mant bewailed his fate, but none felt constrained to do anything about it Cecil now ruled everything, though Raleigh unsuccessfully tried to

[1] *History of England*, ch. 44. It may be as well to remark that Lytton Strachey's *Elizabeth and Essex* is perhaps best left unread.

dispute the ascendancy with him. As for the queen, it appears that she was certainly growing old and rather weary. But not yet: it was not Essex's death that depressed her, but the gradual disappearance of all those with whom she had lived a long lifetime together. Her old skill and vigour appeared undimmed in the story of the 1601 parliament. She continued to enjoy dancing and hunting with an energy remarkable in one approaching her seventieth year and only to be explained by her persistent refusal of her physicians' ministrations. Nevertheless, everyone saw that the reign was drawing to a close and began to make preparations. With the skill which had enabled him to ride out several storms and make his way despite physical handicaps, Cecil established himself in the good graces of the only really likely heir, James VI of Scotland. Though he feared the queen's anger and therefore tried very hard to keep the negotiations secret, she knew what went on but said nothing. It is probable that she favoured the Stuart succession—indeed, it is difficult to see whom else she could have favoured—but true to her principle of naming no successor she kept silent, until on her deathbed she pronounced for James—if she did and was not only said to have done so by those in whose hands lay the management of a quiet succession. As the year 1602 progressed, melancholy and a sense of being unwell took possession of her, though in reality her health continued good; her mind remained unaffected to the very end, but she preferred devotion and 'old Canterbury tales' to politics. In March 1603 it became plain that she had lost the desire to live; everyone waited for the end, with sorrow, but also with a lively anticipation of the future. At last, on 24 March 1603, sixty-nine years and six months old, the great queen died quietly, at rest with this world.

The Tudor age was over, for there were no more Tudors. The new reign about to open inherited its problems, and 1603 is a date of only limited significance in the history of England. But it remains true that much of the Stuart trouble was due to Stuart incompetence, and that much of the Tudor success had been due to the skill of the dynasty. It was a wonderful family, and its achievements—aided by the work of many others—were impressive. A country once ravaged by internal war and depression was now, despite external war and more depression, on the way to becoming a major power. Peace at home had brought order and law, a rising prosperity, a spreading over the globe, great things in the arts, a remarkable people. No one would pretend that the sixteenth century was an ideal age. Poverty and disease and cruelty abounded; life was hard and often short for high and low alike. Its politics were too often violent and repulsive, though also full of intelligent vigour. Its religion, though in the end more sincere than that of the late middle ages, also indulged in more intolerance and persecution. Its people were too often hard of face and harder of heart. Yet the state was built anew, government restored and reformed, enterprise encouraged, faith rekindled. The good past survived, the bad past died. In those hundred and twenty years of unremitting labour by monarchs and ministers, merchants and mariners, gentlemen and yeomen, writers and poets and thinkers, a new and greater England emerged from the day-to-day turmoil of life.

BIBLIOGRAPHY

THIS is no attempt at an exhaustive bibliography but only a collection of the more important writings in which the subject may be pursued further. I have tried to give particular attention to recent publications not to be found in earlier lists. I see no point in attempting to choose among the many printed sources for the sixteenth century, but three books shall be mentioned because they will offer an easy and painless introduction to contact with the age. *The Thought and Culture of the English Renaissance*, ed. Elizabeth M. Nugent (Cambridge 1956) assembles a great variety of excellent Tudor prose; the introductory prefaces vary in value but are in general helpful. R. H. Tawney and E. Power, *Tudor Economic Documents* (3 vols., London 1924), supply much detail to illumine the complexities of economic affairs. And any edition of Shakespeare's *Works*, supplemented perhaps by the *Oxford Book of Sixteenth Century Verse*, is a *sine qua non*. For a full discussion of the literature I refer to Conyers Read, *Bibliography of British History: Tudor Period* (2nd ed., Oxford 1959). Useful lists are found in (4), (5), and (13) below.

A. GENERAL
1. S. T. Bindoff, *Tudor England* (London 1950).
   The best short survey and a brilliant achievement of compression. Particularly good on economic questions.
The Political History of England:
2. H. A. L. Fisher, *Vol. V: 1485–1547* (London 1913).
3. A. F. Pollard, *Vol. VI: 1547–1603* (London 1910).
   Still in some ways the best account, though both detail and general interpretation require revision.
The Oxford History of England:
4. J. D. Mackie, *The Earlier Tudors 1485–1558* (Oxford 1952).
5. J. B. Black, *The Reign of Elizabeth* (2nd ed., Oxford 1960).
   Include sections on economic, constitutional, and cultural matters not found in (2) and (3). Certainly worth consulting, especially for the sake of their excellent bibliographies.
6. J. A. Williamson, *The Tudor Age* (2nd ed., London 1959).
   Good on maritime affairs.

B. POLITICAL HISTORY
(a) Henry VII
7. W. Busch, *England under the Tudors: Henry VII* (London 1895).
   Remains the best detailed history, but is seriously out of date in its discussion of government and finance.
8. K. Pickthorn, *Early Tudor Government: Henry VII* (Cambridge 1934).
   Analytical discussion of government, mainly from a lawyer's point of view. Though not superseded, clearly in parts no longer acceptable in the light of more recent research.
9. G. R. Elton, 'Henry VII: Rapacity and Remorse', *Hist. Journal* 1958.
   Elaborates approach of chapters I and II above. Has led to a controversy: J. P. Cooper, 'Henry VII's Last Years Reconsidered', *ibid.* 1959; G. R. Elton, 'Henry VII: A Restatement', *ibid.* 1960.
   See also (32), (34), (35).

(b) *Henry VIII*
10. K. Pickthorn, *Early Tudor Government: Henry VIII* (Cambridge 1934).
This exchanges the analytical for the chronological method and in effect becomes a history of the reign with some valuable *obiter dicta* on government.
11. G. R. Elton, *Star Chamber Stories* (London 1958).
Six cases of Henry VIII's reign, throwing light on several aspects of its history.
12. A. F. Pollard, *Henry VIII* (London 1905).
The best life. Tends to overestimate the king's ability and to sentimentalise the constitutional problems.
13. A. F. Pollard, *Wolsey* (London 1929).
P.'s greatest work: embodies vast knowledge and penetrating judgment. Particularly good on Wolsey's activities as a judge.
14. R. W. Chambers, *Thomas More* (London 1935).
Of the many lives of More, this is certainly the one best worth reading. Imaginative and sympathetic, but also fair.
15. A. G. Dickens, *Thomas Cromwell and the English Reformation* (London 1959).
To this brief but excellent modern appraisal, which destroys many false views, add three papers by G. R. Elton, the basis for much said in chapters VI and VII above: 'King or Minister? The Man behind the Henrician Reformation', *History* 1954; 'Thomas Cromwell's Political Creed', *Trans. R. Hist. Soc.*; 1956 'Thomas Cromwell's Decline and Fall', *Cambridge Historical Journal* 1951.
16. J. A. Muller, *Stephen Gardiner and the Tudor Reaction* (London 1926)
Workmanlike, but tends to take Gardiner at his own valuation.

(c) *Edward and Mary*
The best outline is in (3); (1) is valuable for a summary of the economic background.
17. A. F. Pollard, *England Under the Protector Somerset* (London 1900).
Much too kind to Somerset and the author's weakest book—but that still makes it a good one.
18. S. T. Bindoff, *Ket's Rebellion* (Historical Association Pamphlet 1949).
19. H. F. M. Prescott, *Mary Tudor* (London 1952).
Rather crowded and a trifle romantic, but sound and readable.
20. E. H. Harbison, *Rival Ambassadors at the Court of Queen Mary* (Princeton 1940).
Detailed discussion of foreign affairs and the activities of the French and Imperial ambassadors; based on much useful material, but it does go on.
21. F. G. Emmison, *Tudor Secretary* (London 1961).
Painstaking biography of Sir William Petre; throws much light on politics and government, as well as on the notorious new gentry of the age.

(d) *Elizabeth*
22. A. L. Rowse, *The England of Elizabeth* (London 1950).
Discusses, with an overwhelming wealth of detail, the land, people, government, and Church of the period. Indispensable for the social structure and history of the time. The author's obtrusive prejudices must be discounted.
23. M. Creighton, *Queen Elizabeth* (London 1899).
Judicious: by a notable historian of the last pontifical school. Interpretation perhaps too purely political.
24. J. E. Neale, *Queen Elizabeth* (London 1934).
The outstanding modern life. A little indulgent towards Elizabeth.
25. J. E. Neale, *Elizabeth I and her Parliaments* (2 vols.; London 1953, 1957).
A brilliant and remarkably full narrative of parliamentary affairs, indispensable to an understanding of the political, constitutional, and ecclesiastical history of the reign.

26. E. P. Cheyney, *History of England, from the Defeat of the Armada to the Death of Elizabeth* (2 vols.; New York 1914, 1926).
   Intended as a continuation of J. A. Froude's great *History of England 1529–88*, but both much sounder and much duller. Good on the agencies of government; unduly hostile to Elizabeth.

27. *Elizabethan Government and Society*, ed. S. T. Bindoff, J. Hurstfield, C. H. Williams (London 1961).
   A collection of valuable papers by various authors; the most important ones are separately noted in the right place. Note here: W. T. Maccaffery, 'Place and Patronage in Elizabethan Politics'; J. Hurstfield, 'The Succession Struggle in Late Elizabethan England'.

28. Conyers Read, *Mr Secretary Walsingham and the Policy of Queen Elizabeth* (3 vols.; Oxford 1925).
   The main study of Elizabethan foreign policy; also useful on the office of secretary. Exceedingly detailed with very full quotations.

29. Conyers Read, *Mr Secretary Cecil and Queen Elizabeth* (Oxford 1955); *Lord Burghley and Queen Elizabeth* (Oxford 1960).
   Despite its enormous detail and vast quotations, this is not the badly needed biography of Burghley, but rather a companion work to (28). Concentrates predominantly on foreign affairs and Scotland.

30. L. Stone, *An Elizabethan: Sir Horatio Palavicino* (Oxford 1956).
   Interesting life of an out-of-the-way character—merchant, financier, diplomatist, gentleman, upstart.

C. GOVERNMENT

31. G. R. Elton, *The Tudor Constitution: Documents and Commentary* (Cambridge 1960).
   Replacing J. R. Tanner's *Tudor Constitutional Documents* (Cambridge; 2nd ed. 1930), this contains a concise analytical account of Tudor government and its instruments, with a detailed guide to the bibliography.

(a) *Finance*
32. F. C. Dietz, *English Government Finance 1485–1558* (Univ. of Illinois 1920).
33. F. C. Dietz, *English Public Finance 1558–1642* (New York 1932).
   The only comprehensive studies of revenue and expenditure. However, both leave too many administrative questions unanswered and are often unreliable in their figures; a new study would not come amiss. There is much on finance in (26), (34), (35), (36).

(b) *Administration*
34. G. R. Elton, *The Tudor Revolution in Government* (Cambridge 1953).
   Deals with financial administration, the seals and secretaries, the council, and the king's household, mainly during Thomas Cromwell's tenure of office.

35. W. C. Richardson, *Tudor Chamber Administration 1485–1547* (Baton Rouge 1952).
   Product of much difficult research and especially useful for Henry VII. Conclusions differ somewhat from (34).

36. G. R. Elton, 'The Elizabethan Exchequer: War in the Receipt', in (27).
37. H. C. Bell, *Introduction to the Court of Wards and Liveries* (Cambridge 1953).
   Deals thoroughly with the administrative but not with the social aspects of this court.

38. J. Hurstfield, *The Queen's Wards* (London 1958).
   More than a history of the court of wards under Elizabeth: rather an important study of Elizabethan social history. For other aspects of the subject see the same author's 'The Revival of Feudalism in Early Tudor England', *History* 1952; 'Lord Burghley as Master of the Court of Wards', *Trans. R. Hist. Soc.* 1949.

39. F. M. G. Evans, *The Principal Secretary of State* (Manchester 1923).
In the main after 1580. See also (28) and (34).

(c) *The Law*
40. W. H. Holdsworth, *History of English Law* (13 vols.; London 1903 onwards).
Vol. i contains the best account of the various courts; vols. iv and v the history of law in the sixteenth century. Vol. iv also includes a remarkable survey of the constitution, which, however, needs ample correction in many parts.
41. J. P. Dawson, *A History of Lay Judges* (Harvard 1960).
Although the book ranges from the ancient Greeks to the nineteenth century, its core consists of excellent studies of English central and local jurisdiction in the fifteenth to seventeenth centuries.

(d) *The Council*
The older accounts of the privy council are practically worthless, at least as far as the history of the council is concerned: they still offer something towards an understanding of its working. E. R. Turner, *The Privy Council*, vol. i (Baltimore 1927) needs a red flag of warning. The subject is dealt with in (31); it may be pursued further in (34) and (26), together with the following:
42. *Cases in the Council of Henry VII*, ed. C. G. Bayne (London, Selden Society 1958).
Valuable introduction; for a criticism see G. R. Elton in *Eng. Hist. Rev.* 1959.
43. A. F. Pollard, 'Council, Star Chamber, and Privy Council under the Tudors', *English Historical Review* 1922 and 1923.
44. W. H. Dunham, Jr., 'Henry VIII's Whole Council and Its Parts', *Huntington Library Quarterly* 1943.

(e) *Parliament*
A. F. Pollard's *Evolution of Parliament* (2nd ed., London 1925) is interesting and contains some valuable points, but it is so unreliable in parts and so badly constructed that its use is not recommended except to the expert. Thus there are no books on parliament before 1558, but useful discussions will be found in (8), (10), (12), and (31). The following articles, the basis of several points made in this book, may help further:
45. G. R. Elton, 'Parliamentary drafts 1529–40', *Bulletin of the Institute of Historical Research* 1952 (classifies the surviving drafts into aspects of government planning and examples of private enterprise); 'The Evolution of a Reformation Statute', *Eng. Hist. Rev.* 1949 (discusses the growth of the act of appeals and Cromwell's drafting of legislation); 'The Commons' Supplication of 1532', *ibid.* 1951 (describes the development of the measure and analyses the parliamentary manoeuvres involved; has been subjected to some partially constructive criticism by J. P. Cooper, 'The Supplication against the Ordinaries Reconsidered', *ibid.* 1957).
About the parliaments of Elizabeth we are well informed thanks to J. E. Neale (also [25] above).
46. J. E. Neale, *The Elizabethan House of Commons* (London 1949).
Very important. An analysis of elections, membership, and procedure.
47. J. E. Neale, 'The Commons' Privilege of Free Speech in Parliament', *Tudor Studies presented to A. F. Pollard* (London 1924).
48. W. Notestein, *The Winning of the Initiative by the House of Commons* (London 1924).
Changes in Commons' procedure late in the reign.

(f) *Local Government*
On this much has been written; there are good summaries in (8), (25), and (34).
49. G. Scott Thompson, *Lords Lieutenants in the Sixteenth Century* (London 1923).

50. C. A. Beard, *The Office of Justice of the Peace* (New York 1924).
   No more than a bare introduction.
51. R. R. Reid, *The King's Council of the North* (London 1921).
   Exhaustive and sound. A useful short account is F. W. Brooks, *The Council of the North* (Historical Association Pamphlet 1953).
52. P. Williams, *The Council in the Marches of Wales under Elizabeth I* (Cardiff 1958).
   Gives also a succinct account of the council's earlier history and an excellent description of the social situation in the Marches.
53. J. A. Youings, 'The Council of the West', *Trans. R. Hist. Soc.* 1960.

(g) *Thought on Government and Politics*
54. Sir Thomas Smith, *De Republica Anglorum* (ed. L. Alston, Cambridge 1906).
   A most valuable contemporary survey. In English, despite its title.
55. C. Morris, *Political Thought in England from Tyndale to Hooker* (Oxford 1953).
   A brilliant summary with many original and interesting suggestions to make. Contains a really first-class bibliography which makes a long list superfluous here.
56. J. W. Allen, *Political Thought in the Sixteenth Century* (London 1928).
   Weighty and authoritative. Covers thought in all Western Europe.
57. F. Le V. Baumer, *Early Tudor Theory of Kingship* (Yale 1940).
   Full survey, rather cut and dried.
58. W. G. Zeeveld, *Foundations of Tudor Policy* (Harvard 1948).
   A study of the obscure men who defended the Cromwellian revolution. Z. probably overestimates their importance, but the book is most interesting and revealing.
59. E. T. Davies, *The Political Ideas of Richard Hooker* (London 1946).
   Not in (55) and therefore worth mentioning separately:
60. J. H. Hexter, *More's Utopia: the biography of an idea* (Princeton 1952).
   The sanest and least engaged analysis of a famous book. But see also (14).
61. C. H. McIlwain, *Constitutionalism Ancient and Modern* (New York 1947).
   Often splendid essays by an old master which the present writer finds progressively less convincing. Chapter 5 deals with the transition from 'medieval' to 'modern'.
62. G. L. Mosse, *The Struggle for Sovereignty in England* (Michigan State College Press 1950).
   Mostly on the early Stuarts, but with a useful though controversial summary of late Tudor thought.

D. ECONOMIC HISTORY
   At present there is no full-scale economic history of this period, but (63) and (64) provide something like a survey.

(a) *General*
63. E. Lipson, *An Economic History of England*, vol. ii (London 1931).
   Unreliable on agrarian and social questions; still useful on trade and industry.
64. J. H. Clapham, *Concise Economic History of Britain* (Cambridge 1949).
   An admirable introduction.

(b) *Agriculture*
65. R. H. Tawney, *The Agrarian Problem in the Sixteenth Century* (London 1912).
   Much of this famous pioneering work now needs supplementing with later studies, but the book remains the basis of all agrarian history in the period.

66. M. Beresford, *The Lost Villages of England* (London 1954).
Tries to trace the sites of deserted villages, as well as the occasion and cause of their abandonment. Seeks to re-establish the view that enclosure for sheep-farming resulted in widespread depopulation c. 1450–1520 and makes some telling points; but the question remains fairly open.

67. Joan Thirsk, *Tudor Enclosures* (Historical Association Pamphlet 1959).
Best recent summary of the present position.

68. W. G. Hoskins, *Essays in Leicestershire History* (Liverpool 1950).
An outstanding example of the growing body of 'local' historical writing directly relevant to large national problems. Important for the effects of enclosure and the fate of the yeoman.

69. M. Campbell, *The English Yeoman under Elizabeth and the Early Stuarts* (Yale 1942).
Deals in detail with the social and economic circumstances of the subject.

70. E. Kerridge, 'The Movement of Rents 1540–1640', *Economic History Review* 1953.
Perhaps the beginning of a new view on rack-renting, but so far has remained in somewhat doubtful isolation.

(c) The Gentry

71. R. H. Tawney, 'The Rise of the Gentry', *Economic History Review* 1941.

72. H. R. Trevor-Roper, *The Gentry 1540–1640* (Cambridge 1953).
The two main contributions to the controversy outlined above, pp. 255ff. There have been further moves since that section was written, on the whole bearing out the tentative verdict there recorded. See e.g.: M. Finch, *Five Northamptonshire Families* (Oxford 1956); A. R. Batho, 'The Finances of an Elizabethan Nobleman', *Econ. Hist. Rev.* 1957; H. R. Trevor-Roper, 'The General Crisis of the Seventeenth Century', *Past and Present* 1959; P. Zagorin, 'The Social Interpretation of the English Revolution', *Journal of Economic History* 1959. The business has ceased to be fruitful.

(d) Trade

73. G. D. Ramsay, *English Overseas Trade during the Centuries of Emergence* (London 1957).
Extends beyond the sixteenth century, but provides the best introduction to Tudor trade.

74. G. Schanz, *Englische Handelspolitik gegen Ende des Mittelalters* (Leipzig 1881).
Despite its age still the standard account of early Tudor commercial affairs. Some of its tables and arguments are corrected by P. Ramsay, 'Overseas Trade in the Reign of Henry VII', *Econ. Hist. Rev.* 1954.

75. A. A. Ruddock, *Italian Merchants and Shipping in Southampton 1270–1600* (Southampton 1951).
The last part covers the decline of Southampton's Italian trade under the early Tudors.

76. G. Connell-Smith, *Forerunners of Drake* (London 1954).
A thorough investigation of Anglo-Spanish trade from the treaties of Henry VII to its decline in the 1540s.

77. F. J. Fisher, 'Economic Trends and Policy in the Sixteenth Century', *Economic History Review* 1940.
Important analysis of the ups and downs of the cloth trade.

78. W. R. Scott, *The Constitution and Finance of English, Scottish, and Irish Joint Stock Companies* (3 vols.; Cambridge 1910–12).
A badly arranged monumental work which contains a vast deal of information on trade.

79. G. Unwin, 'The Merchant Adventurers' Company in the Reign of Elizabeth', *Studies in Economic History* (London 1927).
   The classic deflation of the M.A. For a different but unconvincing view see (22). The great days of the M.A. in the early sixteenth century still await their historian.
80. T. S. Willan, *The Early History of the Russia Company* (Manchester 1956).
81. A. C. Wood, *A History of the Levant Company* (London 1935).
82. T. S. Willan, *Studies in Elizabethan Foreign Trade* (Manchester 1959).
   In addition to a detailed study of the Morocco Company, this contains valuable essays on interlopers and the outports.
83. A. E. Feavearyear, *The Pound Sterling* (Oxford 1931).
   The best account of the coinage and its manipulation. See also appendix in (4).

(e) Industry
84. G. Unwin, *Industrial Organisation in the Sixteenth and Seventeenth Centuries* (Oxford 1904).
   Mostly on the seventeenth, but important, especially together with the same author's *Guilds and Companies of London* (London 1908).
85. J. U. Nef, 'Technology and Industry, 1540–1640', *Economic History Review* 1934).
   Controversial, as are the same author's 'Prices and Industrial Capitalism in France and England, 1540–1640', *ibid.* 1937; 'War and Economic Progress 1540–1640', *ibid.* 1942; and *Industry and Government in France and England 1540–1640* (American Philosophical Society Memorials, Philadelphia 1940).
86. E. Lipson, *English Woollen and Worsted Industries* (2nd ed., London 1953).
87. J. U. Nef, *The Rise of the British Coal Industry* (2 vols., London 1932).

(f) Social Policy
88. G. R. Elton, 'State Control in Early Tudor England', *Economic History Review* 1961.
   Throws doubt on the present state of knowledge and confident assertions based on it.
89. S. T. Bindoff, 'The Making of the Statute of Artificers', in (27).
90. R. K. Kensall, *Wage Regulation under the Statute of Artificers* (London 1938).
91. R. H. Tawney, 'The Assessment of Wages in England by the Justices of the Peace', *Vierteljahrschrift f. Sozial–u. Wirtschaftsgeschichte* 1913
92. M. G. Davies, *The Enforcement of English Apprenticeship* (Harvard) 1956.
   Between them, these last four make the statute of artificers one of the better known Tudor topics; (92) has wider implication for the whole problem of law enforcement.
93. E. M. Leonard, *The Early History of English Poor Relief* (Cambridge 1900).
   It is time that this old standard work were superseded, at least for the period before 1572 and especially as to the practical working of poor relief. See also G. R. Elton, 'An Early Tudor Poor Law', *Econ. Hist. Rev.* 1953.
94. W. K. Jordan, *Philanthropy in England 1480–1660* (London 1959).
   Contains a vast deal of most valuable (and largely unsuspected) information concerning testamentary charity and charitable foundations. Unfortunately the argument raised on the facts, supported by statistics which take no account of the changing value of money, cannot be accepted without serious reservations.
95. R. H. Tawney, *Religion and the Rise of Capitalism* (London 1926).
   The fundamental work on economic thought in the period. Has led to much controversy and is, indeed, more convincing for the seventeenth than the sixteenth century. But remains one of the outstanding historical works of the present century.

96. Thomas Wilson, *A Discourse on Usury*, ed. R. H. Tawney (London 1925).
The long introduction provides the fundamental study of money and credit in the sixteenth century.

E. THE CHURCH
A small selection from a huge mass of writings.

97. J. Gairdner, *The English Church in the Sixteenth Century from Henry VIII to Mary* (London 1903).
98. W. H. Frere, *The English Church in the Reigns of Elizabeth and James I* (London 1904).
These two volumes, part of a series, cover the period. Both are sound enough on fact, but while (98) is judicious and to be recommended, (97) is marked by a distorting dislike of the Reformation, and its opinions and interpretations must be used with great care. The same applies more forcibly still to Gairdner's *Lollardy and the Reformation* (4 vols., London 1908–13).

(a) *The Reformation*
See also n.2 on p. 99 above.
99. T. M. Parker, *The English Reformation to 1558* (Oxford 1950)
The best brief survey, questionable here and there on the constitutional side.
100. H. Maynard Smith, *Pre-Reformation England* (London 1938).
101. H. Maynard Smith, *Henry VIII and the Reformation* (London 1948).
Both these are interesting and lucid accounts, rather lightweight in treatment and only ordinary on the political side. (100) gives a good view of the state of the Church, for which see also (13) and (102).
102. P. Hughes, *The Reformation in England* (3 vols., London 1950–4).
The inevitable bias of this catholic history does nothing to lessen the importance of vol. i; the other two volumes need more critical care in use. However, throughout it contains much important and unusual discussion not found elsewhere.
103. G. Constant, *The Reformation in England* (2 vols., London 1934), 1942; translated from the French).
Sound account of little independent value; based on very wide reading among printed materials; commonly rated too high. Vol. ii (on Edward VI), with valuable analyses of theological questions, is the more important.
104. A Ogle, *The Tragedy of the Lollards' Tower* (Oxford 1949).
Mainly a study of the case of Richard Hunne. Proves that he was murdered, and argues that his case was the basis of the commons' attitude and work in 1529–32. Its thesis has some support from (45).
105. A. G. Dickens, *Lollards and Protestants in the Diocese of York* (Oxford 1959).
Throws a quite new light on the religious situation and attitude of Yorkshire.
106. F. W. Maitland, 'The Anglican Settlement and the Scottish Reformation', *Old Cambridge Modern History*, vol. ii.
Still in many ways far and away the best account of the years 1558–68; part of the story must be revised in accordance with J. E. Neale's 'The Elizabethan Acts of Supremacy and Uniformity', *Eng. Hist. Rev.* 1951.
107. J. V. P. Thompson, *The Supreme Governor* (London 1940).
A useful, if rather slight, summary of Elizabeth's policy towards the the Church.
108. J. Mozley, *William Tyndale* (London 1937).
109. A. F. Pollard, *Thomas Cranmer and the English Reformation* (London 1905).
The best of several lives of Cranmer.

110. H. Darby, *Hugh Latimer* (London 1953).
Straightforward; interesting on account of its subject.

(b) The Monasteries and the Deprivations
F. A. Gasquet's *Henry VIII and the Monasteries*, despite the notion, not so long ago expressed by Cardinal Gasquet's biographer, that it still sets the standard in the field, is best ignored.
111. D. Knowles, *The Religious Orders in England: The Tudor Age* (Cambridge 1959).
Not only just the best book on the subject, but a truly excellent one.
112. G. Baskerville, *English Monks and the Suppression of the Monasteries* (London 1937).
Marred slightly by too ready a hostility to the monks, and heavily by a needless flippancy, this book still retains some independent value by the side of (111) because it is more able to see the anti-monastic point of view.
113. A. Savine, *English Monasteries on the Eve of the Dissolution* (Oxford 1909).
Very important. A detailed investigation of the condition of the houses, based in the main on an analysis of the *Valor Ecclesiasticus*.
114. H. Grieve, 'The Deprived Married Clergy in Essex', *Trans. R. Hist. Soc.* 1940).
115. C. H. Garret, *The Marian Exiles* (Cambridge 1938).
Valuable facts, doubtful deductions.

(c) Catholic, Puritan, and Anglican
116. A. O. Meyer, *England and the Catholic Church under Elizabeth* (London 1916; translated from the German).
A scholarly investigation—thorough, unimpassioned, and in a neutral tone; but readable. Easily the best thing on the subject.
117. A. C. Southern, *Elizabethan Recusant Prose* (London, n.d.).
Mainly a study of writings, but also a valuable contribution to the history of Elizabethan Catholicism.
118. M. M. Knappen, *Tudor Puritanism* (Chicago 1939).
Now the standard work. Deals with the subject in all its forms, from Tyndale to the Separatist movement.
119. A. F. Scott Pearson, *Thomas Cartwright and Elizabethan Puritanism* (Cambridge 1925).
120. P. Collison, 'John Field and Elizabethan Puritanism', in (27).
121. R. G. Usher, *The Reconstruction of the English Church* (2 vols., New York 1910).
Book I of vol. i deals with the state of the clergy and the attack on puritanism late in the reign.
122. R. G. Usher, *The Rise and Fall of the High Commission* (Oxford 1913).
Fair example of the constitutional history of a court.

(d) Special Studies suggested for Reading
123. E. G. Rupp, *Studies in the Making of the Protestant Tradition* (Cambridge 1947).
Admirable essays on the Lutheran influence in the Henrician Reformation.
124. E. T. Davies, *Episcopacy and the Royal Supremacy in the Church of England in the XVI Century* (Oxford 1950).
Interesting analysis of the teaching of the formularies; weak on the actual working of the relationship.
125. H. C. Porter, *Reformation and Reaction in Tudor Cambridge* (Cambridge 1958).
Goes well beyond the implications of the title in investigating the nature and effect of theological disputes.

126. F. D. Price, 'Gloucester Diocese under Bishop Hooper 1551–3', *Transactions of the Bristol and Glos. Archaeol. Soc.* 1938; 'An Elizabethan Church Official—Thomas Powell, Chancellor of Gloucester Diocese', *Church Quarterly Review* 1939; 'Abuses of Excommunication and the Decline of Ecclesiastical Discipline under Queen Elizabeth', *Eng. Hist. Rev.* 1942.
These three papers give a very good idea of the state of the Church in a badly run diocese, but though Gloucester may have been particularly bad it was not untypical.
127. C. Hill, *Economic Problems of the Church from Archbishop Whitgift to the Long Parliament* (Oxford 1956).
Though mainly concerned with the early Stuart period, this book is valuable for the condition of the Elizabethan Church and clergy.

F. NAVAL AND MILITARY MATTERS
A good general account may be extracted from (6)

(a) The Navy
128. M. Oppenheim, *History of the Administration of the Royal Navy* (London 1896).
The fundamental study.
129. W. Monson, *Naval Tracts*, ed. M. Oppenheim (6 vols., Navy Record Society 1902–14).
Important Introductions.
For the navy under Elizabeth see also (135), 137), and (141).

(b) The Army
130. C. G. Cruickshank, *Elizabeth's Army* (Oxford 1946).
Good introductory study, with useful bibliography. The first chapters of (144) add important detail on the army in Ireland; and see (49) for the militia.

(c) Explorations
131. J. A. Williamson, *Maritime Enterprise 1485–1558* (Oxford 1913).
An older standard work, now to be amended and extended by (132), (133), and especially (76) which shows that naval depredations by Englishmen began much sooner than used to be thought.
132. J. A. Williamson, *The Voyages of the Cabots and the English Discovery of North America under Henry VII and Henry VIII* (London 1929).
133. E. G. R. Taylor, *Tudor Geography 1485–1583* (London 1931).
Important study of geographical learning and practice. Must be read, even though the material has hardly been turned into a book.
134. A. L. Rowse, *The Expansion of Elizabethan England* (London 1955).
Valuable for its picture of the countries on the fringe of England.
135. J. A. Williamson, *The Age of Drake* (London 1946).
The best survey of the second half of the century, rather more critical of Drake than—
136. J. S. Corbett, *Drake and the Tudor Navy* (2 vols., London 1898–9).
Still a very important work much of which cannot be found elsewhere. Undoubtedly prejudiced in Drake's favour.
137. J. A. Williamson, *Hawkins of Plymouth* (London 1946).
Probably the author's masterpiece, it supersedes his own earlier *Sir John Hawkins* (Oxford 1927). Particularly good for the history of the navy.
138. A. L. Rowse, *Sir Richard Grenville* (London 1937).
Good both as biography and history; throws much light as well on the social structure of the south-west (for which see also the same author's *Tudor Cornwall* [London 1947]).

139. D. B. Quinn, *Raleigh and the British Empire* (London 1947).
Very useful on both subjects, and lists the more important of the many lives of Raleigh, to which might now be added W. M. Wallace, *Sir Walter Raleigh* (Princeton 1959).
140. J. A. Williamson, *The Ocean in English History* (Oxford 1941).
Less narrative than this author's other work, it contains in particular a fine summary of the work of the propagandists.

(d) *The War*
Thoroughly dealt with in (26) and (134); much detail also in (135–9).
141. G. Mattingly, *The Defeat of the Spanish Armada* (London 1959).
Exciting, in part overdone; a brilliant synthesis of English and Spanish contributions which places the campaign in the larger setting of war and politics.
142. R. B. Wernham, 'Queen Elizabeth and the Portugal Expedition of 1589', *English Historical Review* 1951.
Important revision of the traditional version, as given, e.g., in (26).
143. R. B. Wernham, 'Elizabethan War Aims and Strategy', in (27).
Continues the rehabilitation of the queen's policy.
144. C. Falls, *Elizabeth's Irish Wars* (London 1950).
Thorough and fascinating, with a good bibliography.

G. SCOTLAND, WALES, AND IRELAND
(a) *Scotland*
Both (4) and (5) are strong on this.
145. P. Hume Brown, *History of Scotland* (3 vols., Cambridge 1911).
The standard history.
146. G. Donaldson, *The Scottish Reformation* (Cambridge 1960).
Important revision of traditional views; stresses the gradual establishment of the Reformation and the initial absence of presbyterianism.
147. Lord Eustace Percy, *John Knox* (London 1937).
148. T. F. Henderson, *Mary Queen of Scots* (London 1905).
Generally accepted as the best biography: there are many. Read's *Bibliography* lists well over a hundred items directly concerned with the Queen.
149. D. H. Willson, *King James VI and I* (London 1956).

(b) *Wales*
See especially (52).
150. C. A. J. Skeel, 'Wales under Henry VII', *Tudor Studies presented to A. F. Pollard* (London 1924).
151. W. Ll. Williams, *Making of Modern Wales* (London 1919).
Collection of important studies on Tudor Wales.
152. J. F. Rees, 'Tudor Policy in Wales', *Studies in Welsh History* (Cardiff 1947).
A lucid summary with an excellent map. See also W. Rees, 'The Union of England and Wales', *Transactions of the Cymmrodorion Society* 1937.

(c) *Ireland*
153. R. Bagwell, *Ireland under the Tudors* (3 vols., London 1885–90).
Another standard work.
154. B. Fitzgerald, *The Geraldines* (London 1953).
Brief and rather popular, but sound.
155. R. Dudley Edwards, *Church and State in Tudor Ireland* (Dublin 1935).
The impact of the Reformation on Ireland; see also the same author's 'Ireland, Elizabeth I, and the Counter-Reformation', in (27).
156. E. W. L. Hamilton, *Elizabethan Ulster* (London 1919).
Together with (144), a good account of Ireland under Elizabeth.

H. LITERATURE AND THE ARTS

(4) and (5) give adequate summaries and good biographies.

157. F. Caspari, *Humanism and the Social Order in Tudor England* (Chicago 1954).
Discusses, fully and in detail, the educational thought of some leading Tudor humanists; valuable bibliographical footnotes.

158. E. M. W. Tillyard, *The Elizabethan World Picture* (London 1943).
A polished account of the traditional element in Elizabethan thinking.

159. *The Cambridge History of English Literature* (reprint of 1932), vols. iii–vi.
A most valuable compilation, covering all aspects of literature in considerable detail. The chapters, written by different people, vary enormously: some are excellent, others the last word in literary murder.

160. C. S. Lewis, *English Literature in the Sixteenth Century, excluding Drama* (Oxford 1954).
A brilliant, often provocative, survey which illumines much darkness.

161. F. P. Wilson, *Elizabethan and Jacobean* (Oxford 1945).
A highly illuminating analysis of the great age.

162. F. S. Boas, *An Introduction to Tudor Drama* (Oxford 1933).
Deals with the drama before Shakespeare.

163. M. M. Reese, *Shakespeare: his world and his work* (London 1952).
A discussion of all aspects of Shakespeare and a useful introduction to the enormous literature of the subject. For this see also the annual surveys edited by A. Nicol.

164. E. Walker, *A History of Music in England* (3rd ed., revised by J. A. Westrup, Oxford 1952).
The standard work, not exciting, but sound.

165. T. Garner and A. Stratton, *The Domestic Architecture of England during the Tudor Period* (2 vols., London 1929).
Plentiful pictures and illuminating comment; jejune off the field of architecture.

166. Erna Auerbach, *Tudor Artists* (London 1954).
Important. Concentrates on miniature painting, but gives also summaries of portrait painting on a larger scale and the work done by artists in heraldry and for the royal revels. Valuable biographical details and a very full bibliography.

167. Erna Auerbach, *Nicholas Hillyard* (London 1961).

INDEX